Microprocessor/Hardware Interfacing and Applications

Barry B. Brey
DeVry Institute of Technology—Columbus, Ohio

Charles E. Merrill Publishing Company
A Bell & Howell Company
Columbus Toronto London Sydney

Merrill's International Series in Electrical and Electronics Technology

BATESON	*Introduction to Control System Technology, 2nd Edition, 8255-2*
BOYLESTAD	*Introductory Circuit Analysis, 4th Edition, 9938-2* *Student Guide to Accompany Introductory Circuit Analysis, 4th Edition, 9856-4*
BOYLESTAD/KOUSOUROU	*Experiments in Circuit Analysis, 4th Edition, 9858-0*
NASHELSKY/BOYLESTAD	*BASIC Applied to Circuit Analysis, 20161-6*
BREY	*Microprocessor/Hardware Interfacing and Applications, 20158-6*
FLOYD	*Digital Fundmentals, 2nd Edition, 9876-9* *Electronic Devices, 20157-8* *Essentials of Electronic Devices, 20062-8* *Principles of Electric Circuits, 8081-9* *Electric Circuits, Electron Flow Version, 20037-7*
STANLEY, B.H.	*Experiments in Electric Circuits, 9805-X*
GAONKAR	*Microprocessor Architecture, Programming and Applications With the 8085/8080A, 20159-4*
ROSENBLATT/FRIEDMAN	*Direct and Alternating Current Machinery, 2nd Edition, 20160-8*
SCHWARTZ	*Survey of Electronics, 2nd Edition, 8554-3*
SEIDMAN/WAINTRAUB	*Electronics: Devices, Discrete and Integrated Circuits, 8494-6*
STANLEY, W.D.	*Operational Amplifiers With Linear Integrated Circuits, 20090-3*
TOCCI	*Fundamentals of Electronic Devices, 3rd Edition, 9887-4* *Electronic Devices, 3rd Edition, Conventional Flow Version, 20063-6* *Fundamentals of Pulse and Digital Circuits, 3rd Edition, 20033-4* *Introduction to Electric Circuit Analysis, 2nd Edition, 20002-4*
WARD	*Applied Digital Electronics, 9925-0*

Published by
Charles E. Merrill Publishing Company
A Bell & Howell Company
Columbus, Ohio 43216

This book was set in Times Roman and Helvetica.
Production coordination and text design: Tracey E. Dils
Cover Design: Tony Faiola
Cover photo courtesy of Western Electric.

Library of Congress Catalog Card Number: 83-62909
International Standard Book Number: 0-675-20158-6
Printed in the United States of America
4 5 6 7 8 9 10—88 87 86

To my wife Virginia
and our children Robert, Kim, and Brenda.

Preface

This text can be used in a one- or two-term course towards a two- or four-year engineering technology degree, a computer science degree, or an engineering degree. It is also readily usable by the practicing technologist or engineer who desires updating in microprocessor hardware interfacing.

To ensure success with this text, it is strongly recommended that the reader know the fundamentals of digital electronics and machine or assembly language programming. Helpful is familiarity with the MC6800 or 8085A microprocessor, or Zilog Z80* if the reader can translate the 8085A code used in this text.

Chapter one compares and contrasts the mainframe computer system with the microprocessor and introduces the reader to the text's terminology. It also describes how software and hardware development relates to a total system design approach.

Chapter two introduces the architecture of the microprocessor by describing the internal operation of each functional unit. It offers information on the wide variety of available microprocessors and describes commonly used microprocessor system bus standards, such as IEEE–696/S100 and the STD–BUS.

Chapters three and four cover the Motorola and Intel series of microprocessors. A knowledge of both is worthwhile, but covering just one should suffice for understanding the book's remaining chapters.

Chapter five studies memory interface. It examines how memory devices operate and looks at memory address decoding, development of memory systems (including both static and dynamic elements), and an example of a STD–BUS memory interface.

Chapter six and seven detail the Input/Output fundamentals that are built upon in the remaining chapters of the text: programmable interface components, keyboards, displays, solenoid operated devices, Analog to Digital Converters, Digital to Analog Converters, and stepper motors.

Chapter eight offers percise coverage of interrupt structures and interrupt processed I/O techniques. It compares interrupt structures of the commonly available microprocessors, including a discussion of applications such as a real time clock, a priority interrupt scheme, a Centronics type printer interface, and a software FIFO or Queue memory.

Chapter nine introduces digital communications, with information on both serial and parallel techniques along with standard interface components. It covers

*I would like to acknowlege that Zilog and Z80® are trademarks of Zilog, Inc., with whom I am not associated.—Barry B. Brey

RS–232C, IEEE–488, current loops, FSK and PSK data transmission, and MODEMs.

Chapter ten is about Direct Memory Access, which, although heavily used in industry, has been all but ignored by most textbooks. It compares DMA structures of different microprocessors and DMA controllers. An application of direct memory access has been presented in the form of a CRT refresh circuit.

Chapters eleven and twelve deal strictly with applications. They examine for each application how and why various system components were selected and what software is required.

Appendix A provides a glimpse of the Z80 microprocessor for comparative purposes. It then could be the processor used throughout this text instead of the MC6800 or Intel 8085A, at the instructor's option.

Appendix B contains data sheets that might be useful in designing projects at the ends of chapters eleven and twelve. (These projects, much longer than the normal homework assignment, are best suited to a lab.)

A recommended sequence of study would be chapters one and two, followed by either chapter three or four. The choice of chapter and microprocessor is completely up to the user; almost any microprocessor can be used with this text. Once the processor and its timing have been thoroughly studied, the remainder of the text may be covered in numeric order (with Chapter 11 or 12 or both selected based on whether Chapter 3 or 4 were studied earlier).

This book provides a sound foundation in microprocessor system development that can be used in more advanced courses covering communications, computer systems, and modern digital control systems.

Acknowledgments

With gratitude, I wish to acknowledge the assistance of the following reviewers: John Blankenship, of DeVry Institute of Technology in Atlanta, Ramakant A. Gayakwad, DeVry Institute of Technology in Los Angeles, John L. Morgan, DeVry Institute of Technology in Dallas, Ralph Folger of Hudson Valley Community College (N.Y.), David Hata, Portland Community College (Oregon), Peter Holsberg, Mercer County Community College (N.J.), Eldon W. Husband, University of Houston at Clear Lake City.

A special thank you is given to David Leitch, of DeVry Institute of Technology—Columbus, whose figure-by-figure and word-by-word checking of the galley proofs have been invaluable.

Contents

1

Introduction to Microprocessors

Almost all forms of consumer, industrial, and military electronics equipment use microprocessors. Thus all electronics professionals need a firm grasp of microprocessor hardware interfacing.

To provide some insight into this exploding field, chapter 1 introduces the student to the past, present, and possible future of the computer and the microprocessor.

1-1 MAINFRAME COMPUTER SYSTEMS

The first electronic digital computer systems, built in the late 1940s, were developed to solve complex scientific problems. These systems were massive and power hungry, with relatively low speeds and small memories. It's hard to believe they are related to efficient mainframe computers of today.

It was in the early 1950s, when business applications were realized, that the boom began. Computers could handle vast amounts of information at relatively high speeds, making them ideal for accounting and record handling in large businesses. Drawbacks to their use were expense and a significant space requirement.

Since these beginnings, the large mainframe computer systems have made continuous and tremendous strides. The areas of improvement are all-encompassing. For example, memory size and speed increased significantly with the advent of the integrated circuit. Whereas the old machines ran at a few thousand operations per second, systems now accomplish well over ten million operations per second. Data transfer has become much more efficient through new methods of "human interface," through printers for hardcopy and CRT terminals for softcopy.

Modernizing changes were due largely to the expansion of knowledge about digital technology. Progress in vacuum tubes, diode switching logic, small- and medium-scale integration, and finally large- and very-large-scale integration followed closely.

Memory is a good example of how this progress was achieved. In the beginning, memory consisted of two vacuum tubes that were required to store one binary bit of information. Today millions of bits can be stored in the area once occupied by a vacuum tube. Even more amazing is that power consumption is less than that required for the filament in a vacuum tube. No wonder the field has exploded.

The programming environment has changed, too. In the early days, a programmer had to communicate with the machine in *its* own language, machine language. This cumbersome method required hours just to be able to print a list of numbers. Now the programmer enters commands in a pseudo-English language, and a device called a *compiler* translates it into a fairly efficient machine-language program. Without these strides in communication, we would still be working on a program to generate the telephone company's monthly bills!

The large mainframe computer (see figure 1–1) solves problems for both the business and scientific communities. Today they handle data processing and accounting for most companies, model all types of business ventures, solve extremely complex scientific problems, and help design many products. One additional area of use is the dedicated task application: processes such as automated board testing, system testing, production line control, and products such as microwave ovens, automobile emission control systems, CRT terminals, and printers. Some of these applications have given way to smaller computer systems as they have been developed. (Few large computer systems are included in dedicated task functions because of their cost.)

FIGURE 1–1 A typical large mainframe computer system.
SOURCE: Courtesy of Amdaul Corporation.

To be sure, the large mainframe computer will remain vital to businesses because of its massive storage capacity and speed. The future certainly also holds new language development, possibly an English language compiler, so that anyone can direct large systems easily. The most significant changes will probably come in this area of human interface. Even now, "networking" (talking to the large system through a smaller computer) is becoming commonplace because of the time it saves the computer. As you can imagine, the new trend is small computer systems for a variety of tasks, including networking or data entry into large computer systems.

MINICOMPUTER SYSTEMS 1-2

As the previous section indicates, the cost and size of the mainframe computer made it impossible to use in certain dedicated task applications. To this end, the industry developed a scaled-down version, dubbed the *minicomputer.* The main differences between the mainframe computer and the minicomputer are word size and processing speed. Mainframes can typically manipulate 32-bit binary numbers, while minicomputers typically manipulate 16-bit binary numbers. The logic circuitry incorporated in the minicomputer also reduces its speed.

Minicomputers, such as the VAX-11 in figure 1–2, typically handle such applications as board testing, system testing, automation, networking, and a variety of other fairly complex tasks. As technology advanced, minicomputers became more powerful and compact. Today minicomputers are performing, at greater speeds, tasks as complex as those performed by the early mainframe computers.

FIGURE 1–2 The VAX-11/730 minicomputer system, foreground; the VAX-11/750 (left); the VAX-11/780 (right); and the VAX-11/782 (rear).

SOURCE: Photo courtesy of Digital Equipment Corporation.

Eventually, the minicomputer will undoubtedly be replaced by the superminicomputer. In fact, there is significant evidence that this is occurring today. The DEC PDP-11 is now made with the LSI-11 microprocessor, the TI 990 minicomputer uses the TMS-9900 microprocessor, and this list continues as manufacturers flock to microprocessors.

The superminicomputer with the structure, speed, and capacity of the current mainframe computer, will probably perform network control and file management functions in the future.

1-3 THE MICROPROCESSOR BASED MICROCOMPUTER

In the beginning, microprocessor fabrication mainly used medium-scale integrated circuits. These circuits typically consisted of a 4-bit arithmetic unit, a control read only memory, and some simple control logic. The arithmetic unit was capable of incrementing and decrementing a number and performing binary coded decimal addition. The control read only memory held microcode, which directed the arithmetic unit and hardware attached to the system through the control logic circuitry. The control logic directed the control read only memory by providing a memory address and various other control signals in the system. These early microprocessors were employed in devices such as cash registers, calculators, and a variety of other fundamental digital systems.

The first integration of these devices into single component microprocessors was in the four function calculator. In fact, today's calculator chips have retained much from their early medium-scale integrated circuit beginnings. They are still binary coded decimal processors, using programmable logic arrays to direct and control the calculator.

The current microprocessor has evolved in several areas. The arithmetic unit has been modified into an arithmetic and logic unit, functioning with both binary and binary coded decimal numbers. Register arrays incorporated into the microprocessor allow for more efficient programming. Finally, a special form of memory, the *last-in, first-out stack,* permits more orderly handling of subroutines.

The Early Microprocessors

The first integrated microprocessor was a 4-bit processor, designed to handle a nibble of data. These early microprocessors were implemented using PMOS technology, which made them slow and fairly awkward to interface to standard TTL logic circuitry. Instructions were executed in about 20 μs, extremely slow by today's standards.

The Intel 4004, the first microprocessor, was designed for a few limited applications. It could only address 4K nibbles of memory, which severely limited its program and data storage capabilities. Some of the early Intel 4004 applications were games, test equipment, and other simple digital systems.

The next phase of development for the microprocessor was the Intel 8008, a more powerful version of the Intel 4004. The 8008 could manipulate an entire byte of data, making it more flexible in application. The amount of program storage space was increased from 4K nibbles to 16K bytes, which allowed for more powerful software based systems. Since most data handled in computer applications is 8 bits wide, the 8008 saw much more application than the earlier 4004 microprocessor. The relatively low speed of the 8008, which was capable of only about fifty thousand operations per second, created problems and limited its application.

N-Channel MOSFET Breakthrough

In the early 1970s, MOSFET integrated circuit technology experienced a breakthrough with the then-new N-channel technology. N-channel technology was faster than P-channel technology, which led to its quick rise in popularity. It also worked from a positive power supply, making it easier to interface to TTL logic circuitry.

Intel announced and sampled the Intel 8080 microprocessor in late 1973. It was constructed from NMOS logic, which allowed it to outperform the earlier 8008 by a factor of ten. The 8080 microprocessor could execute 500,000 operations per second and address 64K bytes of memory. It also maintained an upward software compatibility with the 8008. All of the 8008 instructions will function on the 8080. Since then, the 8080 has become an extremely widely used and applied microprocessor.

Other integrated circuit manufacturers began producing a wide variety of microprocessors but never seemed to narrow the lead of the Intel 8080. Examples of other early microprocessors are National Semiconductor's IMP-4 and SC/MP, Rockwell International's PPS-4 and PPS-8, Motorola's MC6800, and Fairchild's F-8. Most microprocessors used either N- or P-channel MOSFET technology, some used CMOS technology, and still others used TTL and IIL technologies. Today there are basically two types of microprocessors in production, the single component microprocessor and the bit slice microprocessor. Bit slice microprocessors can be cascaded to allow functioning systems with word widths from 4 bits to 200 bits.

Single Component Microcomputer

In the mid 1970s, a new form of microprocessor entered the marketplace, the single component microcomputer. This device contained a processor, read only memory for program storage, read/write memory for data storage, input/output connections for interfacing to the outside world, and (in some) a timer/events counter. Two of the single component microcomputers are the Intel 8048 and the Motorola 6805R2. This new breed of microcomputer allowed many systems to be built with one integrated circuit. Some applications currently include microwave ovens, washing machines, CRT terminals, and printers.

This device is found in an increasing number of applications and deserves more discussion. Unfortunately, more coverage at this time would be impossible without first developing an understanding or a good general knowledge of microprocessor interfacing. The transition to this device is extremely easy once interfacing has been mastered.

Modern Microprocessors

Currently the mainstays of the modern microprocessor are the 8- and 16-bit versions of microprocessors. The current heavyweights in this area are the Intel 8085A and the Intel 8088. The 8085A is an 8-bit microprocessor; the 8088 is a 16-bit microprocessor, handling data transfers 8 bits at a time. The main reason for Intel Corporation's success is its ability to maintain programming compatibility with earlier products and to provide a wide range of peripheral interface components. Other current-technology microprocessors available are the Intel 8086, Zilog Z8000, the Motorola MC68000, and the Texas Instruments TMS9900. These current-technology microprocessors have few differences in the instruction sets, architecture, and memory structures. The main ingredient for success seems to be an upward compatibility from one generation to the next and a wide variety of hardware interface components.

Microprocessors of the Future

The future may bring 32-bit architectures with essentially the same speed and throughput as modern mainframe computer systems. In fact, Intel has released such a system, the iAPX-432, which is even called a *micromainframe!* Future architectures will include space for massive program and data storage with capacity for machine and human interface. This text will emphasize the importance of interfacing, which will continue to be an important function of the computer engineer.

THE SOFTWARE DEVELOPMENT TASK 1-4

Software design for the modern microprocessor based system has become too complex to be accomplished efficiently by a single individual. A team of software specialists is generally required for implementing most designs in a reasonable amount of time.

The software specialist has changed over the years. At one time a programmer needed little knowledge of hardware; today the specialist develops the software to replace once-standard hardware circuitry such as counters and multiplexers. Developing modern microprocessor based software requires in-depth understanding of digital hardware circuitry.

The technique of software development has changed tremendously over the years. At one time the programmer developed software using an assembly language program that accepted information in symbolic machine language and converted it into binary machine code. This, of course, still required many hours and was little improvement over writing a program in binary machine language. The only real advantages of the assembler were that they reduced coding errors and were self-documenting.

Today more high-level languages are being used in the development task to generate programs for microprocessor based systems. PASCAL and PL/M, both fairly efficient generators of binary machine language, are two high-level languages in current use. Unfortunately, high-level languages cannot generate all the machine language required.

Hardware interface control usually involves considerable binary bit manipulation, for which most higher-level languages have little capacity. The assembler, which allows the programmer to manipulate the data more efficiently at the bit level, is still applicable in this area and may remain so for quite a few more years. Another limitation of the high-level languages, which is sometimes overlooked, is the fact that the machine code generated by these languages is not as efficient as code developed by an experienced programmer. In many cases coding efficiency is not critical, except in hardware interface. An example of critical code is the software used to time an event, such as the length of time the magnatron in a microwave oven remains on to defrost an item of food. Since each instruction and the time it takes to execute are important, an assembler would be used to generate this type of code.

Modular Programming

The modular approach is an efficient method for developing system software. A *module,* or small portion of an entire system, allows a programmer to concentrate on one area of the program at a time. This allows the programmer to develop, test, and debug small portions of the total program. The software manager assigns the modules to the programmers most qualified to develop each, thus making the most effective use of the programming staff.

Once all modules have become operational, the manager links them together to form the system program. This seems to be the most sensible and often-used approach to software development. Its main drawback is the interface between software modules. Sometimes data flows among modules are not exactly as predicted, causing problems that are fairly hard to detect and correct.

Built-in Diagnostic Tests

In today's sophisticated microprocessor based systems, it is often difficult or impossible for the technician to enter a program for the purpose of system testing. System test or diagnostic programs must be included whenever a system's software is developed. If a fault is detected, the software should indicate the fault by lighting LED indicators or displaying a particular code number on the screen of the CRT, if one is available.

This diagnostic software must be able to test the system RAM and ROM and also exercise the hardware. *RAM testing* involves running a functional test or a static test of the memory whenever power is first applied to the system. ROMs and their programs can be tested by running a checksum on their contents, by exclusive ORing all of the bytes of data on the ROM together and checking against the correct checksum stored on the ROM. The hardware testing is system dependent. To test a printer, the printer can print all of the characters; to test a CRT terminal, the software can display all of the characters on the screen. A more complete discussion of this type of testing is included in chapters 5 and 6.

Software Development Tools

The software development aide is a critical portion of the software development function. A typical software development aide, as pictured in figure 1–3, should contain several CRT terminals for program module entry, a shared disk for module storage, a printer for hardcopy documentation, a ROM programmer to place the developed software on a ROM, and finally some method of connection to the actual hardware circuitry of the system. The aide is tied to the hardware during system testing so that part of the developed software or the entire system can be tested on the actual hardware.

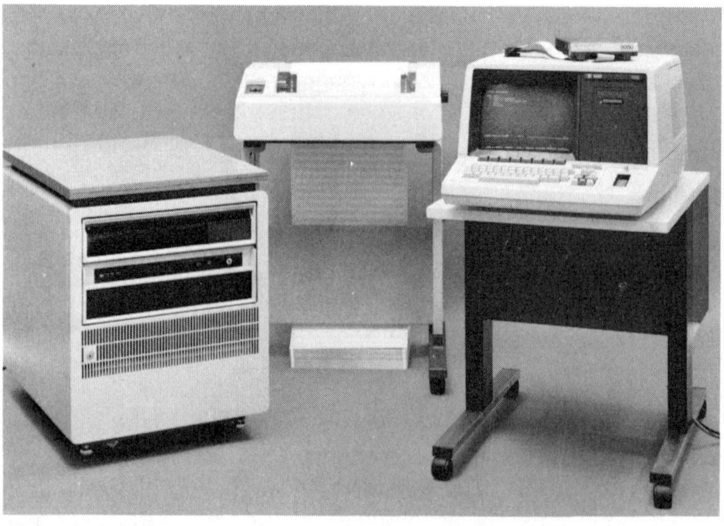

FIGURE 1–3 The 64000 logic development system.
SOURCE: Courtesy of Hewlett-Packard, Inc.

This aide must also be able to link modules together, assemble symbolic code, compile high-level languages, and debug faulty software.

The Development Task

To use the software development aide, the software specialist creates the program module through the CRT terminal. Once the module is operational, it is saved on the disk for later use in developing the entire system program. Once all modules have been developed, the software manager links them together, tests them as a system, and debugs any faults that appear.

After testing is completed, the final step in the development process is *emulation:* either running the program in a different computer system or actually connecting the prototype model of the hardware to the software development system. The latter is the best possible test, since it actually tests or exercises the hardware and the software together as a unit.

During software analysis, the software development aide should be capable of indicating faults as they occur to the programmer. At times, this may be difficult, and in certain cases a software driver must be written to test every aspect of the program module under development. To test a subroutine that would add together ten different numbers one would write a short program that uses the subroutine. This short program is called a *software driver,* since it is specifically written to test the subroutine. It is interesting to note that software drivers are often longer and more involved than the software under test.

Once the entire system is debugged and emulated, it can be burned or programmed into an EPROM. Since most development systems incorporate an EPROM programmer, this is usually a very easy task. Once the EPROMs are programmed, the final test is executed by placing them into the prototype model and running the system. Hardware testing usually requires fairly sophisticated test equipment, which will be discussed in the next section.

THE HARDWARE DEVELOPMENT TASK 1-5

Hardware design methodology differs from software design methodology, since components must be found to implement the desired system. The first and most obvious task is to select a microprocessor for the system. This is often the first step, but it is premature when a microprocessor that cannot adequately handle the hardware is selected. The first item to examine is the type of hardware interface components that have been chosen or designed; then the most applicable microprocessor for the task can be selected.

Since the software may be developed by a separate team of individuals, they receive the hardware specifications at this point. After analyzing the hardware specifications, the software team estimates the amount of ROM space required for program storage and the amount of RAM space required for data storage. Once this information is available, it is possible to develop a complete logic diagram for the hardware. From it, a prototype can be built and tested as thoroughly as possible until the software has been developed and debugged.

Microprocessor Trainers

If the microprocessor selected is foreign to the engineering staff, time is allocated to training, commonly by microprocessor trainers produced by the microprocessor manufacturers. Figure 1–4 illustrates the 8086A based SDK-86 trainer from Intel. In some cases, training may include seminars to introduce the engineering staff to the new microprocessor.

A typical microprocessor training system contains a keyboard, a grouping of alphanumeric displays, a serial interface for a CRT terminal, and software located in a ROM. The keyboard allows access to the microprocessor and its hardware interface components, which are usually provided on the training aide. The displays allow the user to scan through the memory, display the contents of the internal registers, and single step through a program. The single step feature allows the user to learn the operation of the microprocessor. The trainer enables the user to develop a proficiency with both the hardware and the software. It is not intended as a system-designing tool, since most aides are fairly limited. This is one of the most effective methods for mastering a new microprocessor, since the unit can be taken home in most cases.

In-circuit Emulators

In a discussion of hardware development aides, it is important to mention the in-circuit emulator. An *in-circuit emulator,* such as the one illustrated in figure 1–5, allows the engineer to plug the hardware into the software development system for complete testing with the actual software to be used in the completed system. One other important feature is that the hardware can often be tested before the system software has been completed, identifying simple hardware faults that may not normally surface until final testing. In most applications, the software development station will contain the software until both the software and the hardware have been completely debugged and appear to be functional.

FIGURE 1–4 The SDK-86 Intel 8086 based microprocessor training aide.

SOURCE: Courtesy of Intel Corporation.

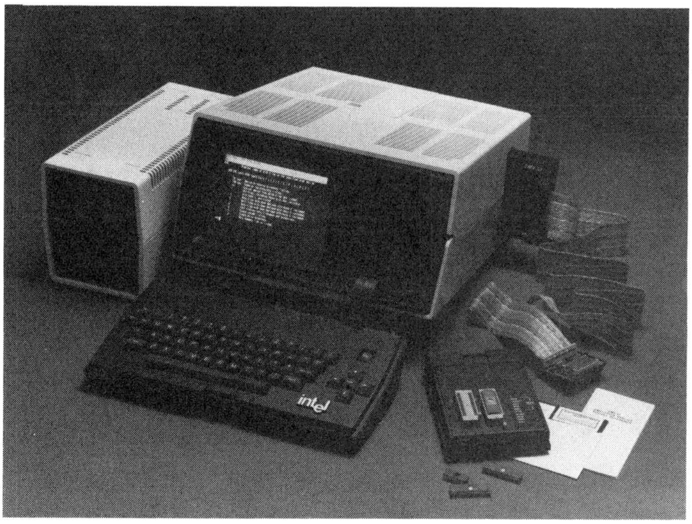

FIGURE 1–5 A personal development system that includes an in-circuit emulator.
SOURCE: Courtesy of Intel Corporation.

Data Analyzers

Another important tool for the hardware engineer is the *digital data analyzer,* which is essentially a multichannel digital storage oscilloscope. Most modern data analyzers can capture data in increments of in time in nanoseconds (ns). This allows the designer to view timing changes with unprecedented accuracy.

The *logic,* or *data, analyzer* stores a snapshot of many digital signals over a specific period of time, allowing the user to view very complex timing without the problem of synchronization associated with the analog oscilloscope. Figure 1–6 shows a 16-channel digital logic analyzer. This is possible because most data analyzers contain some form of storage element. This *storage element,* or *memory,* can be used to sample a period of time and save it for later comparisons. In fact, the analyzer can take a snapshot of a complex set of timing waveforms and automatically compare the content of its internal memory with a new set of waveforms. This feature can be used to accomplish a very efficient automatic test.

Synchronization in data analyzers is accomplished by externally triggering on key binary bit patterns. This allows the user to search an incoming data stream for a particular binary bit pattern. Once the analyzer triggers, it begins storing data in an internal memory that can be viewed by the user at any time.

Data is viewable in many different formats: binary, octal, hexadecimal, ASCII, and as waveforms on the face of the CRT. Some newer data analyzers will display 48 different waveforms at one time. Another display mode that is sometimes useful is the mapped mode. *Mapped mode operation* causes the screen to be filled with dots representing bits of information stored in the memory. This map will normally contain a pattern that, in some cases, can be used to test a system. If the software were to hang up in an infinite loop, this would become apparent on the CRT screen.

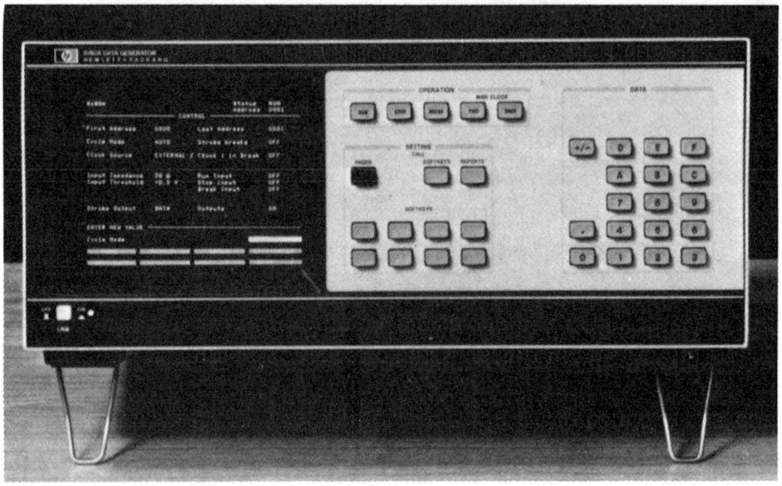

FIGURE 1–6 The 8182A data analyzer.
SOURCE: Courtesy of Hewlett-Packard, Inc.

Data analyzers are also, in some cases, capable of performing signature analysis. Signature analysis is normally used by a technician to test a faulty digital system. A data stream normally has a unique binary bit pattern, called its *signature*. If this pattern is known, the technician can determine whether a product is functioning properly by comparing the measured signature with a predetermined signature. If there is no match, the technician must then locate the faulty component.

Another important role of the data analyzer is in production testing. Since it contains memory, it can be used to test a newly manufactured system by comparing known data from a good system with the data sampled from the newly manufactured system. Since most data analyzers will automatically indicate a data match, virtually anyone can learn to handle automated testing in this manner.

Summary

In thirty years, computer technology has progressed from colossal mainframe computers to the microprocessor, which can easily be balanced on the end of a pencil. Such a tremendous change is truly incredible.

What will the future bring? Eventually, most products will contain a microprocessor, be designed by a microprocessor, or be assembled and tested by a microprocessor. People will function only with their microprocessors at hand. This will be the Symbiotic Age—the age where human and machine merge to become one newer and more powerful creature. The individual will no longer be able to function independently of the computer. Pure speculation? Are we already at the verge of this frontier? Are some professionals already in the Symbiotic Age?

New test equipment, the data (or logic) analyzer, has been developed to test microprocessor based systems; by all predictions, it will be more common than the ordinary oscilloscope in a few years. Future software will allow the masses access to the microprocessor. This may even be voice-directed software, with voiced responses. The entire field of electronics feels the impact of the changes thrust upon it by the microprocessor. We are entering an age of the microprocessor. No phase of electronics will remain untouched or unchanged by this new device.

Glossary

Assembler A program that converts symbolic machine language into binary machine language.

Byte Generally a grouping of eight binary bits.

Compiler A program that converts or translates a high-level language into binary machine language.

Computer A machine that can receive, transmit, store, and manipulate information.

Data analyzer A multichannel digital oscilloscope that can process the data and display it in many different forms.

Diagnostics Programs that have been expressly written to test the memory or the system hardware.

Emulator A device that can imitate either partially or completely the operation of a given microprocessor.

Hard copy The printed output of a computer.

Hardware A computer system's electronic circuitry.

Interpreter A computer program that generates a pseudocoded or tokenized language that is not machine language. BASIC is often this type of system.

Large-scale integration A microcircuit containing between one hundred and one thousand logic elements.

Logic analyzer See Data Analyzer.

Machine language The binary bit patterns that direct a computer's operation.

Mainframe computer A large computer system designed for general-purpose data processing.

Medium-scale integration A microcircuit containing between 11 and 99 logic elements.

Microcomputer A computer system integrated on one integrated circuit or a small computer system based on a microprocessor.

Minicomputer A scaled down mainframe computer system.

Modular programming This type of programming divides the software design task into modules that are easy to develop and debug.

Nibble Generally, a grouping of four binary bits.

Program A grouping of instructions that direct the operation of a computer system.

Signature A unique number that indicates the data contained in a serial stream of digital data.

Signature analyzer A device that can accumulate binary bits of information in order to develop a signature of the data.

Small-scale integration A microcircuit containing ten or fewer logic elements.

Soft copy The displayed output of a computer system on a CRT terminal.

Software A computer's program is often referred to as *software*.

Symbiotic age The age when human and machine will merge into a new and more powerful working unit.

Very-large-scale integration A microcircuit containing over one thousand logic elements.

Questions and Problems

1 Contrast the main differences between a microprocessor and a mainframe computer system.

2 In what situation would an assembler be preferred to a compiler?

3 In what situation would a compiler be preferred to an assembler?

4 What major breakthrough allowed microprocessors to function at a faster rate?

5 List two different commonly found high-level languages.

6 What is the first step in hardware development?

7 What is the significance of the software module in software development?

8 Why are diagnostics used in a microprocessor based system?

9 Outline the steps that are normally followed in the software development task.

10 List the component parts of a software development system.

11 List four applications for microprocessors.

12 List an application suitable for a 4-bit microprocessor.

13 List an application suitable for an 8-bit microprocessor.

14 Will the world ever see a 128-bit microprocessor? Explain your answer.

15 Cite at least two examples of human-machine symbiosis.

2

Microprocessor Architecture

Before we can discuss a particular microprocessor, it is a good idea to examine computer architecture in general. This provides a context for understanding the architecture of a particular microprocessor.

This chapter discusses the component parts of the microprocessor as well as the ancillary components in the microprocessor based system. It also contrasts, in brief, some of the features found in modern microprocessors, including the various types in production and the instructions available to the programmer.

2-1 GENERAL COMPUTER ARCHITECTURE

The block diagram of a computer system, illustrated in figure 2–1, depicts the typical layout for almost all bus oriented digital computer systems. The central unit controls the flow of information between itself and the memory or input/output equipment. This central unit is called the *central processing unit* (CPU) in a mainframe or minicomputer and the *microprocessing unit* (MPU), in a microcomputer.

The CPU communicates with the memory and the I/O through a few control lines attached to each unit. These control lines basically control the reading and writing of information and comprise the computer system's *control bus*. In addition to the control bus, there exists a group of wires, the *system data bus,* that convey the information to and from memory and I/O. A third set of connections, the *address bus,* points to a specific memory location or to a unique I/O device.

Through these three buses, the central unit manipulates information in the memory and passes information out to an external device. All bus oriented digital computer systems use the same three buses to process information. The data bus carries the information; the address bus points to the location of the information; and the control bus controls the direction, flow, origin, and destination of the data. In fact, most computer system functioning is similar, allowing a detailed description of interfacing to be presented without undue detail about a specific microprocessor.

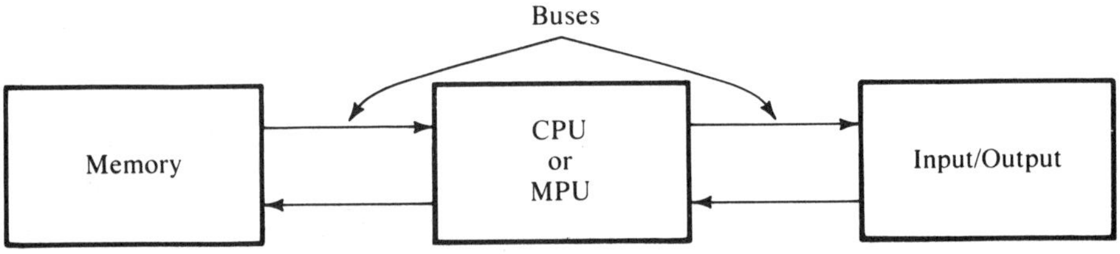

FIGURE 2–1 The basic block diagram of an electronic digital computer system.

2-2 THE MPU

Data transfer, arithmetic and logic operations, and decision making are the three main functions shared by all MPUs. The main differences between an MPU and a CPU are the speed at which these three basic functions can be performed and the binary bit size of the data. Data size, or width, in some of the newer microprocessors has equaled that of many mainframe computer systems. The CPU in a mainframe computer system is about one hundred times faster than the typical microprocessor. If this appears to be a minor difference, imagine a single day's worth of data processing taking one hundred days on a microprocessor based computer system. It should be fairly clear why mainframe computer systems are still in use and will probably continue to be for quite some time.

Data Transfer Operations

Data transfer is the most important function, since the MPU spends at least 95 percent of its time transferring data. Data transfers can follow many different paths in most microprocessors. The most common path is to and from the memory in the system, since fetching instructions for a program demands a lot of time. The rest of the time, data is transferred to and from the I/O and passed around inside the processor itself. Most microprocessors include a scratch pad memory, or register array, for this last purpose.

Arithmetic and Logic Operations

About 4 percent of the MPU's time is spent on simple arithmetic and logic operations. The arithmetic function that is most often performed is addition. Through the addition operation, the microprocessor can subtract, by first complementing a number and adding it to a second number to generate a difference. This complement in most microprocessors is a 2's complement, so that one is actually performing 2's complement addition to obtain the difference. The main advantage of the 2's complement method—as compared to the 1's complement method—is the fact that a negative zero cannot occur, and signed numbers present no major problem in the 2's complement system. Therefore, most processors are capable of adding and subtracting (by adding).

Many of the newer microprocessors are also capable of multiplication and division. These operations are actually performed by shifting and adding for multiplication and by shifting, comparing, and subtracting for division.

Microprocessors can also perform some basic logic operations. These operations often include logical multiplication (AND), logical addition (INCLUSIVE-OR), inversion (NOT), EXCLUSIVE-OR, and various forms of shifting and rotating. The most commonly used logic operation is the AND function, which is used to mask, or clear to zero, a portion of a binary number. In fact, complete bit control over a binary quantity is possible by using the AND function to clear bits to zero; the OR function to set bits to ones; and the EXCLUSIVE-OR function to complement or invert bits. Some microprocessors actually have a special TEST or BIT TEST instruction, which may be used to test bits in the accumulator. This instruction usually performs the AND operation without changing the number under test.

Decision-making Operations

The least used, but nonetheless important, function of the MPU is its ability to make some form of decision. All of the decisions that a microprocessor is capable of performing are based upon numerical tests. For example, a number can be tested and the result can indicate a negative quantity. The microprocessor can make a decision based upon this negative result by modifying its instruction flow. Instruction flow modification is accomplished by a form of conditional branch or conditional jump instruction. Other commonly testable conditions are positive, zero, not zero, carry after an addition, borrow after a subtraction, parity even, parity odd, overflow and equality.

The Mainframe Computer Versus the Microprocessor

What arithmetic operations can a mainframe computer system perform that a microprocessor cannot directly accomplish? One is floating point arithmetic, which can only be performed through software or by using a floating point arithmetic processor, which is actually a special purpose microprocessor. Such a device is interfaced to the microprocessor in chapter 7.

Basic Microprocessor Architecture

The diagram in figure 2–2 represents the general architecture of many of the microprocessors that are available today. The internal architecture is composed of an instruction register, an arithmetic and logic unit (ALU), a register array, and a control circuit that coordinates the operation of the microprocessor.

The control logic causes the microprocessor to perform its two main functions, the *fetch,* or *acquisition,* and *execution* phases of operation. The fetch phase causes the microprocessor to send the address of the next instruction to be executed out of the device through the address bus. The control logic then causes the memory to read information from the addressed location by sending a MEMORY READ signal out through the control bus. Data is fetched into an internal register called an *I,* or *instruction register,* which holds the instruction while the control logic decodes it and begins executing it. One other very important event occurs during the fetch sequence: the program counter is incremented so that the next fetch phase will fetch the next sequential instruction from the memory. This is the basic sequence of events required to fetch an instruction from the memory and to begin executing it.

The ALU is responsible for performing the arithmetic and logic operations inside the microprocessor. The control logic directs the operation of the ALU and causes it to perform an arithmetic or logic operation on data from the memory or the register array. The result of this operation is passed back to the memory or the register array to complete the operation.

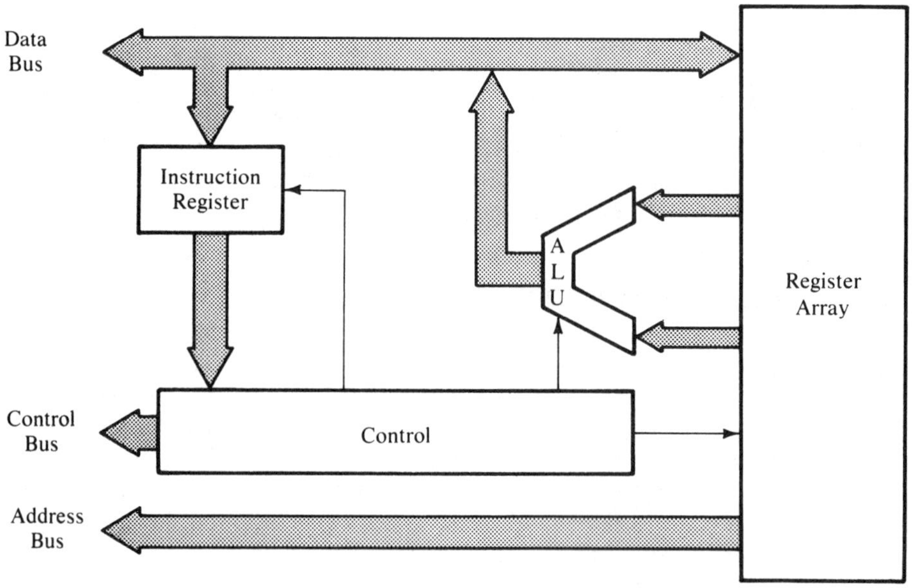

FIGURE 2–2 The internal representation of a microprocessor.

The register array contains one or more general-purpose registers, at least one accumulator that holds the result from the ALU, a program counter that keeps track of which instruction is to be executed next, and, in almost all cases, a stack pointer register responsible for tracking the last-in, first-out stack memory.

MEMORY 2-3

The memory in a computer system stores the data and instructions of the programs. Instructions are stored in the computer system's memory for quick access. The calculator normally cannot store its instructions in memory, so that it requires the operator's memory to enter a sequence of instructions through the keyboard. In the computer, the operator must still enter the instructions, but when they have been stored in the memory, the computer can go through them at a very high rate of speed. It can also use the same sequence of instructions with many different sets of data over and over again. The calculator would require the operator to reenter the entire program with each new set of data. This stored program concept has led to the tremendous processing power of the modern computer.

Program Storage

In microprocessor based systems, the program and system diagnostics are customarily stored in a read only memory (ROM). Various forms of ROMs have been developed over the years for this purpose. The ROM must be programmed at the factory while it is being manufactured; the PROM is programmed by burning open fusible links; the EPROM is programmed electrically and erased with ultraviolet light; and the EEPROM and EAROM are programmed and erased electrically.

In most systems the ROM stores the program and diagnostics, while the PROM or EPROM is used to develop the prototype system. The role of the EEPROM and EAROM is to store important data for extended periods of time. This long-term storage is not subject to power failures and is also reprogrammable by the user of the system. These features make it extremely useful for storing tax tables in electronic cash registers, tab positions in CRT terminals, and similar features in other types of equipment.

Data Storage

Data is commonly stored in semiconductor RAM, which is fabricated from bipolar transistors or MOSFETs. The most common type is the NMOS memory, which can access data in 100 ns or less. NMOS memory is available in two forms: the dynamic form (DRAM), which requires periodic refreshing; and the static form (SRAM), which retains data as long as power is applied. Since dynamic memory requires additional circuitry to accomplish refreshing, it is normally used only in memory systems of over 16K bytes in size.

2-4 INPUT/OUTPUT

The main purpose of the input/output block (figure 2–1) is to allow the microprocessor to communicate directly with people or with another computer or machine. The most familiar types of I/O equipment are CRT terminals and printers. Other forms include indicator lamps, switches of all types, solenoids, relays, disk systems, and speakers.

Typical microprocessor I/O equipment includes the analog-to-digital converter, digital-to-analog converter, photosensitive device, and the microphone. In fact, any device that responds to an electrical signal or produces an electrical signal can be, and often is, used as an I/O device in a microprocessor based system.

2-5 BUS STRUCTURES

The Address Bus

Address buses are present and basically the same in all microprocessors. They are incorporated into the system to address the memory and the I/O equipment. Address buses in various microprocessors differ only in width. The most common number of address connections available today is 16, with some of the newer microprocessors containing either 20 or 24 connections. Most of these buses are three-state connections, which will go to their high impedance state at some time during normal microprocessor operation.

In some cases the address bus connections are shared or multiplexed with other buses or signals at the microprocessor. In microprocessors where the address bus is multiplexed, the manufacturer provides a signal to demultiplex the bus. Figure 2–3 illustrates the Intel 8085A, which has a multiplexed address/data bus.

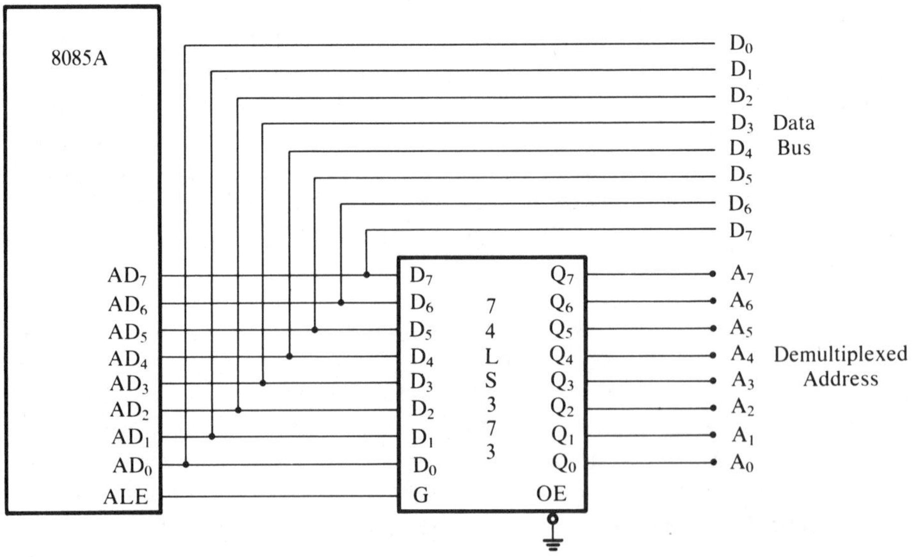

FIGURE 2–3 The Intel 8085A microprocessor with a circuit to demultiplex its address data bus.

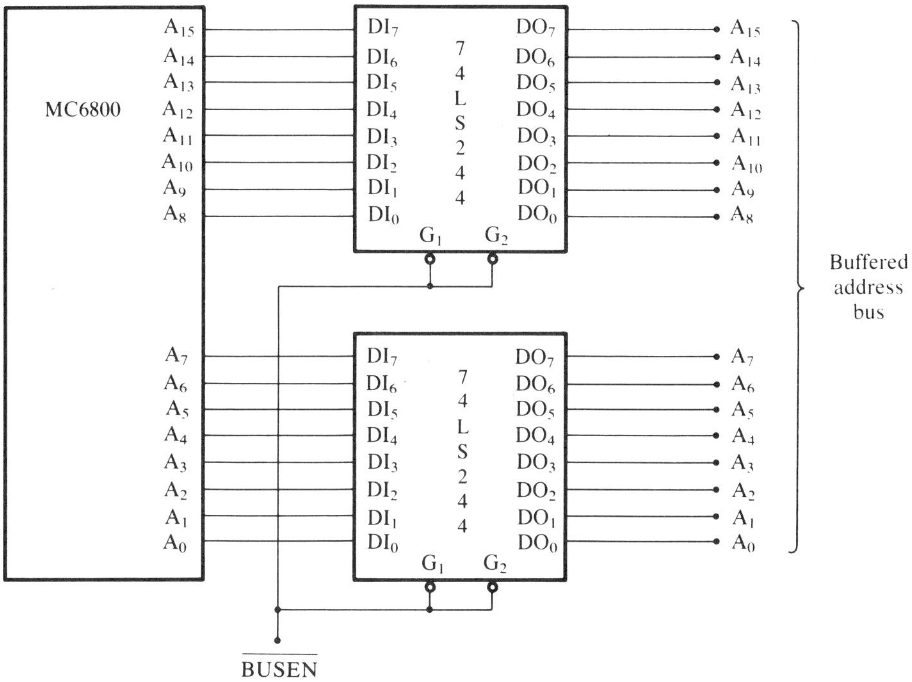

FIGURE 2–4 The Motorola MC6800 microprocessor with a circuit to buffer the address bus.

In the 8085A, the processor sends out the least significant half of the memory address on the address/data bus, along with the address latch enable (ALE) signal. The 74LS373 transparent octal latch captures this portion of the address and holds it until the processor sends out another address along with ALE. The gate (G) input to the latch causes it to accept data when high and to remember or capture data when low. This latch will also provide additional drive capability to the address pins.

In many microprocessors today, the address bus and other output pins are capable of driving only one standard TTL unit load. This will, in many systems, be insufficient to drive the system bus, so that additional buffering is often required.

The Address Bus Buffers

Figure 2–4 illustrates how the address bus connections on the Motorola MC6800 can be buffered to provide additional drive. This circuit uses two 74LS244 octal three-state buffers to provide additional drive capability to the address bus. Before the addition of these buffers, the MC6800 was capable of driving one standard TTL unit load or five low-power Schottky-clamped TTL unit loads. With the addition of these buffers, it can now drive twenty standard TTL unit loads or about one hundred low-power Schottky-clamped TTL unit loads.

The $\overline{BUSEN}$ connection allows the buffered outputs to be floated or placed in their high impedance state during some of the processor's operations. Besides providing additional drive, the buffered outputs present a lower output impedance to the bus than do the original pins on the MC6800.

This impedance is nearly the same as the characteristic impedance of the bus itself, which helps to eliminate noise that might otherwise be generated.

In most single board systems, excluding the very large single board or multiple board systems, output buffers are not normally required because of the relatively short buses and light loading. Under most circumstances, buffers are present only when driving heavy TTL loads or more than ten MOSFET loads.

If additional buffers are required, as in figure 2–4, propagation delay times of these buffers must be taken into account when developing a system. For example, with the address bus, the propagation delay time of the buffer is subtracted from the access time allowed to the memory by the microprocessor. If, in addition to the buffers on the address bus, buffering is added to the data bus, time allowed to access memory is decreased by the sum of both propagation delay times. It is important to consider these delay times when using memory or I/O devices with access times that are nearly equal to the time allotted by the microprocessor.

Data Bus

The data bus is typically a bidirectional bus that may, in some processors, also be multiplexed with some other information. If an external buffer is required on this bus, it takes the form of a bidirectional bus buffer or bus transceiver. The circuit of figure 2–5 illustrates the Intel 8088, which contains a multiplexed bidirectional data bus. In this diagram, an octal latch demultiplexes the address/data bus, and an octal bus transceiver buffers the data bus. The $\overline{RD}$ signal from the processor is an active low signal that changes

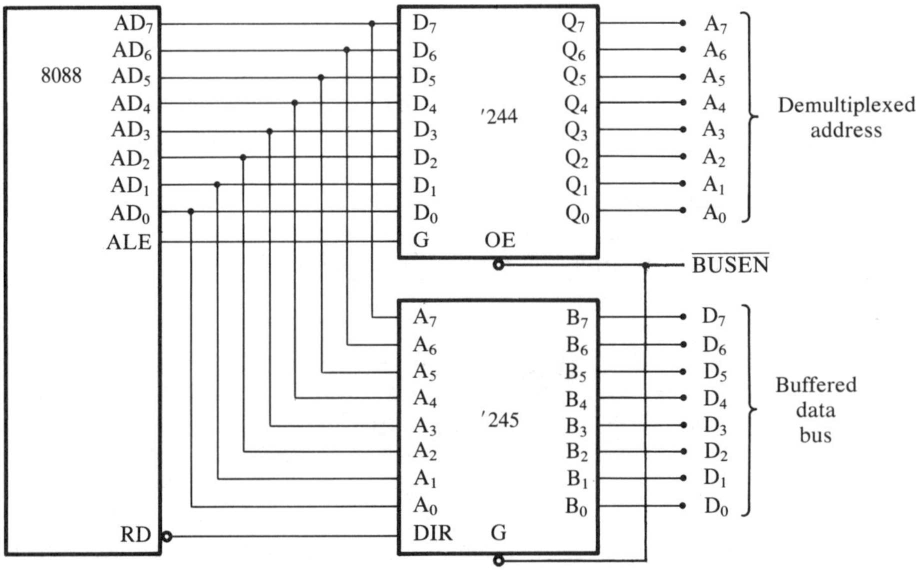

FIGURE 2–5 The Intel 8088 microprocessor with a circuit to buffer the data bus and demultiplex the address/data bus.

the direction of data flow through the bus transceiver. When this signal is active, data will flow toward the microprocessor. The $\overline{\text{RD}}$ signal only becomes active whenever the processor anticipates data from the memory or the I/O. During a write to I/O or memory, the $\overline{\text{RD}}$ pin is inactive, allowing data to flow out to the system through the bus transceivers.

The $\overline{\text{BUSEN}}$ connection is used during a direct memory access or bus request operation in the system. In a direct memory access operation, these buses are normally placed in their high impedance state. $\overline{\text{BUSEN}}$ accomplishes this by disabling the buffers.

Control Bus

The control bus is one of the most important buses in the system, since it actually controls the memory and I/O equipment. Each microprocessor in production today has a slightly different control bus configuration. The most important control bus signals are the read and write signals, since these are the basic functions of the memory and the input/output circuitry.

In some microprocessors these are actually separate lines; in others, they are incorporated into a single control line. The Intel 8080A uses $\overline{\text{MEMR}}$, $\overline{\text{MEMW}}$, $\overline{\text{IOR}}$, and $\overline{\text{IOW}}$ to control memory and I/O; the Commodore (formally MOS Technology) 6502 uses R/$\overline{\text{W}}$ and phase two of the clock; the Intel 8085A uses $\overline{\text{RD}}$, $\overline{\text{WR}}$, and IO/$\overline{\text{M}}$; and the Motorola MC6800 uses VMA, R/$\overline{\text{W}}$, and phase two of the clock. Although many different control signals are in use, they all essentially indicate read and write.

I/O Control

There are two different techniques for handling the control of I/O devices, which examining the control signals of different microprocessors will illustrate. One of these techniques is the *memory mapped I/O,* in which I/O devices are treated as memory. In fact, with regard to software and hardware control signals, the I/O is indeed memory.

The other technique is *isolated I/O* or *I/O mapped I/O,* in which the I/O device is a separate I/O device. That is, the I/O device has a unique I/O address, not a memory address. Processors that use this type of I/O have special instructions, IN and OUT, to transfer data to and from this separate I/O space. Both techniques have advantages and disadvantages.

In the memory mapped I/O scheme, there are two basic control signals, memory read and memory write. In the isolated I/O scheme, there are four basic control signals: memory read, memory write, I/O read, and I/O write. The main advantage of the memory mapped I/O system is that it requires only two control signals to function. The isolated I/O scheme requires four, but it does not require any of the memory space to function. Which one of these schemes is better? It depends upon the application and the microprocessor chosen for the application.

In addition to these basic memory and I/O control signals, there are special inputs and outputs, such as interrupt control, direct memory access control, ready, reset, and various other processor dependent control signals.

This text will not discuss in detail processor dependent control signals, only those that apply to all microprocessors in general. The reader will find more information on the Intel control signals in chapter 3, the Motorola control signals in chapter 4, and the Zilog control signals in the Appendix on the Z80.

Interrupts

The interrupt input on most microprocessors will, when placed at its active level, interrupt the program and CALL up a subroutine from the memory. The purpose of this subroutine is to service the interrupt, and it is for this reason that this type of subroutine is called an *interrupt service subroutine*. Interrupts handle extremely slow external I/O devices, such as keyboards, in order to improve the performance of the microprocessor based system. They also free microprocessor execution time in applications such as real time clocks. This discussion will be expanded in chapter 8.

Direct Memory Access

The hold, or bus request, input on many microprocessors facilitates the I/O technique of *direct memory access*. The main function of this input is to cause the microprocessor to relinquish control of the memory and I/O by disconnecting itself from the address, data, and control buses. Once the processor is disconnected, another processor takes over the memory and I/O space. This is useful in systems where more than one controller or processor must have access to the memory and I/O. This input, along with acknowledgment outputs, will be discussed in chapter 10.

Reset

The reset input on most microprocessors allows the microprocessor to be initialized whenever power is applied or at the discretion of the operator. Power on clearing is normally accomplished by using a simple RC circuit, as illustrated in figure 2–6. Whenever Vcc, or 5 V, is applied, the capacitor, which is initially discharged, begins to charge toward 5 V. This takes some time because the RC time constant of the circuit allows the microprocessor ample time to feel a logic zero on its reset pin while Vcc is applied to reset itself. The push button switch allows the operator to reset the microprocessor whenever it might be required. Upon resetting, many microprocessors are internally initialized, so that they function at a predefined memory location fetching an instruction. This reset location, in some microprocessors a vector, is very important because it is at this location that the system program must begin. In the case of a vector, the vector points to the beginning of the system software.

Wait States

The READY or MRDY pin provided on many microprocessors indicates to the microprocessor that the memory and/or the I/O circuitry is ready to function. If a slow memory device, a device with a longer than normal access time, is to be connected to the microprocessor, the ready input causes the microprocessor to enter into waiting states. Wait states are multiples of the system clock pulses that cause the system to allow more time for the memory to access data. Because of the wide range of timing among microprocessors, the

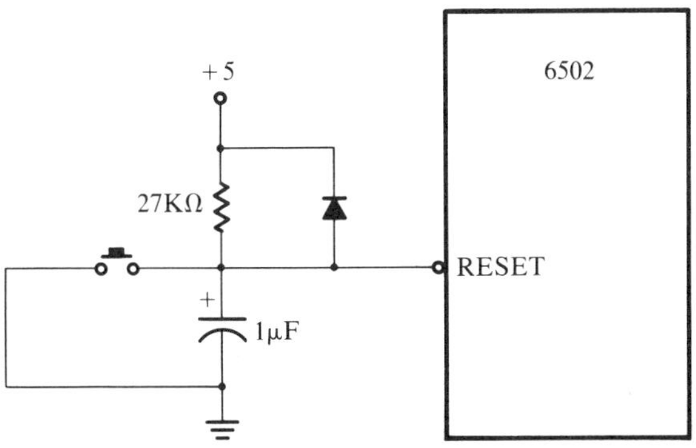

FIGURE 2–6 The reset circuitry for a Commodore 6502 microprocessor.

best source of information about the operation and timing of this pin is the literature provided by the manufacturer, including, in some cases, the circuit recommended to cause wait states.

Bus Timing

Bus timing is extremely important to the hardware engineer, who mainly concentrates on the timing required to achieve a particular result. Some of these times are memory access time, read or write pulse widths, memory cycle time, clock pulse width, and clock period. Most of these timing signals will be discussed in greater detail in chapters 3 and 4.

Clock Period

The clocking period will be discussed at this point, since it does not depend on understanding memory and I/O interfacing. There are normally two discrete limits to the clocking period that are determined by the internal structure of the microprocessor and must be observed for proper operation: The shortest clocking period depends on the type of logic family that comprises the microprocessor and is caused by internal propagation delay times. The longest allowable clocking period is determined by the fact that most microprocessors use dynamic storage in their register arrays. Dynamic registers require periodic refreshing to maintain the integrity of the data stored in them. If the clocking period is longer than that recommended by the manufacturer, the integrity of the data stored internally is lost.

The clock waveform or waveforms are normally generated by a crystal controlled oscillator that is incorporated into the microprocessor or available as an ancillary component from the manufacturer. The system hardware generally governs the operating period within the constraints allowed by the manufacturer.

Bus Contention

Since memory components have one pin that controls reading and writing of data, why do some microprocessors provide two control signals for the memory? These signals prevent what is often referred to as *bus conflict* or *bus contention*.

A bus contention occurs whenever the bus is driven from two points at the same time. This condition does not damage any of the devices connected to the bus, but it may cause a temporary loss of data at a critical point in the microprocessor timing. To prevent this conflict, it is important to use all of the supplied control signals when interfacing memory and/or I/O devices. Bus contention is discussed further in chapters 5 and 6 on memory and I/O interface.

2-6 A COMPARISON OF TYPICAL MICROPROCESSORS

Four-bit Microprocessors

The TMS 1000 (Texas Instruments) dominates the 4-bit microprocessor market. In large quantities, its price has dropped to about one dollar, with applications in such systems as microwave ovens, washing machines, and dishwashers.

Eight-bit Microprocessors

The area of heaviest competition and application is the 8-bit microprocessor, and in this area there are several competitors. In comparing 8-bit microprocessors, one finds that their function and application are about the same. For example, virtually all 8-bit microprocessors have a 16-bit address bus. Some microprocessors share a portion of the address bus connections with the data bus, and others share the data bus connections with information about microprocessor function. In every case the data bus is 8 bits in width, and it is always bidirectional. There is little variation in speed among microprocessors, with all operating within a range between 1 μs and 0.20 μs.

Eight-bit microprocessors differ most in availability of ancillary components. Some microprocessor manufacturers supply a wide variety of interface components, while others provide virtually none. Microprocessor interfacing is simplified when most of the intricate design work has already been accomplished by the manufacturer. The more successful microprocessors have a vast line of interface components.

Another feature that is often overlooked in comparing microprocessors is the interrupt structure of the processor. Interrupt inputs vary from one to up to five. In all cases the interrupt scheme can be expanded by adding external hardware, but in small systems requiring only a few interrupt inputs, it is useful to have a processor with more than one such input. Most modern applications of the microprocessor can be improved by using one or more interrupts to speed information processing. Therefore, this is an important aspect of selecting the right microprocessor to do the job.

Sixteen-bit Microprocessors

Variation in 16-bit architectures is greater than in standard 8–bit architectures. One significant variation is the width of the data bus. The data bus is either 8 or 16 bits in width, which presents a problem in selecting a particular 16-bit microprocessor. The 8-bit bus architecture is appropriate for the user who has invested time and money in 8-bit peripherals. Designing a system by eliminating the need to develop new memory and I/O interfaces significantly reduces the expense.

The 16-bit microprocessor that employs an 8-bit data bus preserves this investment and allows a significant increase in performance due to the internal 16-bit architecture. All 16-bit microprocessors incorporate instructions for multiplication, division, and block data manipulation, thus reducing software coding time. These new instructions reduce the time required to develop a new system and correspondingly reduce the development cost.

The user who requires more speed selects a 16-bit data bus version of the 16-bit microprocessor or possibly a 32-bit microprocessor. The 32-bit microprocessor is normally reserved for high technology applications and may eventually replace the smaller mainframe computer systems.

Bit Slice Microprocessors

Bit slice technology is appropriate only when an application requires extremely high speed, very wide word widths, or a tailored instruction set. Since the instruction set of the bit slice microprocessor is more basic than the fixed word width microprocessor, it requires more time for software development. A typical fixed word width microprocessor, such as the Intel 8085A, has a few hundred instructions; whereas the bit slice processor may contain tens of thousands of instructions. Developing a bit slice technology system requires significant increases in cost and training time.

Single Component Microcomputers

Single component microcomputers, available from various manufacturers, are useful in less complex applications. These contain a microprocessor, ROM or EPROM for program storage, and RAM for data storage. In most cases, they also contain connections for input and output operations. Often small- and medium-sized systems can be implemented by using one of these processors and very few other components. This, of course, decreases the expense of development time for both hardware and software. In addition, the fewer components in a system, the easier it is for the field service technician to maintain.

Microprocessor Selection

As the previous discussion suggests, it is difficult to select a microprocessor for an application without first researching the hardware aspects of the system to be designed. Once the hardware is specified, software to implement the system is analyzed for proper processor operation. If the application requires complex arithmetic operations, a 16-bit microprocessor is appropriate. If the application requires simple arithmetic and many string manipulations, an 8-bit microprocessor is chosen. Its application in the system dictates the choice of microprocessor.

Table 2–1 lists some of the available microprocessors, including package size, address bus width, data bus width, basic processor word size, and special features.

TABLE 2–1 A comparison of microprocessors.

Part	Manufacturer	Type	Word Bit Size	Address Bus Width	Number of Pins	Speed	Clock	Date
2901	Advanced Micro Devices	Bit Slice	4	Varies	40	0.115	9	1975
6502	Commodore	MPU	8	16	40	3	1	1975
mN602	Data General	MPU	16	16	40	2.4	8.3	1979
T-11	Digital Equipment Corp.	MPU	16	16	40	1.2	7.5	1982
F8	Fairchild	MPU	8	16	40	2	2	1974
4040	Intel	MPU	4	13	24	12.3	2	1974
8048	Intel	Single Chip	8	12	40	6	2.5	1977
8080	Intel	MPU	8	16	40	2	2	1973
8085	Intel	MPU	8	16	40	1.3	3	1976
8086	Intel	MPU	16	20	40	0.6	5	1978
8088	Intel	MPU	16	20	40	0.6	5	1979
iAPX-432	Intel	MPU	32	32	64	0.4	8	1981
6100	Intersil	MPU	12	15	40	5	2.5	1974
3870	MOSTEK	Single Chip	8	12	40	2	4	1977
6800	Motorola	MPU	8	16	40	2	1	1974
6805	Motorola	Single Chip	8	8	28	2	4	1979
6809	Motorola	MPU	8	16	40	1.5	2	1979
68000	Motorola	MPU	16	24	64	0.6	6	1980
16016	National Semiconductor	MPU	16	24	48	0.4	6	1983
1802	RCA	MPU	8	16	40	5	3.2	1978
PPS-4	Rockwell	MPU	4	10	40	8.3	4	1974
2650	Signetics	MPU	8	15	40	1.5	3	1975
TMS1000	Texas Instruments	MPU	4	9	28	15	0.4	1974
TMS9900	Texas Instruments	MPU	16	16	64	4.7	3	1976
Z80	Zilog	MPU	8	16	40	1.6	2.5	1976
Z8001	Zilog	MPU	16	16	48	0.4	4	1981

NOTE: Clock = CPU clock frequency in megahertz (MHz).
Speed = shortest instruction execution time in microseconds (μs)

A COMPARISON OF MICROPROCESSOR INSTRUCTION SETS 2-7

Figure 2–7 illustrates the internal structure of a variety of microprocessors. All include an accumulator, an index register or pointer, some general-purpose registers, a stack pointer, and a program counter. The number of internal registers varies widely, but generally the more registers a microprocessor contains, the more flexible it becomes. It is generally easier to write efficient software—in terms of memory utilization, speed, and cost—with a larger number of internal registers.

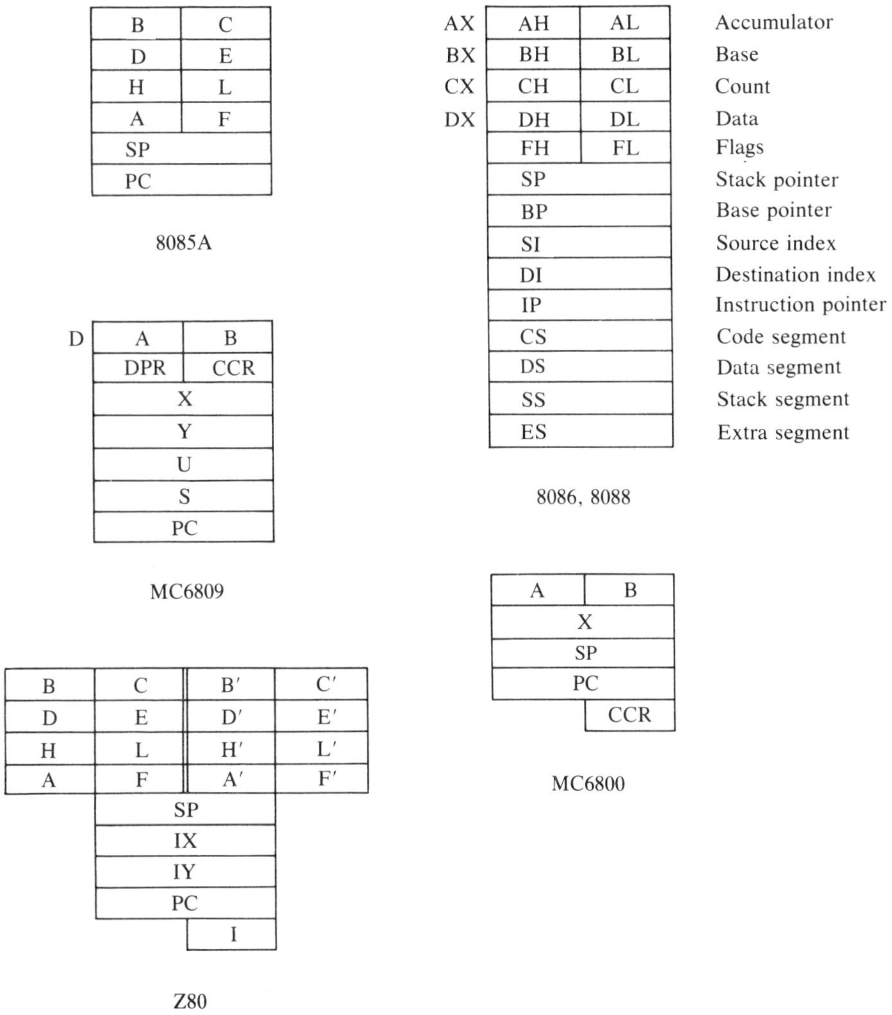

FIGURE 2–7 The internal programming models or structures for the 8085A, 8086, 8088, MC6800, MC6809, and the Z80 microprocessors.

Base Page Addressing

Some microprocessors with a limited number of internal registers use a portion of the memory as an extension of the internal register structure. This extension is called a *base page* or *scratch pad memory*.

The base page, which is usually 256 bytes in length, is usually located at the beginning of the memory system. This extension of the internal register array (addressed by the numbers 00 through FF) effectively increases the amount of register storage from a few bytes to more than 256 bytes. The only disadvantage of this type of addressing is that it normally takes more time to reference memory than it does to reference an internal register.

In the MC6809 microprocessor, the base page can be located in any area of the memory through a base page pointer register. This is a tremendous asset in processing large quantities of data, since more than one set of base page registers is available.

Indexed Addressing

Index registers, or pointers, are a very important portion of the makeup of the internal register structure. The pointer or pointers reference lists of data in the microcomputer's memory system. Without this ability, programming would be cumbersome, if not impossible. Many programs require at least two index registers or pointers, since it is often necessary to manipulate two sets of information at one time. If fewer than two are available, problems of this nature are much more difficult to solve.

Relative Addressing

Another form of addressing often found in microprocessors is relative addressing. In most cases, this form of addressing is not essential, but when it is available, it reduces the number of bytes required to implement a particular task. The major problem of relative addressing is that it is rather difficult to determine the displacement when one is coding with binary machine language. If an assembler is to be used for program development, this presents no problem.

Displacement is a number that indicates how far away from the location of the next instruction the address or data is located. For example, to refer to a byte of information that is 4 bytes after the next instruction, one uses a displacement of four.

Indirect Addressing

Less common is *indirect addressing,* in which an indirect instruction allows the programmer to refer to a byte of data through a location stored in another memory location or register. For example, if memory location 12 contains a 6 and the instruction loads the accumulator indirectly from 12, the contents of location "6" are actually placed in the accumulator.

Indirectly addressing memory through another memory location has its application, but little in the type of software normally associated with hardware control. It is most useful for implementing jump tables in systems such as interpreters and more complex software.

Immediate Addressing

Immediate addressing loads an internal register or a memory location with the byte of data that immediately follows the op-code in the memory. In most cases, many arithmetic and logic instructions are available in this form. Immediate addressing is useful whenever a program deals with constants. The data can be stored with the instruction, allowing the program to be written more easily.

Variable Length Instructions

All microprocessors are able to address a byte or word of data in the memory directly by using different length instructions. Some use a 3-byte-long instruction, while others address a base page of memory by a 2-byte-long instruction.

Input/Output Techniques

Input/output techniques are available in the memory mapped I/O scheme and the isolated I/O scheme. In the *memory mapped* scheme, all instructions that deal with the memory are available to handle data transfer to or from the I/O equipment. In the *isolated,* or *I/O mapped,* I/O scheme, two instructions, input and output, handle I/O transfer. Though the isolated I/O technique of transfer sounds cumbersome, in many cases it is at least as efficient as memory mapped I/O. Also, if the machine has isolated I/O, it can also accomplish memory mapped I/O; but a machine designed without isolated I/O can never accomplish isolated I/O.

Stacks

Stack memory schemes are basically the same in all microprocessors: they store data and *return addresses* from subroutines without regard to memory address. They perform these functions through a special register, the *stack pointer,* which tracks the stack automatically. When the stack pointer register is initialized in a program, the processor maintains the stack if proper syntax is followed.

Many microprocessors require that data be placed on the stack and retrieved from the stack in pairs of bytes. Some microprocessors store and retrieve single bytes of data, and others store both single and double byte numbers on their stacks.

Another major consideration for the programmer is the direction of the data flow to and from the stack. Since the stack is a last-in, first-out memory, the data is reversed in order by the stack. For example, if a 4 followed by a 2 is placed onto the stack, the 2 followed by the 4 is extracted from the stack.

Complex Instructions

Some of the complex instructions available on newer microprocessors include multiplication, division, translation, and various forms of character string manipulation. Certain microprocessors perform ASCII arithmetic, which is often quite useful. As the need for newer and more complicated instructions arises, manufacturers will develop new microprocessors to meet the demand of the industry.

2-8 MICROCOMPUTER SYSTEM BUSES

Two fairly common bus standards, the IEEE-696/S100 BUS and the STD-BUS, have gained wide acceptance throughout the industry. These standards define the pin configurations and card sizes of microcomputer interface printed circuit boards. The S100 standard is a 100-pin standard, and the STD-BUS is a 56-pin standard. Both are adaptable to a wide variety of 8-bit microprocessors, and the S100 standard is also adaptable to the newer 16-bit microprocessors.

The IEEE-696/S100 Bus Standard

MITS Inc. developed the S100 bus for their Altair 8800 microcomputer system in 1974. It soon became the de facto standard, with a large number of other microcomputer manufacturers adopting it as their system bus. Since that time about one hundred manufacturers have been producing boards for this bus. S100 boards can accomplish most tasks from additional memory to boards that synthesize speech.

In 1978, a committee of the Institute of Electrical and Electronics Engineers (IEEE) drafted a proposal making the S100 bus a standard bus for microcomputer systems. Some of the changes from the original bus included a wider data bus of 16 bits, a wider memory address bus of 24 bits, and extended direct memory access control.

The most current version of the IEEE-696/S100 standard is illustrated in table 2–2. The standard requires three power supply voltages on the bus. These voltages are +8 V, −16 V, and +16 V. These supply voltages generate +5 V, −5 V, +12 V, and −12 V, which are developed by local regulators on each plug-in printed circuit board. The standard limits the current from each of these power supplies on each board to no more than 1 A.

TABLE 2-2 The IEEE-696/S100 bus standard pin assignments.

Pin No.	Signal	Description
1	+8 V	Power supply input for the +5 V regulators. Must be between +7 V and +25 V, with an average of no more than +11 V.
2	+16 V	Power supply input for the +12 V regulators. Must be between +14.5 V and +35 V with an average of no more than +21.5 V.
3	XRDY	XRDY must be true along with RDY (pin 72) to indicate that the bus is ready.
4	$\overline{\text{VI0}}$	Vectored interrupt line 0.
5	$\overline{\text{VI1}}$	Vectored interrupt line 1.
6	$\overline{\text{VI2}}$	Vectored interrupt line 2.
7	$\overline{\text{VI3}}$	Vectored interrupt line 3.
8	$\overline{\text{VI4}}$	Vectored interrupt line 4.
9	$\overline{\text{VI5}}$	Vectored interrupt line 5.
10	$\overline{\text{VI6}}$	Vectored interrupt line 6.
11	$\overline{\text{VI7}}$	Vectored interrupt line 7.
12	$\overline{\text{NMI}}$	Nonmaskable interrupt input.
13	$\overline{\text{PWRFAIL}}$	Power failure signal.

TABLE 2–2 (continued)

Pin No.	Signal	Description
14	$\overline{\text{DMA3}}$	Direct memory access address bit 3.
15	A18	Address bit position 18.
16	A16	Address bit position 16.
17	A17	Address bit position 17.
18	$\overline{\text{SDSB}}$	The status bit disable control bit.
19	$\overline{\text{CDSB}}$	The control signal disable control bit.
20	GND	Signal ground.
21	—	Not defined at this time.
22	$\overline{\text{ADSB}}$	The control signal that disables the address bus.
23	$\overline{\text{DODSB}}$	The control signal that disables the data output bus.
24	ϕ	Status valid strobe signal.
25	$\overline{\text{pSTVAL}}$	Status bits valid strobe.
26	pHLDA	The hold acknowledge signal used to acknowledge a direct memory access.
27	—	Not defined at this time.
28	—	Not defined at this time.
29	A5	Address bit position 5.
30	A4	Address bit position 4.
31	A3	Address bit position 3.
32	A15	Address bit position 15.
33	A12	Address bit position 12.
34	A9	Address bit position 9.
35	DO1	Data output bus bit position 1 or bidirectional data bus bit 1.
36	DO0	Data output bus bit position 0 or bidirectional data bus bit 0.
37	A10	Address bit position 10.
38	DO4	Data output bus bit position 4 or bidirectional data bus bit 4.
39	DO5	Data output bus bit position 5 or bidirectional data bus bit 5.
40	DO6	Data output bus bit position 6 or bidirectional data bus bit 6.
41	DI2	Data input bus bit position 2 or bidirectional data bus bit 10.
42	DI3	Data input bus bit position 3 or bidirectional data bus bit 11.
43	DI7	Data input bus bit position 7 or bidirectional data bus bit 15.
44	sM1	The status bit that indicates the current bus cycle is an op-code fetch.
45	sOUT	The status bit that indicates the current bus cycle is an output.
46	sINP	The status bit that indicates the current bus cycle is an input.
47	sMEMR	The status bit that indicates the current bus cycle is a memory read.
48	sHLTA	The status bit that indicates the processor is currently halted.

TABLE 2–2 (continued)

Pin No.	Signal	Description
49	CLOCK	A 2-MHz squarewave.
50	GND	Signal ground.
51	+8 V	See pin 1.
52	−16 V	See pin 2 except for the polarity.
53	GND	Signal ground.
54	$\overline{\text{SLAVE CLR}}$	Used to reset bus slave devices.
55	$\overline{\text{DMA0}}$	Direct memory access address bit 0.
56	$\overline{\text{DMA1}}$	Direct memory access address bit 1.
57	$\overline{\text{DMA2}}$	Direct memory access address bit 2.
58	$\overline{\text{sXTRQ}}$	The status bit that requests 16-bit slaves to assert $\overline{\text{SIXTN}}$.
59	A19	Address bit position 19.
60	$\overline{\text{SIXTN}}$	The signal asserted by 16-bit slaves in response to the $\overline{\text{sXTRQ}}$ signal.
61	A20	Address bit position 20.
62	A21	Address bit position 21.
63	A22	Address bit position 22.
64	A23	Address bit position 23.
65	—	Not defined at this time.
66	—	Not defined at this time.
67	$\overline{\text{PHANTOM}}$	A signal that disables the normal slave devices and enables the phantom slave devices.
68	MWRT	Memory write control signal derived from the logical combination of pWR and sOUT.
69	—	Not defined at this time.
70	GND	Signal ground.
71	—	Not defined at this time.
72	RDY	See pin 3.
73	$\overline{\text{INT}}$	Main processor interrupt input.
74	$\overline{\text{HOLD}}$	Used to request a direct memory access.
75	$\overline{\text{RESET}}$	Used to reset bus master devices.
76	pSYNC	This control signal identifies BS1.
77	$\overline{\text{pWR}}$	Indicates the presence of valid data on the data output bus or the bidirectional data bus.
78	pDBIN	Indicates that the bus master is waiting for data on its input data bus or bidirectional data bus.
79	A0	Address bit position 0.
80	A1	Address bit position 1.
81	A2	Address bit position 2.
82	A6	Address bit position 6.
83	A7	Address bit position 7.
84	A8	Address bit position 8.
85	A13	Address bit position 13.
86	A14	Address bit position 14.
87	A11	Address bit position 11.
88	DO2	Data output bus bit position 2 or bidirectional data bus bit 2.

TABLE 2–2 (continued)

Pin No.	Signal	Description
89	DO3	Data output bus bit position 3 or bidirectional data bus bit 3.
90	DO7	Data output bus bit position 7 or bidirectional data bus bit 7.
91	DI4	Data input bus bit position 4 or bidirectional data bus bit 12.
92	DI5	Data input bus bit position 5 or bidirectional data bus bit 13.
93	DI6	Data input bus bit position 6 or bidirectional data bus bit 14.
94	DI1	Data input bus bit position 1 or bidirectional data bus bit 9.
95	DI0	Data input bus bit position 0 or bidirectional data bus bit 8.
96	sINTA	The signal that identifies an interrupt acknowledge.
97	$\overline{\text{sWO}}$	The status bit that identifies a write bus cycle.
98	$\overline{\text{ERROR}}$	The bus signal that indicates a bus error in the current bus cycle.
99	$\overline{\text{POC}}$	Used to initialize all devices whenever power is applied to the system.
100	GND	Signal ground.

This bus allows up to eight vectored interrupt inputs, greatly extending the computational power of the bus and microcomputer system. In addition to these vectored interrupt inputs, there are provisions to allow up to 16 direct memory access devices to function in the system. The data bus connections are provided for unidirectional or bidirectional capabilities of 8 or 16 bits in width. The address bus has been widened, so that the microprocessor can directly address up to 16 megabytes of system memory, as opposed to the original 64K bytes of memory. The control signals are flexible to allow most microprocessors to adapt well to this bus.

The STD-BUS

The STD-BUS was developed in 1978 as a low cost original equipment manufacturer (OEM) microcomputer system bus. Most of the 8-bit microprocessors adapt well to this bus, but the 16-bit microprocessor, excluding the Intel 8088, cannot use it. Figure 2–8 illustrates both the S100 bus card and the STD-BUS card for comparison. As the figure demonstrates, the S100 bus card is much larger than the STD-BUS card, so that it is often more useful for microcomputer implementation.

Table 2–3 presents the STD-BUS pin configuration as a comparison with the S100 bus of table 2–2. The STD-BUS was designed to implement the Z80, 8080, 8085, 8088, MC6800, and the MC6809. The S100 bus is capable of supporting the aforementioned microprocessors and the 6502, Z8000, MC68000, and both the 8086 and 8088.

TABLE 2–3 The STD-BUS pin connections.

Pin No.	Signal	Description
1	+5 V	Regulated +5 V into the board.
2	+5 V	Regulated +5 V into the board.
3	GND	Signal ground.
4	GND	Signal ground.
5	−5 V	Regulated −5 V into the board.
6	−5 V	Regulated −5 V into the board.
7	D3	Bidirectional data bus bit 3.
8	D7	Bidirectional data bus bit 7.
9	D2	Bidirectional data bus bit 2.
10	D6	Bidirectional data bus bit 6.
11	D1	Bidirectional data bus bit 1.
12	D5	Bidirectional data bus bit 5.
13	D0	Bidirectional data bus bit 0.
14	D4	Bidirectional data bus bit 4.
15	A7	Address bit position 7.
16	A15	Address bit position 15.
17	A6	Address bit position 6.
18	A14	Address bit position 14.
19	A5	Address bit position 5.
20	A13	Address bit position 13.
21	A4	Address bit position 4.
22	A12	Address bit position 12.
23	A3	Address bit position 3.
24	A11	Address bit position 11.
25	A2	Address bit position 2.
26	A10	Address bit position 10.
27	A1	Address bit position 1.
28	A9	Address bit position 9.
29	A0	Address bit position 0.
30	A8	Address bit position 8.
31	$\overline{\text{WR}}$	Write strobe to memory or I/O.
32	$\overline{\text{RD}}$	Read strobe to memory or I/O.
33	$\overline{\text{IORQ}}$	Input/output selection bit.
34	$\overline{\text{MEMRQ}}$	Memory selection bit.
35	$\overline{\text{IOEXP}}$	Input/output expansion bit.
36	$\overline{\text{MEMEX}}$	Memory expansion bit.
37	$\overline{\text{REFRESH}}$	Signal that indicates a refresh address is present on the address bus.
38	$\overline{\text{MCSYNC}}$	Machine cycle sync signal.
39	$\overline{\text{STATUS 1}}$	CPU status signal one.
40	$\overline{\text{STATUS 0}}$	CPU status signal zero.
41	$\overline{\text{BUSAK}}$	Bus acknowledge signal.
42	$\overline{\text{BUSRQ}}$	Bus request signal.
43	$\overline{\text{INTAK}}$	Interrupt acknowledge signal.
44	$\overline{\text{INTRQ}}$	Interrupt request signal.
45	$\overline{\text{WAITRQ}}$	Wait request signal.
46	$\overline{\text{NMIRQ}}$	Nonmaskable interrupt request signal.

TABLE 2–3 (continued)

Pin No.	Signal	Description
47	$\overline{\text{SYSRESET}}$	System reset signal.
48	$\overline{\text{PBRESET}}$	Operator pushbutton reset signal.
49	$\overline{\text{CLOCK}}$	System clock.
50	$\overline{\text{CNTRL}}$	AUX timing.
51	PCO	Daisy chain output
52	PCI	Daisy chain input.
53	AUXGND	AUX signal ground.
54	AUXGND	AUX signal ground.
55	AUX + V	+ 12 V power supply input.
56	AUX − V	− 12 V power supply input.

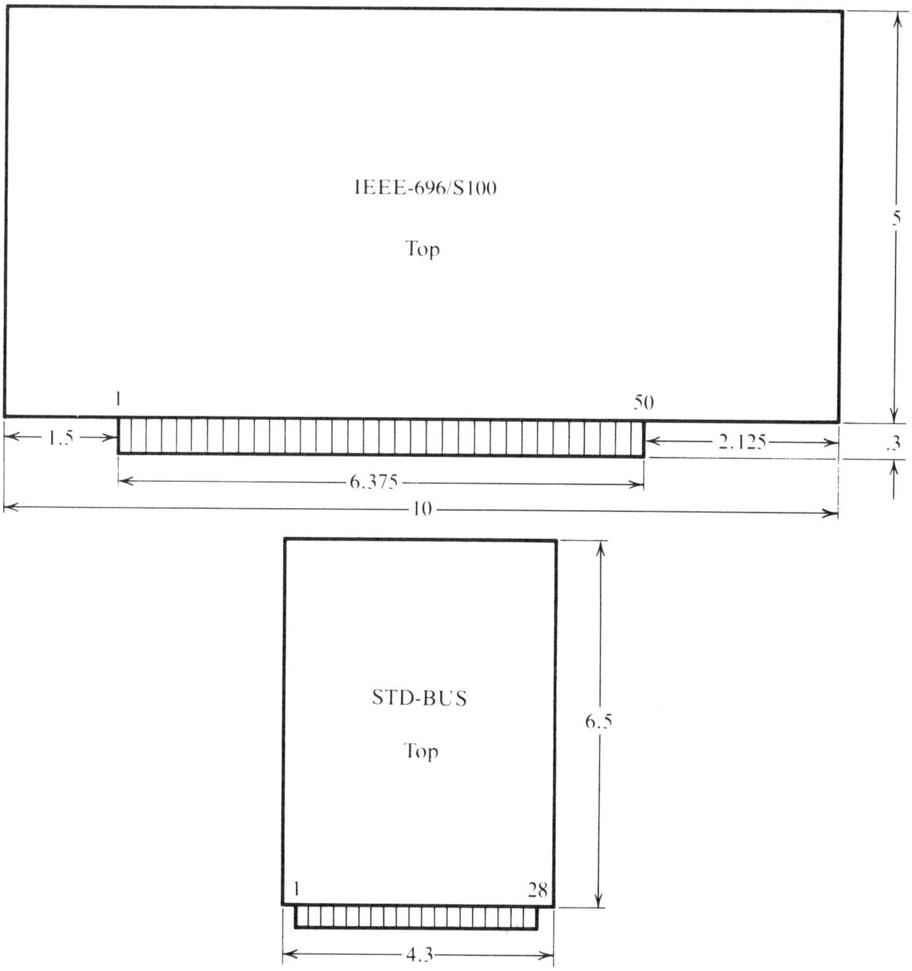

FIGURE 2–8 Top views of the IEEE-696/S100 and STDBUS printed circuit plug boards.

Bus Considerations

It is very important to understand these two buses, since they find wide application in industry. Some important considerations to take into account in designing a card for either bus standards follow.

Bus Drivers The bus drivers for both buses require that the driver is capable of being three-stated, sinking at least 24 mA of current at no more than 0.5 V and sourcing at least 2 mA of current at no fewer than 2.4 V. These requirements are easily achieved today with devices such as the 74LS240 and 74LS244 octal bus drivers. The bus receivers should exhibit some hysteresis to help eliminate any noise picked up on the buses.

Power Supply Decoupling It is also extremely important to decouple each board from the power distribution network by using a ferite bead and a capacitive decoupling network. Each component on the board should also be decoupled from the local power distribution grid if it is subject to generating switching transients. Totem pole output TTL logic gates, for example, generate switching transients and should therefore be bypassed, using a 0.01–0.1 μF capacitor placed as closely as possible to their power supply input pins. Most NMOS devices must also be bypassed, since they have output circuitry that can also generate switching transients.

Component Placement Component placement on the board itself is also critical in some instances. All devices should be placed as closely as possible to the bus connections to reduce lead lengths. This procedure reduces the amount of noise generated on the bus which can be coupled into other printed circuit cards in the system.

Standard Waveforms

The waveforms pictured in figure 2–9 illustrate the standard set of memory read and memory write waveforms available in the S100 bus system. Each of these waveform sets is divided into bus states or clocking periods. During bus state one (BS1), the memory address and status information are placed on the bus by the microprocessor. At bus state two (BS2), the control signals for the memory appear on the system bus. During bus state three (BS3), the data is written into memory or extracted from the memory by the microprocessor. Since each of these bus states is 500 ns in length, the S100 system is capable of one bus transfer every 1.5 μs. The standard clock frequency for the S100 standard is defined in the specification as a 2-MHz clock. Timing on the STD-BUS is almost identical to the S100 bus since they are based on similar microprocessors. The S100 bus was based on or designed around the Intel 8080, and the STD-BUS was designed around the Zilog Z80, which is almost identical with respect to signals to the 8080.

Other Bus Standards

Other bus standards, such as the Q-bus (Motorola) and the Multibus (Intel), have been developed by various microcomputer manufacturers. Since they are used by very few microcomputer systems, they will not be discussed here. A comparison of the S100 bus or the STD-BUS with almost any of these buses reveals basically the same set of connections and timing.

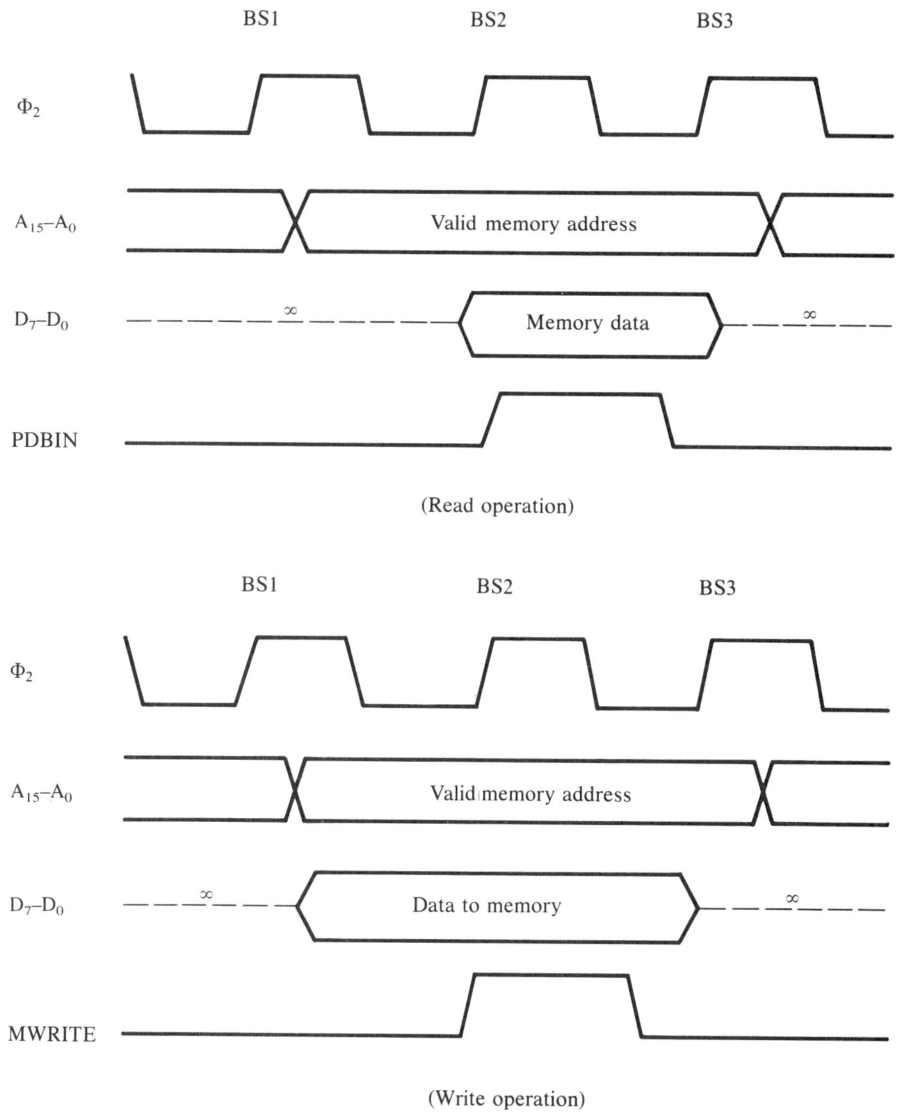

FIGURE 2–9 IEEE-696/S100 bus read and write timing diagrams.

Summary

This chapter presents a basic description of microprocessor architecture and details the functional components of the microprocessor. It is important to note that all microprocessors are essentially the same: all contain a data bus, an address bus, and a control bus. No improvements have been made to this basic structure, and none is contemplated. It is important to understand the roles of the address bus, the data bus, and the control bus in the system.

The more common microprocessors are compared to produce a broader knowledge of what is available. Chapters 3 and 4 and Appendix A (on the Z80) provide more detail.

It is also important to develop a basic knowledge of the signals available on the S100 bus and the STD-BUS. Although the student may never work with either bus, the same basic type of bus and information in the system will appear in any system used.

Glossary

Address bus A group of wires that carry an address to the memory and to the input/output devices in a computer system.

ALU The arithmetic and logic unit of a microprocessor performs all of the arithmetic and logic operations.

Base page Generally the first 256 bytes of the memory, which are used as a scratch pad.

Bus contention Also called a *bus conflict,* this occurs whenever two or more devices drive any bus at the same time.

Control bus A group of wires that control the memory and input/output devices in a computer system.

CPU The central processing unit that controls the memory and the input/output equipment in a computer system.

Data bus A group of wires used by the microprocessor to transfer data to and from memory and I/O.

Decoupling capacitor A capacitor that decouples an integrated circuit from the power supply. This is normally required to prevent problems with power supply transients.

DMA An input/output technique that transfers data directly into or out of the memory without the intervention of the microprocessor.

EAROM An electrically alterable read only memory can be programmed and erased while resident in a computer system; it will retain data even after the power has been removed from the system.

EEPROM An electrically erasable programmable read only memory (see EAROM).

EPROM An erasable programmable read only memory can be programmed electrically, but must be erased under an ultraviolet lamp.

Ferrite bead A small inductor that is often used in decoupling circuitry.

LIFO A last-in, first-out memory has data stored and retrieved in the order indicated.

Interrupt An input/output technique by which the hardware in the system can call a subroutine in the computer's memory.

MPU A microprocessing unit.

OEM An acronym for original equipment manufacturer.

Parity A count of the number of ones in a binary number, expressed as even or odd.

PROM A programmable read only memory is programmed by burning open small fusible links.

Propagation delay The time required for a signal to move from one point to another, usually through a logic element.

RAM A random access memory can be written into or read from in an equal amount of time.

ROM A read only memory is programmed by the manufacturer and cannot be written into or erased by the user.

Stack A portion of the memory commonly used to store data and return addresses for subroutines in a computer.

Wait condition When a microprocessor has stopped executing instructions and is waiting for information from a slow device.

Questions and Problems

1. What three main components comprise all digital computer systems?
2. What are the three functions of the MPU?
3. What are the two functions of the memory in a computer system?
4. What useful task is performed by the input/output equipment in a computer system?
5. Programs are often stored in which type of memory?
6. Where would the use of an EAROM be desirable?
7. What is a transparent latch?
8. Output pins on most microprocessors are capable of driving how many standard TTL unit loads?
9. Propagation delay times can normally be ignored in microprocessor based systems. Explain your answer.
10. What is a bus transceiver?
11. How is an input/output device treated in a system that uses memory mapped I/O?
12. Interrupts are particularly useful in handling which type of external input/output devices?
13. Whenever a HOLD is asserted in a microprocessor, which events will occur?
14. Explain how the circuit in figure 2–6 functions.
15. Contrast the IEEE-696/S100 bus standard with the STD-BUS standard.
16. Local regulation would be used with which one of the bus standards mentioned in question 15?
17. Describe the significance of power supply decoupling.
18. How does the hysteresis of a bus receiver reduce noise problems?

3

The 8085A, 8086, and 8088 Microprocessors

This chapter provides hardware detail on the 8085A, 8086, and 8088 to enable the reader to use any of these microprocessors throughout the rest of this text. The student is advised to concentrate on the 8085A; after it is mastered, the 8086 and 8088 can be studied next.

Most of the discussion emphasizes the 8085A, with references to the 8086 and 8088 for comparison. The Intel user's manuals can provide additional detail on these microprocessors.

3-1 PINOUTS

Figure 3–1 illustrates the 8085A, 8086, and 8088 microprocessor pinouts. All three microprocessors are packaged in 40-pin integrated circuits requiring a single 5V power supply for proper operation. The 8085A uses a maximum of 170 mA of current, the 8086 uses a maximum of 360 mA, and the 8088 uses a maximum of 340 mA.

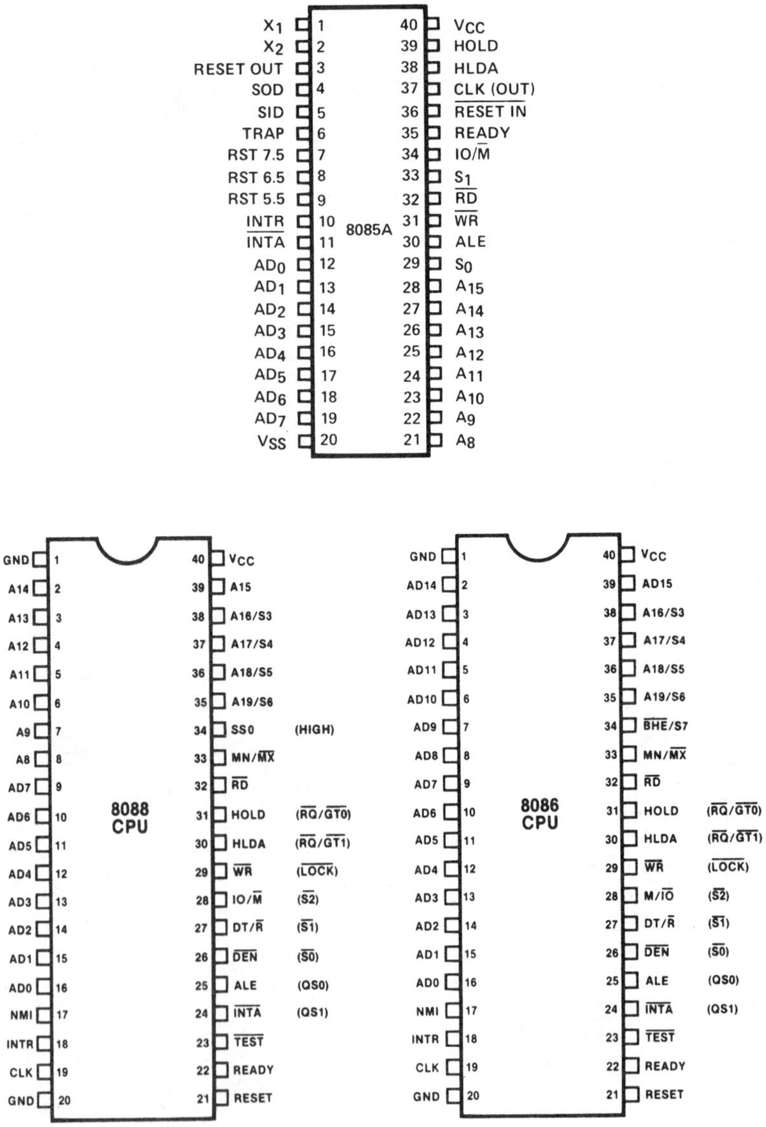

FIGURE 3–1 Pin diagrams or pinouts of the Intel 8085A, 8086, and 8088 microprocessors.

SOURCE: Reprinted by permission of Intel Corporation, Copyright 1978 and 1981.

Drive Capabilities

All three microprocessors can provide 2.0 mA of sink current and 400 μA of source current at any of the output pin connections. This is enough current to drive one 74XXX TTL unit load, one 74SXXX TTL unit load, five 74LSXXX TTL unit loads, or about ten NMOS or CMOS unit loads. Table 3–1 illustrates the sink and source current requirements for all of these logic types. Normally no more than ten MOS loads are connected because each MOS input places a fairly large amount of capacitance on an output connection.

Family	Type	Sink Current	Source Current
TTL	74XXX	1.6 mA	40 μA
TTL	74LSXXX	0.39 mA	20 μA
TTL	74SXXX	2.0 mA	50 μA
CMOS	—	10 μA	10 μA
NMOS	—	10 μA	10 μA

TABLE 3–1 Unit loading of various logic families.

Since excessive bus capacitance degrades the timing signals from the microprocessor, it is a poor practice to connect more than about ten MOS loads to any single output.

Input Loading

Input connections sink and source a maximum of only 10 μA of current. In addition, they present approximately 10 pF of capacitance. Input voltages are directly TTL compatible and therefore present no problem when interfacing to standard TTL logic circuitry.

Noise Immunity

The system noise immunity for any of these microprocessors is about 350 mV, due to a derated logic zero output voltage of 0.45 V maximum. Some systems require special attention when interfacing external circuitry to these microprocessors. If a higher noise immunity is desired, it can be achieved by adding buffers to all of the output connections.

3-2 CLOCK CIRCUITRY

The 8085A contains an internal oscillator that, in most cases, generates the basic timing for this microprocessor. The 8086 and 8088 require the addition of an external clock generator to provide their basic timing.

8085A Clock Circuitry

Under normal operation, a crystal of either 6.0 MHz or 6.144 MHz is attached to the X1 and X2 inputs of the 8085A, as pictured in figure 3–2(a). The crystal frequency is internally divided by two to produce the basic microprocessor timing and the clock out signal from the clock out pin. Permissible crystal frequencies for the 8085A range between 1.0 MHz and 6.2 MHz for reliable operation. If a frequency is chosen outside of this range, Intel does not guarantee proper operation.

Figures 3–2(b) and 3–2(c) illustrate two other less commonly used methods for obtaining a microprocessor clock signal for the 8085A. The main disadvantage of the RC or LC timing network is its lack of accuracy and stability. In most cases, the microprocessor clock times external events; since it must be fairly accurate, a crystal clock is generally used.

An external clock input may be found in a system that already has a TTL compatible clock waveform present. This clock waveform can and often does drive the microprocessor, as illustrated in figure 3–2(d).

8086 and 8088 Clock Circuitry

The 8086 and 8088 require an external clock generator or an external TTL compatible clock for operation. In most applications, the 8284A clock generator supplies the clock waveform and provides synchronization for the READY and RESET inputs to these microprocessors. Figure 3–3 illustrates the 8284A clock generator attached to the clock inputs of either an 8086 or an 8088. The 8284A divides the crystal frequency by three for the clock input to

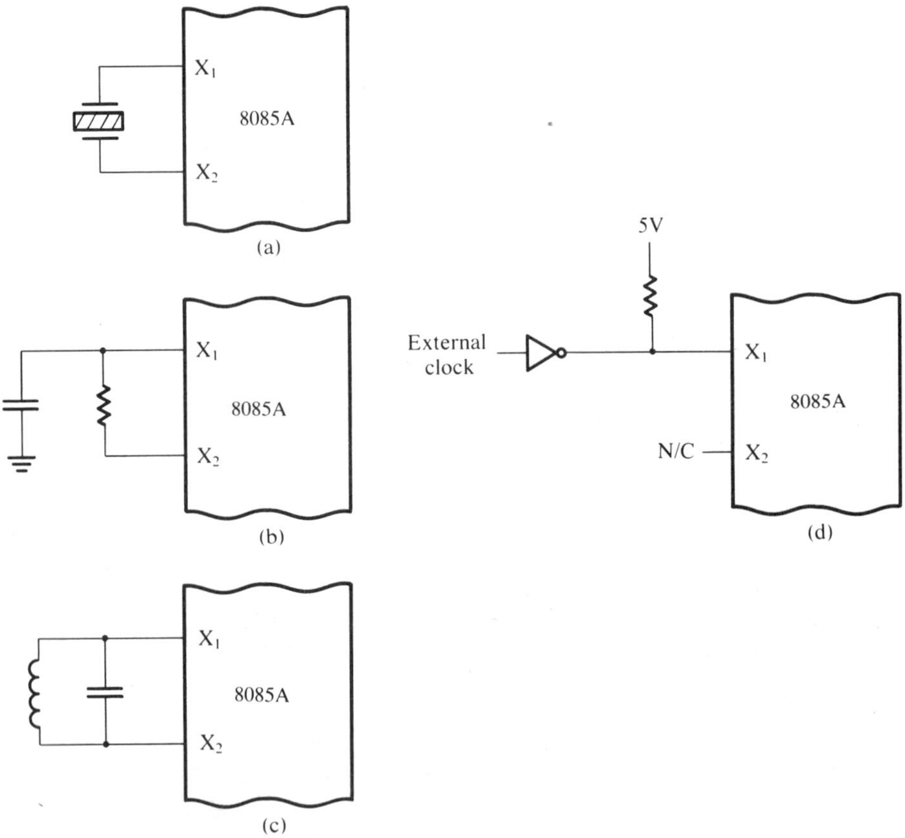

FIGURE 3–2 Methods of obtaining a clock for the Intel 8085A microprocessor: (a) crystal, (b) RC timing, (c) LC timing, (d) external clock.

the microprocessor and develops a peripheral clock signal one-sixth the crystal frequency. The 8086 and 8088 both typically use a clock frequency of 5.0 MHz, so that a 15-MHz crystal is attached to the 8284A to achieve this clock frequency.

ADDRESS BUS CONNECTIONS 3-3

The 8085A, 8086, and 8088 all use a multiplexed address bus. The 8085A multiplexes the least significant half of its 16-bit address bus with the data bus. The 8086 multiplexes all 20 of its address bus connections with the data

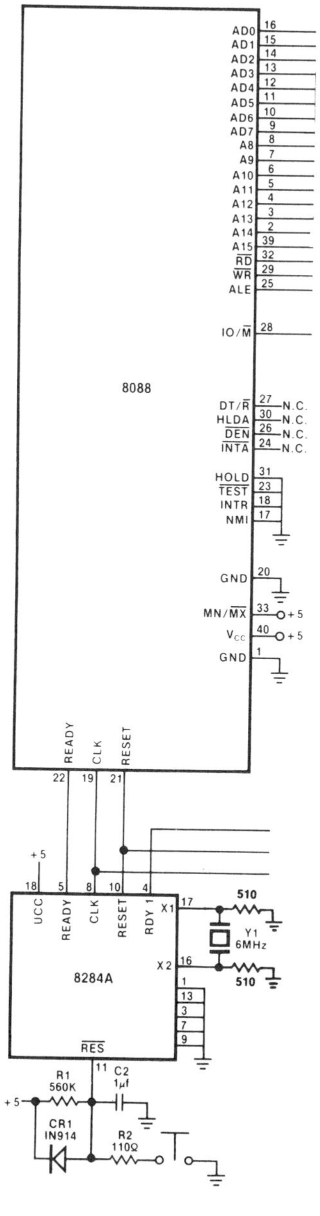

FIGURE 3–3 Obtaining the clock for the Intel 8086/8088 microprocessor using the Intel 8284A clock generator.

SOURCE: Reprinted by permission of Intel Corporation, Copyright 1981.

bus and some status information. The 8088 is a cross between the 8085A and the 8086 in the way that its address bus is multiplexed. The least significant 8 bits of the 20 bits of the address bus are multiplexed with the data bus, and the most significant 4 bits are multiplexed with status information. Refer to figure 3–4 for a more detailed view of this bus in all three microprocessors.

The 8085A can address 64K of memory and 256 different I/O devices through its address bus. Both the 8086 and the 8088 can directly address 1024K bytes of memory and 64K different I/O devices. The 8088 directly addresses bytes of memory, and the 8086 can directly address either bytes or 16-bit words of memory.

3-4 DATA BUS CONNECTIONS

The data bus connections in all three microprocessors are multiplexed with other address information. This is allowable since data flows on this bus only after the memory is given sufficient time to access data. The overall effect of this multiplexed bus has been to reduce the total number of pin connections on these microprocessors. The 8085A and 8088 multiplex the data bus with the least significant half of the address bus, and the 8086 multiplexes its 16-bit data bus with the least significant 16 bits of the address bus.

The address latch enable (ALE) signal in all three cases allows the address bus information to be separated from the data bus information for use in the system. Figure 3–5 illustrates all three processors and the methods used to demultiplex this information. The data bus in these schematics actually still contains memory addressing information, but since it is not used for data, it can be ignored.

Figure 3–6 depicts a method that is sometimes required for buffering the data bus, since the 8088 and 8086 are often used in a large system.

The data bus buffer's direction of data flow is controlled by the microprocessor's Data Transmit/Receive (DT/$\overline{R}$) signal. Normally the direction of data flow is out of the microprocessor through the bus buffers unless a read is occurring. In this case, the DT/$\overline{R}$ signal becomes a logic zero for a read and switches the direction of the data flow through the data bus buffers into the microprocessor. The data enable ($\overline{DEN}$) connection from the 8088 becomes active only when the data bus is to be used by the processor. At all other times, this output is inactive, keeping the 8256 bus transceiver in its high impedance state.

Buffers decrease the amount of time allowed for memory access by 10–20 ns. If this degree of reduction is objectionable, the 74S series TTL circuits (which have a shorter propagation delay time) reduce the time below 10 ns.

3-5 CONTROL BUS CONNECTIONS

The control bus structures of the 8085A and the 8086 and 8088 in the minimum mode are almost identical if the major control signals that accomplish memory and I/O references are compared. In the maximum mode, which

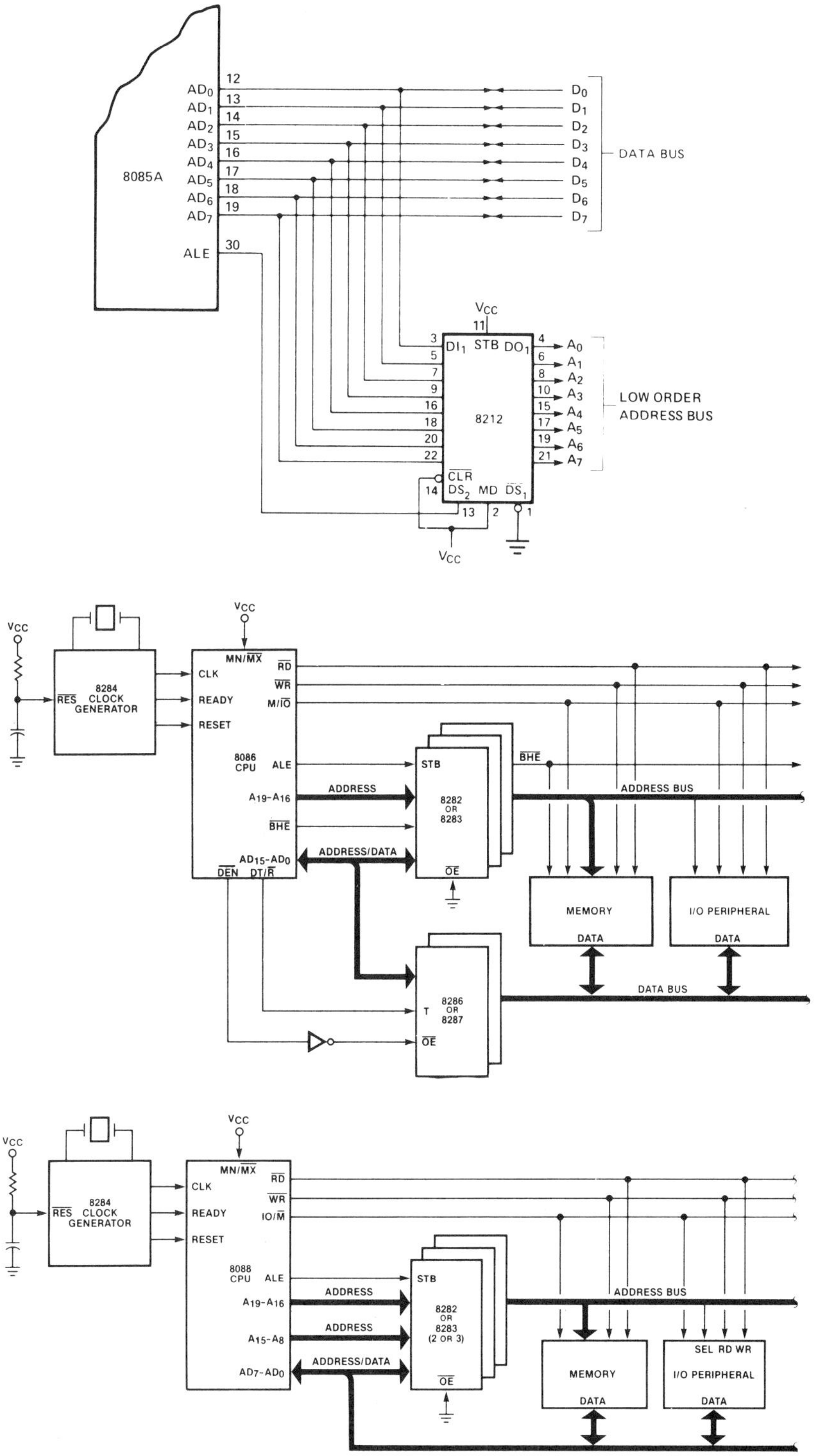

FIGURE 3–4 Bus demultiplexers and buffers for the Intel microprocessors: (a) demultiplexing the 8085A address/data bus, (b) demultiplexing and buffering the 8086 address and data buses, (c) demultiplexing the 8088 address/data bus.

SOURCE: Reprinted by permission of Intel Corporation, Copyright 1978, 1981.

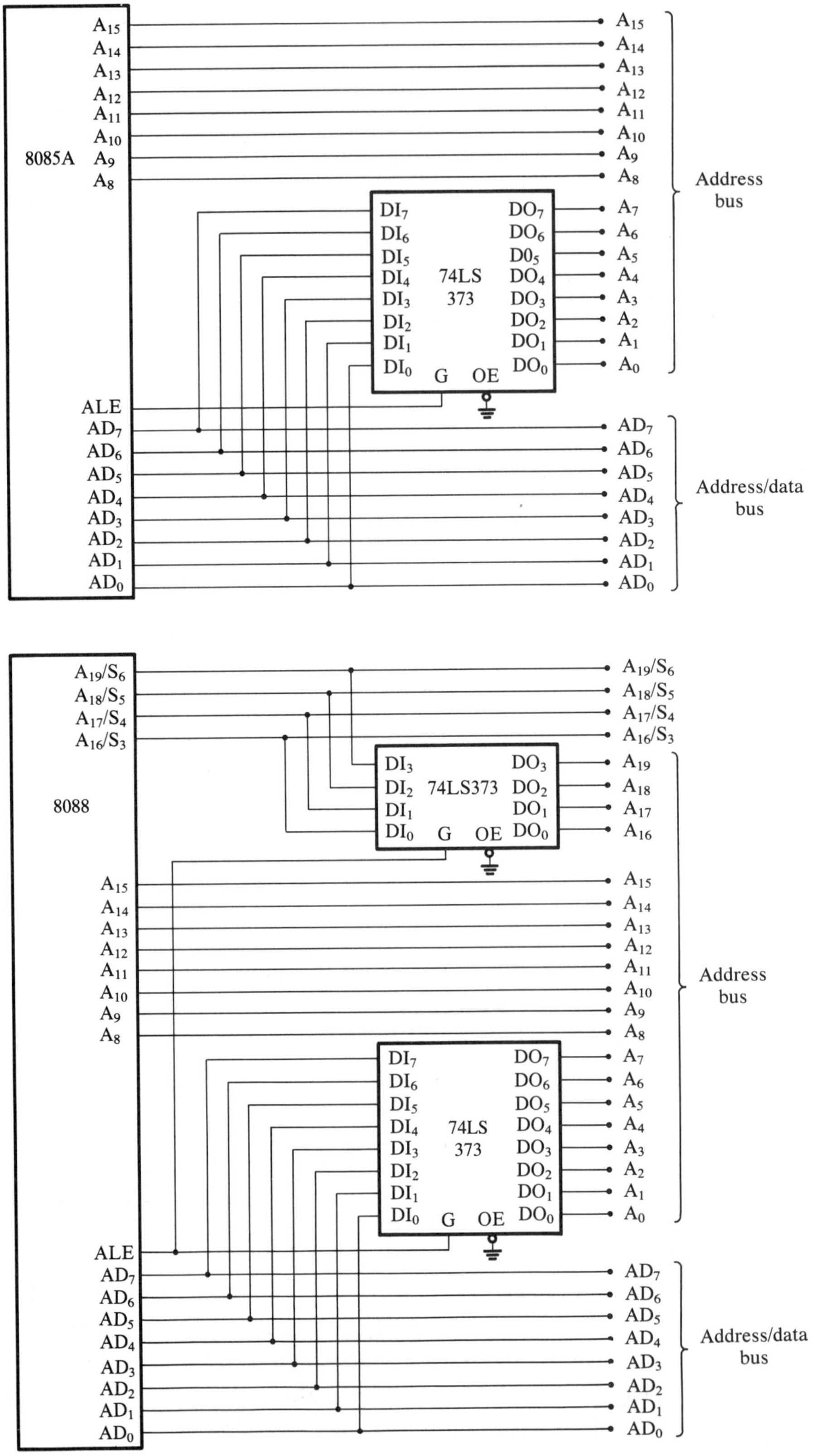

FIGURE 3–5 (a) 8085A and (b) 8088 address/data and address buses.

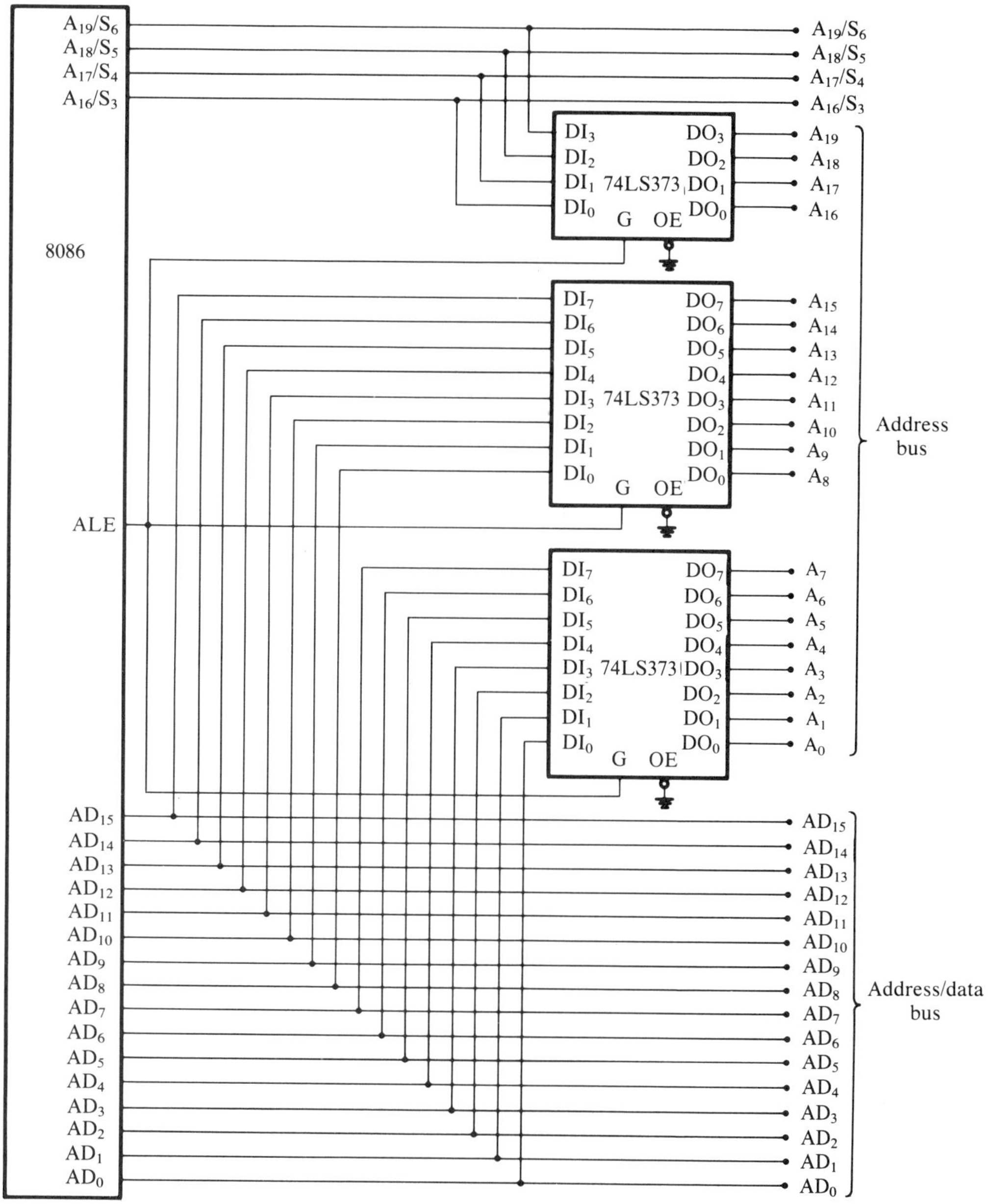

FIGURE 3–5 (c) 8086 address/data and address buses.

requires an external bus controller, the 8086 and 8088 resemble the now-obsolete 8080A. Maximum mode operation allows the 8086 and the 8088 to function in a very large system. Minimum mode operation allows these processors to be used in a smaller dedicated task application. Table 3–2 contrasts the control signals of the 8085A, 8086, and 8088.

In the minimum mode the HOLD and HLDA signals cause and acknowledge a direct memory access (see chapters 8–10).

The $\overline{WR}$ pin is identical in all three cases and times the writing of data to either memory or an I/O device.

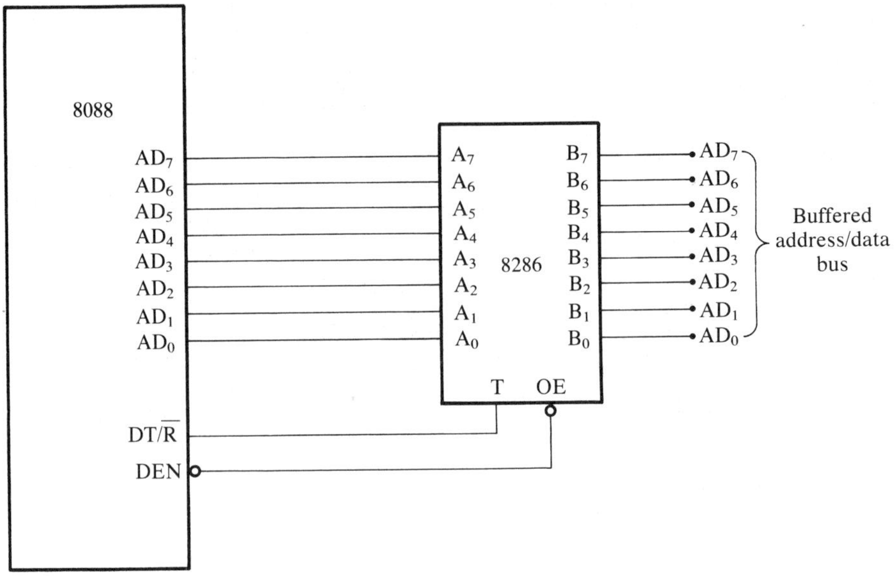

FIGURE 3–6 The 8088 connected to an 8286 octal bus transceiver to create a buffered address/data bus.

The $IO/\overline{M}$ signal is present on all three microprocessors, but it is inverted on the 8086. The 8085A and the 8088, which are 8-bit data bus microprocessors, use the same $IO/\overline{M}$ signal; the 8-bit peripherals designed for the 8085A also function without additional circuitry with the 8088.

Figure 3–7 illustrates the 8085A connected to a 3-to-8 line decoder that generates the four control signals: $\overline{MEMR}$ (memory read), $\overline{MEMW}$ (memory write), $\overline{IOR}$ (I/O read), and $\overline{IOW}$ (I/O write). These control signals appear elsewhere in this book and are, in certain cases, an important change from the standard control bus signals, $\overline{RD}$ (read), $\overline{WR}$ (write), and $IO/\overline{M}$ (I/O or memory).

The $DT/\overline{R}$ and $\overline{DEN}$ signals are only present on the 8086 and the 8088 and control external data bus buffers when the system requires them. $DT/\overline{R}$ controls the direction of the data flow, and $\overline{DEN}$ enables or disables the external buffers. These buffers are normally disabled for a direct memory access.

The $\overline{RD}$ signal, which appears on all three microprocessors for all modes of operation, times the transfer of data into the microprocessor from an external memory or I/O device.

ALE is used to demultiplex the address/data bus and appears in the first clocking period of every bus transfer machine cycle. A *bus transfer machine cycle* is one in which data actually flows into or out of the microprocessor through the data bus. It is important to note that there are some machine cycles that do nothing. These do-nothing cycles are called *bus idle,* or *passive,* cycles during which the bus is idle and can be used for some other operation.

In the 8088 an additional minimum mode control signal, $\overline{SS0}$, has been provided. $\overline{SS0}$, with the $DT/\overline{R}$ and $IO/\overline{M}$ signals, can be decoded to indicate the type of machine cycle that the microprocessor is currently executing (as pictured in table 3–3).

TABLE 3–2 A comparison of the control signals for the 8085A and the 8086/8088.

Signal	8085A	8086/8088
ALE	Used to latch A0 through A7.	Used to latch A0 through A7 in the 8088 and A0 through A15 in the 8086.
$\overline{\text{WR}}$	Write strobe to the bus.	Write strobe to the bus.
$\overline{\text{RD}}$	Read strobe to the bus.	Read strobe to the bus.
HOLD	Input used to request a DMA.	Input used to request a DMA.
HLDA	Output used to acknowledge a DMA.	Output used to acknowledge a DMA.
$\overline{\text{DEN}}$	—	Used to enable the system data bus if external bus buffers are present.
DT/$\overline{\text{R}}$	—	Used to change the direction of data flow through external data bus buffers if present.
IO/$\overline{\text{M}}$	Indicates an I/O or memory operation.	Indicates an I/O or memory operation in the 8088 only.
$\overline{\text{IO}}$/M	—	Indicates an I/O or memory operation in the 8086 only.
INTR	Interrupt request.	Interrupt request.
$\overline{\text{INTA}}$	Acknowledges the INTR.	Acknowledges the INTR.
NMI	(TRAP) on the 8085 is a nonmaskable interrupt input.	Is a nonmaskable interrupt input.
RST 7.5 RST 6.5 RST 5.5	Maskable interrupt inputs.	—
READY	Indicates the bus is ready for a transfer.	Indicates the bus is ready for a transfer.
RESET	$\overline{\text{RESET}}$ causes program execution from 0000H.	Causes program execution from FFFF0H.
MN/$\overline{\text{MX}}$	—	Selects minimum or maximum mode operation.

TABLE 3–3 8086 and 8088 machine cycle types.

IO/$\overline{\text{M}}$	DT/$\overline{\text{R}}$	$\overline{\text{SS0}}$	Function
0	0	0	Code access
0	0	1	Memory read
0	1	0	Memory write
0	1	1	Passive
1	0	0	Interrupt acknowledge
1	0	1	I/O read
1	1	0	I/O write
1	1	1	Halt

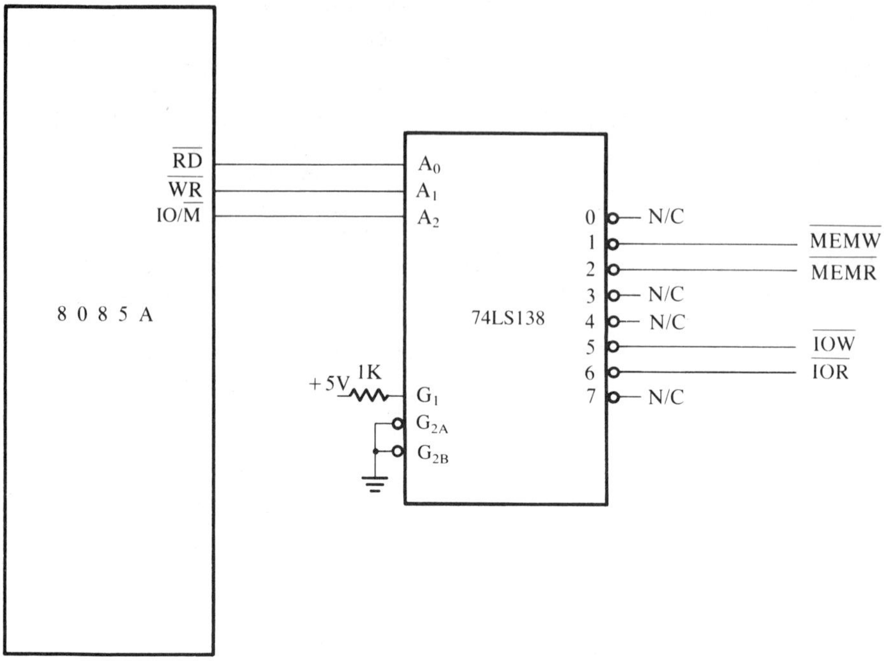

FIGURE 3–7 The 8085A configured to generate the four system control signals $\overline{MEMW}$, $\overline{MEMR}$, $\overline{IOW}$, and $\overline{IOR}$.

In maximum mode operation, both the 8086 and the 8088 require an additional component to function. The 8288 bus controller is needed to generate an expanded set of system control signals. Figure 3–8 compares a minimum mode system with a maximum mode system.

The major difference between these two systems is the memory and I/O control signals. In the minimum mode system, $\overline{RD}$ and $\overline{WR}$ are used to control both the I/O and the memory. In the maximum mode system, four new control signals have been developed for this purpose by the 8288 bus controller. $\overline{MRDC}$ and $\overline{MWTC}$ control the memory, and $\overline{IORC}$ and $\overline{IOWC}$ control the I/O devices. Notice that these signals perform the same functions as the signals developed in figure 3–7 for the 8085A.

The advanced memory and I/O write signals $\overline{AMWC}$ and $\overline{AIOWC}$ are not connected in this example but do find application if the memory or I/O device needs more time to accomplish a write. These advanced signals are issued to allow an external device to begin an early access.

TABLE 3–4 Segment register selection.

S4	S3	Function
0	0	Alternate data
0	1	Stack
1	0	Code
1	1	Data

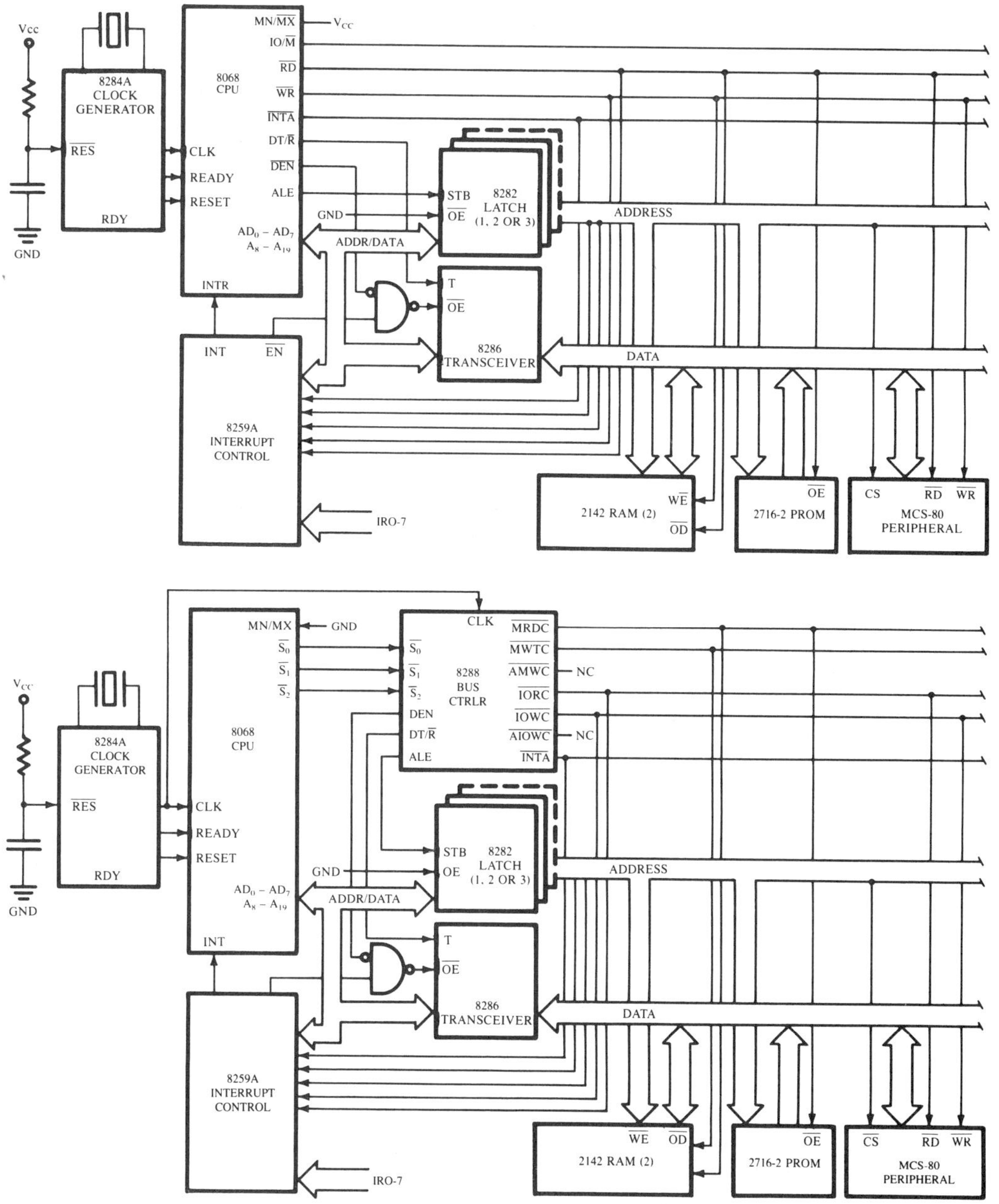

FIGURE 3–8 (a) The 8088 connected to a system in minimum mode operation, (b) the 8088 connected to a system in maximum mode operation.

SOURCE: Reprinted by permission of Intel Corporation, Copyright 1981.

In addition to the new signals generated by the bus controller, four status signals have also been provided. The S3 and S4 status bits indicate which segment register forms the current memory address, as indicated in table 3–4. S5 is exactly the same as the PSW interrupt enable bit, and S6 is always zero.

The $\overline{\text{INTA}}$ signal is used as a strobe whenever an interrupt takes effect. It is used in the 8086 and 8088 to read the interrupt vector from the external hardware and in the 8085 to read a RST or a CALL instruction from the external hardware.

3-6 RESET

The 8085A Reset

The 8085A is reset by placing a logic zero on the active low $\overline{\text{RESET IN}}$ pin. This input must be held at a logic zero level for at least 10 ms after the power supply connection to Vcc has reached 5 V; if it is not held low for this length of time, Intel does not guarantee a reset. In addition to the reset input, Intel provides a RESET OUT connection to reset other devices in a system. Table 3–5 illustrates the internal circuits initialized by the $\overline{\text{RESET IN}}$ signal. It is important to note that the program counter is cleared to zero on a reset. This causes the instruction at memory location zero to be executed after a $\overline{\text{RESET IN}}$.

TABLE 3–5 The effect of the 8085A $\overline{\text{RESET IN}}$ signal.

Circuit	Reset/Set
Program counter	Reset
Instruction register	Reset
INTE flip-flop	Reset
RST 7.5 flip-flop	Reset
TRAP flip-flop	Reset
SOD flip-flop	Reset
Machine state flip-flop	Reset
Machine cycle flip-flop	Reset
Internally latched flip-flops for HOLD, INTR, and READY	Reset
RST 5.5 mask	Set
RST 6.5 mask	Set
RST 7.5 mask	Set

The 8086 and 8088 Reset

The 8086 and the 8088 are reset by placing a logic one on the active high RESET pin. This pin must be held at this level for at least four clocking periods, except after power on, where it must be held for 50 μs to guarantee a reset. Table 3–6 illustrates the internal effect of a reset. The first instruction executed after a reset is at location FFFF0 because the code segment register is set to an FFFF and the instruction pointer is cleared to a zero.

A Typical Power on Clearing Circuit

The output of the power on clearing circuit (see figure 3–9) is connected to the active low reset input of an 8085A or to the $\overline{\text{RES}}$ input of the 8284A clock generator of the 8086 or 8088 system. The 8284A clock generator contains a circuit that inverts this signal and generates the RESET input for the 8086 or 8088.

TABLE 3–6 The effect of the 8086 and 8088 RESET signal.

Circuit	Condition
Flags	Cleared
Instruction pointer	0000
Code segment register	FFFF
Data segment register	0000
Stack segment register	0000
Extra segment register	0000
Queue	Empty

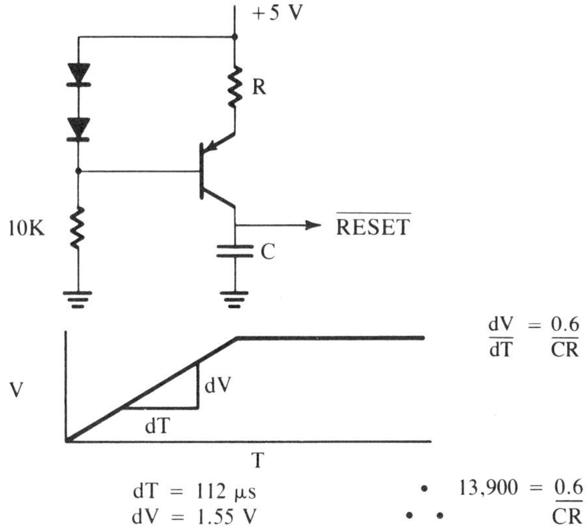

FIGURE 3–9 A typical power on clearing circuit for a microprocessor.

BUS TIMING 3-7

If the 8085A is operated with a 3 MHz clock, it takes 1 μs to transfer a byte of information to or from the I/O or the memory. It takes the 8085A three of its clocking cycles to transfer a byte of information. The 8086 and 8088 require four clocking periods to accomplish the transfer of a byte for the 8088 and 16 bits for the 8086. It would seem that these microprocessors are slower than the 8085A, but this is not the case since the clocking period is typically 200 ns. At this rate a bus transfer occurs in 800 ns, rather than the 1 μs rate for the 8085A.

8085A Read Timing

Figure 3–10 pictures the basic read timing diagrams for the 8085A. It also illustrates the AC timing characteristics for these waveforms. The read timing diagram is divided into clocking states (labeled T1, T2, and T3). These three states comprise one 8085A bus cycle.

During clocking state T1 the memory address or an I/O port number is issued to the system. During this state the microprocessor also sends out the ALE signal to demultiplex the address/data bus. It is important to note that

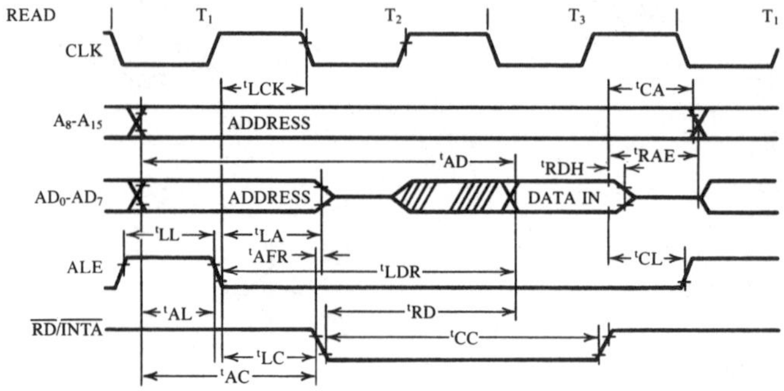

8085AH, 8085AH-2: (T_A = 0°C to 70°C, V_{CC} = 5V ±10%, V_{SS} = OV)*
8085AH-1: (T_A = 0°C to 70°C, V_{CC} = 5V ±5%, V_{SS} = 0V)

Symbol	Parameter	8085AH[2] (Final)		8085AH-2[2] (Final)		8085AH-1 (Preliminary)		Units
		Min.	Max.	Min.	Max.	Min.	Max.	
t_{CYC}	CLK Cycle Period	320	2000	200	2000	167	2000	ns
t_1	CLK Low Time (Standard CLK Loading)	80		40		20		ns
t_2	CLK High Time (Standard CLK Loading)	120		70		50		ns
t_r, t_f	CLK Rise and Fall Time		30		30		30	ns
t_{XKR}	X_1 Rising to CLK Rising	25	120	25	100	20	100	ns
t_{XKF}	X_1 Rising to CLK Falling	30	150	30	110	25	110	ns
t_{AC}	A_{8-15} Valid to Leading Edge of Control[1]	270		115		70		ns
t_{ACL}	A_{0-7} Valid to Leading Edge of Control	240		115		60		ns
t_{AD}	A_{0-15} Valid to Valid Data In		575		350		225	ns
t_{AFR}	Address Float After Leading Edge of $\overline{READ}$ ($\overline{INTA}$)		0		0		0	ns
t_{AL}	A_{8-15} Valid Before Trailing Edge of ALE [1]	115		50		25		ns

***Note:** For Extended Temperature EXPRESS use M8085AH Electricals Parameters.

FIGURE 3–10 The 8085A read timing diagram and AC characteristics.

SOURCE: Reprinted by permission of Intel Corporation, Copyright 1983.

ALE becomes a logic one before the address is available, which means that a positive edge triggered latch cannot demultiplex this information. Instead most systems use a positive gated transparent latch.

During timing state T2 the read control signal $\overline{RD}$ is sent to the system. In this state the 8085A also samples the READY input to see whether or not a wait state is required for the current bus transfer. This state allows the memory time to access data and to accomplish some internal operations.

Data is transferred through the data bus connections during state T3 and the microprocessor samples or reads the data present on the data bus at this time. This data comes either from a memory device or an external input device.

Symbol	Parameter	8085AH[2] (Final)		8085AH-2[2] (Final)		8085AH-1 (Preliminary)		Units
		Min.	Max.	Min.	Max.	Min.	Max.	
t_{ALL}	A_{0-7} Valid Before Trailing Edge of ALE	90		50		25		ns
t_{ARY}	READY Valid from Address Valid		220		100		40	ns
t_{CA}	Address (A_{8-15}) Valid After Control	120		60		30		ns
t_{CC}	Width of Control Low ($\overline{\text{RD}}$, $\overline{\text{WR}}$, $\overline{\text{INTA}}$) Edge of ALE	400		230		150		ns
t_{CL}	Trailing Edge of Control to Leading Edge of ALE	50		25		0		ns
t_{DW}	Data Valid to Trailing Edge of $\overline{\text{WRITE}}$	420		230		140		ns
t_{HABE}	HLDA to Bus Enable		210		150		150	ns
t_{HABF}	Bus Float After HLDA		210		150		150	ns
t_{HACK}	HLDA Valid to Trailing Edge of CLK	110		40		0		ns
t_{HDH}	HOLD Hold Time	0		0		0		ns
t_{HDS}	HOLD Setup Time to Trailing Edge of CLK	170		120		120		ns
t_{INH}	INTR Hold Time	0		0		0		ns
t_{INS}	INTR, RST, and TRAP Setup Time to Falling Edge of CLK	160		150		150		ns
t_{LA}	Address Hold Time After ALE	100		50		20		ns
t_{LC}	Trailing Edge of ALE to Leading Edge of Control	130		60		25		ns
t_{LCK}	ALE Low During CLK High	100		50		15		ns
t_{LDR}	ALE to Valid Data During Read		460		270		175	ns
t_{LDW}	ALE to Valid Data During Write		200		120		110	ns
t_{LL}	ALE Width	140		80		50		ns
t_{LRY}	ALE to READY Stable		110		30		10	ns
t_{RAE}	Trailing Edge of $\overline{\text{READ}}$ to Re-Enabling of Address	150		90		50		ns
t_{RD}	$\overline{\text{READ}}$ (or $\overline{\text{INTA}}$) to Valid Data		300		150		75	ns
t_{RV}	Control Trailing Edge to Leading Edge of Next Control	400		220		160		ns
t_{RDH}	Data Hold Time After $\overline{\text{READ}}$ $\overline{\text{INTA}}$	0		0		0		ns
t_{RYH}	READY Hold Time	0		0		5		ns
t_{RYS}	READY Setup Time to Leading Edge of CLK	110		100		100		ns
t_{WD}	Data Valid After Trailing Edge of $\overline{\text{WRITE}}$	100		60		30		ns
t_{WDL}	LEADING Edge of $\overline{\text{WRITE}}$ to Data Valid		40		20		30	ns

FIGURE 3–10 *continued*

8085A Read Control Signal Timing

In the 8085A the amount of time allowed for the memory or the I/O to access data is TAD time, which amounts to 575 ns at the highest allowable clocking rate. Most memory devices have an access time of 450 ns or less, making them compatible with the 8085A.

Another critical time in most memory devices is TRD time in the 8085A timing diagram. The 8085A allows 300 ns for the memory device to respond from the leading edge, one-to-zero transition, of the $\overline{RD}$ signal. Most memory devices require a minimum of 150 ns to interface easily with the 8085A.

The last timing interval of importance to memory or I/O interface is the turn off delay time of the memory device's output buffers. Most memory devices have a turn off delay time no greater than 120 ns. Examining the timing diagram for the 8085A shows the allowable turn off time TRAE, which is 150 ns, will leave a 30-ns margin.

8085A Write Timing

Figure 3–11 illustrates the basic write timing for the 8085A microprocessor. The trailing edge of the write pulse $\overline{WR}$ is usually the portion of the waveform that causes a write to occur and is a reference in RAM memory timing diagrams.

The data is valid on the data bus 450 ns before the trailing edge of the $\overline{WR}$ strobe in the 8085A. This same data is valid only 100 ns after the trailing edge of $\overline{WR}$. Fortunately the data hold time requirement in most memory devices is 0 ns, so that this time presents no problem when selecting a RAM. The duration of time that data must be present before the trailing edge of $\overline{WR}$ varies from RAM to RAM.

Minimum Mode 8086 and 8088 Read Timing

Figure 3–12 illustrates the basic read timing diagram and the AC characteristics for the 8086 and 8088 microprocessors. These microprocessors differ from the 8085A in that it takes four clock states for a bus cycle, as opposed to three for the 8085A.

State T1 provides the system with the ALE pulse and memory address on both the address bus and the address/data bus. In addition to ALE, DT/$\overline{R}$ becomes a logic zero for data receive.

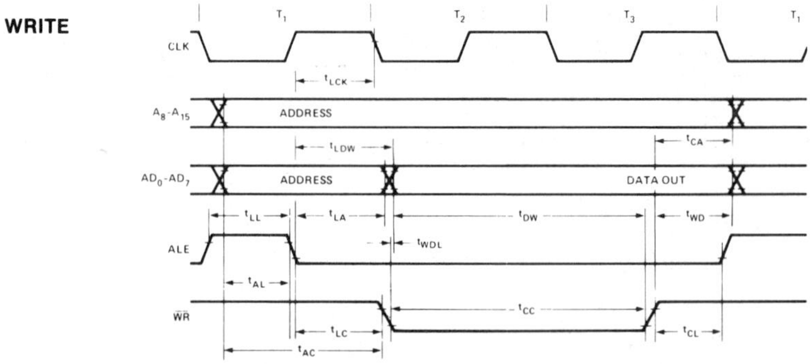

FIGURE 3–11 The 8085A write timing diagram.

SOURCE: Reprinted by permission of Intel Corporation, Copyright 1983.

BUS TIMING—MINIMUM MODE SYSTEM

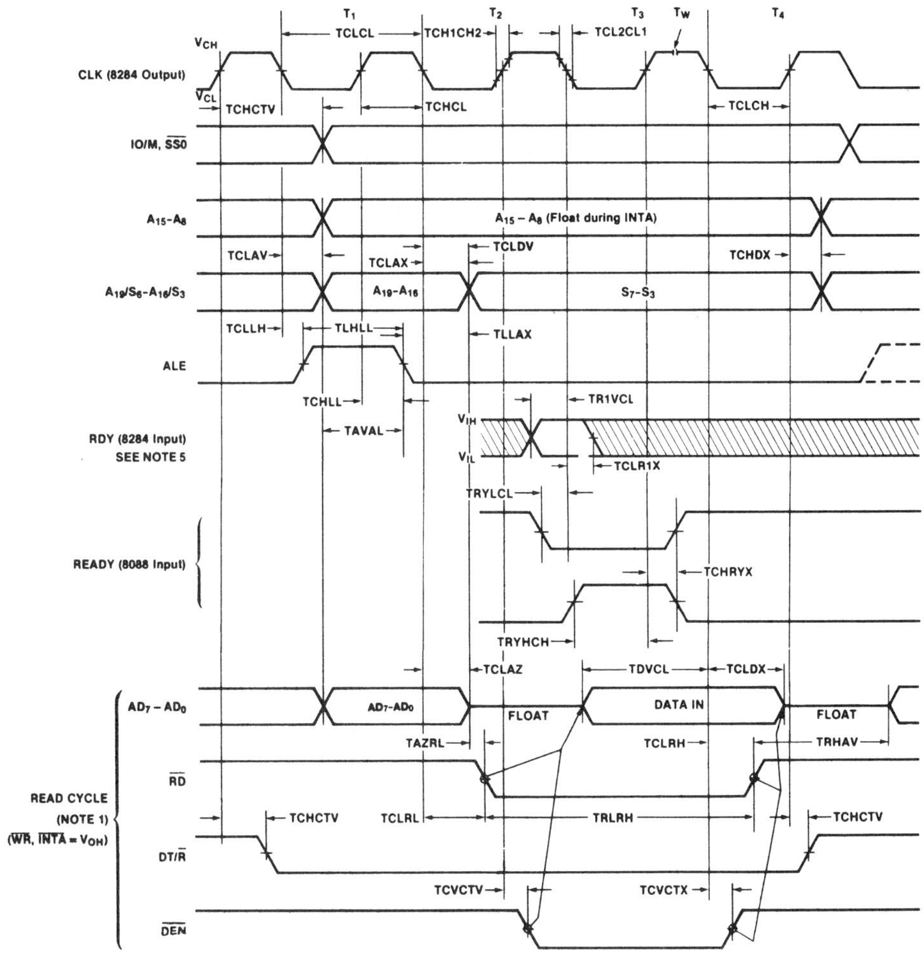

FIGURE 3–12 The 8086 read timing diagram and AC characteristics.
SOURCE: Reprinted by permission of Intel Corporation, Copyright 1983.

In state T2, the $\overline{RD}$ signal is issued to the memory or I/O to begin a memory or I/O read. The $\overline{DEN}$ signal is also activated during this clock cycle, activating the external data bus buffer.

States T3 and T4 provide time for the information to be read from the external memory or I/O device. The data bus is sampled by the microprocessor in the middle of T3 and on into T4. This is required by the increased speed of these processors.

Minimum Mode 8086 and 8088 Read Control Signal Timing

The access times allowed for the memory and I/O devices are understandably shorter for these microprocessors than for the 8085A because of the increased clock frequency. The time allowed to the memory or I/O by the 8086 or 8088 microprocessor is approximately 460 ns at the highest allowable

(8086: T_A = 0°C to 70°C, V_{CC} = 5V ± 10%)
(8086-1: T_A = 0°C to 70°C, V_{CC} = 5V ± 5%)
(8086-2: T_A = 0°C to 70°C, V_{CC} = 5V ± 5%)

MINIMUM COMPLEXITY SYSTEM TIMING REQUIREMENTS

Symbol	Parameter	8086		8086-1 (Preliminary)		8086-2		Units
		Min.	Max.	Min.	Max.	Min.	Max.	
TCLCL	CLK Cycle Period	200	500	100	500	125	500	ns
TCLCH	CLK Low Time	118		53		68		ns
TCHCL	CLK High Time	69		39		44		ns
TCH1CH2	CLK Rise Time		10		10		10	ns
TCL2CL1	CLK Fall Time		10		10		10	ns
TDVCL	Data in Setup Time	30		5		20		ns
TCLDX	Data in Hold Time	10		10		10		ns
TR1VCL	RDY Setup Time into 8284A (See Notes 1, 2)	35		35		35		ns
TCLR1X	RDY Hold Time into 8284A (See Notes 1, 2)	0		0		0		ns
TRYHCH	READY Setup Time into 8086	118		53		68		ns
TCHRYX	READY Hold Time into 8086	30		20		20		ns
TRYLCL	READY Inactive to CLK (See Note 3)	−8		−10		−8		ns
THVCH	HOLD Setup Time	35		20		20		ns
TINVCH	INTR, NMI, $\overline{\text{TEST}}$ Setup Time (See Note 2)	30		15		15		ns
TILIH	Input Rise Time (Except CLK)		20		20		20	ns
TIHIL	Input Fall Time (Except CLK)		12		12		12	ns

FIGURE 3–12 *continued*

clocking frequency. Since the access time is barely longer than 450 ns, some problems may occur in interfacing standard 450 ns memory. A margin of about 20 ns must be maintained between the actual access time of the memory component and the access time allowed to the memory component by the processor. If not, reliable operation is doubtful. In this case, it is wise to choose a memory component with an access time of less than 450 ns.

These processors allow the memory 285 ns of time to be enabled from the $\overline{\text{RD}}$ strobe signal; whereas the 8085A allows 300 ns. Any of these is adequate, since most memory devices require 150 ns or less from the $\overline{\text{RD}}$ strobe.

The 8086 and 8088 allow the memory output buffers TRHAV time, or 255 ns, to turn off or three-state. Most memory devices require only 120 ns.

Minimum Mode 8086 and 8088 Write Timing

Figure 3–13 illustrates the basic write timing for the 8086 and 8088 microproc-

TIMING RESPONSES

Symbol	Parameter	8086		8086-1 (Preliminary)		8086-2		Units
		Min.	Max.	Min.	Max.	Min.	Max.	
TCLAV	Address Valid Delay	10	110	10	50	10	60	ns
TCLAX	Address Hold Time	10		10		10		ns
TCLAZ	Address Float Delay	TCLAX	80	10	40	TCLAX	50	ns
TLHLL	ALE Width	TCLCH−20		TCLCH−10		TCLCH-10		ns
TCLLH	ALE Active Delay		80		40		50	ns
TCHLL	ALE Inactive Delay		85		45		55	ns
TLLAX	Address Hold Time to ALE Inactive	TCHCL−10		TCHCL−10		TCHCL−10		ns
TCLDV	Data Valid Delay	10	110	10	50	10	60	ns
TCHDX	Data Hold Time	10		10		10		ns
TWHDX	Data Hold Time After WR	TCLCH−30		TCLCH−25		TCLCH−30		ns
TCVCTV	Control Active Delay 1	10	110	10	50	10	70	ns
TCHCTV	Control Active Delay 2	10	110	10	45	10	60	ns
TCVCTX	Control Inactive Delay	10	110	10	50	10	70	ns
TAZRL	Address Float to READ Active	0		0		0		ns
TCLRL	$\overline{RD}$ Active Delay	10	165	10	70	10	100	ns
TCLRH	$\overline{RD}$ Inactive Delay	10	150	10	60	10	80	ns
TRHAV	$\overline{RD}$ Inactive to Next Address Active	TCLCL−45		TCLCL−35		TCLCL−40		ns
TCLHAV	HLDA Valid Delay	10	160	10	60	10	100	ns
TRLRH	$\overline{RD}$ Width	2TCLCL−75		2TCLCL−40		2TCLCL−50		ns
TWLWH	$\overline{WR}$ Width	2TCLCL−60		2TCLCL−35		2TCLCL−40		ns
TAVAL	Address Valid to ALE Low	TCLCH−60		TCLCH−35		TCLCH−40		ns
TOLOH	Output Rise Time		20		20		20	ns
TOHOL	Output Fall Time		12		12		12	ns

NOTES:
1. Signal at 8284A shown for reference only.
2. Setup requirement for asynchronous signal only to guarantee recognition at next CLK.
3. Applies only to T2 state. (8 ns into T3).

FIGURE 3–12 *continued*

essors, which differs little from that of the 8085A. The main difference is the extra clocking state T4, which allows more writing time to the memory.

The only significant differences in read and write timing are the logic level of the DT/$\overline{R}$ signal and the activation of the $\overline{WR}$ strobe instead of the $\overline{RD}$ strobe. The data is valid at the data bus for 340 ns before the trailing edge of the $\overline{WR}$ strobe and 39 ns after the trailing edge. These times present no major problem in interfacing, since the data hold time on a memory component is usually 0 ns. The data setup time, of course, will vary from one memory component to another.

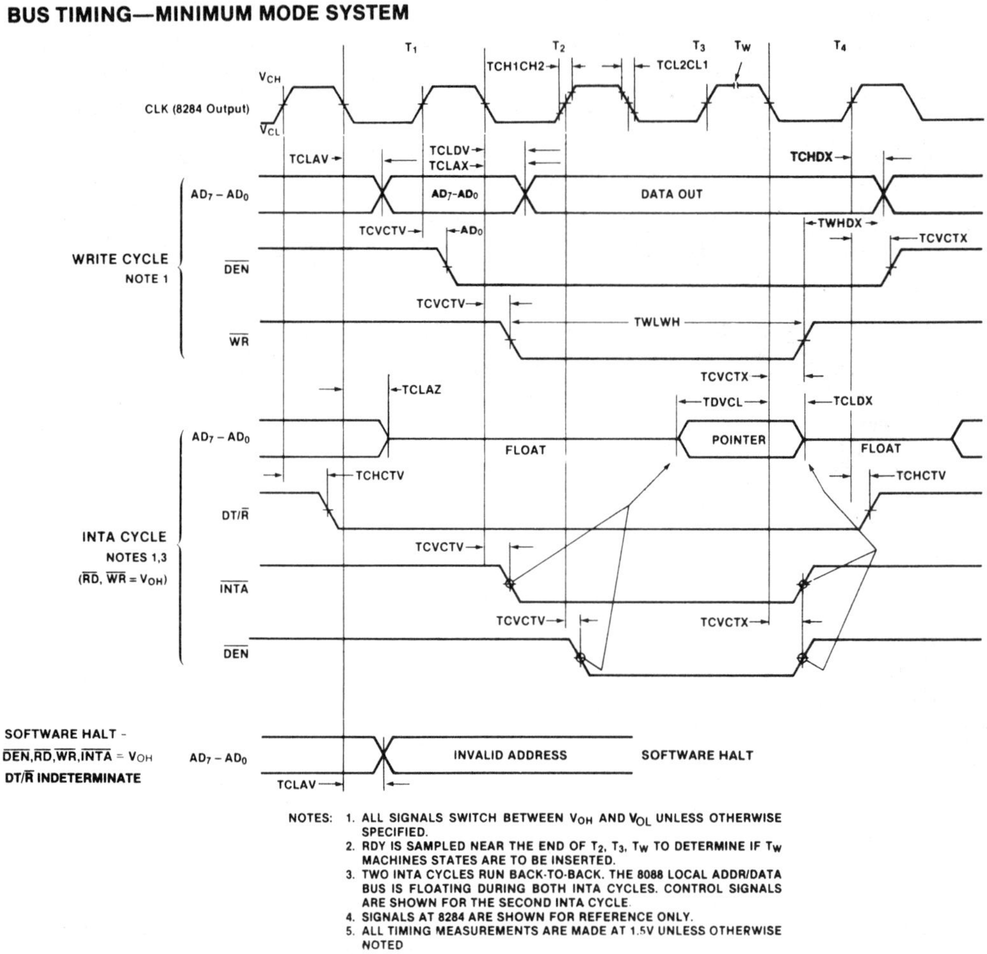

FIGURE 3–13 The 8086 write timing diagram.

SOURCE: Reprinted by permission of Intel Corporation, Copyright 1983.

3-8 MAXIMUM MODE 8086/8088 OPERATION

In the maximum mode the 8284 bus controller develops the control bus signals discussed earlier. The timing for these control signals is illustrated in figure 3–14 and is almost identical to the timing in the minimum mode illustrated in the last section.

New signals that are used for systems with multiple processors on the system bus have replaced the HOLD and HLDA connections on the 8086 and 8088. The $\overline{RQ}/\overline{GT0}$ and $\overline{RQ}/\overline{GT1}$ interface either the 8089 I/O coprocessor or the 8087 arithmetic coprocessor to the microprocessor. Since these request/grant signal lines are synchronous control lines, all processors must be referenced to the same system clock.

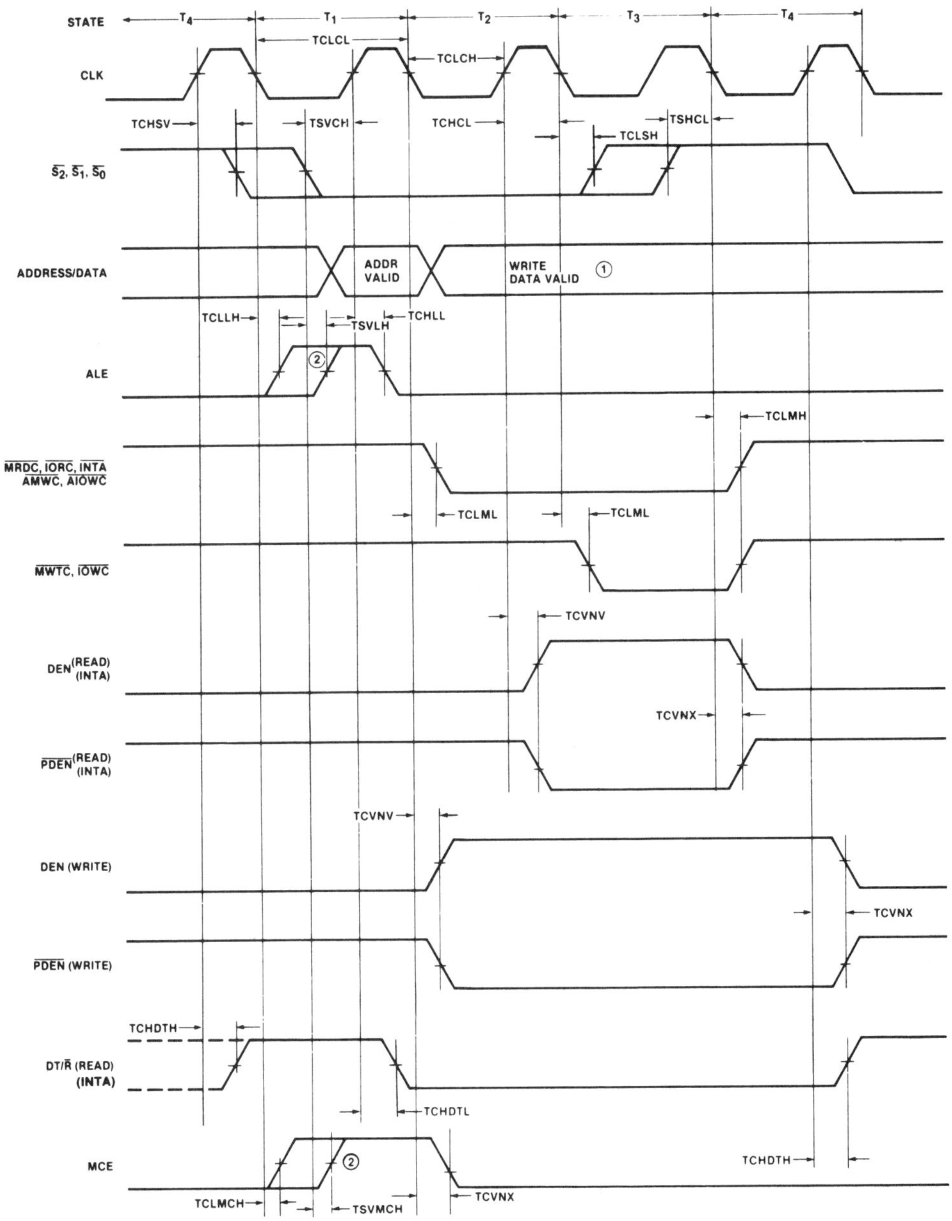

NOTES:
1. ADDRESS/DATA BUS IS SHOWN ONLY FOR REFERENCE PURPOSES.
2. LEADING EDGE OF ALE AND MCE IS DETERMINED BY THE FALLING EDGE OF CLK OR STATUS GOING ACTIVE, WHICHEVER OCCURS LAST.
3. ALL TIMING MEASUREMENTS ARE MADE AT 1.5V UNLESS SPECIFIED OTHERWISE.

FIGURE 3–14 The timing diagram of the 8288 Bus Controller.

SOURCE: Reprinted by permission of Intel Corporation, Copyright 1983.

Another connection provided in maximum mode is the $\overline{\text{LOCK}}$ connection. This output is used with the 8289 bus arbiter in shared bus systems to lock the bus so that an instruction can be completely executed without intervention from the arbiter. The lock is induced under software control by prefixing an instruction with the lock prefix.

Finally, there are two outputs to track the internal queue, if required. The QS1 and QS0 pins indicate the condition of the internal FIFO or queue register after the indicated activity occurs. Table 3–7 illustrates the bit decoding pattern for these two status signals.

TABLE 3–7 Queue status.

QS1	QS0	Function
0	0	No operation
0	1	First byte of op-code
1	0	Empty queue
1	1	Subsequent byte

3-9 INTERRUPTS

8085A Interrupts

The 8085A microprocessor has a very powerful interrupt structure capable of handling five different external interrupting devices. One of these inputs is nonmaskable while the other four are maskable. They all have a fixed priority scheme, which is presented in table 3–8.

TABLE 3–8 8085A interrupt information.

Name	Priority	Address	Sensitivity
TRAP	1	24H	Rising edge and high level
RST 7.5	2	3CH	Rising edge
RST 6.5	3	34H	High level
RST 5.5	4	2CH	High level
INTR	5	*	High level

NOTE: *The address CALLed by this input is determined by the external hardware.

Each of the interrupt inputs, except INTR, causes the 8085A to generate internally a 1-byte CALL instruction called a *RESTART*. The addresses for these restarts are listed in the table with the type of triggering required to activate each of the interrupt inputs.

Whenever the 8085A accepts an interrupt, all future interrupts are disabled except TRAP, the nonmaskable interrupt. Unless the interrupt service subroutine reenables the interrupts before a return occurs, no more interrupts can ever take effect.

The INTR input is internally decoded to produce a pulse on the $\overline{\text{INTA}}$ output whenever it is accepted. This strobe occurs in lieu of an internally generated input and is used to fetch a RESTART or CALL instruction from external hardware. Figure 3–15 pictures a simple circuit for gating an RST 5 into the microprocessor in response to an INTR pulse.

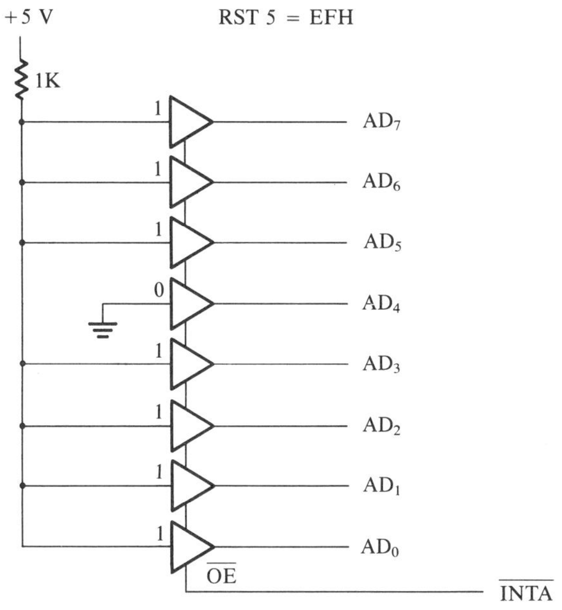

FIGURE 3–15 A circuit that will force a RST 5 onto the data bus in response to an interrupt request.

8086 and 8088 Interrupts

The interrupt structure of the 8086 and 8088 is more powerful than that of the 8085A, which has many more levels of interrupts. The 8086 and 8088 have two hardware interrupt inputs, a nonmaskable interrupt input (NMI) and INTR, which is similar to the interrupt input of the 8085A.

The NMI input is always active; whenever it is pulsed high, it causes an interrupt to the interrupt service subroutine pointed to by Vector 2. When this interrupt is accepted, it disables the INTR pin, pushes the contents of the flag register onto the stack, and calls the interrupt service subroutine.

An interrupt vector is a 4-byte-long entry into a table in memory locations 00000H through 003FFH. Two values are stored in this table at each active interrupt vector: the instruction pointer (IP) in the first 2 bytes, followed by the code segment (CS) register. Intel reserves interrupt vectors 5 through 31 for use in present and future Intel products; these should not be used if an Intel product will ever be connected to the 8086 or 8088. Table 3–9 illustrates the interrupt vectors.

The INTR interrupt input is level sensitive and must be held active until recognized by the microprocessor. It works in the same manner that the INTR pin functions on the 8085A. When accepted, the $\overline{INTA}$ output or acknowledge signal pulses twice. During the first pulse the processor locks out all other arbiters in the system, so that the bus is not accessed by another processor. During the second pulse of the $\overline{INTA}$ pin, the external hardware must provide an 8-bit interrupt vector to the microprocessor. The vector is applied to the least significant half of the data bus during the second pulse of $\overline{INTA}$. Figure 3–16 pictures a simple circuit for causing an interrupt vector 128 base ten to the data bus.

TABLE 3–9 8086/8088 interrupt vector table.

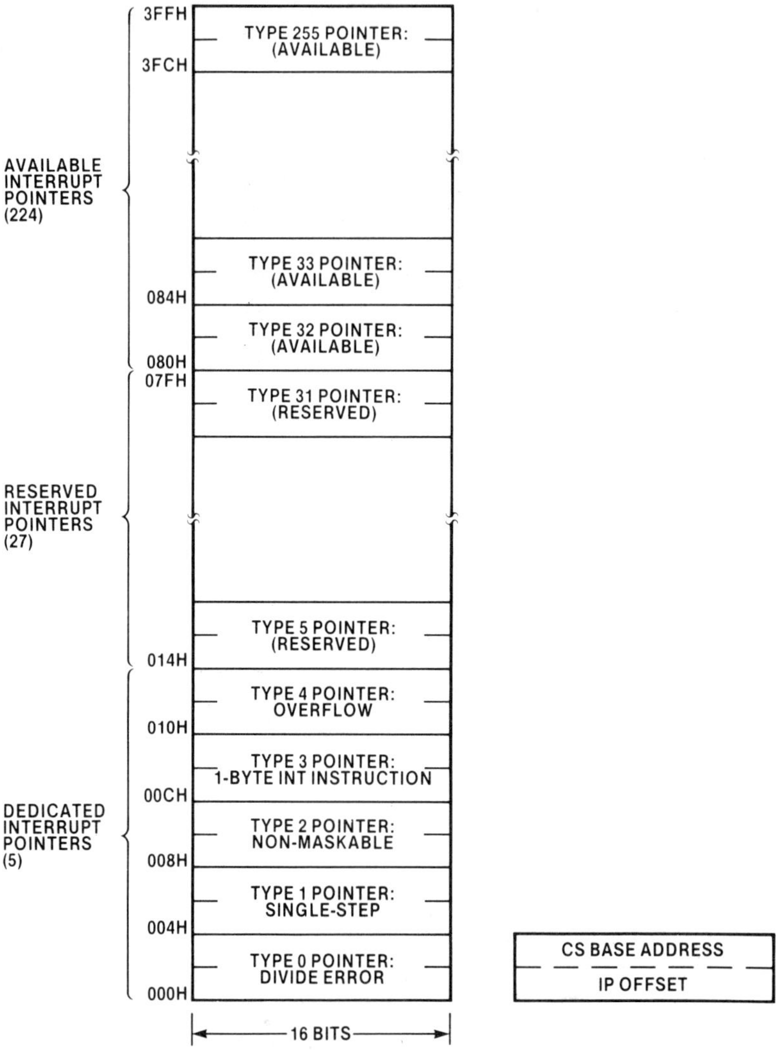

SOURCE: (Reprinted by permission of Intel Corporation, copyright 1981)

3-10 DIRECT MEMORY ACCESS CONNECTIONS

The 8085A uses the same type of control signals for DMA as the 8086 or 8088 in minimum mode. The HOLD input and the HLDA output are used to gain access to the microprocessor buses for a DMA.

When the HOLD input is accepted by the microprocessor, it relinquishes control of the memory and I/O connected to its buses by floating the address

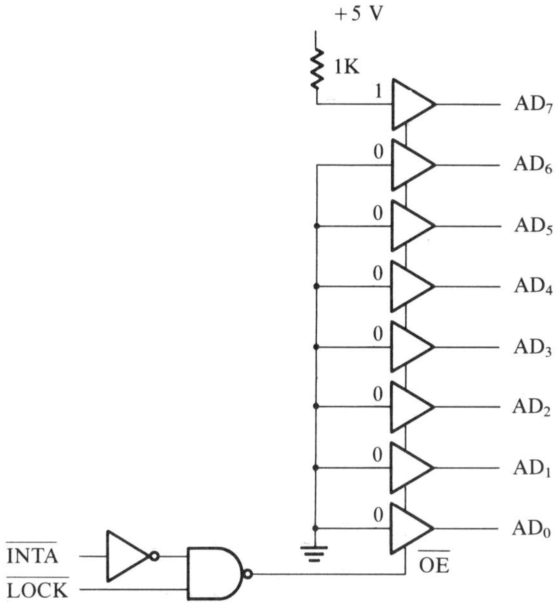

FIGURE 3–16 A circuit that will force interrupt vector 128 onto the data bus in response to an interrupt request.

bus, data bus, and control bus to their high impedance state. This effectively disconnects the microprocessor from the system.

Once the microprocessor has three-stated its buses, the external device is signaled through the HLDA output. HLDA indicates that the microprocessor has indeed released the memory and I/O for external usage. Once HLDA is active, the external device gains complete control of the microprocessor's address and I/O space. The external device is then free to manipulate the I/O circuitry and the memory.

MISCELLANEOUS 8085A PIN CONNECTIONS 3-11

SID and SOD

The SID and SOD connections on the 8085A are used as 1-bit I/O ports. Serial input data (SID) can be sampled by executing the RIM instruction. This leaves the value of the SID pin in the sign bit position of the accumulator after a RIM instruction.

Serial output data (SOD) is controlled by placing the desired level in the sign bit of the accumulator and a logic one in the next bit position. When the SIM instruction is executed, the content of the sign bit is latched into the SOD pin.

S0 and S1

S0 and S1 are two status bits provided on the 8085A. These bits indicate, in conjunction with the IO/$\overline{M}$ signal, the current type of machine cycle, as listed in table 3–10.

TABLE 3–10 8085A machine cycle status.

IO/$\overline{M}$	S1	S0	Status
0	0	0	Halt
0	0	1	Memory write
0	1	0	Memory read
0	1	1	Op-code fetch
1	0	0	Halt
1	0	1	I/O write
1	1	0	I/O read
1	1	1	Interrupt acknowledge

READY

The READY input slows the microprocessor so that a slower memory or I/O device can be used in the system. In normal operation, this pin is held at a logic one level.

If the READY pin is held at a logic zero level, the microprocessor will wait for an indefinite period of time. This waiting period is measured in multiples of the processor clock. When the pin is returned to its logic one state, all processing continues in the normal mode.

This pin can cause single step operation and implement the run/stop function. Figure 3–17 illustrates its use in the run/stop function on an 8085A microprocessor.

3-12 MISCELLANEOUS 8086 AND 8088 PIN CONNECTIONS

The $\overline{\text{TEST}}$ input is tested by the WAIT instruction. If the $\overline{\text{TEST}}$ pin is a logic one, or inactive, the WAIT instruction will cause the microprocessor to stop executing instructions until the $\overline{\text{TEST}}$ pin is grounded. Although in most applications this pin is grounded, it has interesting uses.

FIGURE 3–17 A circuit that will allow the 8085A to be stopped at any instant in time without the loss of data.

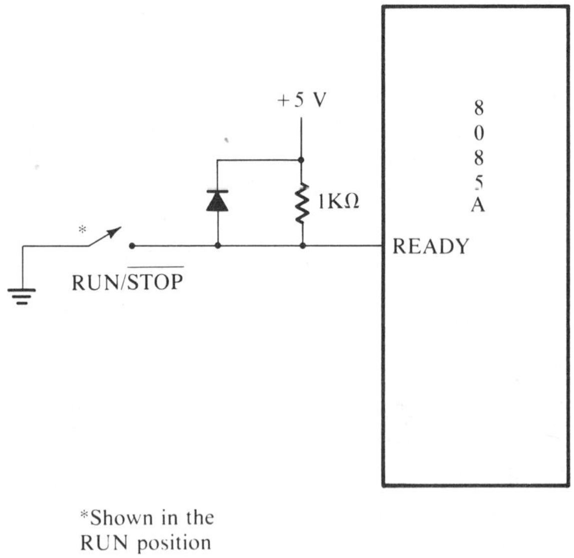

The $\overline{BHE}$ signal, only present on the 8086, indicates which byte in the memory is to be selected by the microprocessor. This signal is combined with address bit A0 to select a whole word, upper byte, lower byte, or no byte of information. Table 3–11 illustrates the logical combinations of A0 and $\overline{BHE}$.

$\overline{BHE}$	A0	Function
0	0	Whole word
0	1	Upper byte
1	0	Lower byte
1	1	None

TABLE 3–11 Memory byte selection.

INSTRUCTION TIMING 3-13

To calculate the time required to execute a program or wasted in a delay loop, it is necessary to know the execution times for each instruction. The times for the 8085A are illustrated in table 3–12 as clock cycle times. To determine the time required to execute an instruction, multiply the number of clock cycles by the basic operating frequency of the microprocessor. For example, if it takes 7 clock cycles to execute a MVI A,02 at a clock cycle time of 0.333 μs, then it takes the 8085A 2.333 μs to execute this instruction.

The table illustrates that a few instructions require either 7 or 11 clock cycles to execute (7/11). For example, with JNC DOG, it takes 11 cycles on no carry and 7 cycles on a carry condition.

MICROPROCESSOR TESTING WITH A LOGIC ANALYZER 3-14

The logic analyzer is extremely useful in microprocessor testing. In fact, it is the only device that can be used to view the timing of a processor functioning in a system. It is even possible to view the program execution path or track with the logic analyzer, which is extremely useful in debugging complicated software.

Instruction Tracking with the Logic Analyzer

The op-codes of an instruction can be stored with the memory addresses in the memory of the logic analyzer for later viewing as hexadecimal op-codes. In some newer analyzers, it is even possible to store the mnemonics of these op-codes in the memory of the analyzer and to display a symbolic listing. This, of course, would not be a program listing; it would be a dynamic listing of the instructions as actually executed in the system.

To track the op-codes in an operating system with a logic analyzer, three signal components must be connected to the analyzer. The data input connection for the analyzer is connected to the address/data bus in order to view the op-codes as they are fetched. In addition to data, a logic analyzer needs

TABLE 3–12 Instruction execution times for the 8080/8085A microprocessor.

8080A/8085A INSTRUCTION SET INDEX

Instruction		Code	Bytes	T States		Machine Cycles
				8085A	8080A	
ACI	DATA	CE data	2	7	7	F R
ADC	REG	1000 1SSS	1	4	4	F
ADC	M	8E	1	7	7	F R
ADD	REG	1000 0SSS	1	4	4	F
ADD	M	86	1	7	7	F R
ADI	DATA	C6 data	2	7	7	F R
ANA	REG	1010 0SSS	1	4	4	F
ANA	M	A6	1	7	7	F R
ANI	DATA	E6 data	2	7	7	F R
CALL	LABEL	CD addr	3	18	17	S R R W W*
CC	LABEL	DC addr	3	9/18	11/17	S R•/S R R W W*
CM	LABEL	FC addr	3	9/18	11/17	S R•/S R R W W*
CMA		2F	1	4	4	F
CMC		3F	1	4	4	F
CMP	REG	1011 1SSS	1	4	4	F
CMP	M	BE	1	7	7	F R
CNC	LABEL	D4 addr	3	9/18	11/17	S R•/S R R W W*
CNZ	LABEL	C4 addr	3	9/18	11/17	S R•/S R R W W*
CP	LABEL	F4 addr	3	9/18	11/17	S R•/S R R W W*
CPE	LABEL	EC addr	3	9/18	11/17	S R•/S R R W W*
CPI	DATA	FE data	2	7	7	F R
CPO	LABEL	E4 addr	3	9/18	11/17	S R•/S R R W W*
CZ	LABEL	CC addr	3	9/18	11/17	S R•/S R R W W*
DAA		27	1	4	4	F
DAD	RP	00RP 1001	1	10	10	F B B
DCR	REG	00SS S101	1	4	5	F*
DCR	M	35	1	10	10	F R W
DCX	RP	00RP 1011	1	6	5	S*
DI		F3	1	4	4	F
EI		FB	1	4	4	F
HLT		76	1	5	7	F B
IN	PORT	DB data	2	10	10	F R I
INR	REG	00SS S100	1	4	5	F*
INR	M	34	1	10	10	F R W
INX	RP	00RP 0011	1	6	5	S*
JC	LABEL	DA addr	3	7/10	10	F R/F R R†
JM	LABEL	FA addr	3	7/10	10	F R/F R R†
JMP	LABEL	C3 addr	3	10	10	F R R
JNC	LABEL	D2 addr	3	7/10	10	F R/F R R†
JNZ	LABEL	C2 addr	3	7/10	10	F R/F R R†
JP	LABEL	F2 addr	3	7/10	10	F R/F R R†
JPE	LABEL	EA addr	3	7/10	10	F R/F R R†
JPO	LABEL	E2 addr	3	7/10	10	F R/F R R†
JZ	LABEL	CA addr	3	7/10	10	F R/F R R†
LDA	ADDR	3A addr	3	13	13	F R R R
LDAX	RP	000X 1010	1	7	7	F R
LHLD	ADDR	2A addr	3	16	16	F R R R R

Instruction		Code	Bytes	T States		Machine Cycles
				8085A	8080A	
LXI	RP,DATA16	00RP 0001 data16	3	10	10	F R R
MOV	REG,REG	01DD DSSS	1	4	5	F*
MOV	M,REG	0111 0SSS	1	7	7	F W
MOV	REG,M	01DD D110	1	7	7	F R
MVI	REG,DATA	00DD D110 data	2	7	7	F R
MVI	M,DATA	36 data	2	10	10	F R W
NOP		00	1	4	4	F
ORA	REG	1011 0SSS	1	4	4	F
ORA	M	B6	1	7	7	F R
ORI	DATA	F6 data	2	7	7	F R
OUT	PORT	D3 data	2	10	10	F R O
PCHL		E9	1	6	5	S*
POP	RP	11RP 0001	1	10	10	F R R
PUSH	RP	11RP 0101	1	12	11	S W W*
RAL		17	1	4	4	F
RAR		1F	1	4	4	F
RC		D8	1	6/12	5/11	S/S R R*
RET		C9	1	10	10	F R R
RIM (8085A only)		20	1	4	–	F
RLC		07	1	4	4	F
RM		F8	1	6/12	5/11	S/S R R*
RNC		D0	1	6/12	5/11	S/S R R*
RNZ		C0	1	6/12	5/11	S/S R R*
RP		F0	1	6/12	5/11	S/S R R*
RPE		E8	1	6/12	5/11	S/S R R*
RPO		E0	1	6/12	5/11	S/S R R*
RRC		0F	1	4	4	F
RST	N	11XX X111	1	12	11	S W W*
RZ		C8	1	6/12	5/11	S/S R R*
SBB	REG	1001 1SSS	1	4	4	F
SBB	M	9E	1	7	7	F R
SBI	DATA	DE data	2	7	7	F R
SHLD	ADDR	22 addr	3	16	16	F R R W W
SIM (8085A only)		30	1	4	–	F
SPHL		F9	1	6	5	S*
STA	ADDR	32 addr	3	13	13	F R R W
STAX	RP	000X 0010	1	7	7	F W
STC		37	1	4	4	F
SUB	REG	1001 0SSS	1	4	4	F
SUB	M	96	1	7	7	F R
SUI	DATA	D6 data	2	7	7	F R
XCHG		EB	1	4	4	F
XRA	REG	1010 1SSS	1	4	4	F
XRA	M	AE	1	7	7	F R
XRI	DATA	EE data	2	7	7	F R
XTHL		E3	1	16	18	F R R W W

Machine cycle types:

F	Four clock period instr fetch	
S	Six clock period instr fetch	
R	Memory read	
I	I/O read	
W	Memory write	
O	I/O write	
B	Bus idle	
X	Variable or optional binary digit	
DDD	Binary digits identifying a destination register	B = 000, C = 001, D = 010 Memory = 110
SSS	Binary digits identifying a source register	E = 011, H = 100, L = 101 A = 111
RP	Register Pair	BC = 00, HL = 10 DE = 01, SP = 11

*Five clock period instruction fetch with 8080A.

†The longer machine cycle sequence applies regardless of condition evaluation with 8080A.

•An extra READ cycle (R) will occur for this condition with 8080A.

*All mnemonics copyrighted © Intel Corporation 1976.

(Reprinted by permission of Intel Corporation, copyright 1983)

a clock signal to acquire the information from the data bus. In the case of the 8085A, a clock signal must be provided when S1 and S0 are both high at the same time that $\overline{\text{RD}}$ is a logic zero. The clock input must be set so that it is active on the zero-to-one transition of the $\overline{\text{RD}}$ strobe. The circuitry required to generate this clock is illustrated in figure 3–18.

In addition to the data and clock inputs, the analyzer must also be triggered at the proper point. This is accomplished by using the beginning address of the software under test. Many analyzers have a set of 16 trigger qualifying inputs that can be attached to the address bus for this purpose.

Once the analyzer is triggered, it stores the op-codes for each subsequent memory location until its internal memory is full. At this time, the listing of the op-codes is displayed and checked.

In many cases it is desirable to display not only the instruction, but also the data as it leaves or enters the processor. In this case, the circuit of figure 3–18 is modified into the circuit of figure 3–19. This change would capture each byte of data written to or read from the memory or the I/O equipment in the system.

Displaying the Timing Diagram of the Microprocessor

If the hardware in a system or its timing is suspect, the logic analyzer can display the complete timing diagram or a portion of it. To display the complete timing diagram, a logic analyzer capable of displaying more than 16 channels of information is necessary.

To display the timing diagram, the clock input to the analyzer is normally connected to the clock of the microprocessor under test; if desired, it can also be set to internal clocking. The problem with this is that there may be an anomaly in the timing diagram.

The data inputs are connected to the $\overline{\text{RD}}$ and $\overline{\text{WR}}$ signals and a few of the data and address bus connections to provide a timing diagram for the system that can detect timing problems.

Summary

This chapter has been developed to provide a workable knowledge of the hardware signals of the 8085A, 8086, and 8088. It is by no means an exhaustive study of these microprocessors and their timing. The student who

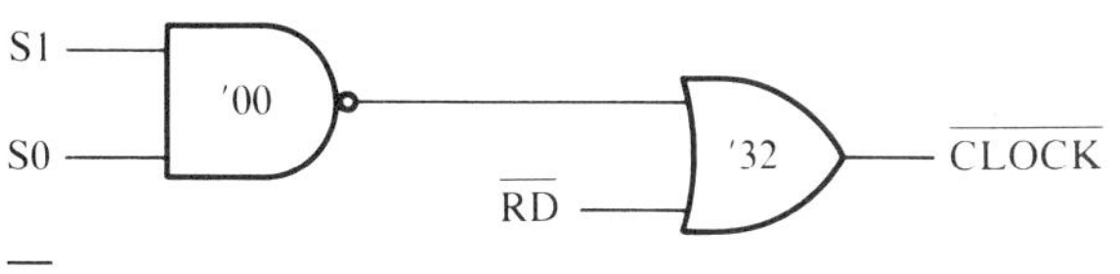

FIGURE 3–18 The circuitry required to generate an op-code acquisition clock for a logic analyzer.

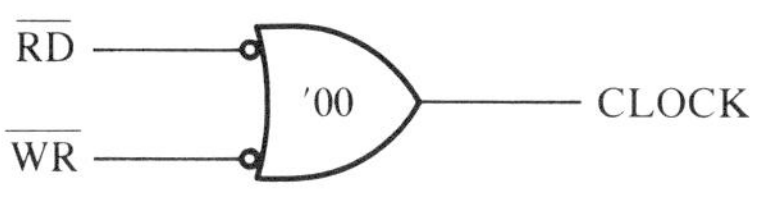

FIGURE 3–19 The circuit required to generate a clock for acquisitioning all data bus transfers.

requires additional information should refer to Intel's THE MCS-80/85 FAMILY USER'S MANUAL (January 1983) and the IAPX 86,88 USER'S MANUAL (August 1981).

This chapter provides the reader the information needed to complete a course based on this text. It is also applicable to a course based on Motorola or other microprocessor products.

Glossary

Access time The time required to access data in a memory device.

Bus cycle A grouping of clock states used to access the memory or I/O through the microprocessor buses.

Clock cycle time One clocking period.

Clock state One clocking period.

DMA An acronym for "Direct Memory Access," a technique to transfer data directly to or from the memory or an external device.

FIFO A type of memory in which the first piece of information in is the first to come out.

Instruction cycle The time required to fetch and execute one machine language instruction.

Interrupt A technique whereby the hardware can initiate a subroutine CALL.

Machine cycle A grouping of clock periods used to perform a task, such as op-code fetch.

Nonmaskable interrupt An interrupt input that cannot be disabled or turned off.

Queue See FIFO.

Single step The ability to execute a program one bus cycle or one instruction at a time.

Wait state A period of time equal to one clocking period caused by the READY input pin.

Questions and Problems

1 What is the noise immunity for the Intel series of microprocessors?

2 What is the maximum number of MOS loads that can be connected to the microprocessor?

3 How many low power Schottky TTL unit loads can be connected to an output pin safely?

4 What is the maximum clock frequency allowable for the 8085A?

5 What is the clock cycle time whenever a 4 MHz crystal is attached to the 8085A?

6 An RC circuit can generate the clock for an 8085A. Why is it not normally used in place of a crystal?
7 By what factor will the 8284A clock generator divide the crystal frequency?
8 How many bytes of memory can the 8085A address directly?
9 How many bytes of memory can the 8088 address directly?
10 What is the purpose of the ALE signal?
11 Whenever the data bus is buffered, will the memory access time increase or decrease?
12 What is the purpose of the $\overline{\text{RD}}$ signal?
13 What is the purpose of the $\overline{\text{WR}}$ signal?
14 Which edge of the $\overline{\text{WR}}$ strobe can write the information to the memory or an I/O device?
15 What is the purpose of the DT/$\overline{\text{R}}$ and $\overline{\text{DEN}}$ signals in the 8088 microprocessor?
16 What do status bits generally indicate?
17 When the 8085A microprocessor is RESET, it begins executing the program stored at which memory location?
18 When the 8088 microprocessor is RESET, it begins executing the program stored at which memory location?
19 What memory access time does the 8085A allow if operated at its maximum clock frequency?
20 Which memory access time does the 8086 allow if operated at its maximum clock frequency?
21 List each interrupt input pin for the 8085A and indicate each interrupt vector location.
22 Redraw the diagram illustrated in figure 3–15 so that the 8085A will respond to a RST 3 instruction.
23 Redraw the diagram illustrated in figure 3–16 so that the 8088 will respond to interrupt vector 100 decimal.
24 Which 8085A interrupt inputs are level sensitive?
25 Describe what happens to the buses during a HOLD.
26 Which Intel microprocessor has the ability to accomplish serial I/O directly?
27 List two results that the READY input can accomplish.
28 Given the following 8085A sequence of instructions, determine how many clock cycles are required to execute it.

```
        MVI  A,10H
LOOP:   DCR  A
        JNZ  LOOP
```

29 How many microseconds are required to execute the sequence of instructions above if the 8085A clock cycle time equals 1 μs?
30 What would be the maximum execution time for these instructions if the number moved into the accumulator could be changed? (Assume a 1 μs clock period.)

31 Why would a logic analyzer be a good software debugging tool?

32 Would it be possible to use the ALE signal as a clock pulse to the logic analyzer? If so, explain which information could be captured for the 8085A microprocessor.

4

The MC6800, MC6809, and MC68000 Microprocessors

This chapter introduces the current line of Motorola microprocessors. It is important to learn the operation and interfacing of either the MC6800 or MC6809 microprocessor first, since the remainder of this text emphasizes these microprocessors. Once they are learned, transition to the MC68000 or any other microprocessor manufactured by any of the IC houses is easy. For example, the 8085A is also covered in some detail.

Whichever microprocessor you choose to study, you will find subsequent chapters interesting and useful.

4-1 PINOUTS

Figure 4–1 illustrates the MC6800, MC6809, and MC68000 microprocessors' pinouts. The MC6800 and MC6809 are both packaged in 40-pin dual in-line packages, while the MC68000 is integrated into a 64-pin dual in-line package. All three devices operate from a single 5V power supply with power dissipations of less than 1.5 W.

Output Loading

The MC6800 and MC6809 microprocessors are capable of providing 1.6 mA of sink current and 400 μA of source current at any of the output pins. This current will drive one 74XXX TTL unit load, four 74LSXXX TTL unit loads, or about ten NMOS or CMOS unit loads. Only ten NMOS or CMOS unit loads may be connected because each MOS input places a fairly large amount of capacitance on an output connection. Too much bus capacitance will degrade the timing signals issued by the microprocessor, causing performance problems. To prevent this, MOS loads are limited to ten or less. Refer to table 3–1 in chapter 3 for a detailed look at unit loading.

The MC68000 is capable of sinking 1.6 mA on the HALT pin, 3.2 mA on the address pins, and about 5.0 mA on the data bus connections. With this de-

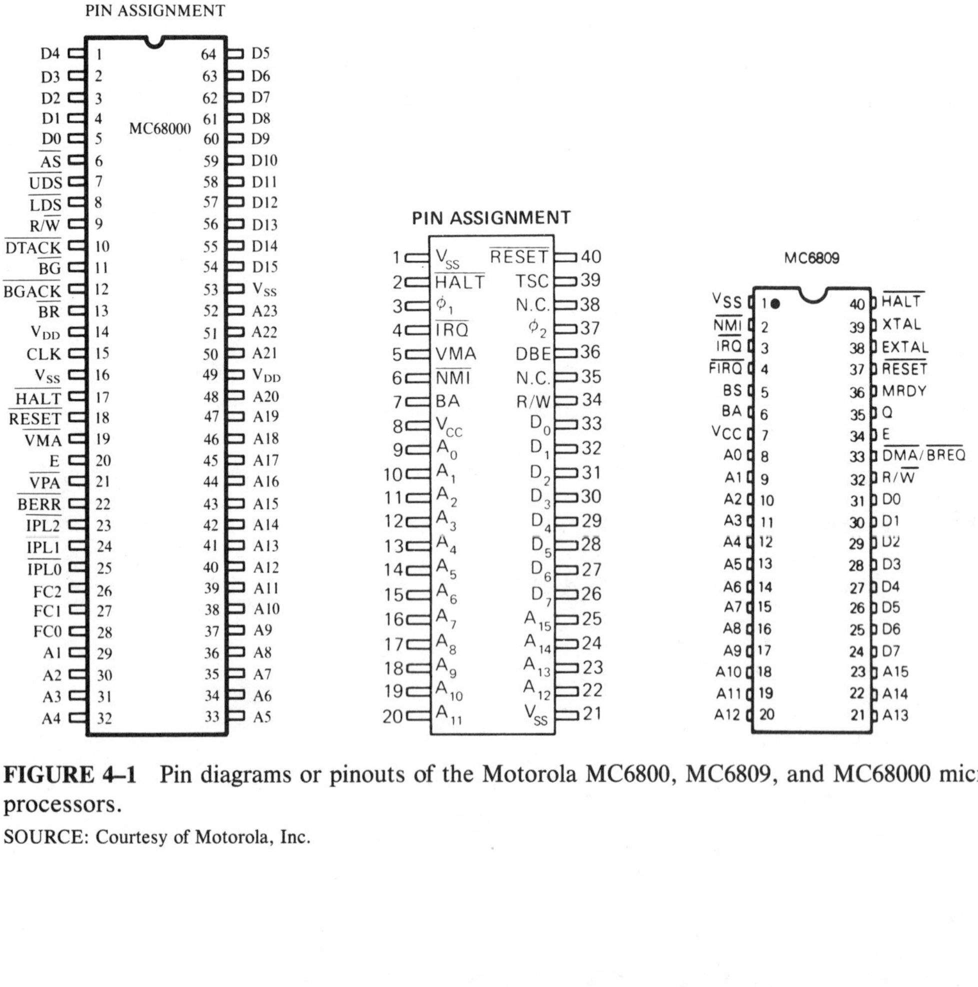

FIGURE 4–1 Pin diagrams or pinouts of the Motorola MC6800, MC6809, and MC68000 microprocessors.

SOURCE: Courtesy of Motorola, Inc.

vice, more TTL components can be driven directly from the output pins of the microprocessor. This means that a larger system may be connected directly to the MC68000 without the addition of external bus buffers. Since the source current at these outputs remains at 400 μA, the maximum number of MOS loads remains at ten or less.

It is interesting to note that the MC6800 and MC6809 microprocessors will not drive a 74SXXX series TTL load. This limitation can be overcome by using a 74ASXXX series gate or a FAST gate from Fairchild.

Input Loading

Input connections on all three microprocessors sink and source a maximum of 2.5 μA of current and present about 10 pF of capacitance. In addition to low loading, they are also compatible with the standard TTL voltage levels.

Noise Immunity

The system noise immunity in any of the Motorola processors is about 400 mV and is directly compatible with standard TTL noise immunities. In systems that contain heavy capacitive loads, long bus connections, or excessive current loads, bus buffers at the output connections are recommended. With additional buffering, it is possible to connect up to 100 MOS or 74LSXXX TTL unit loads to an output connection. Most buffers contain an enhanced pullup network that has been designed to drive capacitive loads.

CLOCK CIRCUITRY 4-2

The MC6809 contains an internal clock generator that, in most cases, generates the basic timing for the microprocessor. The MC6800 and the MC68000 both require the addition of an external clock generator to provide their basic timing.

MC6809 Clock Circuitry

Under normal operation, a crystal with a frequency of 8 MHz would be attached between the EXTAL and XTAL input pins of the MC6809 (as pictured in figure 4–2). The crystal is internally divided by a factor of four to produce the 2 MHz basic operating frequency. The range of allowable crystal frequencies is between 8.0 MHz and about 400 kHz for reliable operation. If

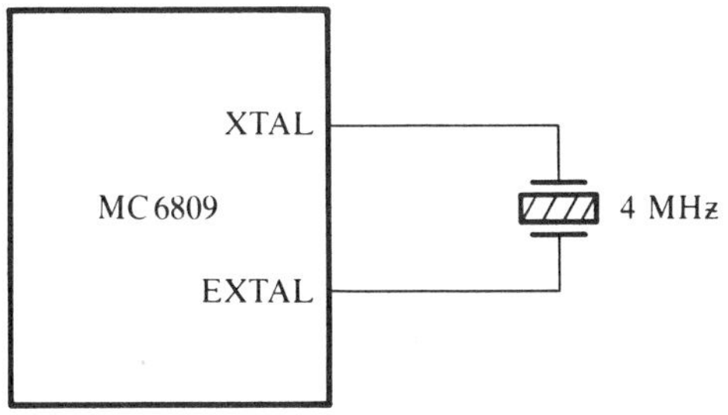

FIGURE 4–2 The MC6809 clock generation circuitry.

an operating frequency outside this range is chosen, Motorola will not guarantee the proper operation of the MC6809.

In addition to a crystal, the MC6809 may be driven from an external TTL source. This is accomplished by grounding the XTAL pin and connecting the external TTL clock signal to the EXTAL connection. This method of operation is used in multiple processor systems, where one timing source drives all of the processors.

MC6800 and MC68000 Clock Circuitry

The MC6800 and MC68000 require an external clock generator for proper operation. The MC6875 clock generator, as illustrated in figure 4–3, can generate the required multiphase clock inputs for the MC6800. The MC68000 requires a TTL compatible clock input of up to 8.0 MHz for proper operation. A circuit that can be used to generate this clock is illustrated in figure 4–4.

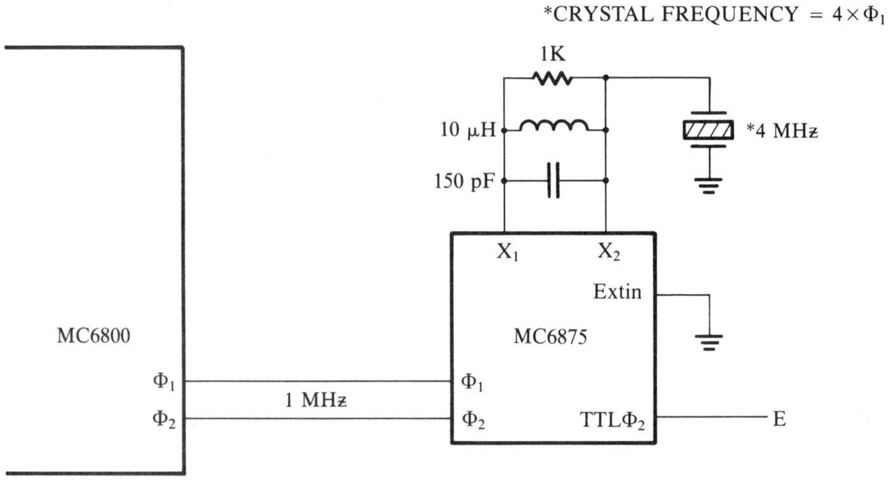

FIGURE 4–3 The MC6875 clock generator connected to the MC6800 microprocessor.

FIGURE 4–4 The MC68000 clock generation circuitry.

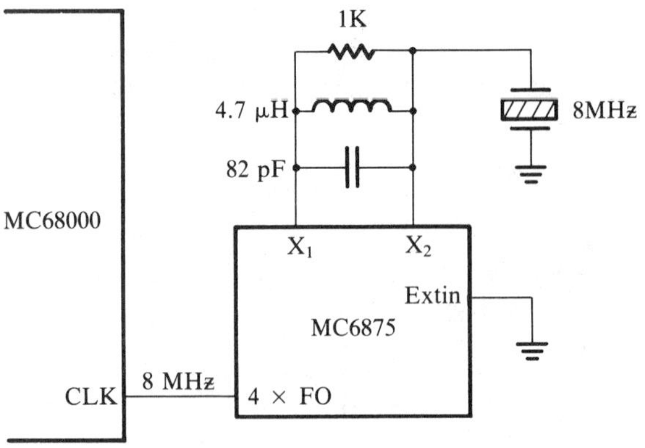

ADDRESS AND DATA BUS CONNECTIONS 4-3

The Address Bus

Both the MC6800 and the MC6809 contain 16 pins that have been dedicated to addressing the memory and I/O. This feature allows either of these microprocessors to address 64K bytes of memory and I/O space directly.

The MC68000 contains 23 address connections, which allow it to access an astounding 16M bytes of memory and I/O directly. This is equal to eight million 16-bit words of memory information. In addition to the number of address connections present, the amount of drive current available is triple that of the MC6800 or MC6809.

The Data Bus

The data bus of the MC6800 and MC6809 microprocessors is 8 bits in width; whereas the MC68000 uses a 16-bit data bus. This bus, in all three cases, is a bidirectional, three-state bus that passes information out of, or into, the microprocessor.

As with the address bus, the data bus on the MC68000 possesses an enhanced drive capability. This capability allows the microprocessor to be structured into a larger system before bus buffering is required.

MC68000 Bus Buffering

Figure 4–5 illustrates the inclusion of a set of data and address bus buffers for the MC68000 microprocessor. The $\overline{AS}$, or address strobe, output is connected to the enable ($\overline{G}$) input on the address buffers. The $\overline{AS}$ signal becomes a logic zero whenever the address bus contains a valid memory address. In this circuit, $\overline{AS}$ switches the three-state buffers to their *enabled,* or on, condition.

The bidirectional bus transceivers, which are connected to the data bus, are controlled by the R/$\overline{W}$ control signal. Since the R/$\overline{W}$ signal selects the direction of data flow on the data bus, it is usable as a directional control input to the transceivers. During a memory or I/O read, R/$\overline{W}$ is high and causes the data to flow in from the data bus; during a memory or I/O write, this line is low and causes the data to flow out to the memory and I/O.

CONTROL BUS CONNECTIONS 4-4

The control bus structures of the MC6800, MC6809, and the MC68000 are almost identical when only the major control signals are examined. If the MC6800 and MC6809 are compared, they differ only in the way that direct memory access I/O is controlled. Comparing all three demonstrates many more differences. Table 4–1 contrasts these differences.

The Basic Memory and I/O Control Signals

All three microprocessors use the R/$\overline{W}$ signal to command the memory or I/O to read or write data. In the MC68000 this signal also works in conjunction

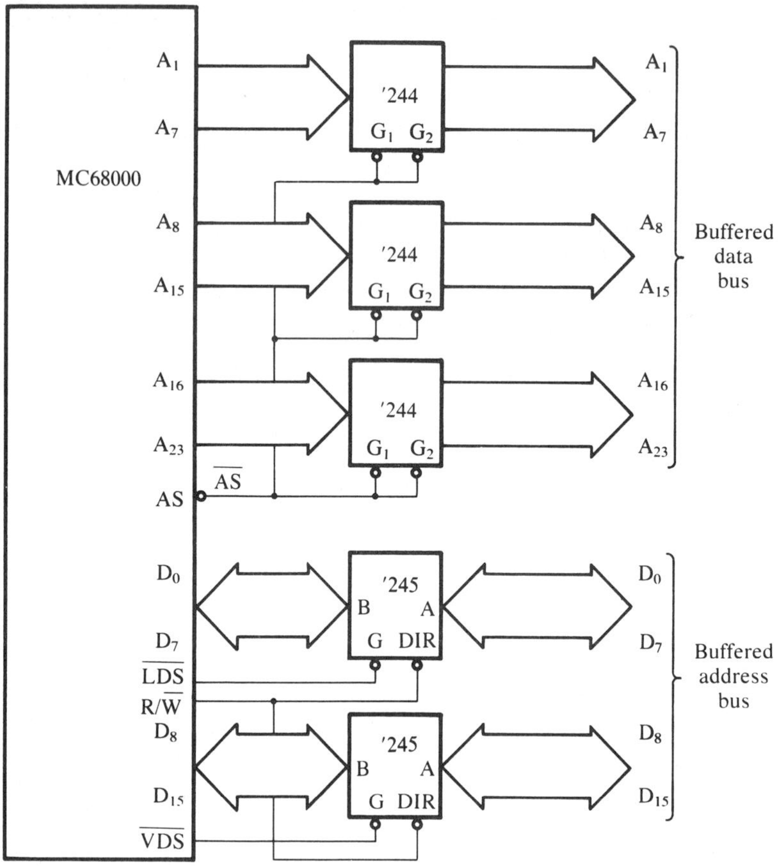

FIGURE 4–5 A fully buffered MC68000 microprocessor.

with the $\overline{LDS}$ and $\overline{UDS}$ data strobes, which indicate how the microprocessor will react with the data bus during the current bus cycle. Table 4–2 illustrates how the MC68000 interprets the data bus for each combination of the R/$\overline{W}$, $\overline{LDS}$, and $\overline{UDS}$ signals.

In addition to these three control signals, the $\overline{VMA}$ and $\overline{E}$ signals are also present on all three microprocessors. The $\overline{VMA}$ signal indicates that the address bus contains a "valid memory address"; the $\overline{E}$ signal, or *enable,* is used to enable the memory or I/O device. The $\overline{E}$ signal is actually not present on the MC6800, but it is the phase two TTL output of the clock generator circuitry.

Additional MC6809 Control Signals

The MC6809 has a few other control signals that are not present on the MC6800. These include BS, $\overline{FIRQ}$, MRDY, and $\overline{DMA/BREQ}$. The BA and BS signals indicate the present state of the MC6809, as illustrated in table 4–3.

The MRDY signal extends the access time provided for the memory by extending the current read or write cycle. The extension may be anything

TABLE 4–1 Comparative control signals.

MC6800/MC6809	MC68000	Function
R/$\overline{\text{W}}$	R/$\overline{\text{W}}$	Controls reading or writing to memory or I/O
VMA	$\overline{\text{AS}}$,$\overline{\text{VMA}}$	Valid memory address present on the address bus
ϕ2,E	$\overline{\text{UDS}}$,$\overline{\text{LDS}}$,$\overline{\text{E}}$	Enables data bus so that no contention can occur
$\overline{\text{NMI}}$	LEVEL 7	Nonmaskable interrupt
$\overline{\text{IRQ}}$,$\overline{\text{FIRQ}}$	LEVEL 0–6 TRAPS	Maskable interrupts
$\overline{\text{MRDY}}$	$\overline{\text{DTACK}}$	Slow memory control
$\overline{\text{DMA/BREQ}}$,BA BS,DBE,TSC	$\overline{\text{BR}}$,$\overline{\text{BG}}$ BGACK	DMA control and bus arbitration

TABLE 4–2 MC68000 bus control strobes.

$\overline{\text{UDS}}$	$\overline{\text{LDS}}$	R/$\overline{\text{W}}$	Function
0	0	0	Valid data bus
0	0	1	Valid data bus
0	1	0	Bits 8–15 appear on both halves of bus
0	1	1	Bits 8–15 appear on upper half of bus. Lower half contains unknown information
1	0	0	Bits 0–7 appear on both halves of bus
1	0	1	Bits 0–7 appear on lower half of bus. Upper half contains unknown information
1	1	X	Data bus contains unknown information

from one clocking period up to 10 μs in duration. This is most useful if a slower external device is to be interfaced to the MC6809. An example is an analog-to-digital converter, as illustrated for the 8085A in chapter 6.

The $\overline{\text{DMA/BREQ}}$ input is used for a direct memory access or bus arbitration; it is covered, along with the $\overline{\text{FIRQ}}$ input, later in this chapter.

Additional MC68000 Control Signals

The advanced architecture of the MC68000 microprocessor includes some additional control pins, such as $\overline{\text{BGACK}}$, $\overline{\text{VPA}}$, $\overline{\text{DTACK}}$, $\overline{\text{BERR}}$, $\overline{\text{BR}}$, $\overline{\text{BG}}$,

TABLE 4–3 BA and BS processor state signals.

BA	BS	Processor State
0	0	Normal
0	1	Interrupt or reset acknowledge
1	0	Sync acknowledge
1	1	Halt/bus grant acknowledge

$\overline{\mathrm{IPL0}}$, $\overline{\mathrm{IPL1}}$, $\overline{\mathrm{IPL2}}$, FC0, FC1, and FC2. These pins control such features as interrupts and direct memory access or bus arbitration.

The FC0, FC1, and FC2 signals indicate the status of the MC68000 as depicted in table 4–4.

TABLE 4–4 MC68000 bus function control signals.

FC2	FC1	FC0	Cycle Type
0	0	0	Undefined
0	0	1	User data
0	1	0	User program
0	1	1	Undefined
1	0	0	Undefined
1	0	1	Supervisor data
1	1	0	Supervisor program
1	1	1	Interrupt acknowledge

FC0, FC1, and FC2 are basically used to indicate the mode of operation, either supervisor or user. In the supervisor state, the MC68000 can control an external memory management device and system software. This capacity provides security, since the memory management unit and system software cannot be accessed by the normal user. The access requires a shift to the supervisor state, which is a privileged state.

The $\overline{\mathrm{BERR}}$ input signal informs the processor of a bus error and is provided by the external hardware. The type of hardware most likely to generate this signal is a memory parity checking circuit. If a parity error is detected, this signal becomes active, and the processor executes an exception sequence or an interrupt. This sequence reads the address of the user supplied bus error handling subroutine from memory address $00008. Control is then transferred to this error-handling subroutine for a possible repeat of the bus cycle.

The $\overline{\mathrm{BR}}$, $\overline{\mathrm{BG}}$, and $\overline{\mathrm{BGACK}}$ signals are used when more than one MC68000 or a DMA controller is connected in a system. $\overline{\mathrm{BR}}$ is an input that requests the use of the bus. $\overline{\mathrm{BG}}$ is an output that indicates that the MC68000 will release bus control at the end of the current cycle. The $\overline{\mathrm{BGACK}}$ input indicates that some other device has become the bus master. These signals are discussed in greater detail in the section on bus arbitration.

The $\overline{\mathrm{VPA}}$ input is activated whenever an external MC6800 peripheral device is addressed. This is provided so that the wealth of MC6800 8-bit peripheral devices can function with the MC68000. It also signals the processor to use automatic vectoring for an interrupt, as described in the interrupt section of this chapter.

4-5 RESET OR RESTART

If the MC6800 or MC6809 microprocessors are reset, they look at memory location $FFFE for the restart vector. The restart vector holds the starting address of the system program.

Resetting or restarting the MC68000 is completely different because two vectors apply to this function. When the MC68000 is first powered up, locations zero through three must contain the supervisor stack pointer (SSP). Locations four through seven must contain the location of the first instruction to be executed after a reset. These vectors are used only during a power up sequence.

The RESET instruction in the MC68000 will not cause the reset vectors to be called. This instruction will only cause the $\overline{\text{RESET}}$ output pin to become active for 124 clocking periods after it has been executed. This instruction and the resulting signal on the $\overline{\text{RESET}}$ pin are only used for reinitializing the external peripheral components in the system. It has absolutely no effect on the internal registers of the MC68000.

If repowering the processor is desirable, it can be accomplished by using the reset vectors stored in the vector table.

BUS TIMING 4-6

The standard operating frequency for the MC6800 and the MC6809 is 1 MHz. At this rate they are capable of transferring 1 byte of information per clocking period or 1 byte every microsecond. The MC68000 works with an internal clock frequency of 8 MHz and can transfer 1 byte of data every 500 μs since the internal timing is set up so that four external clock pulses are required for a bus transfer.

MC6800 Read and Write Timing

Figure 4–6 illustrates the basic read and write timing diagrams of the MC6800 microprocessor and its AC characteristics. In the MC6800 timing diagrams, the address is presented to memory and I/O during the logic zero portion of the phase two clock. When the phase two clock becomes a logic one, data is transferred into the processor or sent out from it.

The time allowed for a memory access (Tacc) is equal to 540 ns worst case. In other words, the memory, plus the time delay introduced by buffers, should have an access time of no longer than 540 ns. In addition to this time constraint, it is also important to note that data must be held for 10 ns minimum after the phase two clock returns to the logic zero level. If the phase two clock is used as an enable (or E) signal, the amount of time required to enable the memory device must not exceed 350 ns. Since the output buffers in a memory device typically take 120 ns to enable, this is generally ample time.

MC6800 Memory Read and Write Signals

The circuit depicted in figure 4–7 allows the MC6800 or MC6809 to be used with most of this text. It also allows it to be used, without effort, with most of the industrywide standard memory components, such as the 2114 RAM, 2716 EPROM, and others.

By combining the phase two TTL signal or E signal with the VMA output and the R/$\overline{\text{W}}$ signal, we obtain the $\overline{\text{MEMR}}$ or $\overline{\text{RD}}$ and $\overline{\text{MEMW}}$ or $\overline{\text{WR}}$ control signals that are used throughout this book. These pulses are approxi-

MAXIMUM RATINGS

Rating	Symbol	Value	Unit
Supply Voltage	V_{CC}	-0.3 to +7.0	Vdc
Input Voltage	V_{in}	-0.3 to +7.0	Vdc
Operating Temperature Range—T_L to T_H	T_A		^oC
MC6800, MC68A00, MC68B00		0 to +70	
MC6800C, MC68A00C		-40 to +85	
MC6800BQCS, MC6800CQCS		-55 to +125	
Storage Temperature Range	T_{stg}	-55 to +150	^oC
Thermal Resistance	θ_{JA}		$^oC/W$
Plastic Package		70	
Ceramic Package		50	

ELECTRICAL CHARACTERISTICS (V_{CC} = 5.0 V, ± 5%, V_{SS} = 0, T_A = T_L to T_H unless otherwise noted)

Characteristic		Symbol	Min	Typ	Max	Unit
Input High Voltage	Logic	V_{IH}	V_{SS} + 2.0	–	V_{CC}	Vdc
	$\phi1,\phi2$	V_{IHC}	V_{CC} - 0.6	–	V_{CC} + 0.3	
Input Low Voltage	Logic	V_{IL}	V_{SS} - 0.3	–	V_{SS} + 0.8	Vdc
	$\phi1,\phi2$	V_{ILC}	V_{SS} - 0.3	–	V_{SS} + 0.4	
Input Leakage Current		I_{in}				μAdc
(V_{in} = 0 to 5.25 V, V_{CC} = max)	Logic*		–	1.0	2.5	
(V_{in} = 0 to 5.25 V, V_{CC} = 0.0 V)	$\phi1,\phi2$		–	–	100	
Three-State (Off State) Input Current	D0-D7	I_{TSI}	–	2.0	10	μAdc
(V_{in} = 0.4 to 2.4 V, V_{CC} = max)	A0-A15, R/$\overline{W}$		–	–	100	
Output High Voltage		V_{OH}				Vdc
(I_{Load} = -205 μAdc, V_{CC} = min)	D0-D7		V_{SS} + 2.4	–	–	
(I_{Load} = -145 μAdc, V_{CC} = min)	A0-A15, R/$\overline{W}$, VMA		V_{SS} + 2.4	–	–	
(I_{Load} = -100 μAdc, V_{CC} = min)	BA		V_{SS} + 2.4	–	–	
Output Low Voltage (I_{Load} = 1.6 mAdc, V_{CC} = min)		V_{OL}	–	–	V_{SS} + 0.4	Vdc
Power Dissipation		P_D	–	0.5	1.0	W
Capacitance		C_{in}				pF
(V_{in} = 0, T_A = 25°C, f = 1.0 MHz)	$\phi1$		–	25	35	
	$\phi2$		–	45	70	
	D0-D7		–	10	12.5	
	Logic Inputs		–	6.5	10	
	A0-A15, R/$\overline{W}$, VMA	C_{out}	–	–	12	pF

CLOCK TIMING (V_{CC} = 5.0 V, ± 5%, V_{SS} = 0, T_A = T_L to T_H unless otherwise noted)

Characteristics		Symbol	Min	Typ	Max	Unit
Frequency of Operation	MC6800	f	0.1	–	1.0	MHz
	MC68A00		0.1	–	1.5	
	MC68B00		0.1	–	2.0	
Cycle Time (Figure 1)	MC6800	t_{cyc}	1.000	–	10	μs
	MC68A00		0.666	–	10	
	MC68B00		0.500	–	10	
Clock Pulse Width	$\phi1,\phi2$ – MC6800	$PW_{\phi H}$	400	–	9500	ns
(Measured at V_{CC} - 0.6 V)	$\phi1,\phi2$ – MC68A00		230	–	9500	
	$\phi1,\phi2$ – MC68B00		180	–	9500	
Total $\phi1$ and $\phi2$ Up Time	MC6800	t_{ut}	900	–	–	ns
	MC68A00		600	–	–	
	MC68B00		440	–	–	
Rise and Fall Times (Measured between V_{SS} + 0.4 and V_{CC} - 0.6)		$t_{\phi r}$, $t_{\phi f}$	–	–	100	ns
Delay Time or Clock Separation (Figure 1)		t_d				ns
(Measured at V_{OV} = V_{SS} + 0.6 V @ t_r = t_f ≤ 100 ns)			0	–	9100	
(Measured at V_{OV} = V_{SS} + 1.0 V @ t_r = t_f ≤ 35 ns)			0	–	9100	

FIGURE 4–6 The read and write timing diagrams and charcteristics of the MC6800 microprocessor.

SOURCE: Courtesy of Motorola, Inc.

READ/WRITE TIMING (Reference Figures 2 through 6)

Characteristic	Symbol	MC6800			MC68A00			MC68B00			Unit
		Min	Typ	Max	Min	Typ	Max	Min	Typ	Max	
Address Delay	t_{AD}										ns
C = 90 pF		–	–	270	–	–	180	–	–	150	
C = 30 pF		–	–	250	–	–	165	–	–	135	
Peripheral Read Access Time $t_{ac} = t_{ut} - (t_{AD} + t_{DSR})$	t_{acc}	–	–	530	–	–	360	–	–	250	ns
Data Setup Time (Read)	t_{DSR}	100	–	–	60	–	–	40	–	–	ns
Input Data Hold Time	t_H	10	–	–	10	–	–	10	–	–	ns
Output Data Hold Time	t_H	10	25	–	10	25	–	10	25	–	ns
Address Hold Time (Address, R/$\overline{W}$, VMA)	t_{AH}	30	50	–	30	50	–	30	50	–	ns
Enable High Time for DBE Input	t_{EH}	450	–	–	280	–	–	220	–	–	ns
Data Delay Time (Write)	t_{DDW}	–	–	225	–	–	200	–	–	160	ns
Processor Controls											
Processor Control Setup Time	t_{PCS}	200	–	–	140	–	–	110	–	–	ns
Processor Control Rise and Fall Time	t_{PCr}, t_{PCf}	–	–	100	–	–	100	–	–	100	ns
Bus Available Delay	t_{BA}	–	–	250	–	–	165	–	–	135	ns
Three-State Delay	t_{TSD}	–	–	270	–	–	270	–	–	220	ns
Data Bus Enable Down Time During ϕ1 Up Time	t_{DBE}	150	–	–	120	–	–	75	–	–	ns
Data Bus Enable Rise and Fall Times	t_{DBEr}, t_{DBEf}	–	–	25	–	–	25	–	–	25	ns

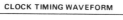

CLOCK TIMING WAVEFORM

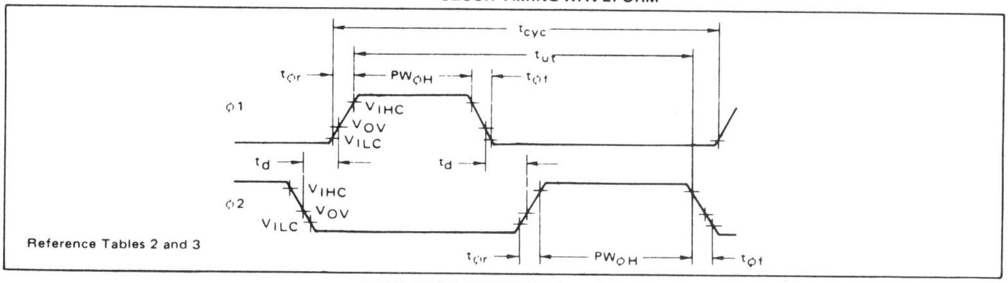

READ DATA FROM MEMORY OR PERIPHERALS

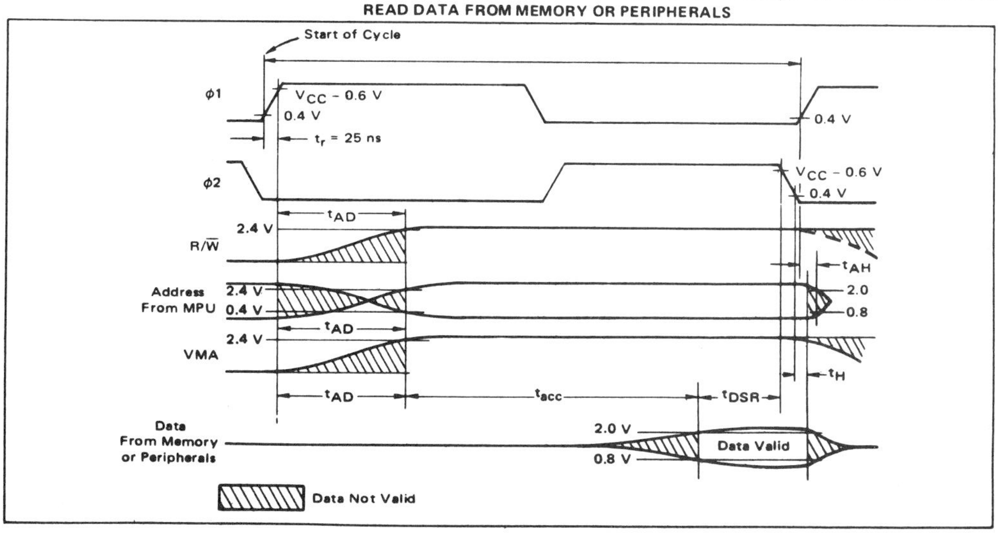

FIGURE 4–6 *continued*

WRITE IN MEMORY OR PERIPHERALS

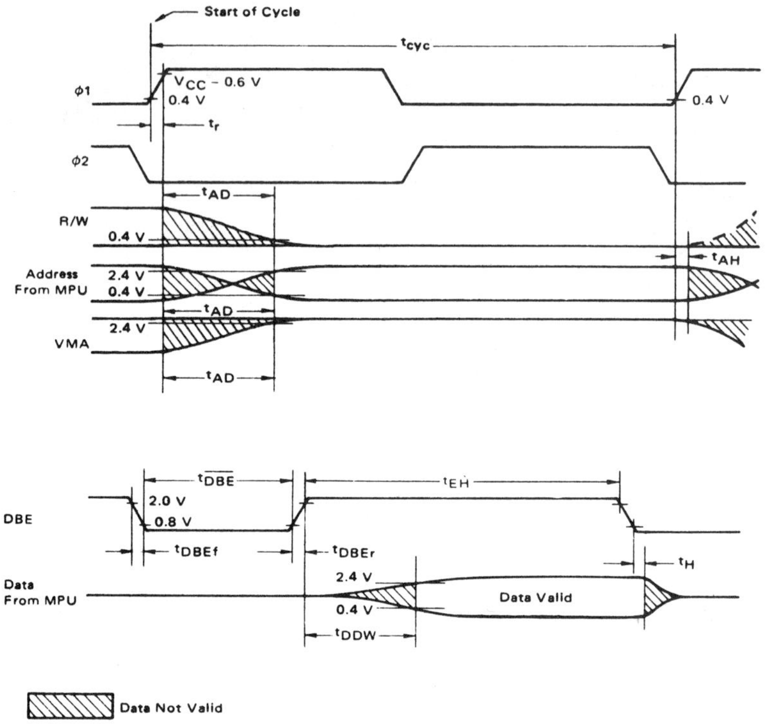

TYPIÇAL DATA BUS OUTPUT DELAY versus CAPACITIVE LOADING (T_{DDW})

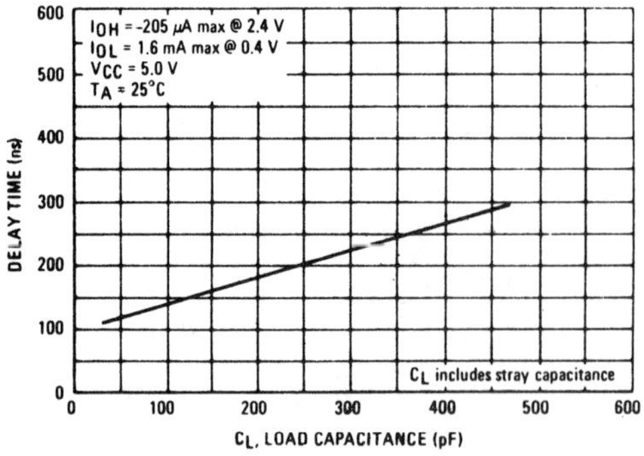

TYPICAL READ/WRITE, VMA, AND ADDRESS OUTPUT DELAY versus CAPACITIVE LOADING (T_{AD})

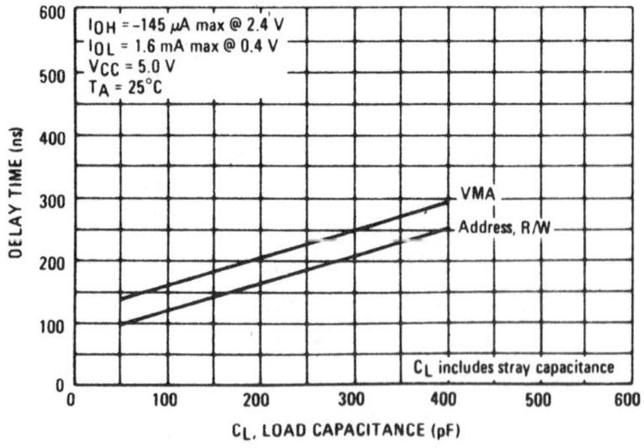

FIGURE 4–6 *continued*

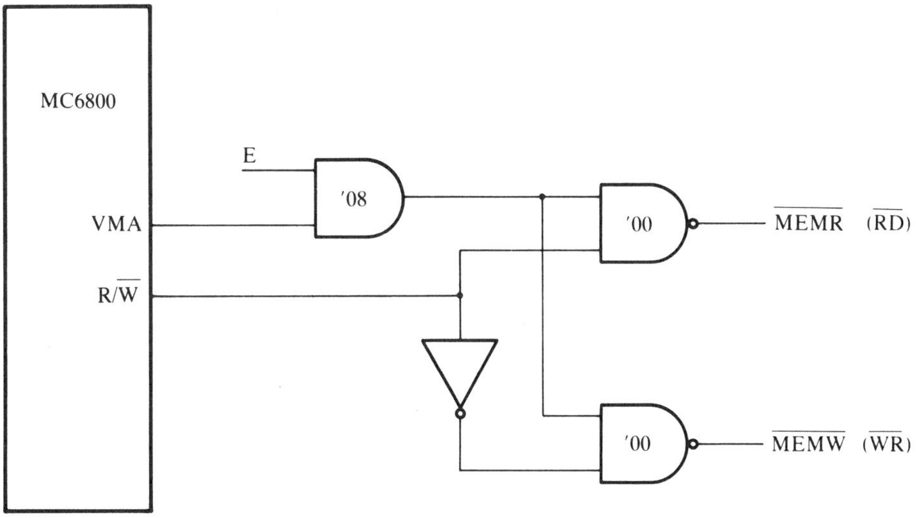

* E is the phase 2 TTL CLOCK

FIGURE 4–7 Using the MC6800 to generate the $\overline{\text{MEMR}}$ and $\overline{\text{MEMW}}$ control signals.

mately 500 ns in width and are compatible with many standard memory components. Since the 680XX series microprocessors do not support isolated I/O, no attempt has been made to develop the I/O control signal $\overline{\text{IOR}}$ and $\overline{\text{IOW}}$. For I/O control and its application, refer to the section in chapter 6 on memory mapped I/O.

MC68000 Read and Write Timing

Figure 4–8 illustrates the timing diagrams for the MC68000 microprocessor. The MC68000 will transfer one word, or 16 bits, of information every 500 ns, since it operates at a basic clock frequency of 8 MHz. The amount of time allowed to the memory component attached to the MC68000 is approximately 300 ns. This means that higher-speed memory components must be selected for use with this processor.

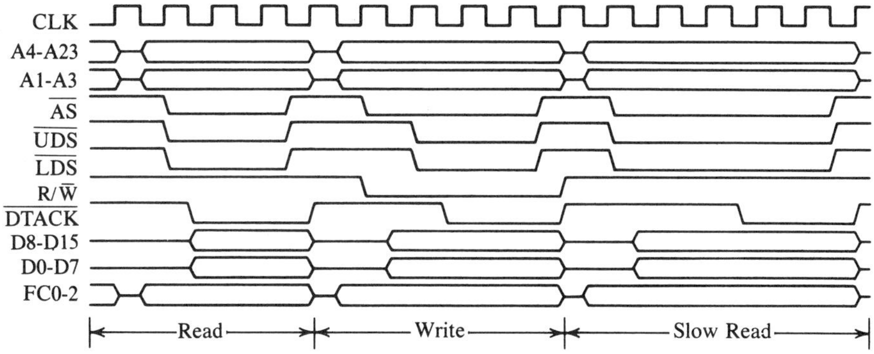

FIGURE 4–8 Basic read and write timing for the MC68000 microprocessor.
SOURCE: Courtesy of Motorola, Inc.

The $\overline{AS}$, or address strobe, signal activates a memory component. It is normal to use this signal to supply the MC68000 with its $\overline{DTACK}$ signal in systems that contain memory that can access data within 350 ns.

The MC6809 MRDY and the MC68000 $\overline{DTACK}$

The MRDY connection on the MC6809 prolongs the processor bus cycle for low-speed memory or I/O devices. This input can be held at a logic zero level for up to 10 μs for these slower devices. If held longer than 10 μs, Motorola will not guarantee the validity of the data stored in the MC6809 internal register array.

The $\overline{DTACK}$ input, or *data acknowledge,* of the MC68000 can serve about the same purpose as the MRDY input of the MC6809. The difference is that the MRDY input is an optional feature that can be ignored by connecting it to a logic one, while the $\overline{DTACK}$ input must be used.

During a read operation, for example, the MC68000 sends out the control signals and waits for the external device (usually memory) to send the $\overline{DTACK}$ signal back to the microprocessor. In fact, if the $\overline{DTACK}$ signal does not occur, the system waits just as it does with MRDY. Once the processor accepts the information, the $\overline{DTACK}$ signal must be returned to its inactive state before another bus cycle can occur. Without this timing, the MC68000 will not function.

4-7 MC6809 AND MC68000 BUS ARBITRATION (DMA)

MC6809 Bus Arbitration

The MC6809 microprocessor has an input labeled $\overline{DMA/BREQ}$ that requests access to the MC6809 system bus. When this pin is active, the microprocessor releases control of the system bus by three-stating the address, data, and control buses. This allows an external device to access the memory and I/O connected to the MC6809 directly.

The BA and BS signals grant or acknowledge the bus request when they are both at logic one levels. This same level also indicates that the microprocessor may be halted.

MC68000 Bus Arbitration

If more than one microprocessor or similar device is to function on the same bus system, a need for bus arbitration arises. The set of connections described in this segment determines which device will control the bus so that no conflict can occur. Bus conflicts will almost always result in a loss of data if they are allowed to occur.

The $\overline{BR}$, or *bus request* signal, is an input to the MC68000 that asks for or requests the system bus. If the MC68000 is at the end of its current bus cycle, it will grant the bus request by sending out the $\overline{BG}$, or *bus grant* signal. Once the requesting device notices the $\overline{BG}$ signal, it returns a $\overline{BGACK}$, or *bus grant acknowledge* signal, back to the MC68000 to indicate that it has taken over the system buses.

This arbitration dialog is normally carried out between the MC68000 and an external DMA controller. During the bus grant, the MC68000 relinquishes control of the system by floating the address, data, and control bus. This of course will allow the external device to gain complete control over the system buses. The typical three wire handshake is illustrated in the timing diagram of figure 4–9.

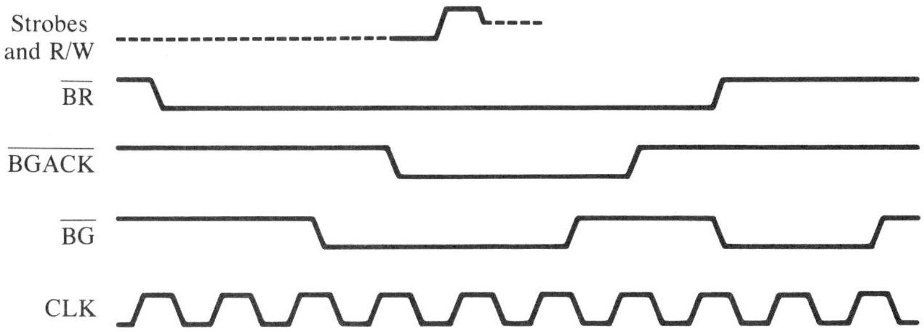

FIGURE 4–9 MC68000 bus arbitration timing.
SOURCE: Courtesy of Motorola, Inc.

INTERRUPT STRUCTURES 4-8

MC6800 Interrupt Structure

The MC6800 microprocessor has two hardware and one software interrupt that are vectored through the top part of the memory. Table 4–5 illustrates the interrupt vectors for the MC6800 microprocessor. These vectors contain the location of the software that will be executed in response to these input signals.

TABLE 4–5 MC6800 interrupt vectors.

Vector Location	Signal
$FFFE, $FFFF	Reset
$FFFC, $FFFD	$\overline{NMI}$
$FFFA, $FFFB	SWI
$FFF8, $FFF9	$\overline{IRQ}$

MC6809 Interrupt Structure

The MC6809 microprocessor has three hardware interrupts and three software interrupts that are vectored through the top portion of the memory. A new hardware interrupt, labeled $\overline{FIRQ}$, has been added to the $\overline{IRQ}$ and $\overline{NMI}$ inputs of the MC6800. The only difference between the new interrupt and the two old interrupts is that the $\overline{FIRQ}$ input will only store the program counter and the status register on the stack. The $\overline{IRQ}$ and $\overline{NMI}$ inputs place all of the internal registers, except the hardware stack pointer, on the stack.

Table 4–6 illustrates the vector locations for the interrupt inputs to the MC6809.

MC68000 Interrupt Structure

The interrupt structure for the MC68000 is quite different from the structure for the MC6800 and MC6809. A complete listing of the many different interrupts appears in table 4–7.

TABLE 4–6 MC6809 interrupt vectors.

Vector Location	Signal
$FFFE, $FFFF	Reset
$FFFC, $FFFD	$\overline{\text{NMI}}$
$FFFA, $FFFB	SWI
$FFF8, $FFF9	$\overline{\text{IRQ}}$
$FFF6, $FFF7	$\overline{\text{FIRQ}}$
$FFF4, $FFF5	SWI2
$FFF2, $FFF3	SWI3
$FFF0, $FFF1	Reserved

TABLE 4–7 MC68000 interrupt vectors.

Vector Number	Address	Assignment
0	00000	Reset initial SSP
	00004	Reset initial PC
2	00008	Bus error
3	0000C	Address error
4	00010	Illegal instruction
5	00014	Divide by zero
6	00018	CHK instruction
7	0001C	TRAPV instruction
8	00020	Privilege violation
9	00024	Trace
10	00028	Line 1010 emulator
11	0002C	Line 1111 emulator
12–23	00030–0005F	Reserved by Motorola
24	00060	Spurious interrupt
25	00064	Level 1 interrupt
26	00068	Level 2 interrupt
27	0006C	Level 3 interrupt
28	00070	Level 4 interrupt
29	00074	Level 5 interrupt
30	00078	Level 6 interrupt
31	0007C	Level 7 interrupt
32–47	00080–000BF	TRAP instruction vectors
48–63	000C0–000FF	Reserved by Motorola
64–255	00100–003FF	USER interrupt vectors

This vector table occupies the first 1024 bytes of memory or first 512 words of memory. Seven of these vectors are used for external interrupts; the remaining vectors are used for reset, for various Motorola system functions, and for TRAPS.

TRAPS are used by the system program to call up error handling routines; they may also be used as short form subroutine jumps if so desired. The trap number references a vector in the vector table that indicates the address of the TRAP subroutine.

External interrupts are caused by applying the interrupt device number, one through seven binary, on the three interrupt inputs IPL0, IPL1, and IPL2. Level seven has the highest priority, while level one has the lowest. A zero binary on these 3 pins indicates that no interrupt is being requested.

These interrupts reference the seven vectors listed in table 4–7 if the $\overline{\text{VPA}}$ input is asserted. Notice that these vectors are only 1 byte in length. One-byte vector locations are normally used for interrupts and contain memory address 0000 0000 0000 00XX XXXX XX00, where XXXX XXXX is the vector stored at autovector locations one through seven.

If desired, the external hardware may apply the interrupt vector location by not asserting the $\overline{\text{VPA}}$ input. If an external interrupt vector is supplied through the least significant 8 bits of the data bus, a vector to any of the 256 possible table entries can occur. This is useful if multiple interrupt processed I/O devices exist at each interrupt priority level.

Masking various interrupt levels is accomplished through the status register and the 3 bits assigned to perform this function. Interrupts are prohibited if the masks are the same priority level or greater than the currently requested interrupt level. The level seven interrupt cannot be inhibited or masked by the mask bits. It is equivalent to the $\overline{\text{NMI}}$ interrupt input on the MC6800 and MC6809.

INSTRUCTION TIMING 4-9

This section includes a list of the instructions and the number of clock cycles required to execute them. Only the MC6800 instructions are provided in this chapter. They are given to allow the student to calculate some of the time delays required for homework problems or outside development. The complete instruction set for the MC6800 is listed in table 4–8. To calculate the amount of time required to execute an instruction, multiply the number of instruction cycles by 1 μs. This is, of course, for the standard 1 MHz version of the MC6800.

THE MC6800 AND THE LOGIC ANALYZER 4-10

The logic analyzer is an extremely useful device in microprocessor testing. In fact, it is the only device that can be used to view the timing of a microprocessor while it is functioning in a system. It is even possible to view the pro-

TABLE 4–8 MC6800 instruction timing.

	(Dual Operand)	ACCX	Immediate	Direct	Extended	Indexed	Implied	Relative		(Dual Operand)	ACCX	Immediate	Direct	Extended	Indexed	Implied
ABA		•	•	•	•	•	2	•	INC		2	•	•	6	7	•
ADC	x	•	2	3	4	5	•	•	INS		•	•	•	•	•	4
ADD	x	•	2	3	4	5	•	•	INX		•	•	•	•	•	4
AND	x	•	2	3	4	5	•	•	JMP		•	•	•	3	4	•
ASL		2	•	•	6	7	•	•	JSR		•	•	•	9	8	•
ASR		2	•	•	6	7	•	•	LDA	x	•	2	3	4	5	•
BCC		•	•	•	•	•	•	4	LDS		•	3	4	5	6	•
BCS		•	•	•	•	•	•	4	LDX		•	3	4	5	6	•
BEA		•	•	•	•	•	•	4	LSR		2	•	•	6	7	•
BGE		•	•	•	•	•	•	4	NEG		2	•	•	6	7	•
BGT		•	•	•	•	•	•	4	NOP		•	•	•	•	•	2
BHI		•	•	•	•	•	•	4	ORA	x	•	2	3	4	5	•
BIT	x	•	2	3	4	5	•	•	PSH		•	•	•	•	•	4
BLE		•	•	•	•	•	•	4	PUL		•	•	•	•	•	4
BLS		•	•	•	•	•	•	4	ROL		2	•	•	6	7	•
BLT		•	•	•	•	•	•	4	ROR		2	•	•	6	7	•
BMI		•	•	•	•	•	•	4	RTI		•	•	•	•	•	10
BNE		•	•	•	•	•	•	4	RTS		•	•	•	•	•	5
BPL		•	•	•	•	•	•	4	SBA		•	•	•	•	•	2
BRA		•	•	•	•	•	•	4	SBC	x	•	2	3	4	5	•
BSR		•	•	•	•	•	•	8	SEC		•	•	•	•	•	2
BVC		•	•	•	•	•	•	4	SEI		•	•	•	•	•	2
BVS		•	•	•	•	•	•	4	SEV		•	•	•	•	•	2
CBA		•	•	•	•	•	2	•	STA	x	•	•	4	5	6	•
CLC		•	•	•	•	•	2	•	STS		•	•	5	6	7	•
CLI		•	•	•	•	•	2	•	STX		•	•	5	6	7	•
CLR		2	•	•	6	7	•	•	SUB	x	•	2	3	4	5	•
CLV		•	•	•	•	•	2	•	SWI		•	•	•	•	•	12
CMP	x	•	2	3	4	5	•	•	TAB		•	•	•	•	•	2
COM		2	•	•	6	7	•	•	TAP		•	•	•	•	•	2
CPX		•	3	4	5	6	•	•	TBA		•	•	•	•	•	2
DAA		•	•	•	•	•	2	•	TPA		•	•	•	•	•	2
DEC		2	•	•	6	7	•	•	TST		2	•	•	6	7	•
DES		•	•	•	•	•	4	•	TSX		•	•	•	•	•	4
DEX		•	•	•	•	•	4	•	TSX		•	•	•	•	•	4
EOR	x	•	2	3	4	5	•	•	WAI		•	•	•	•	•	9

NOTE: Interrupt time is 12 cycles from the end of the instruction being executed, except following a WAI instruction. Then it is 4 cycles.

SOURCE: Courtesy of Motorola, Inc.

gram execution path or track with the logic analyzer, which can be extremely useful in debugging complicated software.

Instruction Tracking with the Logic Analyzer

The op-codes of an instruction can be stored with the memory addresses in the memory of the logic analyzer for later viewing as hexadecimal op-codes. In some of the newer logic analyzers, it is even possible to view this information in mnemonic form as a listing on the screen of the analyzer. This, of course, is not a listing of the program; it is a dynamic listing of the instructions as they are actually executed in the system.

To track the program in an operating system with a logic analyzer, three signal components must be connected to the analyzer. The data input connections for the analyzer are connected to the MC6800 data bus, allowing the instructions and data to be displayed as they appear on the data bus. In addition to the data, a logic analyzer needs a clock signal to acquire the information from the data bus. This signal is obtained by logically combining the VMA signal with phase two of the clock. It is important that the analyzer clock is set on the negative edge of the output of the circuit in figure 4–10.

In addition to the data and clock inputs, the analyzer must also be triggered at the proper point by using the beginning address of the software under test as a trigger. Many analyzers have a 16-channel trigger producing circuit for this purpose.

Once the analyzer is triggered, it stores the information from the data bus in its internal memory until it is full. At this time the listing of the program can be viewed and checked for errors.

Displaying the Timing Diagram of the MC6800

To test the entire system, it is a good idea to view the timing of the microprocessor on the logic analyzer. To display the complete timing diagram, you need an analyzer capable of displaying more than 24 signals at one time. In many cases the analyzer that you use may have only 8 or 16 channels. If this is the case, you have to be more selective with the signals viewed on the analyzer.

To display the timing diagram for the MC6800, you may want to use the internal clock set to sample the information at the rate of every 20–50 ns. This procedure generates a fairly accurate timing diagram. The data inputs may consist of the VMA, R/$\overline{W}$, and the clock signal plus a few data bus bits and a few address bus bits. This will not display a complete timing diagram, but at least you can determine if the memory or I/O is functioning properly.

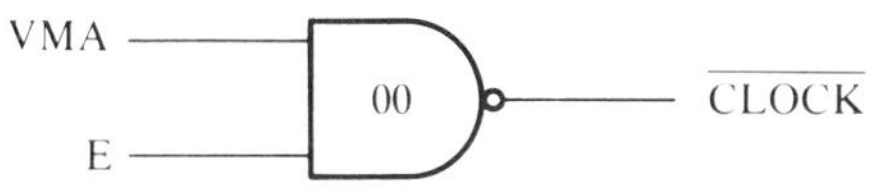

FIGURE 4–10 Circuitry required to generate a clock pulse for the logic analyzer.

Summary

This chapter provides a working knowledge of the hardware signals and major timing of the microprocessor. The MC6800, MC6809, and MC68000 Motorola microprocessors were covered in fair detail, but less comprehensively than in the data sheets from the manufacturer. If more detail is required on any of these or other microprocessors manufactured by Motorola, please refer to *The Complete Motorola Microcomputer Data Library* published by Motorola.

This chapter, of course, does supply enough detail so that you can explore the wonders of these fantastic devices. This book also allows a glimpse of another microprocessor, if you happen to be studying the Intel 8085A microprocessor discussed in chapter 3. In fact, I would strongly urge the student to make a comparative analysis of both Intel and Motorola microprocessors by perusing both chapters.

Glossary

Access time The amount of time required by a memory component to access or retrieve information.

Bus arbitration An access technique used when more than one bus controller or microprocessor exists on the same memory and I/O bus structure.

Bus cycle Whenever information is moved out of or into the microprocessor through its bus.

Direct memory access (DMA) A computer's ability to store or retrieve information directly from the memory without the intervention of the microprocessor.

Instruction cycle Equal to one clocking period in the MC6800, MC6809, and MC68000.

Interrupt An I/O technique that allows a slower external I/O device to interrupt the instruction flow of the microprocessor. This is accomplished through a hardware subroutine jump.

Memory management A technique whereby available memory space can be increased to an unlimited amount.

Parity A technique used to check for the validity of data.

Pinout The pictorial view of an integrated circuit defining each pin connection.

Read cycle Whenever the microprocessor reads data from the memory or an I/O device.

Sink current The amount of current available at an output whenever that output is a logic zero.

Source current The amount of current available at an output whenever that output is a logic one.

Transceiver A digital device that can either drive a bus line or receive data from a bus line.

Vector A number stored in the memory that is used to point to another location in the memory.

Write cycle Whenever the microprocessor writes information to a memory or an I/O device.

Questions and Problems

1 List the number of pin connections on each of the following microprocessors: MC6800, MC6809, and MC68000.

2 How many TTL unit loads can the MC6800 or MC6809 microprocessor directly drive?

3 How many TTL unit loads can the MC68000 microprocessor directly drive? Explain your answer.

4 What is the noise immunity for the MC6800, MC6809, and MC68000?

5 Which crystal frequency would be selected to operate the MC6800 at 1 MHz?

6 Which crystal frequency would be selected to operate the MC6809 at 1 MHz?

7 How many memory locations can the MC6800 or MC6809 directly address?

8 How many memory locations can the MC68000 directly address?

9 How many data bus connections are available on the MC68000 microprocessor?

10 Which MC6800 bus is a bidirectional bus?

11 What is the purpose of the $\overline{AS}$ pin on the MC68000?

12 What is the purpose of the $\overline{LDS}$ and $\overline{UDS}$ strobes on the MC68000?

13 The $\overline{BERR}$ signal on the MC68000 indicates which condition?

14 Which three signals control a DMA action on the MC68000 microprocessor?

15 Which signals control the DMA action of the MC6809 microprocessor?

16 Where must the RESET vector be stored in the MC6800 or MC6809 microprocessor?

17 Where must the RESET vector be stored in the MC68000 microprocessor?

18 How much time is allowed for memory access in a MC6800 based system?

19 How much time is allowed for memory access in a MC68000 based system?

20 Explain the operation of the circuit in figure 4–7.

21 What is the purpose of the $\overline{DTACK}$ signal in the MC68000 microprocessor?

22 List the types of interrupts available for the MC6800 microprocessor.

23 List the types of interrupts available for the MC6809 microprocessor.

24 List the types of interrupts available for the MC68000 microprocessor.

25 What is the difference between the $\overline{FIRQ}$ and the $\overline{IRQ}$ inputs on the MC6809?

26 Which MC68000 interrupt input level has the highest priority?

27 How long does it take the MC6800 to execute the LDAA instruction if a clock frequency of 1 MHz has been selected?

28 Given the following MC6800 program, determine how long it takes to execute if a 1 MHz clock is used.

```
        LDAA   #$10
LOOP    DECA
        BNE    LOOP
```

29 The logic analyzer can monitor the instruction flow in a subroutine or a program. Write a short program to test I/O location $C000.

30 If you were to use the internal clock on the logic analyzer and you set it for a 1 μs sample rate, what would you view on the screen if the data bus were connected to the analyzer's data inputs?

5

Memory Interface

This chapter introduces memory interfacing, a very important portion of microprocessor system design that develops an understanding of decoding. Decoding is extremely important because it is used in both memory and I/O interfacing.

This chapter provides a detailed study of the various types of memory devices, including ROM, EPROM, SRAM, and DRAM. Since these devices will be included in most future systems, a complete understanding is definitely an asset.

In addition to interfacing the above devices, decoding of completely and incompletely specified memory address is presented. These techniques and their proper application will almost always reduce the overall cost of a memory system.

5-1 CHARACTERISTICS OF MEMORY DEVICES

The ROM, or read only memory, and the RAM, or random access read and write memory, are the two general categories of memory devices in common use today. Both types have many features in common, including address connections, data bus connections, and similar control connections. The read only memory is commonly used to store programs and long-term data nonvolatilely; the semiconductor random access memory stores temporary data, since it is a volatile memory.

Read Only Memory (ROM)

Read only memory can be subdivided into many different categories, such as the PROM, EPROM, EAROM, and EEPROM. The ROM is a device that is mask programmed at the factory by the manufacturer in the last phase of fabrication. It is most often used in large production runs because the manufacturer charges thousands of dollars for the initial mask.

The PROM is a field programmable device programmed by a machine called a *PROM burner* or *PROM programmer.* The PROM burner received its name from the action required to program a PROM. This type of ROM is programmed by burning open small fuses located inside the integrated circuit. Since a fuse is burned open during programming, this device may only be programmed one time.

The EPROM has an advantage over the PROM because it can be erased. The EPROM is erased by exposing it to a high-intensity ultraviolet light for approximately 6–40 min. When programmed, fuses are not burned as with the PROM; instead an electrical charge is trapped in an insulated gate region. This trapped or programmed charge will be held for many years in this gate region. The charge is erasable through a quartz crystal window using ultraviolet light, which causes a photocurrent to flow, neutralizing the trapped charge. The main problem with the EPROM is that it takes a considerable amount of time to erase it.

The EAROM or EEPROM is a device that can be programmed and erased electrically. It is often called a *read mostly memory* (RMM) since it is often used to store data for an extended period of time. It typically requires about 4 to 10 ms to erase and another 4 to 10 ms to write new information, giving it a clear advantage over the EPROM. Its main disadvantage is the fact that it can only be erased and reprogrammed about ten thousand times.

Random Access Memory (RAM)

Random access memory can be divided into two major categories, the *static RAM* (SRAM) and the *dynamic RAM* (DRAM). Static random access memory is capable of storing information statically for as long as power is applied to the device. Dynamic memory will only store information for a few milliseconds before it is lost. A few milliseconds of time may not seem like much, but in this amount of time a microprocessor is able to accomplish quite a few tasks.

When dynamic memory is used in a system, additional circuitry is required to refresh the information periodically. When a DRAM is refreshed, the data from a group of memory locations is read and rewritten. If a memory system is small, static devices are used because of the additional cost of the refreshing circuitry. The breakeven point seems to be at about 16K bytes of memory. Memory systems containing more than 16K bytes will generally be dynamic, while systems containing less memory will be static.

Memory Size

The device illustrated in figure 5–1 is a 2K byte EPROM. Notice that 11 of the pin connections are used for memory addressing, 8 for data output connections, 3 for control, and 2 for the power supply connections. This particular EPROM is very commonly used today because of the single 5-V power supply requirement, its byte-sized capacity, and the ease at which it is interfaced to most commonly available microprocessors.

How do you determine how much memory is available in a device with 11 address connections? The number of locations on the memory device can be computed by raising two to a power equal to the number of address connections, as illustrated in example 5–1.

EXAMPLE 5–1

$$2^{11} = 2048 \text{ or 2K locations}$$

Likewise you can determine how much memory can be addressed or connected to a microprocessor if the number of address connections is known. The Intel 8085A has 16 address connections; it is capable of directly addressing 2^{16}, or 65,536, different memory locations.

Figure 5–2 illustrates the 4564 dynamic RAM, which is capable of storing 64K bits of information. Notice that it has been integrated into a 16-pin integrated circuit. It appears that the manufacturer has made a mistake or exam-

PIN CONFIGURATION

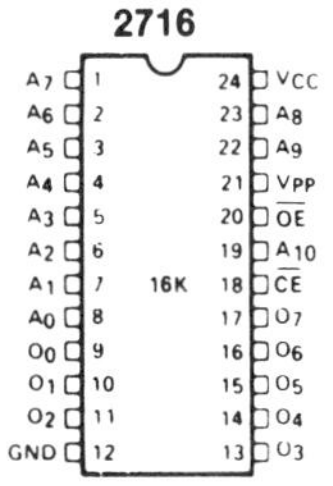

MODE SELECTION

PINS / MODE	$\overline{CE}$/PGM (18)	$\overline{OE}$ (20)	V_{PP} (21)	V_{CC} (24)	OUTPUTS (9-11, 13-17)
Read	V_{IL}	V_{IL}	+5	+5	D_{OUT}
Standby	V_{IH}	Don't Care	+5	+5	High Z
Program	Pulsed V_{IL} to V_{IH}	V_{IH}	+25	+5	D_{IN}
Program Verify	V_{IL}	V_{IL}	+25	+5	D_{OUT}
Program Inhibit	V_{IL}	V_{IH}	+25	+5	High Z

BLOCK DIAGRAM

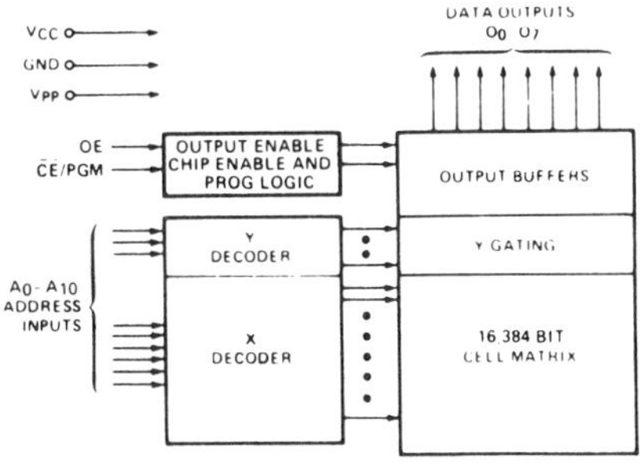

PIN NAMES

A_0–A_{10}	ADDRESSES
$\overline{CE}$/PGM	CHIP ENABLE/PROGRAM
$\overline{OE}$	OUTPUT ENABLE
O_0–O_7	OUTPUTS

FIGURE 5–1 The pinout of the Intel 2716 2K x 8 EPROM.

SOURCE: Reprinted by permission of Intel Corporation, Copyright 1979.

PIN FUNCTIONS

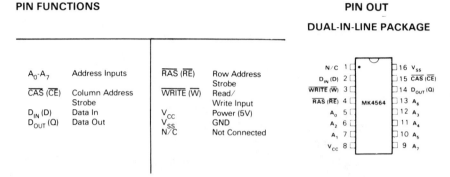

A_0-A_7	Address Inputs	$\overline{RAS}$ ($\overline{RE}$)	Row Address Strobe
$\overline{CAS}$ ($\overline{CE}$)	Column Address Strobe	$\overline{WRITE}$ ($\overline{W}$)	Read/ Write Input
D_{IN} (D)	Data In	V_{CC}	Power (5V)
D_{OUT} (Q)	Data Out	V_{SS}	GND
		N/C	Not Connected

PIN OUT

DUAL-IN-LINE PACKAGE

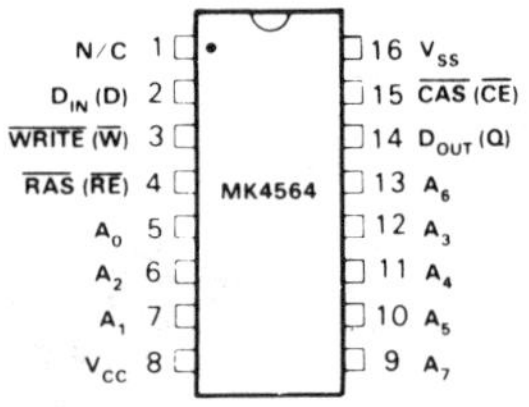

FIGURE 5–2 The pinout for the MK4564 64K x 1 dynamic RAM.
SOURCE: Courtesy of MOSTEK, Inc.

ple 5–1 is incorrect. Sixteen address connections are required to address this amount of memory and only 16 pins are available. To help reduce the size of the component, the manufacturer has elected to multiplex the address connections so that only 8 pins are actually needed to address this amount of memory. Multiplexed address connections have been in use since the early 1970s. To use this device, the $\overline{CAS}$ (or *column address strobe*) and $\overline{RAS}$ (or *row address strobe*) inputs strobe the address into internal address registers, where it is held to address the memory array.

Memory Data Connections

In figure 5–2 you will notice that the device uses separate pins for input and output data. This is one method of connecting a memory device to a system that has two data buses, one for input data and one for output data. Today very few microprocessor based systems use two buses; instead they use bidirectional data buses and memory devices that are capable of functioning with a bidirectional bus.

The 4564 can be used as a bidirectional device by connecting its input and output data pins. This connection effectively produces a bidirectional bus, since the data output pin is normally at its high impedance state. It is important that devices connected in this manner have three-state output connections. If additional drive is required, it can be obtained by connecting a three-state buffer between the data output connection and the bidirectional bus, as illustrated in figure 5–3. The $\overline{READ}$ signal is activated to drive the bus with data from this device.

FIGURE 5–3 Connecting a memory device that contains separate I/O pins as a common I/O memory device.

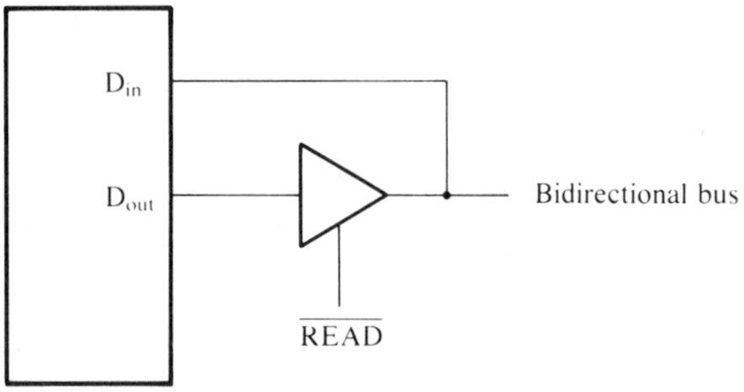

Memory Control

The control connections on memory devices are nearly the same for all devices. Figure 5–1 used 2 pins for its control, the $\overline{\text{OE}}$ and $\overline{\text{CE}}$ pins. $\overline{\text{OE}}$, or *output enable,* causes the internal three-state output buffers to drive the output pins, provided that $\overline{\text{CE}}$, or *chip enable,* has also been activated. All memory devices have some form of chip enable or chip selection logic. Even the circuit in figure 5–2 has this logic but it is hidden in the function of the $\overline{\text{CAS}}$ pin. Normally a memory device will contain either a $\overline{\text{CE}}$ or a $\overline{\text{CS}}$ pin for control.

Some devices, such as the one shown in figure 5–4, have multiple chip enable logic. Whenever more than 1 chip enable pin is present, it aids the hardware designer in interfacing the device to a microprocessor. When multiple chip selection pins exist, all must be activated to enable the memory component. In figure 5–4, $\overline{\text{CS1}}$ and $\overline{\text{CS2}}$ must both be grounded and CS3 must be pulled up to a logic one to select the device. Once selected, data will appear at the output connections within a short period of time.

Another control pin found on RAM memory devices is the $\overline{\text{WE}}$ or R/$\overline{\text{W}}$ pin. Figure 5–5 pictures the 4118 static RAM, which contains a $\overline{\text{WE}}$ pin and an $\overline{\text{OE}}$ pin. Both pins can facilitate the device's connection to a bidirectional data bus. This memory has been organized as a bytewide memory device with 1024 memory locations. The $\overline{\text{WE}}$, or *write enable,* pin causes a write into this memory component.

As discovered in this section, memory devices are nearly all alike in function and application. More detail will be provided later, along with the design methodology for their connection to microprocessors.

TIMING CONSIDERATIONS OF MEMORY DEVICES 5-2

To interface a memory device to a microprocessor, a thorough understanding of the memory device itself must be grasped. Operation of a memory component can only be understood by reading the timing diagrams provided by the manufacturer. Along with the timing diagram is a listing of electrical characteristics that describe the times required to control and utilize the device. These times and the timing diagram must be understood to ensure a device's proper operation with a particular microprocessor. It is important to note that not all memory components are compatible with all microprocessors.

Basic Timing Diagrams

A few words about timing diagrams before looking deeply into one of them: The first thing to be noticed, in figure 5–6, is that the address connections are not shown individually but as a composite waveform of all the address inputs. This arrangement has been chosen to conserve space and to make it easier to understand the waveforms.

The only thing that a composite waveform can indicate is a change in bit patterns. This is viewed as an *X,* or *crossover point,* on the timing diagrams. Another common practice on timing diagrams is to show a line halfway between a logic one and a logic zero for a high impedance condition. It does *not*

PIN CONFIGURATION

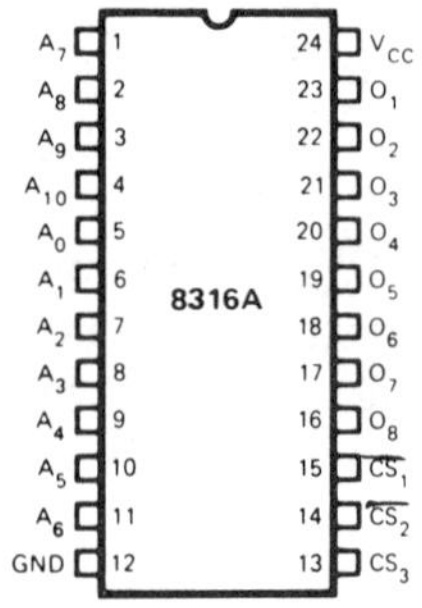

BLOCK DIAGRAM

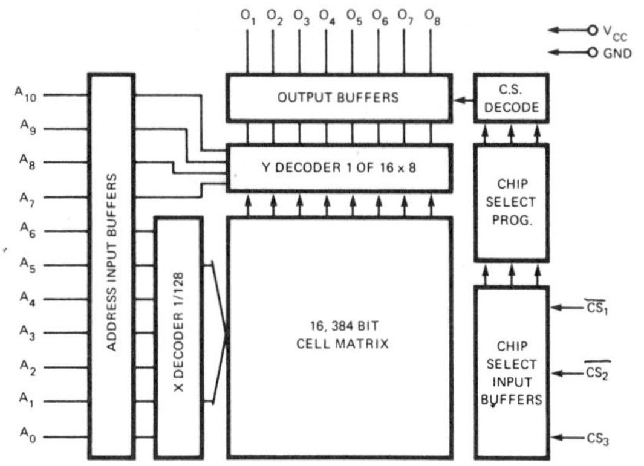

A.C. CHARACTERISTICS T_A = 0°C to +70°C, V_{CC} = +5V ±5% unless otherwise specified

SYMBOL	PARAMETER	LIMITS			UNIT
		MIN.	TYP.(1)	MAX.	
t_A	Address to Output Delay Time		400	850	nS
t_{CO}	Chip Select to Output Enable Delay Time			300	nS
t_{DF}	Chip Deselect to Output Data Float Delay Time	0		300	nS

CONDITIONS OF TEST FOR A.C. CHARACTERISTICS

Output Load . . . 1 TTL Gate, and C_{LOAD} = 100 pF
Input Pulse Levels . . . . 0.8 to 2.0V
Input Pulse Rise and Fall Times . (10% to 90%) 20 nS
Timing Measurement Reference Level
Input 1.5V
Output . . . . 0.45V to 2.2V

CAPACITANCE (2) T_A = 25°C, f = 1 MHz

SYMBOL	TEST	LIMITS	
		TYP.	MAX.
C_{IN}	All Pins Except Pin Under Test Tied to AC Ground	4 pF	10 pF
C_{OUT}	All Pins Except Pin Under Test Tied to AC Ground	8 pF	15 pF

(2) This parameter is periodically sampled and is not 100% tested.

A.C. WAVEFORMS

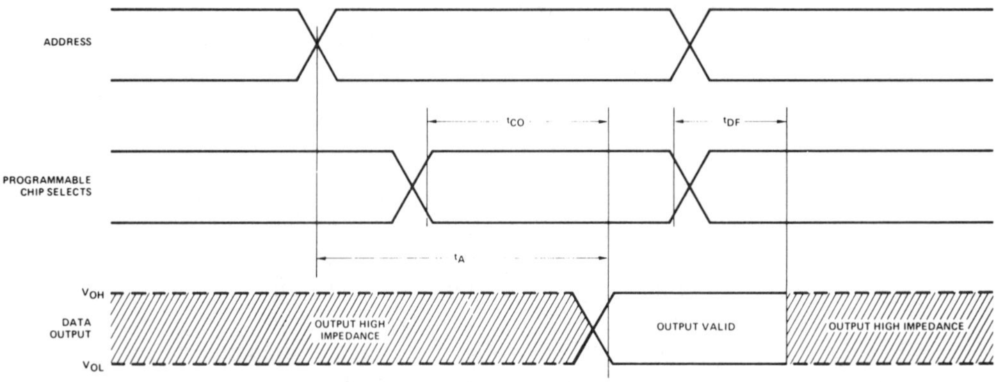

FIGURE 5–4 The 8316 ROM, which contains multiple chip enable inputs.

SOURCE: Reprinted by permission of Intel Corporation, Copyright 1978.

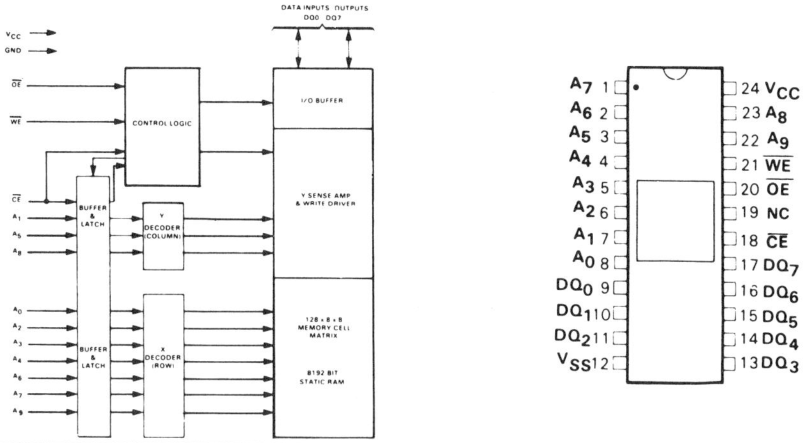

TRUTH TABLE

$\overline{CE}$	$\overline{OE}$	$\overline{WE}$	Mode	DQ
V_{IH}	X	X	Deselect	High Z
V_{IL}	X	V_{IL}	Write	D_{IN}
V_{IL}	V_{IL}	V_{IH}	Read	D_{OUT}
V_{IL}	V_{IH}	V_{IH}	Read	High Z

X = Don't Care

PIN NAMES

A_0-A_9	Address Inputs	$\overline{WE}$	Write Enable
$\overline{CE}$	Chip Enable	$\overline{OE}$	Output Enable
V_{SS}	Ground	NC	No Connection
V_{CC}	Power (+5V)	DQ_0-DQ_7	Data In/Data Out

FIGURE 5–5 The MK4118 static 1K x 8 RAM.
SOURCE: Courtesy of MOSTEK, Inc.

indicate that the voltage level is 2.5 V. This type of waveform most often appears on data output connections from memory devices and microprocessors.

EPROM Timing

A complete set of timing diagrams for the 2716 EPROM is provided in figure 5–7, along with its electrical characteristics. Refer to this figure for the following discussion of read timing, which applies to all memory devices.

The first change that occurs when reading information from a memory device is the application of the memory address. This application triggers an external decoder that generates the $\overline{CE}$ (chip enable) input to the memory. After this step, the microprocessor issues the read signal to place the $\overline{OE}$ input at a logic zero. The memory then, in a short period of time, begins to drive the data bus with information for the microprocessor.

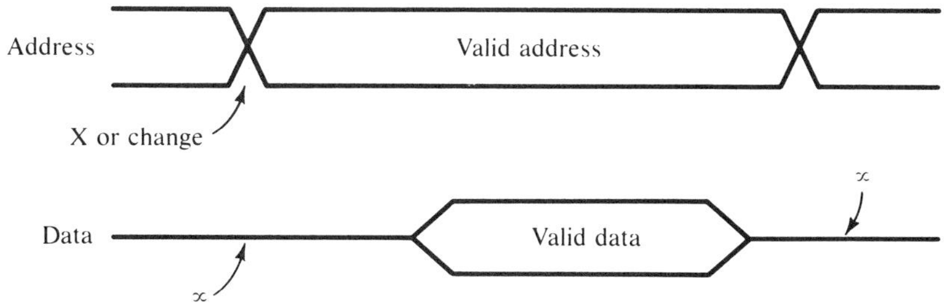

FIGURE 5–6 Interpreting general memory timing diagrams.

A.C. Characteristics

Symbol	Parameter	2716 Limits			2716-1 Limits			2716-2 Limits			Unit	Test Conditions
		Min	Typ[4]	Max	Min	Typ[4]	Max	Min	Typ[4]	Max		
t_{ACC}	Address to Output Delay			450			350			390	ns	$\overline{CE} = \overline{OE} = V_{IL}$
t_{CE}	$\overline{CE}$ to Output Delay			450			350			390	ns	$\overline{OE} = V_{IL}$
t_{OE}	Output Enable to Output Delay			120			120			120	ns	$\overline{CE} = V_{IL}$
t_{DF}	Output Enable High to Output Float	0		100	0		100	0		100	ns	$\overline{CE} = V_{IL}$
t_{OH}	Address to Output Hold	0			0			0			ns	$\overline{CE} = \overline{OE} = V_{IL}$

Capacitance[5] $T_A = 25°C$, f = 1 MHz

Symbol	Parameter	Typ.	Max.	Unit	Conditions
C_{IN}	Input Capacitance	4	6	pF	$V_{IN} = 0V$
C_{OUT}	Output Capacitance	8	12	pF	$V_{OUT} = 0V$

A.C. Test Conditions:

Output Load: 1 TTL gate and $C_L = 100$ pF
Input Rise and Fall Times: ≤20 ns
Input Pulse Levels: 0.8V to 2.2V
Timing Measurement Reference Level:
Inputs 1V and 2V
Outputs 0.8V and 2V

A.C. WAVEFORMS

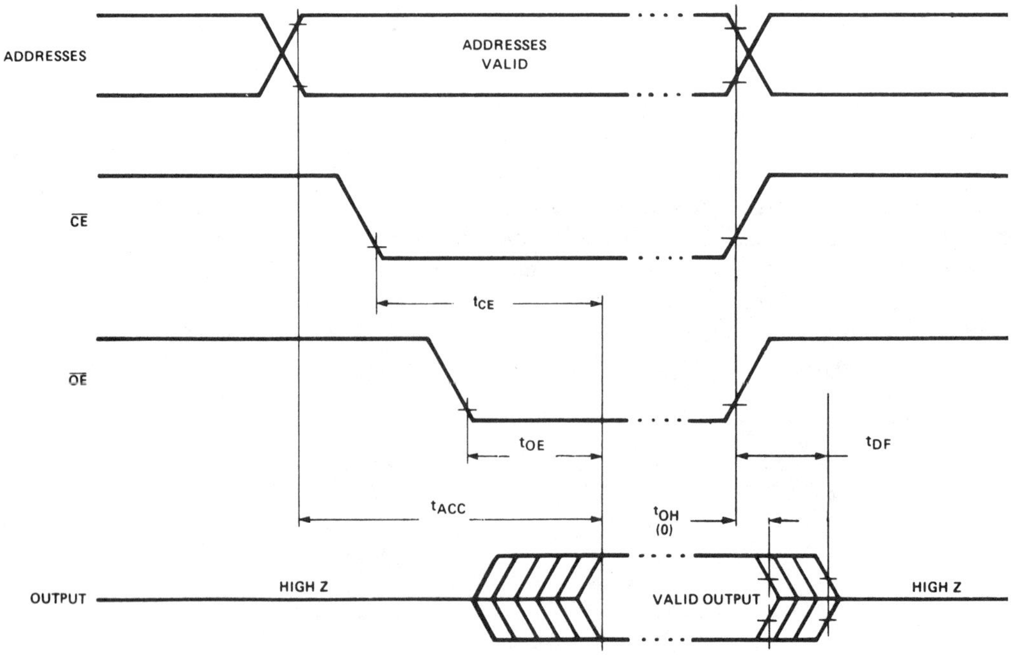

FIGURE 5–7 The timing diagram and AC characteristics for the Intel 2716 EPROM.
SOURCE: Reprinted by permission of Intel Corporation, Copyright 1978.

Access time, the amount of time required to access information, varies considerably from memory device to memory device. In the memory device in figure 5–7, it takes 450 ns for data to be accessed from the address inputs or the $\overline{CE}$ input. (This is by definition the access time for a memory component.) Since the $\overline{CE}$ input is developed by an external memory address decoder, the decoder propagation delay time is added to the access time of the memory device. How long it takes the data to be accessed would then be 450 ns plus the decoder's propagation delay time.

Another critical time is the period required for the output buffers to be activated. The output buffers are enabled by the application of a logic zero to the $\overline{OE}$ connection of this memory device. The electrical characteristics indicate that this procedure requires 120 ns. The $\overline{OE}$ connection prevents bus conflicts or contentions in microprocessors that use a multiplexed data bus. In microprocessors without a multiplexed data bus, this pin can be treated as an additional chip enable input. Whenever more than one chip enable is present, all must be placed at their active levels to obtain information at the output of the memory.

To summarize, the microprocessor sends a memory address that is decoded by an external decoder to the memory. The output of the decoder activates the $\overline{CE}$ input and starts to access data inside the memory component. Finally, the microprocessor sends out some form of memory read signal, which activates $\overline{OE}$ and causes the memory to apply data to the data bus.

Static RAM Timing

Figure 5–8 illustrates the timing diagram and specifications for the 2114, 1K by 4, SRAM. You will notice that the timing diagram is very similar to the one for the 2716 EPROM with one exception: the $\overline{WE}$ input replaces the $\overline{OE}$ input. The number of address inputs is reduced by 1 pin because this device contains only 1024 memory locations (instead of the 2048 memory locations in the 2716). The 2716 has eight output connections; the 2114, because of a change in internal organization, only has four. The I/O pins input data to the memory and also extract data from the memory. These are common I/O pins, which are present on quite a few RAM memory devices.

In figure 5–8(a), you will notice that only the address information, the $\overline{CS}$ (or *chip selection*) information, and the data output information are provided. It is understood that $\overline{WE}$ (write enable) input is at its inactive level because a read operation is being illustrated. The microprocessor outputs a memory address to the address pins, and an external decoder generates a logic zero for the $\overline{CS}$ pin. Then, after some prescribed access time, data will appear at the I/O pins.

One significant change to note is that the access time for the 2114 RAM is much shorter than the access time for the 2716 EPROM, as denoted in figure 5–7. This reduction in access time is required in a system that uses a multiplexed data bus since the bus is not available for use until some time after the memory address is sent out to the memory. This decrease in access time allows the read signal to be combined logically with the memory address to activate the $\overline{CS}$ input for the RAM. This procedure is necessary to avoid a bus conflict.

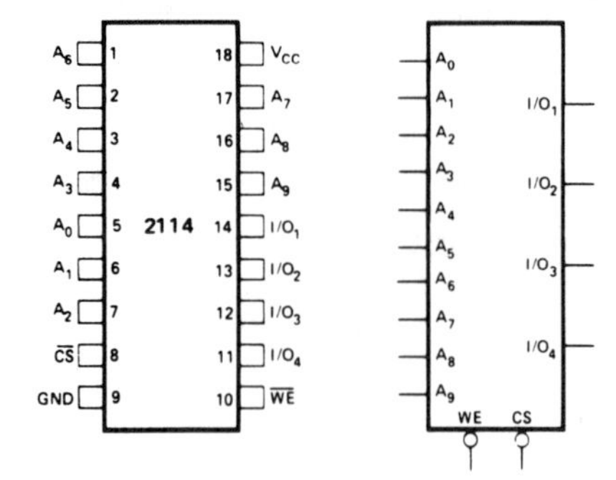

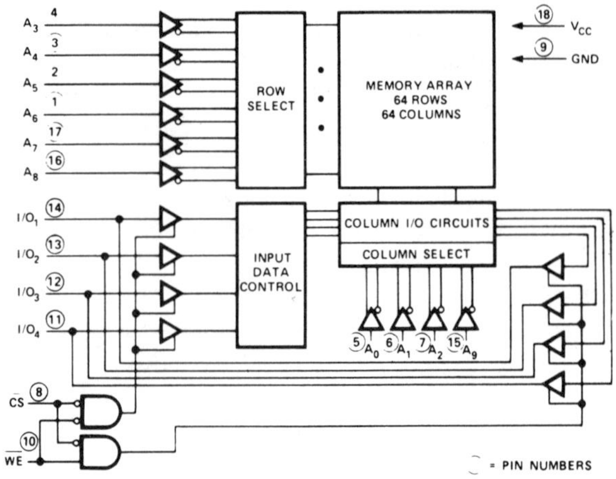

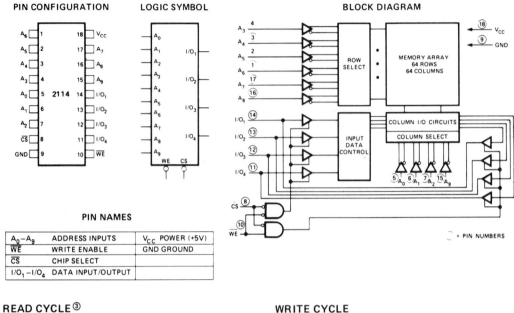

PIN NAMES

A_0–A_9	ADDRESS INPUTS	V_{CC} POWER (+5V)
$\overline{WE}$	WRITE ENABLE	GND GROUND
$\overline{CS}$	CHIP SELECT	
I/O_1–I/O_4	DATA INPUT/OUTPUT	

READ CYCLE ③

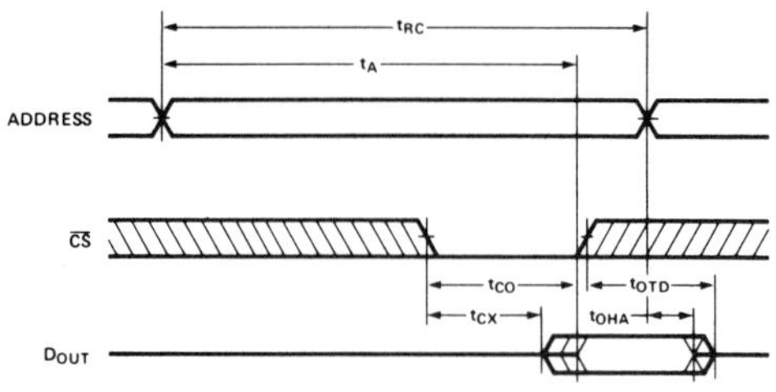

WRITE CYCLE

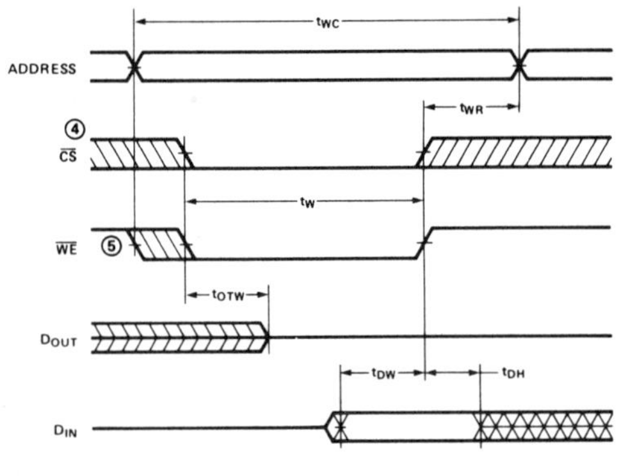

NOTES:

③ $\overline{WE}$ is high for a Read Cycle.

④ If the $\overline{CS}$ low transition occurs simultaneously with the $\overline{WE}$ low transition, the output buffers remain in a high impedance state.

⑤ $\overline{WE}$ must be high during all address transitions.

FIGURE 5–8 The Intel 2114 1K x 4 static RAM pinout, timing, and AC characteristics.

SOURCE: Reprinted by permission of Intel Corporation, Copyright 1978.

Figure 5–8(b) illustrates the write timing for the 2114 RAM. Here, unlike in figure 5–8(a), the $\overline{WE}$ signal is illustrated because it is used by the memory to accomplish a memory write. In some memory devices, this pin is labeled R/$\overline{W}$ and has exactly the same function as $\overline{WE}$.

For the microprocessor to write information into the 2114, it first sends out a memory address that is decoded to enable the device. The write signal that follows indicates that the data to be written into the memory is available on the data bus.

The time required to write information is normally equal to or less than that required to read information. In the case of the 2114, the period required to write information is about 150 ns from the $\overline{WE}$ signal; the time required to read information is about 250 ns.

A.C. CHARACTERISTICS $T_A = 0°C$ to $70°C$, $V_{CC} = 5V \pm 5\%$, unless otherwise noted.

READ CYCLE [1]

SYMBOL	PARAMETER	2114-2, 2114L2 Min.	Max.	2114-3, 2114L3 Min.	Max.	2114, 2114L Min.	Max.	UNIT
t_{RC}	Read Cycle Time	200		300		450		ns
t_A	Access Time		200		300		450	ns
t_{CO}	Chip Selection to Output Valid		70		100		120	ns
t_{CX}	Chip Selection to Output Active	20		20		20		ns
t_{OTD}	Output 3-state from Deselection		60		80		100	ns
t_{OHA}	Output Hold from Address Change	50		50		50		ns

WRITE CYCLE [2]

SYMBOL	PARAMETER	2114-2, 2114L2 Min.	Max.	2114-3, 2114L3 Min.	Max.	2114, 2114L Min.	Max.	UNIT
t_{WC}	Write Cycle Time	200		300		450		ns
t_W	Write Time	120		150		200		ns
t_{WR}	Write Release Time	0		0		0		ns
t_{OTW}	Output 3-state from Write		60		80		100	ns
t_{DW}	Data to Write Time Overlap	120		150		200		ns
t_{DH}	Data Hold From Write Time	0		0		0		ns

NOTES:
1. A Read occurs during the overlap of a low $\overline{CS}$ and a high $\overline{WE}$.
2. A Write occurs during the overlap of a low $\overline{CS}$ and a low $\overline{WE}$.

FIGURE 5–8 *continued*

Memory Cells

Figure 5–9 illustrates the 4116 dynamic RAM. Dynamic RAMs differ from static RAMs in that they require periodic refreshing. A static RAM stores information for an indefinite amount of time, while a dynamic RAM stores information for only a few milliseconds. This is due to the internal structure of the dynamic RAM.

Figure 5–10(a) illustrates a basic static RAM memory element or cell, while figure 5–10(b) illustrates a basic dynamic cell. These illustrations show that the DRAM cell only requires half the transistors of the SRAM cell. Although this suggests that a DRAM can accommodate twice as much memory as the SRAM, actually many more than twice as many DRAM cells can be placed in the same area. The DRAM cell dissipates much less power than the SRAM cell. Power is dissipated in a DRAM cell only when data is written, read, or refreshed.

Again referring to figure 5–9, notice that there are only 7 pins devoted to memory addressing. How is this possible when this memory device has 16K bits of information stored inside? It's possible because the address pins are used for 14 bits of address information that are strobed or multiplexed into the 7 pins, 7 bits at a time. A much more detailed discussion of DRAM and its timing is presented in a later section of this chapter.

FUNCTIONAL DIAGRAM

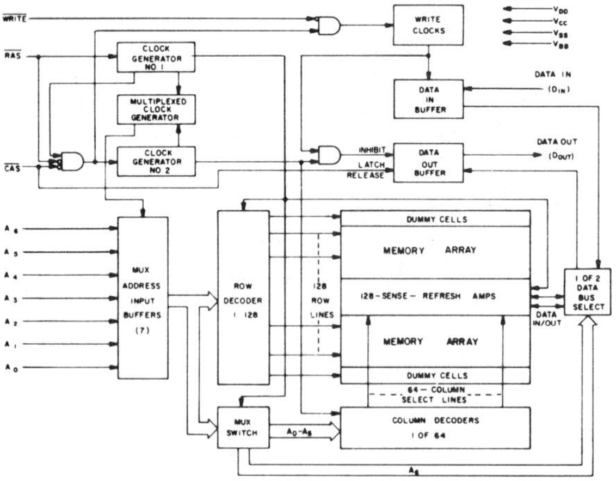

PIN CONNECTIONS

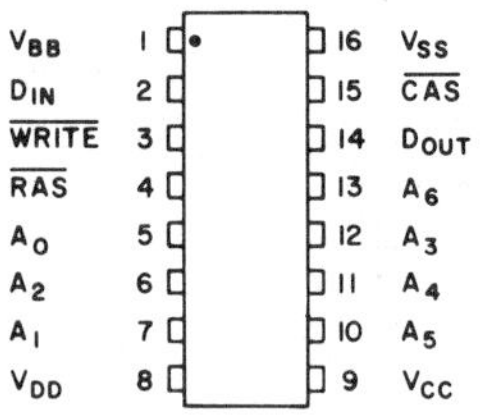

PIN NAMES

A_0-A_6	ADDRESS INPUTS	WRITE	READ/WRITE INPUT
CAS	COLUMN ADDRESS STROBE	V_{BB}	POWER (−5V)
D_{IN}	DATA IN	V_{CC}	POWER (+5V)
D_{OUT}	DATA OUT	V_{DD}	POWER (+12V)
RAS	ROW ADDRESS STROBE	V_{SS}	GROUND

FIGURE 5–9 The MK4116 16K x 1 dynamic RAM.
SOURCE: Courtesy of MOSTEK, Inc.

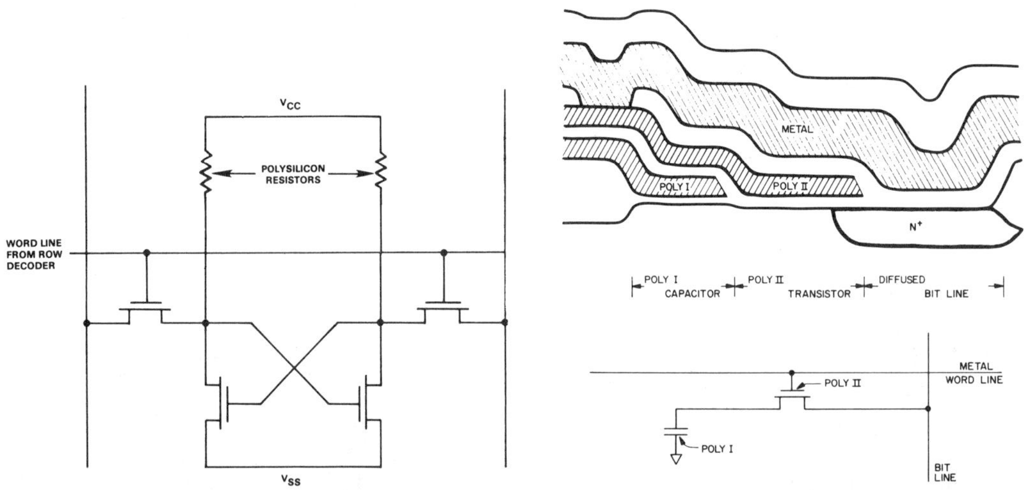

FIGURE 5–10 RAM Memory Cells: (a) the MK4108 static memory cell, (b) the MK4116 dynamic memory cell.
SOURCE: Courtesy of MOSTEK, Inc.

EEPROM Timing

The last memory device to be discussed is the 2816 EEPROM in figure 5–11, which is receiving wide application because of its nonvolatility. This device is often called a *nonvolatile RAM*. It can be written and erased electrically without losing information when disconnected from the power supply. The 2816 EEPROM is very useful for storing information that is changed only occasionally.

In the past a battery was required with standard RAM to create a nonvolatile RAM. The main timing difference between EEPROM and RAM is that erasure or writing takes much more time in the EEPROM. The 2816, for exam-

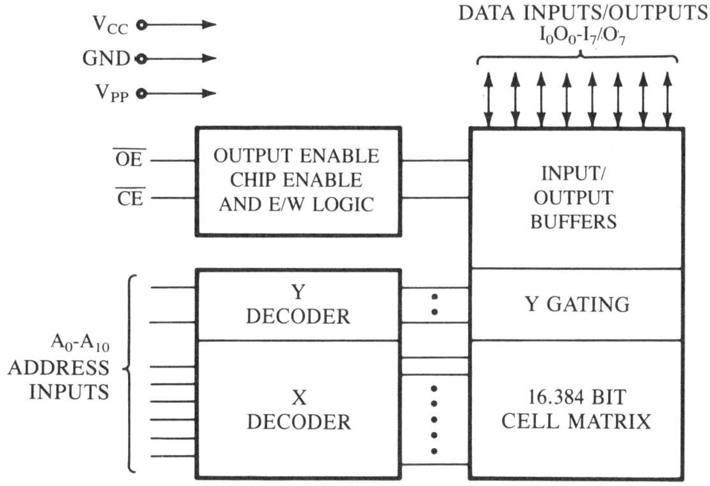

2816 Functional Block Diagram

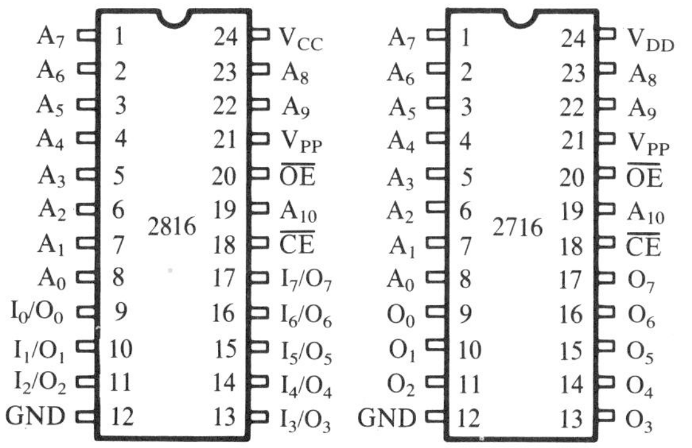

PIN NAMES

A_0-A_{10}	ADDRESSES
$\overline{CE}$	CHIP ENABLE
$\overline{OE}$	OUTPUT ENABLE
O_0-O_7	DATA OUTPUTS
I_0-I_7	DATA INPUTS
V_{PP}	PROGRAM VOLTAGE

FIGURE 5–11 The Intel 2816 2K x 8 EEPROM.
SOURCE: Reprinted by permission of Intel Corporation, Copyright 1982.

ple, requires 10 ms to write or to erase information. This may seem to be too much time, but if data is only written occasionally, it presents no problem in most systems.

Another difference is that the 2816 requires a 21-V power supply for programming, so that a system incorporating this device requires an additional power supply.

Applications for this type of memory usually include tab positions on CRT terminals, sales tax look-up tables in electronic cash registers, and a variety of other applications. In fact, it may eventually replace other forms of ROM since a change in software can be accomplished in the machinery without removing the integrated circuits from the system. The software can even be changed remotely through a telephone line or a data link to the manufacturer.

5-3 ADDRESS DECODING

An *address decoder* is a device or digital circuit that indicates that a particular area of memory is being addressed, or pointed to, by the microprocessor. In other words, an address decoder is a simple combinational logic circuit. Most address decoders have one or more outputs that become active for a particular area of memory.

The Basic Address Decoder

The circuit of figure 5–12 uses a simple 4 input NAND gate as a memory address decoder. The output of the NAND gate is active low, so that its output only becomes a logic zero whenever all of the inputs are pulled high. In this example, a microprocessor with a 16-bit address bus is connected to the NAND gate. The output of the NAND gate will go low whenever the microprocessor addresses a memory location that begins with an A hexadecimal. As example 5–2 indicates, the first four bits of the address bus are decoded by the NAND gate, with the remaining bits illustrated as *X*s (don't cares). They are called *don't cares* because as far as this circuit is concerned we are not interested in their logic levels. If all zeros are inserted for the don't cares, we can locate the lowest numbered memory location decoded by the circuit. In this case the lowest numbered memory address decoded is A000H. Notice that a capital letter *H* following a number denotes a hexadecimal quantity. With some microprocessors, a dollar sign ($) preceding the number indicates a hexadecimal quantity.

EXAMPLE 5–2

A15	A14	A13	A12	A11	A10	A9	A8	A7	A6	A5	A4	A3	A2	A1	A0	
1	0	1	0	X	X	X	X	X	X	X	X	X	X	X	X	(A X X X H)
							or									
1	0	1	0	0	0	0	0	0	0	0	0	0	0	0	0	(A 0 0 0 H)
							to									
1	0	1	0	1	1	1	1	1	1	1	1	1	1	1	1	(A F F F H)

The highest location decoded by the decoder can be determined by substituting all logic ones for the don't cares. In this case, the highest location decoded is AFFFH. This decoder will produce a logic zero at its output for any memory location between A000H and AFFFH. We have decoded a 4K-byte segment of the microprocessor's address space. It is very important to remember that 1000H is equal to 4K and that 400H is equal to 1K. This relationship makes developing memory address decoding circuitry easier.

Let's suppose that a particular application requires a 2K-byte segment of ROM using the 2716 EPROM. The engineering department has indicated only that this device must function at memory location 2000H through and

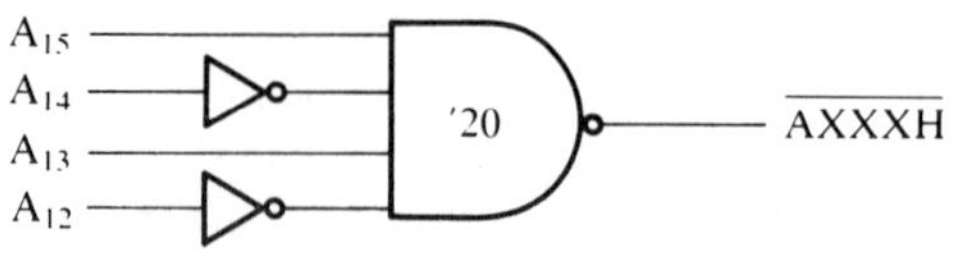

FIGURE 5–12 Basic circuit for decoding an address beginning with an A hexadecimal.

including 27FFH. The first step (see example 5–3) is to write down both extremes of the memory locations in binary. The binary representations indicate that the right-hand 11 address bits, A0 through A10, change from all zeros to all ones within this area of memory; the left-hand 5 address bits, A11 through A15, remain the same. In fact, if you were to compare the next lowest and the next highest binary memory addresses, 1FFFH and 2800H, you would notice that the first 5 bits would change. In other words, the first five bits of the address are unique to this area of memory.

EXAMPLE 5–3

A15	A14	A13	A12	A11	A10	A9	A8	A7	A6	A5	A4	A3	A2	A1	A0		
0	0	1	0	0	0	0	0	0	0	0	0	0	0	0	0	or	2000H
							to										
0	0	1	0	0	1	1	1	1	1	1	1	1	1	1	1	or	27FFH

Since the output of this circuit must generate a logic zero to ground the enable input of the 2716, a truth table, table 5–1, is developed. From the truth table we can write a Boolean logic expression for the logic zero output. The expression for this range of addresses is depicted in equation 5–1. This expression can be implemented with a five input OR gate if one is available.

$$A15 + A14 + \overline{A13} + A12 + A11 = \overline{2000H \text{ to } 27FFH} \qquad \textbf{5–1}$$

Since only a five or more input NAND gate is available, DeMorgan's theorem is used on the left-hand side of equation 5–1 to convert it to NAND gate form as shown in equation 5–2. Figure 5–13 illustrates this Boolean expression

$$\overline{\overline{A15} \cdot \overline{A14} \cdot A13 \cdot \overline{A12} \cdot \overline{A11}} = \overline{2000H \text{ to } 27FFH} \qquad \textbf{5–2}$$

implemented with an eight input NAND gate (the 74LS30 eight input NAND) and inverters (the 74LS04 hex inverter).

Integrated Decoder Circuits

In most applications, more than one memory device is usually required for system operation. It would be extremely wasteful to use an eight input NAND gate for each memory device. To this end, a decoder, selected from the variety in production by the IC houses, is used.

An extensive search for the ideal decoder suggests that for many applications the 74LS138 or Intel 8205 3-to-8 line decoder is ideal. In fact, after examining many pieces of microprocessor based equipment, it appears that the entire industry has also discovered this device. The most useful features of this device are the multiple enable inputs.

Figure 5–14 depicts this decoder, along with a truth table describing its operation. This decoder has active low outputs that only become active when all of the enable inputs are at their active levels. Whenever this device is enabled, the 3-bit binary number present at the address inputs causes one of the output pins to become active.

Using Decoder Circuits

Suppose that a given system requires eight EPROMs of the 2716 type to function at memory address 0000H through 3FFFH. This can be accomplished

TABLE 5–1 2000H to 27FFH address decoder truth table.

A15	A14	A13	A12	A11	Out
0	0	0	0	0	1
0	0	0	0	1	1
0	0	0	1	0	1
0	0	0	1	1	1
0	0	1	0	0	0
0	0	1	0	1	1
0	0	1	1	0	1
0	0	1	1	1	1
0	1	0	0	0	1
0	1	0	0	1	1
0	1	0	1	0	1
0	1	0	1	1	1
0	1	1	0	0	1
0	1	1	0	1	1
0	1	1	1	0	1
0	1	1	1	1	1
1	0	0	0	0	1
1	0	0	0	1	1
1	0	0	1	0	1
1	0	0	1	1	1
1	0	1	0	0	1
1	0	1	0	1	1
1	0	1	1	0	1
1	0	1	1	1	1
1	1	0	0	0	1
1	1	0	0	1	1
1	1	0	1	0	1
1	1	0	1	1	1
1	1	1	0	0	1
1	1	1	0	1	1
1	1	1	1	0	1
1	1	1	1	1	1

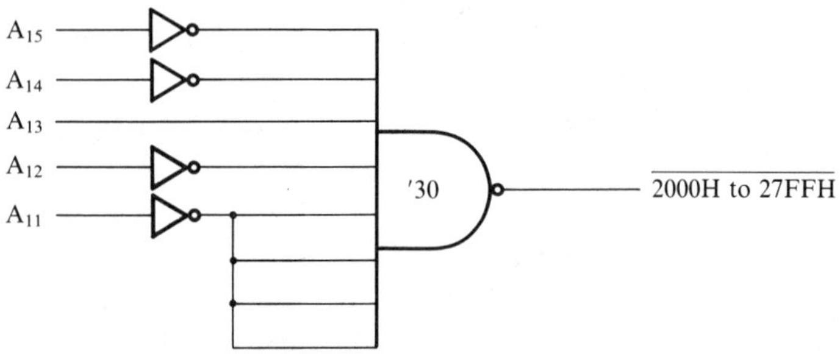

FIGURE 5–13 A circuit to implement equation 5–2.

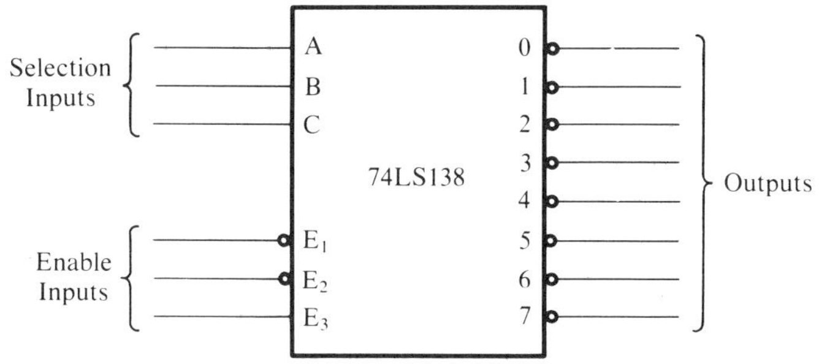

Inputs						Outputs							
Enable			Select										
$\overline{E_1}$	$\overline{E_2}$	E_3	C	B	A	$\overline{0}$	$\overline{1}$	$\overline{2}$	$\overline{3}$	$\overline{4}$	$\overline{5}$	$\overline{6}$	$\overline{7}$
1	X	X	X	X	X	1	1	1	1	1	1	1	1
X	1	X	X	X	X	1	1	1	1	1	1	1	1
X	X	0	X	X	X	1	1	1	1	1	1	1	1
0	0	1	0	0	0	0	1	1	1	1	1	1	1
0	0	1	0	0	1	1	0	1	1	1	1	1	1
0	0	1	0	1	0	1	1	0	1	1	1	1	1
0	0	1	0	1	1	1	1	1	0	1	1	1	1
0	0	1	1	0	0	1	1	1	1	0	1	1	1
0	0	1	1	0	1	1	1	1	1	1	0	1	1
0	0	1	1	1	0	1	1	1	1	1	1	0	1
0	0	1	1	1	1	1	1	1	1	1	1	1	0

FIGURE 5–14 The 74LS138 3-to-8 line decoder and truth table.

by using eight 8 input NAND gates and a multitude of inverters; or it can be accomplished with one 74LS138 decoder. Sounds hard to believe, doesn't it?

The first step in designing this interface is to write the binary address with A10 through A0 as don't cares, as illustrated in example 5–4. We don't care about these address bits since the memory devices themselves internally decode these address bit positions. Remember that the 2716 has 11 address pins.

EXAMPLE 5–4

A15	A14	A13	A12	A11	A10	A9	A8	A7	A6	A5	A4	A3	A2	A1	A0	
0	0	0	0	0	X	X	X	X	X	X	X	X	X	X	X	or 0000H
							to									
0	0	1	1	1	X	X	X	X	X	X	X	X	X	X	X	or 3FFFH

Observe that A15 and A14 are the only binary bit positions in this range of addresses that remain unchanged. These 2 bits enable the 74LS138 decoder. The next three address bit positions (A13, A12, and A11) do change; in fact, they change or vary through every binary combination from 000 to 111. These 3 bits are ideal candidates for the address inputs of the decoder. The completed circuit is illustrated in figure 5–15.

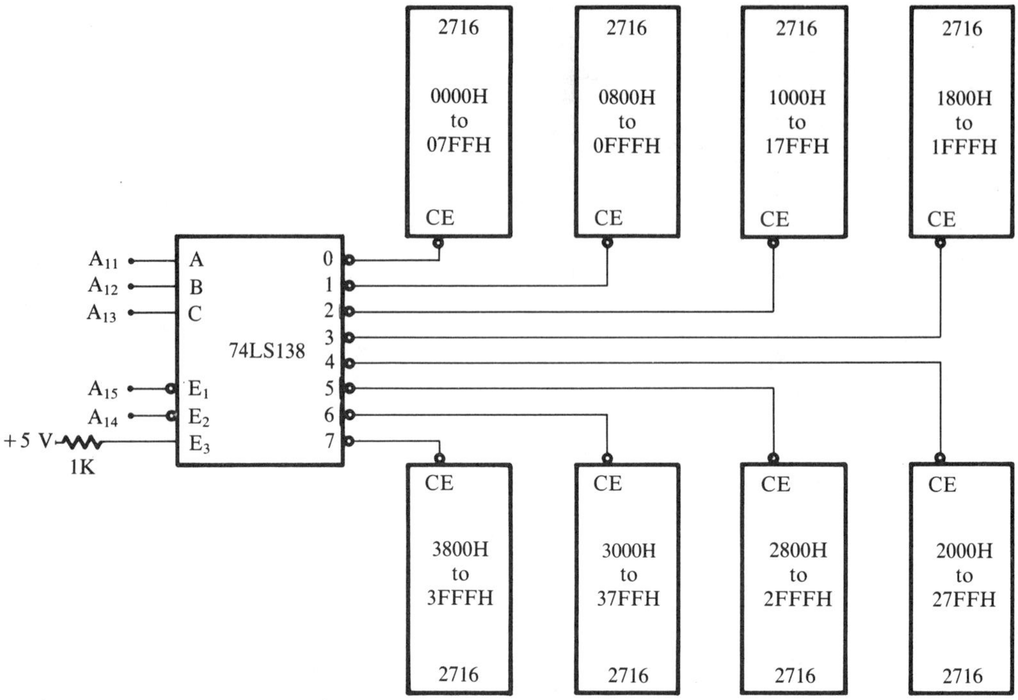

FIGURE 5–15 A circuit that will select one of the eight EPROMs if the correct address appears on the inputs of the 74LS138 3-to-8 line decoder.

Notice that only the 74LS138 decoder and eight EPROMs appear in the complete circuit. Again this is by far the most efficient method of decoding memory addresses that the author has encountered. It is even an effective approach if only one or two devices are to be selected or enabled with their outputs.

The rule followed in industry today is to minimize the component count. The fewer the integrated circuits in a system, the more reliable and the easier it is to maintain or troubleshoot.

PROM Decoders

Another device that may be found as a memory address decoder is the TTL bipolar PROM. For example, the 74S288 PROM, which has five address inputs and eight outputs, can be used in the same way the 74LS138 was used in figure 5–15. The only difference is that each of the PROM's 32 memory locations must be programmed with the correct output bit patterns to enable the eight memory devices. This is a much more costly approach to memory device selection but one that is used on occasion. Its main advantage is that the decoded address range can be changed at some point in the future by changing the PROM — not by rewiring the circuit. Figure 5–16 illustrates the 74S288, which selects eight 2716 EPROMs, and the contents of the PROM.

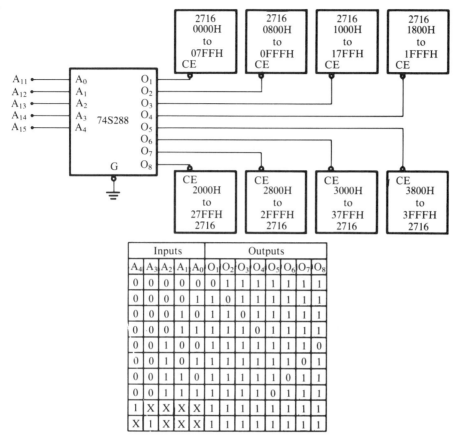

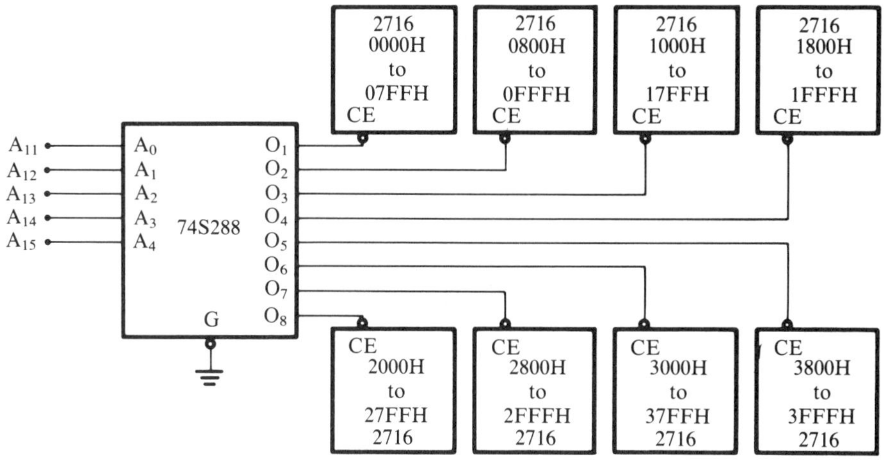

Inputs					Outputs							
A_4	A_3	A_2	A_1	A_0	O_1	O_2	O_3	O_4	O_5	O_6	O_7	O_8
0	0	0	0	0	0	1	1	1	1	1	1	1
0	0	0	0	1	1	0	1	1	1	1	1	1
0	0	0	1	0	1	1	0	1	1	1	1	1
0	0	0	1	1	1	1	1	0	1	1	1	1
0	0	1	0	0	1	1	1	1	1	1	1	0
0	0	1	0	1	1	1	1	1	1	1	0	1
0	0	1	1	0	1	1	1	1	1	0	1	1
0	0	1	1	1	1	1	1	1	0	1	1	1
1	X	X	X	X	1	1	1	1	1	1	1	1
X	1	X	X	X	1	1	1	1	1	1	1	1

FIGURE 5–16 A circuit that will select one of the eight EPROMs if the correct address appears on the inputs of the 74LS288 PROM decoder.

STATIC MEMORY SYSTEMS 5-4

Static memory systems are found in applications requiring only a small amount of RAM for implementation. Because ROM is always static, the principles in this section also apply to the ROM section in any system. The first step in developing any system memory is the memory map. A *memory map* illustrates which segments are to be used for RAM, and, in some cases, where the I/O resides.

Memory Maps

Figure 5–17 illustrates a typical memory map of a small system. This particular system requires 12K bytes of memory for program storage in ROM and 2K bytes of memory for data storage in RAM. The segments for both types of memory were arbitrarily chosen for this example problem.

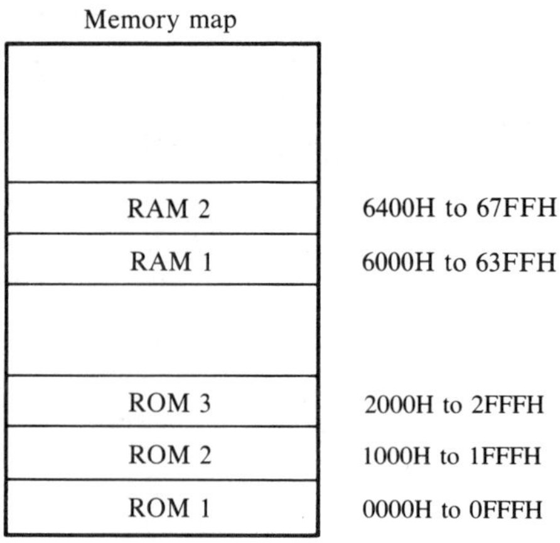

FIGURE 5–17 The memory map of a small memory system consisting of two segments of RAM and three segments of EPROM.

	A_{15} A_{14} A_{13} A_{12}	A_{11} A_{10} A_9 A_8	A_7 A_6 A_5 A_4	A_3 A_2 A_1 A_0
ROM	0 0 0 0	X X X X	X X X X	X X X X
		to		
ROM	0 0 1 0	X X X X	X X X X	X X X X
RAM	0 1 1 0	0 0 X X	X X X X	X X X X
		to		
RAM	0 1 1 0	0 1 X X	X X X X	X X X X

As illustrated in the figure, ROM1 resides at memory locations 0000H through 0FFFH; ROM2 resides at memory locations 1000H through 1FFFH; and ROM3 resides at memory locations 2000H through 2FFFH. RAM1 resides at memory 6000H through 63FFH, and RAM2 resides at memory locations 6400H through 67FFH. The ROM and RAM in this system are contiguous by themselves, but not together as a unit. In most cases it may not be necessary to construct a memory that is contiguous, but for this example it is assumed to be a system requirement.

Once the memory has been mapped, the ROM and RAM boundary addresses are written in binary, so that a decoder can be selected for the system. This is illustrated at the bottom of the figure. In both cases, the address bits that are internally decoded by the memory devices are drawn as don't cares. The remaining address bit positions must be decoded by an external memory address decoder to select or enable the memory devices at the appropriate time. Since these ROM and RAM sections have different numbers of address bits to be externally decoded, two decoders are required for this application.

Multiple Memory Device Decoders

The circuit depicted in figure 5–18 shows the result using two 3-to-8 line (74LS138) decoders. The first decoder, which is connected to the four most significant address bit positions, generates signals whenever the microprocessor addresses data in the bottom half of the memory. Each one of the eight outputs will become active for a 4K-byte segment of the memory.

In this application, the first three 4K-byte segments are used for ROM1, ROM2, and ROM3, which are connected to the first three outputs. Output zero will go low for memory addresses 0000H through 0FFFH; output one will go low for memory addresses 1000H through 1FFFH; and output two will go low for memory addresses 2000H through 2FFFH.

In addition to these three connections to the ROMs, you will notice that the $\overline{\text{MEMR}}$ signal is also connected to their $\overline{\text{OE}}$ pins. This synchronizes the transfer of data from the ROMs to the microprocessor. More detail on where the $\overline{\text{MEMR}}$ signal comes from and how it is generated is provided in chapters 3 and 4.

Output six of the first decoder enables the second decoder whenever the microprocessor points to a memory location 6XXXH. The second decoder then generates an output for the two RAM devices because it decodes address bits A10 and A11.

Output zero, of the second decoder, becomes active whenever address 6000H through 63FFH is sent out of the microprocessor. Output one becomes active whenever the microprocessor presents memory address 6400H through 67FFH. These outputs select or enable the two RAM devices.

In addition to selection inputs, the RAMs also contain a $\overline{\text{WE}}$ connection and an $\overline{\text{OE}}$ connection. These inputs control the application of data to the memory and also control when data is sent to the microprocessor from the memory. $\overline{\text{MEMW}}$ causes the write to occur and $\overline{\text{MEMR}}$ causes the read to occur.

Since the number of integrated circuits used in a system is important, the circuit in figure 5–18 is redesigned, using a TTL PROM for memory address decoding rather than two 74LS138 decoders. By reducing the number of integrated circuits used in a system, we improve its reliability, reduce its power consumption, reduce its size, and make it easier for a technician to troubleshoot for faults.

Figure 5–19 illustrates the same system, using the 3624A PROM in place of the two 74LS138 decoders. This PROM is organized as a 512-byte memory device and can be used in almost any memory decoder circuit imaginable.

To understand how the outputs of the PROM function, peruse table 5–2, which illustrates the data stored on this PROM. For example, the first output of the PROM (O1) will become active whenever the memory address begins with four zeros. This occurs whenever memory addresses 0000H through 0FFFH appear on the address bus. Output two becomes active whenever 00001 binary appears on the address bus. The remaining bit patterns are easily calculated by looking at the truth table and writing down the binary bit patterns for these outputs.

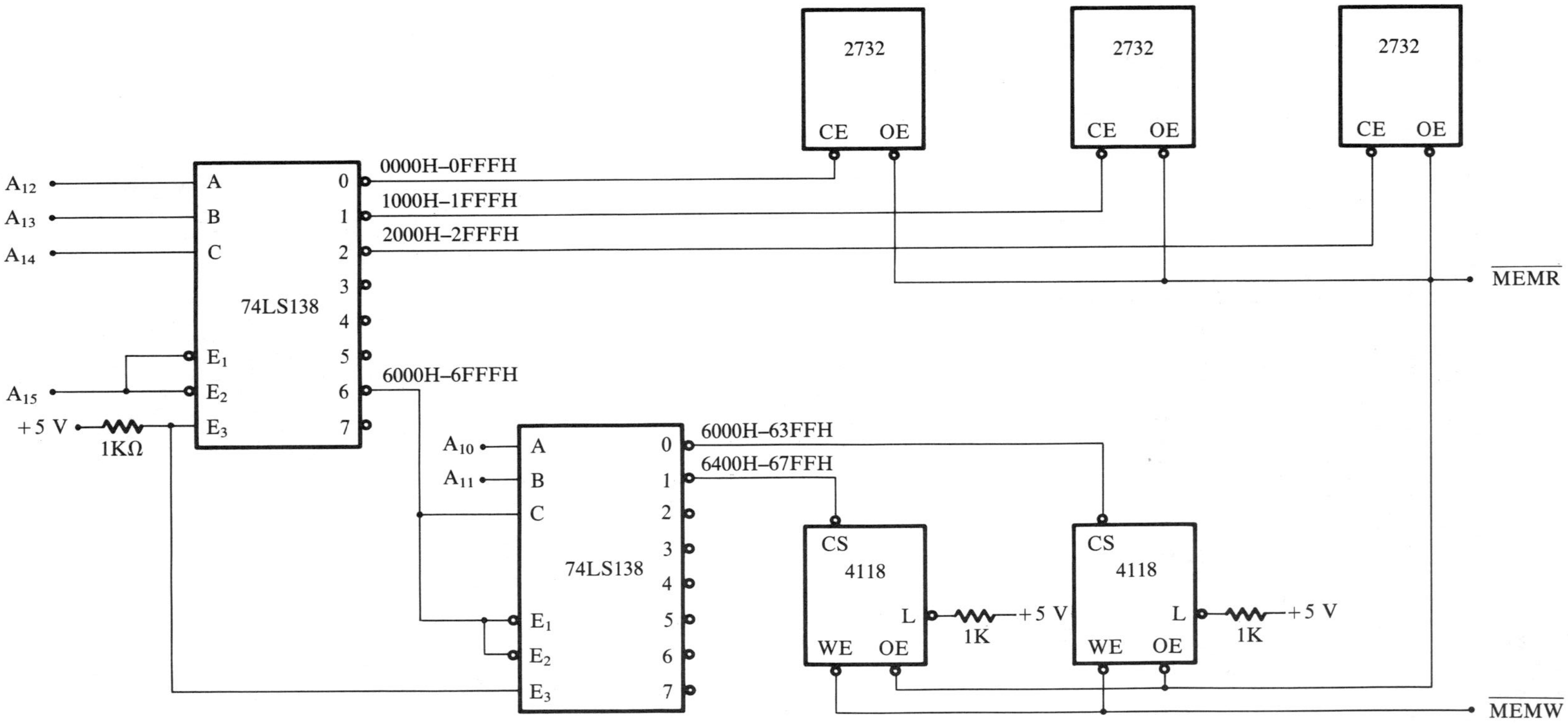

FIGURE 5–18 A circuit constructed from the memory map of figure 5–17 using 3-to-8 line decoders for memory address selection.

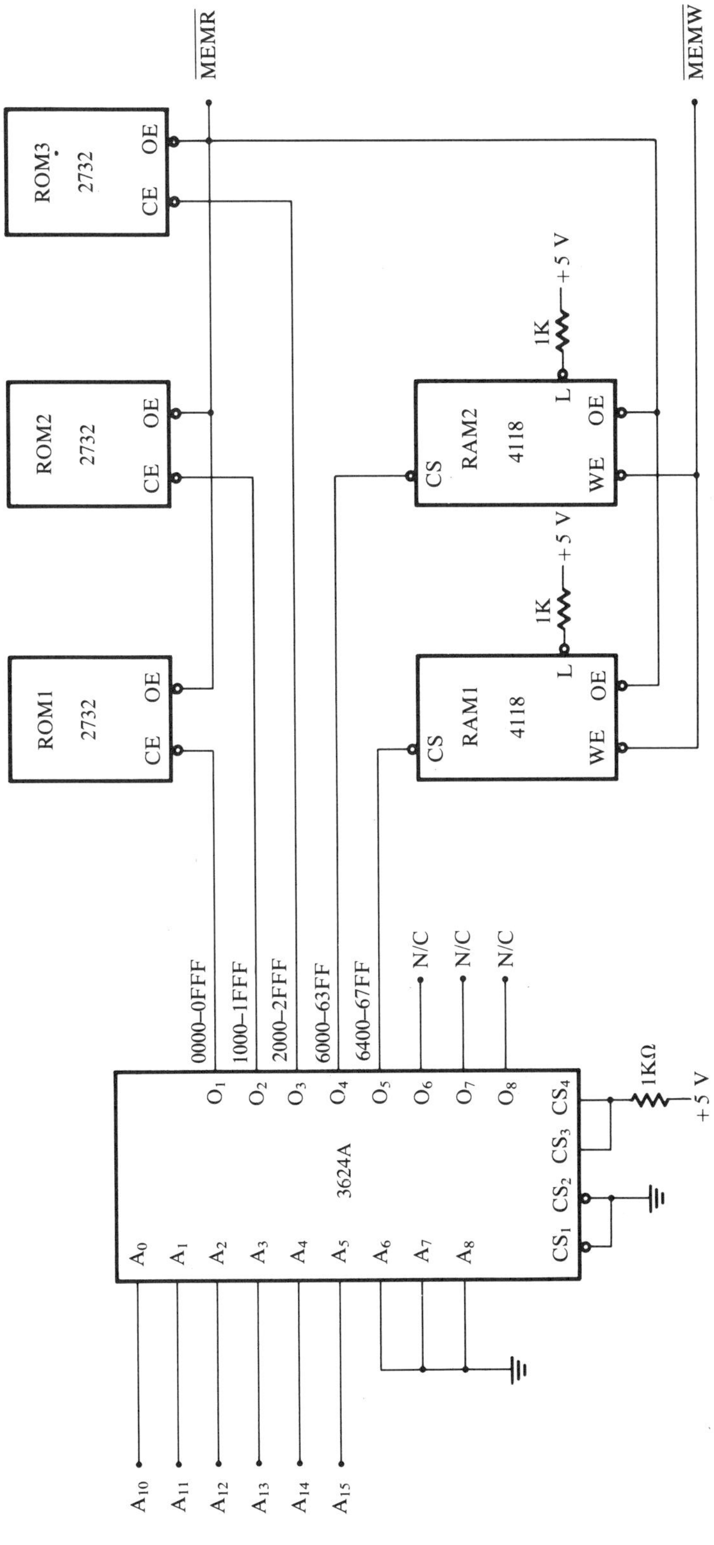

FIGURE 5–19 A circuit constructed from the memory map of figure 5–17 using a 3624A PROM decoder for memory address selection.

TABLE 5–2 The 3624A programmed logic for the circuit in Fig. 5–19.

Inputs									Outputs							
A8	**A7**	**A6**	**A5**	**A4**	**A3**	**A2**	**A1**	**A0**	**O8**	**O7**	**O6**	**O5**	**O4**	**O3**	**O2**	**O1**
0	0	0	0	0	0	0	0	0	X	X	X	1	1	1	1	0
0	0	0	0	0	0	0	0	1	X	X	X	1	1	1	1	0
0	0	0	0	0	0	0	1	0	X	X	X	1	1	1	1	0
0	0	0	0	0	0	0	1	1	X	X	X	1	1	1	1	0
0	0	0	0	0	0	1	0	0	X	X	X	1	1	1	0	1
0	0	0	0	0	0	1	0	1	X	X	X	1	1	1	0	1
0	0	0	0	0	0	1	1	0	X	X	X	1	1	1	0	1
0	0	0	0	0	0	1	1	1	X	X	X	1	1	1	0	1
0	0	0	0	0	1	0	0	0	X	X	X	1	1	0	1	1
0	0	0	0	0	1	0	0	1	X	X	X	1	1	0	1	1
0	0	0	0	0	1	0	1	0	X	X	X	1	1	0	1	1
0	0	0	0	0	1	0	1	1	X	X	X	1	1	0	1	1
0	0	0	0	1	1	0	0	0	X	X	X	1	0	1	1	1
0	0	0	0	1	1	0	0	1	X	X	X	0	1	1	1	1
All other combinations									X	X	X	1	1	1	1	1

The main advantage of using the PROM to decode the memory address is the reduction in component count. The main disadvantage is that a PROM must be programmed, and programming PROMs requires special equipment and time. These advantages and disadvantages are weighed whenever a system is being developed.

Another option that deserves investigation is incompletely specified memory address decoding. Up until now, we have been using all of the memory address bits to select a memory device. This is only applicable in a system that will eventually contain every memory location. Most applications do not use the entire memory; therefore, the technique covered in the first portion of this section is useful only in a handful of applications.

This time, let's suppose that the system memory will only contain three 4K-byte ROMs and two 1K-byte RAMs. This assumption makes memory address decoding a lot simpler, since we do not need to decode all of the bits of the memory address to select five different devices. In fact, to select five different devices, we need only have available a 3-bit binary address, since it offers eight different combinations.

Starting with the memory map as we did before, we can segment it into eight different sections. Each section can be a memory device. In this example, five of the eight sections are used for memory, as illustrated in figure 5–20.

ROM1 is enabled whenever the memory address begins with 000, ROM2 whenever the memory address begins with 001, and so forth. The three most significant address bit positions are connected to a 3-to-8 line decoder (as illustrated in figure 5–21) to produce the required chip selection outputs for the memory devices.

Output one of the decoder becomes active for memory addresses 0000H through 1FFFH, which is not 4K bytes of memory. This would seem to cre-

A_{15}	A_{14}	A_{13}
	1	1	1
	1	1	0
RAM2	1	0	1
RAM1	1	0	0
	0	1	1
ROM3	0	1	0
ROM2	0	0	1
ROM1	0	0	0

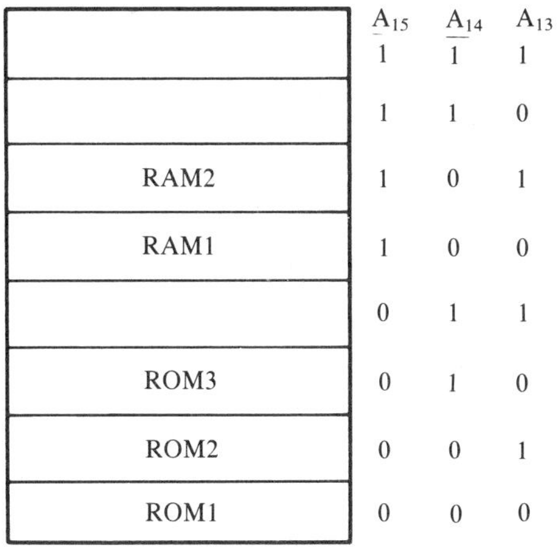

FIGURE 5–20 A memory map for an incompletely specified memory system.

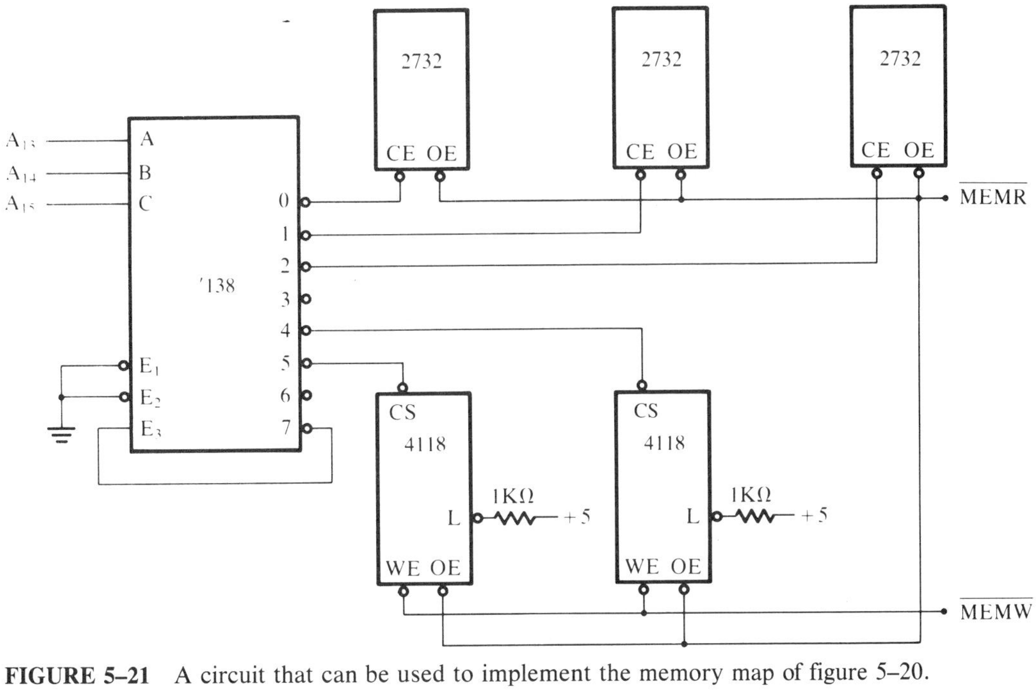

FIGURE 5–21 A circuit that can be used to implement the memory map of figure 5–20.

ate a problem when connecting a 4K-byte memory device to this output, but it doesn't. The memory device will respond to locations 0000H through 0FFFH or locations 1000H through 1FFFH. In other words, the data in the ROM will appear at the outputs twice in this range of memory. ROM1 is said to *overlay* 8K bytes of memory, of which only 4K bytes will be used. If the program is written to function in memory locations 0000H through 0FFFH, that is exactly where it will function. The fact that it also appears at locations 1000H through 1FFFH is not important, since this area of memory is never addressed by the program.

The remaining ROMs also overlay 8K bytes of memory each, again creating no problem for the programmer developing the software for the system. Address assignments for the ROMs can be as follows: ROM1 (0000H–0FFFH), ROM2 (3000H–3FFFH), and ROM3 (4000H–4FFFH). Notice that the ROM storage is not contiguous storage, which can present a slight problem in developing the software for the system. To bypass this difficulty, the program is required to jump or branch from memory location 0FFFH to memory location 3000H for a continuation of the program.

Each of the RAM devices also overlays an 8K-byte block of the memory and appears eight times in the block. Again this does not present a problem, since the memory can be made contiguous by proper selection of the memory addresses. The RAMs can reside at locations 9C00H through 9FFFH for RAM1 and A000H through A3FFH for RAM2. As can be seen, this is contiguous memory that will function perfectly.

As far as simplicity is concerned, this last implementation is by far the best for a small system since it only requires one decoder. Output seven, which is never active under normal usage, is a pullup for active high input E3. This practice saves the cost of the resistor and is common. This procedure reduces the total cost of the system. The connection may cause a problem in a system that has not been completely debugged if this area of memory is addressed. If this area of memory is addressed by the processor, it can lock out all of the memory.

A word on memory access times at this point is appropriate. The propagation delay time through the 74LS138 decoder is approximately 22 ns, and the propagation delay time through the 2364A PROM is approximately 70 ns. Comparing these two times, which subtracts from the time allowed by the microprocessor for the memory to access data, indicates that it is wise to use the decoder instead of the PROM.

For example, if the microprocessor allows 575 ns of time for the memory to access data and the memory device itself requires 450 ns to access the data, the system has a 125-ns *margin:* The decoder can use up to 125 ns of time before the system becomes inoperative. In this case, using the decoder or the PROM creates no problem; but if the memory access time is longer or the time allowed by the processor is shorter, the PROM cannot decode the address. The margin should always be at least 20 ns or longer.

STD-BUS Memory Interface

The next example problem, illustrated in figure 5–22, depicts a buffered printed circuit card for use in the STD-BUS system. Notice that all connections into or out of this card are buffered; that is, inputs represent one LS unit load and outputs are buffered to drive a considerable number of unit loads. The 12 least significant address inputs are buffered through two 74LS244 octal bus buffers, and the remaining address bits are connected to a dual 2-to-4 line decoder.

The microprocessor in the STD-BUS system sends out a memory address along with the $\overline{\text{MEMEX}}$ signal and the $\overline{\text{MEMRQ}}$ signal. For normal memory operation the $\overline{\text{MEMEX}}$ signal is a logic one and the $\overline{\text{MEMRQ}}$ signal is a logic zero. The $\overline{\text{MEMEX}}$ signal is applied to the $\overline{\text{1G}}$ input of the decoder, which causes the two most significant address bits to be decoded and produce a logic zero on one of the four $\overline{\text{1Y}}$ outputs of the decoder. The strapping pro-

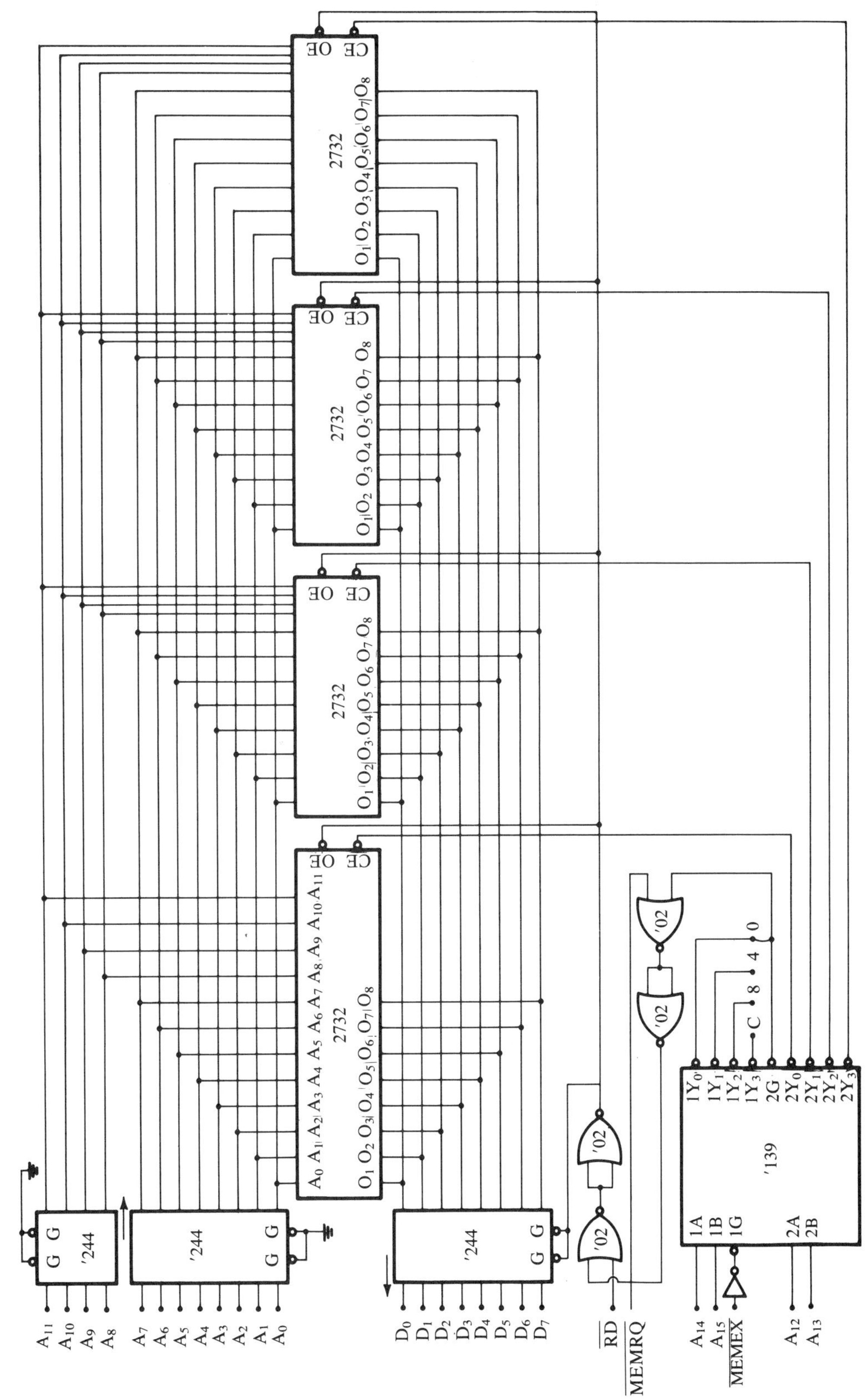

FIGURE 5–22 A fully buffered 16K x 8 EPROM printed circuit card for the STD-BUS standard microcomputer bus.

vided at these outputs selects the 16K block of memory at which the board will function: 0 (0000H–3FFFH); 4 (4000H–7FFFH); 8 (8000H–BFFFH); and C (C000H–FFFFH). The diagram illustrates that the strapping has connected this board to function at memory locations 0000H through 3FFFH. The output of the strap is connected to two points in the circuit: One enables or selects the other half of the decoder through $\overline{2G}$; and the other point gates the $\overline{MEMRQ}$ signal through, to be combined with the $\overline{RD}$ strobe.

The second section of the decoder, if enabled, decodes address bits A13 and A12 to select one of the four EPROMs. The outputs of this decoder function as follows: $\overline{2Y0}$ for memory address 0000H through 0FFFH, $\overline{2Y1}$ for memory address 1000H through 1FFFH, $\overline{2Y2}$ for memory address 2000H through 2FFFH, and $\overline{2Y3}$ for memory address 3000H through 3FFFH. In this example, the decoding scheme reduces the access time by about 44 ns, which is the time required for the address to propagate (1) through the top portion of the decoder, (2) down through the strap, and (3) through the bottom section of the decoder.

Once the appropriate EPROM is selected by the decoder, the microprocessor issues a $\overline{RD}$ signal so that the data can be read from the memory without a bus conflict. The $\overline{RD}$ signal is gated through to the $\overline{OE}$ connection on each EPROM and also to the active low gate input of the data bus buffer (74LS244). If the board is enabled by the proper or selected range of addresses, data is applied to the data bus by the data bus buffers.

This particular board has been implemented with a minimal number of integrated circuits to make maintenance easier and to increase the reliability of the board. Some important portions of this board do not appear in the schematic diagram and are worth mentioning at this point.

Power supply inputs and decoupling are not shown but are extremely critical to the proper operation of this board. A general rule of thumb to follow when decoupling ICs from the power supply is that each totem-pole output requires about 2000 pF of capacitance for proper operation. The capacitors are required since totem-pole outputs generate noise at the power supply connections that can be coupled into another device in the system. It is also important not to lump this capacitance together at one point. It should be distributed about the board in smaller 0.1- or 0.01-μF capacitors.

5-5 DYNAMIC MEMORY SYSTEMS

Dynamic memory is normally used whenever the amount of RAM required for the system is 16K bytes or larger. The main disadvantage of dynamic memory is that it must be periodically refreshed or rewritten since it can only retain stored data for a few milliseconds.

Refreshing is typically accomplished by either the microprocessor, through some internal hardware (as in the Zilog Z80), or through an external dynamic RAM controller. *Pseudo static RAM* devices, or PSRAM, are now becoming available with most of the refreshing logic built into the memory device. Until they become commonly available, it will be the circuit designer's responsibility to connect the dynamic devices up to large systems. This section will focus on the standard dynamic RAM.

64K-Bit Dynamic RAM

The 4564, illustrated in figure 5–2, is a typical dynamic RAM used in many newer applications. This device is organized as a 64K by 1-bit memory device; therefore, eight such devices are required to develop a 64K-byte DRAM memory.

Several problems arise when attempting to use one of these devices. With most DRAMs an address multiplexer must be incorporated into the system to provide the address at the proper time. Since refreshing must be accomplished for all memory locations, a refresh counter may be required. Also, an external refresh logic circuit must be provided to accomplish refresh timing for the DRAM.

The Address Multiplexer

The address can be multiplexed using two 74157 quad 2-to-1 line multiplexers, as illustrated in figure 5–23. In this circuit the least significant portion of the memory address is presented to the DRAM until $\overline{RAS}$ goes low, when the most significant portion of the address is presented.

The output pins on the multiplexer are connected to the memory address pins of the 4564 through 33-Ω resistors that dampen the amount of negative undershoot on these pins. If only one of a set of 8 MK4564s is in use, these resistors are optional.

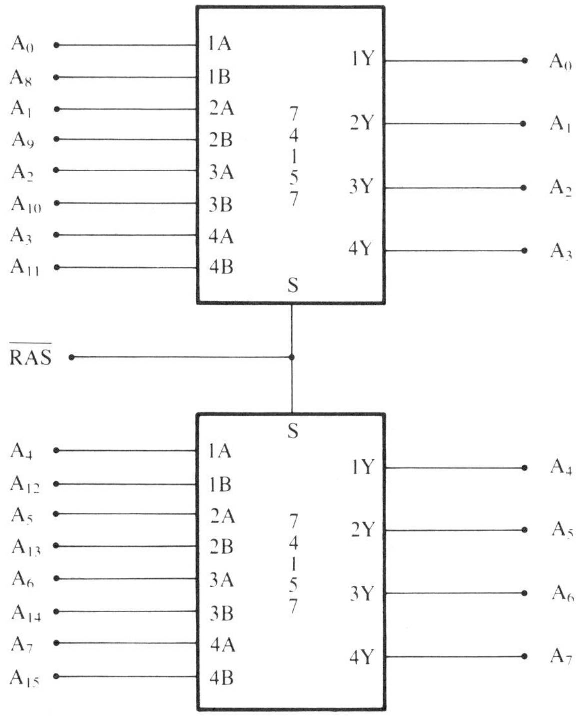

FIGURE 5–23 A circuit used to multiplex the address inputs to a dynamic RAM.

The Refresh Counter

The refresh counter can be a discrete counter located in the microprocessor; in a DRAM controller; or built into the memory, as with the PSRAM. The counter for this type of DRAM must be a 7-bit binary counter. Because of the internal structure of the DRAM, 128 refresh cycles are required because it is organized with 128 rows of memory and each row must be refreshed during a read or a write, 128 refresh cycles are required. The counter, located on the circuit board with the 4564, will most likely be used in a system employing this type of DRAM. The counter is connected to the DRAM during a refresh cycle and incremented at the end of the refresh period.

Control Signal Timing

The external logic required to operate the DRAM must contain some form of time delay to generate the $\overline{\text{CAS}}$ signal from the $\overline{\text{RAS}}$ signal. This can be accomplished by using a TTL delay line or by developing an external timing circuit. The delay line technique may or may not be used, since it is a fairly expensive piece of hardware.

Hidden Refresh

Since most microprocessors require more time to fetch and decode an opcode than to read from memory, this is the ideal time to refresh a dynamic memory. In some cases there is actually enough time for refreshing after a read or a write. This type of refresh is called a *hidden refresh* because it takes no additional time from the microprocessor to accomplish it. Another method of refreshing memory that is sometimes used requires that the READY input to the microprocessor be controlled to cause a WAIT state. The WAIT occurs while the external circuit refreshes the memory. This text will discuss and develop the hidden refresh technique because of its efficiency and wide application.

Dynamic RAM Timing

Figure 5–24 illustrates the timing for the 4564 dynamic RAM. The row address is applied to the address connections by the $\overline{\text{RAS}}$, or row address strobe, signal. This strobe enters the row address into an internal latch, where it is held during a memory cycle. After tRCD time, which is quite critical, from a 30 ns minimum to a 65 ns maximum, the column address and the $\overline{\text{CAS}}$ (column address strobe) must be applied. This strobe sends the column address into an internal register where it is also held for the current memory cycle. $\overline{\text{CAS}}$ performs one other important task: it causes the memory device to begin to access data.

If the read signal is applied during the current cycle, the contents of the selected location appear at the output pin within 150 ns after the $\overline{\text{RAS}}$ input becomes a logic zero. The data at the output pin remains valid and stable until the $\overline{\text{CAS}}$ pin returns to a logic one. The time required for the output buffer to return to its high-impedance state is 40 ns from the trailing edge of the $\overline{\text{CAS}}$ signal.

The main difference between a read cycle and a write cycle is the level of the write input. This input must be placed low before $\overline{\text{CAS}}$ goes high and

"$\overline{RAS}$-ONLY" REFRESH CYCLE

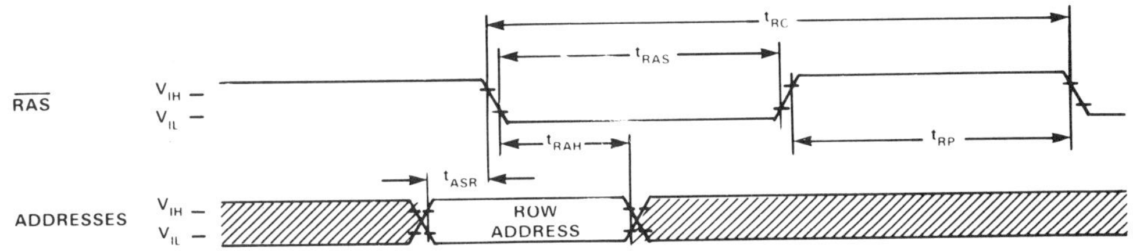

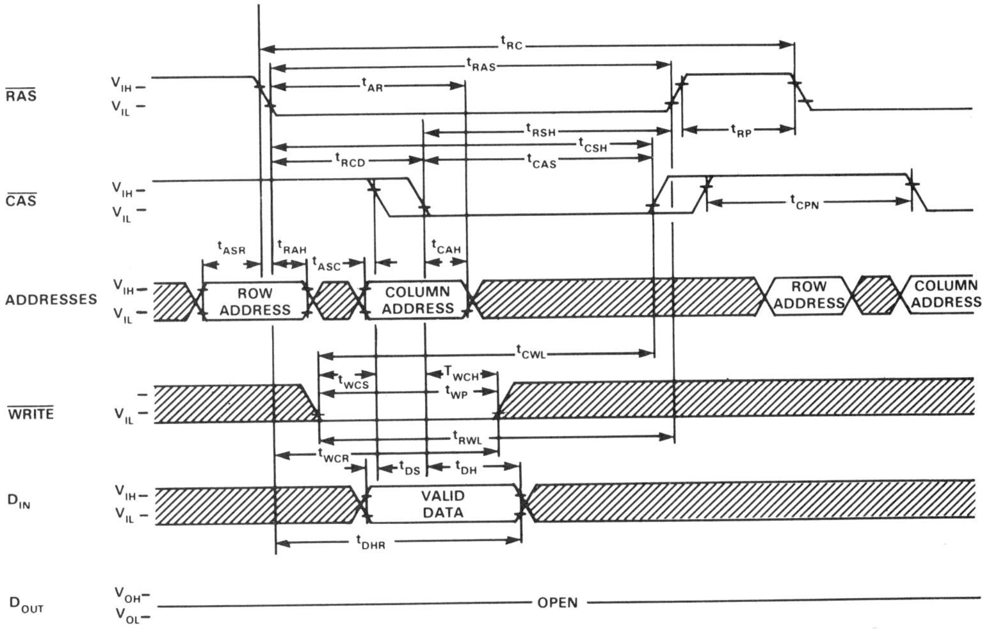

READ CYCLE

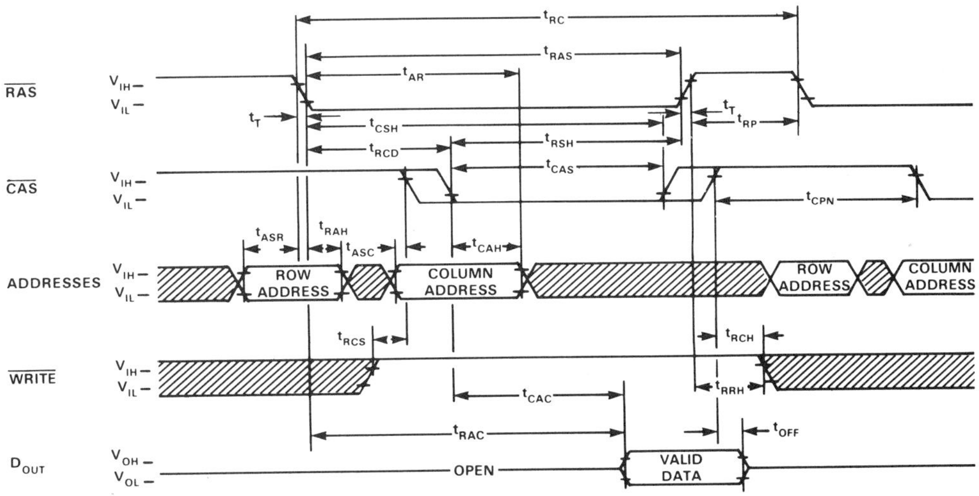

FIGURE 5–24 Timing and AC characteristics for the MK4564 64K x 1 dynamic RAM.

SOURCE: Courtesy of MOSTEK, Inc.

NOTES:

1. All voltages referenced to V_{SS}.
2. I_{CC} is dependent on output loading and cycle rates. Specified values are obtained with the output open. Only one MK4564 is active.
3. An initial pause of 500 μs is required after power-up followed by any 8 $\overline{RAS}$ cycles before proper device operation is achieved. Note that $\overline{RAS}$ may be cycled during the initial pause.
4. AC characteristics assume $t_T = 5$ ns.
5. V_{IH} min. and V_{IL} max. are reference levels for measuring timing of input signals. Transition times are measured between V_{IH} and V_{IL}.
6. The minimum specifications are used only to indicate cycle time at which proper operation over the full temperature range ($0°C \leq T_A \leq 70°C$) is assured.
7. Load = 2 TTL loads and 50 pF.
8. Assumes that $t_{RCD} \leq t_{RCD}$ (max). If t_{RCD} is greater than the maximum recommended value shown in this table, t_{RAC} will increase by the amount that t_{RCD} exceeds the value shown.
9. Assumes that $t_{RCD} \geq t_{RCD}$ (max).
10. t_{OFF} max defines the time at which the output achieves the open circuit condition and is not referenced to V_{OH} or V_{OL}.
11. Operation within the t_{RCD} (max) limit insures that t_{RAC} (max) can be met. t_{RCD} (max) is specified as a reference point only; if t_{RCD} is greater than the specified t_{RCD} (max) limit, then access time is controlled exclusively by t_{CAC}.
12. Either t_{RRH} or t_{RCH} must be satisfied for a read cycle.
13. These parameters are referenced to $\overline{CAS}$ leading edge in early write cycles and to $\overline{WRITE}$ leading edge in delayed write or read-modify-write cycles.
14. t_{WCS}, t_{CWD}, and t_{RWD} are restrictive operating parameters in READ/WRITE and READ/MODIFY/WRITE cycles only. If $t_{WCS} \geq t_{WCS}$ (min) the cycle is an EARLY WRITE cycle and the data output will remain open circuit throughout the entire cycle. If $t_{CWD} \geq t_{CWD}$ (min) and $t_{RWD} \geq t_{RWD}$ (min) the cycle is a READ/WRITE and the data output will contain data read from the selected cell. If neither of the above conditions are met the condition of the data out (at access time and until $\overline{CAS}$ goes back to V_{IH}) is indeterminate.
15. In addition to meeting the transition rate specification, all input signals must transmit between V_{IH} and V_{IL} (or between V_{IL} and V_{IH}) in a monotonic manner.
16. Effective capacitance calculated from the equation $C = I \frac{\Delta t}{\Delta V}$ with $\Delta V = 3$ volts and power supply at nominal level.
17. $\overline{CAS} = V_{IH}$ to disable D_{OUT}.
18. Includes the DC level and all instantaneous signal excursions.
19. $\overline{WRITE}$ = don't care. Data out depends on the state of $\overline{CAS}$. If $\overline{CAS} = V_{IH}$, data output is high impedance. If $\overline{CAS} = V_{IL}$, the data output will contain data from the last valid read cycle.

ELECTRICAL CHARACTERISTICS AND RECOMMENDED AC OPERATING CONDITIONS

(3,4,5,15) ($0°C \leq T_A \leq 70°C$), $V_{CC} = 5.0V \pm 10\%$

SYMBOL			MK4528-15		MK4528-20		MK4528-25			
STD	ALT	PARAMETER	MIN	MAX	MIN	MAX	MIN	MAX	UNITS	NOTES
t_{RELREL}	t_{RC}	Random read or write cycle time	260		345		425		ns	6,7
t_{RELREL} (RMW)	t_{RMW}	Read modify write cycle time	310		405		490		ns	6,7
t_{RELREL} (PC)	t_{PC}	Page mode cycle time	155		200		240		ns	6,7
t_{RELQV}	t_{RAC}	Access time from $\overline{RAS}$		150		200		250	ns	7,8
t_{CELQV}	t_{CAC}	Access time from $\overline{CAS}$		85		115		145	ns	7,9
t_{CEHQZ}	t_{OFF}	Output buffer turn-off delay	0	40	0	50	0	60	ns	10
t_T	t_T	Transition time (rise and fall)	3	50	3	50	3	50	ns	5,15
t_{REHREL}	t_{RP}	$\overline{RAS}$ precharge time	100		135		165		ns	
t_{RELREH}	t_{RAS}	$\overline{RAS}$ pulse width	150	10,000	200	10,000	250	10,000	ns	
t_{CELREH}	t_{RSH}	$\overline{RAS}$ hold time	85		115		145		ns	
t_{RELCEH}	t_{CSH}	$\overline{CAS}$ hold time	150		200		250		ns	
t_{CELCEH}	t_{CAS}	$\overline{CAS}$ pulse width	85	10,000	115	10,000	145	10,000	ns	
t_{RELCEL}	t_{RCD}	$\overline{RAS}$ to $\overline{CAS}$ delay time	30	65	35	85	45	105	ns	11
t_{REHWX}	t_{RRH}	Read command hold time referenced to $\overline{RAS}$	20		25		30		ns	12
t_{AVREL}	t_{ASR}	Row address set-up time	0		0		0		ns	
t_{RELAX}	t_{RAH}	Row address hold time	20		25		30		ns	
t_{AVCEL}	t_{ASC}	Column address set-up time	0		0		0		ns	
t_{CELAX}	t_{CAH}	Column address hold time	30		40		50		ns	
$t_{RELA(C)X}$	t_{AR}	Column address hold time referenced to $\overline{RAS}$	100		130		160		ns	

FIGURE 5–24 *continued*

ELECTRICAL CHARACTERISTICS AND RECOMMENDED AC OPERATING CONDITIONS (Continued)
(3,4,5,15) (0°C $\leq T_A \leq$ 70°C), V_{CC} = 5.0V ± 10%

SYMBOL			MK4528-15		MK4528-20		MK4528-25			
STD	ALT	PARAMETER	MIN	MAX	MIN	MAX	MIN	MAX	UNITS	NOTES
t_{WHCEL}	t_{RCS}	Read command set-up time	0		0		0		ns	
t_{CEHWX}	t_{RCH}	Read command hold time referenced to $\overline{CAS}$	0		0		0		ns	12
t_{CELWX}	t_{WCH}	Write command hold time	45		55		70		ns	
t_{RELWX}	t_{WCR}	Write command hold time referenced to $\overline{RAS}$	115		150		185		ns	
t_{WLWH}	t_{WP}	Write command pulse width	35		45		55		ns	
t_{WLREH}	t_{RWL}	Write command to $\overline{RAS}$ lead time	45		55		65		ns	
t_{WLCEH}	t_{CWL}	Write command to $\overline{CAS}$ lead time	45		55		65		ns	
t_{DVCEL}	t_{DS}	Data-in set-up time	0		0		0		ns	13
t_{CELDX}	t_{DH}	Data-in hold time	45		55		70		ns	13
t_{RELDX}	t_{DHR}	Data-in hold time referenced to $\overline{RAS}$	115		150		190		ns	
t_{CEHCEL} (PC)	t_{CP}	$\overline{CAS}$ precharge time (for page-mode cycle only)	60		75		85		ns	
t_{RVRV}	t_{REF}	Refresh Period		2		2		2	ms	
t_{WLCEL}	t_{WCS}	$\overline{WRITE}$ command set-up time	-10		-10		-10		ns	14
t_{CELWL}	t_{CWD}	$\overline{CAS}$ to $\overline{WRITE}$ delay	55		80		100		ns	14
t_{RELWL}	t_{RWD}	$\overline{RAS}$ to $\overline{WRITE}$ delay	120		165		205		ns	14
t_{CEHCEL}	t_{CPN}	$\overline{CAS}$ precharge time	30		35		45		ns	

AC ELECTRICAL CHARACTERISTICS
(0°C $\leq T_A \leq$ 70°C) (V_{CC} = 5.0V ± 10%)

SYM	PARAMETER	MAX	UNITS	NOTES
C_{I1}	Input Capacitance (A_0 - A_7), D_{IN}	10	pF	16
C_{I2}	Input Capacitance RAS, CAS	10	pF	16
C_{I3}	Input Capacitance $\overline{WRITE}$	20	pF	16
C_O	Output Capacitance (D_{OUT})	14	pF	16,17

FIGURE 5–24 *continued*

must remain low for at least 45 ns before $\overline{\text{CAS}}$ goes high to cause a memory write.

A refresh cycle may be accomplished at any time after a read or a write. The cycle itself is accomplished by placing a logic zero on the $\overline{\text{RAS}}$ pin of this dynamic memory. This refresh pulse must be at least 150 ns in width and must not occur until $\overline{\text{RAS}}$ has been high for at least 100 ns.

One other timing requirement is that the refresh pulse must return to a logic one at least 100 ns before $\overline{\text{RAS}}$ again becomes a logic zero. As you can see, refresh timing is critical; it will be discussed further in the next section.

128K-Byte Dynamic Memory Interface

The circuit illustrated in figure 5–25 pictures a typical 128K-byte dynamic memory system for use with the Intel 8088 microprocessor. The array itself contains sixteen 4564 DRAMS, for a total of 128K bytes of storage. The data in and data out pins are connected to a pair of 8216 bidirectional bus transceivers that interface the data connections to the 8088 data bus. The normal direction of data flow through these transceivers is into the memory array. The array only drives the 8088 data bus when the appropriate memory address is present with the $\overline{\text{RD}}$ or read signal.

The address bus is connected to a pair of 74157 multiplexers controlled by $\overline{\text{RAS}}$. $\overline{\text{RAS}}$ determines whether A0 through A7 or A8 through A15 are connected to the memory array through a second set of multiplexers. This second set selects a memory address or a refresh address from a 7-bit refresh counter. The refresh count is applied to the array during the refresh period, as controlled by the $\overline{\text{RFSH}}$ signal. At the end of a refresh period, the counter is incremented by the positive transition of the $\overline{\text{RFSH}}$ signal. The remaining four address connections are attached to the 74LS138 decoder, which enables the appropriate bank or segment of dynamic RAMs.

In the diagram, the decoder is hard wired to select memory locations 00000H through 1FFFFH or the first 128K bytes of memory. Other connections are possible, allowing the user to select any area of the 1M-byte memory space.

The timing for this memory interface is developed in the circuit of figure 5–26. This circuit contains a crystal controlled clock that generates a 25-MHz clock pulse train that is applied to the clock input of the 74S163 binary synchronous counter. This counter is cleared to zero whenever the microprocessor requests a memory cycle.

Since the most significant 2 bits of the counter are connected to an OR gate, $\overline{\text{RAS}}$ is generated for four clocking periods after the memory request. This and the other signals generated by the timing circuit are illustrated in figure 5–27.

The falling edge of $\overline{\text{RAS}}$ causes the $\overline{\text{Q}}$ output of the JK flip-flop to become a logic one, in turn causing $\overline{\text{CAS}}$ to become a logic zero. The time between the falling edge of $\overline{\text{RAS}}$ and the falling edge of $\overline{\text{CAS}}$ is approximately 25–35 ns, which is well within specifications for this device. $\overline{\text{CAS}}$ is returned to a logic one at the end of the current memory cycle when the $\overline{\text{RD}}$ or $\overline{\text{WR}}$ pulse, which caused the cycle, returns to a logic one. This return is accomplished through the asynchronous $\overline{\text{SET}}$ input of the JK flip-flop.

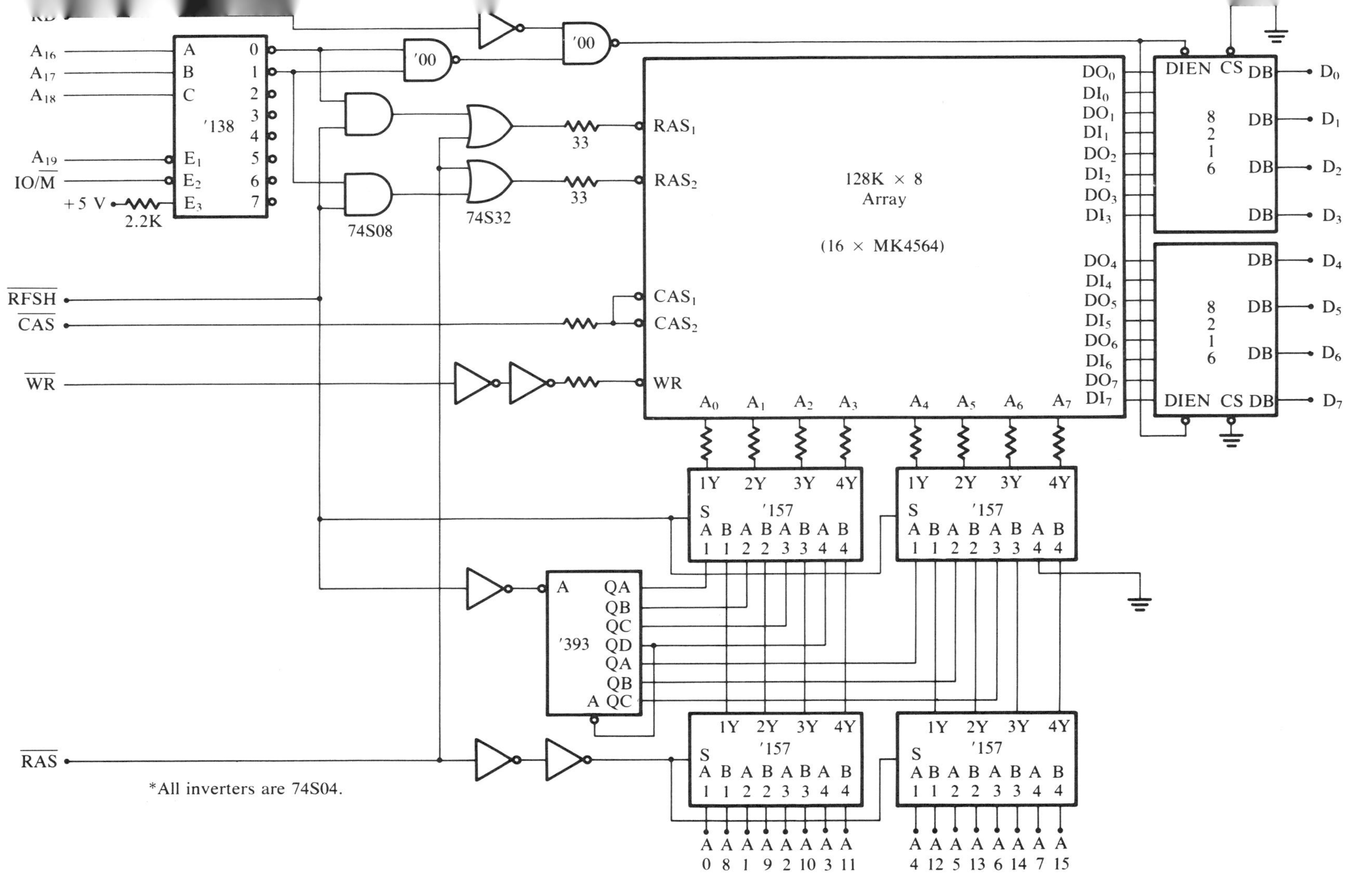

FIGURE 5–25 A 128K x 8 dynamic memory system using an array of 16 MK4564 dynamic memory devices.

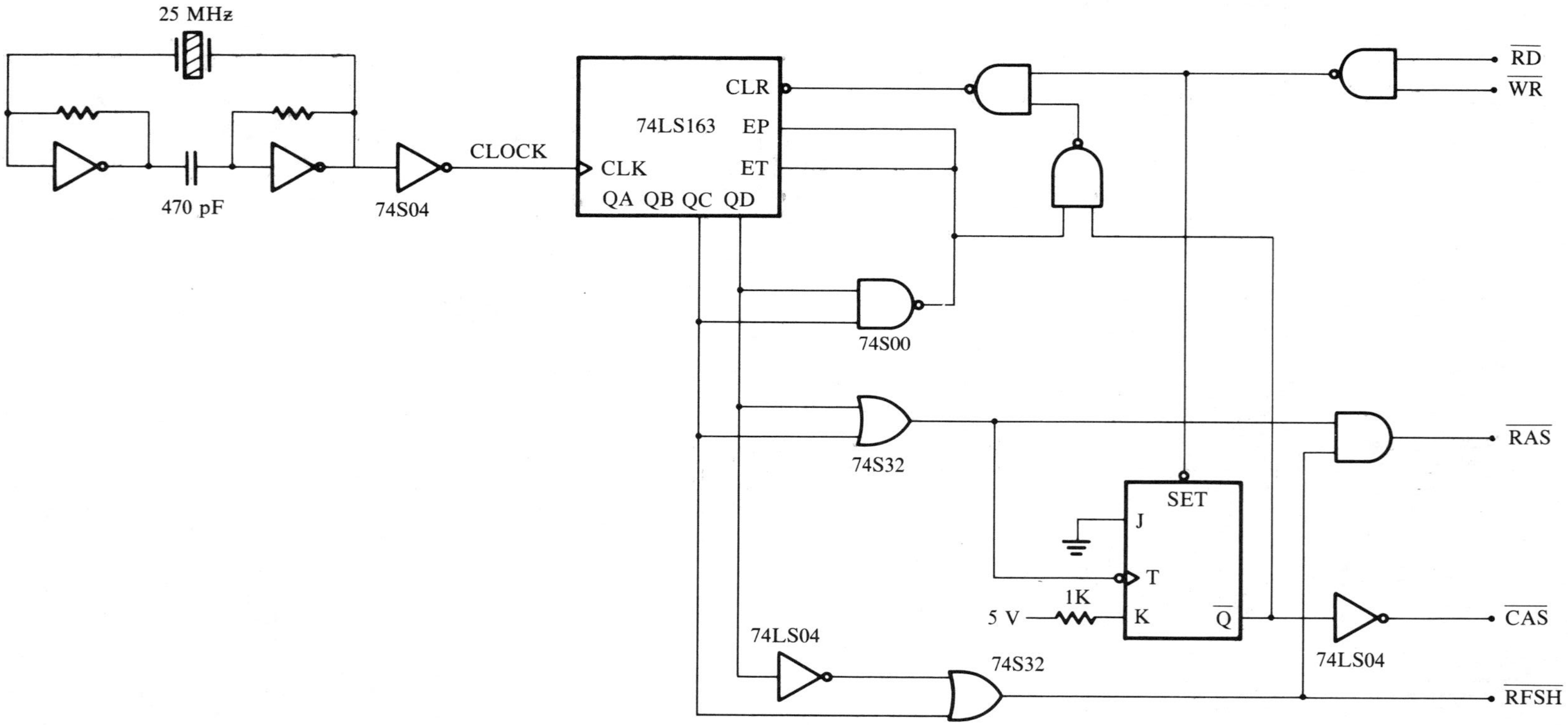

FIGURE 5–26 The circuit to generate the control signals $\overline{RAS}$, $\overline{CAS}$, and $\overline{RFSH}$ for the schematic of figure 5–25.

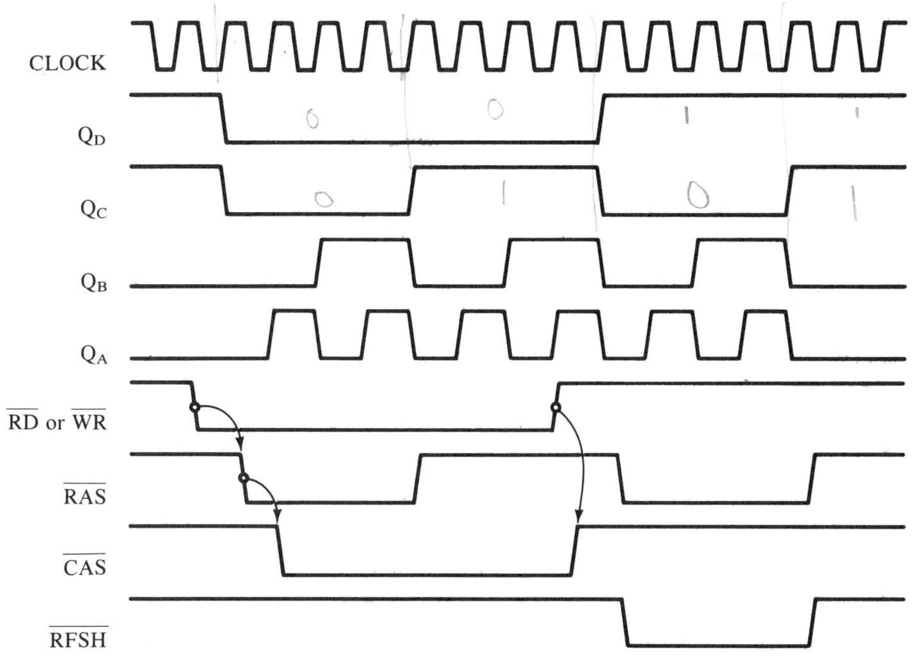

FIGURE 5–27 The signal timing diagram for the circuit of figure 5–26.

The refresh ($\overline{RFSH}$) signal is generated when the counter's outputs are 10XX binary, about 140 ns after $\overline{RAS}$ returns to a logic one. When the counter reaches a count of 1100 binary, it stops counting and remains in this state until the next $\overline{RD}$ or $\overline{WR}$ arrives from the 8088.

Since a memory cycle occurs at most once every 800 ns, all timing requirements for refreshing, reading, and writing for this memory are easily met. The type of refreshing employed is called *hidden refresh,* since a refresh occurs with every read or write and does not require any extra time from the microprocessor.

There is only one problem that can arise with this type of refreshing. If the microprocessor is halted, no memory read or write cycle occurs and the information stored in the memory is lost. A halt instruction or a DMA of long duration can cause the loss of data. It is necessary to include a circuit to detect this condition if the program is halted by the microprocessor. Since the halt instruction is seldom used in practice, this type of circuitry is not included in the previous dynamic memory interface.

MEMORY TESTING 5-6

An important portion of system design and repair is the ability to test a memory component. Memory testing involves determining whether a memory device and/or the memory selection logic is functioning properly. Memory testing software is found in many cases today in the system program. Many systems perform a memory self test every time that power is applied to the system. Self tests will normally test the RAM and the ROM in a system. The self test software is stored at the very beginning of the system program at the microprocessor's reset location. In addition to the self test program, maintenance software is often included to perform a more complex test of the memory. Most self test software is often called *static* testing, whereas most maintenance test software is called *dynamic* testing.

ROM Self Testing

How can a ROM be tested in a system? It is actually very simple if you think a little. The ROM contains a known set of data that can be checked numerically either by adding or exclusively-ORing all of the bytes together and checking the result. The result is stored in one of the memory locations on the ROM for this purpose. This procedure will not catch every possible ROM failure, but it will catch a vast majority of them. Figure 5–28 illustrates the flowchart for a typical ROM self test program. If an error is detected, the system program is aborted and some type of error indication is presented to the operator. In a system that contains a CRT terminal, a number may appear on the screen. If no visual display for the operator is present, an error code can be displayed on a set of LED indicators for the repairperson. This code indicates that a ROM is faulty; in fact, it can indicate which ROM is faulty.

RAM Self Testing

RAM self testing in a system is not much more complicated than ROM testing. The only major difference is that the RAM doesn't have a known set of data when power is applied. The data is provided by the test routine.

One simple static test of the system RAM is to test whether or not each memory location is capable of storing ones and zeros. The test program can set all of the bits of the RAM and test them to see if they are actually set. If

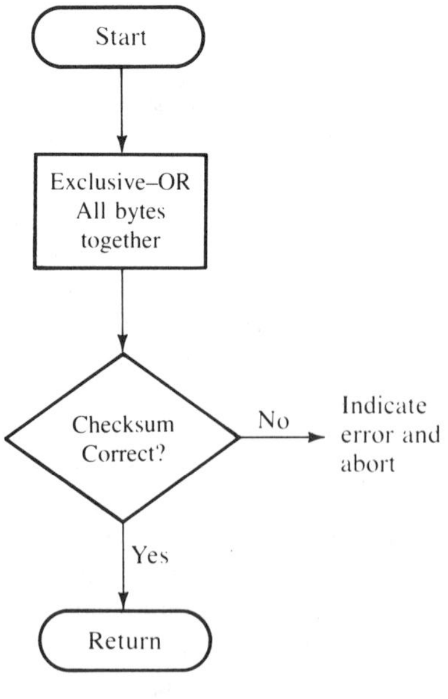

FIGURE 5–28 The flowchart for a ROM self-test subroutine.

that checks, the program can then clear all of the bits and check to see if they cleared. If both tests are passed, chances are excellent that all of the RAM is good. A flowchart for a RAM test is provided in figure 5–29. It is important to set or clear all of the bits before checking. Sometimes a memory cell will remember the information for a few hundred microseconds, giving the memory time to forget if it is faulty. As with the ROM, if the RAM fails the test, there is some type of indication for the operator or repairperson.

Fully Testing a RAM for Maintenance

In many cases the static testing described for self testing RAMs finds the faulty component. It always finds the bad or burned out memory cell. Other errors that occur in memory devices are not revealed by static testing. Sometimes internally generated noise changes the contents of a memory cell. This type of change can only be detected by the appropriate test sequence.

Dynamic testing most often consists of storing data into some of the memory locations. Once this data is stored, the software attempts to disrupt it by writing to other locations in the memory. If noise were to cause any of the original locations to change, the component might malfunction occasionally at some future time.

Checkerboard Testing

One such test is the *checkerboard test,* which stores alternate ones and zeros into each location in the memory. After this is accomplished, the program checks the memory to see if any change has occurred. The next step is to

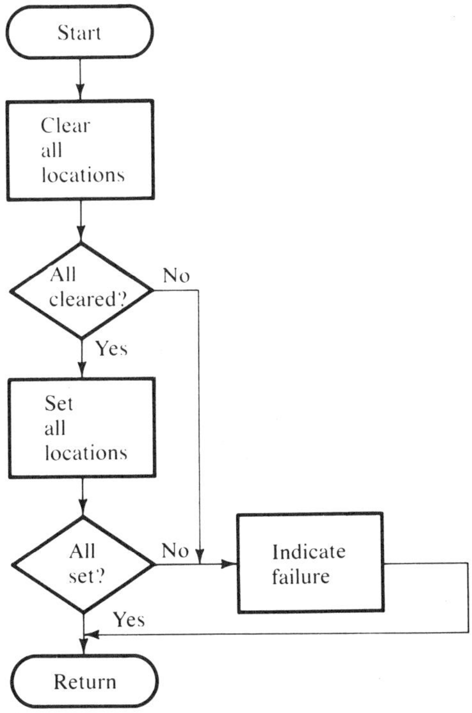

FIGURE 5–29 The flowchart for a functional RAM test subroutine.

complement one location and test the rest. Next complement the next location and test the rest. This procedure is repeated until every memory location is complemented and tested. At the end of this sequence, the program begins again, complementing the first location and testing the next. A flowchart for this type of dynamic test is illustrated by figure 5–30.

Memory Decoder Testing

In some cases the memory devices are functional but appear to be bad because of a decoder failure. Figure 5–31 shows a 74LS138 4-to-8 line decoder that is connected to a memory array. A flowchart for the test program is pictured in figure 5–32, along with the waveforms that are generated at the output pins of the decoder. These outputs can be checked on an oscilloscope or, more easily, tested with a digital logic probe. If the waveforms are present, the decoder is probably functioning properly and the memory indeed is bad.

Summary

This chapter introduced the student to memory interface, including both static and dynamic memory devices. Some types of memory omitted from this chapter will be covered later. The EEPROM, for example, will be discussed in chapter 7, because it requires an understanding of input/output techniques to interface properly. Another popular memory technique is bank

FIGURE 5–30 The flowchart for a checkerboard RAM test.

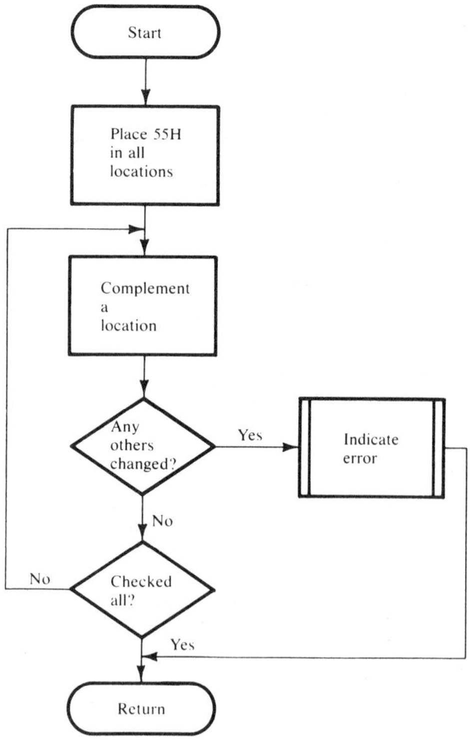

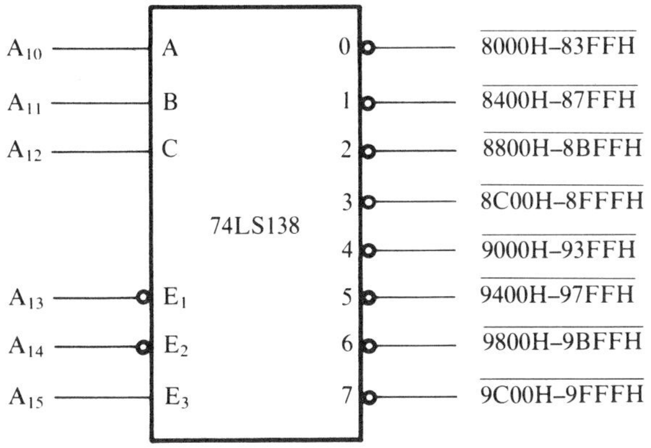

FIGURE 5–31 A decoder circuit that decodes 1K blocks of the memory address from 8000H through 9FFFH.

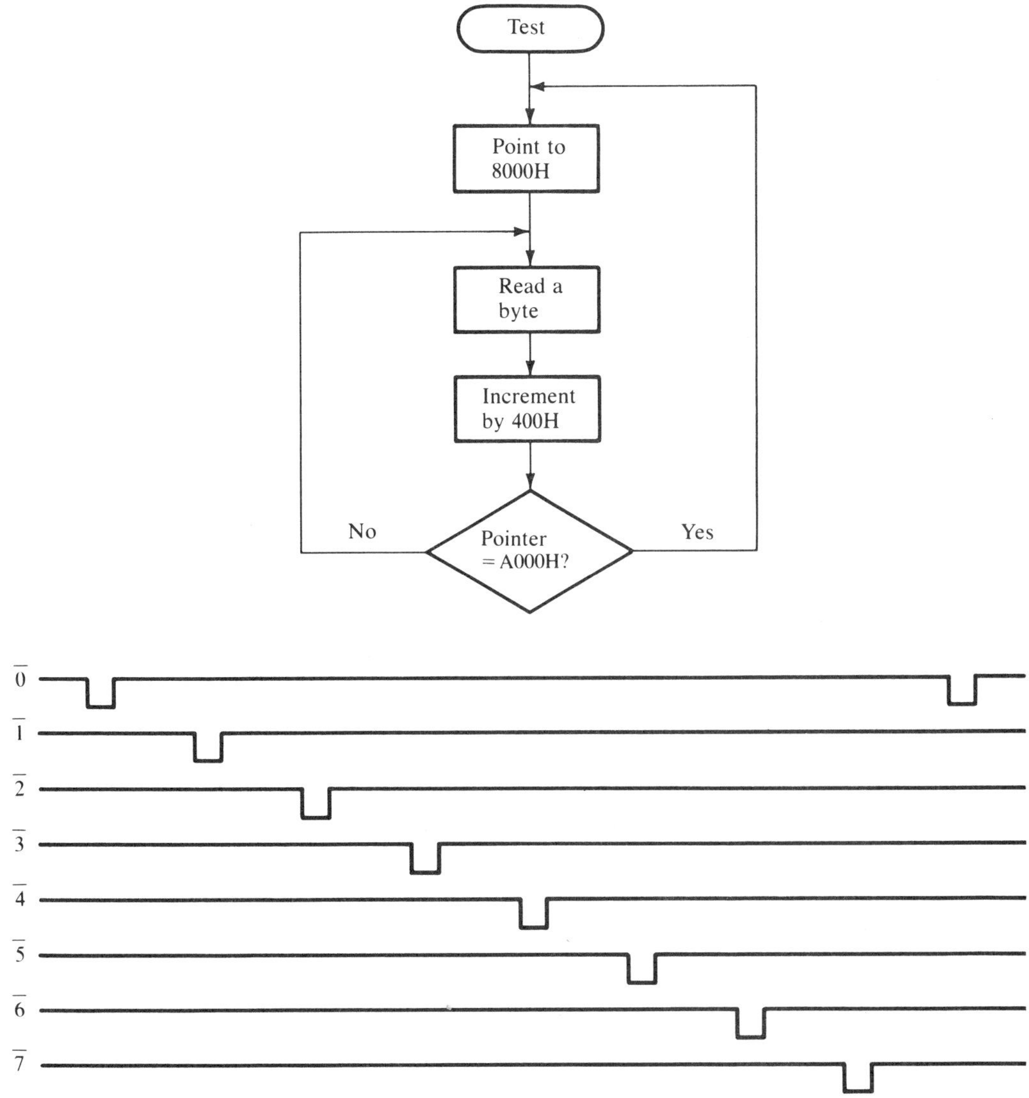

FIGURE 5–32 The flowchart of the test program and output waveforms for the decoder in figure 5–31.

selection. This too requires understanding of input/output techniques and will be covered in a subsequent chapter.

The most important item introduced in this chapter is memory address decoding. Both types, completely and incompletely specified decoding, find wide application. These techniques will be used for input/output interfacing; so make sure that you're familiar with them.

Glossary

Address decoder A device that decodes the memory address presented on the address bus by the microprocessor to select memory devices.

Access time The time required for a memory component to produce the addressed information at its output pins.

Common I/O The same pin on a memory device is used to input and output data.

Completely specified When memory devices populate the entire memory space and the decoder treats it accordingly, the memory is said to be completely specified.

Contiguous memory A block of memory in which one location touches the next location without any gaps.

Dynamic RAM (DRAM) A memory device that stores information for a brief period of time, usually only about 2 ms.

Dynamic memory testing A memory test designed to cause error to occur inside the memory device, if possible.

Hidden refresh A technique in which a memory refresh requires none of the microprocessor's time. It is hidden within the op-code fetch in many cases.

Incompletely specified When a memory will never be completely filled and some of the address bits are ignored by the address decoder.

Memory map A drawing of the proposed structure of the memory system.

Nonvolatile When a memory device is able to retain data whenever the power is removed from the system.

Refresh The act of periodically rewriting information in a dynamic RAM.

Separate I/O When data into and out of a memory device uses separate pins.

Static memory testing A memory testing technique that checks each location for functionality.

Static RAM A device that stores information as long as the power is applied to the system.

Volatile A device that loses data whenever power is removed from the system.

Questions and Problems

1 List three commonly available types of read only memory.

2 Describe the difference between static and dynamic memory.

3 How many address pins would be found on a nonmultiplexed 16K memory device?

4 Why do some memory devices have more than one chip enable or chip select input?

5 What is a bus contention or conflict?

6 Which connection present on most memory devices can be used to prevent a bus contention?

7 Describe the difference between common and separate I/O as it applies to memory.

8 Explain the term *memory access time.*

9 Why is the dynamic RAM so much more dense than the static RAM?

10 Why is an EEPROM called a *read mostly memory?*

11 Develop the circuitry required to select an EPROM for memory locations 3000H through 3FFFH.

12 Why aren't NAND gates normally used as decoders?

13 Find a better decoder than the 74LS138. At least *try* to find a better decoder.

14 What is meant by the term *contiguous memory?*

15 Develop a memory system using six 2716 EPROMs located in a contiguous block of memory from location 5000H through memory location 7FFFH.

16 Develop a memory system using two 2716 EPROMs and three 2732 EPROMs located in memory location 0000H through and including memory location 3FFFH.

17 Develop a memory system using four 2732 EPROMs for program storage at memory locations C000H through FFFFH and three 4118 RAMs at memory locations 0000H through 0BFFH.

18 Develop a memory system that uses one 2716 EPROM and one 4118 RAM. Locate them anywhere you wish. (HINT: Use incompletely specified decoding.)

19 Develop a memory system that uses two 2716 EPROMs, three 2732 EPROMs, and one 4118 RAM. Locate them anywhere you wish.

20 Why is it important to minimize the number of integrated circuits used in a design?

21 Why is it important to bypass integrated circuits?

22 Why is a resistor connected in series with various pins in a dynamic memory interface?

23 What is the purpose of the $\overline{\text{RAS}}$ input on a dynamic RAM?

24 What is hidden refresh? Why would it be used in a memory system?

25 The decoder in the circuit of figure 5–25 could be used to select any bank of memory up to which memory location?

26 The 74S163 illustrated in figure 5–26 will count up to which binary count?

27 Once the counter of figure 5–26 has been cleared it cannot be cleared again until what occurs?

28 What problem may occur in the operation of the circuit in figure 5–25?

29 Develop a ROM test program from the flowchart of figure 5–28. This program must test a 2K-byte ROM, beginning at location zero. The checksum is stored at the last location of this ROM.

30 From the flowchart of figure 5–29 develop a program that will test a 1k-byte RAM residing at locations 1000H through 13FFH.

31 Develop the software required to test the decoders of figure 5–18.

6

Basic Input/Output Interface Circuitry

This chapter introduces the basic input/output interface circuitry found in most applications. As stated previously, I/O interfacing is a very important portion of microprocessor design. A complete understanding is critically important for success in this field.

Basic interface components, along with their connection to the microprocessor, are described in this chapter. These basics are then used as a foundation for learning more complex I/O systems in the next and subsequent chapters of this text.

6-1 SIMPLE INPUT/OUTPUT DEVICES

Simple input/output devices that are commonly found in most systems include switches, numeric displays, relays, and solenoids. Most of these are very easy to understand but may require some circuit detail for their proper interfacing. This section will cover all of these devices, including solenoids and relays. Solenoids and relays will be covered again in other sections of this chapter, since they require some software and hardware to interface properly.

Switches

Almost all switches in use today are single pole, single throw toggle or push button switches. In the past, digital electronic circuitry used the single pole, double throw switch because of a problem with contact bounce. Contact bouncing occurs in any mechanical switch and produces many connections or contacts when thrown. They bounce in the same way that a hammer bounces when dropped on a hard surface, and this can cause serious problems in most digital systems.

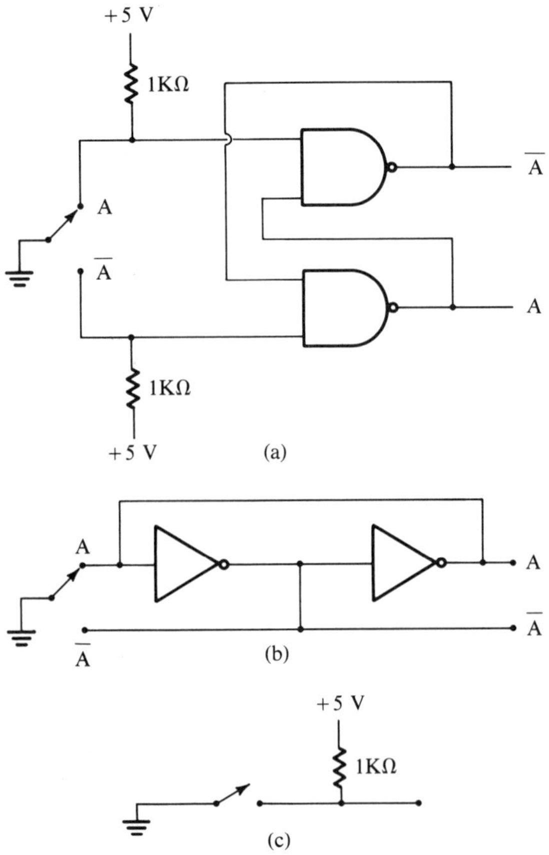

FIGURE 6–1 Switch interface circuitry: (a) a SPDT switch connected to a NAND gate contact bounce eliminator, (b) a SPDT switch connected to an inverter contact bounce eliminator, (c) a SPST switch setup to be connected to a microprocessor based system with software contact bounce elimination.

The circuits of figures 6–1(a) and 6–1(b) illustrate two different types of contact bounce eliminators. These circuits are required to debounce mechanical switch contacts if a microprocessor does not read the switches. Their major disadvantage is the type of switch required and the additional circuitry needed to debounce the switches.

Today the switch and accompanying resistor, pictured in figure 6–1(c), are all that are required to connect a switch to a microprocessor-based digital system. The contact bounce is handled by software inside the microprocessor. In certain instances the pullup resistor may actually be incorporated inside the microprocessor interface circuit.

LED Displays

The display devices in common use today vary considerably from those of the past. One of the most common is the simple light emitting diode, or *LED*. Figure 6–2 illustrates a typical digital to LED interface. Notice that a standard TTL component drives the LED. Most single LEDs require approximately 10 mA of current flow to be illuminated at full brilliance. Since the forward voltage drop across an LED is approximately 1.65 V, the value of the current limiting resistor would be 330 Ω in this example.

A standard TTL component is used instead of a low-power Schottky TTL device because the low-power Schottky device is not capable of sinking the required amount of current. The standard TTL gate can safely sink 16 mA of current; the low-power Schottky TTL device can only sink 4 mA of current. Whenever any digital circuit is to be interfaced to an LED, make sure that it will be capable of sinking enough drive current.

Figure 6–3 illustrates a common anode seven segment LED display whose internal structure is nothing more than a single LED for each of the lettered

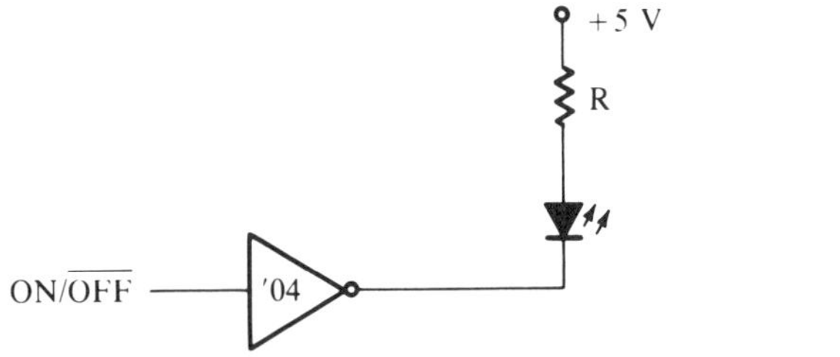

$$R = \frac{5\text{ V}-1.65\text{ V}}{\text{Iave}} = \frac{3.35\text{v}}{\text{Iave}}$$

FIGURE 6–2 A single light emitting diode (LED) connected to an inverter driver.

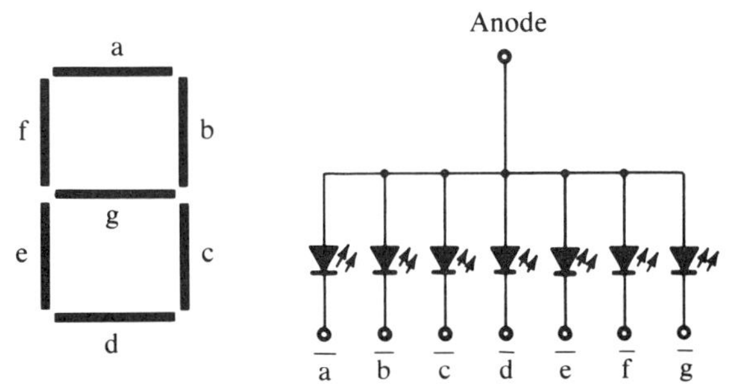

FIGURE 6–3 A seven segment common anode LED display.

segments. Drivers for this device can be the same as those indicated in figure 6–2. In many cases displays are multiplexed and may require a lot more current. In such cases, you are most likely to find high current drivers such as transistors or Darlington pairs used in place of the TTL logic gate drivers.

Fluorescent Displays

Fluorescent display devices, such as the one pictured in figure 6–4, have become more popular in recent years because they have a higher intensity than the seven segment LED displays and can be filtered to a wider variety of different colors. The only disadvantages of the fluorescent display (in comparison to the LED display) are its requirements for a filament voltage, a negative grid voltage, and a drive voltage of 15–30 V, and its much shorter life span. This type of display emits a blue-green light instead of the characteristic red light emitted by most LEDs.

It is operated by applying a 15–30 V signal to each anode that is to be illuminated. At the same time the grid voltage must be changed from a negative voltage to a slightly positive voltage. This procedure causes the tube to begin conduction, and the electrons that strike the anode excite it into producing light.

The Negative Grid Supply

Since this device requires a negative grid supply voltage to turn a segment on and off, the interface circuit must contain a negative power supply. When one is available, this presents no problem in the design of the display; but when it is not, it can involve additional cost. To minimize the added cost, a charge pump can supply this negative voltage.

A *charge pump,* as illustrated in figure 6–5, is an oscillator followed by a differentiator, which produces positive and negative pulses. The negative pulses can be rectified and regulated to produce a negative DC voltage. In most cases the amount of current available from this type of supply is small. For this application the grid current is very small, making it an ideal candidate for a charge pump.

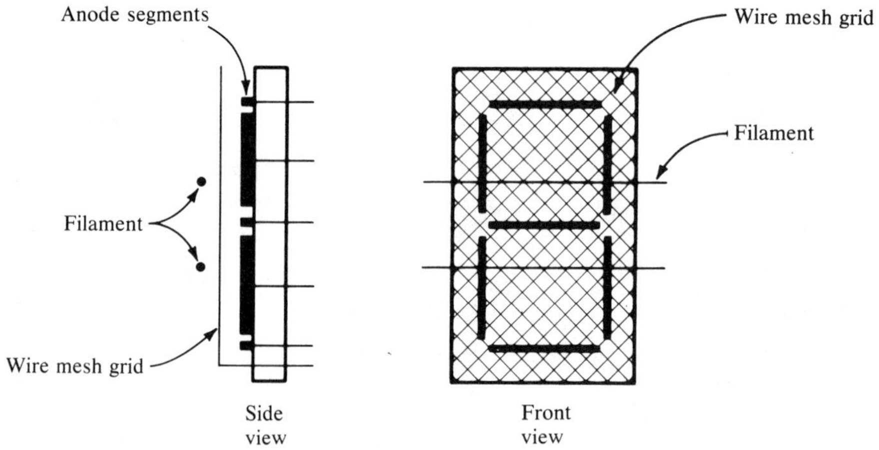

FIGURE 6–4 A seven segment fluorescent display tube.

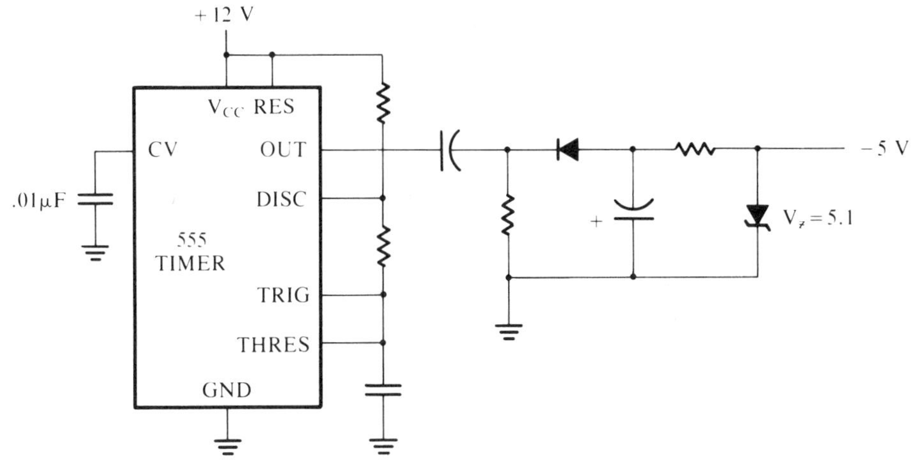

FIGURE 6–5 A charge pump and oscillator that can provide a low current negative supply voltage.

Anode Switch

Figure 6–6 illustrates a typical anode driver for a fluorescent display. This driver happens to be a PNP transistor that has been made TTL compatible with an NPN transistor. A logic one applied to the base of the NPN transistor causes it to saturate. This in turn causes base current to flow in the PNP transistor, which also saturates. The 30 V applied by the PNP transistor to the anode cause the segment to light.

Liquid Crystal Displays

The last type of display device to be discussed is the liquid crystal display, or LCD. This type of device is more common in calculators and digital watches than in other areas because it is commonly available in only these formats. It has the advantage of being highly visible in bright light where other devices are extremely difficult to see. It also uses an extremely low amount of power, which makes it ideal for most applications.

This type of display device is by far the hardest to use, since it requires AC excitation voltages rather than DC excitation voltages. These AC voltages must be between 30 Hz and 1000 Hz and are normally TTL logic levels. Figure 6–7 depicts the internal structure of the LCD and the required excitation

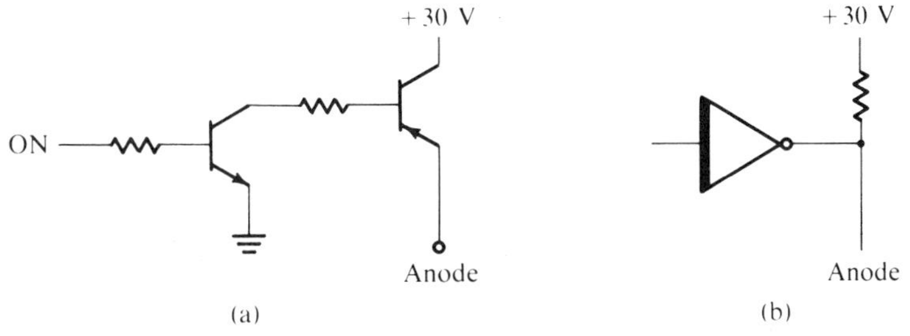

FIGURE 6–6 (a) An anode driver using discrete transistor logic, (b) an anode driver using a high voltage open collector TTL inverter and a current limiting resistor.

waveforms. The electrostatic field developed between the electrodes aligns the liquid crystal molecules, which allow light to pass through the material to the mirror below. Since the mirror is exposed to light, it reflects more light than the surrounding area and appears to light up. This type of display is a *reflective LCD*.

Another type, the *absorption* type, absorbs light when a voltage is placed across its electrodes. A piece of black paper behind it absorbs most of the light, so it appears to darken. This type is most often found in digital watches and other consumer products.

Relays and Solenoids

The last types of simple input/output devices to be discussed are the relay and solenoid. Relays are primarily used to switch many different voltages at

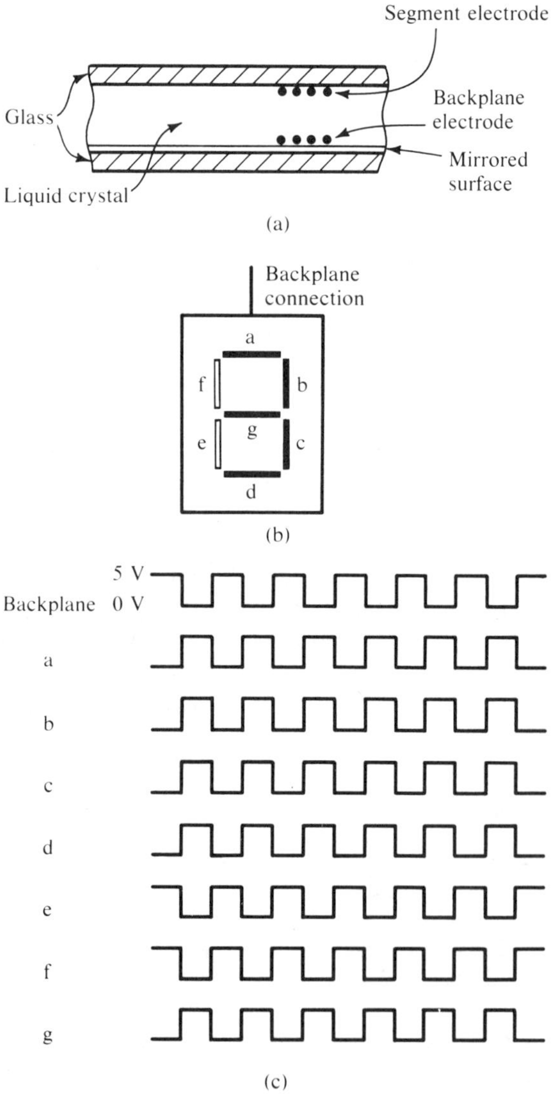

FIGURE 6–7 (a) The internal structure of a reflective liquid crystal display (LCD), (b) the segment and backplane connections of an LCD, (c) the TTL compatible waveforms required to display the number three.

one time or to switch very high voltages. Applications for solenoids include moving mechanical devices such as printing characters on printers.

Figure 6–8 shows how a typical solenoid or relay is interfaced to a digital system. In most cases the Darlington pair illustrated is prepackaged in one three-terminal transistorlike device. Notice that the circuit requires very few components to implement, since in most cases the Darlington pair has sufficient gain to allow a direct TTL connection to its input. If not, an external pullup or helper resistor can provide increased bias current sufficient to activate the device. This resistor can allow a current flow of up to I_{SINK} of the TTL device.

THE INTERFACE POINT 6-2

What is the *interface point?* It is the point at which a TTL compatible input or output device releases or accepts data. An input device releases data to the microprocessor, and an output device accepts data from the microprocessor. All input and output devices require the same basic interface circuitry.

The Basic Input Interface

Most microprocessors accept data from an input device through the data bus connections and therefore require some form of switch to connect this data to the bus at the appropriate time. The most effective digital switch available is the three-state buffer. Figure 6–9 illustrates a set of eight buffers, the 74LS244 octal buffer, connected to an 8-bit TTL compatible input device. Examples of TTL compatible input devices are binary switches, the output of an analog-to-digital converter, and many other types of peripheral interface components.

The decoder selects the device by producing a logic zero at its output, which enables (turns on) the three-state buffers. In most microprocessors, this strobe is normally active for about 300–1000 ns.

Once enabled, these buffers connect the data from the input device to the microprocessor's data bus for processing. The device decoder, as discussed in the next section, indicates that the microprocessor has executed an input instruction.

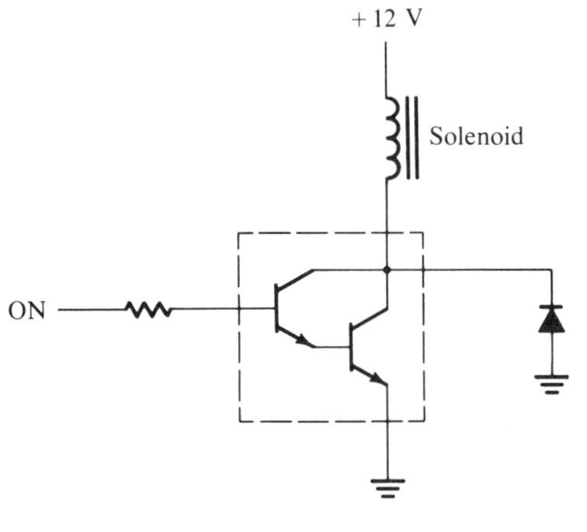

FIGURE 6–8 A DC solenoid and its Darlington pair driver.

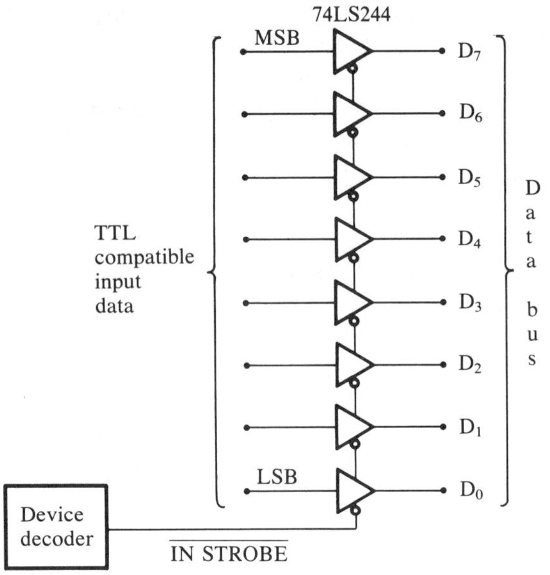

FIGURE 6–9 A typical TTL compatible input interface circuit illustrating the three-state bus buffers that drive the microprocessor bus.

All input devices must either use this circuit or have a similar circuit built into them. In many cases the decoder is an external circuit and the three-state buffers are internal to the I/O circuit.

The Basic Output Interface

Whenever data is sent out of the microprocessor to an external output device, it appears on the data bus for only a brief period of time. It is during this window that the external device must capture the information. In almost all instances, the external output device uses some form of latch to grab onto and hold the data bus information.

Figure 6–10 illustrates a typical output interface circuit. A device decoder generates a strobe pulse that provides a clock pulse for the 74LS374 octal latch in this circuit. For more complete details on this timing, refer to the section on *memory write* in chapters 3 and 4. Additional information on this strobe is provided in the next section. Information from the data bus, which has been applied to the D inputs of the latch, is held for the external TTL compatible device. Notice that the clock pulse input is a positive edge triggered input to the latch.

In most microprocessors, information is only available to the external device for a microsecond or less without the external latch. Suppose you were required to display a binary number on eight LEDs. If the latch was not present, the information might flash on the displays for a microsecond, hardly enough time to observe the number. As you can imagine, without this latch few devices can be effectively connected to the processor.

As with the input circuitry, the decoder is usually a separate circuit and the latches are quite often built into the external device. In fact, it is very difficult to find a microprocessor peripheral component that doesn't contain a latch for the output data. Some devices actually contain a latch for the input data, as well.

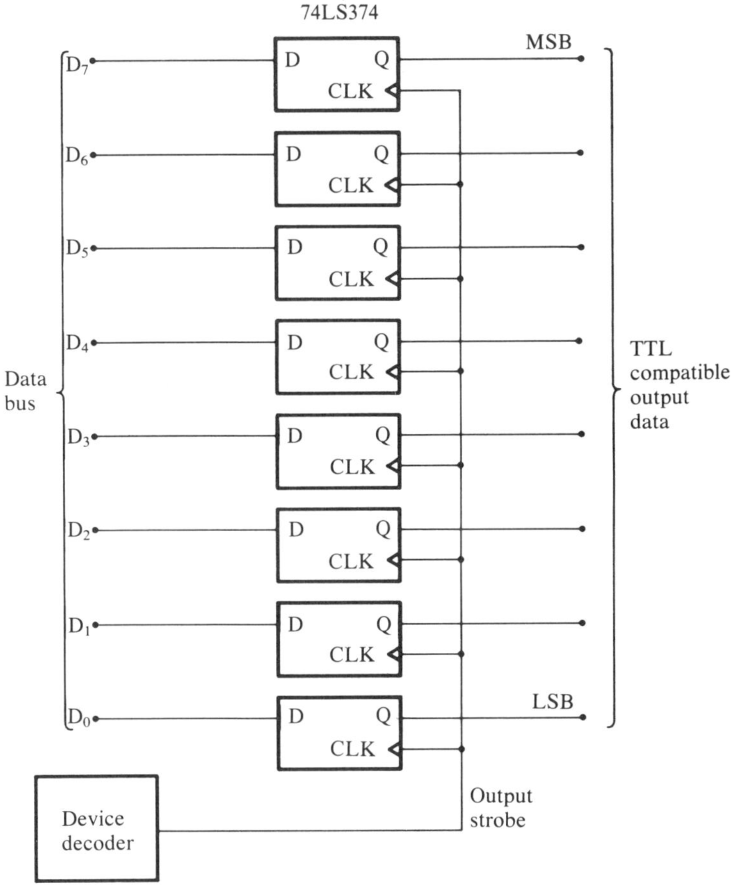

FIGURE 6–10 A typical TTL compatible output interface illustrating the data latches required to capture the data bus information for the external circuitry.

INPUT/OUTPUT DEVICE SELECTION 6-3

Memory mapped I/O and isolated I/O are the two basic input/output schemes in use today. Memory mapped I/O treats the input/output device as if it were a location in the memory. Isolated I/O treats it separately from the memory. Both schemes are quite usable in most applications, since it is rare that the entire memory is used for program and data storage. Intel and Zilog microprocessors use either isolated I/O or memory mapped I/O; Motorola microprocessors can only use memory mapped I/O.

The Memory Mapped I/O Decoder

Let's suppose that eight different I/O devices are required for a particular application, and the memory mapped I/O technique is to be employed. Since we have decided to use this scheme, we must first set aside a portion of memory for the input/output devices. Figure 6–11 illustrates the proposed memory and input/output maps for this system. Maps are a very useful method of looking at a memory and I/O structure before the appropriate decoders are designed.

Memory locations CF00H through CFFFH, a page in the memory, are employed for the input/output area. You may argue that this is a lot of memory for eight input/output devices unless you consider the entire memory. Only a very small portion of the available memory is used for I/O. We typically do this to reduce the number of address bits that must be decoded to produce the device selection strobes.

1100 1111 0000 0000 or CF00H
to
1100 1111 1111 1111 or CFFFH

After examining this I/O address range, it is apparent that CFXXH, which is common to all of the I/O devices, is the bit pattern that must be decoded.

An eight input NAND gate would most likely be used to decode this address range and develop the page selection strobe ($\overline{\text{PAGE CF}}$). This strobe would enable a decoder to select one of the eight different I/O devices. The page selection logic and the page decoder appear in figure 6–12.

The most significant eight address connections are decoded to produce the page selection strobe, but we still have 8 address bits to decode to select the eight different I/O devices. A 3-to-8 line decoder develops the device strobes because we plan to connect only eight devices in this region of memory.

Five of the eight remaining address bits can be ignored, since they are not needed to produce the strobes. It is decided to use A7, A6, and A5 for the decoder inputs; but any of the remaining 8 address bits can be used for this purpose.

Each location that is decoded overlays 32 different I/O device addresses. Output zero of the decoder is active for locations CF00H through CF1FH or for 32 different addresses. As with the memory, this presents no problem

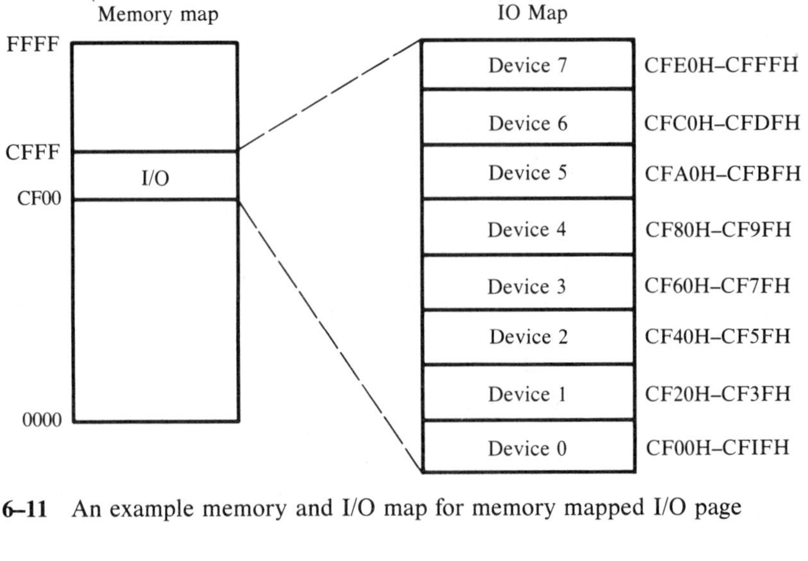

FIGURE 6–11 An example memory and I/O map for memory mapped I/O page CFXX.

since the program can be written to use only one of these locations. The same is true about the remaining seven outputs.

Isolated I/O Decoder

Figure 6–13 depicts the memory and input/output maps for a microprocessor capable of using isolated I/O. With this technique, the entire memory is al-

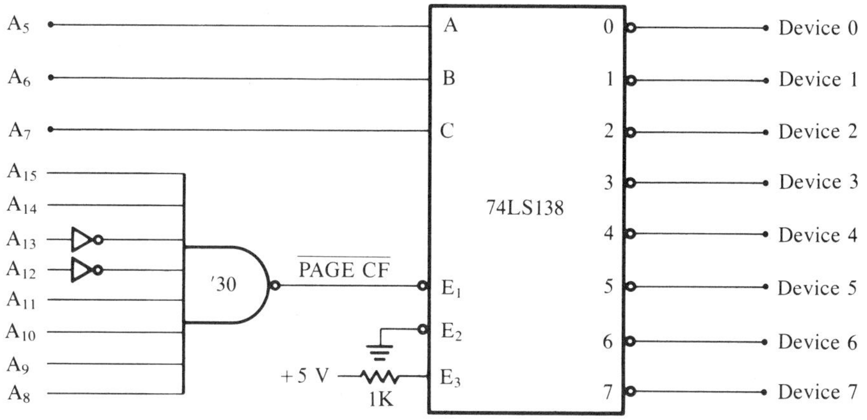

FIGURE 6–12 The memory mapped I/O port decoder for the map illustrated in figure 6–11.

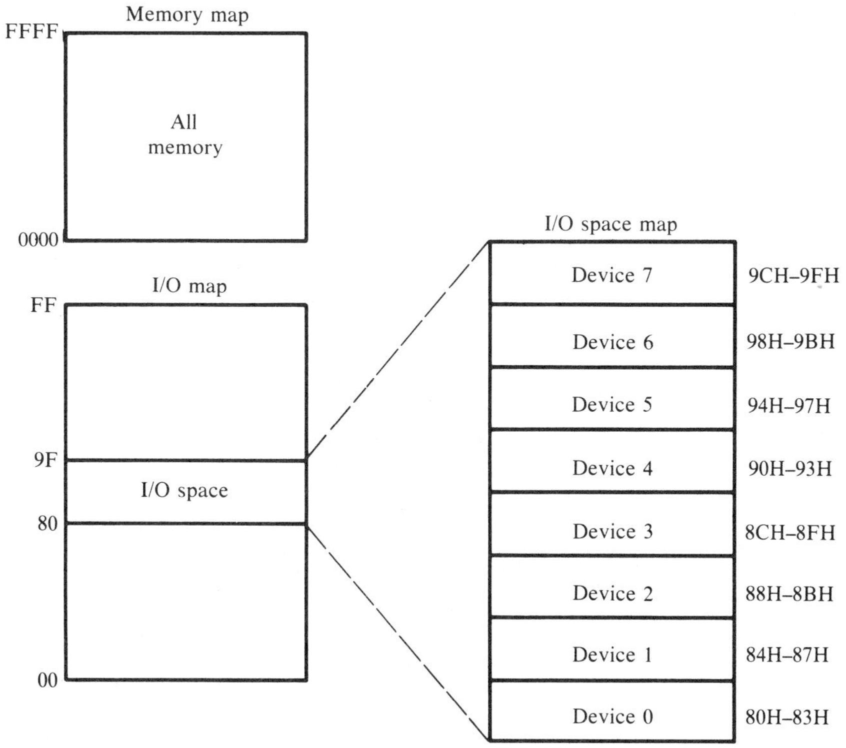

FIGURE 6–13 An example memory map and I/O map for an isolated I/O system.

ways available for the system. The I/O map can be viewed as a miniature memory for the purpose of I/O device selection and control.

In this example, the input/output devices exist at I/O port locations 80H through 9FH. This arrangement leaves a large space in the I/O map for other input/output devices that may also be included in the system at a later time.

Where does the I/O port or device number appear on a microprocessor that uses isolated I/O? It appears on the address bus in the same manner that a memory address appears. The only difference is that the port number, an 8-bit number, appears twice on the 8085A address bus. Example 6–1 shows the binary bit pattern present on the address bus for I/O port number 7AH.

EXAMPLE 6–1

0 1 1 1   1 0 1 0   0 1 1 1   1 0 1 0 = 7A7AH

The circuit in figure 6–14 illustrates the way port numbers 80H through 9FH can be decoded. In this example the most significant half of the address bus enables the 3-to-8 line decoder. The most significant half is normally used with the 8085A because it is not multiplexed. The Z80 has its port number appear on the least significant part of the address bus. If this processor is to be interfaced, you must use that half of the address bus. The 8086 and 8088 use a 16-bit port number, which appears on the least significant sixteen address bus connections.

Once the decoder is enabled, its outputs become active as dictated by address connections A12, A11, and A10. The choice of these address connections is arbitrary; other connections could be selected.

Output zero becomes a logic zero for the instructions IN 80H through an IN 83H or for an OUT 80H through an OUT 83H. These I/O port locations overlay four different port addresses. This procedure, of course, presents no problem in almost all systems since the program is written for only one location.

A Comparison of Isolated and Memory Mapped I/O Decoders

Comparing the circuits of figures 6–12 and 6–14, we notice that both decoders appear to be decoding a memory address. This is true; without completing the timing required to accomplish either memory mapped or isolated I/O,

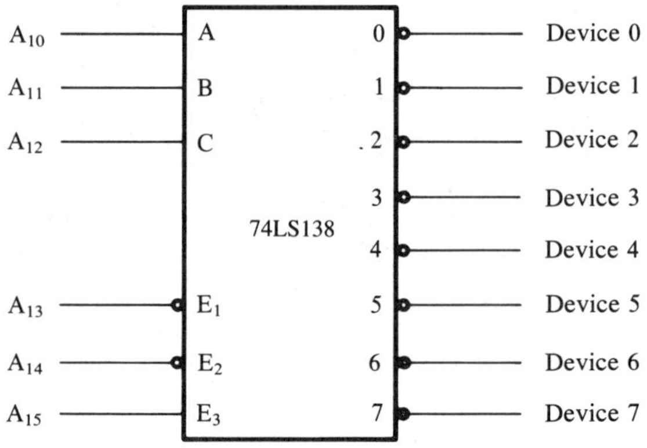

FIGURE 6–14 The isolated I/O port decoder for the I/O map illustrated in figure 6–13.

this is all they accomplish. These circuits only develop signals that can be used to select an input/output device; they do not generate the strobes required to transfer any of the data.

Memory Mapped I/O Strobe Generation

Figure 6–15 illustrates a circuit that generates eight different memory mapped I/O input strobes. If you compare this circuit with the circuit of figure 6–12, you see two changes: The page select strobe is changed to page D4H and the $\overline{\text{MEMR}}$ (memory read) signal is attached to an enable input. This decoder will now only function for a memory read from page D4H. It also develops one of the eight different input strobe signals for this page of I/O. Each of the input strobes becomes a logic zero for a period of time equal to the $\overline{\text{MEMR}}$ signal, and this is when the processor expects to receive information from the external device.

If output strobes are required in a system, the circuit of figure 6–15 can be modified to produce them by replacing the $\overline{\text{MEMR}}$ signal with the $\overline{\text{MEMW}}$ signal. This change enables the decoder for a memory write into the selected page. At this time the microprocessor has data available for the external device.

Isolated I/O Strobe Generation

The circuit in figure 6–16 shows how a decoder can be used in an isolated I/O scheme to generate both input and output strobes. The decoder in this circuit is only enabled for I/O port numbers 00H through 3FH and only at the time of an I/O read or an I/O write. Once enabled, input C selects outputs 0 through 3 for an input instruction and outputs 4 through 7 for an output instruction. This circuit will generate four input strobes and four output strobes.

After examining both I/O schemes, it appears that the amount of circuitry required to implement isolated I/O is much less than with memory mapped

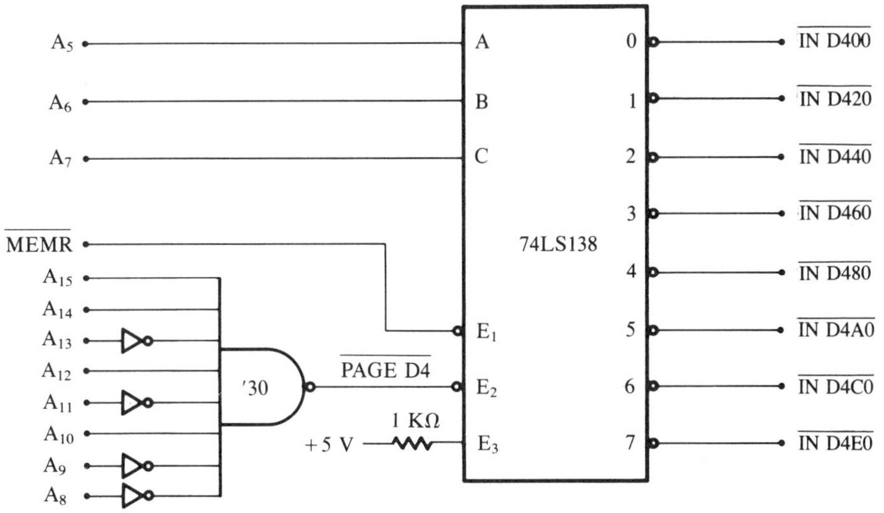

FIGURE 6–15 A circuit that will develop eight different memory mapped I/O strobes. These signals will only go low for a read from the indicated ranges of memory.

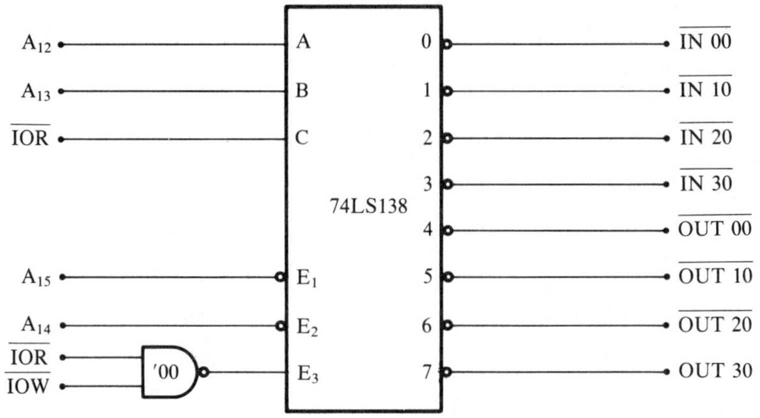

FIGURE 6–16 A circuit that will generate four isolated I/O output strobes and four isolated I/O input strobes.

I/O. Whether or not isolated I/O is used depends on the microprocessor, the type of hardware control software needed in a system, and the circuit designer's preference.

6-4 THE PERIPHERAL INTERFACE ADAPTER (PIA)

A peripheral interface adapter contains two or three parallel I/O ports or locations that can be programmed to handle input or output data. Some of these adapters also contain either RAM or ROM memory. Still others contain a timer or programmable modulus counter that can generate a variety of different signals. The timer is also used to count external events in some applications.

These devices allow almost any TTL compatible input or output device to be interfaced to the microprocessor. They contain the basic input and output circuitry discussed previously in this chapter. In addition to the basic I/O circuitry, PIAs contain a handshaking or synchronization mechanism that is typically used with asynchronous external I/O devices to synchronize them with the microprocessor.

This section will discuss two different types of PIAs. One contains I/O ports, memory, and a timer; the other contains I/O ports alone. The 8155 is discussed because of its ease in interfacing to a multiplexed bus microprocessor, and the MC6821 because of its wide application with the MC6800. Granted there are many other PIA components on the market today, but these two devices are representative of all of them.

A Typical Port Pin Connection

Figure 6–17 illustrates the typical circuit for a bidirectional parallel port pin. Bidirectional port pins are programmable as inputs or outputs, or, if the application requires it, they can be used as truly bidirectional I/O lines.

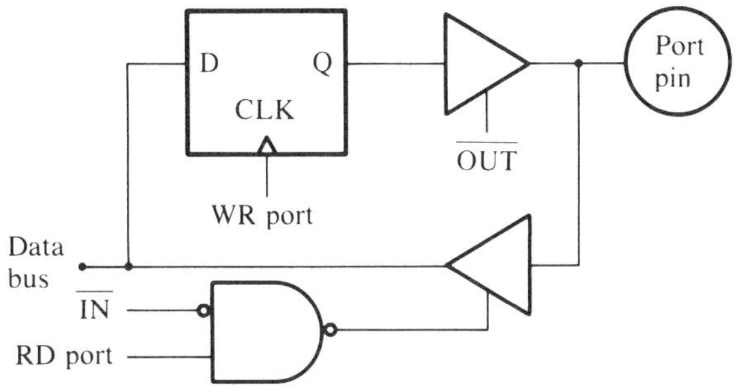

FIGURE 6–17 A typical internal representation of a programmable bidirectional PIA port pin connection.

The RD port and WR port signals are developed by the internal control logic of the adapter. These signals become active only when the device is enabled and the correct I/O address is present to select this particular bit of the port.

The $\overline{OUT}$ and $\overline{IN}$ signals are also developed internally and are used to program the port pin as either an input or an output. If the port pin is programmed as an output, $\overline{OUT}$ is a logic zero and $\overline{IN}$ is a logic one. In this mode, the signal from the three-state buffer, which is connected to the Q output of the flip-flop, is passed through to the port pin. The data is held in an internal latch for this port pin and remains there until new information is outputted to the pin.

In the input mode, $\overline{OUT}$ is a logic one and $\overline{IN}$ is a logic zero. This causes the buffer, which has been connected to the flip-flop, to be disabled and allows the RD port signal to pass through to the other three-state buffer. So whenever data is read from this port pin, the RD port strobe goes high, causing the control input to the buffer to become zero when reading the port pin. Once the data is read, it is often held in an internal latch for the microprocessor.

The 8155 Combination I/O, RAM, and Timer

Peripheral interface adapters are available for multiplexed data buses or standard nonmultiplexed data buses. The multiplexed bus version is normally set up to work with isolated I/O, and the nonmultiplexed version works with either isolated or memory mapped I/O.

The 8155, which is designed to work with isolated I/O and a multiplexed address/data bus, is illustrated in figure 6–18. The 8155 contains two 8-bit bidirectional I/O ports, one 6-bit multipurpose I/O port, 256 bytes of RAM, and a 14-bit programmable modulus counter or timer. The timer is capable of producing either a square wave or a pulse at its output.

8155 Selection

Devices are selected through the active low $\overline{CE}$ input of the 8155, which controls both the I/O and memory selection. If an active high CE is required, the 8156 can be used, since it is identical to the 8155 except in the logic level of the selection input. The selection of I/O or memory is controlled by the IO/$\overline{M}$ control signal present on some of the microprocessors designed for isolated

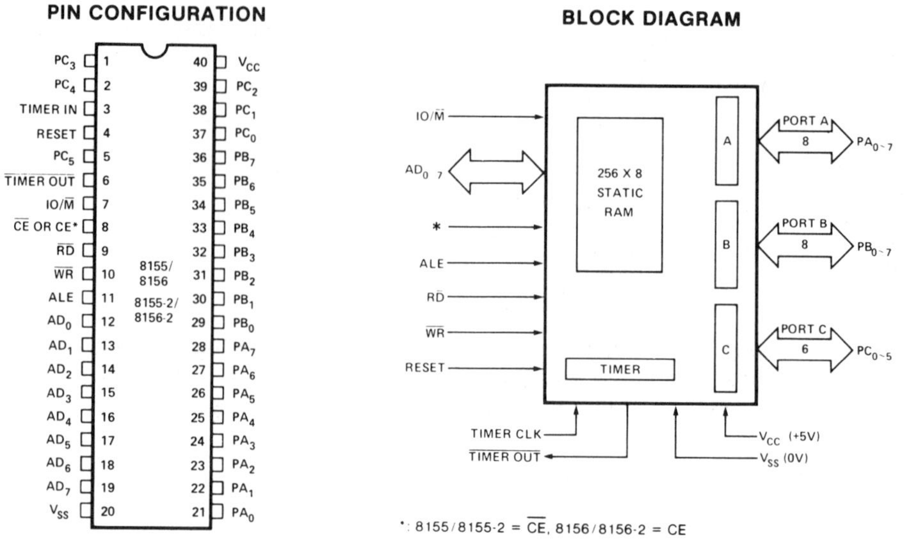

FIGURE 6–18 The block diagram and pinout of the 8155/8156 combination RAM, I/O, and timer integrated circuit.

SOURCE: Reprinted by permission of Intel Corporation, Copyright 1983.

I/O. Since both the I/O space and the memory space are enabled by $\overline{CE}$, much of the following text will discuss device selection.

Table 6–1 indicates the internal I/O ports or I/O addresses for the 8155. This device contains six different usable I/O port addresses. The most significant 5 bits of the port address are don't cares and enable the device through an external decoder. These don't cares are often fixed at some logic level by the external decoder. The external decoder generates the $\overline{CE}$ signal for the 8155 by decoding these 5 address bits.

A simple decoder is connected to the $\overline{CE}$ input in the circuit of figure 6–19. This decoder has fixed both the I/O port addresses and the addresses of the internal memory. The internal memory overlays memory addresses A000H through BFFFH because the decoder enables the 8155 for any mem-

TABLE 6–1 8155 I/O port assignments.

Port Address A15 or A7	A14 or A6	A13 or A5	A12 or A4	A11 or A3	A10 or A2	A9 or A1	A8 or A0	Selected Device
X	X	X	X	X	0	0	0	Command/Status
X	X	X	X	X	0	0	1	Port A
X	X	X	X	X	0	1	0	Port B
X	X	X	X	X	0	1	1	Port C
X	X	X	X	X	1	0	0	LSB of timer
X	X	X	X	X	1	0	1	MSB of timer

ory operation whose address begins with a 101 binary. The IO/$\overline{M}$ signal, which controls the selection of I/O or memory, is at a logic zero level to generate a memory reference. So the internal memory is activated whenever an address occurs with this bit pattern. Since there are only 256 bytes of RAM, the actual range of addresses may be A000H through A0FFH or any one of 32 possible ranges. The choice of the actual address range depends on the system and preoption of the system designer.

MEMORY	=	101X XXXX XXXX XXXX	= A000H to BFFFH
I/O	=	101X XXXX	= A0H to BFH

The I/O overlays I/O addresses A0H through BFH. Any time that the first 3 bits of the address bus contain a 101 binary, the decoder's output activates the 8155. If at the same time the IO/$\overline{M}$ signal is a logic one, an I/O device is activated. Notice that the I/O and the memory address spaces are not independent of each other with this integrated circuit. Because of this, care must be exercised in planning the I/O port numbers and the memory addresses.

The I/O addresses also overlay a large portion of the I/O address space, and the actual values may be A0H through A5H, A8H through ADH, BOH through B5H, or B8H through BDH. Again the choice of the actual I/O port numbers is the preoption of the system designer.

8155 Command Register

The 8155 is a programmable I/O device that must be programmed for normal operation so that the I/O pins can be controlled and the timer can be set with a count and started if needed. The command register, which accomplishes

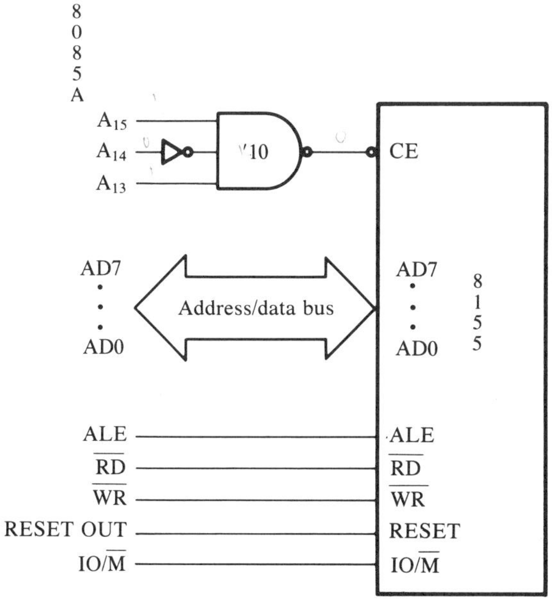

FIGURE 6–19 An example decoder and interconnection diagram from the 8155 to the 8085A microprocessor.

the programming, is the internal register that directs the operation of the 8155. Bits 7 and 6 of the command register, as illustrated in table 6–2, program the operation of the internal timer; bits 5 and 4 control the interrupts; bits 3 and 2 control the operation of port C; and bits 1 and 0 control the operation of ports B and A.

Port C can be programmed to operate in two alternate modes that will be discussed later in this section. Once the correct bit pattern for the command register is determined, it is loaded into the accumulator and sent out to the command register with an OUT instruction. Programming the command register normally occurs at the system reset location or whenever a change in operation is required.

The Timer

The internal timer must normally be loaded with the correct count before it is started or reprogrammed during a program. If it isn't, the timer will still operate; but its first counting sequence will be random. Loading is accomplished by sending the least significant 8 bits of the count to I/O port number XXXX X100 and the most significant portion, along with the the mode bits

TABLE 6–2 8155 command register bit assignments.

Command Register

7	6	5	4	3	2	1	0

Bit Positions	Function
7 and 6	Program the operation of the Timer
	0 0 = Timer NOP
	0 1 = Stop timer
	1 0 = Stop timer after terminal count
	1 1 = Start timer
5	Programs the port B interrupt function
	0 = Disable interrupt port B
	1 = Enable interrupt port B
4	Programs the port A interrupt function
	0 = Disable interrupt port A
	1 = Enable interrupt port A
3 and 2	Program the operation of port C
	0 0 = Input
	0 1 = ALT mode 3
	1 0 = ALT mode 4
	1 1 = Output
1	Programs the operation of port B
	0 = Input
	1 = Output
0	Programs the operation of port A
	0 = Input
	1 = Output

M2 and M1, to I/O port number XXXX X101. The timer ports and the bit patterns for M1 and M2 are illustrated in table 6–3. Once the timer is loaded with the count and mode, it may be started by storing a new command in the command/status register of the 8155. If the timer is being reprogrammed for a different count or mode of operation, it must be stopped and restarted to generate the new output. If you skip this step, the count will not change.

The timer count can range in value from 2H to 3FFFH and can generate a square wave or pulse. The duration of the pulse output is equal to one input clock period, while the square wave is symmetrical.

For example, if the timer is programmed to divide by 7 as a square wave, the output is high for four input clock periods and low for three. If pulse mode is selected, the output remains a logic one until the seventh clock pulse. At this time, it becomes a logic zero for one clocking period.

8155 Reset

Whenever the 8155 is reset by applying a logic one to the active high RESET pin, it is programmed so that the three I/O ports are setup as inputs, the output latches are cleared, and the timer is stopped. The contents of the internal memory will not be modified by a RESET.

8155 Example Problem

To help the reader gain a complete understanding of the 8155, figure 6–20 illustrates an example circuit programmed to function as indicated.

First the I/O port numbers to be used in this example must be determined. The decoder, connected to the $\overline{CE}$ pin of the 8155, enables the device whenever the first 3 address bits are high. The I/O ports then have addresses 111X X000 through 111X X101, so that they overlay ports E0H through F5H and also F0H through F5H. The port numbers used in this example are E0H through E5H.

TABLE 6–3 8155 timer ports.

Port XXXX X100 (LSB)

C7	C6	C5	C4	C3	C2	C1	C0

Port XXXX X101 (MSB)

M2	M1	C13	C12	C11	C10	C9	C8

Bit Assignment	Function
C13 to C0	14-bit count
M2 and M1	Timer waveform control
	0 0 = Single square wave
	0 1 = Continuous square wave
	1 0 = Single pulse
	1 1 = Continuous pulse

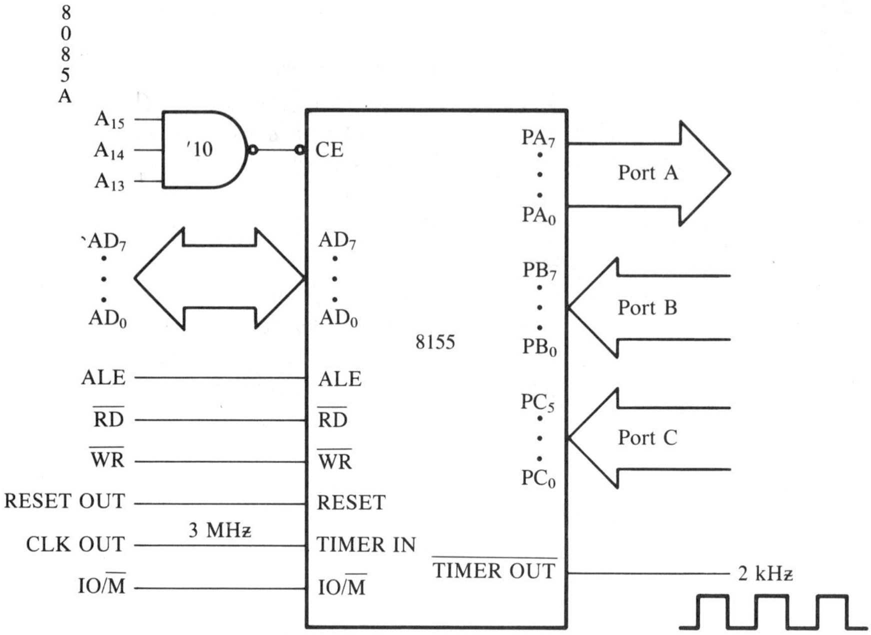

FIGURE 6–20 An example 8155 interface with Port A designated as an output, Ports B and C designated as inputs, and the timer set up to divide the clock by 1500.

When gathering the information from the illustration, notice that port A is an output port, port B and C are input ports, and the timer must be programmed to divide by 1500. Also notice that the timer must produce a continuous squarewave at 2000 Hz. Since the count must be programmed into the timer before it is started, this is the first step of the initialization dialog. Once the count and mode are programmed, the timer may be started and the remaining I/O port functions may be programmed. The initialization dialog is normally placed at the RESET location in the system's memory or location 0000H for the 8085A.

```
;8155 INITIALIZATION DIALOG FOR THE 8085A
;THIS SOFTWARE MUST BE EXECUTED BEFORE ANY
;8155 OPERATION CAN BE PERFORMED
;
RESET: MVI A,0DCH
       OUT 0E4H          ;SET LSB OF COUNT
       MVI A,45H
       OUT 0E5H          ;SET MODE AND MSB OF COUNT
       MVI A,11000001B
       OUT 0E0H          ;PROGRAM COMMAND REGISTER
           .
           .
           .
```

When the 8155 is programmed as illustrated, it will continue to function in this fashion until it is reprogrammed or RESET.

Handshaking with the 8155

The ALT3 and ALT4 modes operation for port C provide handshaking for external I/O devices, including printers that indicate when they are ready for the next character and keyboards that indicate that they have a character available for the microprocessor.

What is a handshake? *Handshaking* is a term that describes a communications protocol between two separate digital systems. This handshake, in many cases, is accomplished through two wires or signal lines. You and an automobile exhibit this type of handshake everytime that you start the car. You turn the ignition key and the starter begins to turn the engine. This can be thought of as one of the handshaking signals. In response the engine starts and signals you by making some noise; this is the other signal path in the handshake. One signal goes from you to the engine through the starter and the other goes from the engine to you through the sound of the engine's starting. If either of these signals is lost, you cannot reliably start the automobile.

Handshaking synchronizes a device such as a printer to the microprocessor. This synchronization is accomplished, in many cases, with a pair of wires and some software. A wire from the microprocessor signals the printer that data is being sent to the printer. The printer, when ready to receive more data, sends a signal back to the microprocessor. This "handshake" between the microprocessor and printer synchronizes their operation. The microprocessor waits for the ready signal from the printer before sending another byte of information.

Alternate Modes of Operation

Table 6–4 lists the pin assignments for port C whenever it is programmed for either alternate modes ALT3 or ALT4. Notice that the port C pins take on a meaning other than as input or output pins.

The $\overline{STB}$, or strobe signal, strobes data into or out of a port; the BF, or buffer full signal, indicates whether or not data is present inside the I/O port; and INTR, or interrupt request, becomes a one after the arrival of the $\overline{STB}$ signal. INTR causes an interrupt to occur in a microprocessor; interrupts will be discussed in detail in chapter 8.

8155 Strobed Input Operation

Strobed input operation of the 8155 is illustrated in figure 6–21(a). The strobe input, which comes from the external device, causes the data to be held in an internal latch; forces the buffer full flag (BF) high; and forces the INTR

Pin #	ALT3 Pin Name	ALT4 Pin Name
PC0	Port A INTR	Port A INTR
PC1	Port A BF	Port A BF
PC2	Port A $\overline{STB}$	Port A $\overline{STB}$
PC3	Output pin	Port B INTR
PC4	Output pin	Port B BF
PC5	Output pin	Port B $\overline{STB}$

TABLE 6–4 8155 port C alternate modes ALT3 and ALT4.

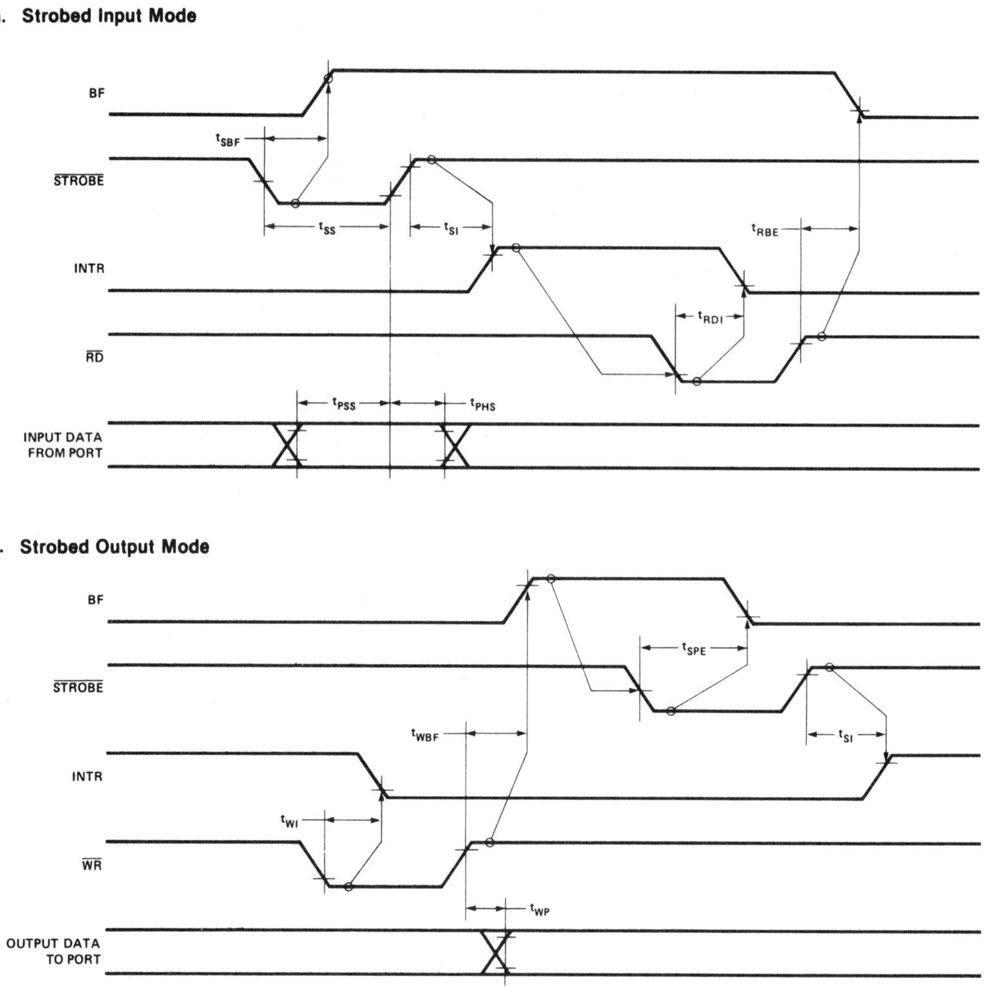

FIGURE 6–21 (a) Timing diagrams for strobed input operation of the 8155, (b) timing diagrams for strobed output operation of the 8155.

SOURCE: Reprinted by permission of Intel Corporation, Copyright 1983.

signal high. The software provided by the user tests BF to determine if data has been strobed into the port by the $\overline{STB}$ signal.

When BF is detected high, the software reads or inputs data from this port. The data is then transferred into the accumulator of the microprocessor, and the buffer full flag is cleared by the 8155. Buffer full is cleared whenever the data is read from the port.

8155 Strobed Output Operation

Strobed output operation is pictured in the timing diagram of figure 6–21(b). The order of operation for strobed output is the reverse of strobed input. The data is first written into the port by the microprocessor, which causes the data to be held in an internal latch, clears INTR, and forces buffer full (BF) high.

Buffer full indicates to the external device that data is present in the port. The external device responds by sending a strobe to the port, which indicates that it has received the information. The strobe then forces buffer full low and also sets the INTR signal.

The software associated with this port checks the buffer full flag to determine if the external device has removed the data from the port. If not, the software waits for the buffer full flag to be cleared by the external strobe signal. This type of operation is useful with the printer interface discussed earlier in the text.

8155 Keyboard Interface

The circuit of figure 6–22 indicates the way a keyboard may be connected to the 8155 by using the strobed input mode of operation for port A.

Whenever a key is depressed on the keyboard, ASCII data is presented to port A, along with a 1.5-μs pulse from $\overline{DAV}$, or data available. The $\overline{DAV}$ pulse, connected to the strobe input of port A, stores the ASCII character in port A and forces the buffer full flag high.

The buffer full flag must be detected by the software to determine if a key on the keyboard is depressed. Detection is accomplished by polling the BF flag bit, as illustrated in the software for this example. Once the keystroke is detected, the data is input to the microprocessor, clearing the buffer full flag.

The buffer full then indicates to the keyboard that the data is accepted. The keyboard looks for the negative edge of BF to acknowledge the receipt of the ASCII character.

8155 Status Register Bit Assignment

Table 6–5 illustrates the contents of the accumulator after data is input or read from the 8155 status register. The bits in the register indicate the current conditions of the timer, interrupts, and buffer full signals. This register is important in developing the software polling for the keyboard.

Accumulator After Status Read							
X	T I M	I E B	B B F	I R B	I E A	A B F	I R A

TABLE 6-5 8155 status register bit assignment.

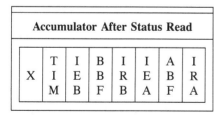

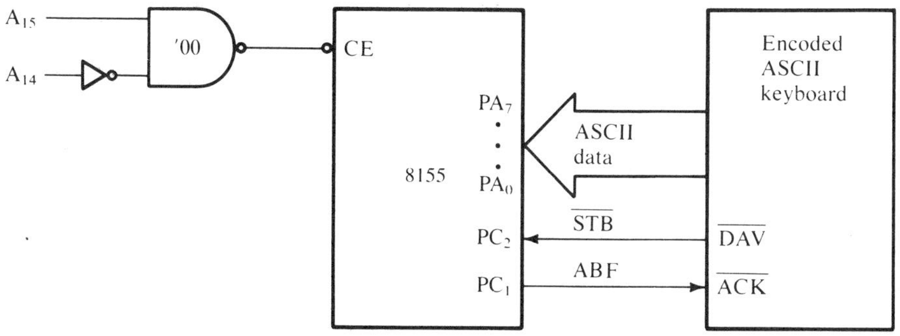

FIGURE 6–22 An example of the 8155 connected to an ASCII encoded keyboard using strobed input operation.

A brief explanation of each of the status register bit positions follows:

TIM Whenever the internal timer reaches its terminal count, this bit position becomes a logic one. For example, if the timer is programmed to divide by ten, this bit becomes a logic one on the tenth clock pulse.

IEB Whenever this bit position is a logic one, it indicates that the port B interrupt has been enabled through the command register.

BBF The port B buffer full flag (BBF) indicates that data has been strobed into the port B latch for an input operation or that data has been extracted from the port for an output operation.

IRB The *interrupt request bit* reflects the condition of the port B INTR pin.

IEA This position indicates that interrupt port A has been enabled using the command register. Whenever this bit position is a logic one, it indicates that the port B interrupt has been enabled through the command register.

ABF The port A buffer full flag (ABF) indicates that data has been strobed into port A for an input operation or extracted from port A for an output operation.

IRA This position reflects the condition of the port A INTR signal.

The Keyboard Software

To develop the software for this keyboard, the port A buffer full flag must be located. This flag bit is located in the status register of the 8155 and can be examined by inputting the status register at port number XXXX X000. In this example, figure 6–22, the I/O port assignment is 10XX X000 (80H) for the command/status register.

```
;8155 INITIALIZATION DIALOG
INIT:    MVI  A,00000100B ;SELECT ALT3 AND
         OUT  80H         ;PORT A = INPUT
          .
          .
;INKEY SUBROUTINE
INKEY:   IN   80H     ;GET STATUS WORD
         ANI  02H     ;ISOLATE ABF
         JZ   INKEY   ;LOOP IF NO DATA
         IN   81H     ;GET DATA
         RET          ;RETURN FROM THE SUBROUTINE
```

The INKEY subroutine provides the necessary software to read an ASCII coded character from the keyboard. The status word is input and ABF is checked or polled to see whether data has been strobed into port A from the keyboard; if it has not, the subroutine begins again. It continues to repeat until a character finally arrives from the keyboard. Once a character is strobed into port A, the subroutine detects ABF and inputs the data to the accumulator. It then returns to the program that called it with the ASCII data in the accumulator.

The MC6821 Peripheral Interface Adapter (PIA)

Figure 6–23 depicts the block diagram and pinout of the MC6821 peripheral interface adapter (PIA), which is fairly popular in systems that utilize memory mapped I/O. It contains two 8-bit bidirectional programmable parallel I/O ports that may be programmed as any combination of inputs and outputs. For example, the MC6821 can be programmed so that it functions with 12 output pins and 4 input pins.

In addition to the two 8-bit I/O ports or peripheral data registers, the MC6821 contains two data direction registers. The data direction registers program the direction of data flow in the two I/O ports. They also control two control registers, which direct the operation of the MC6821.

Selection

The MC6821 is selected by the chip selection inputs CS0, CS1, and $\overline{CS2}$, and the enable input E or phase two clock. For the MC6821 to perform an operation, all chip enable and selection pins must be active.

For example, if information is to be written into the PIA, $\overline{CS2}$ and R/$\overline{W}$ are grounded. CS0 and CS1 are placed at a logic one. The data from the microprocessor's data bus is then written into the PIA on E or phase two of the clock.

In addition, the internal registers must also be selected. This selection is accomplished through two external register selection pins, RS0 and RS1, and two internal bits in control registers A and B. Normally the RS0 and RS1 pins are connected to two of the address bus connections from the microproces-

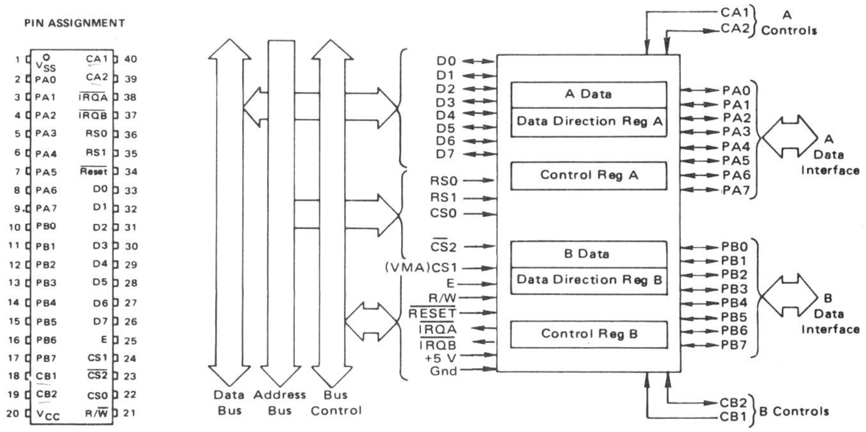

FIGURE 6–23 The pinout and block diagram of the MC6821 PIA.

SOURCE: Courtesy of Motorola, Inc.

sor so that the I/O port address selects the desired register. Table 6–6 indicates which registers are selected with RS0 and RS1.

TABLE 6–6 MC6821 register selection bits.

RS1	RS0	CRA-2	CRB-2	Function
0	0	1	X	Peripheral register A
0	0	0	X	Data direction register A
0	1	X	X	Control register A
1	0	X	1	Peripheral register B
1	0	X	0	Data direction register B
1	1	X	X	Control register B

The control registers, as illustrated in table 6–7(a) through 6–7(e), select either the DDR or the peripheral data register and the function of several pins on the MC6821. The DDR access bit, bit 2 in both registers, selects the DDR for the respective port whenever it is a zero. If the DDR access bit is a one, it selects the peripheral data register. The remaining bits control the interrupt requests and the function of the CA2, CB2, CA1, and CB1 handshaking or control pins.

TABLE 6–7 (a) MC6821 Control Register bit assignment.

Control Register A

7	6	5 4 3	2	1 0
IRQA1	IRQA2	CA2 Control	CRA-2	CA1 Control

Control Register B

7	6	5 4 3	2	1 0
IRQB1	IRQB2	CB2 Control	CRB-2	CB1 Control

If the control register is read by the microprocessor, interrupt status bits CRA6, CRA7, CRB6, and CRB7 are the only bits that convey information. More information regarding interrupt operation of this device appears in chapter 8.

MC6821 Reset

Whenever the MC6821 is reset by applying a logic zero on the active low $\overline{\text{RESET}}$ input, all of the internal registers are cleared. This procedure programs peripheral registers A and B as input devices. It also disables $\overline{\text{IRQA}}$ and $\overline{\text{IRQB}}$.

TABLE 6–7 (b) MC6821 control inputs CA1 and CB1.

CRA-1 (CRB-1)	CRA-0 (CRB-0)	Interrupt Input CA1 (CB-1)	Interrupt Flag CRA-7 (CRB-7)	MPU Interrupt Request $\overline{\text{IRQA}}$ ($\overline{\text{IRQB}}$)
0	0	↓ Active	Set high on ↓ of CA1 (CB1)	Disabled — $\overline{\text{IRQ}}$ remains high
0	1	↓ Active	Set high on ↓ of CA1 (CB1)	Goes low when the interrupt flag bit CRA-7 (CRB-7) goes high
1	0	↑ Active	Set high on ↑ of CA1 (CB1)	Disabled — $\overline{\text{IRQ}}$ remains high
1	1	↑ Active	Set high on ↑ of CA1 (CB1)	Goes low when the interrupt flag bit CRA-7 (CRB-7) goes high

NOTES: 1. ↑ indicates positive transition (low to high)
2. ↓ indicates negative transition (high to low)
3. The Interrupt flag bit CRA-7 is cleared by an MPU Read of the A Data Register, and CRB-7 is cleared by an MPU Read of the B Data Register.
4. If CRA-0 (CRB-0) is low when an interrupt occurs (Interrupt disabled) and is later brought high, $\overline{\text{IRQA}}$ ($\overline{\text{IRQB}}$) occurs after CRA-0 (CRB-0) is written to a "one".

(Courtesy of Motorola, Inc.)

TABLE 6–7 (c) Control of CA2 and CB2 as interrupt inputs.

CRA-5 (CRB-5)	CRA-4 (CRB-4)	CRA-3 (CRB-3)	Interrupt Input CA2 (CB-2)	Interrupt Flag CRA-6 (CRB-6)	MPU Interrupt Request $\overline{\text{IRQA}}$ ($\overline{\text{IRQB}}$)
0	0	0	↓ Active	Set high on ↓ of CA2 (CB2)	Disabled — $\overline{\text{IRQ}}$ remains high
0	0	1	↓ Active	Set high on ↓ of CA2 (CB2)	Goes low when the interrupt flag bit CRA-6 (CRB-6) goes high
0	1	0	↑ Active	Set high on ↑ of CA2 (CB2)	Disabled — $\overline{\text{IRQ}}$ remains high
0	1	1	↑ Active	Set high on ↑ of CA2 (CB2)	Goes low when the interrupt flag bit CRA-6 (CRB-6) goes high

NOTES: 1. ↑ indicates positive transition (low to high)
2. ↓ indicates negative transition (high to low)
3. The Interrupt flag bit CRA-6 is cleared by an MPU Read of the A Data Register, and CRB-6 is cleared by an MPU Read of the B Data Register.
4. If CRA-3 (CRB-3) is low when an interrupt occurs (Interrupt disabled) and is later brought high, $\overline{\text{IRQA}}$ ($\overline{\text{IRQB}}$) occurs after CRA-3 (CRB-3) is written to a "one".

(Courtesy of Motorola, Inc.)

TABLE 6–7 (d) Control of CA2 as an output.

CRA-5	CRA-4	CRA-3	CA2 Cleared	CA2 Set
1	0	0	Low on negative transition of E after an MPU Read "A" Data operation.	High when the interrupt flag bit CRA-7 is set by an active transition of the CA1 signal.
1	0	1	Low on negative transition of E after an MPU Read "A" Data operation.	High on the negative edge of the first "E" pulse which occurs during a deselect.
1	1	0	Low when CRA-3 goes low as a result of an MPU Write to Control Register "A".	Always low as long as CRA-3 is low. Will go high on an MPU Write to Control Register "A" that changes CRA-3 to "one".
1	1	1	Always high as long as CRA-3 is high. Will be cleared on an MPU Write to Control Register "A" that clears CRA-3 to a "zero".	High when CRA-3 goes high as a result of an MPU Write to Control Register "A".

(Courtesy of Motorola, Inc.)

TABLE 6–7 (e) Control of CB2 as an output.

CRB-5	CRB-4	CRB-3	CB2 Cleared	CB2 Set
1	0	0	Low on negative transition of first E pulse following an MPU Write "B" Data Register operaton.	High when the interrupt flag bit CRB-7 is set by an active transition of the CB1 signal.
1	0	1	Low on the positive transition of the first E pulse after an MPU Write "B" Data Register operation.	High on the positive edge of the first "E" pulse following an "E" pulse which occurred while the part was deselected.
1	1	0	Low when CRB-3 goes low as a result of an MPU Write in Control Register "B".	Always low as long as CRB-3 is low. Will go high on an MPU Write in Control Register "B" that changes CRB-3 to "one".
1	1	1	Always high as long as CRB-3 is high. Will be cleared when an MPU Write Control Register "B" results in clearing CRB-3 to "zero".	High when CRB-3 goes high as a result of an MPU Write into Control Register "B".

(Courtesy of Motorola, Inc.)

MC6821 Interface

The MC6821 is specifically designed to function with Motorola microprocessors, but it can also be used with other microprocessors. A typical interface for the MC6821 is illustrated in figure 6–24. VMA, which becomes a logic one for a valid memory address, activates CS0, and address bus connections A14 and A15 complete the selection of this device. In other words, the device is selected for valid memory locations $4000 through $7FFF, or one-fourth of the available memory ($ = hexadecimal).

Address bits A0 and A1 determine which internal register is selected for the data transfer: $4000 selects data direction register A or port A, $4001 control register A, $4002 data direction register B or port B, and $4003 control register B.

The phase 2 ($\phi 2$) TTL connection, or E, times the transfer to or from the MC6821, while the R/$\overline{W}$ signal selects the direction of the transfer.

MC6821 Interfaced to an 8085A

Figure 6–25 pictures the MC6821 wired to function as an 8085A memory mapped or isolated I/O peripheral device. S1 provides an advanced write signal for the proper operation and the NAND gate enables the MC6821 at the appropriate time in the 8085A timing. Interchanging the $\overline{MEMR}$ and $\overline{MEMW}$ with the $\overline{IOR}$ and $\overline{IOW}$ signals selects either memory mapped operation or isolated I/O operation.

The only problem with this interface is the timing required by the 8085A on a read operation. The 8085 requires information within 300 ns from the $\overline{MEMR}$ signal, and the MC6821 provides the information within 320 ns. This mismatch can be corrected in two different ways: The clock frequency of the 8085A can be reduced slightly from its maximum; or a higher speed version of the PIA, the MC68A21, can be substituted.

As an isolated I/O device, ports 60H through 63H can be used; as a memory mapped I/O device, address 6000H through 6003H can be used. The memory mapped version requires an overlay area from location 6000H through 7FFFH, and the isolated I/O version requires an overlay area from port 60H through 7FH.

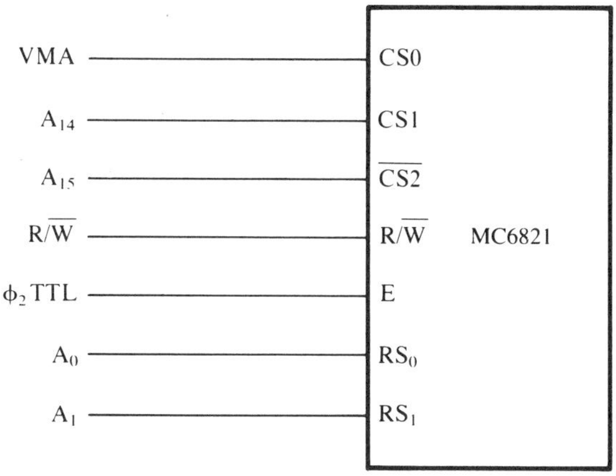

FIGURE 6–24 A typical MC6821 interface to a MC6800 or MC6809 microprocessor.

FIGURE 6–25 A typical MC6821 interface to an 8085A microprocessor.

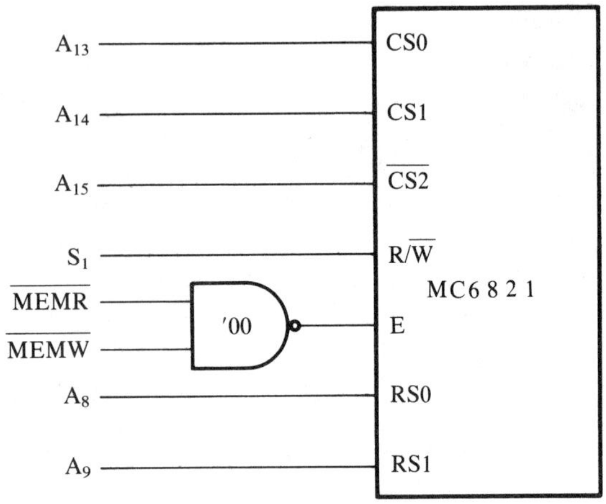

MC6821 Keyboard Interface

This time the keyboard interface described with figure 6–22 is connected to an MC6821 and an MC6800 microprocessor (figure 6–26). The memory space decoded by the chip select inputs is from location \$8000 through \$BFFF.

Initialization Dialog

The first step that must be accomplished is initialization of the MC6821 at the reset location, which is pointed to by the reset vector of the MC6800. Looking at table 6–7, we can determine the correct bit pattern for the command register for this application. The following initialization dialog would program both the command register for the MC6821 and the data direction register.

```
1 *INITIALIZATION DIALOG
2  RESET     CLR  $8001 SELECT DATA DIRECTION REG.
3            CLR  $8000 PROGRAM (A) AS INPUT
4            LDAA #$2C  SETUP CONTROL PATTERN
5            STAA $8001 SELECT DATA REG.
             .
             .
             .
```

The data direction register is selected for port A in line 2. Next, port A is programmed as an input port by line 3. This is not necessary when the MC6821 is RESET; it is illustrated for an application in which this is not the case. Next, lines 4 and 5 load the control register with a \$2C that disables interrupts, programs pin CA1 as a negative edge triggered input for $\overline{DAV}$, programs pin CA2 as a negative going output for the $\overline{ACK}$, and allows access to peripheral data register A.

Keyboard Input Subroutine

Finally a subroutine must be written to poll or check bit position seven of CRA to determine when data is available at port A. The return line 10 occurs whenever data is detected and the data is found in accumulator B after the return.

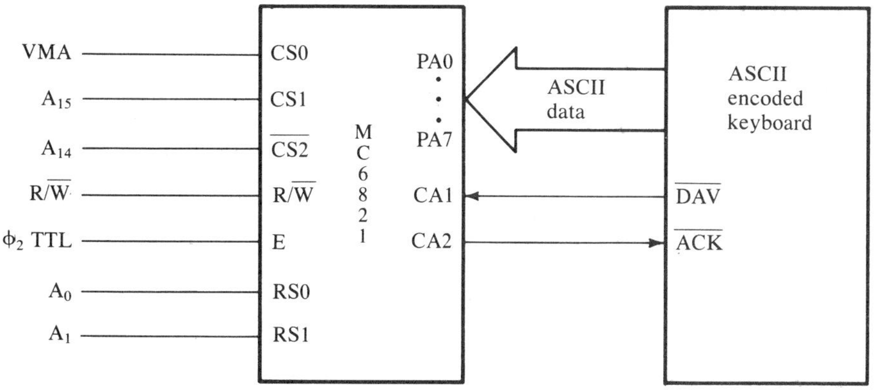

FIGURE 6–26 An MC6800 microprocessor interfaced to an ASCII encoded keyboard through an MC6821 PIA.

```
*INKEY SUBROUTINE
 INKEY TST  $8001  TEST CRA 7
       BPL  INKEY  WAIT FOR CRA 7 = 1
       LDAB $8000  GET DATA FROM PORT A
       RTS         RETURN FROM SUBROUTINE
```

When both examples are compared in this section of the text, it is apparent that the initialization dialog for the MC6821 (11 bytes) is longer than for the 8155 (4 bytes). The subroutines in both examples are approximately equivalent in length. The subroutine for the 8155 takes 11 bytes of memory, and the subroutine for the MC6821 takes ten bytes. Which of the two devices and their respective microprocessors is more suitable depends on the application at hand.

SOLENOID OPERATED DEVICES 6-5

Many output devices use a solenoid or relay to accomplish some form of work. For example, a dot matrix printer uses seven or nine solenoids to print information on the paper and may also use a solenoid to advance the paper to the next line. Another example is a point of sales terminal (POS), which uses a solenoid to open the cash drawer, advance paper, print information on its ticket printer, and—if equipped with a coin changer—return the correct denominations of coins for change.

Solenoid Interface

Solenoids usually demand a considerable amount of current from the controlling source. Since the controlling source is often a microprocessor, some form of buffer or current driver must be connected between the microprocessor's output circuitry and the solenoid. Figure 6–27 depicts a Darlington driver and an optical coupler that is used for isolation between the microprocessor and the solenoid's DC power supply.

FIGURE 6–27 (a) A typical TTL compatible Darlington solenoid driver using a helper resistor, (b) an optically isolated TTL compatible solenoid driver.

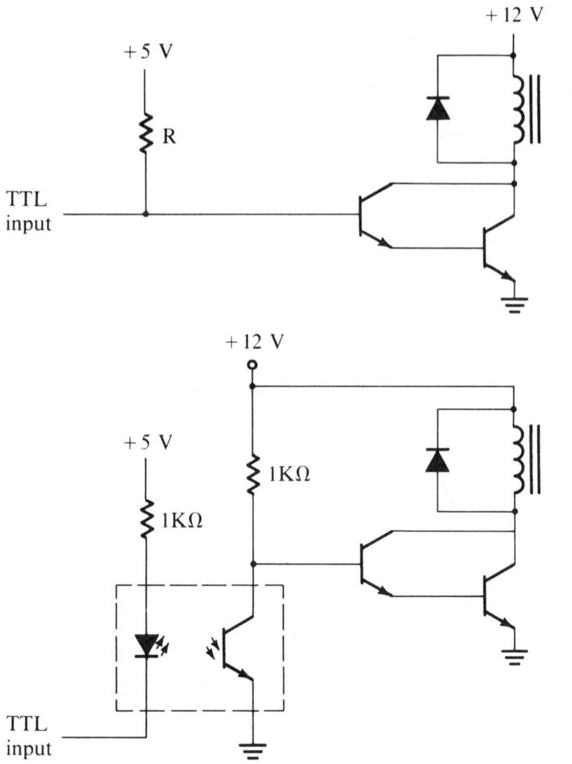

The source current available for the Darlington pair from most output ports is about 400 μA. If more current is required, an external pullup resistor can be included to increase the amount of source current for the Darlington pair. This can increase the current to 400 μA plus the sink current handling capability of the output port.

For example, the amount of available source current for the Darlington pair can be boosted to 2.4 mA for an 8155 output pin. This equals the sink current of the output pin plus the source current (400 μA).

Darlington Driver

The circuit illustrated in figure 6–27(a) uses a Darlington pair with a gain of 2000 minimum and a solenoid that requires 2 A of current. Without an external resistor, the Darlington pair can only drive a solenoid requiring 800 mA of current. In this case a pullup resistor to boost the drive current to the required 1.0 mA is required. At an output voltage of 1.4 V, the resistor must supply 600 μA of current, which, in addition to the 400 μA of current from the port, is 1.0 mA. This means that with a voltage drop of 3.6 V, the difference between 1.4 and 5 V, across the resistor, a current of 600 μA must flow. In this case the calculated value would be 6K Ω. Since 6K is not a standard resistor value, a 5.6K ohm resistor is used.

Does this create a problem with the current sinking capability of the I/O port? The amount of sink current that will flow in this circuit is 5.6K divided by the supply voltage of 5 V. This amount of current does not exceed the 2 mA sink capability, so the circuit will function properly.

Optical Isolation

The optical isolator depicted in figure 6–27(b) separates the power supplies of the microprocessor and the external solenoid. In many cases this is desirable because of the large fluctuation in load currents found at the solenoids. This fluctuation can be coupled back to the logic power supply, causing major problems in the reliability of the microprocessor based system.

8155 Solenoid Software

Figure 6–28 illustrates a solenoid attached to the 8155 PIA. The I/O port number for this solenoid is decoded as 61H which is bit position 7 of port A.

In this example the timer is used to generate the required amount of time delay for the solenoid. In practice, this may be done or a simple software time delay subroutine can be used.

The solenoid selected for this application requires an activation time of 4 ms for proper operation. To accomplish this, the timer develops the required amount of delay. Since the clock cycle time of the 8085A is 0.333 μs with a 6-MHz crystal, the timer count has to be 12,000 or 2E18H. The subroutine for activating the solenoid for this amount of time follows:

```
SOLE:  MVI   A,01000011B ;STOP TIMER
       OUT   60H
       IN    60H         ;CLEAR TERMINAL COUNT FLAG
       MVI   A,18H       ;LOAD TIME DELAY COUNT
       OUT   64H
       MVI   A,6EH
       OUT   65H
       MVI   A,80H       ;ACTIVATE SOLENOID
       OUT   61H
```

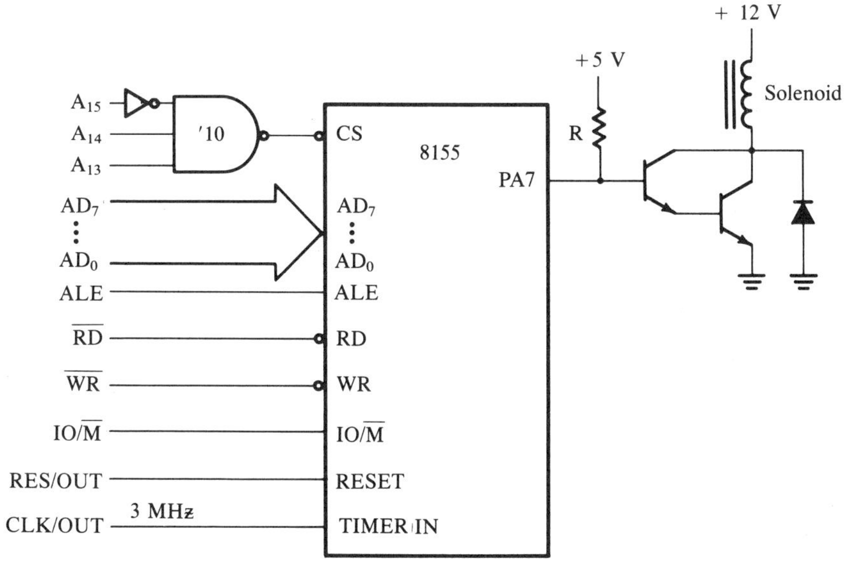

FIGURE 6–28 An 8085A microprocessor interfaced to a solenoid through the 8155 PIA.

```
        MVI   A,11000011B ;START TIMER
        OUT   60H
TEST:   IN    60H         ;GET 8155 STATUS BYTE
        ANI   40H         ;TEST TC FLAG
        JZ    TEST        ;IF DELAY NOT TIMED OUT
        MVI   A,00H       ;DEACTIVATE SOLENOID
        OUT   61H
        RET
```

This subroutine stops the timer to ensure that it is not already counting and then clears the terminal count flag. The TC flag has to be cleared since it is latched high whenever a TC is reached. In this application there is no method of knowing whether or not this flag is cleared. The act of reading the status register in the 8155 will always clear the TC flag.

The remaining portion of this subroutine loads the timer, fires the solenoid, and waits for it to time out. Polling tests the TC flag bit in the status register. Once a TC is detected, the solenoid is deenergized and a return from the subroutine occurs.

MC6821 Solenoid Software

The MC6800 and the MC6821 are illustrated in figure 6–29, driving a solenoid that is connected to a pin on the PIA. Memory locations $E000 through $E003 are decoded to control this interface.

Unlike the 8155, the MC6821 does not contain a timer; a timer either must be added to the system or a software time delay must be utilized. The latter technique is chosen for this application.

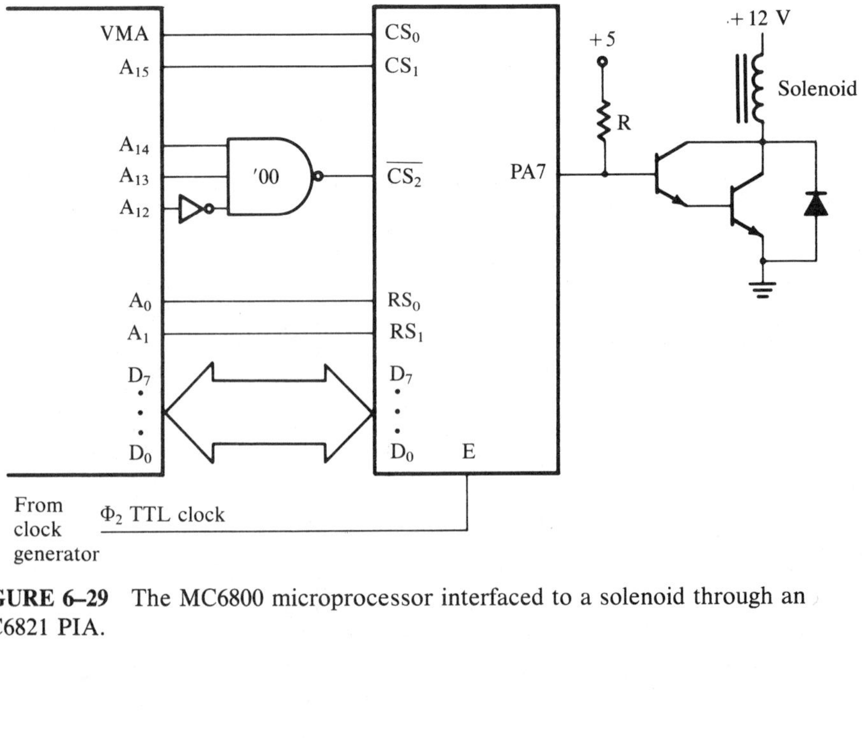

FIGURE 6–29 The MC6800 microprocessor interfaced to a solenoid through an MC6821 PIA.

```
SOLE:  LDAA #$80 TURN SOLENOID ON
       STAA $E001
       LDAA #$1E  COUNT A = 30
LOOP1  LDAB #$32  COUNT B = 50
LOOP2  DECB
       BNE  LOOP2 THIS LOOP DELAYS 300 MICROSECONDS
       DECA
       BNE  LOOP1 GOES THROUGH LOOP2 TIMES 30
       CLR  $E001 TURN SOLENOID OFF
       RTS
```

This subroutine wastes 9 ms between the time that the solenoid is turned on and off. The technique uses two nested time delay loops, with the inner loop wasting 300 μs of time. The outer loop goes through the inner loop 30 times, so that the total delay is 30 times 300 μs, or 9 ms. This is the time required to ensure the proper operation of the solenoid. Refer to chapter 4 for the information required to calculate this time delay sequence.

AC Solenoid

In certain applications it may be necessary to control an AC relay or solenoid, and a different interface must be used. In most cases isolation is more important when interfacing to an AC solenoid than to a DC solenoid, so an optical isolator is more likely to be used. Isolation is more important when AC control is considered, since a shorted TRIAC can apply 115 VAC to the logic circuitry. If this happens, most of it is destroyed and a fire may even result.

A simple circuit for interfacing an AC solenoid is illustrated in figure 6–30. An optically isolated TRIAC is connected to the output of a port pin. This TRIAC in turn controls a larger power TRIAC, since most optically isolated TRIACs cannot handle a large amount of current. To activate the solenoid, (1) a logic zero is placed on the input of the optically isolated TRIAC, (2) causing it to conduct and in turn (3) causing the power TRIAC to conduct, which (4) activates the solenoid.

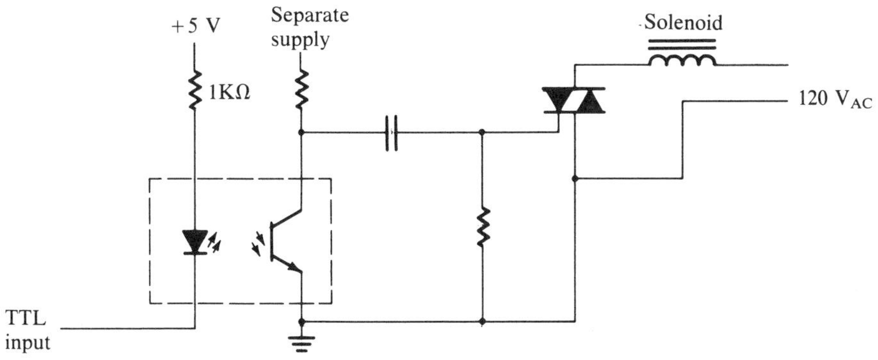

FIGURE 6–30 An optically coupled interface to an AC solenoid.

Summary

This chapter introduced the fundamental input/output building blocks used to construct most microprocessor based systems. The basic input and output interface points were illustrated along with a description of memory mapped and isolated I/O. These fundamental areas were built upon to include a coverage of the 8155 and MC6821 PIAs. Finally the solenoid operated device was discussed, illustrating more uses for the 8155 and the MC6821.

With this foundation, chapter 7, which uses the PIA extensively, leads us into the real world of microprocessor interface.

A keyboard application that introduced the idea of polled I/O was illustrated; it will be built upon in the remainder of this text. It is critical that this technique is fully understood, since it is widely used for many different types of I/O devices.

Glossary

ASCII code An alphanumeric code used with almost all microprocessor based computer systems.

Command register A register that controls a programmable I/O device.

Contact bounce Whenever a mechanical contact is made, it physically bounces, producing erroneous pulses.

Contact bounce eliminator A circuit that removes or eliminates the electrical contact bounces.

8155 A programmable I/O device that contains three separate I/O ports, 256 bytes of RAM, and a programmable 14-bit modulus counter.

Fluorescent display A device that emits a blue-green light.

Handshaking The act of synchronizing the microprocessor with an external circuit through software or hardware.

Initialization dialog A program that initializes all of the programmable I/O devices in a system.

LED A light emitting diode that emits light whenever a small current is passed through it.

Liquid crystal display A device that displays information by either blocking or passing light.

MC6821 A programmable interface adapter that contains two I/O ports and handshaking signals for the two ports.

Page An area of memory equal to 256 bytes.

Peripheral interface adapter A circuit that connects an external device to the microprocessor.

Port Another name for the I/O memory address or isolated I/O location.

Status The condition of an I/O device.

Timer A programmable modulus counter.

Questions and Problems

1 Describe the operation of the contact bounce eliminator of figure 6–1(b).

2 What is a disadvantage of the fluorescent numeric display?

3 All input devices require which type of circuitry for proper operation?

4 All output devices require which type of circuitry for proper operation?

5 How is the strobe produced in I/O circuitry?

6 Compare isolated I/O with memory mapped I/O.

7 What is a page of memory?

8 What is one advantage of isolated I/O?

9 What is one advantage of memory mapped I/O?

10 Develop a decoder that will generate a logic one for page EDH.

11 Develop a decoder that will generate a logic one for isolated I/O ports AXH.

12 Design a circuit that will develop eight I/O strobes at memory mapped I/O locations 10XXH. Make certain to label the address ranges of your output strobes.

13 Design a circuit that will generate 16 I/O strobes at isolated I/O addresses 9XH. Make certain to label the strobes.

14 Compare the 8155 and MC6821 programmable interface components.

15 Interface an 8155 to function at isolated I/O space CXH.

16 How many 8155s can be interfaced to a single microprocessor?

17 Interface a MC6821 to function at page $7X.

18 How many 6821s can be interfaced to a single microprocessor?

19 Develop initialization dialog for the 8155 in problem 15 if port A and C were to function as inputs, port B as an output, and the timer were to produce a series of pulses at 1/374 of the input rate.

20 Develop the initialization dialog for the MC6821 in problem 17 if port A is to function as a simple input device and port B is to function as a simple output device.

21 Develop a decoder that will enable the 8155 for I/O ports 6XH and memory address 2000H through 2FFFH.

22 Explain the way the control register in the MC6821 selects either the DDR or port register.

23 Describe the operation of the buffer full flag for the strobed input mode of operation of the 8155.

24 Which two MC6821 pins select an internal register?

25 Connect seven solenoids to an output port of the 8155 and develop the hardware and software to control these seven 10 ms solenoids. Your subroutine should fire the solenoids in the pattern passed to it in the accumulator register.

26 Connect seven solenoids to the MC6821 and develop the hardware and software to operate them for 10 ms. The parameter controlling which solenoids are to be activated is passed to the subroutine through accumulator B.

7

Input/Output Systems

This chapter uses the PIA, introduced in the last chapter, in many common applications. These include keyboards, displays, digital-to-analog converters, analog-to digital converters, arithmetic processors, EEPROMs, and stepper motors. All of these systems are component portions of larger systems. Understanding them makes developing a large system much easier.

In addition to the above systems, this chapter develops a scheme for expanding the memory in a system. This technique has become known as *memory management.* With this technique it is possible to extend the available memory in any microprocessor to an unlimited amount.

7-1 KEYBOARDS

Keyboards are interfaced in two different ways in most microprocessor based systems. The first method uses a keyboard encoder that detects keystrokes, converts the keystrokes into ASCII code, and signals the microprocessor that information is available. The second method requires an input port and an output port, which are used with some software to multiplex the keys in a keyboard matrix.

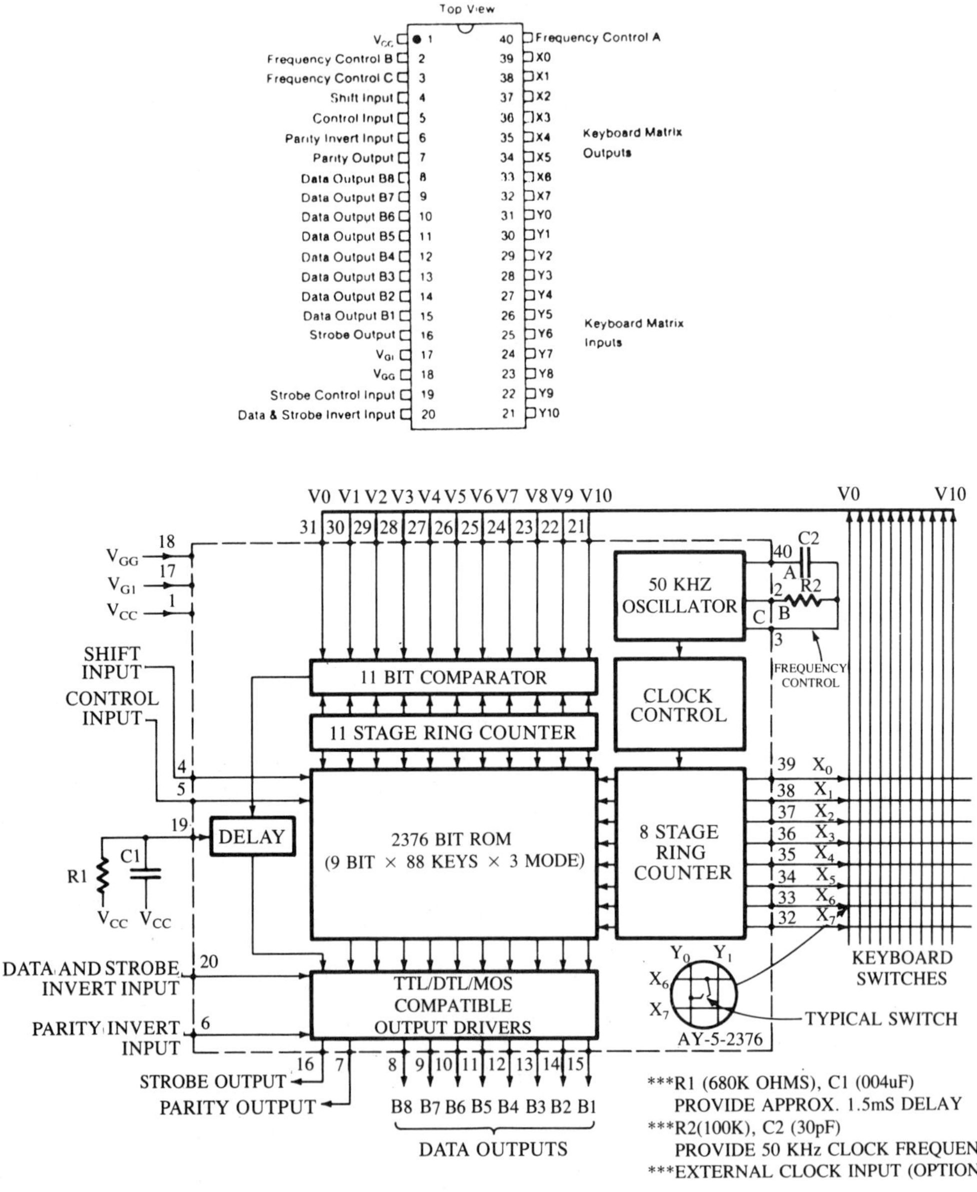

FIGURE 7–1 The pinout and block diagram of the AY-5-2376 keyboard encoder.

SOURCE: Courtesy of General Instruments, Inc.

Keyboard Encoder

The AY-5-2376, a typical keyboard encoder, is illustrated in figure 7–1. The keys are attached to the encoder through an eleven by eight keyboard matrix, which allows 88 keys to be connected to the encoder.

The encoder, under normal operation, scans the keyboard matrix for a key closure. Once the closure is detected, the internal circuitry addresses a ROM, which provides the ASCII address of the key at the data output connections. This information is not considered valid until the AY-5-2376 generates the output strobe signal after time is allowed for the key switch to stop bouncing.

In addition to the 88 key switches connected in the keyboard matrix, 2 additional switch connections accomplish the shift and the control functions. These additional inputs select different ASCII codes for the key switches. The internal ROM is a 264 word read only memory, which provides three sets of ASCII codes, depending upon the conditions of shift and control.

Keyboard Encoder to 8155 Interface

Figure 7–2 pictures the AY-5-2376 connected to an 8155 peripheral interface adapter. The strobe output, which becomes active after a valid keystroke, strobes the keyboard data into the I/O port for use by the microprocessor. Once the software detects this event, data is input to the microprocessor and

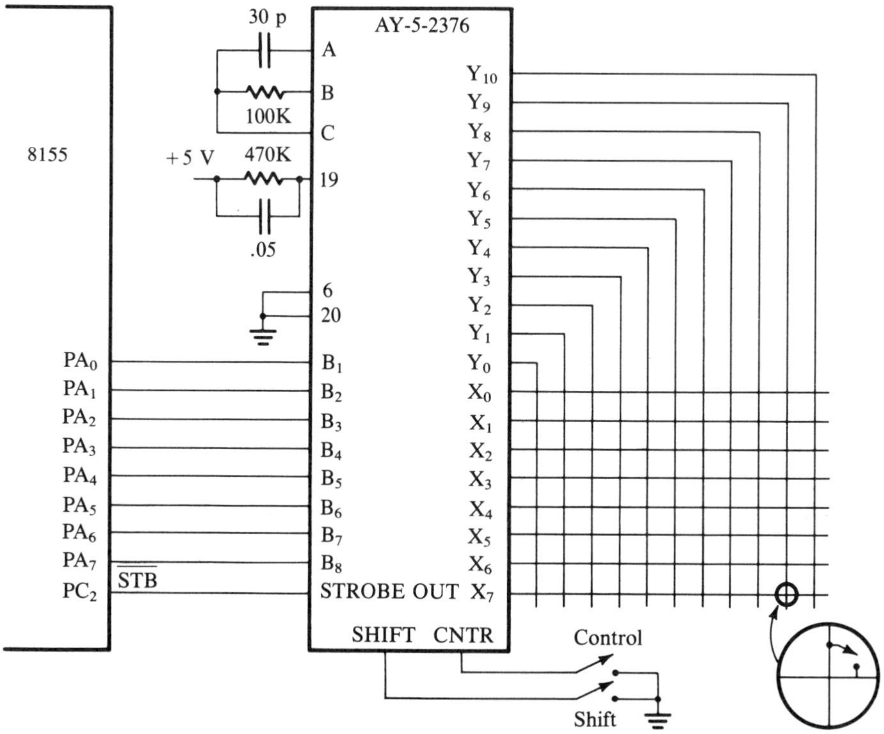

FIGURE 7–2 An AY-5-2376 interface to the 8155 through Port A using the strobed input mode of operation.

the I/O port is again ready for another byte of information from the keyboard.

Pins A, B, and C on the AY-5-2376 are used as timing inputs for an internal oscillator. This oscillator times the basic keyboard scanning rate. The SC pin connection develops a time delay internally, which debounces the keys on the keyboard.

The subroutine that is used to test the AY-5-2376 for data follows:

```
;THIS SUBROUTINE CHECKS FOR KEYBOARD DATA
;IF DATA IS FOUND IT RETURNS WITH IT IN THE ACC
;IF NO DATA IS FOUND IT WAITS FOR THE DATA
;
;THE ACC AND FLAGS ARE DESTROYED
;
INKEY:   IN    STATUS   ;GET THE BUFFER FULL FLAG
         ANI   02H      ;ISOLATE ABF
         JZ    INKEY    ;LOOP IF THERE IS NO DATA
         IN    PORTA    ;INPUT THE ASCII DATA
         RET            ;RETURN FROM THE SUBROUTINE
```

Hexadecimal Keypad Interface

The keyboard encoder is only used when a full keyboard is connected to the microprocessor. Most applications do not require a complete keyboard, so this circuit is not found. In its place you would probably find the circuit of figure 7–3 with a small keyboard matrix of 16 keys.

For this interface to fit many different types of parallel interface adapters, the diagram identifies only port A and port B.

This keyboard is organized as a 2-by-8-bit matrix. Port A must be programmed as an input port, while the 2 bits used in port B must be programmed as outputs. This is accomplished with the initialization dialog discussed in the last chapter and with the subroutines for this circuit.

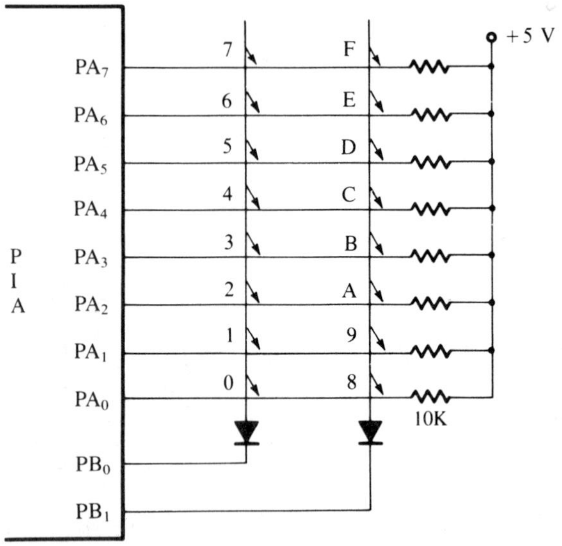

FIGURE 7–3 A hexadecimal keypad connected to Port A of a PIA.

The subroutines that will scan the keyboard must be capable of selecting a column of eight keys, detecting if any of the eight keys is depressed, debouncing the keystroke, and providing a code to identify the key's location. The flowchart provided in figure 7–4 illustrates this sequence of events.

8085A Keypad Software

When developing the software for this application, binary bit patterns 0000 0010 and 0000 0001 are chosen as codes to select the columns, and binary bit patterns 0000 0000 and 0000 1000 are chosen as an indicator for the first key in the selected column.

The time required for debouncing the keys depends upon the type of push button switches selected for the keyboard. In general, push button switches will stop bouncing after 10–20 ms.

The 8155 is initialized by programming the command register so that port A is an input port and port B is an output port. The initialization dialog is placed at the start of the system software at the reset location.

```
;INITIALIZATION DIALOG FOR THE 8155 KEYBOARD INTERFACE
;
RESET: MVI   A,00000010B ;SET PORT A = INPUT
       OUT   COMMAND     ;SET PORT B = OUTPUT
              .
              .
              .
```

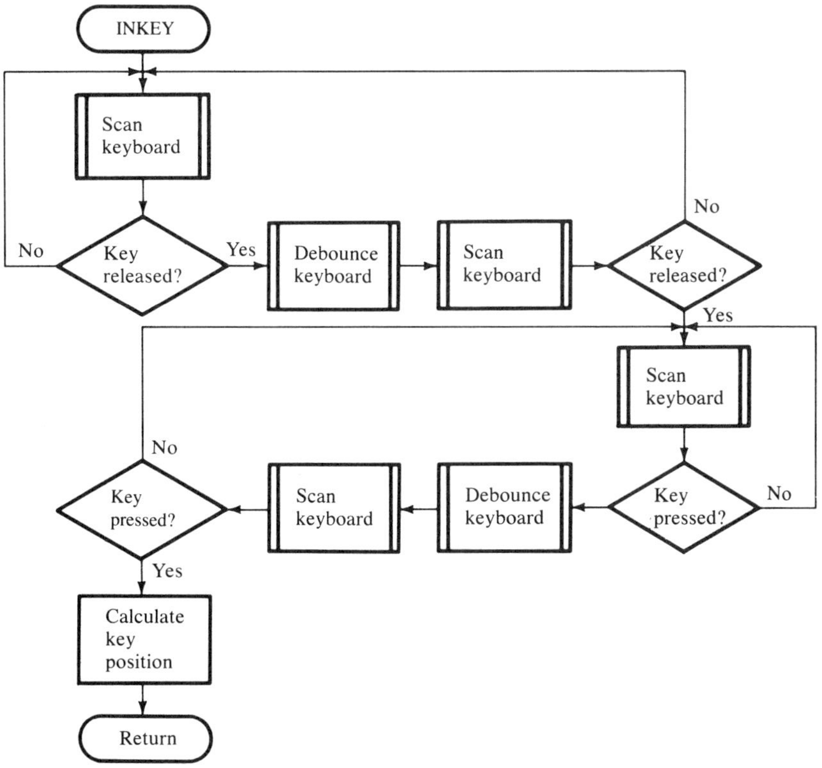

FIGURE 7–4 The flowchart for scanning the keyboard illustrated in figure 7–3.

After the 8155 is initialized, it can be controlled to scan the keyboard. The INKEY subroutine that scans this keyboard follows:

```
 1 ;8085A ASSEMBLY LANGUAGE VERSION
 2 ;SUBROUTINE TO DETECT A KEYSTROKE AND RETURN
 3 ;WITH THE KEY CODE IN THE C-REGISTER.
 4 ;
 5 ;ALL REGISTERS EXCEPT HL ARE DESTROYED
 6 ;USES THE SCAN AND DELAY SUBROUTINES
 7 ;
 8 ;CHECK FOR KEY RELEASE
 9 INKEY: CALL SCAN      ;CHECK ALL KEYS
10        JNZ  INKEY     ;IF KEY IS DEPRESSED
11        CALL DELAY     ;DEBOUNCE
12        CALL SCAN      ;CHECK ALL KEYS
13        JNZ  INKEY     ;IF KEY IS DEPRESSED
14 ;CHECK FOR A KEY
15 LOOP:  CALL SCAN      ;CHECK ALL KEYS
16        JZ   LOOP      ;IF NO KEY IS DEPRESSED
17        CALL DELAY     ;DEBOUNCE
18        CALL SCAN      ;CHECK ALL KEYS
19        JZ   LOOP      ;IF IT WAS NOISE
20 ;DETERMINE WHICH KEY WAS DEPRESSED
21 LOOP1: RRC            ;LOCATE ROW
22        RNC            ;RETURN IF FOUND
23        INR  C         ;MODIFY KEY CODE
24        JMP  LOOP1     ;CONTINUE TO LOOK
```

Lines 9 through 13 in the 8085A version of the keyboard software check whether the previous key has been released. This check is necessary because the software that uses this subroutine may call it before the person using the keyboard has had time to remove a finger from the button. If the key is released, lines 15 through 19 scan, or search, for another key closure. Once a key closure is detected, the subroutine searches the binary bit pattern for the closed contact; as it does, it modifies the key code in the C-register. When the code of the keystroke has finally been calculated, a return occurs with C equal to the key's code number.

```
;20 MSEC. TIME DELAY SUBROUTINE
;CLOCK CYCLE TIME = 333 NSEC.
;ACC, F, D AND E ARE DESTROYED
;
DELAY:  LXI  D,1568D   ;LOAD COUNT
DELAY1: DCX  D         ;DECREMENT COUNT
        MOV  A,D       ;TEST DE FOR A ZERO
        ORA  E
        JNZ  DELAY1    ;COUNT = ZERO?
        RET
```

The amount of time used for the contact debounce delay is left up to the user, since it varies with different switches. The count 1568 in the DELAY subroutine is chosen for a 20 ms time delay for this example.

```
;KEYBOARD SCANNING SUBROUTINE
;MODIFIES B AND C, DESTROYS ACC AND F
;RETURN ZERO = NO KEYSTROKE
;RETURN NOT ZERO = KEYSTROKE
;
SCAN:   MVI  A,02H      ;SELECT A COLUMN
        MVI  C,00H      ;SET ROW STARTING KEY CODE
        OUT  PORTB
        IN   PORTA      ;CHECK ROWS
        CPI  0FFH
        RNZ             ;RETURN ON KEY
        MVI  A,01H      ;SELECT NEXT COLUMN
        OUT  PORTB
        MVI  C,08H      ;SET ROW STARTING KEY CODE
        IN   PORTA      ;CHECK ROWS
        CPI  0FFH
        RET
```

The keyboard scanning subroutine selects a column by modifying the data at port B. Once a column of eight keys is selected, port A is input and checked for a keystroke. If 1 or more bits are logic zeros at this time, it indicates that a key is depressed and the subroutine returns with the accumulator containing the row bit pattern. If no key is depressed, the column selection bit pattern and the row beginning key code are modified and the next column of eight keys is checked.

6800 Keypad Software

To implement the hex keypad with the MC6800 and MC6821 PIA, the PIA must first be programmed or initialized at the reset location for the system program. The dialog that follows programs port A as an input port and port B as an output port.

```
*6821 HEX KEYPAD INITIALIZATION DIALOG
*
RESET   CLR  CRA     SELECT PORT A DDR
        CLR  PORTA   PORT A = INPUT
        CLR  CRB     SELECT PORT B DDR
        LDAA #$FF    PORT B = OUTPUT
        STAA PORTB
        LDAA #$04
        STAA CRA     SELECT PORT A DATA REGISTER
        STAA CRB     SELECT PORT B DATA REGISTER
          .
          .
          .
```

The keypad scanning subroutine, which follows, checks to see whether a key is released. This is done because the software jumping to this subroutine may execute in a very short period of time. If it jumps to the subroutine before the operator releases the key, multiple keystrokes are entered into the system. Once the key is released, the INKEY subroutine detects which key has been pressed and returns with the code of the key in accumulator B.

```
*6800 ASSEMBLY LANGUAGE VERSION
*SUBROUTINE TO DETECT A KEYSTROKE AND RETURN
*WITH THE KEY CODE IN ACCUMULATOR B.
*
*WAIT FOR KEY RELEASE
INKEY  JSR    SCAN      CHECK ALL KEYS
       BNE    INKEY     IF KEY IS DEPRESSED
       JSR    DELAY     DEBOUNCE
       JSR    SCAN      CHECK ALL KEYS
       BNE    INKEY     IF KEY IS DEPRESSED
*WAIT FOR A NEW KEYSTROKE
LOOP   JSR    SCAN      CHECK ALL KEYS
       BEQ    LOOP      IF NO KEY DEPRESSION
       JSR    DELAY     DEBOUNCE
       JSR    SCAN      CHECK ALL KEYS
       BEQ    LOOP      IF NO KEY DEPRESSION
*DETERMINE KEY CODE
LOOP1  LSRA             LOCATE KEYSTROKE
       BCC    RET       RETURN WHEN FOUND
       INCB             MODIFY KEY CODE
       JMP    LOOP1     KEEP CHECKING
```

The time delay subroutine uses nested loops to achieve a time delay of 20 ms. This time delay is required to debounce the mechanical key switches in the keyboard matrix.

```
*20 MSEC. TIME DELAY SUBROUTINE
*
DELAY  LDAA   #$14     LOAD COUNT
DELAY1 LDAB   #$A5
DELAY2 DECB            DECREMENT B COUNT
       BNE    DELAY2   COUNT B = ZERO?
       DECA            DECREMENT A COUNT
       BNE    DELAY1   COUNT A = ZERO?
       RTS             RETURN FROM DELAY
```

The SCAN subroutine selects a column of eight keys and determines whether or not a key is depressed. If a key is detected, a return equal occurs; if no key is detected, a return not equal occurs.

```
*CHECK FOR ANY KEY SUBROUTINE
*RETURN EQUAL = KEYSTROKE DETECTED
*RETURN NOT EQUAL = NO KEYSTROKE DETECTED
*
SCAN   LDAA   #$02     SELECT COLUMN
```

```
          STAA    PORTB
          CLRB            SET KEY CODE
          LDAA    PORTA   CHECK KEYS
          CMPA    #$FF    CHECK FOR KEY
          BNE     RET     RETURN ON KEY
          LDAA    #$01    SELECT COLUMN
          STAA    PORTB
          LDAB    #$08    SET KEY CODE
          LDAA    PORTA   CHECK KEYS
          CMPA    #$FF    CHECK FOR KEY
RET       RTS             RETURN FROM SUBROUTINE
```

MULTIPLEXED DISPLAYS 7-2

Display devices are normally multiplexed to reduce the component count in a microprocessor based system. In microprocessors, the seven segment code is developed with software to further reduce the amount of external hardware required in the system.

BCD to Seven Segment Code Conversion

Code conversion from binary coded decimal to seven segment code is usually done via a table lookup subroutine. The BCD coded number forms the address of the seven segment coded character stored in a table in the memory. This method of code conversion is widely used because of its speed and relatively low cost. Table 7–1 illustrates the typical lookup table for a common anode seven segment display. The display and driver circuitry is pictured in figure 7–5. When a logic one is applied to the base of the segment driver, it becomes forward biased. This sinks current for the cathode of the display, which then lights.

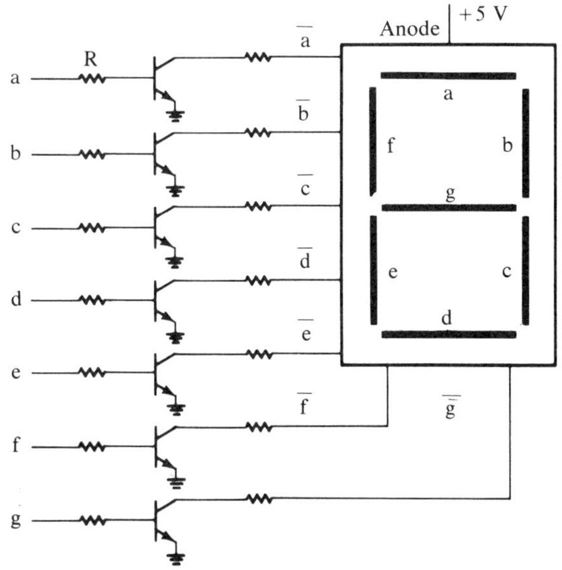

FIGURE 7–5 A seven segment LED display illustrating the segment drivers.

TABLE 7–1 Common anode seven segment lookup table.

Address	Data								Displayed Data
	X	a	b	c	d	e	f	g	
TABLE	0	1	1	1	1	1	1	0	0
TABLE+1	0	0	1	1	0	0	0	0	1
TABLE+2	0	1	1	0	1	1	0	1	2
TABLE+3	0	1	1	1	1	0	0	1	3
TABLE+4	0	0	1	1	0	0	1	1	4
TABLE+5	0	1	0	1	1	0	1	1	5
TABLE+6	0	1	0	1	1	1	1	1	6
TABLE+7	0	1	1	1	0	0	0	0	7
TABLE+8	0	1	1	1	1	1	1	1	8
TABLE+9	0	1	1	1	1	0	1	1	9

8085A Table Lookup Software

Software to convert the unpacked or single BCD digit in the accumulator of an 8085A into a seven segment coded number follows:

```
 1   ;8085A ASSEMBLY LANGUAGE PROGRAM
 2   ;SUBROUTINE TO CONVERT THE ACCUMULATOR FROM
 3   ;BCD TO SEVEN SEGMENT CODE
 4   ;HL IS DESTROYED
 5   ;REFERENCES TABLE 7-1
 6   ;
 7   CONVERT: ANI    0FH       ;MASK LEFT NIBBLE
 8            LXI    H,TABLE   ;POINT TO LOOKUP TABLE
 9            ADD    L         ;ADD BCD TO ADDRESS (HL)
10            MOV    L,A
11            MOV    A,H
12            ACI    00H
13            MOV    H,A
14            MOV    A,M       ;GET SEVEN SEGMENT CODE
15            RET
```

6800 Table Lookup Software

Software to convert the contents of accumulator B in the MC6800 from a single unpacked BCD digit into seven segment code follows:

```
 1   *6800 ASSEMBLY LANGUAGE PROGRAM
 2   *SUBROUTINE TO CONVERT ACCUMULATOR B FROM BCD
 3   *INTO SEVEN SEGMENT CODE.
 4   *X IS DESTROYED
 5   *REFERENCES TABLE 7-1
 6   *
 7   CONVERT: ANDB   #$0F      MASK LEFT NIBBLE
 8            LDX    #TABLE    GET TABLE ADDRESS
```

```
        STX   TEMP     SAVE TABLE ADDRESS
        ADDB  TEMP+1   DEVELOP ADDRESS
        STAB  TEMP+1
        BCC   CONV1
        INC   TEMP
CONV1   LDX   TEMP     GET TABLE ADDRESS
        LDAB  X        GET 7 SEGMENT CODE
        RTS
```

Location TEMP in the above software is 2 bytes of memory somewhere in the base page. This reduces the length of this subroutine. The extra work allows this subroutine to be stored in a ROM. If a ROM will not be used, the subroutine can be shortened considerably.

Multiple Digit Display

The table lookup technique for code conversion, along with other software, multiplexes the two digit display illustrated in figure 7–6. Port A supplies both displays with seven segment code through a set of drivers, and port B selects either digit zero or digit one. Again the type of peripheral interface adapter is not specified, so that any can be utilized.

Port A provides seven segment data for both displays through a set of current amplifiers. These amplifiers are required to provide enough drive current for the displays, which typically require 10 mA per segment. Since this is a two digit multiplexed display, each display segment requires twice this amount of current to remain illuminated at normal intensity. A three digit display requires three times the current, and so forth.

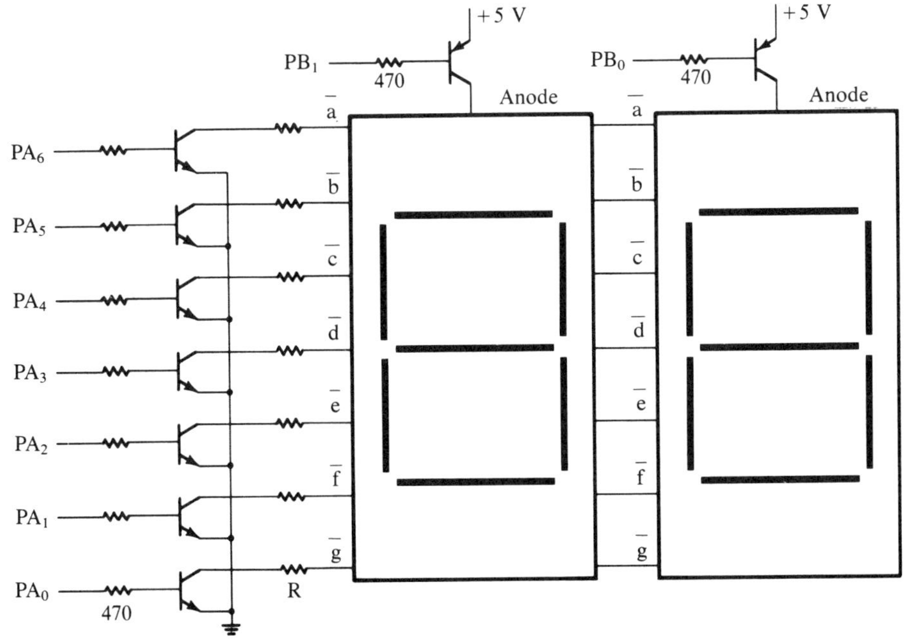

FIGURE 7–6 A two digit multiplexed seven segment LED display.

The software developed to drive the displays will make one pass only; that is, it will display each digit only one time. It is the responsibility of the software using this subroutine to call it continually to maintain a constantly displayed number. If you wish to do quite a bit of processing between calls, it is important to blank the displays to prevent damage. The displays may be blanked by turning off both displays.

Figure 7–7 illustrates the flowchart for the DISP subroutine. Port B selects the digit that displays the information at port A. The two "digit" selection

FIGURE 7–7 A flowchart of the subroutine required to multiplex the two LED displays pictured in figure 7–6.

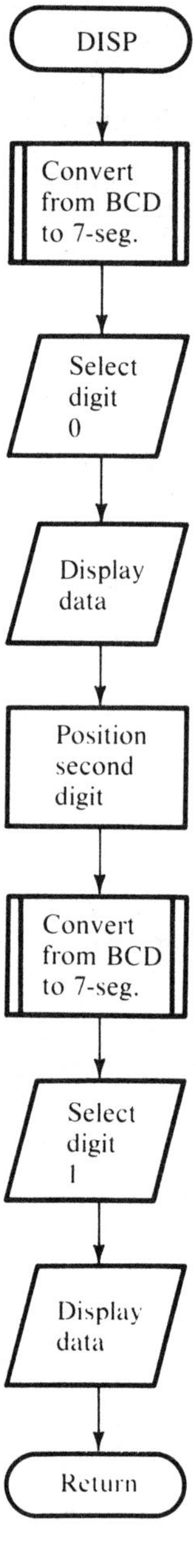

pins at port B are connected to transistor switches that select a digit. These switches must be capable of passing the current from all seven segments in the selected display. In this circuit that amounts to 140 mA peak for each seven segment display, with an average current of 70 mA.

The subroutine that causes the 1 ms time delay is not illustrated but can be developed in the same manner as the DELAY subroutine in the section on keyboards. The DELAY subroutine is included to reduce the switching time to the displays. Without it, RF is generated and propagated from the displays, causing a problem with the Federal Communications Commission (FCC).

8085 Version of the Display Software

Before the display can be used, the 8155 must be programmed. In this application, ports A and B must be programmed as output ports for the display. As with the prior software, the initialization dialog is found at the reset location.

```
;8155 INITIALIZATION DIALOG
;
RESET: MVI   A,00000011B   PROGRAM PORT A & B
       OUT   COMMAND       AS OUTPUT PORTS
        .
        .
        .
```

Once the 8155 is programmed, the DISP subroutine can be used whenever data is to be displayed on the two digit display.

```
;8085 ASSEMBLY LANGUAGE PROGRAM
;SUBROUTINE TO DISPLAY THE PACKED BCD NUMBER
;IN THE ACCUMULATOR ON THE TWO DIGIT DISPLAY.
;
DISP:   PUSH PSW        ;SAVE BCD
        CALL CONVERT    ;CONVERT TO SEVEN SEG.
        OUT PORTA       ;SEND DATA
        MVI A,02H       ;SELECT DIGIT 0
        OUT PORTB
        CALL DELAY      ;WAIT 1 MSEC.
        POP PSW         ;GET BCD
        RRC             ;POSITION NEXT DIGIT
        RRC
        RRC
        RRC
        CALL CONVERT    ;CONVERT TO SEVEN SEG.
        OUT PORTA       ;SEND DATA
        MVI A,01H       ;SELECT DIGIT 1
        OUT PORTB
        CALL DELAY      ;WAIT 1 MSEC.
        RET             ;RETURN FROM DISP
```

6800 Version of the Display Software

Before the display can be used, the MC6821 must be programmed. In this application ports A and B must be programmed as output ports for the display. As with the prior software, the initialization dialog is found at the reset location. Steps 3 and 4 are only required if the MC6821 is not reset. This may be the case in some systems; so it may be better to include these steps as a matter of practice.

```
 1 *6821 INITIALIZATION DIALOG
 2 *
 3 RESET CLR  CRA        SELECT DDR PORT A
 4       CLR  CRB        SELECT DDR PORT B
 5       LDAA #$FF       SET ALL BITS TO OUTPUT
 6       STAA DDRA       PROGRAM PORT A
 7       STAA DDRB       PROGRAM PORT B
 8       LDAA #$04       SELECT DATA FOR PORT A
 9       STAA CRA
10       STAA CRB        SELECT DATA FOR PORT B
           .
           .
           .
```

After the MC6821 is programmed, the DISP subroutine can be used whenever data is to be displayed on the two digit display.

```
*6800 ASSEMBLY LANGUAGE PROGRAM
*SUBROUTINE THAT TAKES THE PACKED BCD FROM
*ACC B AND DISPLAYS IT ON THE DISPLAYS.
*
DISP    PSHB               SAVE BCD DATA
        JSR   CONVERT      CONVERT TO SEVEN SEG.
        STAB  PORTA        SEND DATA
        LDAB  #02          SELECT DIGIT 0
        STAB  PORTB
        JSR   DELAY        WAIT FOR 1 MSEC.
        PULB               RESTORE BCD
        LSRB               POSITION NEXT DIGIT
        LSRB
        LSRB
        LSRB
        JSR   CONVERT      CONVERT TO SEVEN SEG.
        STAB  PORTA        SEND DATA
        LDAB  #01          SELECT DIGIT 1
        STAB  PORTB
        JSR   DELAY        WAIT FOR 1 MSEC.
        RTS                RETURN FROM DISP
```

DIGITAL-TO-ANALOG AND ANALOG-TO-DIGITAL CONVERTERS 7-3

Many microprocessor based systems require the generation or reception of analog voltages. Today this is a simple task with the many types of prepackaged digital-to-analog and analog-to-digital converters. In fact some of the newer microprocessors are manufactured with built-in analog-to-digital converters.

Eight-Bit Digital-to-Analog Converters

Figure 7–8 illustrates a microprocessor compatible 8-bit digital-to-analog converter. This particular device will generate an output voltage of 0–2.55 V in steps of 0.01 V, with a full-scale accuracy of plus or minus 0.6 percent. The output settles, or becomes valid, within 1.5 μs after a new 8-bit code is strobed into its internal latch.

Memory-Mapped Connections of the AD558 DAC

Figure 7–9 pictures the AD558 DAC connected to a microprocessor as a memory mapped I/O device. $\overline{CE}$ is connected to the active low write signal from the microprocessor, and $\overline{CS}$ is connected to the output of a simple address decoder. The data bus from the microprocessor is joined to the data bus connections. Any time that the microprocessor writes information into a mem-

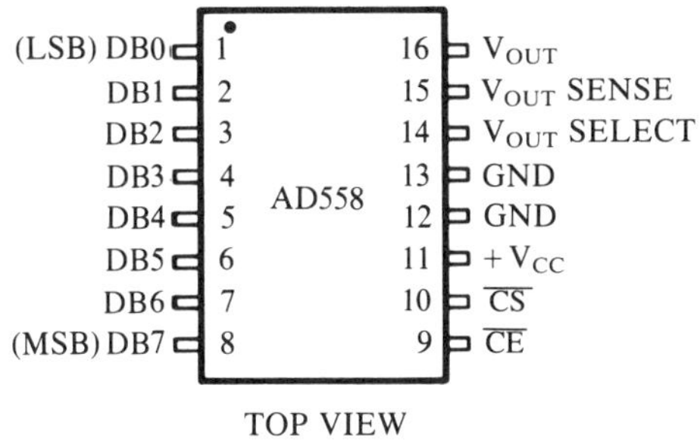

FIGURE 7–8 The AD558 microprocessor compatible 8-bit digital to analog converter.

SOURCE: Courtesy of Analog Devices, Inc.

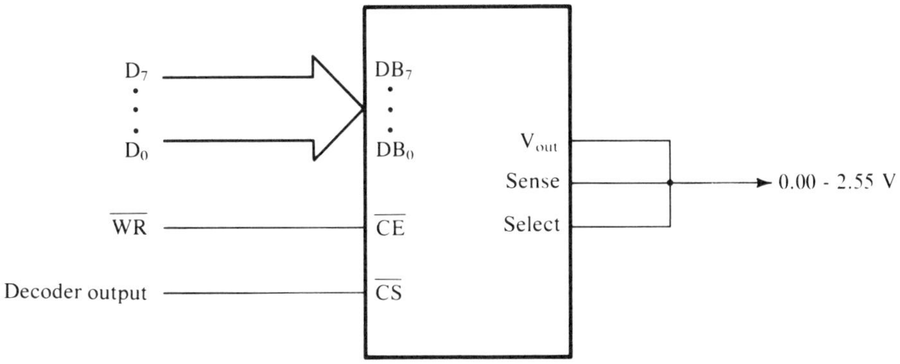

FIGURE 7–9 The AD558 digital to analog converter connected to a microprocessor data bus and control signals.

ory location decoded by the decoder, the contents of the data bus are latched into the DAC. This procedure generates an analog output voltage that is proportional to the digital input in about 1.5 μs.

Eight-Bit Analog-to-Digital Converters

Analog-to-digital converters in data acquisition systems monitor external analog voltages. Figure 7–10 pictures the AD7574 8-bit analog-to-digital converter, which functions with a single 5 V power supply and is directly compatible with virtually all microprocessors. It converts the analog input into an 8-bit digital output within 15 μs.

AD7574 ADC

The AD7574 is controlled through two connections to the microprocessor, $\overline{RD}$ and $\overline{CS}$. The $\overline{RD}$ input, on the zero to one transition, clears the converter and begins a new conversion; on the one to zero transition, data appears on the output pins if $\overline{CS}$ is also active. $\overline{CS}$ blocks data from appearing at the output connections and a busy signal on the $\overline{BUSY}$ pin but doesn't prevent the converter from being internally reset. Because of this, extreme care must be taken in the use of this device.

8085A to ADC Interface

Figure 7–11 pictures an INTEL 8085A connected to the AD7574 ADC, using the READY input for slowing the microprocessor to match the speed of this converter. Whenever data is read from I/O device FXH with an IN FXH instruction, the output of the decoder forces $\overline{RD}$ and $\overline{CS}$ on the converter to become active. This initiates a conversion and causes the $\overline{BUSY}$ signal to become a logic zero during the conversion process. The logic zero on the $\overline{BUSY}$ output causes the 8085A to enter into WAIT states because of the zero presented at its READY input. The $\overline{BUSY}$ line remains a logic zero until the converter finishes converting the analog input to digital. When $\overline{BUSY}$ returns to a logic one, it allows the 8085A to continue executing instructions. To ensure that the converted data is fresh, the first IN FXH is ignored.

MC6800 to ADC Interface

The MC6800 must be interfaced to the AD7574 in a different manner, since it does not possess a READY input or any comparable input. An example of a

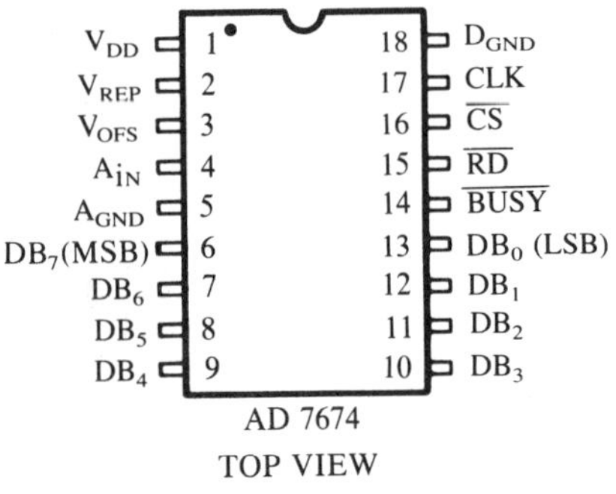

FIGURE 7–10 The AD7574 8-bit microprocessor compatible analog to digital converter.

SOURCE: Courtesy of Analog Devices, Inc.

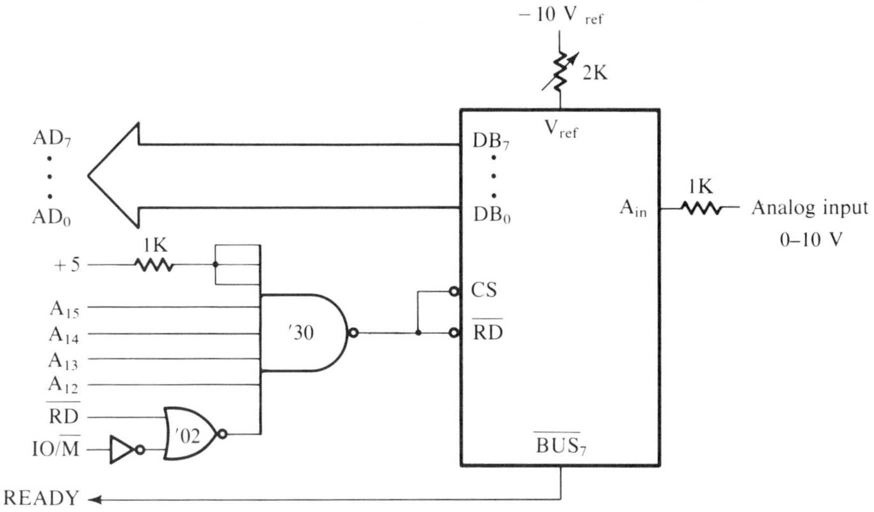

FIGURE 7–11 The AD7574 analog to digital converter interfaced to an Intel 8085A microprocessor.

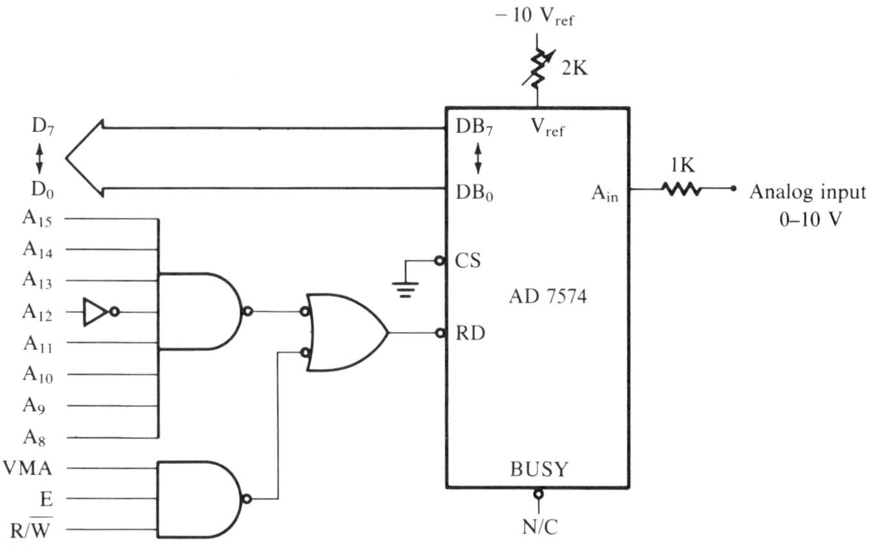

FIGURE 7–12 An AD7574 analog to digital converter interfaced to a Motorola MC6800 or MC6809 microprocessor.

possible connection is pictured in figure 7–12. In this example the $\overline{CS}$ pin is grounded and the converter is controlled from its $\overline{RD}$ input.

When the MC6800 reads data from memory location $EFXX, the $\overline{RD}$ pin on the converter becomes a logic zero forcing data to be read from the converter. After the $\overline{RD}$ returns to a logic one, the converter is reset and takes another sample of the analog input data. The only problem that arises with this interface is that the first ADC read contains old information and 15 μs must be allowed for the converter to complete a conversion.

MC6800 Subroutine to Read the ADC

```
*SUBROUTINE TO READ A NUMBER FROM THE AD7574 ADC
*RESULT IS RETURNED IN ACCUMULATOR A
*6800 CLOCK = 1 MHZ.
*
ADC     LDAA $EF00      START CONVERSION
        PSHA            WAIT 16 MICROSECONDS
        PULA
        PSHA
        PULA
        LDAA $EF00      READ DATA
        RTS
```

7-4 STEPPER MOTORS

Stepper motors are digital motors that are becoming extremely common in "low torque" digital applications. They are precisely positionable in either a closed or open loop control system with a minimum of circuitry. Some stepper motors can be positioned to within a degree or less of the required position.

A typical schematic representation of a stepper motor is depicted in figure 7–13. This motor has four separate windings to control its relative position. Currents through the coils generate magnetic fields to position the rotor. The rotor is a permanent magnet that is positioned by the magnetic fields generated in the field coils. Once the rotor is moved to its final position, the magnetic fields from these coils keep the rotor at that position. In the example shown, the rotor moves in a clockwise direction.

The Current Driver

Generating the field currents requires a current driver. Figure 7–14 is a schematic diagram of a typical current driver for one of the four stepper motor coils. The driver is capable of generating a current flow through the coil and of reducing the amount of current for holding the coil at a particular position.

FIGURE 7–13 The internal representation of a stepper motor.

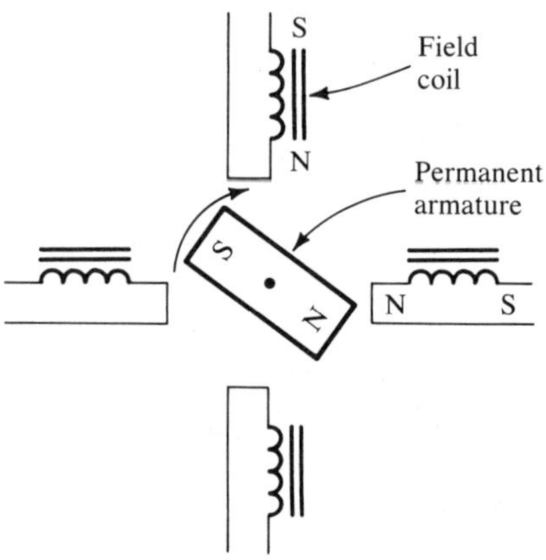

Moving the rotor requires more current than holding it at a constant position requires.

The direction of rotation is determined by the pattern of current flows through the coils in a sequence. This sequence determines the speed and direction of the rotation. The STEP input is provided by the software that controls the stepper motor and causes the current through the coils to increase so that a step occurs.

Stepper Control

The control of a stepper motor requires four separate current drivers and one step control signal. If the step interval is equal to 1.8 degrees, 200 steps or pulses are required to rotate the rotor through one revolution. By sending the drivers the binary bit patterns illustrated in table 7–2, the direction and speed of the rotor can be easily controlled. This bit pattern causes two of the four stepper motor coils to be energized at a time. Moving the bit patterns in the directions indicated rotates the magnetic field inside the motor. The faster a pattern is moved, the faster the motor turns.

Counterclockwise Pattern	Clockwise Pattern
0 0 1 1	1 1 0 0
0 1 1 0	0 1 1 0
1 1 0 0	0 0 1 1
1 0 0 1	1 0 0 1

TABLE 7–2 Stepper motor control bit patterns.

Software to control the stepper motor is required to control both the direction of rotation and the number of steps to be rotated. It must also have the ability to remember the current position of the rotor. Software for controlling the stepper and interface of figure 7–15 has been developed for both the Intel 8085A and the Motorola 6800. A flowchart illustrates this subroutine in figure 7–16. In both cases, memory location LOC indicates the current bit pattern of the previous data sent to the stepper motor. It is this bit pattern that must be modified to cause the proper direction of rotation. The B register in both cases represents both the direction of rotation and the number of steps to be rotated. If B contains a positive number, the rotation is in the clockwise direction; if negative, the rotation is in the counterclockwise direction.

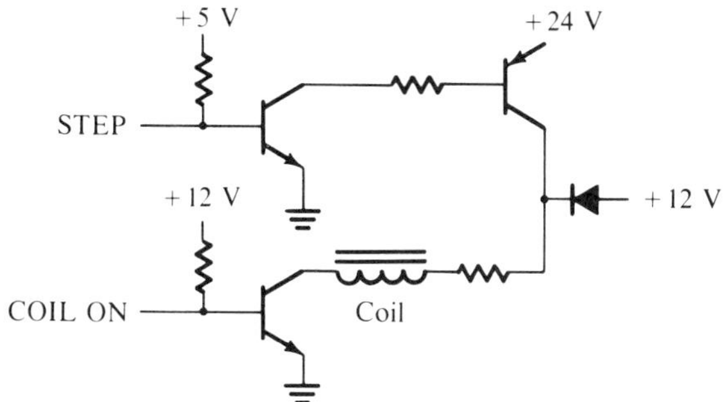

FIGURE 7–14 A typical stepper coil driver. STEP causes 24 V to be applied to the coil, and COIL ON determines whether or not current flows through the coil.

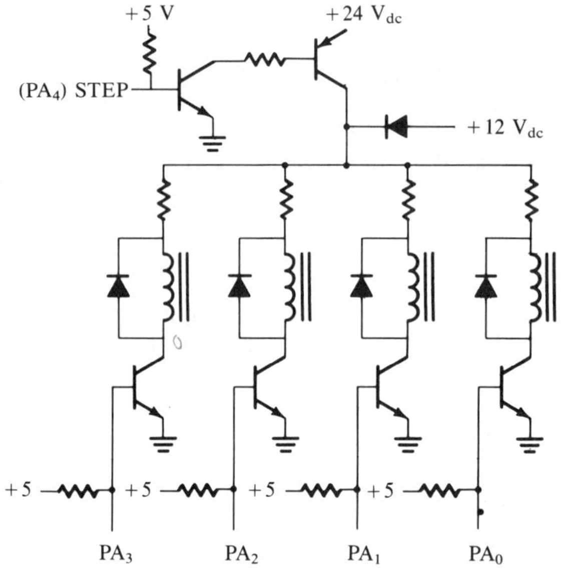

FIGURE 7–15 An interface from TTL compatible circuitry to a four coil stepper motor.

```
;8085A ASSEMBLY LANGUAGE PROGRAM
;SUBROUTINE TO CONTROL A STEPPER MOTOR
;B=NUMBER OF STEPS AND DIRECTION
;CW = + AND CCW = -
;
;TEST FOR DIRECTION
STEP:    MOV  A,B      ;GET DIRECTION
         ADD  A        ;DIRECTION TO CARRY
         LDA  LOC      ;GET PRIOR LOCATION
         JC   STEP2    ;COUNTERCLOCKWISE?
         RRC           ;SETUP NEW POSITION
;ROTATE STEPPER MOTOR
STEP1:   STA  LOC      ;SAVE NEW POSITION
         ORI  10H      ;SETUP STEP BIT
         OUT  PORTA    ;START ROTATION
         CALL DELAY    ;WAIT 1 MSEC.
         MOV  A,B      ;GET COUNT
         ANI  7FH      ;STRIP OFF DIRECTION
         DCR  A        ;DECREMENT COUNT
         JZ   STEP3    ;DONE?
         DCR  B        ;DECREMENT COUNT
         JMP  STEP     ;MOVE ANOTHER STEP
;SETUP FOR COUNTERCLOCKWISE
STEP2:   RLC           ;SETUP NEW POSITION
         JMP  STEP1    ;GO STEP MOTOR
;STOP ROTATION AND END SUBROUTINE
STEP3:   LDA  LOC      ;GET LOCATION
         ANI  15       ;CLEAR STEP BIT
```

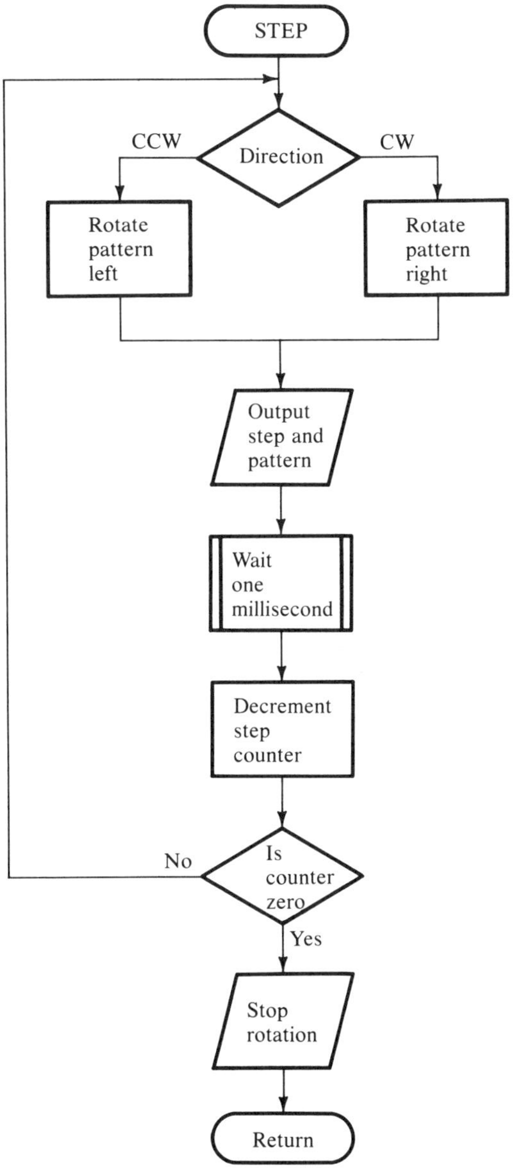

FIGURE 7–16 The flowchart of a subroutine that will control the direction of rotation and the number of steps for the stepper motor interface of figure 7–15.

```
           OUT  PORTA    ;STOP ROTATION
           RET           ;RETURN FROM SUBROUTINE
    LOC:   DB   33H      ;INITIAL POSITION
```

```
    *6800 ASSEMBLY LANGUAGE PROGRAM
    *SUBROUTINE TO CONTROL A STEPPER MOTOR
    *ACC B=NUMBER OF STEPS AND DIRECTION
    *CW = + AND CCW = -
    *
```

```
*TEST FOR DIRECTION
STEP     LDAA   LOC     GET PRIOR POSITION
         TSTB           CHECK FOR DIRECTION
         BMI    STEP2   COUNTERCLOCKWISE?
         LSRA           SETUP NEW POSITION
         BCC    STEP1   NO CARRY?
         ADDA   #$80    ADJUST RESULT
*START ROTATION
STEP1    STAA   LOC     SAVE NEW POSITION
         ORAA   #$10    SETUP STEP BIT
         STAA   PORTA   START ROTATION
         JSR    DELAY   WAIT FOR 1 MSEC.
         TBA            GET COUNT
         ANDA   #$7F    STRIP DIRECTION BIT
         DECA           DECREMENT COUNT
         BEQ    STEP3   COUNT ZERO?
         DECB           DECREMENT COUNT
         BRA    STEP    MOVE ANOTHER STEP
*IF COUNTERCLOCKWISE
STEP2    ASLA           SETUP NEW POSITION
         BCC    STEP1   NO CARRY?
         INCA           ADJUST POSITION
         BRA    STEP1   GO ROTATE
*FINISH SUBROUTINE
STEP3    LDAA   LOC     GET POSITION
         ANDA   #$0F    CLEAR STEP BIT
         STAA   PORTA   STOP ROTATION
         RTS            RETURN FROM SUBROUTINE
LOC      FCB    #$33    INITIAL VALUE
```

Positional Feedback

The position of the stepper motor may or may not be critical to a particular application. For example, if paper is being fed in a printer with the stepper motor, the position is not important. Feeding one line of paper may merely mean that the stepper must be pulsed 20 times for each line of paper. Pulsing it 10 times would move the paper one-half of a line.

On the other hand, if the stepper positions the dot matrix print head in a printer, positional feedback may indeed be important. One method of obtaining this feedback is to sense a home position. In printers the home position is normally the left-hand margin of the page. This is most often accomplished with an optical device that includes an LED and a phototransistor. When the head is homed, the beam of light is broken and this can be sensed with the hardware and software.

Once this home position is known, the printer software can step over the required steps to any printing position without any further feedback. Granted, errors can occur without further feedback, but with today's modern stepper motors, they happen very rarely.

EEPROM INTERFACE 7-5

The EEPROM, as discussed in the chapter on memory systems, is a device capable of retaining information once the power has been removed. This feature is very useful in many applications where setup information is tedious to enter into a system. This device allows this type of data to be stored for an extended period of time without the application of system power. It is not suited for all applications, since it has a limited life span of only 10,000 write and erase cycles per byte.

Unfortunately this device is not as easy to interface to a microprocessor as a ROM or RAM because it requires much more time to write or erase information. It also requires a special 21 V pulse to accomplish the erase or write.

2816 EEPROM

Figure 7–17 illustrates the pinout of the 2816 2K-byte EEPROM from Intel. This device is similar to the 2716 EPROM that was interfaced in the chapter on memory. About the only difference is that it contains I/O pins rather than output pins. The I/O pins read information and program data, when required.

Programming and erasing take 10 ms per byte. They are accomplished by applying the data to be stored in a location on the I/O pins, the address on the address pins, and a 21 V pulse on the programming pin. This programming pulse must be present for 9–15 ms.

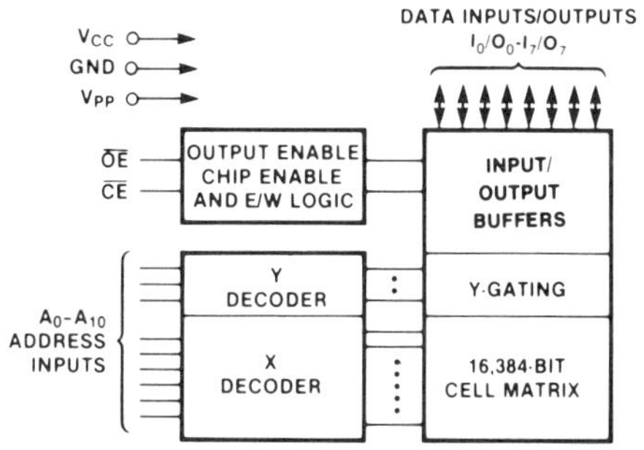

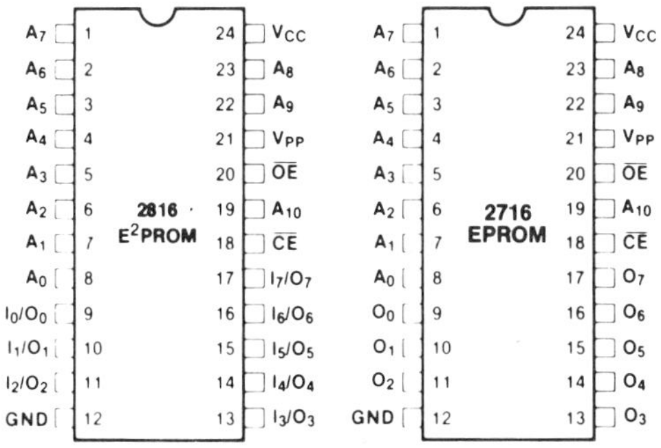

PIN NAMES

A_0-A_{10}	ADDRESSES
$\overline{CE}$	CHIP ENABLE
$\overline{OE}$	OUTPUT ENABLE
O_0-O_7	DATA OUTPUTS
I_0-I_7	DATA INPUTS
V_{PP}	PROGRAM VOLTAGE

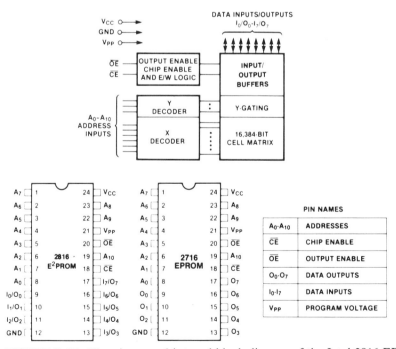

FIGURE 7–17 The pinout and internal block diagram of the Intel 2816 EEPROM.

SOURCE: Reprinted by permission of Intel Corporation, Copyright 1982.

Basic High-Speed Interface

Figure 7–18 illustrates the basic circuitry required to program or read the EEPROM without a large investment in hardware or software. The 8155 programs the device by timing the basic sequence and applying the programming pulse. It also provides the data and address for the purpose of programming the 2816.

The system progresses at full speed while programming or erasing a byte in the EEPROM. The only time that any delay in accessing the 2816 is observed is when a read is attempted as the device is being programmed. If this occurs, the processor READY line is pulled low, causing it to wait until the current programming is completed.

The 8155

Ports A, B, and C of the 8155 are programmed as input devices until a program cycle begins. Then port A and a portion of C supply the address to the 2816, and port B supplies the data. The busy flip-flop develops the READY signal for the system, controls the buffers, and allows the V_{PP} switch to be activated.

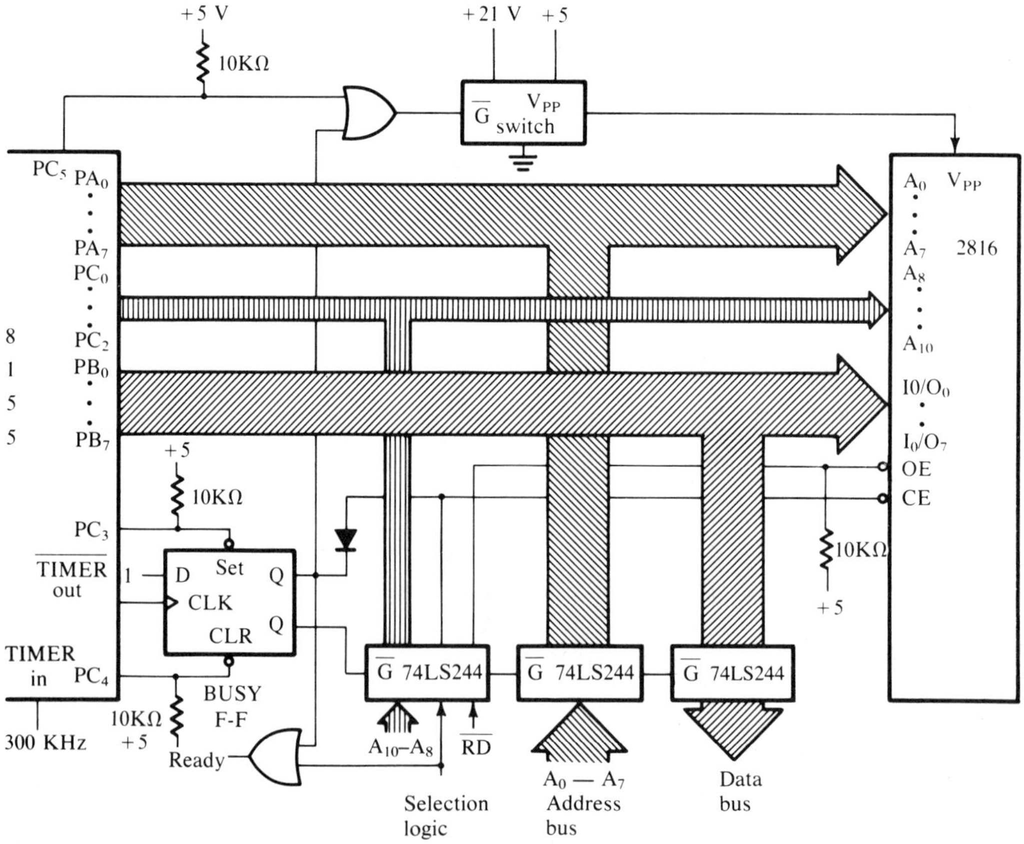

FIGURE 7–18 The circuit required to program the 2816 EEPROM and to read it in a system.

The timer within the 8155 develops a 10-ms programming pulse for the EEPROM. In this example it doesn't directly generate the pulse; it sets the busy flip-flop, which ends the programming or erase sequence.

The Generation of the Programming Pulse

The programming pulse is generated from the output of the busy flip-flop, which is turned on by the software at the beginning of a write cycle and PC5. Once activated, it applies a 21 V pulse to the V_{PP} pin of the EEPROM. At the end of the timing sequence, the output of the timer sets the busy flip-flop, which ends the application of the programming pulse to V_{PP}. This interface assumes that 21 V is available in the system. If it is not, some type of switching regulator that will develop approximately 15 mA of current can be included.

The Software

The software for this application can be broken down into three portions: initialization dialog, a programming subroutine or erase subroutine, and a polling subroutine.

The polling subroutine tests the timer's terminal count bit to determine whether or not a byte is programmed or erased.

```
POLL:   IN STATUS       ;GET 8155 STATUS WORD
        ANI 40H         ;TEST TC FLAG
        RET
```

As you can see, this is a very short subroutine, which returns "zero" if TC is not reached. If the TC is reached, a return "not zero" occurs and is tested if the system program is to access the 2816.

The initialization dialog is required to setup the 8155 ports so that all ports are input ports. In addition, the busy flip-flop must be set initially so that data can be read from the EEPROM until a programming sequence or erase sequence is required.

```
INIT    MVI  A,01001100B    ;PROGRAM PORTS AND
        OUT  COMMAND        ;STOP TIMER
        MVI  A,0F7H         ;SET BUSY F-F
        OUT  PORTC
        IN   STATUS         ;CLEAR TC FLAG
        MVI  A,0FFH         ;DEACTIVATE SET
        OUT  PORTC
        MVI  A,00000000B    ;PORT C = INPUT
        OUT  COMMAND
          .
          .
```

The programming subroutine and erase subroutine must be capable of sending the address to the EEPROM, as well as the data to be programmed into it. This is accomplished by sending some parameters to these subroutines through register B for the programmed data and the DE pair for the address of the data. Erasure is obtained by programming all ones into a location.

This subroutine must also be able to clear the busy flip-flop and program the timer for the 10 ms pulse that sets the busy flip-flop at the end of the programming sequence.

```
;THIS SUBROUTINE WILL PROGRAM OR ERASE A BYTE IN
;REGISTER B AT THE ADDRESS INDICATED IN DE
PROG:   CALL SETUP      ;CLEAR BUSY F-F AND SEND ADDR
        CALL TIME       ;START THE TIMER
        MOV  A,B        ;GET DATA
        CALL VPP        ;SEND DATA AND START VPP
        RET
;
;SETUP SUBROUTINE
;
SETUP   MVI  A,0FH      ;SETUP PORTS AS OUTPUTS
        MVI  A,0EFH     ;CLEAR BUSY F-F
        OUT  PORTC
        MOV  A,E        ;SEND ADDRESS
        OUT  PORTA
        MOV  A,D
        ORI  0F8H
        OUT  PORTC
        RET
;
;START TIMER
;
TIME:   MVI  A,B8H      ;PROGRAM TIMER
        OUT  TIMEL      ;TIMER PORT LSB
        MVI  A,8BH      ;SET COUNT AND SINGLE PULSE
        OUT  TIMEH      ;TIMER PORT MSB & MODE
        MVI  A,0CFH     ;SETUP B AS OUTPUT
        OUT  COMMAND    ;START TIMER
        RET
;
;SEND DATA AND START VPP
;
VPP:    OUT  PORTB      ;SEND DATA
        IN   PORTC      ;GET ADDRESS
        ANI  0DFH       ;ENABLE VPP
        OUT  PORTC
        RET
```

7-6 MEMORY EXPANSION TECHNIQUES

There are many techniques for expanding the amount of available space in a memory system. They all seem to hinge on about the same technique, memory bank selection. To expand a memory system all that is required is the addition of some extra memory address pins and a more sophisticated software operating system.

In most cases only a part of the memory system is expandable, as illustrated in the diagram of figure 7–19. In this system the bottom 16K bytes of memory are common to all additional blocks of memory. Only the memory devices above location 3FFFH have additional address inputs. For this reason, many blocks are illustrated for this portion of the memory system. It would be easy to add 8 address bits to any 8-bit microprocessor by adding an 8-bit output port for this purpose. This expands or allows 256 additional blocks of memory to be added, probably enough for most computer systems using an 8-bit microprocessor.

The Hardware

The hardware required for the bank selection is merely a simple 8-bit output port or device that uses either memory mapped or isolated I/O techniques. Figure 7–20 illustrates a 74LS374 latch used as an additional address register for memory banks. This gives the system a 24-bit memory address instead of the original 16 bits.

For isolated I/O port, number 3FH specifies which bank of memory is to be used for locations 4000H through FFFFH. In memory mapped I/O, the address location used to change banks is 3FXXH.

The Software

The bottom portion of this memory system probably contains system software in a read only memory. This software comprises the operating system for the computer and may also contain a high-level language, such as an assembler or compiler. It also contains a subroutine to handle memory management for the multiple banks of memory.

A system might include several CRT terminals that share the same basic system. This arrangement would reduce total system costs, since the software could allocate banks of memory to each different CRT terminal. The alloca-

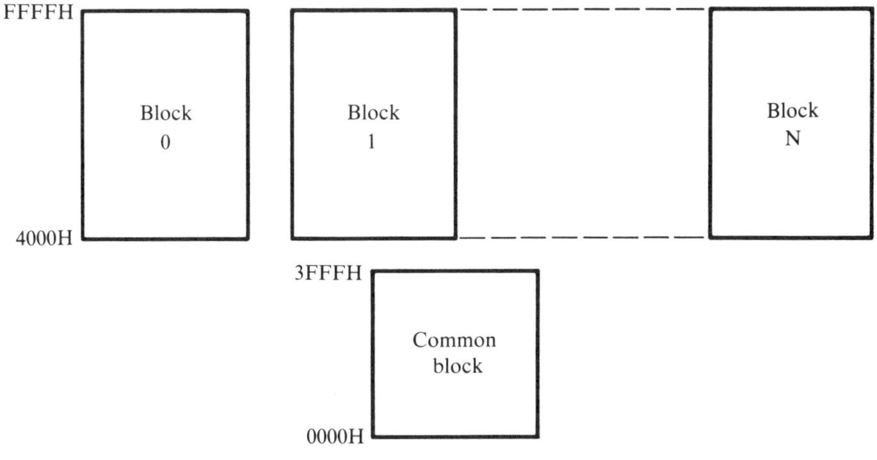

FIGURE 7–19 One possible system configuration for expanding the size of a system memory.

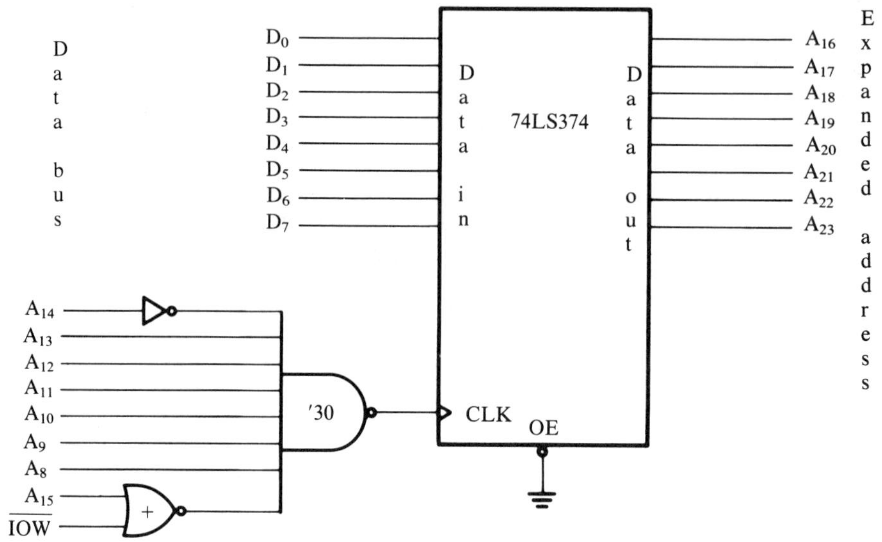

FIGURE 7–20 Address bus expansion latch and the decoder logic for I/O port 3F or memory mapped location 3FXX.

tion could be accomplished dynamically. This scheme of memory utilization assigns only the required amount of memory to each CRT terminal or user.

This is only one of many possibilities for bank selection logic. Most microprocessor manufacturers provide some form of memory management component that will essentially accomplish this type of memory management and bank selection for the user.

7-7 ARITHMETIC PROCESSORS

With the microprocessor used for high-level language compilation, it is often desirable to include an arithmetic processor in the system. Most manufacturers make such a device, which is often capable of accomplishing most floating point arithmetic operations. Since most higher-level languages use this type of arithmetic, a separate dedicated processor can be advantageously applied. Software required to perform this type of arithmetic is extremely long and very slow. This even applies to the newer microprocessors, which contain at least a fixed point multiply and a divide instruction.

The Am9512 Floating Point Processor

This device, illustrated in figure 7–21, is capable of both 32- and 64-bit floating point arithmetic. The operations that it can perform include addition, subtraction, multiplication, and division.

Execution times range from 4 clocking periods to 4560 clocking periods. If a 2-MHz clock is used, that equates to 2–2280 μs. If software is developed to accomplish these operations, it takes quite a bit longer.

TABLE 7–3 Am9512 commands.

Command 7	6	5	4	3	2	1	0	Mnemonic	Description
X	0	0	0	0	0	0	1	SADD	Single precision addition NOS = NOS + TOS
X	0	0	0	0	0	1	0	SSUB	Single precision subtraction NOS = NOS − TOS
X	0	0	0	0	0	1	1	SMUL	Single precision multiply NOS = NOS × TOS
X	0	0	0	0	1	0	0	SDIV	Single precision divide NOS = NOS/TOS
X	0	0	0	0	1	0	1	CHSS	Single precision sign change TOS = −TOS
X	0	0	0	0	1	1	0	PTOS	Single precision push
X	0	0	0	0	1	1	1	POPS	Single precision pop
X	0	0	0	1	0	0	0	XCHG	Single precision exchange Swap TOS with NOS
X	0	1	0	1	1	0	1	CHSD	Double precision sign change TOS = −TOS
X	0	1	0	1	1	1	0	PTOD	Double precision push
X	0	1	0	1	1	1	1	POPD	Double precision pop
X	0	0	0	0	0	0	0	CLR	Clear status
X	0	1	0	1	0	0	1	DADD	Double precision addition NOS = NOS + TOS
X	0	1	0	1	0	1	0	DSUB	Double precision subtraction NOS = NOS − TOS
X	0	1	0	1	0	1	1	DMUL	Double precision multiply NOS = NOS × TOS
X	0	1	0	1	1	0	0	DDIV	Double precision divide NOS = NOS/TOS

Table 7–3 illustrates the complete instruction set for this device, along with the binary op-codes required to perform the indicated tasks. The most significant bit (X) controls the SVREQ pin (discussed under the topic of pin descriptions later in this section). TOS, or *top of stack,* describes the position of data on an internal stack that holds the data for the arithmetic operation of the Am9512. In addition to the references to TOS in table 7–3, you will also notice NOS. NOS, or *next on stack,* refers to the position on the stack that is POPed out of the Am9512. More discussion of TOS and NOS appears later in this text with the description of the internal stack.

Pin Descriptions

CLK an external clock input of up to 2 MHz.

RESET clears the END, ERR, and SVREQ output pins.

C/$\overline{\text{D}}$ defines whether a read or write will occur to the command/status register or the internal data stack.

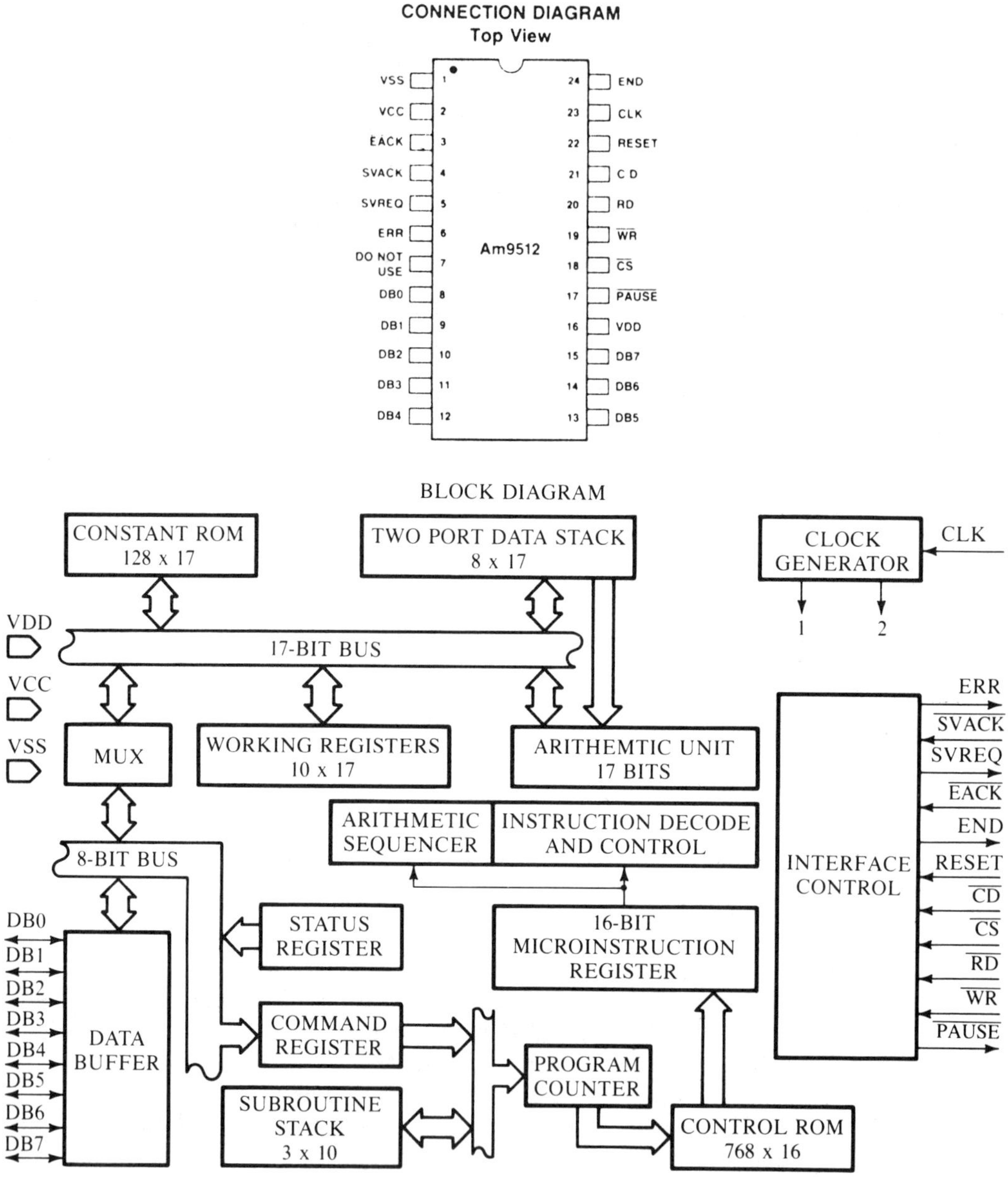

FIGURE 7–21 The pinout and internal block diagram of the Am9512 arithmetic processor.

END an output that indicates the end of the current operation. This output remains high after the end of an operation until an $\overline{\text{EACK}}$.

$\overline{\text{EACK}}$ this input acknowledges an END operation by clearing the END output.

SVREQ this output is essentially the same as END, except that it can be selectively controlled by the eighth bit position in a command.

$\overline{\text{SVACK}}$ clears SVREQ.

ERR indicates that the current command has resulted in an error. Some error conditions that are indicated are divide by zero, exponent overflow, and exponent underflow. Reading the status register clears this error indicator.

PAUSE this output is used for synchronization with some microprocessors. In an 8085A based system, it is connected to the READY pin.

Basic Operation

The Am9512 operates on the data entered into its internal data stack. For this reason, it must be loaded with both operands before an operation can be executed properly. The operands must be placed on the stack with the least significant byte first. This stack can hold up to four single precision or two double precision numbers. The first number placed on the internal stack ends up as the TOS, and the second number ends up as the NOS. A logic zero placed on the C/$\overline{\text{D}}$ pin indicates data entry or extraction from the stack.

Floating Point Data Formats

Table 7–4 illustrates the data format for both the single and double precision floating point numbers. Each type of number has two portions, a mantissa and an exponent. The left-hand bit of both types of data contains the sign bit of the mantissa. If the sign bit is a one, a negative number is contained in the mantissa; if zero, a positive number is contained. Positive and negative numbers differ in sign bit only; the mantissa always contains the magnitude of the number, as described in the following text.

$$2^{exp} \times \text{mantissa} = \text{floating point number} \qquad 7\text{–}1$$

TABLE 7–4 Floating point word formats.

	Single Precision	
31	30 — 23	22 — 0
S	Exponent	Mantissa
	Double Precision	
63	62 — 52	51 — 0
S	Exponent	Mantissa

The next portion of both words contains the exponent of the number. The single precision number contains an 8-bit exponent stored in excess 127 notation. That is, an exponent of 4 is actually stored as an unsigned number equal to 131, or 1000 0011 binary. An exponent of -100 is represented as a 27, or 0001 1011 binary. With a double precision number, the exponent is an 11-bit binary number expressed in excess 1023 notation.

The mantissa is either a 24-bit normalized number for single precision or a 53-bit normalized number for double precision. Each actually contains one less bit, but an implied bit of one is assumed outside of the stored quantity. All mantissas are represented as numbers in the following true magnitude form: 1.XXX, where XXX is the number stored as the mantissa and the one is implied.

EXAMPLE 7–1

Represent a 42 decimal in single precision FPF.

Binary = 101010

Normalized floating point form = 1.0101×2^5

(s) (exp) (mantissa)

FPF = 0 10000100 01010000000000000000000

In example 7–1, the original decimal number 42 is converted to a binary number. This number is then normalized to produce a 1.0101. The exponent of 2 indicated is a 5, since the radix is moved five places to the left during normalization. Finally, this floating point number is formed into a 32-bit number that is compatible with the Am9512. To store a zero in this form, all bits of the number are made zero, including the sign bit, exponent, and the mantissa.

The 8085A Interface

Figure 7–22 illustrates the basic interface to an 8085A microprocessor. The only external hardware required is the port or device decoder. In this case a simple four input NAND gate decodes a port number. Address bit position A8 is connected to the $C/\overline{D}$ input to select command or data.
The port number decoded by this example is EXH. The software illustrated later in this section uses port E0H for data and port E1H for command and status. As you can see, the interface circuitry required is very simple.

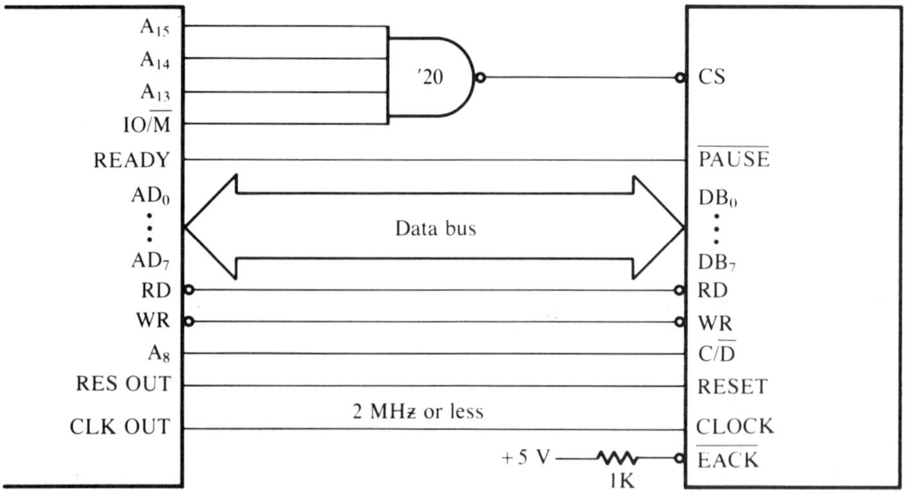

FIGURE 7–22 An Am9512 arithmetic processor interfaced to an Intel 8085A microprocessor.

The Am9512 Status Register

Before the software for this application can be developed, the status word of the Am9512 must be examined. The bit pattern for this register is shown in table 7–5 and a description of each bit follows:

TABLE 7-5 Am9512 status register.

B	S	Z		D	E	E	
U	I	E	X	I	X	X	X
S	G	R		V	P	P	
Y	N	O		E	U	O	

BIT7 (BUSY) indicates that a command is being processed by the Am9512 when high. A zero condition indicates that the device is idle.

BIT6 (SIGN) indicates the sign of the result.

BIT5 (ZERO) indicates that the result is a zero.

BIT3 (DIVIDE EXCEPTION) indicates that an attempt to divide by zero has occurred.

BIT2 (EXPONENT UNDERFLOW) indicates that an exponent underflow has occurred.

BIT1 (EXPONENT OVERFLOW) indicates that an exponent overflow has occurred.

The Am9512 Control Software

The control software for this device consists of subroutines to test the status register, load and unload the internal data stack, and start an operation.

The first subroutine to be illustrated tests the Am9512 to determine whether an operation is complete. A return from this subroutine will only occur for a completed operation, with the type of return indicating whether any errors have occurred. Return zero means no errors and return not zero means that an error has occurred.

```
;STATUS POLLING SOFTWARE
STAT:   IN    0E1H        ;READ STATUS REGISTER
        ORA   A           ;TEST ACCUMULATOR
        JM    STAT        ;IF BUSY
        ANI   0EH         ;ISOLATE ERROR FLAGS
        RET               ;RETURN
```

The next subroutine developed loads the 4-byte-long single precision number, pointed to by the HL pair, into the Am9512. It is assumed that the least significant byte is stored in the lowest numbered memory location.

```
;THIS SUBROUTINE LOADS A SINGLE PRECISION NUMBER
;INTO THE Am9512
LOAD:   MVI   B,4         ;LOAD COUNTER
        MOV   A,M         ;GET A BYTE
        OUT   0E0H        ;SEND IT
```

```
          INX   H            ;INCREMENT POINTER
          DCR   B            ;DECREMENT COUNTER
          JNZ   LOAD+2       ;IF NOT DONE
          RET
```

The next subroutine removes the answer from the Am9512. It again is assumed to be a single precision number that is to be extracted from the floating point processor. The HL pair points to the location in memory where the answer is to be stored.

```
;SUBROUTINE TO EXTRACT THE ANSWER FROM THE Am9512
UNLOAD: MVI   B,4          ;LOAD COUNTER
        IN    0E0H         ;GET BYTE
        MOV   M,A          ;SAVE BYTE
        INX   H            ;POINT NEXT
        DCR   B            ;DECREMENT COUNTER
        JNZ   UNLOAD+2     ;IF NOT DONE
        RET
```

The next step is an example problem. Another subroutine is written to use the three prior subroutines to multiply two single precision numbers together. The numbers are stored at locations NUMB1 and NUMB2, and the answer is stored at location ANS. If an error is detected as a result of this multiplication, a return not zero occurs. If the answer is correct, a return zero occurs.

```
;SUBROUTINE TO MULTIPLY NUMB1 TIMES NUMB2
;AND STORE THE RESULT AT ANS
MULT:   MVI   A,00H        ;CLR COMMAND TO ACC
        OUT   0E1H         ;CLEAR STATUS WORD
        LXI   H,NUMB1      ;POINT TO NUMBERS
        CALL  LOAD         ;LOAD MULTIPLICAND
        CALL  LOAD         ;LOAD MULTIPLIER
        MVI   A,03H        ;SMUL COMMAND TO ACC
        OUT   0E1H         ;START MULTIPLICATION
        CALL  STAT         ;TIME OUT COMMAND
        PUSH  PSW          ;SAVE ERROR FLAG
        CALL  UNLOAD       ;SAVE ANSWER
        POP   PSW          ;GET ERROR CODE
        RET
NUMB1:  DS    4
NUMB2:  DS    4
ANS:    DS    4
```

This appears to be a lot of software just to multiply two numbers together; but if you look at the normal floating point software of approximately six hundred bytes, you form a different opinion. This is just one of many operations that can be performed by the floating point processor.

Summary

This chapter introduced the fundamental input/output systems used to construct most microprocessor based systems. These areas include keyboards, displays, stepper motors, EEPROM memory, ADC and DAC, memory bank selection, and arithmetic processors. With this information, the reader can become capable of developing systems that can perform useful tasks.

Of particular importance in this chapter is the coverage of keyboards, displays, and stepper motors. These mechanisms are found in many microprocessor based applications.

This chapter ignored serial I/O, which is covered in chapter 9 in the discussion of digital communications.

Glossary

Analog-to-digital converter A device that converts an analog voltage into a binary or binary coded decimal number that is proportional to the voltage.

Digital-to-analog converter A device that converts a binary or binary coded decimal number into an analog voltage proportional to the number.

Exponent In floating point numbers, it is the binary power of two that indicates the relative position of the radix point.

Floating point number A number that is stored with a mantissa and an exponent. It typically is capable of storing hundreds of bits of information in only 4–8 bytes of memory.

Floating point processor A device that computes the answers to many floating point arithmetic operations.

Mantissa The normalized fractional portion of a floating point number.

Memory bank An additional area of memory allowed by an additional set of address pins controlled by the I/O structure.

Multiplex To share either a wire or a circuit with more than one signal.

Radix The base of a number: radix two is the same as base two.

Stepper motor A digital motor that is controlled by pulses.

Switching supply A power supply that is operated class C to reduce the power consumption and heat dissipation.

Table lookup A programming technique that draws data from a prestored table in the memory.

Questions and Problems

1 Interface an AY-5-2376 to an 8155 and develop a subroutine that will take data from the keyboard encoder and return with it in the accumulator.

2 Interface an AY-5-2376 to a 6821 and develop the subroutine required to take data from the keyboard encoder and return with it in accumulator B.

3 Modify the circuit of figure 7–4 so that 32 keys can be scanned. After this is accomplished, develop a subroutine to scan all 32 keys.

4 Develop a subroutine for the 8085A that will waste exactly 1.9 ms of time. Assume that the system clock frequency is 3 MHz. (Refer to chapter 3.)

5 Develop a subroutine for the 6800 that will waste exactly 7.8 ms of time. Assume that the system clock frequency is 1.0 MHz. (Refer to chapter 4.)

6 Interface two ADCs and one DAC converter to the microprocessor of your choice and develop the software to receive data from both ADCs and to send the sum of the data out of the DAC. Make sure to scale the sum by a factor of 50 percent, so that it can be sent without distortion.

7 Write a program using the subroutines developed for the stepper motor in this chapter that will rotate the motor in the clockwise direction at the rate of 60 RPM.

8 Write a program using the subroutines developed for the stepper motor in this chapter that will rotate the motor 1 step per second for 150 steps in the clockwise direction and then reset the motor in the counterclockwise direction to its starting point.

9 Using the subroutines provided in the chapter, what is the maximum rotational rate of the stepper motor? (Give the answer in RPMs.)

10 Develop an EEPROM memory system that contains 4K bytes of memory.

11 How much time would be required to program all 4096 bytes of memory?

12 Where would memory bank selection prove useful?

13 What problems do you foresee with software selectable memory bank locations? Should protection be included in this type of scheme for memory management?

14 Develop the software required to divide one single precision number by another. Use the subroutines provided in the chapter.

15 Develop the subroutines required to multiply two double precision numbers together.

16 Most math books contain the required algorithm for calculating the sine of a number using a series. Look up this series expansion and develop the software to generate the sine of a number.

8

Interrupt Processed I/O

Interrupts are extremely important microprocessor hardware. The interrupt allows an external system to gain the attention of the microprocessor through an interruption. The currently executing program can be interrupted by the external system through this technique.

This may sound like a relatively unused feature, but it is used extensively. It attends to the needs of any low-speed external device because the only time that the microprocessor "knows" of the existence of the device is during an interrupt. This frees up a tremendous amount of computer time.

8-1 INTRODUCTION TO INTERRUPTS

An *interrupt* is a hardware initiated subroutine call or jump that interrupts the currently executing program. Normally subroutines are called with the software; with an interrupt, an external device can demand the attention of the microprocessor by calling a subroutine through the interrupt structure of the microprocessor. There are usually pin connections on the microprocessor that, when activated, cause an interrupt to occur.

A good example of the usefulness of an interrupt is the keyboard interface discussed in chapter 7. To read data from the keyboard, the microprocessor devotes all of its time to scanning the keyboard for a key switch closure. It scans the keyboard as long as it takes the operator to strike a key.

If the keyboard uses an interrupt whenever a key switch is closed, the processing time utilized by the keyboard interface is reduced to a minimum. This is because with an interrupt, the only time that the microprocessor pays attention to the keyboard is when a key is actually depressed. Therefore, the microprocessor can accomplish useful tasks while the operator is contemplating the next keystroke.

The Interrupt Service Subroutine

The software used in response to the interrupt signal from the hardware is called an *interrupt service subroutine*. In the prior example, the act of typing on a key causes an interrupt. This interrupt then summons the interrupt service subroutine that determines exactly which key has caused the interrupt.

The interrupt service subroutine differs only slightly from a standard subroutine. It usually includes an instruction that reenables future interrupts and other instructions that save the contents of any register used within the interrupt service subroutine.

It is often the responsibility of the interrupt service subroutine to acknowledge the interrupt or to signal that the interrupt has been accepted. In some microprocessors, this is handled internally and is not the responsibility of the software. This acknowledgment usually occurs when the data is transferred to or from the interrupting device and is often a function of the external hardware.

Faults

The main problem with an interrupt driven I/O is the fact that an interrupt can occur at any instant in time, which can cause errors in a system that are very hard to detect. Troubleshooting in a faulty system is made rather difficult because of the apparent randomness of the interrupt. This difficulty can be overcome by developing proper diagnostic software to aid the technician in the repair of a faulty system. Also, additional external hardware can be provided for fault detection.

Types of Interrupts

Two basic types of interrupt inputs exist on various microprocessors, the *maskable* and the *nonmaskable* interrupt inputs. The nonmaskable interrupt input is always active and therefore handles critical events such as power failures and system restarts. The maskable interrupt input is more useful because it can be turned on and off with the software to fit a particular application. Microprocessors may include one of these inputs or both of them and a few include many interrupt inputs to handle complicated control applications.

Microprocessor Interrupt Connections

Figure 8–1 illustrates the interrupt connections of four commonly used microprocessors: the 8085A, MC6800, MC6809, and Z80. The MC6800, MC6809, and Z80 contain a pin labeled $\overline{\text{NMI}}$ for nonmaskable interrupt; the 8085A contains a TRAP pin that performs the same function. The MC6800 and the Z80 have one maskable interrupt, the MC6809 has two maskable interrupts, and the 8085A has four maskable interrupt inputs. It appears that the 8085A has a more powerful hardware interrupt structure than the MC6800, MC6809, and the Z80. The inclusion of these additional interrupt pins reduces the external hardware overhead required for a multiple interrupt implementation. The more powerful interrupt structure of the Z80 will be discussed in section 8–4.

8085A INTERRUPT STRUCTURE 8-2

The 8085A has four interrupt control instructions: EI (enable interrupts), DI (disable interrupts), RIM (read interrupt masks), and SIM (set interrupt masks). The EI instruction turns on all of the unmasked interrupt pins; DI turns off all except the TRAP, which can never be deactivated. This task is accomplished by controlling the logic state of an internal interrupt enable flip-flop. EI sets it and DI clears it.

The SIM Instruction

The bit pattern that must be placed in the accumulator of the 8085A before a SIM instruction is executed is listed in table 8–1. The SIM instruction performs three separate tasks in the 8085A. SIM can control the SOD (serial output data) pin, reset the internal RST 7.5 interrupt request flip-flop, and mask any of the RST pins.

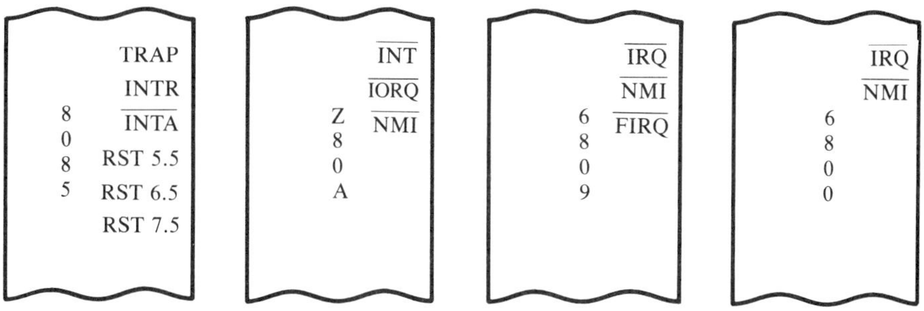

FIGURE 8–1 The interrupt pin connection of four common microprocessors, the Intel 8085A, Zilog Z80, and Motorola MC6800 and MC6809.

TABLE 8–1 Accumulator bit pattern before a SIM.

7	6	5	4	3	2	1	0
SOD	SOE	X	R7.5	MSE	M7.5	M6.5	M5.5

The SOD pin is controlled by placing a logic one in the SOE (SOD enable) bit of the accumulator and the desired logic level to be transferred to the SOD latch in the SOD bit. This is followed by the SIM instruction, which causes SOD to change to whatever was present in the SOD position of the accumulator.

The R7.5 bit, when placed high, will clear any interrupt request that may be pending on the internal RST 7.5 interrupt request flip-flop. The RST 7.5 input is an edge triggered input; in certain applications, it may be necessary to ignore a request on this pin. Figure 8–2 illustrates the internal RST 7.5 interrupt request flip-flop, the logic circuitry for masking, and the EI and DI instructions. The TRAP flip-flop is cleared whenever the processor accepts it or at the time of a reset. The RST 7.5 flip-flop is cleared by the SIM instruction whenever it is accepted or at the time of a reset.

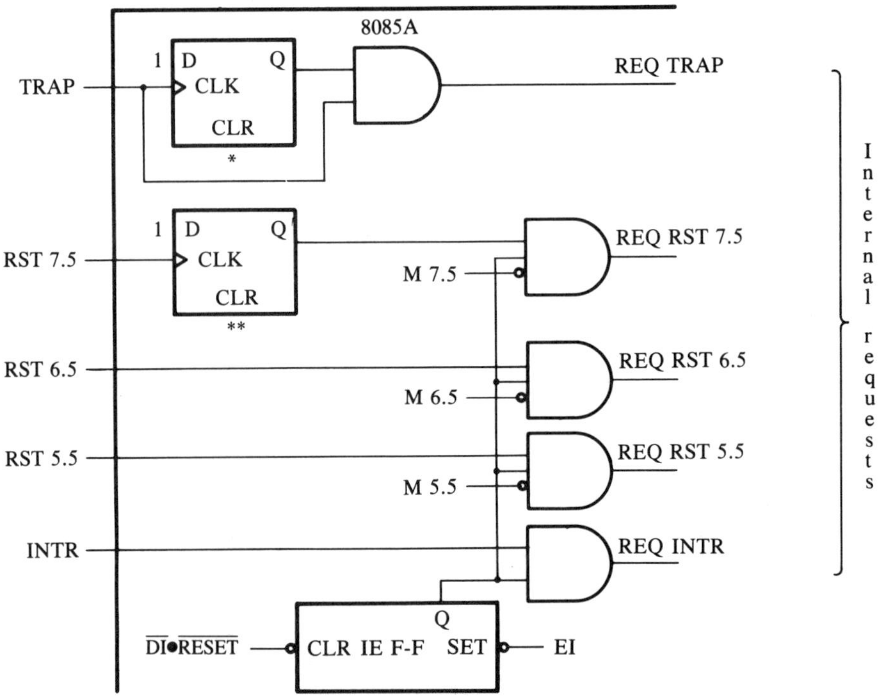

FIGURE 8–2 The internal representation of the Intel 8085A interrupt structure.

*The TRAP flip-flop is cleared on a RESET and when it's accepted by the microprocessor.

**The RST 7.5 flip-flop is cleared on a RESET, when it's accepted by the microprocessor, or with the SIM instruction.

The remaining 4 bits of the SIM control word mask the RST interrupt inputs. To modify these masks, a one is placed in the MSE (mask set enable) bit position; and the appropriate masks are placed in the M7.5, M6.5, and M5.5 bit positions. A logic zero turns on the corresponding RST input and a logic one turns it off. The conditions of these masks are only valid if the interrupt structure is enabled by the EI instruction.

The RIM Instruction

Table 8–2 illustrates the bit pattern found in the accumulator after the RIM instruction is executed. This bit pattern indicates (1) the logic level of the SID (serial input data) pin; (2) which RST interrupts are pending; (3) the state of the internal interrupt enable flip-flop, which is controlled by EI and DI; and (4) the logic levels of the masks.

TABLE 8–2 Accumulator bit pattern after a RIM.

7	6	5	4	3	2	1	0
SID	I7.5	I6.5	I5.5	IE	M7.5	M6.5	M5.5

RIM is most often used to allow a particular interrupt mask to be set or cleared without affecting the other masks. In the example illustrated, the RST 7.5 interrupt input is enabled without affecting the RST 6.5 or RST 5.5 masks.

```
        RIM             ;READ MASKS
        ANI     03H     ;CLEAR ALL BITS EXCEPT M6.5 & M5.5
        ORI     08H     ;SET MSE
        SIM             ;MODIFY MASKS
```

The Interrupt Inputs

Table 8–3 indicates the locations of the subroutines called by the interrupt inputs, the sensitivity of these inputs, and their priority levels. It is important to note that the RST locations are only 4 bytes in length and normally contain a PUSH PSW and a JMP to the interrupt service subroutine.

The TRAP input is both positive edge sensitive and level sensitive for use in power failure detection circuitry. The RST 7.5 input is positive edge sensi-

TABLE 8-3 Interrupt addresses for the 8085A.

Pin Name	Priority	Subroutine	Sensitivity
TRAP	1	0024H	Rising edge and high level
RST 7.5	2	003CH	Rising edge
RST 6.5	3	0034H	High level
RST 5.5	4	002CH	High level
INTR	5	*	High level

NOTE: This input does not have a decoded subroutine address.

tive for any application requiring this type of sensitivity. The RST 6.5, RST 5.5, and INTR inputs are level sensitive; they must be held at their active levels until they are recognized at the end of the current instruction. The time required to recognize these three inputs varies with different instructions and clock speeds of the 8085A. It is also important to note that the HOLD input causes an interrupt to be delayed until after the HOLD condition has ended.

The INTR Input and $\overline{\text{INTA}}$ Output

The INTR input does not call an interrupt service subroutine directly. Instead the 8085A issues an $\overline{\text{INTA}}$ pulse when this input is acknowledged, as illustrated in figure 8–3. It is the designer's responsibility to add hardware that will force an instruction onto the data bus in response to the $\overline{\text{INTA}}$ output of the 8085A. For most applications, a RST 1 through RST 7 is forced onto the data bus; on occasion, a CALL instruction is. (Note that the RST 0 instruction is normally used for a software and hardware RESET.) Figure 8–4 pictures the application of a RST 5 in response to an INTR interrupt request. The RST 5 instruction, an EFH, is hardwired to the inputs of the eight three-state buffers. Whenever the INTR input is placed at the logic one level requesting an interrupt, the microprocessor responds with an $\overline{\text{INTA}}$ pulse. This procedure enables the buffers and applies the EFH or RST 5 op-code on the data bus. The microprocessor responds by executing the RST 5 or it calls the subroutine that begins at memory location 28H.

8-3 MC6800 AND MC6809 INTERRUPT STRUCTURE

The MC6809 has three interrupt inputs: one is a nonmaskable interrupt input, $\overline{\text{NMI}}$, and the others are maskable interrupts, $\overline{\text{IRQ}}$ and $\overline{\text{FIRQ}}$. The MC6800 has all the same inputs except the $\overline{\text{FIRQ}}$. The $\overline{\text{NMI}}$ input causes the MC6809 to look to memory locations $FFFC and $FFFD for the address of the interrupt service subroutine. The $\overline{\text{IRQ}}$ input uses $FFF8 and $FFF9, and the $\overline{\text{FIRQ}}$ input uses $FFF6 and $FFF7 for their service subroutine vectors.

When the interrupt input is accepted by the MC6809 or MC6800, it automatically saves the contents of all internal registers on the stack and looks to the appropriate interrupt vector for the starting location of the interrupt service subroutine. The exception to this rule is the $\overline{\text{FIRQ}}$, or *fast interrupt request* input, which only saves the contents of the program counter and condition code register.

At the end of the interrupt service subroutine, a special return instruction (RTI) reloads the registers saved on the stack and returns to the program that was interrupted. This return instruction is different from RTS, which does not restore any register but the program counter. An extra flag bit in the status register indicates whether the interrupt is a $\overline{\text{FIRQ}}$ or normal interrupt for the MC6809. This is looked at by RTI to determine which registers must be unloaded from the stack.

In the MC6800 the $\overline{\text{IRQ}}$ interrupt input is enabled by the CLI instruction and disabled by the SEI instruction. These instructions control the interrupt

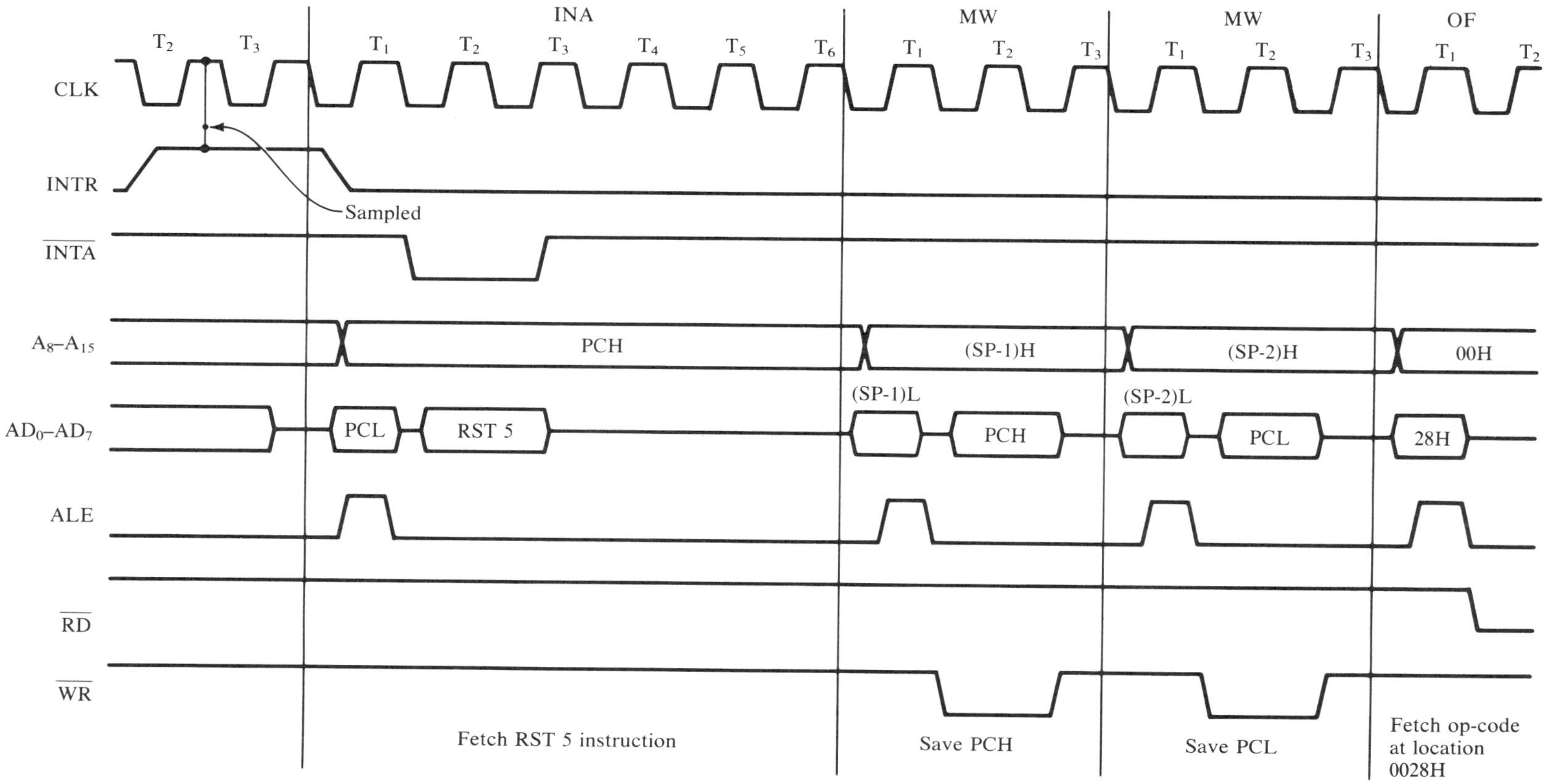

FIGURE 8–3 The timing diagram for an INTR showing the RST 5 instruction in response to the interrupt.

FIGURE 8–4 A circuit that will cause a RST 5 instruction to be gated onto the 8085A data bus in response to an INTR.

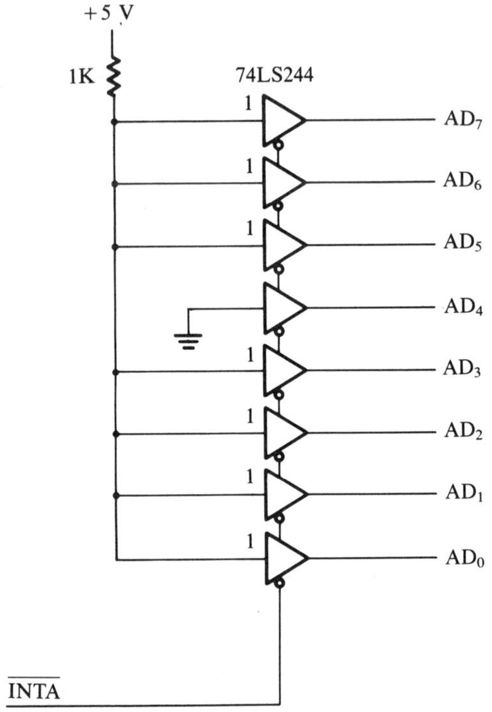

enable bit (I) in the condition code register, which in turn controls whether or not the interrupt is accepted by the microprocessor.

In the MC6809, the (I) and (F) interrupt masks are controlled by the ORCC instruction, which sets or disables them, and the ANDCC instruction, which clears or enables these bits. The (F) condition code bit controls the $\overline{\text{FIRQ}}$ input, and the (I) condition code bit controls the $\overline{\text{IRQ}}$ input.

8-4 Z80 INTERRUPT STRUCTURE

The Z80 has two interrupt inputs, the nonmaskable interrupt input ($\overline{\text{NMI}}$) and the maskable interrupt input ($\overline{\text{INT}}$). The nonmaskable interrupt input CALLs the interrupt service subroutine, which must reside beginning at location 0066H in the memory. Refer to Appendix A on the Z80 for their timing.

Maskable Interrupt

The maskable interrupt input can be used in three different ways by the Z80. The first mode of operation, *mode 0,* is identical to the method used by the INTR pin on the 8085A. The only difference is that to generate $\overline{\text{INTA}}$, the $\overline{\text{IORQ}}$ signal must be logically combined with the M1 signal (as illustrated in figure 8–5). This circuit inserts a RST 4 instruction in response to the $\overline{\text{INT}}$ request. It does this because the RST 4 instruction, an E7H, is hardwired to the buffer inputs. When the processor acknowledges the $\overline{\text{INT}}$ input, the

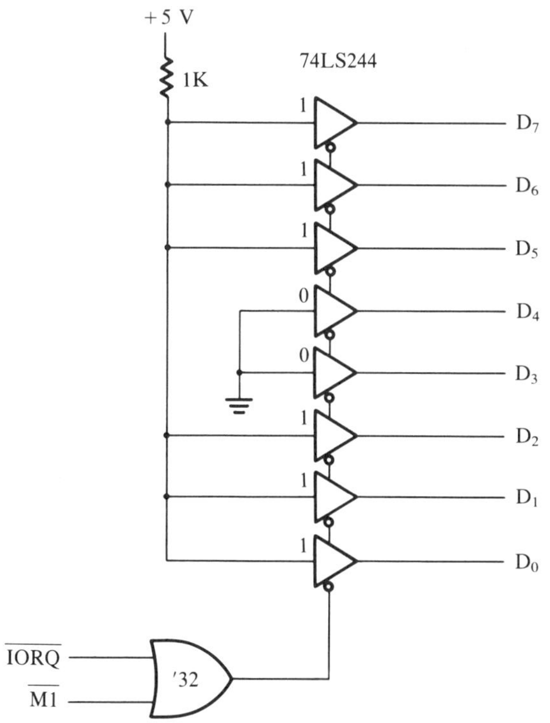

FIGURE 8–5 A circuit that will cause a RST 4 instruction to be gated onto the Z80 data bus in response to an $\overline{INT}$.

buffers gate this op-code onto the data bus for execution by the microprocessor.

A second method, or *mode 1,* causes the Z80 to respond to the $\overline{INT}$ input with a RST 7. This is useful in a small system that requires only one maskable interrupt input. It does not require any additional hardware for implementation.

The third mode of operation, *mode 2,* for the $\overline{INT}$ input is by far the most powerful. This mode allows multiple interrupt inputs for larger systems. When the Z80 responds to this type of interrupt, it reads the least significant portion of the interrupt service subroutine address from the data bus, as illustrated in figure 8–6. This portion of the vector address is combined with the most significant portion, which is stored in a special internal Z80 register called the *I register.* This allows the interrupt service subroutine to be stored anywhere in the Z80 memory address space.

Interrupt Control Instructions

The EI instruction enables the $\overline{INT}$ pin and the DI instruction disables it. This is exactly the same as in the 8085A microprocessor. In addition to these two instructions, three more interrupt control instructions are found in the instruction set. IM 0 selects the first mode, IM 1 selects the second, and IM 2 selects the third and most powerful mode. The interrupt vector location is specified by the LD I,A instruction, which copies the contents of the accumulator into the interrupt vector register. This register, along with the 8 bits of address information fetched during an interrupt acknowledge, forms the interrupt vector address for mode 2 operation.

FIGURE 8–6 This circuit will cause a CALL to memory location XX97H to occur in response to the $\overline{INT}$ input. The XX portion of the address is stored in the I register.

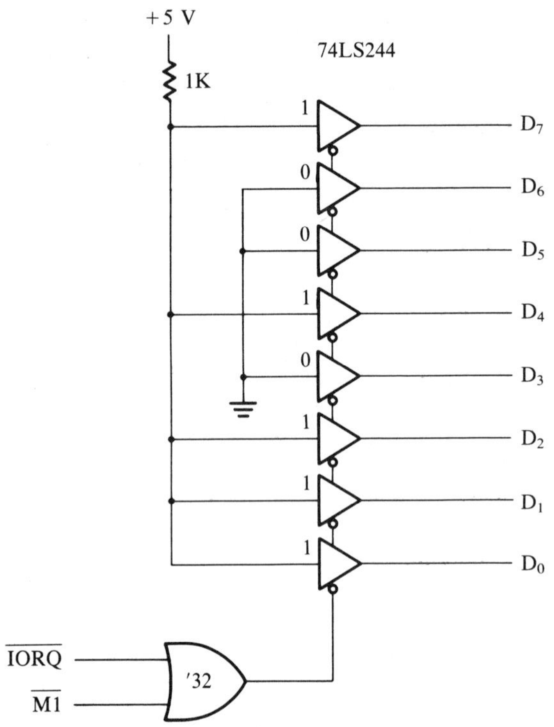

8-5 SIMPLE INTERRUPTS

Most interrupt inputs are level sensitive and must be held high until accepted by the microprocessor. The 8085A RST 7.5 and TRAP inputs are exceptions, since they are edge triggered inputs. To ensure that the interrupt is accepted, a simple latch to accomplish this synchronization may be required. Figure 8–7 illustrates this latch. In certain circumstances the latch is built into the external interrupt device.

The clock input to the D-type latch is a positive edge sensitive input that is pulsed to request an interrupt. The Q output is connected directly to the positive level sensitive interrupt input of the microprocessor, or the $\overline{Q}$ is con-

FIGURE 8–7 A method for converting a level sensitive interrupt input into an edge-triggered interrupt input.

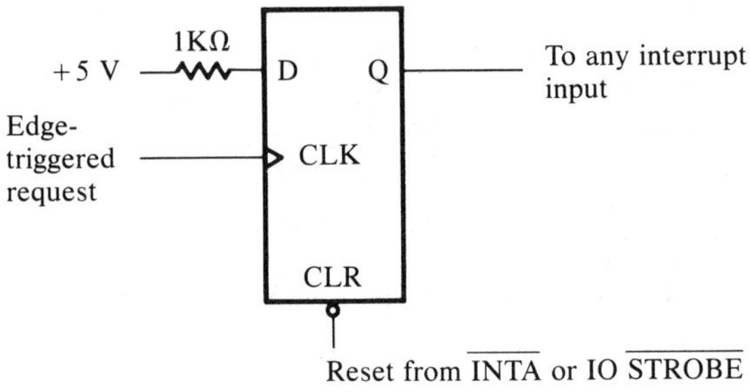

nected to the negative level sensitive input of the microprocessor. When the microprocessor acknowledges the acceptance of the interrupt through either an $\overline{\text{INTA}}$ signal or the act of controlling the interrupting I/O device, the flip-flop is reset to clear the interrupt request.

Real-Time Clock

An application of a simple interrupt is a real-time clock. The clock discussed here is a time of day clock that receives its timing signal from the AC power line. Real-time clocks serve this purpose and clock events in real time.

Clock Hardware

Figure 8–8 illustrates the hardware required to cause a periodic interrupt on the RST 7.5 edge triggered interrupt input of an 8085A microprocessor. A 6.3-V AC signal from the power transformer is rectified and waveshaped by a Schmitt trigger amplifier to produce 60 positive edges per second at the RST 7.5 input. Rectification is accomplished by the clamping diode located within the Schmitt trigger input circuit. The Schmitt trigger is used instead of an inverter because of the rise time requirement of the RST 7.5 input. This guarantees that the interrupt service subroutine, which keeps correct time, will be called exactly 60 times per second.

Clock Software

The time for this clock is kept in four RAM memory locations that contain the binary coded decimal time of day. The first location functions as a divide by 60, or MOD 60, counter to produce 1-s timing pulses for the remainder of the clock. The seconds and minutes locations are also modulus 60 counters, which produce 1-h pulses for the modulus 24 hour counter.

```
TIME:   DB  00      ;1/60 SECONDS COUNTER
        DB  00      ;SECONDS COUNTER
        DB  00      ;MINUTES COUNTER
        DB  00      ;HOURS COUNTER
```

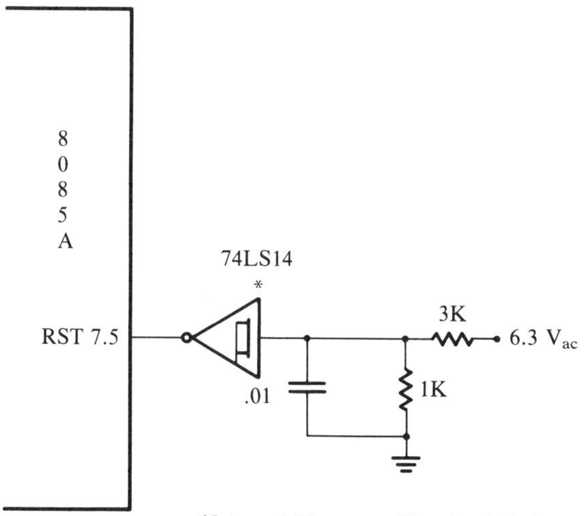

*Internal Clamp rectifies the AC signal.

FIGURE 8–8 A 60-Hz interrupt input for a real time clock.

Update Subroutine

Since there are four counters that must be periodically updated, it is wise to develop a subroutine to handle any one of them. This subroutine must be supplied with the modulus of the counter to be updated and its location in the memory. For this example, the HL pair holds the address of the counter, and the B register holds the modulus of the counter to be incremented. B dictates to the subroutine when a counter will be cleared. This information is supplied by the calling program or, in this case, the interrupt service subroutine.

```
;THIS SUBROUTINE INCREMENTS THE CONTENTS OF THE
;MEMORY LOCATION INDEXED BY THE HL PAIR.
;B INDICATES THE MAXIMUM COUNT PLUS ONE OF
;THIS COUNTER.
;
UPDATE: MOV   A,M    ;GET COUNTER
        INR   A      ;INCREMENT IT
        DAA          ;MAKE RESULT BCD
        MOV   M,A    ;SAVE COUNTER
        SUB   B      ;CHECK FOR TERMINAL COUNT
        RNZ
        MOV   M,A    ;CLEAR COUNTER
        INX   H      ;POINT TO NEXT COUNTER
        RET
```

In the UPDATE subroutine the counter is incremented, and a return not zero occurs if it does not reach its terminal count. If the terminal count is reached, the counter is cleared to zero and the pointer in the HL pair is incremented to the next counter's address. A return zero indicates that the next counter should be incremented because of the overflow, and a return not zero indicates that the next and subsequent counters contain the correct time.

Clock Initialization

The interrupt service subroutine is called 60 times per second if the RST 7.5 interrupt is unmasked and enabled at the RESET location in the system. This initialization sequence follows:

```
RESET: MVI  A,00001011B ;UN-MASK RST 7.5
       SIM
       EI               ;ENABLE INTERRUPTS
       .
       .    (System program starts here)
       .
```

Clock Interrupt Service Subroutine

The interrupt service subroutine itself, as depicted by the flowchart in figure 8–9, must correctly update the BCD clock located in the RAM.

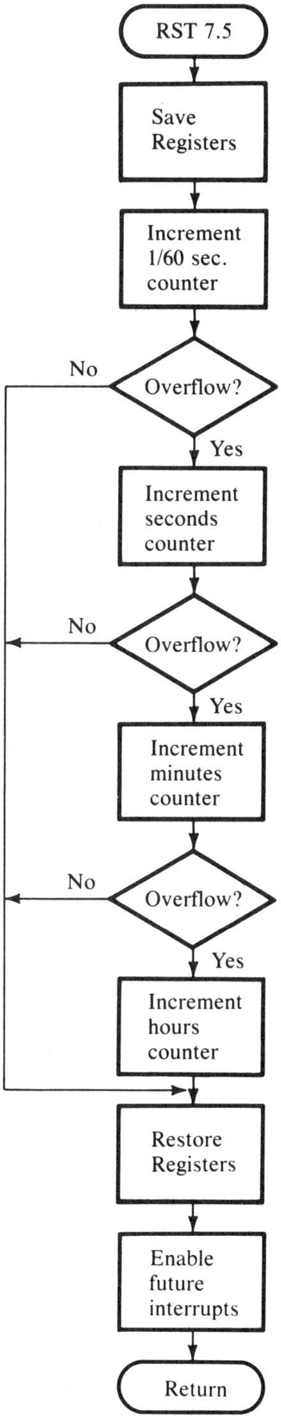

FIGURE 8–9 The flowchart of the interrupt service subroutine that keeps time in the real time clock circuit of figure 8–8.

This is accomplished by updating the 1/60-seconds counter each time an interrupt occurs. If this counter overflows, as it does once per second, the seconds counter is updated. Once per minute, the seconds counter overflows; at this time the minutes counter is updated, and so forth.

```
RST75:  PUSH PSW       ;SAVE AF
        PUSH H         ;SAVE HL
        PUSH B         ;SAVE BC
        MVI  B,60H     ;LOAD MODULUS
        LXI  H,TIME    ;POINT TO CLOCK
        CALL UPDATE    ;INCREMENT 1/60 SECONDS
        JNZ  DONE      ;IF NO OVERFLOW
        CALL UPDATE    ;INCREMENT SECONDS
        JNZ  DONE      ;IF NO OVERFLOW
        CALL UPDATE    ;INCREMENT MINUTES
        JNZ  DONE      ;IF NO OVERFLOW
        MVI  B,24H     ;LOAD NEW MODULUS
        CALL UPDATE    ;INCREMENT HOURS
DONE:   POP  B         ;RESTORE BC
        POP  H         ;RESTORE HL
        POP  PSW       ;RESTORE AF
        EI             ;ENABLE FUTURE INTERRUPTS
        RET
```

A system using this type of clock would seem to become very inefficient since the program or system would be interrupted 60 times per second. This is not the case since this interrupt only consumes less than 0.5 percent of the microprocessor's processing time. In most cases this loss can readily be acceptable for the total system. The interrupt can easily be modified to include the day, month, and year without increasing significantly the time used by the interrupt service subroutine.

One possible pitfall of this type of clock is that another interrupting device may require more time than 1/60 second. If this occurs, the result is a subsequent loss of the correct time. Care must be exercised in using this clock with other interrupts.

8-6 INTERRUPT PRIORITY SCHEMES

On numerous occasions the one or two interrupt inputs provided on most microprocessors prove to be too few. The one exception is the 8085A, which has five of these interrupt inputs. Expanding the number of interrupt inputs is relatively simple because most manufacturers provide an interrupt expansion component.

The Daisy Chain

One interrupt expansion circuit in use is the daisy chain. Figure 8–10 depicts a typical 4-channel daisy chain interrupt system. The interrupt request signal from any of the 4 channels clears the accompanying interrupt request flip-flop, whose output is then logically combined with the outputs of the other three flip-flops to produce an interrupt request signal for the microprocessor. When acknowledging the interrupt, the microprocessor returns an acknowledgment signal through the daisy chain to the nearest requesting device. This acknowledgment signal clears the request, sets the Q output of the flip-flop, and enables the interrupting device. The $\overline{ENX}$ outputs go low for only about 25 ns in this circuit and may therefore need to be latched by the requesting device.

The main shortcoming of this system is that all interrupts remain active at all times, and the priority scheme is fixed. The device nearest the interrupt acknowledge output of the microprocessor, $\overline{REQ1}$, is the one with the highest priority.

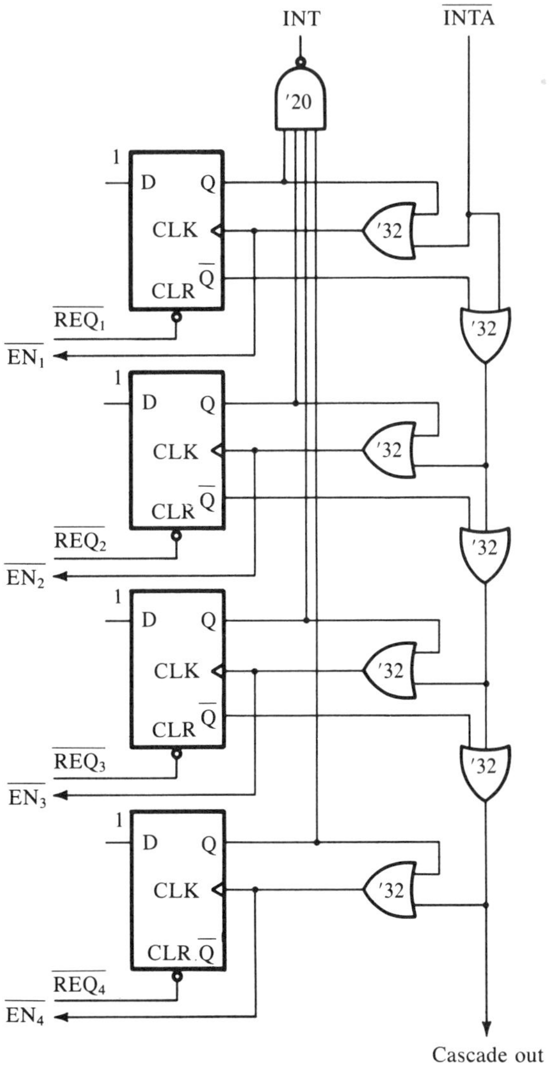

FIGURE 8–10 A daisy chained interrupt expansion circuit.

Restart Priority

Another priority scheme in the Intel or Zilog processors involves using the restart instructions. The circuit in figure 8–11 can be used to expand the interrupt capabilities of these microprocessors easily by causing the microprocessor to execute different restart instructions. The processor accomplishes this by gating the RST instructions onto the data bus for various interrupt input conditions.

Request inputs R1, R2, and R4 cause the microprocessor to execute RST1, RST2, and RST4, respectively. If more than one of these interrupt inputs occurs at a time, different restart subroutines are called. For example, if the R1 and R2 inputs are active at the same time, a RST3 instruction is issued to the microprocessor. The RST3 service subroutine resolves priority between these two request signals. See table 8–4 for the complete list of RST instructions called by this technique.

TABLE 8–4 Vector locations for figure 8–11.

R4	R2	R1	RST Instruction
0	0	0	None
0	0	1	RST 1
0	1	0	RST 2
0	1	1	RST 3
1	0	0	RST 4
1	0	1	RST 5
1	1	0	RST 6
1	1	1	RST 7

This technique is relatively simple but can only be used for the Intel and Zilog 8-bit microprocessors. It also has the limitation of being expandable to only three external interrupts.

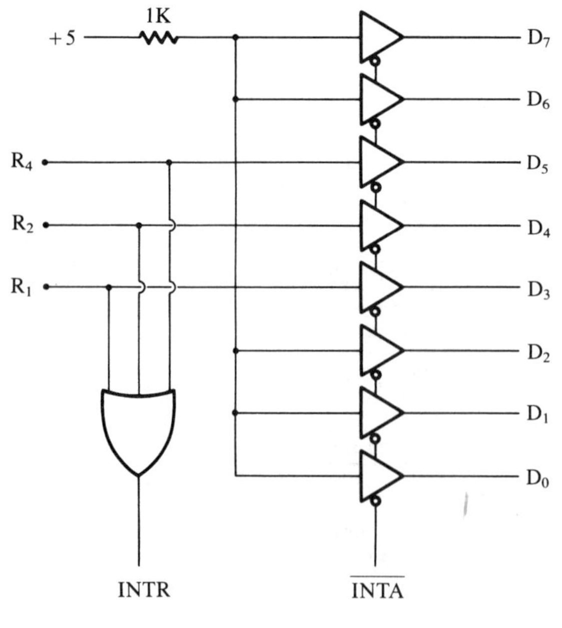

FIGURE 8–11 A circuit for causing multiple RST interrupts in an 8085A or Z80 based system.

Priority Encoder

The priority encoder is the most useful type of interrupt expanding device available today. It may be purchased in IC form and used as desired, or it may be included within an interrupt controller provided by the manufacturer. Generally expansion through this type of device is limited to no fewer than 64 external interrupting devices. A microprocessor based system with so many interrupt processed I/O devices is extremely uncommon.

The 8259A Interrupt Controller

Figure 8–12 illustrates the Intel 8259A programmable interrupt controller, which allows the user to expand the interrupt capabilities of an Intel or Zilog microprocessor to eight or more interrupt inputs. It permits the use of the RST instructions; if required, it inserts CALL instructions in response to an interrupt. This device also allows the user to select the type of priority scheme desired for the interrupt inputs.

8259A Initialization

To use the interrupt controller in a system, four separate command words are used in the initialization process. Figure 8–13 illustrates these four command words, ICW1 through ICW4.

ICW1 indicates whether or not ICW4 is needed, which is discussed further below. It also indicates whether there is a single device or more than one device in the system.

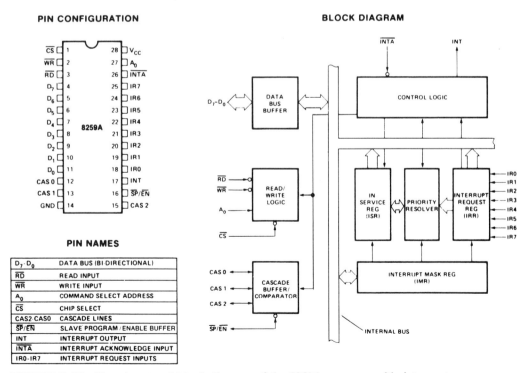

PIN CONFIGURATION

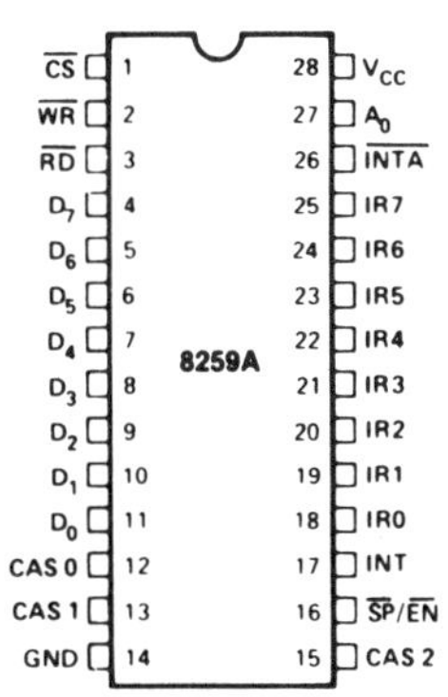

PIN NAMES

D_7-D_0	DATA BUS (BI-DIRECTIONAL)
$\overline{RD}$	READ INPUT
$\overline{WR}$	WRITE INPUT
A_0	COMMAND SELECT ADDRESS
$\overline{CS}$	CHIP SELECT
CAS2-CAS0	CASCADE LINES
$\overline{SP}/\overline{EN}$	SLAVE PROGRAM/ENABLE BUFFER
INT	INTERRUPT OUTPUT
$\overline{INTA}$	INTERRUPT ACKNOWLEDGE INPUT
IR0-IR7	INTERRUPT REQUEST INPUTS

BLOCK DIAGRAM

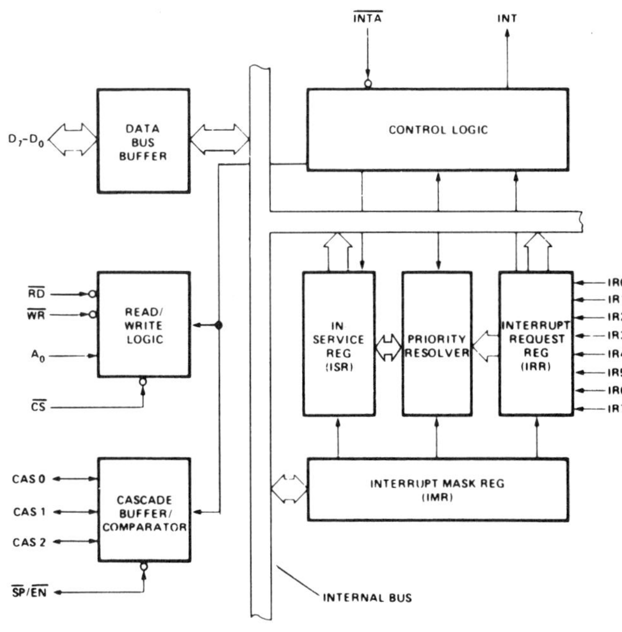

FIGURE 8–12 The pinout and block diagram of the 8259A programmable interrupt controller.

SOURCE: Reprinted by permission of Intel Corporation, Copyright 1983.

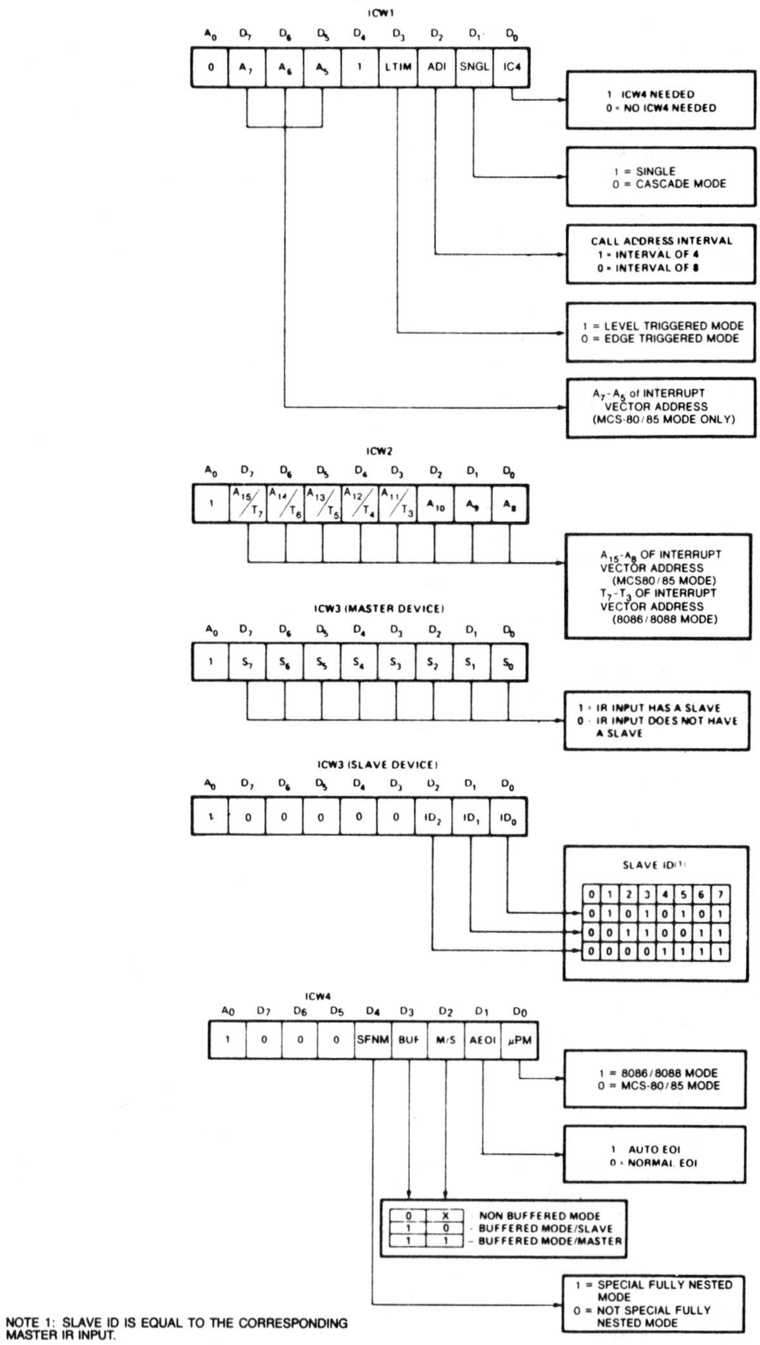

FIGURE 8–13 The four initialization command words for the 8259A programmable interrupt controller.

SOURCE: Reprinted by permission of Intel Corporation, Copyright 1983.

IC4 indicates whether ICW4 is needed.

SNGL indicates whether this is a single 8259A or whether more than one exist in the system.

ADI indicates whether the CALL address interrupt vectors are to be 4 or 8 bytes in length.

LTIM selects level or edge triggering for the eight interrupt request inputs.

A7, A6, and A5 specify part of the address of the second byte of the CALL instruction. (See tables 8–5 and 8–6 for more detail on these bits.)

TABLE 8–5 Second byte of a CALL if vectors are placed four bytes apart.

IR	Interval = 4							
	D7	D6	D5	D4	D3	D2	D1	D0
7	A7	A6	A5	1	1	1	0	0
6	A7	A6	A5	1	1	0	0	0
5	A7	A6	A5	1	0	1	0	0
4	A7	A6	A5	1	0	0	0	0
3	A7	A6	A5	0	1	1	0	0
2	A7	A6	A5	0	1	0	0	0
1	A7	A6	A5	0	0	1	0	0
0	A7	A6	A5	0	0	0	0	0

(Reprinted by permission of Intel Corporation, copyright 1983)

TABLE 8–6 Second byte of a CALL if vectors are placed eight bytes apart.

IR	Interval = 8							
	D7	D6	D5	D4	D3	D2	D1	D0
7	A7	A6	1	1	1	0	0	0
6	A7	A6	1	1	0	0	0	0
5	A7	A6	1	0	1	0	0	0
4	A7	A6	1	0	0	0	0	0
3	A7	A6	0	1	1	0	0	0
2	A7	A6	0	1	0	0	0	0
1	A7	A6	0	0	1	0	0	0
0	A7	A6	0	0	0	0	0	0

(Reprinted by permission of Intel Corporation, copyright 1983)

ICW2 specifies the third byte of the CALL instruction for the 8085A microprocessor. If the 8086 or 8088 is in use, it specifies the interrupt vector.

ICW3 used in a cascaded system only. This initialization command word selects master or slave operation and indicates the slave ID or which slaves are present in the system to the master.

ICW4 normally used in buffered mode. *Buffered mode* is a mode of operation in a system where the data bus contains bidirectional bus buffers. These buffers must be controlled during an interrupt by the 8259A to pass the instruction or vector to the microprocessor. The $\overline{EP}/\overline{EN}$ pin provides this control function to the data bus buffers.

μPM selects which microprocessor is in use with the 8259A.

AEOI controls the automatic end of interrupt operation. If activated, the last $\overline{\text{INTA}}$ pulse automatically internally acknowledges the interrupt request. If not activated, the interrupt service subroutine must clear the interrupt request through an operation command, as described later in this section.

M/S selects master/slave operation. This is used only if the system contains multiple 8259As. The master releases the CALL instruction, and the slave device releases the second and third bytes of the CALL to the 8085A.

BUF used in a large system to enable the buffer control signal $\overline{\text{EP}}/\text{EN}$.

SFNM selects the specially nested mode of operation for the 8259A. This mode is used in a large buffered system with multiple 8259As.

Initialization Example

Figure 8–14 depicts an 8259A attached to an 8085A microprocessor. In this case, it expands the interrupt inputs with eight additional interrupt request inputs. The 8259A is decoded to respond to I/O port numbers 6XH. In this example, it is assumed that this device and its interrupt inputs are to CALL the subroutines that begin in an interrupt vector table at memory location 0800H. Each vector is to be 4 bytes in length. Table 8–7 pictures the interrupts and the interrupt vector locations.

TABLE 8–7 Interrupt vectors for figure 8–14.

Interrupt Pin	Vector Location
IR0	0800H
IR1	0804H
IR2	0808H
IR3	080CH
IR4	0810H
IR5	0814H
IR6	0818H
IR7	081CH

To create a system with these vector locations the 8259A must be initialized. The ICWs, or initialization command words, discussed earlier accomplish the programming.

```
;THIS SEQUENCE OF INSTRUCTION WILL INITIALIZE THE
;8259A
;
INIT:   MVI   A,00010110B      ;SETUP ICW1
        OUT   60H
        MVI   A,00001000B      ;SETUP ICW2
        OUT   61H
          .
          .
          .
```

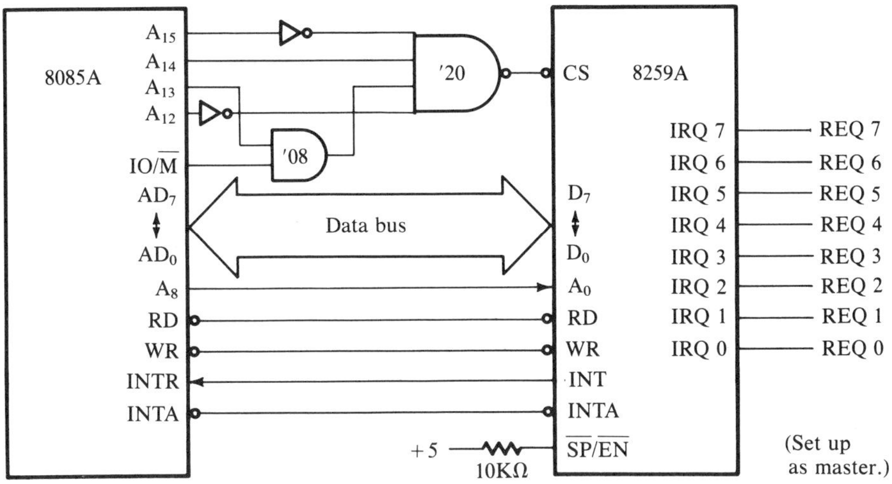

FIGURE 8–14 A typical interface between the 8085A and the 8259A programmable interrupt controller.

The initialization dialog illustrated programs the 8259A so that its interrupt inputs are edge sensitive, the vector interval is 4 bytes, and the vector table begins at location 0800H. From this point forward, a positive edge on any of the interrupt inputs will CALL a subroutine from the vector table.

8259A Operation Command Words

In addition to the initialization commands, it is necessary to program the operation of the 8259A through three separate command words (as pictured in figure 8–15).

Operation command word OCW1 controls the eight interrupt inputs to the 8259A. To mask (1) a channel inhibits it, or prevents an interrupt. To clear a mask (0) enables, or turns on, the corresponding interrupt input.

OCW2 controls the operation of the internal interrupt priority system.

L2, L1, and L0 signals that set the lowest priority interrupt input. If 010 is selected, IR2 has the lowest priority and IR3 has the highest. These bits are also used with the SEOI bit specifically to clear one of the interrupt requests.

EOI clears the interrupt request with the highest priority from the interrupt service subroutine.

SEOI used with the L2, L1, and L0 bits to clear a specific interrupt request.

R causes an automatic priority rotation. The most recently serviced interrupt becomes the lowest priority input.

OCW3 accomplishes the following functions:

RIS and ERIS select which register is read on the next $\overline{RD}$ pulse. The IR register indicates which interrupts are pending, and the IS register indicates which interrupts are masked. These registers are illustrated in figure 8–16 with the Poll register.

P if active, it causes the next read ($\overline{RD}$) to read the highest interrupt input currently requesting service.

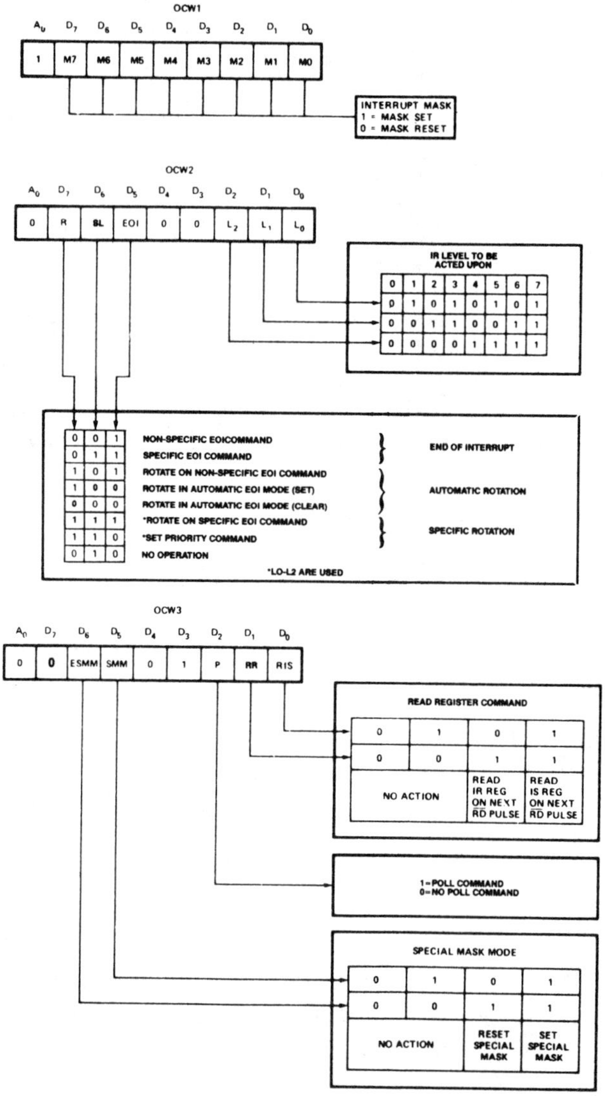

FIGURE 8–15 The operation command word formats for the 8259A programmable interrupt controller.

SOURCE: Reprinted by permission of Intel Corporation, Copyright 1983.

SMM and ESMM control the operation of the special mask mode. When an interrupt is accepted in normal mode, all lower-priority interrupts are disabled. In a case in which a lower-level interrupt is to take effect, the special mask mode is used. This mode allows all other interrupts to take effect when enabled.

More programming is required to operate the interrupt controller pictured in figure 8–16. You will notice that not all of the interrupt inputs are actually connected to an external device. These unused inputs should be turned off,

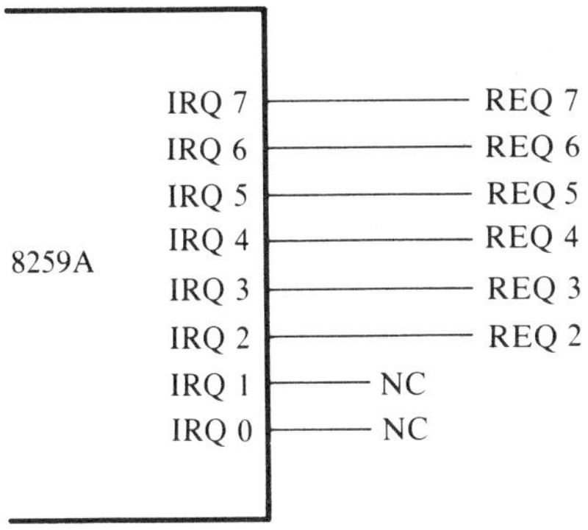

FIGURE 8–16 This interface is identical to the one pictured in figure 8–14, except that two of the eight interrupt inputs are not connected.

or masked. In addition to masking the unused inputs, a rotating priority scheme is employed for the remaining inputs. The remainder of the initialization dialog follows:

```
        MVI   A,00000011B      ;SETUP OCW1
        OUT   61H
        MVI   A,10000010B      ;SETUP OCW2
        OUT   60H
          .
          .
          .
```

From this point forward, the 8259A will function as an interrupt vectoring device.

Interrupt Acknowledge with the 8259A

To acknowledge an interrupt, the interrupt controller must be written into using one of the OCWs described in the preceding paragraphs. Suppose that the IRQ7 input has just taken effect and at this point we are in that interrupt service subroutine. To acknowledge this, we can use OCW2 and the nonspecific end of an interrupt or OCW2 and the specific end of an interrupt. With the nonspecific end of interrupt, it is assumed that it is the latest interrupt, and with the specific EOI we must specify which interrupt. The software illustrated below uses the specific EOI to end the IRQ7 interrupt. It is found at the very tail end of the IRQ7 interrupt service subroutine.

```
;THESE INSTRUCTIONS FORM THE VERY END OF THE IRQ7
;INTERRUPT SERVICE SUBROUTINE.
;
ACK:  MVI   A,11000111B   ;BIT PATTERN TO
;ACKNOWLEDGE THE IRQ7 INTERRUPT IT ALSO MAINTAINS
;ROTATING PRIORITY
      OUT   60H           ;ACKNOWLEDGE THE INTERRUPT
      EI                  ;ENABLE FUTURE INTERRUPTS
      RET                 ;RETURN
```

Polled Interrupts

Still another method of handling multiple interrupt inputs is a polling scheme. This type of interrupt system is adaptable to any microprocessor and uses relatively inexpensive hardware.

Figure 8–17 pictures the schematic diagram of a simple but effective polling scheme. This particular system contains eight interrupt inputs connected to one of the microprocessor's interrupt request inputs. The eight interrupt request lines are connected to a NAND gate, where they are logically combined to produce a logic zero at its output when no request is active. If one or more requests occur, the output of the NAND gate becomes a logic one. (This may or may not be the correct logic level for a particular application, but it can be inverted to produce the correct level.) The eight request lines also connect to an 8-bit input device. This allows the user to determine, through software, which input has caused the interrupt and to assign priority if more than one occurs at the same time.

```
;POLLING INTERRUPT RESPONSE SUBROUTINE
;
POLL:  IN    PORT     ;INPUT INTERRUPT REQUESTS
       LXI   H,TABLE  ;SETUP JUMP TABLE ADDRESS
LOOP:  RLC            ;CHECK INTERRUPT INPUT
       INX   H        ;SETUP NEXT JUMP TABLE ADDRESS
       INX   H
       JC    LOOP     ;CHECK NEXT LEVEL
       MOV   A,M      ;GET LOW ORDER ADDRESS
       INX   H
       MOV   H,M      ;GET HIGH ORDER ADDRESS
       MOV   L,A      ;FORM JUMP ADDRESS
       PCHL           ;JUMP TO SUBROUTINE
;
;INTERRUPT VECTOR TABLE CONTAINS JUMP ADDRESSES
;
TABLE: DW    I7         ;HIGHEST PRIORITY
       DW    I6
       DW    I5
       DW    I4
       DW    I3
       DW    I2
       DW    I1
       DW    I0         ;LOWEST PRIORITY
```

To acknowledge the request, the interrupt service subroutine sends a signal to the requesting device. This signal can clear the appropriate interrupt request in addition to transferring the data. Figure 8–18 illustrates a simple logic circuit that can be used for the request and the data strobe. If A2, A1, and A0 contain 111 at the time of the OUT instruction, the 74LS138 sends the strobe to interrupt device number seven (AK7). If an input device is in use, an IN instruction is used in place of the OUT. Table 8–8 illustrates the I/O port numbers used with this circuit to develop these strobes.

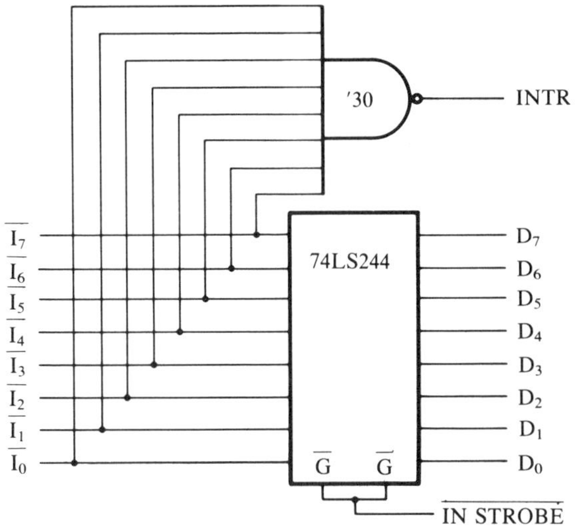

FIGURE 8–17 A circuit for causing an interrupt allowing the system to look at the interrupting inputs.

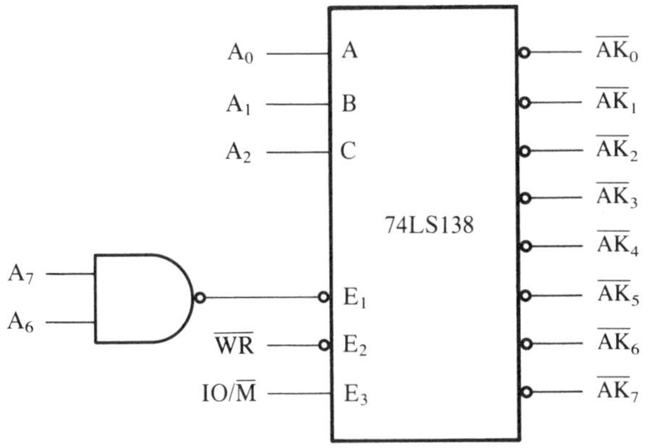

FIGURE 8–18 A circuit that will generate eight different interrupt acknowledge pulses for the interrupting devices. (Refer to table 8–8 for additional detail on these signals.)

TABLE 8–8 Acknowledge strobe ports for figure 8–18.

Port Number	Acknowledge Signal
11XX X000	$\overline{AK0}$
11XX X001	$\overline{AK1}$
11XX X010	$\overline{AK2}$
11XX X011	$\overline{AK3}$
11XX X100	$\overline{AK4}$
11XX X101	$\overline{AK5}$
11XX X110	$\overline{AK6}$
11XX X111	$\overline{AK7}$

8-7 INTERRUPT DRIVEN FIFO

In many applications the data is input or output at a relatively low speed and throughput can be drastically increased by an interrupt. In the example of a printer interface, the speed of the printer itself is relatively low when compared to the microprocessor. It may be able to print an average of 50 characters per second, while the microprocessor can send it information at the rate of about ten thousand characters per second.

In this application the throughput of the computer can be enhanced greatly if an interrupt occurs every time that the printer requires a character to be printed. The only time that the computer has to communicate with the printer is at the time of an interrupt, freeing the microprocessor for more useful tasks.

Centronics Printer Interface

The Centronics parallel printer interface is very commonly used today. Figure 8–19 illustrates the timing diagram for this interface. All of the signals are TTL logic levels, so no special level translation is required between the printer and the computer system.

The $\overline{ACK}$ and $\overline{STROBE}$ signals comprise the control structure of this simple-to-use interface. The acknowledge signal ($\overline{ACK}$) is an output from the printer to the computer indicating that a character has been received and the printer is ready for the next character.

The $\overline{STROBE}$ signal comes from the computer and tells the printer that data is available on the data connections.

In an interrupt processed system, the $\overline{ACK}$ signal causes an interrupt, and the $\overline{STROBE}$ signal is developed by the PIA whenever a character is transmitted to the printer.

8085A Interface

Figure 8–20 depicts a Centronics-type printer interface connected to an 8155 and 8085A. Port A is setup to send the data to the printer as a strobed output port.

The $\overline{STROBE}$ signal for the printer is developed from an output pin on port C. The $\overline{ACK}$ signal from the printer is connected to the $\overline{STB}$ input for port A. In strobed output operation, the $\overline{STB}$ input causes the INTR output of the 8155 to become a logic one. In this case, an interrupt is requested when the printer acknowledges receipt of an ASCII character.

The 8155 in this application is selected whenever the four most significant address connections are at a logic one condition. This means that the 8155

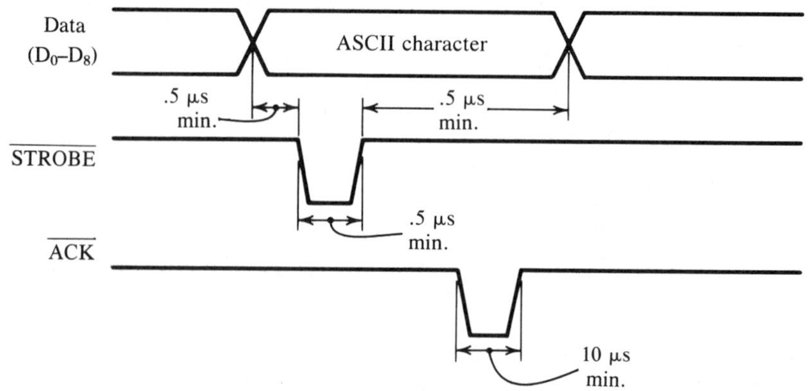

FIGURE 8–19 The timing diagram for the Centronics type printer interface.

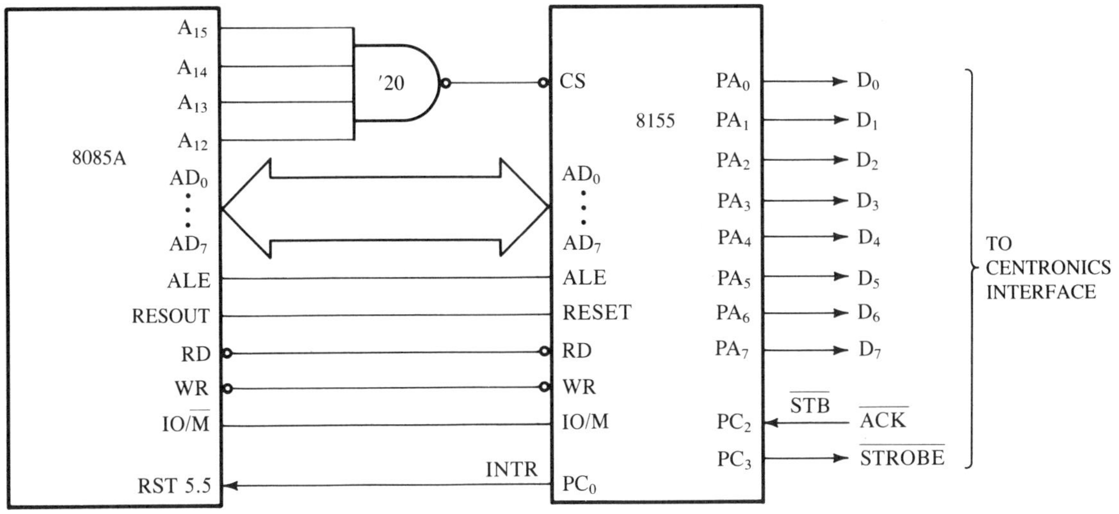

FIGURE 8–20 The Centronics parallel printer interface connected to an 8085A microprocessor through an 8155 PIA.

turns on for I/O port numbers FXH. The software featured later in this section uses ports F0H through F5H for the control of this interface.

MC6800 Interface

See figure 8–21 for a schematic diagram of the MC6800-to-Centronics printer interface. This interface uses the MC6821 to generate an interrupt pulse for the microprocessor along with the data and handshaking for the printer. The

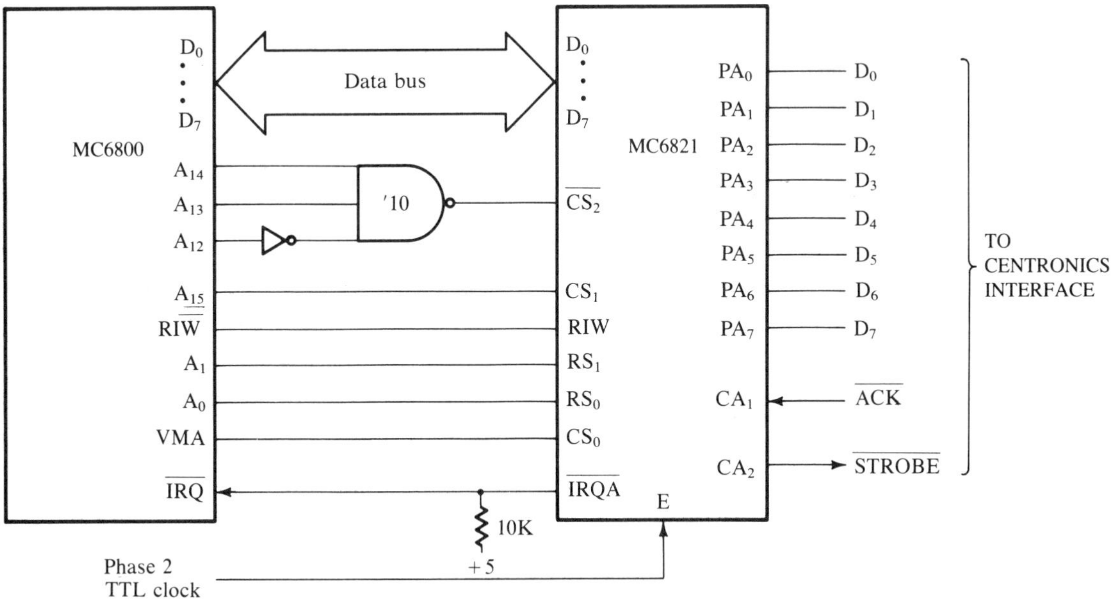

FIGURE 8–21 The Centronics parallel printer interface connected to an MC6800 microprocessor through the MC6821 PIA.

MC6821 responds to memory addresses $EXXX in this example. Addresses $E000 through $E003 are actually used in the software.

Port A is programmed as an output device to transmit data to the printer. Pin CA1 is connected to the $\overline{\text{ACK}}$ signal from the printer to request an interrupt through the $\overline{\text{IRQA}}$ pin. Pin CA2 sends the $\overline{\text{STROBE}}$ signal to the printer whenever data is being transmitted.

The Queue or FIFO

In this type of application, it is customary to use a FIFO or queue to store the data to be sent to the printer. The length of the queue will probably be at least one line in length, or it might be up to several pages. A *queue* or *FIFO* is a special arrangement of the cyclical memory whereby data is addressed through two pointers, an input pointer and an output pointer. It's a cyclical memory, since the same area of memory is used over and over by the system just as the stack uses the same area of memory. In the case of a printer interface, the input pointer is addressed through a subroutine and the output pointer is addressed by the interrupt service subroutine. Since this type of memory system is completely managed by the software, its cost is relatively low.

256-Byte Queue

This example uses 256 bytes (a small portion of the computer memory) for a queue, plus 2 bytes of additional memory for the input and output pointers. In the MC6800 software, 2 bytes per pointer reduce the amount of software. Note that a 256-byte queue is only capable of storing 255 bytes of data; 1 byte is lost because of the full and empty conditions. The queue is depicted in figure 8–22. In this example, if the queue is empty the pointers are equal; if it is full, the output pointer is one less than the input pointer.

Initialization Dialog

The initialization dialog is rather short, since all that is to be accomplished is programming the PIA. The dialog required for both the MC6800 and the 8085A interfaces follows:

FIGURE 8–22 A symbolic presentation of the 256-byte queue or FIFO memory.

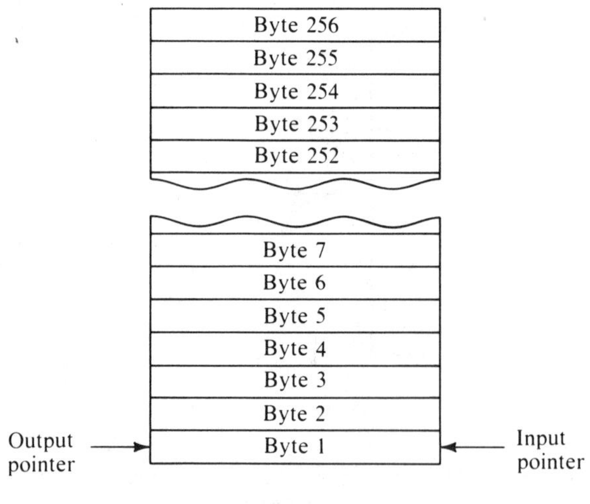

```
*INITIALIZATION DIALOG (MC6800)
*
INIT     CLR  $E001       SELECT DDR PORT A
         LDAA #$FF        SETUP PORT A AS OUTPUT
         STAA $E000
         LDAA #$FD        PROGRAM PINS CA1 AND CA2
         STAA $E001       AND ENABLE PORT A
          .
          .
          .
```

```
;INITIALIZATION DIALOG (8085A)
;
INIT:    MVI  A,15H       PROGRAM PORTS
         OUT  0F0H        AND ENABLE INTERRUPT
         MVI  A,0FFH      SET STROBE HIGH
         OUT  0F3H
          .
          .
          .
```

Queue Software

Subroutines to control the storing and removing of data must be capable of checking the full and empty conditions of the queue. They must also be able to modify the pointer and handle the method of storage required for this type of memory system. The flowchart for this subroutine is depicted in figure 8–23 and the actual subroutines for both the 8085A and MC6800 follow:

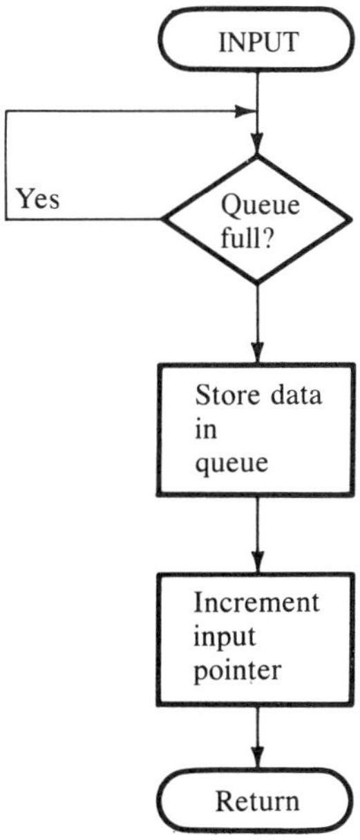

FIGURE 8–23 A flowchart of the INPUT subroutine used to fill the queue.

```
;8085A INPUT SUBROUTINE
;
INPUT:  PUSH PSW        ;SAVE DATA
INP:    LDA  POINTI     ;GET INPUT POINTER
        MOV  L,A        ;SAVE IT
        LDA  POINTO     ;GET OUTPUT POINTER
        DCR  A          ;SETUP POINTER
        CMP  L          ;CHECK FOR FULL
        JZ   INP        ;IF FULL
        MVI  H,PAGE     ;SET PAGE ADDRESS
        POP  PSW        ;GET DATA
        MOV  M,A        ;SAVE DATA
        MOV  A,L        ;GET INPUT POINTER
        INR  A          ;INCREMENT POINTER
        STA  POINTI     ;SAVE POINTER
        RET
```

```
*6800 INPUT SUBROUTINE
*
INPUT   PSHA            SAVE DATA
INP     LDDA POINTI+1   GET INPUT POINTER
        INCA            STEPUP POINTER
        CMPA POINTO+1   COMPARE WITH OUTPUT POINTER
        BEQ  INP        LOOP IF FULL
        LDX  POINT1     RESTORE INPUT POINTER
        PULA            RESTORE DATA
        STAA X          SAVE DATA IN FIFO
        INC  POINTI+1   INCREMENT INPUT POINTER
        RTS             RETURN FROM SUBROUTINE
```

The INPUT subroutine stores information into the queue without pause until the queue is full. When it is full, the subroutine enters into a wait loop until the external interrupting device interrupts this wait loop and extracts data from the queue. (It would be nice to use a HLT (8085A) or a WAI (MC6800), but the subroutine is shorter with a loop.) When data is extracted from the queue, the output pointer is incremented.

The OUTP subroutine is called by the interrupt service subroutine and one of two results occurs. If the queue is empty, a return zero occurs from the OUTP subroutine that must be used by the interrupt service subroutine to disable interrupts. If data is transmitted normally and the queue is not empty, the interrupt service subroutine must allow future interrupts to occur. The flowchart for the OUTP subroutine is illustrated in figure 8–24.

```
;8085A OUTP SUBROUTINE
;
OUTP:   LDA  POINTO     ;GET OUTPUT POINTER
        MOV  L,A        ;SAVE POINTER
        LDA  POINTI     ;GET INPUT POINTER
        CMP  L          ;CHECK FOR EMPTY
```

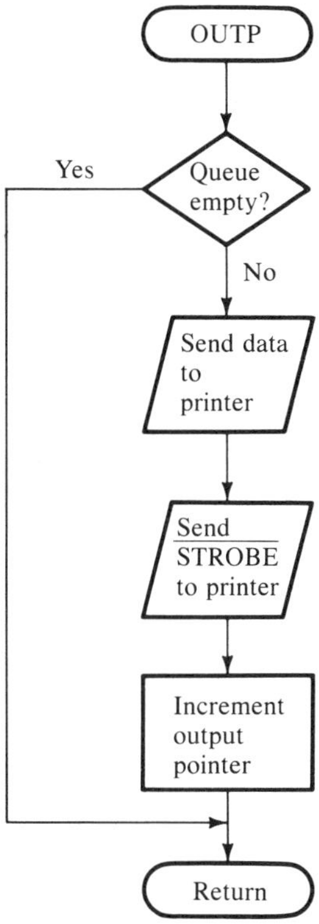

FIGURE 8–24 A flowchart of the OUTP subroutine used to extract data from the queue and print it.

```
        RZ
        MVI  H,PAGE    ;POINT TO QUEUE PAGE
        MOV  A,M       ;GET DATA
        OUT  0F1H      ;SEND IT TO PRINTER
        SUB  A         ;SEND STROBE
        OUT  0F3H
        CMA
        OUT  0F3H
        MOV  A,L       ;GET OUTPUT POINTER
        INR  A         ;INCREMENT POINTER
        STA  POINTO    ;SAVE OUTPUT POINTER
        MVI  A,1
        ORA  A         ;SETUP RETURN NOT ZERO
        RET
```

```
*6800 OUTP SUBROUTINE
*
OUTP    LDX  POINTO     LOAD OUTPUT POINTER
        CPX  POINTI     CHECK FOR EMPTY
        BEQ  OUTE       IF EMPTY
        LDAA X          GET DATA
        STAA $E000      SEND DATA TO PRINTER
        LDAA #$F5       SEND STROBE
```

```
28          STA   $E001
29          LDAA  #$FD
30          STA   $E001
31          INC   POINTO+1    INCREMENT OUTPUT POINTER
32          LDAA  #$01        SET RETURN NOT ZERO
33 OUTE     RTS               RETURN FROM SUBROUTINE
```

Likewise after the INPUT routine is called for the first time, the interrupts must be enabled to allow the interrupt structure to operate and transmit the data to the printer.

The TRANS subroutine sends a string of information to the printer through the queue. The string starting point must be placed in the HL pair for the 8085A and the index register for the MC6800 before this subroutine is called. The string must always terminate with a "$". This works somewhat like the print string subroutine in a CP/M based system. *CP/M* is an acronym for control program microprocessor; this system is found in many business computers and is also becoming popular for home and hobby computers. According to some sources, it is the most popular operating system in use today. Figure 8–25 illustrates the flowchart for the transmission subroutine.

```
51 ;8085A TRANS SUBROUTINE
52 ;
53 TRANS: MOV   A,M    ;GET A BYTE OF DATA
54         CPI   '$'    ;CHECK FOR TERMINATION CHARACTER
55         RZ
56         PUSH  H      ;SAVE HL
57         CALL  INPUT  ;SAVE CHARACTER IN QUEUE
58         MVI   A,0EH  ;ENABLE RST5.5
59         SIM
60         EI           ;ENABLE INTERRUPTS
61         POP   H      ;RESTORE HL
62         INX   H      ;POINT TO NEXT DATA BYTE
63         JMP   TRANS  ;DO IT AGAIN!

34 *6800 TRANS SUBROUTINE
35 *
36 TRANS   LDAA  X            GET DATA
37         CMPA  #$24         CHECK FOR A '$'
38         BEQ   TRANE        WHEN FINISHED
39         STX   TEMP         SAVE POINTER
40         JSR   INPUT        SAVE DATA IN QUEUE
41         CLI                ENABLE INTERRUPTS
42         LDX   TEMP         RESTORE POINTER
43         INX                POINT TO NEXT BYTE
44         JMP   TRANS        LOOP UNTIL DONE
45 TRANE   RTS                END SUBROUTINE
```

The INTS subroutine is used whenever the printer interrupts the microprocessor. This subroutine is flowcharted in figure 8–26. INTS causes a transfer of data through the OUTP subroutine described earlier. If the queue

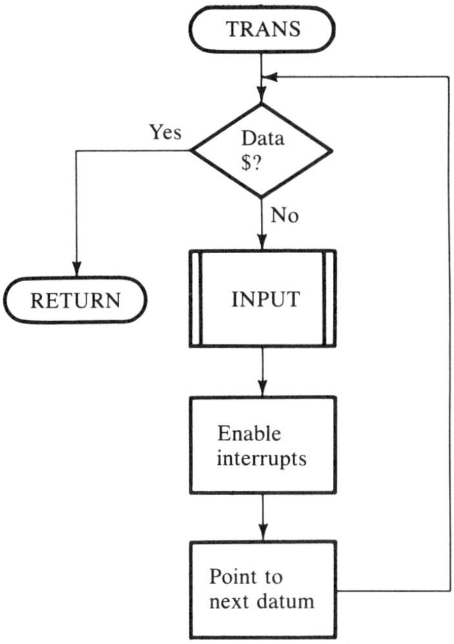

FIGURE 8–25 A flowchart for the TRANS subroutine used to transmit data through the queue to the printer.

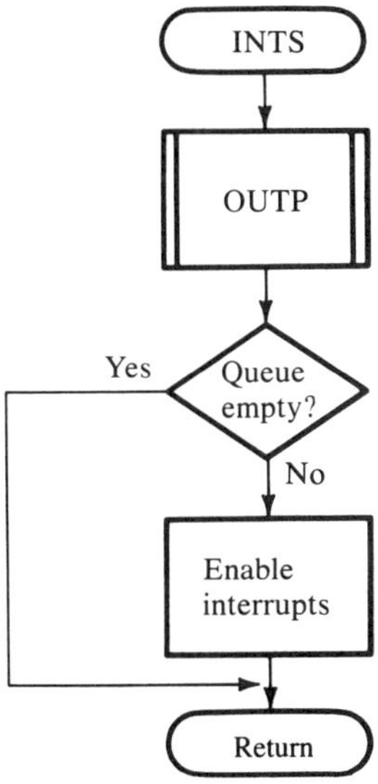

FIGURE 8–26 A flowchart that illustrates the operation of the interrupt service (INTS) subroutine for the queue.

happens to be empty, a return zero from the OUTP subroutine occurs and the interrupt service subroutine is exited through OFF.

```
;8085A INTS SUBROUTINE
;
INTS:   PUSH H
        PUSH PSW
        CALL OUTP  ;SEND CHARACTER TO PRINTER
        JZ   OFF   ;GO TURN IT OFF
        EI         ;ENABLE FUTURE INTERRUPTS
```

```
OFF:    POP   PSW
        POP   H
        RET
```

```
*6800 INTS SUBROUTINE
*
INTS    JSR   OUTP      SEND A CHARACTER TO THE PRINTER
        BEQ   OFF       GO TURN IT OFF
        CLI             ENABLE FUTURE INTERRUPTS
OFF     LDAA  $E000     CLEAR INTERRUPT REQUEST
        RTI             RETURN FROM INTERRUPT
```

As can be perceived through the above software, this application requires a little software overhead; but it is worth it, since the processor continues at full speed at least until the queue fills up. This would give about 4.5 s of additional computing time every time that the printer is accessed; depending upon the application, it can be extremely important.

Summary

This chapter has introduced the interrupt structures of the 8085A, Z80, and MC6800 or MC6809 microprocessors. In a world that requires maximum throughput from its computer systems, interrupts play a very important role.

Interrupts are most useful when interfacing low-speed devices to a microprocessor. In fact, most devices in this world are low-speed devices, when compared to the operating speed of the microprocessor. For this reason, interrupt techniques are used for many applications.

Imagine connecting a printer that can clip along at ten characters per second to a microprocessor without using interrupts. The effective processing power of this sytem would be ten pieces of data per second. With the queue connected, the processing power of the system is increased dramatically.

The only type of I/O device that probably cannot benefit from interrupt processing is a light bulb or a simple on/off sensor.

Glossary

Daisy chain A method of asynchronously coupling and directing a serial signal. In many cases used for directing the interrupt acknowledge signal.

FIFO A first in, first out memory that stores information in this manner.

Interrupt Breaking into a program through the use of an external signal from the hardware, which jumps to an interrupt service subroutine.

Interrupt acknowledge A hardware signal that indicates that an interrupt input has been accepted by the microprocessor.

Interrupt service subroutine A subroutine used by the external hardware to accomplish a task.

Interrupt vector A location or two in the memory or microprocessor that points the way to an interrupt service subroutine.

Maskable interrupt An interrupt input that can be turned off or deactivated.

Nonmaskable interrupt An interrupt input that can never be disabled or turned off.

Polling The act of looking at several interrupt signal lines to determine which are active.

Priority The order in which multiple interrupt inputs are processed.

Programmable interrupt controller A device that is capable of recognizing multiple interrupt inputs and directing the response to these interrupts.

Queue A memory that stores information on a first in, first out basis.

Real time Time as it actually occurs.

Real-time clock A device that keeps track of "real time."

Restart A special 1-byte call instruction in the 8080A, 8085A, and Z80 microprocessors.

Terminal count The state in a modulus counter equal to the modulus. A modulus ten counter's terminal count is a ten.

Questions and Problems

1 What is an interrupt?

2 What is an interrupt service subroutine?

3 Why must interrupts be enabled in the interrupt service subroutine of an 8085A microprocessor?

4 Which special instruction ends an interrupt service subroutine in the MC6809?

5 List three applications in which an interrupt would prove useful.

6 Which three functions are performed by the SIM instruction of the 8085A microprocessor?

7 List what the RIM instruction allows you to determine about the 8085A microprocessor.

8 Which instructions control the maskable interrupt input of the MC6809?

9 Where would a nonmaskable interrupt be useful?

10 Interface a simple push button to a microprocessor as an interrupt input. Develop the software required to allow this button to operate and store zeros in memory locations 1000H through 1FFFH when pressed.

11 For the 8085A develop software that will turn off interrupt input RST 6.5 without affecting the other interrupt inputs.

12 Interface a four key keypad to the microprocessor, using interrupt processing. The system must detect a keystroke; debounce it; and store the data 0,1,2, or 3 into memory location 70H and a zero, to be used as a flag, in memory location 71H.

13 Write the software required to detect a keystroke with the above system.

14 Using programmable timers (as discussed in a previous chapter), cause a periodic interrupt once every second. The interrupt service subroutine should update a binary counter in memory locations 1000H and 1001H to be used as a timer.

15 Write the initialization dialog for an 8259A so that it will refer to an interrupt vector table located at memory location 1000H. This table should contain eight spaces for each vector entry. You are also required to select a rotating priority scheme.

16 Modify the INPUT subroutine in this chapter to function with a 2048-byte queue at locations 1000H through 17FFH.

17 Develop a polled interrupt scheme for the 6800 microprocessor that contains two interrupt inputs. Give these interrupts equal priority in your software.

18 Determine exactly how many bytes per second can be transferred to an I/O device using the 8085A microprocessor. (Refer to chapter 3.)

19 Determine exactly how many bytes per second can be transferred to an I/O device using the 6800 microprocessor. (Refer to chapter 4.)

20 Would an interrupt service subroutine reduce the maximum transfer rate of the microprocessor? Explain your answer.

9 Microprocessor Based Communications

This chapter introduces digital communications from the microprocessor's viewpoint. It doesn't go into lengthy detail on the methods of modulation or the protocols normally associated in the data communications environment. It enables you to make the transition from the purely digital environment to the communications environment.

This chapter develops an understanding of serial and parallel data communications. It then describes some of the many communications interface standards that convey this information to its destination. Many of the more common communications interface standards are explained with a technique or device that will generate the standard form of data communications.

9-1 INTRODUCTION TO DIGITAL COMMUNICATIONS

Serial and parallel data transfer are the two basic methods of communicating digital information between microprocessors and peripheral equipment. Both techniques are in widespread use throughout the industry and each has its advantages and disadvantages.

Serial Data Transfer

Serial data transfer is commonly used whenever digital information must be relayed over a relatively long distance. The data is often transferred through the telephone wires or over the airwaves via some form of radio carrier. The main reason for long-distance serial transfer is the reduction in the number of wires required to carry the information. Unfortunately the speed at which this data can be transferred serially is normally limited to, at present, no more than 4,800 bits per second over commercial voice grade telephone equipment. Leased service is available for rates of 9,600 bits per second. In theory a voice grade channel can carry up to about 20,000 bits per second. Higher speeds are attainable if special digital communications links are leased from the telephone company.

Parallel Data Transfer

Parallel transmission is used for short distances where the speed of information transfer is critical. This form of data communication is found in newer types of computer peripheral equipment with transfer speeds of up to one million characters per second. This equipment includes printers, disk drives, and various other forms of peripheral components.

Asynchronous Serial Data

Serial data is transferred in either the asynchronous or synchronous form. In *asynchronous transmission,* sometimes referred to as *start-stop transmission,* start and stop bit intervals are transmitted with each byte of information for the purpose of synchronization. No clock waveform is transmitted with asynchronous data, since the start and stop bits are used for synchronization.

In *synchronous data transmission,* synchronization is effected by transmitting a synchronization character or two, followed by a large block of data. In addition to the sync characters, a clock waveform must also be transmitted. Therefore, synchronization occurs for a block of data in a synchronous system and for each piece of data in an asynchronous system.

Figure 9–1 illustrates the typical format used for transmitting data asynchronously. Each piece of information is preceded by a start bit that is at a logic zero or, by definition, a *space*. This is followed by data bits that comprise the information that is always transmitted with the least significant bit first. The stop bit, or bits in some older systems, follows the data and is always at the logic one level or, by definition, a *mark*.

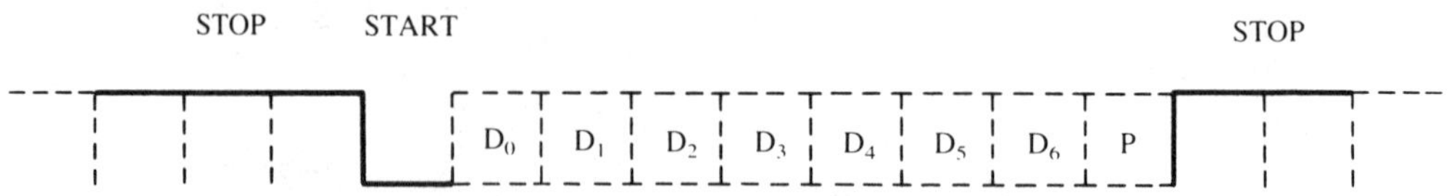

FIGURE 9–1 Asynchronous, or start-stop, serial data.

Baud Rate

The speed at which serial data is transferred is referred to as its *baud rate*. The baud rate is arrived at by taking the reciprocal of the bit time interval for most applications. Refer to the section on PSK (phase shift keying) for a different definition of baud rate as it applies to that form of data. For example, a bit time of 9.09 ms would have a rate of 110 baud, except for PSK. If the serial message consists of a start bit, 8 data bits, and 2 stop bits, a system working at this rate would be capable of transferring 10 bytes of data per second.

Table 9–1 illustrates some commonly used baud rates, along with the number of stop bits and data bits, type of transmission, and the normal application of each rate. Note that all of the baud rates listed are multiples, except 110 baud, which is used for communications between electromechanical teletypewriters (which are quickly disappearing). To my knowledge, the only systems employing 2 stop bits or 1.5 stop bits were designed for mechanical devices. The extra time allowed by additional stops was required for mechanical synchronization in these devices. All other systems use 1 stop bit.

Synchronous Serial Data

In synchronous transmission, data is transmitted with clock pulses, so it is not necessary to send synchronization bits along with the data, as with the asynchronous system. Synchronization can be accomplished by transmitting sync information periodically.

For example, transferring 100 bytes of information by asynchronous methods would take 1000 bit times. This assumes that 1 start and 1 stop bit per byte of data is being transmitted. In a synchronous system that sends 1 sync byte before the start of transmission and an end of message character at the end of transmission, it requires only 816 bit times. If information is transmitted for any extended period of time, synchronous communication is obviously much more efficient.

Since this synchronous communication can take many forms, many computer manufacturers have developed standard communications protocols, such as BISYNC (binary synchronous communications), SDLC (serial data link control), and HDLC (high-level data link control). These types of proto-

TABLE 9–1 Commonly used baud rates.

Baud	Data Bits	Stop Bits	Type	Application
110	5	1.5	Asynchronous	Baudot TTY
110	7 + P*	2	Asynchronous	ASCII TTY
300	7 + P	1	Asynchronous	FSK MODEM
600	7 + P	1	Asynchronous	FSK MODEM
1200	7 + P	1	Asynchronous	FSK MODEM
2400	Variable	–	Synchronous	PSK MODEM
4800	Variable	–	Synchronous	PSK MODEM
9600	Variable	–	Synchronous	PSK MODEM

NOTE: *P = Parity TTY = Teletypewriter
MODEM = MOdulator/DEModulator

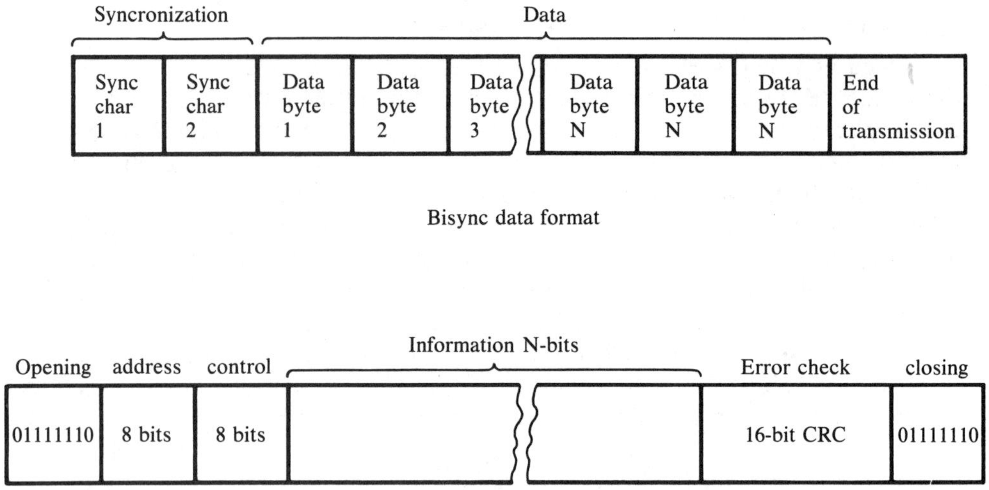

HDLC/SDLC data format

FIGURE 9–2 Two forms of synchronous serial communications protocols.

cols are illustrated in figure 9–2. BISYNC is a byte oriented protocol; SDLC and HDLC are both bit oriented protocols.

9-2 SERIAL COMMUNICATIONS INTERFACE ADAPTERS

There are two basic types of interface adapters for use with serial communications, the universal asynchronous receiver/transmitter (UART) and the universal synchronous receiver/transmitter (USRT). These dev1ces are made by almost all of the integrated circuit manufacturers and are easily interfaced to the microprocessor. Some manufacturers have actually combined the synchronous and asynchronous functions into the same component and coined it a USART, or universal synchronous/asynchronous receiver/transmitter. This book will deal with the two most common microprocessor compatible communications interface adapters, the 8251A from Intel and the MC6850 from Motorola.

Transmission

Data is transmitted from the UART in the serial asynchronous form described in section 9–1. This is accomplished by loading the parallel information into a shift register along with the start, parity, and stop bits. This information is then shifted out of the shift register at the desired baud rate. Figure 9–3 illustrates a simple circuit that transmits 7 data bits along with even parity, 1 start bit, and 1 stop bit.

Reception

Data is received by a UART through a shift register that is clocked at the desired baud rate. The only aspect of its operation that is hard to understand is

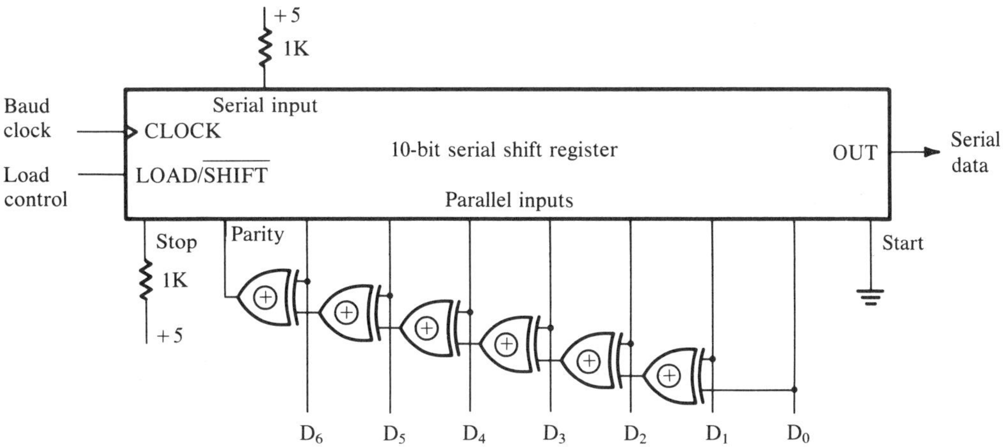

FIGURE 9–3 A circuit that will generate a serial asynchronous message with one stop bit, a parity bit, and a start bit.

that it must determine the correct starting point. This determination is made by searching the incoming data stream for a start bit.

To determine the location of the start bit, this circuit must detect a negative edge. Once a negative edge is found, the circuit takes one more sample of the incoming signal, which is exactly in the middle of the start bit. If the second sample is a logic zero, a start bit has been detected; if not, operation returns to detecting a negative edge. A circuit for detecting this is illustrated in figure 9–4.

Once a valid start is detected, a shift register is clocked at the desired baud rate for eight clock periods. This shifts the 7 data bits and the parity bit into the shift register. The outputs of the shift register now contain the parallel message. After receiving the last stop bit, a signal indicating that data has been received is sent to the computer.

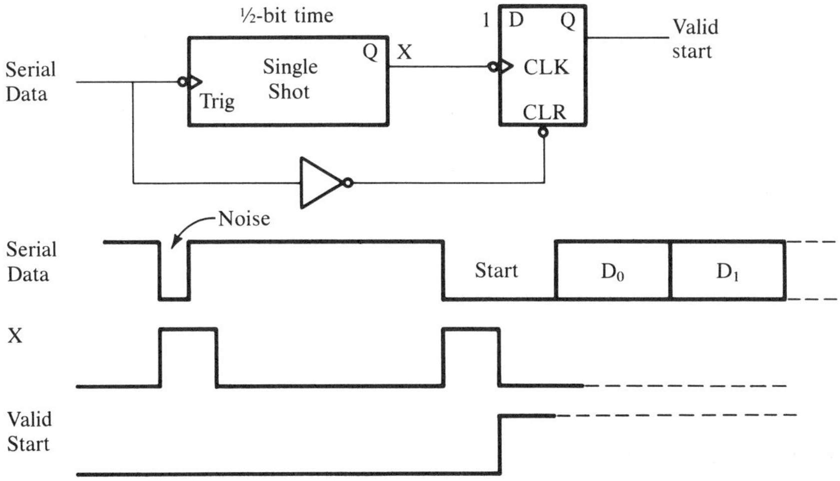

FIGURE 9–4 A logic circuit that will detect a valid start bit.

9-3 THE 8251A COMMUNICATIONS INTERFACE ADAPTER

This device is a combination synchronous/asynchronous receiver/transmitter that is directly compatible with the Intel and Zilog families of microprocessors. Figure 9–5 illustrates the pinout and block diagram of this interface component.

PIN CONFIGURATION

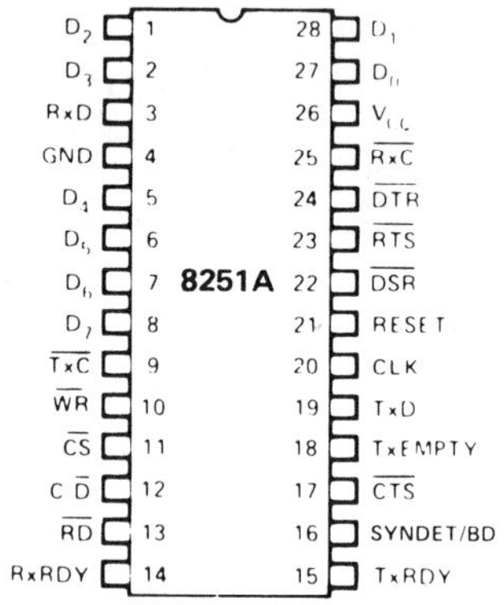

PIN NAMES

D_7/D_0	Data Bus (8 bits)
C/D	Control or Data is to be Written or Read
RD	Read Data Command
WR	Write Data or Control Command
CS	Chip Enable
CLK	Clock Pulse (TTL)
RESET	Reset
TxC	Transmitter Clock
TxD	Transmitter Data
RxC	Receiver Clock
RxD	Receiver Data
RxRDY	Receiver Ready (has character for 8080)
TxRDY	Transmitter Ready (ready for char from 8080)
DSR	Data Set Ready
DTR	Data Terminal Ready
SYNDET/BD	Sync Detect/ Break Detect
RTS	Request to Send Data
CTS	Clear to Send Data
TxE	Trnsmitter Empty
V_{CC}	+5 Volt Supply
GND	Ground

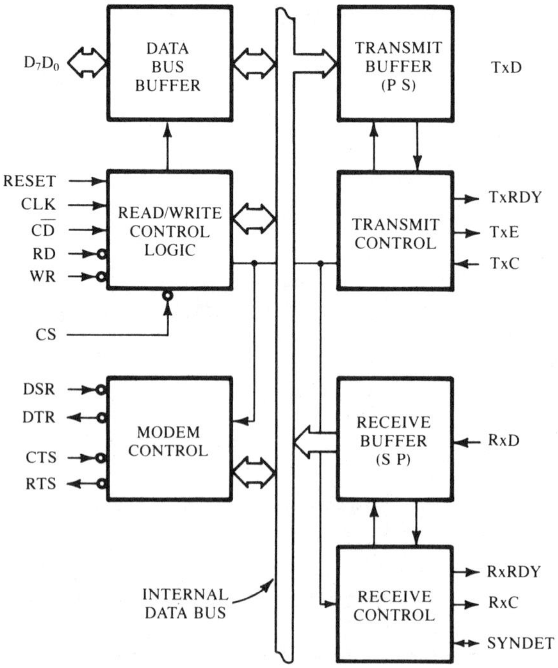

FIGURE 9–5 The pinout and block diagram of the 8251A programmable communications interface adapter.

SOURCE: Reprinted by permission of Intel Corporation, Copyright 1983.

In the asynchronous mode of operation, this device is able to transmit and receive information at baud rates of up to 19,200. This ability makes it usable for just about any application that requires asynchronous serial data. It can also send and detect a break, detect parity, frame and overrun errors, and transmit and receive at different baud rates.

In the synchronous mode of operation, the 8251A can automatically insert one or two sync characters, making it useful for any byte oriented synchronous communications system. It will also transmit and receive data at rates of up to 64,000 baud in this mode. If synchronization is lost, the device automatically enters the hunt mode of operation and searches for the next sync character or character pair to reestablish synchronization.

8251A Hardware Interface

Looking at the block diagram and pinout of the 8251A in figure 9–5, you will notice that the connections have been designed for implementation with an Intel based microprocessor. Figure 9–6 depicts an 8251A interfaced to an 8085A microprocessor so that it functions at I/O port locations D0H and D1H.

The C/$\overline{D}$ connection selects the internal command/status or data register for both the receiver and the transmitter. C/$\overline{D}$ is connected to address connection A8 for the purpose of register selection. Port D0H therefore will specify the data register and port D1H the command/status register.

The $\overline{CS}$ pin is connected to a port decoder that decodes port number D0H and D1H for selecting the 8251A. Once this device is selected and the command/status or data register is specified with C/$\overline{D}$, a $\overline{RD}$ or $\overline{WR}$ signal from the 8085A transfers data to or from the 8251A.

The clock input (CLK) is normally connected to the clock output of the 8085A or any other source that is minimally 30 times the desired baud rate. This input does not determine the baud rate; it is used only for internal timing.

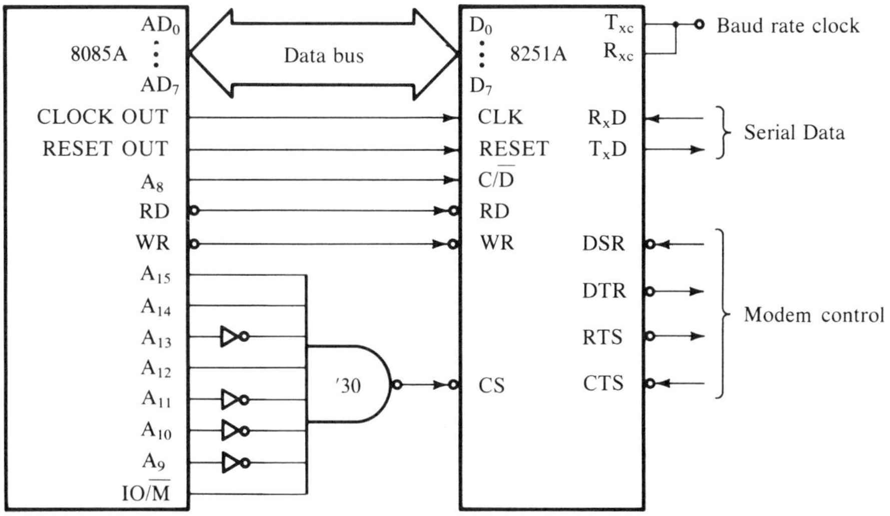

FIGURE 9–6 An 8251A programmable communications interface adapter interfaced to the 8085A.

The baud rate of this device is determined by the $\overline{\text{TxC}}$ input for the transmitter and the $\overline{\text{RxC}}$ input for the receiver. The hardware designer has the option of using a 1X, 16X, or 64X multiplier for this input. In other words, a 19,200-Hz clock can generate 19,200 baud at 1X, 1200 baud at 16X, or 300 baud at 64X.

The $\overline{\text{DSR}}$, $\overline{\text{DTR}}$, $\overline{\text{RTS}}$, and $\overline{\text{CTS}}$ pins are discussed in the section on MODEMS, since these are modem control pins. If no modem is to be used with the 8251A, these pins can be used as simple input and output bits.

8251A Initialization

When power is first applied or the 8251A is RESET, it expects to receive a mode instruction word through the command register. The mode instruction word specifies how the 8251A is to react to future commands and data transfers. Table 9–2 pictures the mode instruction word format for asynchronous operation. Bit positions B2 and B1 select the clock rate multiplier discussed previously. L2 and L1 program the 8251A to transmit and receive either 5, 6, 7, or 8 data bits. Position PEN enables the internal parity generation and detection circuitry, and EP selects even or odd parity if PEN is active. Bits S2 and S1 select the number of stop bits to be used by the USART; this is normally 1 but may be 1.5 for Baudot code or 2 for ASCII coded teletypewriter communications.

TABLE 9–2 Mode instruction word format.

7	6	5	4	3	2	1	0
S2	S1	EP	PEN	L2	L1	B2	B1

Binary Code	S2, S1 Stop Bits	L2, L1 Data Bits	B2, B1 Baud Rate
0 0	–	5	–
0 1	1	6	1X
1 0	1.5	7	16X
1 1	2	8	64X

The short sequence of instructions that follow will program the 8251A to function at a baud rate multiplier of 16X, a character length of 8 bits with odd parity, and 1 stop bit.

```
SETUP: MVI  A,01011110B   ;SETUP THE 8251A
       OUT  0D1H
       MVI  A,00010101B   ;ENABLE RECEIVER AND
       OUT  0D1H          ;TRANSMITTER
```

Once this device is initialized with the mode instruction word, it will not accept another until it is reset by the hardware or the software. In this example, the next time the command register is written into it, it is to control the 8251A, not to initialize it.

Command/Status Register

The command register bit format is pictured in table 9–3; it is used to command the 8251A after initialization. Note that this format is used for both asynchronous and synchronous operation. To transmit and receive information, both the TxEN and RxE bits must be made active and sent out to the command register (see the previous initialization dialog). The other bits are active or inactive, depending upon the utilization requirements of this device.

TABLE 9–3 8251A command register.

7	6	5	4	3	2	1	0
EH	**IR**	**RTS**	**ERN**	**SBRK**	**RxE**	**DTR**	**TxEN**

Bit Name	Function
EH	Enter hunt mode (synchronous operation)
IR	Internal reset
RTS	Written to the $\overline{\text{RTS}}$ pin (inverted)
ER	Resets parity, overrun, and framing errors
SBRK	Send a break character (asynchronous operation)
RxE	Enables the receiver
DTR	Written to the $\overline{\text{DTR}}$ pin (inverted)
TxEN	Enables the transmitter

Table 9–4 pictures the status register bit pattern of the 8251A. This register is read through the command/status register port number, and it indicates the condition of the 8251A. Notice that three types of errors are detected by this integrated circuit. (In practice, these error flags must be reset through the software reset bit of the command register before the reception software can safely continue.)

TABLE 9–4 8251A status register.

7	6	5	4	3	2	1	0
DSR	**SYNDET**	**FE**	**OE**	**PE**	**TxE**	**RxRDY**	**TxRDY**

Bit Name	Function
DSR	Reads the $\overline{\text{DSR}}$ pins (inverted)
SYNDET	SYNC character detection (synchronous operation)
FE	Framing error
OE	Overrun error
PE	Parity error
TxE	Transmitter empty
RxRDY	Receiver ready
TxRDY	Transmitter ready

FE a framing error should not occur under normal operation since it indicates that the received data is missing a stop bit or has an incorrect number of stop bits. This error normally occurs if the data is being received at the wrong baud rate or if the receiver or transmitter frequencies are out of tolerance.

OE an overrun error occurs if the data is not removed from the internal data holding register before the next complete piece of information is received. Again under normal operation this error should not occur. If it does, there is most likely a mistake in the software.

PE a parity error occurs if the received data is determined to contain incorrect parity. This occurs occasionally because of noise on the transmission line; it is the programmer's responsibility, through the software, to indicate an error or somehow plead for a retransmission of the erroneous byte of data.

Data Transfer Software

The data transfer software for this device is extremely simple to write, as illustrated below:

```
5    ;SUBROUTINE TO SEND THE CHARACTER INDEXED BY
6    ;THE HL PAIR.
7    ;ACC AND F ARE DESTROYED
8    ;
9    SEND: IN    0D1H      ;GET STATUS
10          RRC             ;TxRDY INTO CARRY
11          JNC   SEND      ;IF NOT READY
12          MOV   A,M       ;GET DATA
13          OUT   0D0H      ;SEND DATA
14          RET
```

In the SEND subroutine, the TxRDY bit is tested until it indicates that the transmitter is ready to receive another byte of information for transmission. The TxEMPTY bit is not used because it indicates that all bits of data have been completely transmitted. The TxRDY bit indicates that a byte is currently being transmitted and that the internal data holding register is ready for the next byte. This transmitter is buffered so that it can transmit 1 byte while holding a second byte for the transmitter. This increases the throughput of the system slightly by reducing the time required to poll the USART for the first and second transmitted pieces of information.

```
15   ;THIS SUBROUTINE RECEIVES A BYTE OF INFORMATION
16   ;AND STORES IT IN THE LOCATION INDEXED BY HL.
17   ;ACC AND F ARE DESTROYED
18   ;
19   GET:  IN    0D1H      ;GET STATUS
20          ANI   2         ;ISOLATE RxRDY
21          JZ    GET       ;IF NOT READY
22          IN    0D1H      ;GET STATUS
23          ANI   38H       ;CHECK ERRORS
24          JNZ   ERROR     ;IF ERROR
```

```
        IN    ODOH       ;GET DATA
        MOV   M,A        ;STORE DATA
        RET
```

The GET subroutine tests the RxRDY bit to determine whether or not the USART has received a piece of data. If data has not been received, the RxRDY bit is a logic zero, causing the subroutine to loop back to GET. If data is available, RxRDY is a logic one, causing the subroutine to test for error conditions. If an error occurs, a branch is made to a user-defined error handling routine. In many cases, ERROR places a question mark in the location indicated by the HL pair or asks for a retransmission. If no error has occurred, the data is read from the USART and stored in the location indexed by the HL pair.

Interrupts with the 8251A

To use interrupts, the previously described software can be disregarded in favor of hardware connections to the 8085A (as illustrated in figure 9–7). For a transmitter interrupt, the TxRDY pin is connected to RST 5.5; the RxRDY pin is connected to the RST6.5 pin for a receiver interrupt. Interrupt service subroutines are called each time that the transmitter is ready for another byte of information and each time that the receiver contains a byte of information for the computer.

Synchronous Operation

With synchronous operation, the mode instruction word format changes to the one depicted in table 9–5. Here the right two bit positions must both be at the logic zero level to specify synchronous operation. L2 and L1 still specify the number of bits to be transmitted per character, and PEN and EP still control the parity. ESD and SCS are unique to synchronous operation and determine whether sync detect (SD) is an input or an output pin and also whether there is to be a single or double sync character. Once this word is

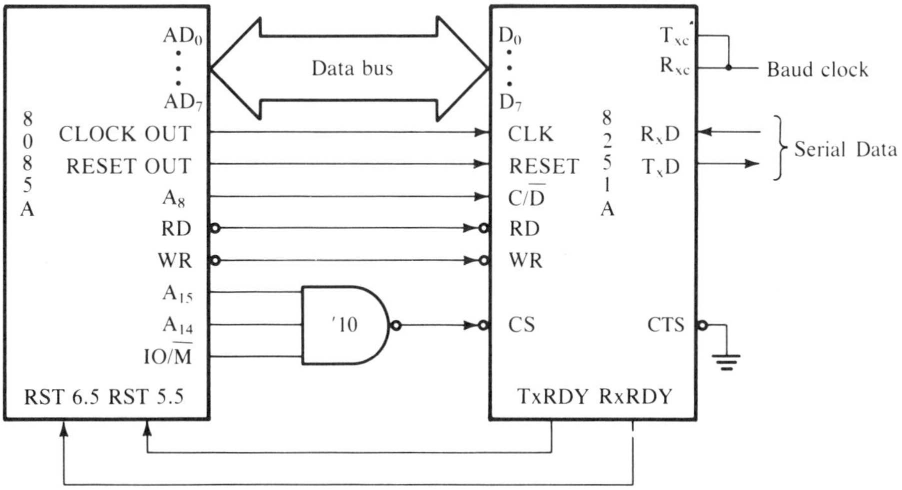

FIGURE 9–7 The 8251A programmable communications interface adapter connected to an 8085A as an interrupt processed I/O device.

sent to the 8251A, it must be immediately followed by the one or two sync characters to be used for synchronization. In other words, this initialization procedure is 1–2 bytes longer than for asynchronous operation.

TABLE 9–5 Synchronous mode instruction format.

7	6	5	4	3	2	1	0
SCS	ESD	EP	PEN	L2	L1	0	0

Bit Name	Function
SCS	Single character SYNC operation
ESD	External SYNC detect (0 = output 1 = input)
EP	Even parity
PEN	Parity enable
L2, L1	Refer to table 9–2 for the bit pattern

The clock inputs for both the receiver and transmitter have no multiplier for synchronous operation: the multiplier is always 1X. Also, it should be noted that synchronous communication is allowed to proceed at a maximum baud rate of 64K.

Synchronous Transmission

In synchronous transmission the one or two sync characters are sent out to the USART using the SEND subroutine listed earlier in the text. This device will only automatically send sync characters at the end of transmitting a block of information; it is up to the user to send them prior to the transmission. The number of bytes sent between sync characters depends upon the type of protocol selected for the system.

Synchronous Reception

To achieve synchronization, an enter hunt command is issued to the 8251A prior to the reception of any information. Once synchronization is achieved, data may then be received in the normal fashion.

```
;SYNCHRONOUS INITIALIZATION DIALOG
SETUP: MVI   A,00011100B   ;SETUP MODE INSTRUCTION
       OUT   0D1H
       MVI   A,SYNC1       ;SETUP SYNC1
       OUT   0D1H
       MVI   A,SYNC2       ;SETUP SYNC2
       OUT   0D1H
       MVI   A,00010101B   ;ENABLE TRANSMITTER
       OUT   0D1H          ;AND RECEIVER
```

A subroutine for asynchronous reception first commands the 8251A to enter the hunt mode to search for the sync characters. Once the sync characters are detected, the subroutine then receives data in the same fashion as in the GET subroutine.

```
;SYNCHRONOUS RECEPTION SUBROUTINE
;RECEIVES A BLOCK OF DATA AND STORES IT BEGINNING
;AT THE LOCATION INDEXED BY HL.
;ACC AND F ARE DESTROYED
;
GETS:   MVI  A,10010101B     ;ENTER HUNT MODE
        OUT  0D1H
GETS1:  IN   0D1H            ;GET STATUS
        ANI  40H             ;ISOLATE SYNDET
        JZ   GETS1           ;IF NOT IN SYNC
GETS2:  IN   0D1H            ;GET STATUS
        ANI  2               ;ISOLATE RxRDY
        JZ   GETS2           ;IF NOT READY
        IN   0D1H            ;CHECK ERROR
        ANI  38H
        JNZ  ERROR
        IN   0D0H            ;GET DATA
        MOV  M,A             ;SAVE DATA
        INX  H
        CPI  EOT             ;CHECK FOR END OF
        JNZ  GETS1           ;NOT END OF TEXT
        RET
```

THE MC6850 COMMUNICATIONS INTERFACE ADAPTER 9-4

The Motorola MC6850 asynchronous communications interface adapter (ACIA), unlike the Intel 8251A, is meant to be used for asynchronous data only. This of course presents no drawback to asynchronous communication.

The MC6850 Pinout and Basic Description

Figure 9–8 illustrates the pinout and block diagram of the ACIA. This device is capable of transmitting and receiving serial data at baud rates of up to 19,200. It is directly compatible with just about any microprocessor that is currently being manufactured but was specifically designed for use with the MC6800 or MC6809 microprocessors.

The clock inputs, R_x and T_x, control the baud rates of the receiver and transmitter sections and are usually tied together. The ACIA, like the 8251A, is programmable, since its baud rate is selectable to some extent by the software. Pin RS, the register selection pin, is used in the same manner as the $C/\overline{D}$ pin on the 8251A, except that the logic levels for selection are inverted. A logic zero selects the control/status register, and a logic one selects the data register.

Modem control is accomplished through the $\overline{RTS}$, $\overline{CTS}$, and $\overline{DCD}$ pins of the ACIA. Although these connections do not completely conform to standard modem control inputs, they can easily be used for this purpose. Modem control will be discussed in the section on modems.

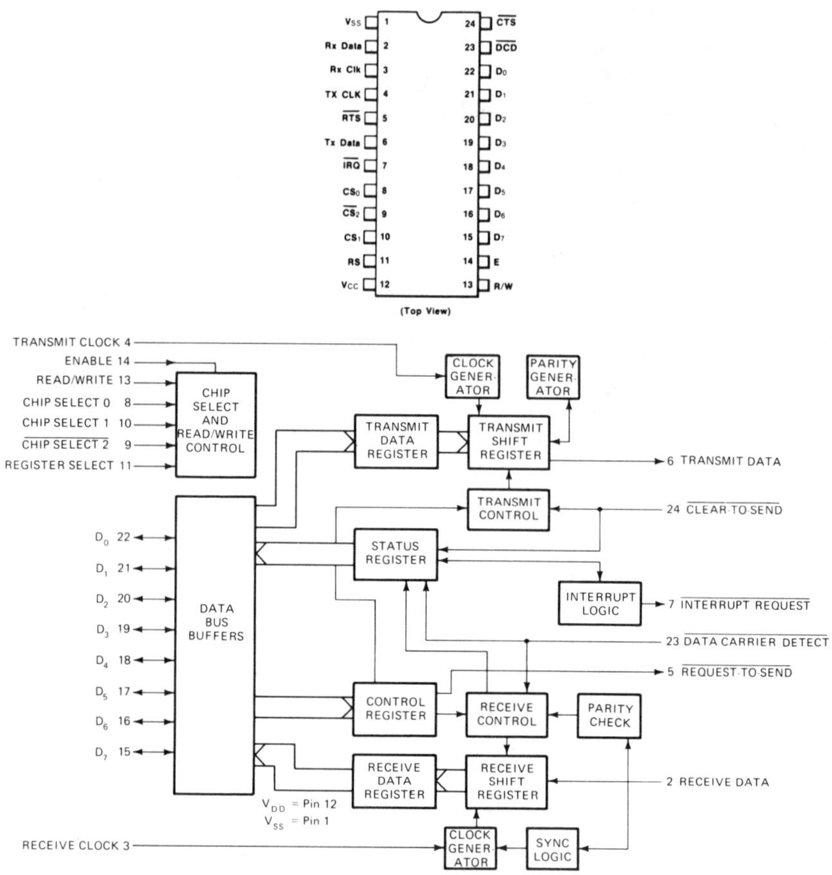

FIGURE 9–8 The MC6850 ACIA pinout and block diagram.
SOURCE: Courtesy of Motorola, Inc.

Programming the ACIA

Programming is accomplished by sending an 8-bit number out to the ACIA control register. Table 9–6 illustrates the bit pattern required for this control register.

Bit positions CR0 and CR1 select the appropriate baud rate multiplier and can also reset the device. For example, if the input clock frequency is 19,200 Hz, divide by 1 would cause operation at 19,200 baud; divide by 16 would cause operation at 1200 baud; and divide by 64 would cause operation at 300 baud. The ACIA is reset to clear any error indications in the status register. These error indicators are discussed in a later section.

Bits CR2, CR3, and CR4 determine the format of the character that will be transmitted and received by the ACIA. For example, if all 3 bits are programmed as zeros, 7 data bits with even parity and 2 stop bits are transmitted and received.

CR5 and CR6 control the transmitter interrupt and the $\overline{\text{RTS}}$ pin and determine whether or not a break character is transmitted. A *break* is, by definition, a space that is transmitted for at least two consecutive character times.

TABLE 9–6 The 6850 ACIA control register.

Control Register

CR7	CR6	CR5	CR4	CR3	CR2	CR1	CR0

CR1	CR0	Function
0	0	÷ 1
0	1	÷ 16
1	0	÷ 64
1	1	Reset

CR4	CR3	CR2	Function
0	0	0	7 bits, even parity, and 2 stops
0	0	1	7 bits, odd parity, and 2 stops
0	1	0	7 bits, even parity, and 1 stop
0	1	1	7 bits, odd parity, and 1 stop
1	0	0	8 bits, no parity, and 2 stops
1	0	1	8 bits, no parity, and 1 stop
1	1	0	8 bits, even parity, and 1 stop
1	1	1	8 bits, odd parity, and 1 stop

CR6	CR5	Function
0	0	$\overline{RTS}$ = 0, Transmit interrupt disabled
0	1	$\overline{RTS}$ = 0, Transmit interrupt enabled
1	0	$\overline{RTS}$ = 1, Transmit interrupt disabled
1	1	$\overline{RTS}$ = 1, Transmit interrupt disabled and transmits a break on transmit data output.

CR7 or RIE enables the $\overline{IRQ}$ pin for the receiver section of the ACIA. An interrupt occurs for a received byte of data, an overrun error, or a positive transition on the $\overline{DCD}$ pin connection.

ACIA Status

The status register, as illustrated in table 9–7, is read by selecting the device and placing a logic zero on the RS pin. This register indicates error conditions, the condition of some of the modem control pins, and the general operating condition of the ACIA.

RDRF indicates that data is available for the microprocessor, which must remove it before the next character is received. If not, the OVRN bit will become active, indicating an overrun error. Other errors detected by the receiver are framing error (FE) and parity error (PE). The framing error indicates that a character is received with an incorrect number of stop bits, and PE indicates that the received data contains the wrong parity.

The $\overline{IRQ}$ status bit indicates that the input buffer is full, there is an overrun error, or there is a positive transition on the $\overline{DCD}$ pin. If the external interrupt pin is connected to the microprocessor's interrupt input, the software checks the status word to determine the cause of the interrupt request.

The remaining bit positions indicate the external conditions of the $\overline{DCD}$ and $\overline{CTS}$ modem control input pins.

TABLE 9–7 ACIA status register.

7	6	5	4	3	2	1	0
IRQ	PE	RO	FE	$\overline{\text{CTS}}$	DCD	TDRE	RDRF

Pin Name	Function
IRQ	Interrupt request
PE	Parity error
RO	Overrun error
FE	Framing error
$\overline{\text{CTS}}$	$\overline{\text{CTS}}$ pin
$\overline{\text{DCD}}$	$\overline{\text{DCD}}$ pin
TDRE	Transmitter empty
RDRF	Receiver full

The MC6850 Hardware Interface

Figure 9–9 pictures the MC6850 ACIA connected to an MC6800 microprocessor. The ACIA is located at I/O locations $E0X0 and $E0X1, as decoded by the page decoder.

For this example, the interrupt input is connected from the MC6850 to the MC6800 to demonstrate an interrupt processing subroutine. The remaining pin connections to the MC6850 are fairly straightforward and will not be discussed here.

ACIA Software Example

In this example the clock input to the ACIA is generated by an external source at a frequency of 4800 Hz. The desired baud rate is 300, so the initialization dialog must set the internal divider to 16 to obtain this baud

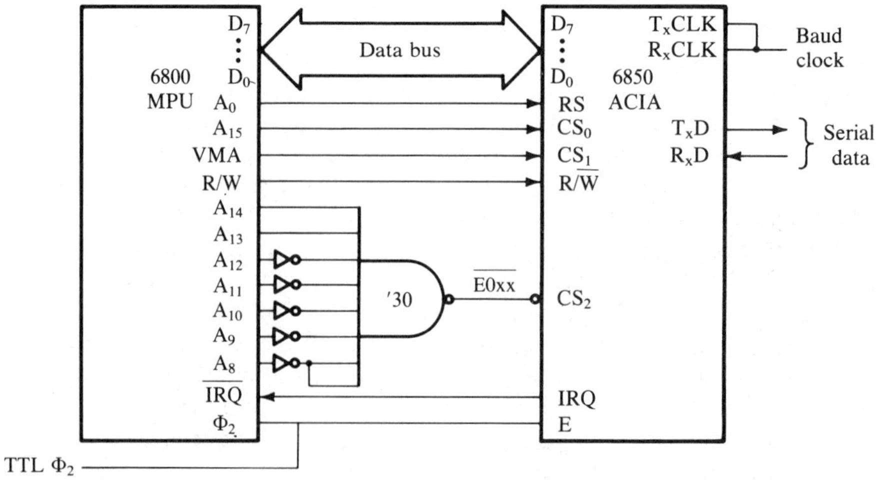

FIGURE 9–9 The Motorola MC6850 ACIA interfaced to the MC6800 microprocessor.

rate. It is also desired that the ACIA send and receive 7 data bits with even parity and 2 stop bits.

```
*INITIALIZATION DIALOG
*
START   LDAA   #3      RESET THE ACIA
        STAA   $E000
        LDAA   #$A1    SETUP ACIA
        STAA   $E000
          .
          .
          .
```

The Interrupt Service Subroutine

The interrupt service subroutine must determine whether the receiver or the transmitter caused the interrupt. It must also determine if the interrupt is caused by an error and, if so, take the appropriate action.

This interrupt service subroutine stores received data at location $D000 and a logic 0 at location $D001. The zero at $D001 is a flag to the system software indicating that a byte of data has been received. The data that is stored at memory location $D002 is transmitted by the interrupt service subroutine, and a zero is placed at location $D003 as a flag.

```
*INTERRUPT SERVICE SUBROUTINE FOR THE ACIA
*
INTER   LDAA   $E000    GET STATUS
        BMI    RECV     IF RECEIVER INTERRUPT
        LDAA   $D002    GET DATA
        STAA   $E001    SEND DATA
        CLR    $D003    CLEAR FLAG
        RTI
RECV    BITA   #$70     TEST ERROR BITS
        BNE    ERR      IF AN ERROR
        LDAA   $E001    GET DATA
        STAA   $D000    SAVE DATA
        CLR    $D001    CLEAR FLAG
        RTI
```

Location ERR in the interrupt service subroutine determines which type of error has occurred and takes corrective action, depending upon the system using the ACIA. The only procedure that occurs in all forms of error handling subroutines is a reset to clear the error flags.

9-5 The RS-232C INTERFACE STANDARD

The EIA RS-232C interface standard is almost universally used for the interconnection of terminal equipment that receives or transmits serial asynchronous data. This standard specifies the pin connections and connector to be employed in this type of application and also the logic levels and protocol used.

Logic Levels

The standard specifies that the logic one level must be no less than −3.0 V and no greater than −25 V; the logic zero level must be no less than +3.0 V and no greater than +25 V. Note that this is negative logic. In addition to voltage levels, the standard specifies that the receiver and transmitter be able to sustain a short circuit to any of these levels for an indefinite period of time. In other words, this particular standard is largely immune to operator abuse.

Since no logic level rides on a zero volt potential, this system is also fairly immune to ground loop problems that often arise in interconnecting terminal equipment. Ground loop currents often flow, causing noise on the ground connection that affects the normal zero volt logic zero level.

Line Characteristics

The transmission line type normally employed is a twisted pair of shielded wire with a line capacitance of no more than 1200 pF and no less than 300 pF. In practice a 300-pF or 330-pF capacitor is often added to the terminal equipment's transmit pin to ensure that the lower capacitance limit is met.

The standard also specifies that the line length be limited to 50 meters if the user expects to receive the same information that was transmitted. If longer line lengths are needed, EIA has other standards that allow line lengths of up to 7 miles.

Connectors

Figure 9–10 depicts the connector specified by EIA for this interface standard. Also listed are the pin definitions for each of the 25 pin connections. In

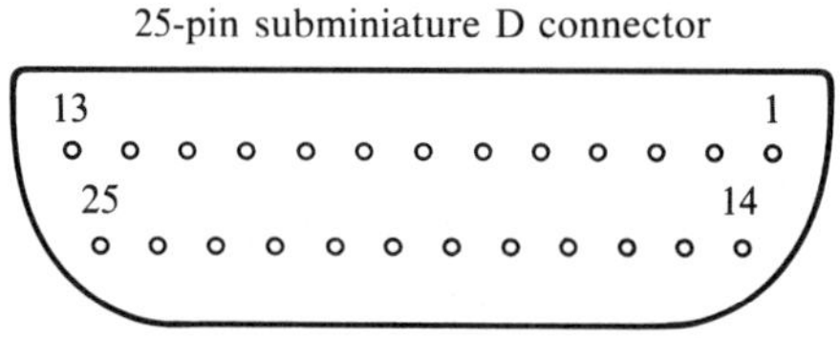

1 – Protective ground	2 – Transmit data
3 – Receive data	4 – RTS
5 – CTS	6 – DSR
7 – Signal ground	8 – Received line signal detector
9 – Test	10 – Test
11 – No assignment	12 – Secondary received line signal detector
13 – Secondary CTS	14 – Secondary transmit data
15 – Transmit signal timing	16 – Secondary received data
17 – Receiver signal timing	18 – No assignment
19 – Secondary RTS	20 – DTR
21 – Signal quality detector	22 – Ring indicator
23 – Data signal rate select	24 – Transmit signal timing
25 – No assignment	

FIGURE 9–10 The EIA RS-232C interface standard connector and pin assignments.

many cases pins 1, 2, 3, and 7 are the only pins that are interconnected between the terminal equipment and computer or modem. Pin 1 is a protective ground that connects the chassis of the equipment together for safety's sake.

In practice, when connecting CRT terminals to computer systems, pins 2 and 3 are twisted in the cable so that transmit is connected to receive. When printers and modems are connected with this standard, the transmit pin (pin 2) is connected on both ends, transmit to transmit. It is best to check the interface wiring diagram before connecting a piece of equipment using this standard.

Drivers and Receivers

Figure 9–11(a) illustrates the typical line driver and figure 9–11(b) the typical line receiver. These devices convert from standard TTL logic levels to RS-232C levels or RS-232C to TTL. Both are 4-channel devices that typically send and receive plus and minus 12-V signals. In some applications, to reduce the cost of power supply, +5 V and −12 V are used. In both cases the noise immunity is the difference between the power supply voltage and the 3-V minimum level set by EIA.

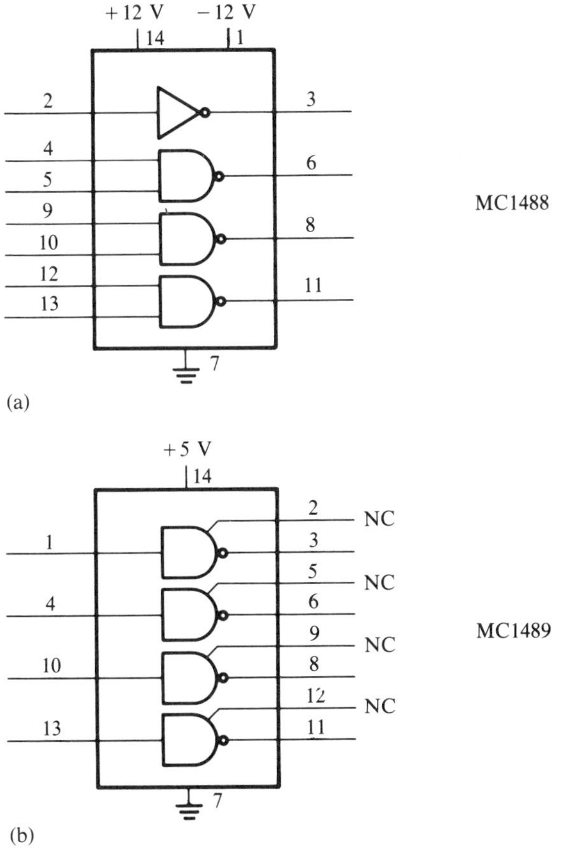

FIGURE 9–11 RS-232C receiver and transmitter: (a) the MC1488 TTL to RS-232C line driver, (b) the MC1489 RS-232C to TTL line receiver.
SOURCE: Courtesy of Motorola, Inc.

If required, the standard input voltage thresholds may be modified by connecting a resistor between the control pin, illustrated in figure 9–11(b), and ground; or between the control pin and one of the power supplies. In most cases this pin is left disconnected to provide the standard plus and minus 3 V thresholds.

9-6 CURRENT LOOPS

Current loops find their application with electromechanical devices such as teletypewriters. The most common form of current loop is the 20-mA current loop; a 60-mA loop is also used by some manufacturers of terminal equipment.

Cable length with a current loop is limited to approximately 2000–3000 feet. This limit is mainly due to IR losses in the cable. Data transmission rates are also limited to no more than 150 baud.

Two types of loops find widespread application: one causes current to flow for a mark and no current for a space and is called a *neutral system*. The other allows current to flow in opposite directions for the space and mark and is called a *polar system*.

Figure 9–12 illustrates both the transmitter and receiver for a 20-mA neutral system: 20 mA of current flows for a mark and no current flows for a space. These circuits translate from TTL voltage levels to current loop levels. This circuitry may not be found in electromechanical applications. In its place a driver may be only a resistor and a series contact, while the receiver may be a solenoid coil.

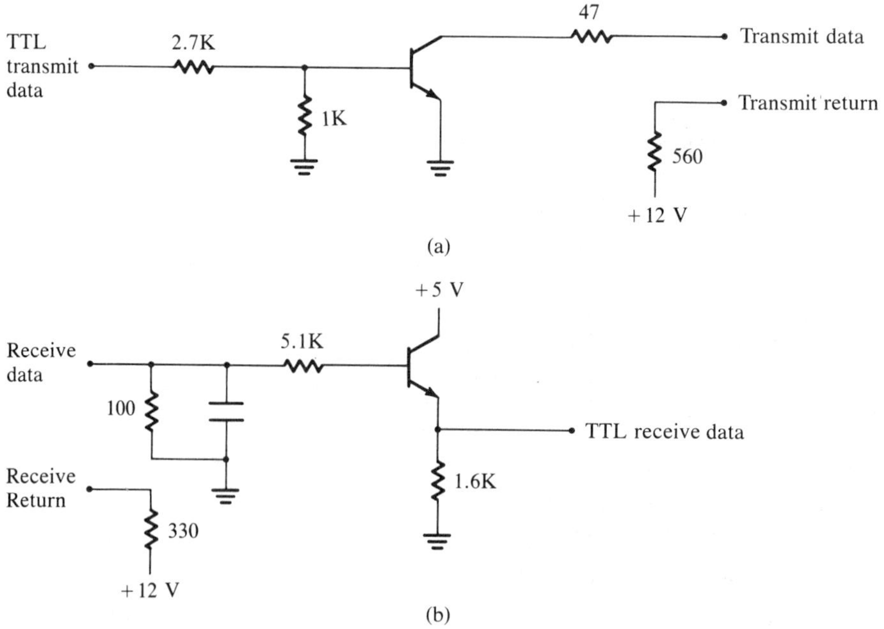

FIGURE 9–12 Two 20 mA current loop translators: (a) a TTL to 20 mA current loop translator, (b) a 20 mA current loop to TTL translator.

This system of serial communications is not very common, mainly because of the low operating speed due to the electromechanical devices that are normally attached to it.

DATA TRANSMISSION METHODS 9-7

There are two basic modulation methods employed in data communications: frequency shift keying (FSK) and phase shift keying (PSK). FSK is used in low-cost, low-speed applications; PSK is used in high-speed data communications. PSK is more efficient but it costs quite a bit more to generate and detect. Figure 9–13 illustrates the waveforms that are obtained from both types of transmissions.

FSK Generation

FSK is extremely easy to generate digitally by microprocessor. All the microprocessor has to do is generate one frequency for a mark and a second frequency for a space by switching two external frequencies or by developing software to generate the two frequencies.

There are two bands of common frequencies in use for FSK digital communications. The low band uses 1070 Hz for a space and 1270 Hz for a mark. The high band uses 2025 Hz for a space and 2225 Hz for a mark. These two bands allow simultaneous two way or full duplex communications over the same pair of wires. FSK is typically used in data communications schemes where the data transmission rate is 300 baud or less. On occasion this technique is employed for simplex, or one way only, communications at baud rates of up to 1200.

Figure 9–14 illustrates a simple system for generating FSK by using a multiplexer. When a logic one is applied to the control input, a 2225-Hz tone is presented at the output; when a logic zero is applied, a 2025-Hz tone appears. In practice this output must be converted to a sine wave for transmission.

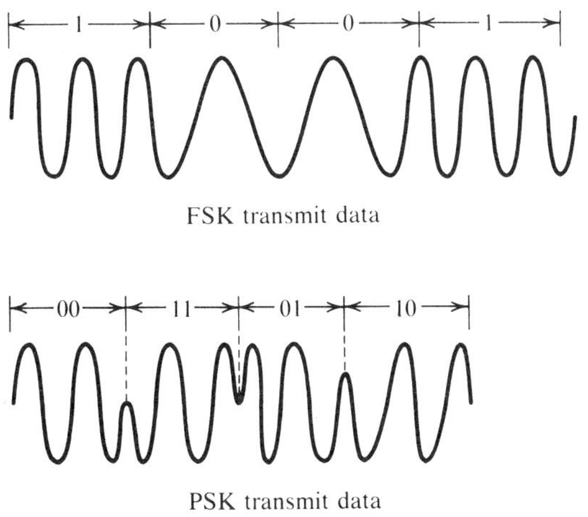

FIGURE 9–13 Frequency shift keying (FSK) and phase shift keying (PSK) data formats.

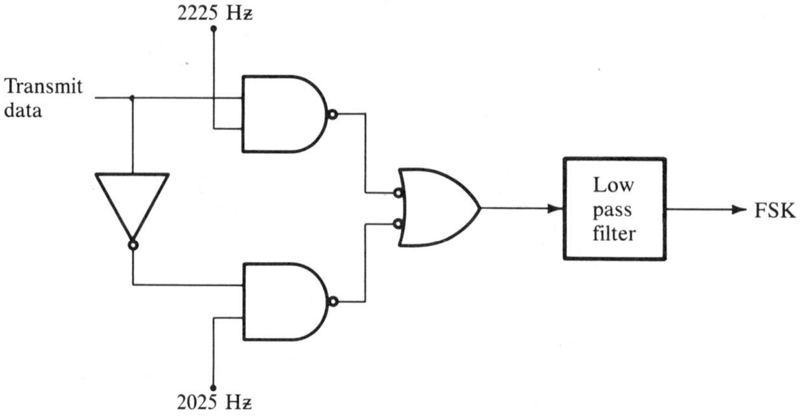

FIGURE 9–14 A circuit that can be used to generate FSK serial data.

FSK Detection

FSK detection is usually accomplished with a phase locked loop or a similar device, such as a tone decoder. Figure 9–15 illustrates a tone decoding phase locked loop that can demodulate the incoming FSK signal to produce a TTL compatible signal. This signal is sampled by the microprocessor to develop an intelligent data word. The phase locked loop is allowed to free run halfway between the logic zero and logic one frequency. The internal phase detector's output can then provide a digital wave corresponding to the two different input frequencies.

PSK

PSK is more commonly used for commercial digital communications because of the speed at which this type of communication can be carried out. In a PSK system 2 bits (a DIBIT) or 3 bits (a TRIBIT) are encoded in the phase angle of the transmitted signal. In other words, during one bit period, it is possible to send either 2 bits or 3 bits of information. This effectively doubles or triples the baud rate. Remember that the baud rate indicates the number of pieces of data transmitted per second, not the frequency of the transmitted signal. In this case the bit rate and the baud rate are different.

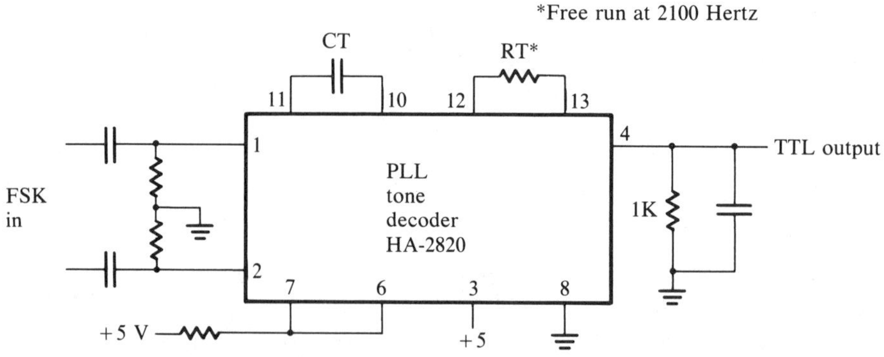

FIGURE 9–15 An FSK detector using a phase locked loop tone decoder.

In a DIBIT system, four phase angles, 0, 90, 180, and 270 degrees, can be transmitted: 0 degrees can represent a 00, 90 degrees a 01, 180 degrees a 10, and 270 degrees an 11. In the TRIBIT system 45, 135, 225, and 315 degrees are used, in addition to the previous phase angles, to allow 3 bits to be encoded at one time.

At the receiver the clock signal that is transmitted along with the data is compared to the data to reveal the phase angle. This phase angle reconstructs the original DIBIT or TRIBIT of data.

Using this type of modulation it is possible to communicate over standard telephone lines at rates of up to 3600 baud. Rates of 9600 baud are obtainable if specially compensated telephone lines are leased from the telephone company.

MODEMS 9-8

A *modem* is a device that translates synchronous or asynchronous digital data stream into an FSK or a PSK signal for use on telephone lines or other media. It will also, in most cases, simultaneously receive data in FSK form or PSK form and convert it back into synchronous or an asynchronous data stream. The word *MODEM* itself is an acronym for MOdulator/DEModulator.

Typical Modem Connection

Modems are normally connected to a computer or terminal equipment through an RS-232C interface connection. The Type D asynchronous modem interface, as specified by EIA, is the most common and easiest to understand and will be discussed for this reason. Figure 9–16 illustrates a typical interface between an asynchronous modem and a computer system.

Pin Functions

Pin 1 Protective ground must be connected from the frames of both the modem and the computer to earth ground.

FIGURE 9–16 A typical modem to computer interconnection diagram.

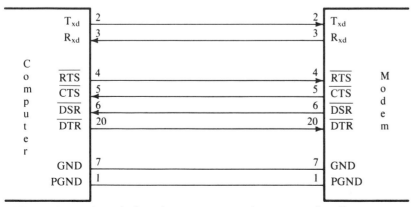

Pin 2 The transmit data pin is an output from the computer or terminal that supplies data for the modem. This pin is an input pin on the modem labeled *transmit*.

Pin 3 The receive data connection presents data to the computer from the modem and is an output pin at the modem.

Pin 4 The $\overline{\text{RTS}}$, or request to send, connection is an input to the modem that must be at the logic zero state to enable the modem to transmit data.

Pin 5 Clear to send, or $\overline{\text{CTS}}$, is a signal from the modem that indicates its transmitter's condition. A logic zero indicates that the modem is ready to transmit.

Pin 6 $\overline{\text{DSR}}$, or data set ready, indicates that the modem is connected to a communications channel and ready to transmit or receive data when a logic zero is present.

Pin 7 Signal ground.

Pin 17 The receiver signal element connection, which is not shown in figure 9–16, is used in synchronous communications to time or clock the reception of data. The one to zero transition on this output pin indicates the center of a bit of information at pin 3.

Pin 20 Data terminal ready, or $\overline{\text{DTR}}$, is an input to the modem that causes it either to connect or disconnect itself from the communications channel. If a logic zero, communication is allowed to proceed; if a logic one, the modem disconnects.

Pin 22 The ring indicator, which is not depicted in figure 9–16, indicates that the modem is receiving a ring signal. This enables automatic answering circuitry present in some modems' interfaces.

Pin 24 The transmitter signal element, which is not shown in figure 9–16, is provided to the modem for synchronous data communications. The one to zero transition must coincide with the center of the transmitted data bit applied to pin 2.

The Modem Handshake

Modem control software has to test the condition of the $\overline{\text{CTS}}$ and $\overline{\text{DSR}}$ signals before transmitting information to the modem. The modem also has to be conditioned by the computer by applying a logic zero on the modem connections $\overline{\text{DTR}}$ and $\overline{\text{RTS}}$.

If one of the two communications interface adapters discussed earlier in this chapter is used, most of the modem control is already accomplished by these devices. For example, the Intel 8251A has all four of the pin connections required for modem control, while the Motorola MC6850 only contains some of the connections.

8251A Modem Control

Figure 9–17 depicts the 8251A connected to a modem. Notice the inclusion of RS-232C line drivers and receivers for both the control and data connections to the modem.

When the 8251A is operated, it checks to see whether the $\overline{\text{CTS}}$ input is at a logic zero; if it is, the TxRDY pin becomes a logic one if the transmitter has been enabled. Before the modem can be used, the condition of the $\overline{\text{DSR}}$

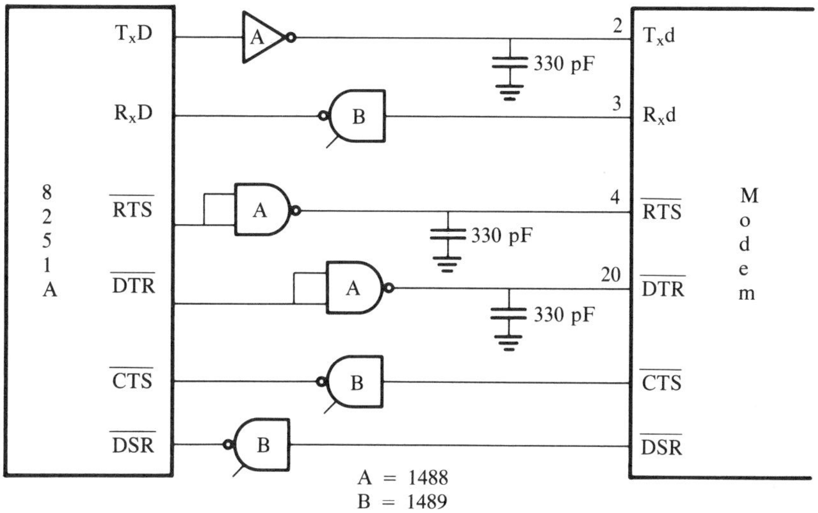

FIGURE 9–17 The 8251A programmable communications interface adapter connected to a MODEM.

must be checked by inputting the status word and testing the DSR bit position. If both pins are active, data transmission can be allowed.

Before the actual transmission occurs, the modem must be conditioned by the 8251A. This is accomplished by activating both the $\overline{\text{DTR}}$ and $\overline{\text{RTS}}$ connections to the modem. $\overline{\text{DTR}}$ is a signal to the modem that indicates that the 8251A has been powered up and is ready to send or receive data. The $\overline{\text{RTS}}$ signal to the modem requests that the modem send data. This signal is important if the modem is operated in simplex mode.

In the *simplex* mode, only the transmission or reception of information can occur at any instant in time. To send data, the 8251A requests that the modem turn the line around for transmission through the $\overline{\text{RTS}}$ signal. It then waits for the modem to signal that it is clear to send information ($\overline{\text{CTS}}$).

If full *duplex* operation is used, as it often is, the $\overline{\text{RTS}}$ and $\overline{\text{CTS}}$ signals really don't have much meaning. $\overline{\text{RTS}}$ and $\overline{\text{CTS}}$ remain at logic zero levels after power is applied to the system.

MC6850 Modem Control

Figure 9–18 illustrates the MC6850 ACIA interfaced to a modem. Control of the modem is accomplished through the $\overline{\text{CTS}}$, $\overline{\text{RTS}}$, and $\overline{\text{DCD}}$ pins on the MC6850. The $\overline{\text{DSR}}$ and $\overline{\text{DTR}}$ signals are not tested or controlled by this device and are controlled externally.

The $\overline{\text{DTR}}$ signal to the modem can be provided by the power supply. When the system is turned on, this pin becomes a logic zero if connected to the output of an inverter, but only if the inverter's input is connected to 5 V. The $\overline{\text{DSR}}$ signal can be tested with a 1-bit input device, or it can be ignored because the modem does not receive or indicate that it is ready to send data through the $\overline{\text{CTS}}$ connection.

The $\overline{\text{RTS}}$ signal from the ACIA conditions the modem for a transmission. It requests that the modem allow a data transmission. If the modem will allow

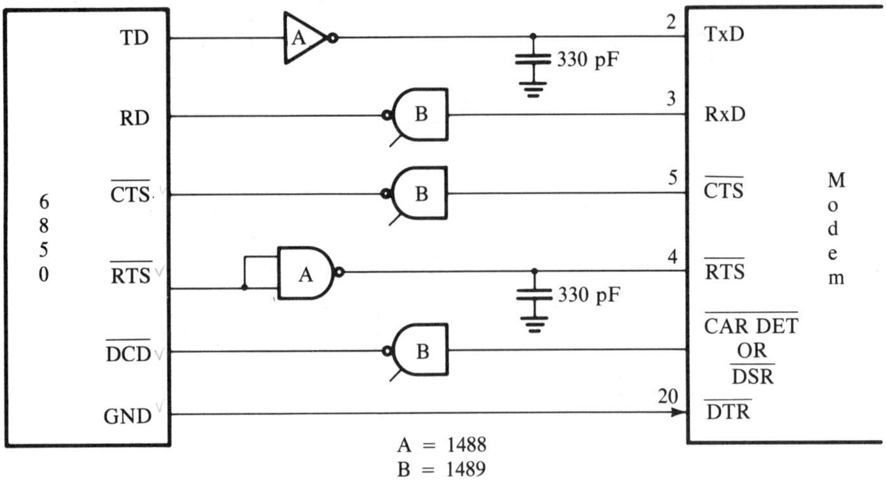

FIGURE 9–18 The MC6850 ACIA connected to a MODEM.

transmission, the $\overline{CTS}$ signal is at a logic zero level. Otherwise, the ACIA must wait until the modem is clear to send data.

Some modems have an output signal that becomes active if a received carrier is detected. This output is connected to the $\overline{DCD}$ input of the ACIA. If the carrier is lost—if the telephone line is disconnected—the $\overline{DCD}$ input goes to a logic one, possibly causing an interrupt.

9-9 IEEE-488 GENERAL PURPOSE INSTRUMENTATION BUS (GPIB)

The IEEE-488 parallel data transfer standard was developed by the Hewlett-Packard Corporation for use in their instruments. It was adopted as a general purpose instrumentation bus (GPIB) by IEEE in 1975. This standard is like the RS-232C standard because it defines the pin connections, protocol, and standard messages for communications.

IEEE-488 allows 8-bit parallel bidirectional communications among as many as 15 devices. These devices must be separated by no more than 2 m per device or 20 m total, whichever is less. Data transfer rates are allowable at up to one million bytes per second. The interface itself consists of eight bidirectional data lines, three handshaking connections, and five interface management connections.

Data Connections

The data connections may be open collector or three-state logic. In most applications these lines use three-state bidirectional data transceivers, as described in earlier chapters, since they increase the usable frequency range of the bus. The frequency range is increased because a three-state driver contains a low impedance pullup network that charges the line capacitance more quickly. This reduction in zero to one transition time allows higher data transmission rates. The data pins are labeled DIO1 through DIO8, where DIO1 is the least significant bit position. The actual pin numbers are illustrated in figure 9–19.

Handshaking Connections

This interface standard uses a three wire handshake to accomplish data transfer.

DAV The DAV, or data available, indicates the availability or validity of data on the data bus connections.

NRFD The NRFD connection, or not ready for data pin, indicates the readiness of the device or devices connected to the bus to receive data.

NDAC The NDAC, or not data accepted, indicates the condition of acceptance by the devices connected to the bus.

The Handshake

Figure 9–20 illustrates the data bus and three handshaking connections to demonstrate the normal handshake that occurs on this bus. When the talker or sending device has information to be placed on the bus, it checks to determine if all devices are ready (NRFD = 1). If they are ready, it places the data on the data bus connections and issues a logic one on the DAV connection to indicate that the bus contains valid data. To complete the handshake, the talker waits for a response from all of the listeners by sampling the NDAC line. When all the devices connected to the bus have received the information, a logic one appears on NDAC to signal the end of the transfer.

Interface Management Connections

These connections, IFC, ATN, SRQ, REN, and EOI, manage the flow of information through the GPIB:

IFC IFC, or interface clear, clears the interface, that is, all of the devices connected to the GPIB.

Pin	Function
1	DI01
2	DI02
3	DI03
4	DI04
5	EOI
6	DAV
7	NFRD
8	NDAC
9	IFC
10	SRQ
11	ATN
12	SHIELD
13	DI05
14	DI06
15	DI07
16	DI08
17	REN
18–23	Wire grounding pairs for pins 6–11
24–	Signal ground

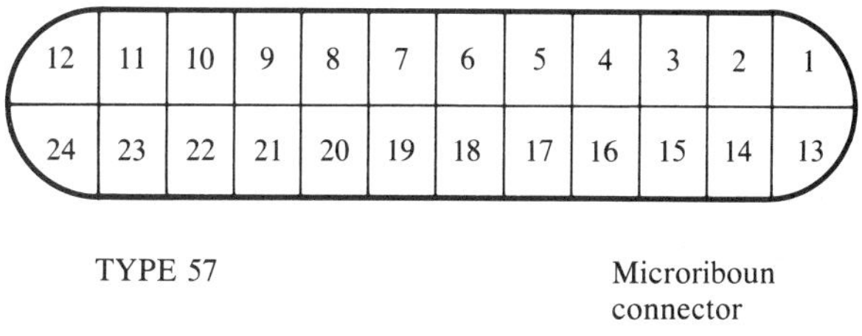

FIGURE 9–19 The IEEE-488 bus connector and connector pin assignments.

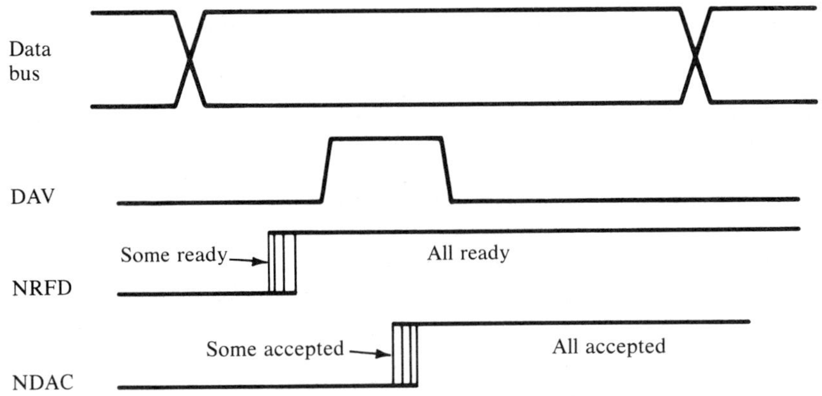

FIGURE 9–20 The IEEE-488 three wire handshake.

ATN The ATN, or attention, line indicates how the data on the data lines is to be interpreted. When ATN is true, the current talker is disabled so that a new device can take over the bus.

SRQ The SRQ, or service request, line indicates that a device connected on the bus needs attention and is requesting an interruption of current events on the bus.

REN The remote enable connection, in conjunction with other messages, selects remote or local control of the device.

EOI EOI, or end or identify, ends a sequence of events or identifies the device during polling.

Interface Functions

Any device connected to the GPIB can assume any one of three identities: the listener, the talker, or the controller. Some devices on the bus can even change their function in midstream, allowing multiple control points on the same bus.

The Listener

The listener is a device that receives data or status information over the bus from other devices in the system. Examples of such devices include printers, disk systems, display devices, and signal generators.

Each listener in a system responds only when addressed. In fact, many listeners can be made receptive at the same time to receive data from a common source. A listener also responds to a variety of other signals in a system.

The Talker

The talker is a device that can provide parallel data or status information to the bus and is used for devices that send information to a computer system. Devices that are often equipped with this interface function include multimeters, frequency counters, disk drives, and data analyzers.

Each talker in a system responds to a unique address or device location that allows the bus controller to select different talkers. Only one talker is allowed to send data down the bus at a time. It also responds to a variety of commands from the GPIB controller.

The Controller

The controller function is the most complicated, since it must be capable of commanding the various talkers and listeners connected to the bus. It must be capable of sending addresses and commands to any or all talkers and listeners on the bus and of conducting polls to see which devices are active.

Provisions have been made so that more than one controller may exist on the GPIB at one time. This is allowed if only one is active at any given moment. Switches between multiple controllers are accomplished through the ATN signal line.

Typical Small GPIB System

The block diagram in figure 9–21 illustrates a small instrumentation system connected to a microprocessor. Device one is the microprocessor, which can command the other devices connected to the bus because it can control, talk, and listen. Device two is a printer, which can accept information from the microprocessor to be printed; therefore, it is a listen only device. Device three is a frequency counter, which is a talk only component.

This simple system can monitor the frequency of an external system, and the microprocessor can print a listing at various periods of time. The microprocessor can also perform a statistical analysis on this information and print it in addition to the readings.

System Controller Communications

Suppose that the controller wishes to read data from the frequency counter to compile a report. It accomplishes this task by commanding the counter to talk by placing the address of the counter on the bus with the my talk address (MTA) command. The counter is now enabled to send data through

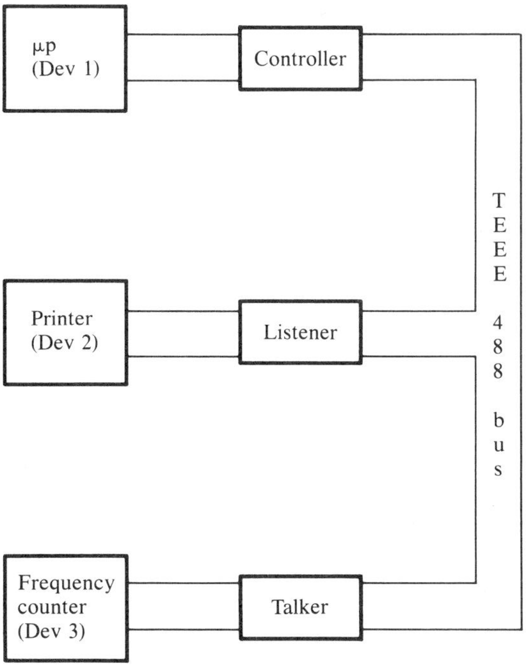

FIGURE 9–21 The block diagram of a small IEEE-488 general purpose instrumentation bus system.

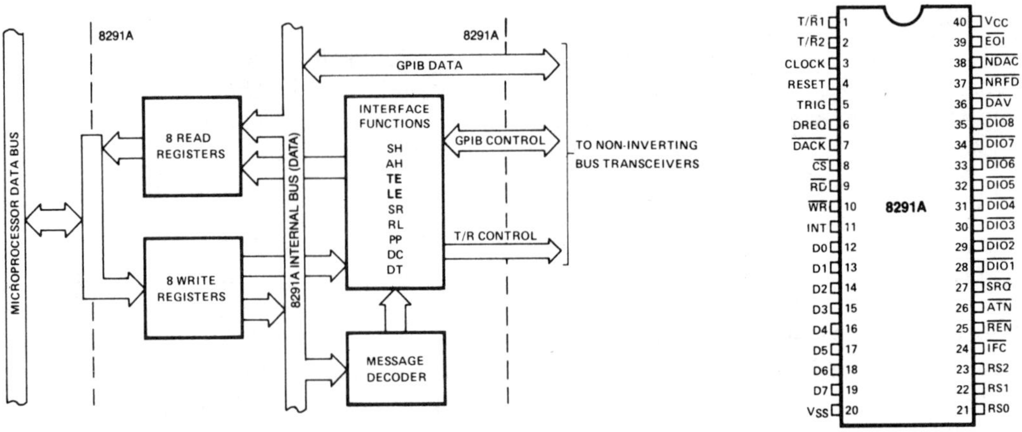

FIGURE 9–22 The 8291A IEEE-488/GPIB talker/listener pinout and block diagram.
SOURCE: Reprinted by permission of Intel Corporation, Copyright 1983.

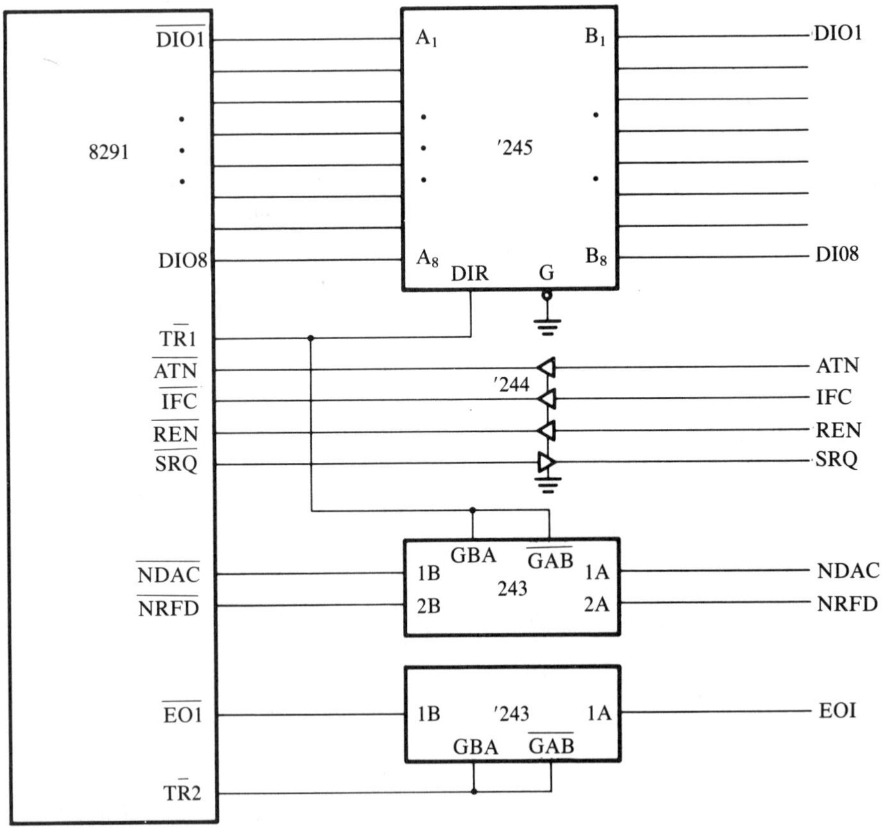

FIGURE 9–23 The 8291A talker/listener interfaced to the IEEE-488 bus through a series of external bus buffers.

the bus to a listener or listeners. If a printed report is to be compiled at the same time, the controller commands the printer, as well as the microprocessor, to begin listening. This procedure is accomplished by addressing them with the my listening address (MLA) command. After all of the devices are programmed by the controller, communications between the counter and the microprocessor and printer proceed unhindered.

The 8291A GPIB Talker/Listener

Figure 9–22 illustrates the pinout and block diagram of the 8291A talker/listener. This device is used with a microprocessor to enact the talk only, listen only or the talker/listener function (illustrated in the block diagram of figure 9–21). This device is capable of implementing the complete system handshaking, extended addressing, and automatic handling of many functions.

Figure 9–23 pictures the 8291A connected to a set of buffers that drive the bus. The only external circuitry required to accomplish this is a set of transceivers for the data bus connections and control pins NRFD, NADC, DAV, and EOI.

The 8292 GPIB Controller

Figure 9–24 pictures the pinout and the block diagram of the 8291A, 8292 GPIB system. The 8292 controller provides the command protocol to enable and disable the various talkers and listeners connected to the bus. It also contains the logic required to pass control to another controller that may or may not be controlling the bus. The controller can also poll the devices in the system to determine which are active.

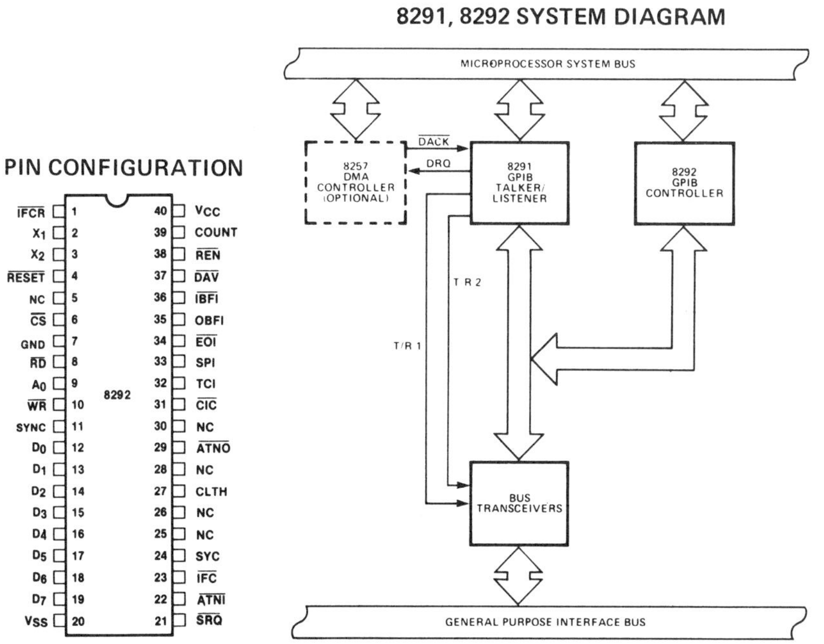

FIGURE 9–24 The 8292 IEEE-488/GPIB bus controller pinout and block diagram.
SOURCE: Reprinted by permission of Intel Corporation, Copyright 1983.

Summary

This chapter is meant to be an introduction to digital communications from the standpoint of the microprocessor. Data is taken from the memory and sent out in the most common forms of both serial and parallel communications. This discussion should prepare the student for a more detailed study of the data as it is sent via common carrier or telephone connections in another course on this vital form of communication.

Modems were briefly introduced, with emphasis on the interface connections rather than on the modulation and switching techniques normally found in these devices. Modem circuit detail has been left for a course in advanced digital communications.

Glossary

ACIA An asynchronous communications interface adapter is a device that receives and transmits asynchronous serial data.

Asynchronous communications These forms of digital communications are carried out by converting parallel information into serial information with the synchronizing bits START and STOP.

Baud rate The number of data bits and synchronizing bits transmitted per second in an FSK digital communications system. In a PSK system, the baud rate represents the number of pieces of information per second. This can be two or three times the bit rate.

BISYNC A synchronous byte oriented communications protocol using 2 synchronization bytes.

DIBIT A pair of bits used to select one of four different phase angles in a PSK communications system.

Duplex A system in which data can be transmitted and received at the same time.

FSK Frequency shift keying is a transmission technique whereby data is encoded as two distinct transmitting frequencies, one for each logic level.

GPIB An acronym for the general purpose instrumentation bus, which is often used to interconnect parallel components to a microcomputer system.

IEEE-488 A parallel interface standard accepted by the Institute of Electrical and Electronic Engineers (see GPIB).

Listener A device that receives information on the GPIB.

MODEM An acronym for MOdulator/DEModulator, a communications device that sends and receives modulated digital data.

Programmable communications interface adapter A programmable device that generates and receives serial data in the asynchronous or synchronous mode.

Protocol A standard method of rules that dictates the way data is transferred.

PSK Phase shift keying is a transmission technique whereby data is encoded in phase angles of the transmitted signal.

RS-232C A serial interface standard developed by the Electronics Industries Association.

SDLC A bit oriented communications protocol that is an acronym for serial data link control.

Simplex Whenever data is communicated in one direction.

Synchronous communications Communications that include a clock pulse for synchronization.

Talker A device that sends data on the GPIB.

TRIBIT Three bits of information that select eight different phase angles in a PSK communications system.

UART A universal asynchronous receiver/transmitter is a device that converts parallel data to serial data and serial data to parallel data.

USART A universal synchronous/asynchronous receiver/transmitter is a device that can communicate by using either asynchronous or synchronous serial data.

USRT A universal synchronous receiver/transmitter is a device that receives and transmits synchronous serial data.

Questions and Problems

1 Describe the basic difference between synchronous and asynchronous digital communications.

2 If an asynchronous communications signal contains 8 bits of data, 1 start bit, and 2 stop bits and each bit time is 9.09 ms, what is the baud rate?

3 Asynchronous data normally has how many stop bits?

4 Sync bytes are used with which type of communication?

5 Asynchronous serial data communications normally occur at baud rates up to which maximum baud rate?

6 Contrast the command structures of the MC6850 and 8251A communications interface adapters.

7 Develop the software required to program the 8251A to function asynchronously with 7 data bits, 2 stop bits, even parity, and a clock divide by rate of 16.

8 Develop the software to program the MC6850 to function with 7 data bits, 2 stop bits, even parity, and a clock divide by rate of 16.

9 How many pin connections exist on the RS-232C interface connector?

10 If a cable has 10 pF of capacitance per meter, what is the longest cable that can be used with RS-232C? (Assume that the driver contains a 300-pF capacitive load.)

11 In a system that uses +12 V and −5 V to power the RS-232C interface, what is the noise immunity of this interface?

12 Why do you suppose that the RS-232C interface standard has been short-circuit- and open-circuit-proofed?

13 What is the main disadvantage of a current loop interface?

14 What is a polar current loop?

15 Explain how FSK data is generated.

16 Explain how PSK data is formed if 2 bits are used to select each phase.

17 Which type of transmission would normally find its place in synchronous communications environments?

18 Describe the purpose of each of the following modem interconnections: $\overline{\text{DSR}}$, $\overline{\text{DTR}}$, $\overline{\text{RTS}}$, and $\overline{\text{CTS}}$.

19 Which modem signal lines must be checked by data terminal or computer before communications can proceed?

20 Which data terminal or computer signal lines must be checked by the modem before communications can proceed?

21 What is the main difference between the interconnections of the modem and data terminal in synchronous and asynchronous systems?

22 Develop the software required to control a modem using the MC6850.

23 Develop the software required to control a modem using the 8251A.

24 Explain the function of a GPIB.

25 Describe the ways the three handshaking signals are applied in the IEEE-488 GPIB.

10 Direct Memory Access

Direct memory access is probably one of the most difficult I/O techniques to understand, but it is worth the extra effort because of its extreme power in a processor based system. This technique is usable for data transfer at extremely high speeds and may, in some cases, be the only technique that can be used.

This chapter introduces the DMA structure of the microprocessor and discusses an application of the technique, CRT screen refreshing, which must occur at a very high rate of speed. CRT screen refreshing is an ideal example of this I/O technique and is also one of the most common.

10-1 INTRODUCTION TO DIRECT MEMORY ACCESS

Direct memory access (DMA) is used whenever data transfer rates exceed the capability of a software transfer. For instance, a typical microprocessor is able to transfer about ten thousand bytes of data per second with a program. This, of course, includes the time it takes to get the information from the memory, send it to an I/O device, and increment a pointer for the next byte. If the required data transfer rates are much faster, a new technique must be found to effect the transfer. The new technique, DMA, is a method whereby the external device goes directly into the memory and either extracts or stores information. The only limitation to the speed of this type of transfer is the speed of the memory system and the speed of the DMA controller.

This I/O technique is found in any system that requires a high data transfer rate. Two common examples are the CRT terminal for screen refreshing and a disk drive for data transfers.

In the CRT terminal, the electron beam moves across the screen at a tremendous rate and requires data at the rate of one character in about every 750 ns maximum. You might think that the microprocessor would have very little processing time with transfers at this rate. It has, because there are times (during retrace and so forth) when the processor is free to do other tasks.

In a disk drive a common data transfer rate is 250,000 bits of information per second. Since over 30,000 bytes of data must be transferred per second, this is also a good application for DMA. Disk drives that are able to store information in double and quad densities are even better candidates for DMA transfers because of their speed.

The Microprocessor DMA Structure

The two connections on almost all microprocessors that are used for controlling the DMA transfer are the HOLD and HLDA pins. The HOLD input requests a DMA cycle. This input causes the microprocessor to suspend operations and to disconnect itself from the data, address, and control buses. This disconnection is accomplished by three-stating or floating these buses. Once the microprocessor has disconnected itself, an external device, usually a DMA controller, can extract from or store information directly into the memory.

To signal the controller that the processor has relinquished control of the buses, the microprocessor sends out a signal that indicates that the buses are indeed at their high impedance state. This HLDA, or hold acknowledge, signal is an indicator that signals the DMA controller or external device to begin transferring the information.

Memory Considerations

The memory in the microprocessor based system is the determining factor on DMA transfer rate. For example, if RAM, which has a cycle time of 500 ns, is used, the memory bandwidth equals 2 MHz. In other words, DMA transfers can be effected at the rate of two million bytes of information per second.

Transfers occur a byte at a time or in bursts of many bytes. The type of transfer selected also affects the maximum transfer rate. For example, if data is burst into the memory, the effective transfer rate is approximately equal to the memory bandwidth. On the other hand, if data is transferred a byte at a time, the rate may be considerably lower because the microprocessor requires some time to acknowledge each DMA request.

The DMA Controller

The DMA controller is almost as complex as a microprocessor and in fact it could be one. It must provide the memory with a memory address and control signals to accomplish a transfer. In addition to the memory control signals and addressing information, it must also control the external DMA controlled I/O device.

Figure 10–1 illustrates the internal structure of a very simple DMA controller. Notice that it contains an address register that selects the desired transfer location. It also contains control logic that provides the memory with its control signals and the I/O device with the appropriate control signals.

A COMPARISON OF DMA SCHEMES 10-2

Most microprocessors have some form of DMA control structure. For example, the Intel 8085A uses a HOLD input and a HLDA output, as does the Zilog Z80. The Motorola MC6800 supports direct memory access with the DBE (data bus enable) and TSC (three-state control) connections. The MC6809 supports DMA through a $\overline{\text{DMA/BREQ}}$ input and a BA and BS output. The BA and BS output must be decoded to produce a DMA acknowledge signal.

The 8085A DMA Structure

In the 8085A, the user can request a DMA transfer by placing a logic one on the HOLD input. This action causes the 8085A to suspend processing instructions. HOLD is recognized at the end of the current bus cycle, which is usually within three clocking periods or 1 μs.

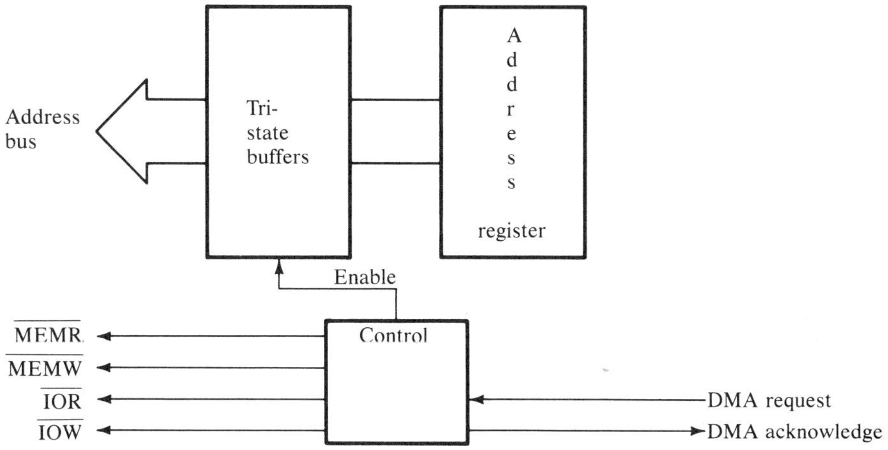

FIGURE 10–1 The block diagram of a simple direct memory access (DMA) controller.

Once operations are suspended, the 8085A floats the address, data, and control bus connections $\overline{RD}$, $\overline{WR}$, and IO/$\overline{M}$ and places a logic one on the HLDA output pin. When HLDA becomes a logic one, the external requesting device can begin transferring data. Refer to figure 10–2 for the 8085A HOLD timing.

It is interesting to note that the HOLD input has a higher priority than any of the interrupt inputs, including the TRAP connection. Therefore, care must be taken when using DMA in conjunction with interrupts, since timing may be affected.

The HOLD input is a level sensitive input and must be held high until it is recognized by the 8085A. This operation may require external synchronization for the proper operation. External synchronization may be accomplished in the same manner used for the level sensitive interrupt inputs discussed in chapter 8.

The MC6800 DMA Structure

The MC6800 uses three inputs to accomplish a DMA: the TSC input; the DBE input, which is normally the phase two clock input to the MC6800; and the phase one clock. Whenever the TSC input and phase one clock are held high and the DBE input is held low, the MC6800's address, data, and R/$\overline{W}$ pin are held in their impedance state. These conditions occur after a short time delay, as illustrated in figure 10–3. The main problem with DMA in this microprocessor is that it completely stops the phase one clock pulse. This clock signal is used to refresh the contents of the dynamic register array internally. The number of bytes that can be burst transferred into or out of the memory during a DMA are thus limited. This clock may only be stopped for 9.5 μs maximum.

The MC6809 DMA Structure

Unlike the MC6800, the MC6809 allows for an unlimited DMA time, making it much more useful in many applications. This prolonged DMA is accom-

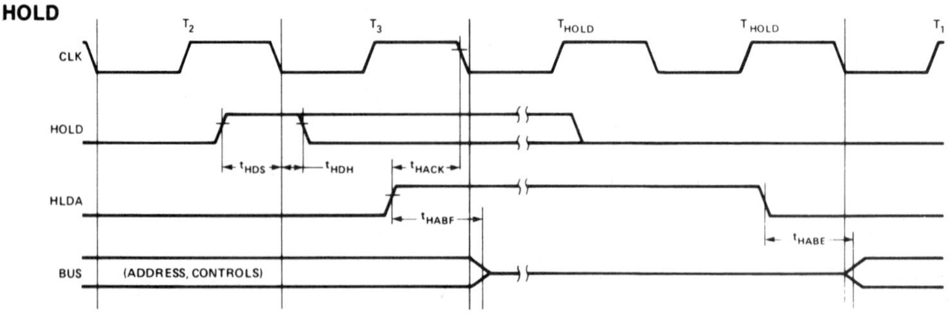

FIGURE 10–2 Intel 8085A microprocessor DMA timing.

SOURCE: Reprinted by permission of Intel Corporation, Copyright 1983.

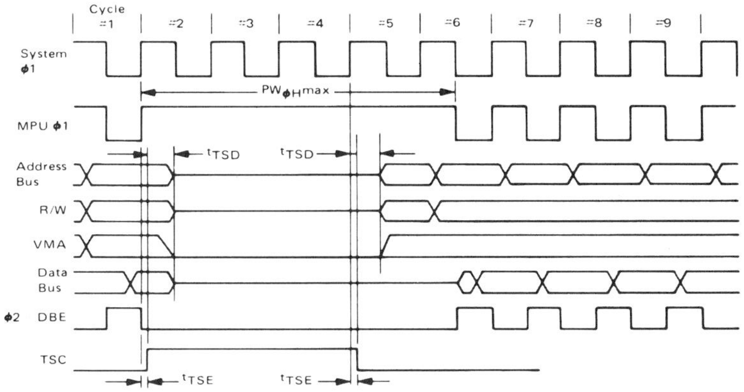

FIGURE 10–3 Motorola MC6800 DMA timing.
SOURCE: Courtesy of Motorola, Inc.

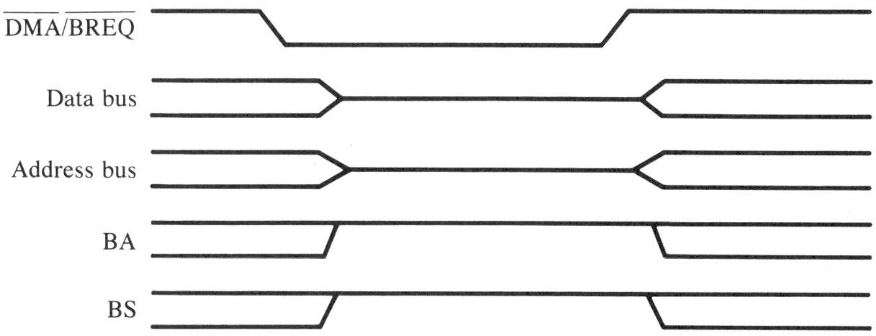

FIGURE 10–4 Motorola MC6809 DMA timing.
SOURCE: Courtesy of Motorola, Inc.

plished because the microprocessor periodically interrupts the DMA cycle to refresh its internal dynamic register array.

When requesting a DMA cycle, the external device places a logic zero on the $\overline{\text{DMA/BREQ}}$ connection (illustrated in figure 10–4). The MC6809 then relinquishes control of the memory by floating the address, data, and control buses. This procedure is indicated to the external controller by the BA and BS lines, which must be logically combined to produce a DMA acknowledge signal. When both BA and BS are at their logic one states, the MC6809 is either halted or acknowledging the DMA request.

Comparison of DMA Schemes

It is fairly easy to see that the DMA structure of the MC6800 microprocessor is extremely awkward or impossible to use if DMA bursts of data are to be accomplished. The MC6809 is more widely applied than the MC6800 because it allows DMA bursts. The only disadvantage of the MC6809 is that it requires an external logic gate to generate the acknowledge signal. The 8085A and Z80 are the most efficient DMA controllable devices because they require no external circuitry and allow unlimited DMA bursting without interrupting the DMA cycle.

10-3 THE 8257-5 DMA CONTROLLER

The 8257-5 DMA controller (figure 10–5) is a 4-channel direct memory access controller compatible with the Intel 8085A and Zilog Z80A microprocessors. This device is capable of single byte transfers or burst transfers with little or no intervention from the microprocessor. It provides not only the memory address for each of the 4 channels but also the control signals for the memory and four different DMA I/O devices.

Each DMA Channel

Each of the four DMA channels contains a programmable address register to indicate the location of the DMA transfer. Each channel also contains a 14-bit counter to indicate how many bytes of data are to be transferred at a time. This counter allows a burst of up to 16K bytes at a time, which is probably the maximum that would ever be transferred in a DMA for an 8-bit microprocessor.

Each channel contains a request input, DRQ, and an acknowledgment output, $\overline{DACK}$. When the DRQ input becomes active for any channel, the 8257-5 checks whether any other DRQ is active and resolves the priority with a

PIN CONFIGURATION

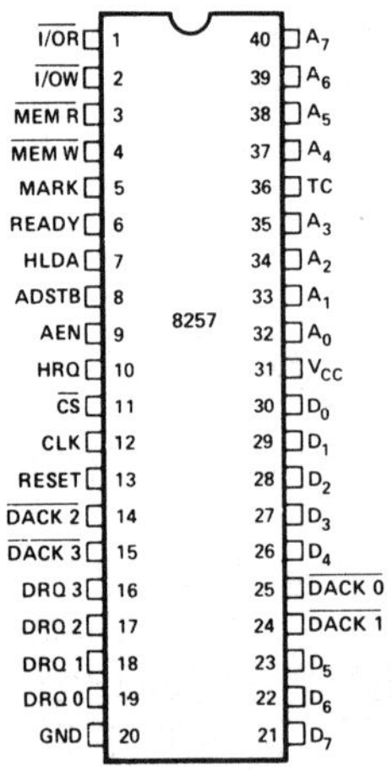

BLOCK DIAGRAM

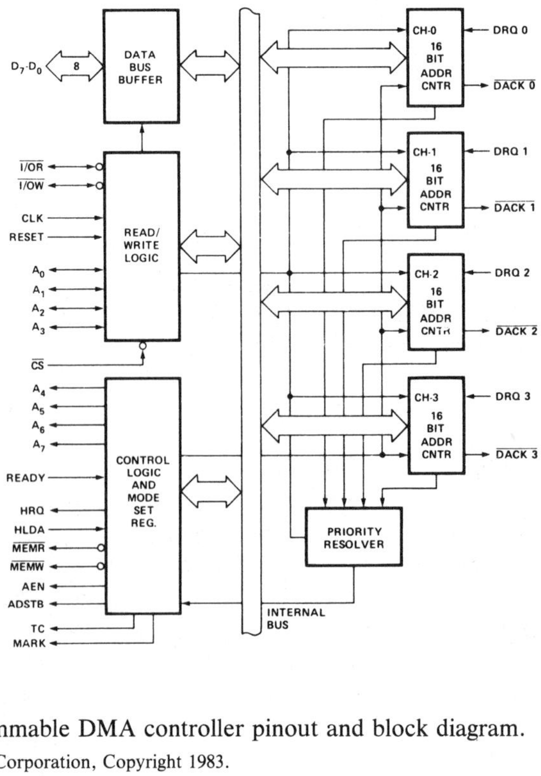

PIN NAMES

D_7-D_0	DATA BUS
A_7-A_0	ADDRESS BUS
$\overline{I/OR}$	I/O READ
$\overline{I/OW}$	I/O WRITE
$\overline{MEMR}$	MEMORY READ
$\overline{MEMW}$	MEMORY WRITE
CLK	CLOCK INPUT
RESET	RESET INPUT
READY	READY
HRQ	HOLD REQUEST (TO 8080A)
HLDA	HOLD ACKNOWLEDGE (FROM 8080A)

AEN	ADDRESS ENABLE
ADSTB	ADDRESS STROBE
TC	TERMINAL COUNT
MARK	MODULO 128 MARK
DRQ_3-DRQ_0	DMA REQUEST INPUT
$\overline{DACK_3}$-$\overline{DACK_0}$	DMA ACKNOWLEDGE OUT
$\overline{CS}$	CHIP SELECT
V_{CC}	+5 VOLTS
GND	GROUND

FIGURE 10–5 The 8257-5 programmable DMA controller pinout and block diagram.
SOURCE: Reprinted by permission of Intel Corporation, Copyright 1983.

multifunction built-in priority encoder. Either rotating or fixed priority can be selected when the 8257-5 is first programmed. With rotating priority, the most recently accepted DRQ input has the lowest priority. This capacity tends to give all of the DRQ inputs equal priority, if desired. When fixed priority is selected, the DRQ0 input has the highest and the DRQ3 input has the lowest.

Channel two can be used in a special mode of operation that is useful for CRT refreshing. This mode automatically reloads the initial address and count after all bytes are transferred, as is required in a CRT terminal. Reloading is accomplished from the channel three DMA address register and counter.

Microprocessor Connections

Figure 10–6 illustrates the connections from an 8085A to the DMA controller. Notice that this device uses the $\overline{MEMR}$, $\overline{MEMW}$, $\overline{IOR}$, and $\overline{IOW}$ control signals. These have been developed with a 74LS257 quad 2-to-1 line multiplexer. The only connection that has not been made is the READY connection, which is sometimes used when slow memory is accessed. Slow memory is virtually nonexistent today because devices are available with access times as low as 80 ns.

The $\overline{CS}$ pin is connected to a simple port decoder so that this 8257-5 is selected for I/O location 7XH. If memory mapping is required, the IO/$\overline{M}$ signal can be inverted so that the device responds to memory address 7XXXH.

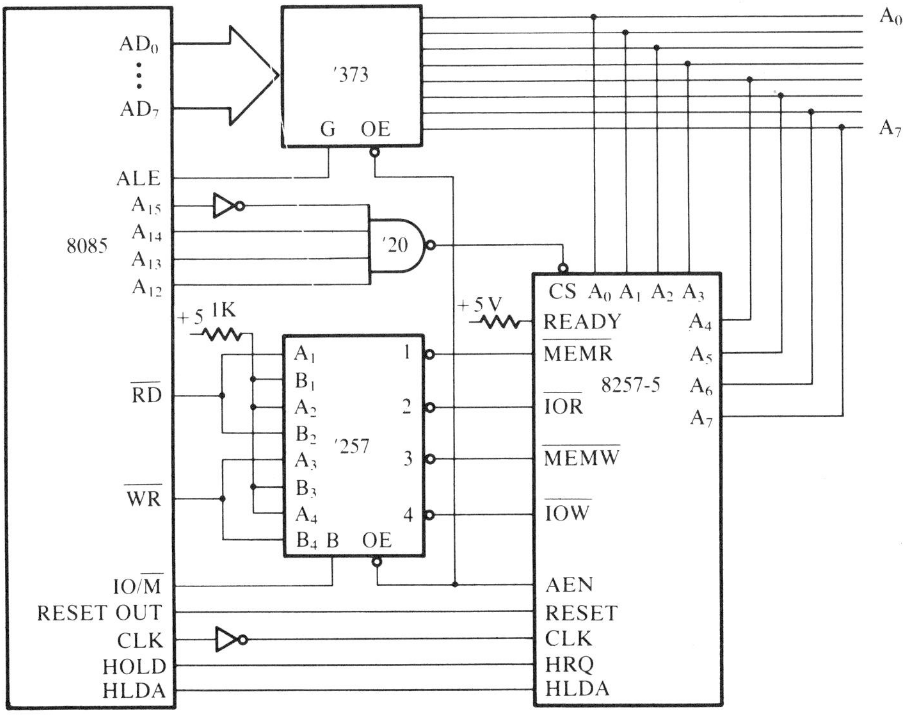

FIGURE 10–6 The 8085A microprocessor portion of the 8257-5 interface.

Unfortunately, Intel failed to include the ALE signal input and accompanying internal address latch; so a 8085A system using this device must include an external address latch. This is also illustrated in figure 10–6.

Memory Connections

Figure 10–7 illustrates the memory side connections of the 8257-5. Notice that an external memory address register is required because the address output from the 8257-5 is multiplexed in order to reduce its pin count. The controller sends out the most significant address bits on data bus connections D0 through D7, where it must be latched into some form of external address latch. Demultiplexing is accomplished in much the same fashion that the 8085A multiplexes its low-order address.

The address latch is controlled by the ADSTB and AEN control signals. AEN enables the outputs of this address latch during the DMA transfer, providing the memory with A8 through A15 during the transfer. Address bits A0 through A7 are provided on the pins labeled A0 through A7. The ADSTB signal is identical to ALE, except that it is used to clock the A8 through A15 into the address latch.

AEN serves one other function in this system; it disables the normal A0 through A7 address latch and the 74LS257 multiplexer. The least significant address is provided by the DMA controller during a DMA cycle, as are the control signals.

I/O Connections

Figure 10–8 pictures the I/O side connections of the DMA controller. Notice that the I/O strobes are developed by logically combining the $\overline{\text{IOR}}$ and $\overline{\text{IOW}}$ signals with the $\overline{\text{DACK}}$ output for a particular channel. The $\overline{\text{DACK}}$ output replaces the device selection logic or port selection logic discussed in previous chapters.

In the drawing, a channel one request is eventually honored by the microprocessor; when it is, the $\overline{\text{DACK1}}$ output becomes a logic zero. This procedure allows the $\overline{\text{IOR}}$ or $\overline{\text{IOW}}$ to be passed on to the DMA controlled device for activation.

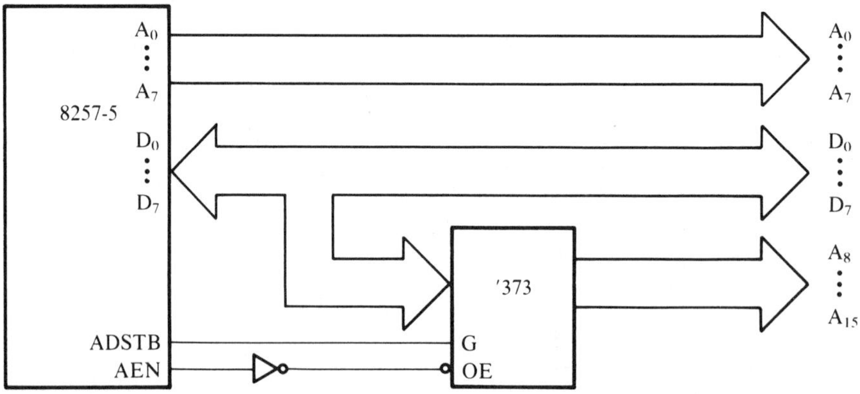

FIGURE 10–7 The memory portion of the 8257-5 DMA controller interface.

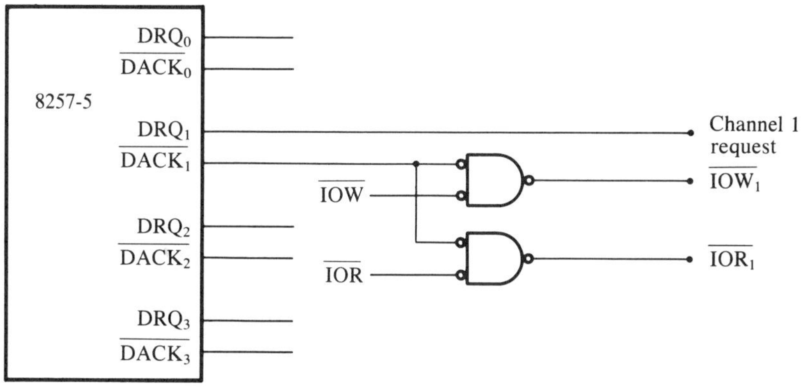

FIGURE 10–8 The I/O portion of the 8257-5 DMA controller interface.

Programming the 8257-5

Programming this device is less difficult than it appears at first once it is understood. Table 10–1 illustrates the port assignments for the 8257-5. When programming this device, the mode set register is programmed first, followed by each active channel's DMA address and the terminal count register. Note that it is important that this order is strictly followed or the programming will be incorrect.

Mode Set Programming

The mode set register, which is depicted in table 10–2, directs the operation of the DMA controller, and it must be programmed. The function of each bit of this register is outlined below:

AL Auto load selects the auto load feature for DMA channel two. The channel two count and address registers are loaded from the channel three count and address registers at a terminal count. This mode therefore reduces the number of channels available from four to three if it is activated.

TCS This terminal count stop bit stops a DMA burst at the terminal count. If TCS is not active, the external DMA device must stop the transfer.

EW The extended write bit extends the length of the $\overline{MEMW}$ and $\overline{IOW}$ signals as required by some slower I/O and memory devices.

RP This rotating priority bit selects a rotating priority scheme. If it is not set, channel zero has the highest priority and channel three the lowest.

ENX The enable DMA bit positions EN0, EN1, EN2, and EN3 enable the respective DMA channels.

Status Register

The status register (table 10–3), which is read by the microprocessor, indicates the condition of the 8257-5. The function of each status bit is characterized in the following list:

TABLE 10–1 8257 register selection.

Register	Byte	Address Inputs A_3	A_2	A_1	A_0	F/L	*Bi-Directional Data Bus D_7	D_6	D_5	D_4	D_3	D_2	D_1	D_0
CH-0 DMA Address	LSB	0	0	0	0	0	A_7	A_6	A_5	A_4	A_3	A_2	A_1	A_0
	MSB	0	0	0	0	1	A_{15}	A_{14}	A_{13}	A_{12}	A_{11}	A_{10}	A_9	A_8
CH-0 Terminal Count	LSB	0	0	0	1	0	C_7	C_6	C_5	C_4	C_3	C_2	C_1	C_0
	MSB	0	0	0	1	1	Rd	Wr	C_{13}	C_{12}	C_{11}	C_{10}	C_9	C_8
CH-1 DMA Address	LSB	0	0	1	0	0	Same as Channel 0							
	MSB	0	0	1	0	1								
CH-1 Terminal Count	LSB	0	0	1	1	0								
	MSB	0	0	1	1	1								
CH-2 DMA Address	LSB	0	1	0	0	0	Same as Channel 0							
	MSB	0	1	0	0	1								
CH-2 Terminal Count	LSB	0	1	0	1	0								
	MSB	0	1	0	1	1								
CH-3 DMA Address	LSB	0	1	1	0	0	Same as Channel 0							
	MSB	0	1	1	0	1								
CH-3 Terminal Count	LSB	0	1	1	1	0								
	MSB	0	1	1	1	1								
MODE SET (Program only)	—	1	0	0	0	0	AL	TCS	EW	RP	EN3	EN2	EN1	EN0
STATUS (Read only)	—	1	0	0	0	0	0	0	0	UP	TC3	TC2	TC1	TC0

*A_0-A_{15}: DMA Starting Address, C_0-C_{13}: Terminal Count value (N-1), Rd and Wr: DMA Verify (00), Write (01) or Read (10) cycle selection, AL: Auto Load, TCS: TC STOP, EW: EXTENDED WRITE, RP: ROTATING PRIORITY, EN3-EN0: CHANNEL ENABLE MASK, UP: UPDATE FLAG, TC3-TC0: TERMINAL COUNT STATUS BITS.

TABLE 10–2 The 8257-5 mode set register.

7	6	5	4	3	2	1	0
AL	TCS	EW	RP	EN3	EN2	EN1	EN0

TABLE 10–3 The 8257-5 status register.

7	6	5	4	3	2	1	0
0	0	0	UP	TC3	TC2	TC1	TC0

UP The update flag indicates when the channel two registers have been reloaded from the channel three registers in the auto load mode of operation.

TC The four TC, or terminal count, status bits indicate that a terminal count has been reached and will remain active until the status register is read. They are cleared when the status register is read by the microprocessor.

Programming the Address and Terminal Count Registers

The address register, which must be programmed before the terminal count register, holds the address of the first byte of information to be transferred. This address is incremented by the controller after each DMA read or write.

The terminal count register is a 14-bit counter that indicates how many bytes are to be transferred in the DMA cycle. This register must always be loaded with the number of bytes to be transferred minus one. The remaining two bit positions of the terminal count register indicate the type of DMA operation to be performed by the channel, read or write (refer to table 10–1).

A DMA write cycle causes data to be read from an external I/O device and written into the memory. A DMA read cycle causes data to be pulled from the memory and written into some external I/O device.

In both cases the least significant portion of the register must be programmed first, followed by the most significant portion. Notice that the I/O port number is the same for both. The direction of data flow is internally controlled by an F/L (first/last) flip-flop that indicates least and most significant data bits or first and last.

Operation

Figure 10–9 depicts the operation of the 8257-5 through a state transition diagram. A series of clock states, each of which is equal to the clock period of the host 8085A, directs the operation of this device.

After a reset, the 8257-5 enters into state SI (initialization state) and remains there until one of the enabled DRQ inputs becomes a logic one. When a DRQ request occurs, the HRQ signal connected to the HOLD input on the 8085A is placed at a logic one, requesting a HOLD.

FIGURE 10–9 The 8257-5 Internal State transition diagram.

SOURCE: Reprinted by permission of Intel Corporation, Copyright 1983.

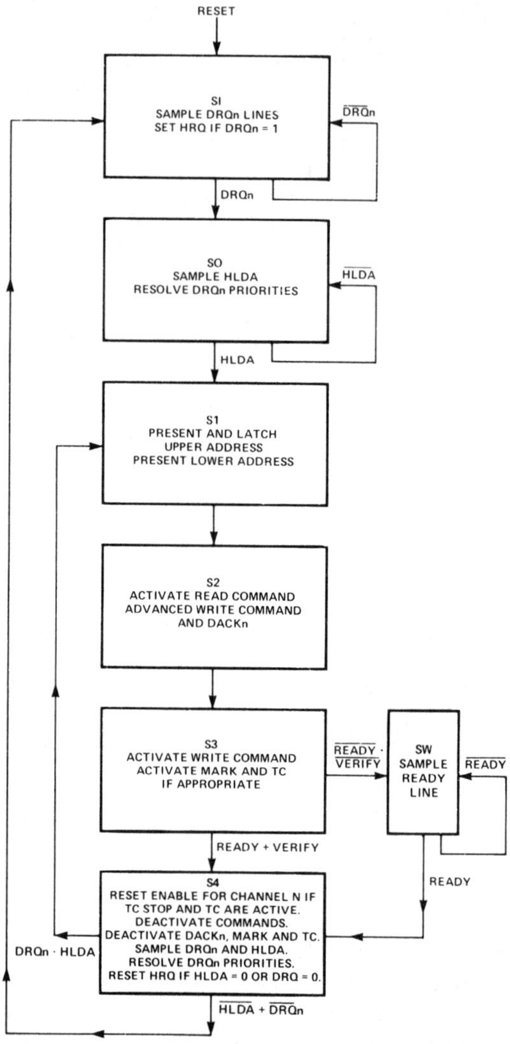

1 DRQn refers to any DRQ line on an enabled DMA channel.

State S0 is entered from SI and waits for the acknowledge signal, HLDA, from the 8085A. If noise on a DRQ input causes the 8257-5 to enter into state S0, it returns to state SI because it is no longer active.

If the DRQ request is still active once the microprocessor acknowledges the request with HLDA, the controller enters clocking state S1. S1 is used by the controller to send out the memory address to the memory system by latching the upper half of the memory address, which is presented on the data bus connections, into an external most significant address latch.

The next state, S2, is mainly used for memory access time; if the controller has been commanded, it issues the advanced $\overline{MEMW}$ or $\overline{IOW}$ signals at this time. Some external devices may require more time to write the information so that the advanced memory or I/O write signals are provided.

In state S3, the data transfer occurs; it is here that the appropriate memory and I/O control signals are activated. During this state the ready line is also sampled to determine whether a slow memory or I/O device is connected to the system.

In the last state, the DMA controller decides whether to transfer another byte of information for burst operation or whether to return to state SI. If the DRQ request is still active, there is a branch to state S1; the entire process of presenting a memory address, followed by the control signals, is repeated for the next byte to be transferred.

This controller can transfer 1 byte of data for every four clock periods in the burst mode and no more than 1 byte of data for every six clock cycles in the single byte mode. If a 3 MHz clock is used for timing, it is able to burst 750,000 bytes of data per second. That rate is quite a bit faster than the rate of the direct I/O techniques discussed in earlier chapters.

Timing

Figure 10–10 pictures the timing diagram for the 8257-5, which should be compared with the description of the operation of the controller. Beginning with the second waveform, DRQ 0–3, you will notice that it causes the 8257-5 to leave state SI and enter into state S0. It also causes the HRQ output, which is connected to the 8085A hold input, to become a logic one. This procedure requests the HOLD or DMA.

Next the controller enters state S1 if the microprocessor has returned the HLDA signal. At this time a flurry of events occurs. The 8257-5 activates the AEN signal to disable the external bus drivers in the system. It also enables the 8257-5 address latch's output. On the positive edge of the S1 clock pulse, the 8257-5 outputs the 16-bit DMA memory address. Half appears on A0 through A7 and the other half appears on the data bus connections. The most significant half of the address is latched into an external address latch using the ADR STB signal that is also present at this time.

During state S2 the 8257-5 sends out the $\overline{\text{DACK 0–3}}$ signal to acknowledge the DMA request to the I/O device.

Finally the data is transferred in state S3. In a DMA write, the $\overline{\text{IOR}}$ and the $\overline{\text{MEMW}}$ signals activate, causing data to be read from an I/O device onto the data bus. The $\overline{\text{MEMW}}$ signal then causes the contents of the data bus, the I/O data, to be written into the selected memory address. If the operation were a DMA read, the $\overline{\text{IOW}}$ and $\overline{\text{MEMR}}$ signals would be active, causing data from the memory to be written into the external I/O device. In the DMA verify mode of operation, no control signal is issued by the 8257-5. All that happens is that the system cycles through the DMA address that can be used by the external device to perform some form of internal verification.

DMA Controlled Data Communications Example

This example, whose hardware is depicted in figure 10–11, automatically transmits a block of information from a portion of the memory out through an 8251A communications interface adapter.

Once the area of memory to be transmitted is loaded with data (by a subroutine that is not illustrated here), the DMA controller can be programmed with the starting location of the data and the length of the block of data. Once these registers are programmed, the mode set register is directed to start the transfer by enabling channel one.

CONSECUTIVE CYCLES AND BURST MODE SEQUENCE

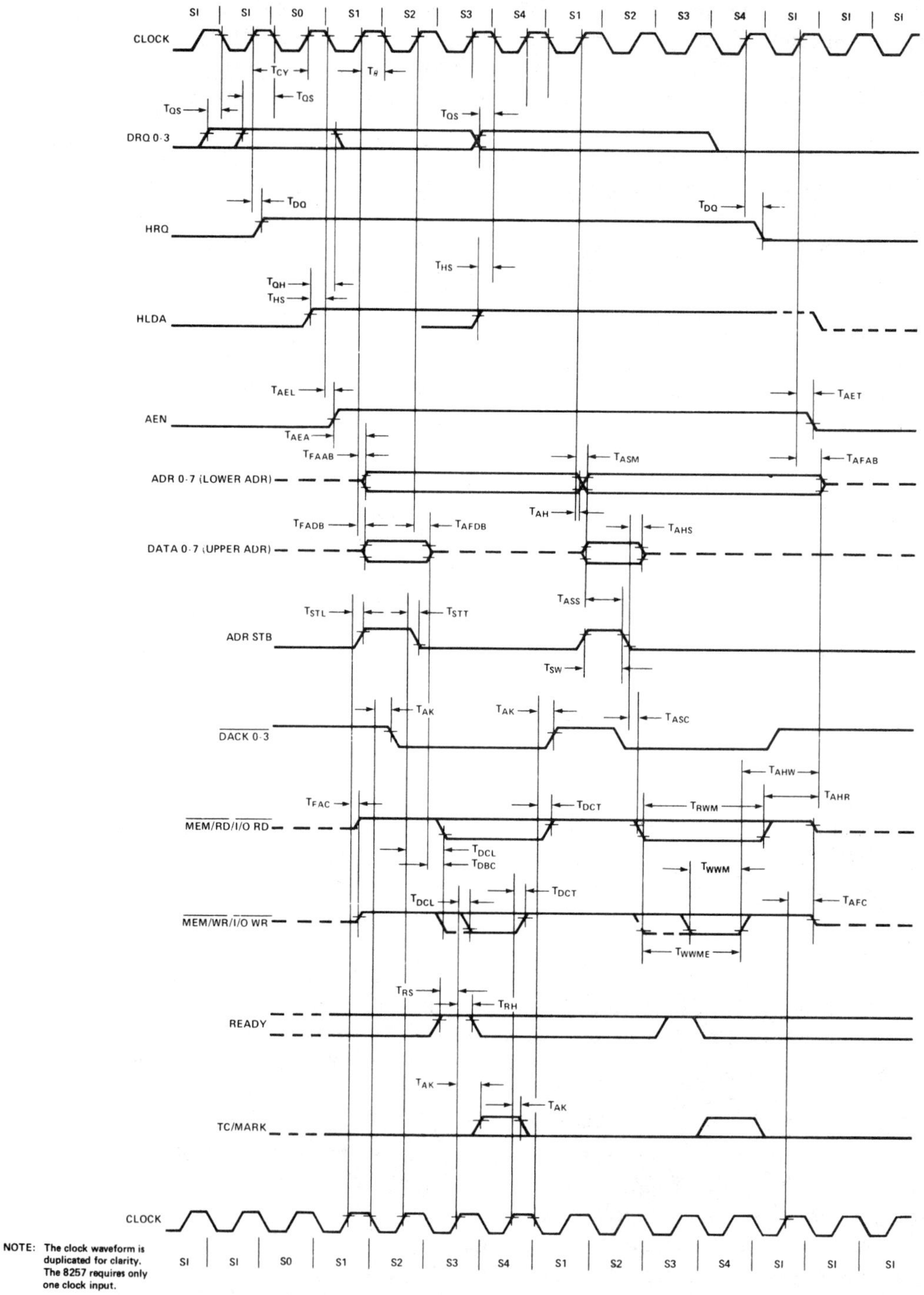

FIGURE 10–10 The timing diagram for the 8257-5 programmable DMA controller.

SOURCE: Reprinted by permission of Intel Corporation, Copyright 1983.

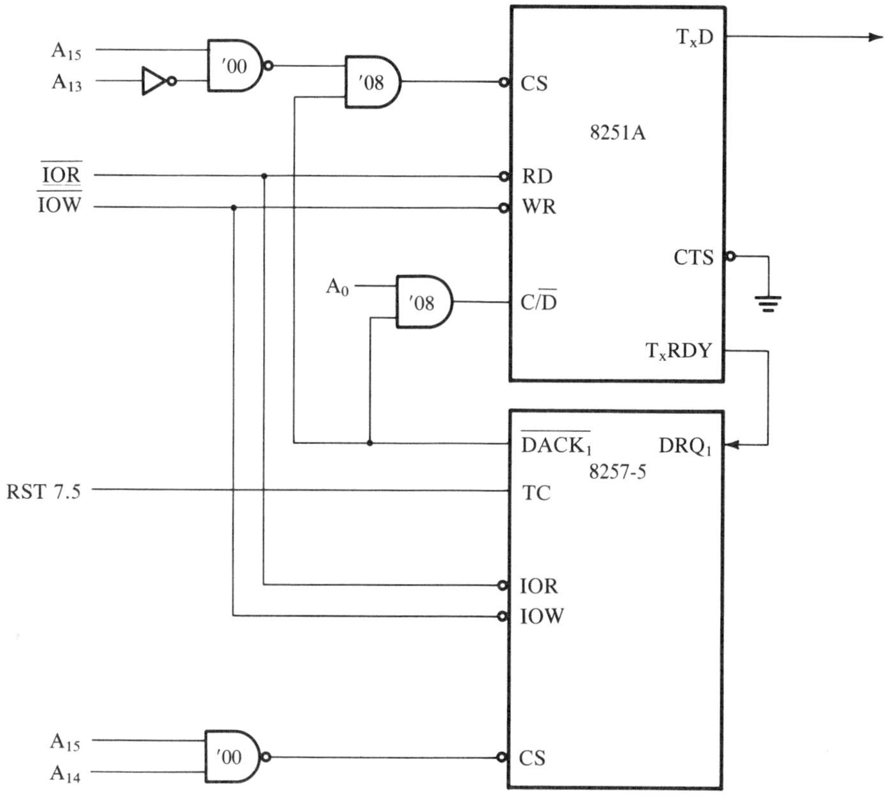

FIGURE 10–11 A DMA controlled data communications interface.

Since the transmitter is probably empty at this time, the transmitter ready pin TxRDY, connected to the DRQ1 input, requests a DMA cycle. When the 8085A grants the cycle, a byte of data is read from the memory and transferred or written to the 8251A.

Since it takes some time to transmit a byte of information, the TxRDY pin remains a logic zero for some time to allow the microprocessor to continue processing other information. In this system, the communication takes only six 8085A clock cycles to transfer a byte of information. Normally some form of subroutine is required to check or poll the status bit of the 8251A. This is probably the most efficient data transfer process possible.

When a terminal count (TC) is reached, all bytes have been transferred and the logic circuitry generates a RST 7.5 interrupt request. This interrupt request signals the 8085A that the transmission is complete and that the DMA controller must be disabled on channel one until the next block transfer.

Software

The software for this example can be broken down into many modules or subroutines for an easier understanding.

A module for the transfer of data into the block of memory to be transmitted is not developed at this time, but all other control software is developed.

Initialization Dialog

The initialization dialog for this example must program both the 8251A and the 8257-5. It must also activate the RST 7.5 interrupt pin used at the end of a transmission. Refer to chapters 7 and 9 for more detailed explanation of some of the initialization dialog that follows:

```
;PROGRAM THE DMA CONTROLLER
;
RESET: SUB   A
       OUT   0F8H        ;CLEAR F/L FLIP-FLOP
;
;PROGRAM THE COMMUNICATIONS CONTROLLER
;7 DATA BITS, ONE STOP BIT, EVEN PARITY
;AND DIVIDE BY 16
;
       MVI   A,7AH       ;PROGRAM THE 8251A
       OUT   081H
       MVI   A,1         ;CONDITION TRANSMITTER
       OUT   081H
       MVI   A,0BH       ;ENABLE RST 7.5
       SIM
       EI                ;ENABLE INTERRUPTS
        .
        .                ;ENTER SYSTEM PROGRAM
        .
```

The Transmit Subroutine

The transmit subroutine is called after the block of data to be transmitted is loaded with information. Its main function is to program the starting location and length of the block into the DMA controller. Since some parameter must accompany the subroutine CALL, two register pairs are elected to handle this function. The DE pair transfers the block address into the subroutine, and the BC pair transfers the length of the block minus one.

```
;TRANSMISSION SUBROUTINE
;BC = LENGTH OF THE BLOCK OF DATA TO BE TRANSMITTED
;DE = BEGINNING ADDRESS OF THE BLOCK OF DATA - 1
;
TRANS:  MOV  A,E         ;LOAD LSB OF ADDRESS
        OUT  0F2H
        MOV  A,D         ;LOAD MSB OF ADDRESS
        OUT  0F2H
        MOV  A,C         ;LOAD LSB OF COUNT
        OUT  0F3H
        MOV  A,B         ;SET UP DMA READ COMMAND
        ORI  80H         ;READ MEMORY, WRITE 8251A
        OUT  0F3H        ;LOAD MSB OF COUNT
        MVI  A,0FFH      ;SET TRANSMIT BUSY FLAG
        STA  TFLAG
```

```
            MVI   A,2          ;ENABLE TRANSMISSION
            OUT   0F8H
            RET
```

The busy flag, or TFLAG, is tested by the system software to determine whether the transmitter is busy. A logic zero indicates not busy, and an FFH indicates a busy condition.

Interrupt Service Subroutine

The interrupt service subroutine has the responsibility of deactivating the channel one DMA and clearing the TFLAG bit to zero.

```
   RST75:   PUSH  PSW          ;SAVE ACC AND FLAGS
            SUB   A            ;TURN CHANNEL ONE OFF
            OUT   0F8H
            STA   TFLAG        ;CLEAR TRANSMITTER BUSY FLAG
            POP   PSW          ;RESTORE ACC AND FLAGS
            EI                 ;ENABLE FUTURE INTERRUPTS
            RET
```

CRT REFRESHING USING DMA 10-4

A CRT terminal requires that data be periodically moved from the memory to the screen through character generation circuitry. This process is most often accomplished through DMA techniques because they allow more time for the microprocessor to process other data.

In an 80-column display, the refresh rate is one character in every 617 ns, a rate that cannot be directly supported by the DMA controller described earlier. This problem can be circumvented by using an external buffer memory to hold one complete line of display information. The display generating circuitry then scans this external memory for displayed data. This technique is fine until it is time to begin displaying the next line of information. Here you find that the horizontal retrace time is too short to load the external buffer with the next 80 characters.

This difficulty can also be overcome if two external 80-character buffers are used in the system: one for the display circuitry to scan and the other to be loaded from the DMA controller. This technique is often referred to as *double buffering*.

Since we are talking about extensive external circuitry, it would be best to search for a microprocessor peripheral component that can handle most of this task. It happens that Intel provides a CRT controller that contains the necessary buffering for the CRT terminal plus a few additional enhancements.

The 8275 CRT Controller

The 8275 CRT controller is illustrated in figure 10–12 with its pinout diagram. This device is very flexible, since it supports graphic character attributes, cursor control, and the light pen screen address.

PIN CONFIGURATION

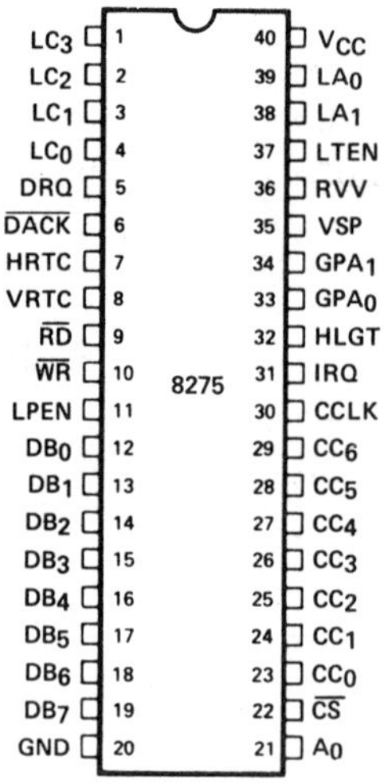

BLOCK DIAGRAM

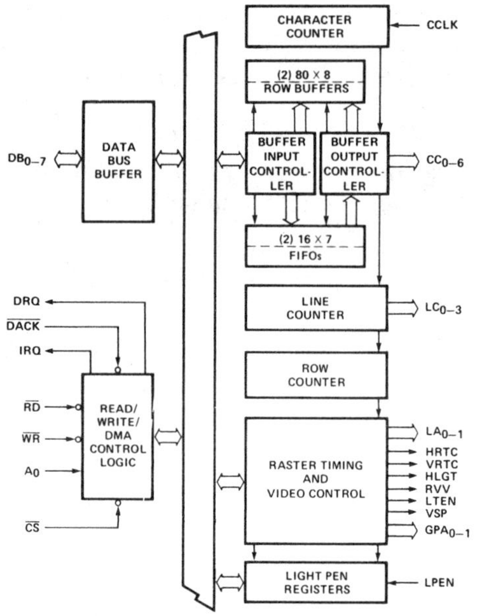

PIN NAMES

DB_{0-7}	BI-DIRECTIONAL DATA BUS	LC_{0-3}	LINE COUNTER OUTPUTS
DRQ	DMA REQUEST OUTPUT	LA_{0-1}	LINE ATTRIBUTE OUTPUTS
$\overline{DACK}$	DMA ACKNOWLEDGE INPUT	HRTC	HORIZONTAL RETRACE OUTPUT
IRQ	INTERRUPT REQUEST OUTPUT	VRTC	VERTICAL RETRACE OUTPUT
$\overline{RD}$	READ STROBE INPUT	HLGT	HIGHLIGHT OUTPUT
$\overline{WR}$	WRITE STROBE INPUT	RVV	REVERSE VIDEO OUTPUT
A_0	REGISTER ADDRESS INPUT	LTEN	LIGHT ENABLE OUTPUT
CS	CHIP SELECT INPUT	VSP	VIDEO SUPPRESS OUTPUT
CCLK	CHARACTER CLOCK INPUT	GPA_{0-1}	GENERAL PURPOSE ATTRIBUTE OUTPUTS
CC_{0-6}	CHARACTER CODE OUTPUTS	LPEN	LIGHT PEN INPUT

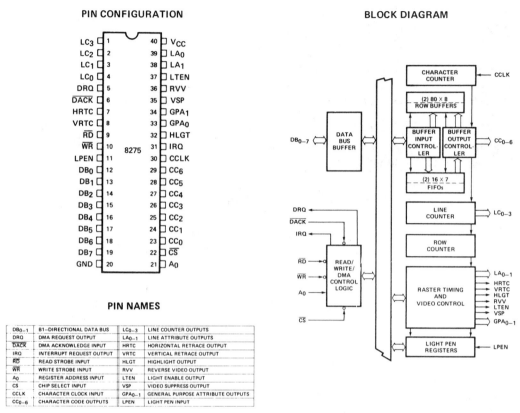

FIGURE 10–12 The pinout and block diagram of the Intel 8275 programmable CRT controller.

SOURCE: Reprinted by permission of Intel Corporation, Copyright 1983.

Figure 10–13 illustrates the 8085A microprocessor interfaced to this component, indicating that little external circuitry is required for this connection. In this example, port number 8XH is decoded for use with the CRT controller.

Internal Registers

Internally the 8275 is a rather simple device containing command, parameter, and status registers. The command register is the means through which the control of this device can be accomplished. There are eight different commands that the 8275 will respond to, and each must be followed by a sequence of between zero and four parameters of information for proper device function.

8275 Commands

START DISPLAY (0 0 1 S S S B B) This command is followed by zero or no parameters and directs the controller to begin displaying data. The DMA requests begin to occur through the DRQ and $\overline{\text{DACK}}$ connections, the interrupts are enabled, and the video is enabled.

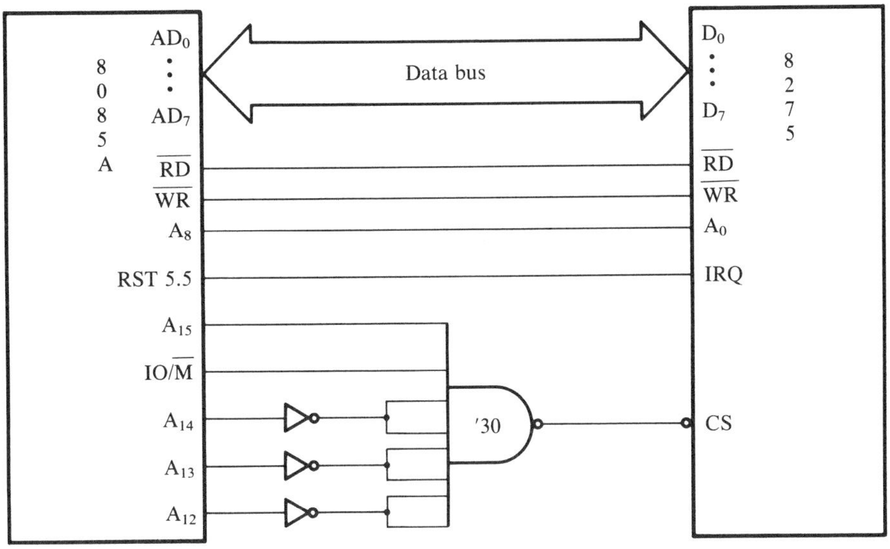

FIGURE 10–13 The 8085A microprocessor interfaced to the 8275 CRT controller.

TABLE 10–4 8275 burst codes.

SSS Burst Space Code				**BB Burst Count Code**		
S	**S**	**S**	**Character Clocks between DMA Requests**	**B**	**B**	**DMA Cycles per Burst**
0	0	0	0	0	0	1
0	0	1	7	0	1	2
0	1	0	15	1	0	4
0	1	1	23	1	1	8
1	0	0	31			
1	0	1	39			
1	1	0	47			
1	1	1	55			

Bits SSS direct the 8275 DMA request circuitry and indicate how many clocks are to occur minimally between DMA requests. The exact number is illustrated in table 10–4. Bits BB indicate how many bytes are to be transferred per DMA burst cycle.

STOP DISPLAY (0 1 0 0 0 0 0 0) This command terminates displaying information by disabling the video signal.

ENABLE INTERRUPT (1 0 1 0 0 0 0 0) This command enables interrupts and sets the enable interrupt status bit.

DISABLE INTERRUPT (1 1 0 0 0 0 0 0) Interrupts are disabled and the interrupt enable status bit is cleared.

PRESET COUNTERS (1 1 1 0 0 0 0 0) Internal counters are preset to the home, or upper left-hand corner, position. These counters remain in this state until another command is issued. This command is usually followed by the START DISPLAY command.

READ LIGHT PEN POSITION (0 1 1 0 0 0 0 0) The position of the light pen is returned on the next two read cycles of the parameter register. The character column is returned on the first read, and the line or row number is returned on the second read. Note that software must be used to supply the correct position because there is a bias of three to four character positions due to internal and external circuitry delays.

LOAD CURSOR POSITION (1 0 0 0 0 0 0 0) The cursor can be directed to any position on the CRT screen by loading the parameter register with the column and row position following this command.

RESET (0 0 0 0 0 0 0 0) The reset command must be followed by four parameters, pictured in figure 10–14, that direct the overall function of the CRT controller.

Status Register

The status indicates the operating condition of the CRT controller. Table 10–5 illustrates this register, and the function of each status bit position is described below:

TABLE 10–5 The 8275 status register.

7	6	5	4	3	2	1	0
0	IE	IR	LP	IC	VE	OU	FO

IE The interrupt enable bit indicates whether or not the last row interrupt will occur.

IR Interrupt request reflects the condition of the IRQ line.

LP The light pen flag bit indicates that the LPEN input pin is activated and the internal light pen registers are loaded with an address.

IC An improper command is received.

VE The video has been enabled.

DU DMA underrun is set whenever a DMA underrun occurs. A DMA underrun occurs whenever the DMA circuitry fails to keep up with the CRT controller. When this happens, the controlled has been programmed for the wrong number of DMA characters per burst or the wrong number of clocks between bursts.

FO The FIFO overrun occurs when the internal attributes FIFO is overrun. This occurs whenever more than sixteen attributes per line are attempted.

Attributes

The CRT controller allows six different field attributes: blink, highlight, reverse video, underline, and two general purpose attributes. The general purpose attributes can be tailored to individual needs because they control two external hardware pins, GPA0 and GPA1.

1. Reset Command:

	OPERATION	A_0	DESCRIPTION	DATA BUS MSB LSB
Command	Write	1	Reset Command	0 0 0 0 0 0 0 0
Parameters	Write	0	Screen Comp Byte 1	S H H H H H H H
	Write	0	Screen Comp Byte 2	V V R R R R R R
	Write	0	Screen Comp Byte 3	U U U U L L L L
	Write	0	Screen Comp Byte 4	M F C C Z Z Z Z

Action — After the reset command is written, DMA requests stop, 8275 interrupts are disabled, and the VSP output is used to blank the screen. HRTC and VRTC continue to run. HRTC and VRTC timing are random on power-up.

As parameters are written, the screen composition is defined.

Parameter — S Spaced Rows

S	FUNCTIONS
0	Normal Rows
1	Spaced Rows

Parameter — HHHHHHH Horizontal Characters/Row

H H H H H H H	NO. OF CHARACTERS PER ROW
0 0 0 0 0 0 0	1
0 0 0 0 0 0 1	2
0 0 0 0 0 1 0	3
.	.
.	.
.	.
1 0 0 1 1 1 1	80
1 0 1 0 0 0 0	Undefined
.	.
.	.
.	.
1 1 1 1 1 1 1	Undefined

Parameter — VV Vertical Retrace Row Count

V V	NO. OF ROW COUNTS PER VRTC
0 0	1
0 1	2
1 0	3
1 1	4

Parameter — RRRRRR Vertical Rows/Frame

R R R R R R	NO. OF ROWS/FRAME
0 0 0 0 0 0	1
0 0 0 0 0 1	2
0 0 0 0 1 0	3
.	.
.	.
.	.
1 1 1 1 1 1	64

Parameter — UUUU Underline Placement

U U U U	LINE NUMBER OF UNDERLINE
0 0 0 0	1
0 0 0 1	2
0 0 1 0	3
.	.
.	.
.	.
1 1 1 1	16

Parameter — LLLL Number of Lines per Character

L L L L	NO. OF LINES/ROW
0 0 0 0	1
0 0 0 1	2
0 0 1 0	3
.	.
.	.
.	.
1 1 1 1	16

Parameter — M Line Counter Mode

M	LINE COUNTER MODE
0	Mode 0 (Non-Offset)
1	Mode 1 (Offset by 1 Count)

Parameter — F Field Attribute Mode

F	FIELD ATTRIBUTE MODE
0	Transparent
1	Non-Transparent

Parameter — CC Cursor Format

C C	CURSOR FORMAT
0 0	Blinking reverse video block
0 1	Blinking underline
1 0	Nonblinking reverse video block
1 1	Nonblinking underling

Parameter — ZZZZ Horizontal Retrace Count

Z Z Z Z	NO. OF CHARACTER COUNTS PER HRTC
0 0 0 0	2
0 0 0 1	4
0 0 1 0	6
.	.
.	.
.	.
1 1 1 1	32

Note: uuuu MSB determines blanking of top and bottom lines (1 = blanked, 0 = not blanked).

FIGURE 10–14 The 8275 RESET command.

SOURCE: Reprinted by permission of Intel Corporation, Copyright 1983.

TABLE 10–6 8275 Attribute codes.

7	6	5	4	3	2	1	0
1	0	U	R	G1	G2	B	H

Bit Name	Function
H	Highlight
B	Blinking
G1, G2	General purpose
R	Reverse
U	Underline

Interrupt Request

The interrupt request output, or IRQ, becomes active at the beginning of the last row of display data. It is used with the autoload feature in a system that does not contain a DMA controller to reset the DMA address. Since the auto load mode is available in the DMA controller, it is not needed with this example.

CRT Connections

Figure 10–15 illustrates the circuitry required to connect a CRT to the CRT controller. The system consists of only a handful of components; five years ago, there would have been approximately fifty SSI, MSI, and LSI components.

The oscillator shown develops an 11.34 MHz dot clock to shift data through the 74166 serial shift register to the screen. It also clocks a modulus six counter that controls the shifting and loading of the 74166. The video signal is a combination of the output of the shift register, VSP, and LTEN. The LTEN signal turns the video signal on and off for certain video attributes, and the VSP signal blanks the video during normal horizontal and vertical retracing and for a blinking character.

The horizontal and vertical retrace drive signals are developed by the circuitry. The control signal circuitry generates the vertical retrace drive pulse; the horizontal drive pulse is developed by a one-shot multivibrator.

Timing

The timing diagram for the circuit in figure 10–15 is illustrated in figure 10–16. The character clock, or output QC, from the divider is a reference signal to the 8275. It must also be used to latch a character into the shift register on the positive transition, as illustrated in the diagram. This edge occurs in coincidence with the decoded state three output of the counter, which latches a character into the shift register.

The CRT Display Initialization Dialog

```
;8275 INITIALIZATION
;
RESET:  SUB  A          ;STOP DISPLAY
```

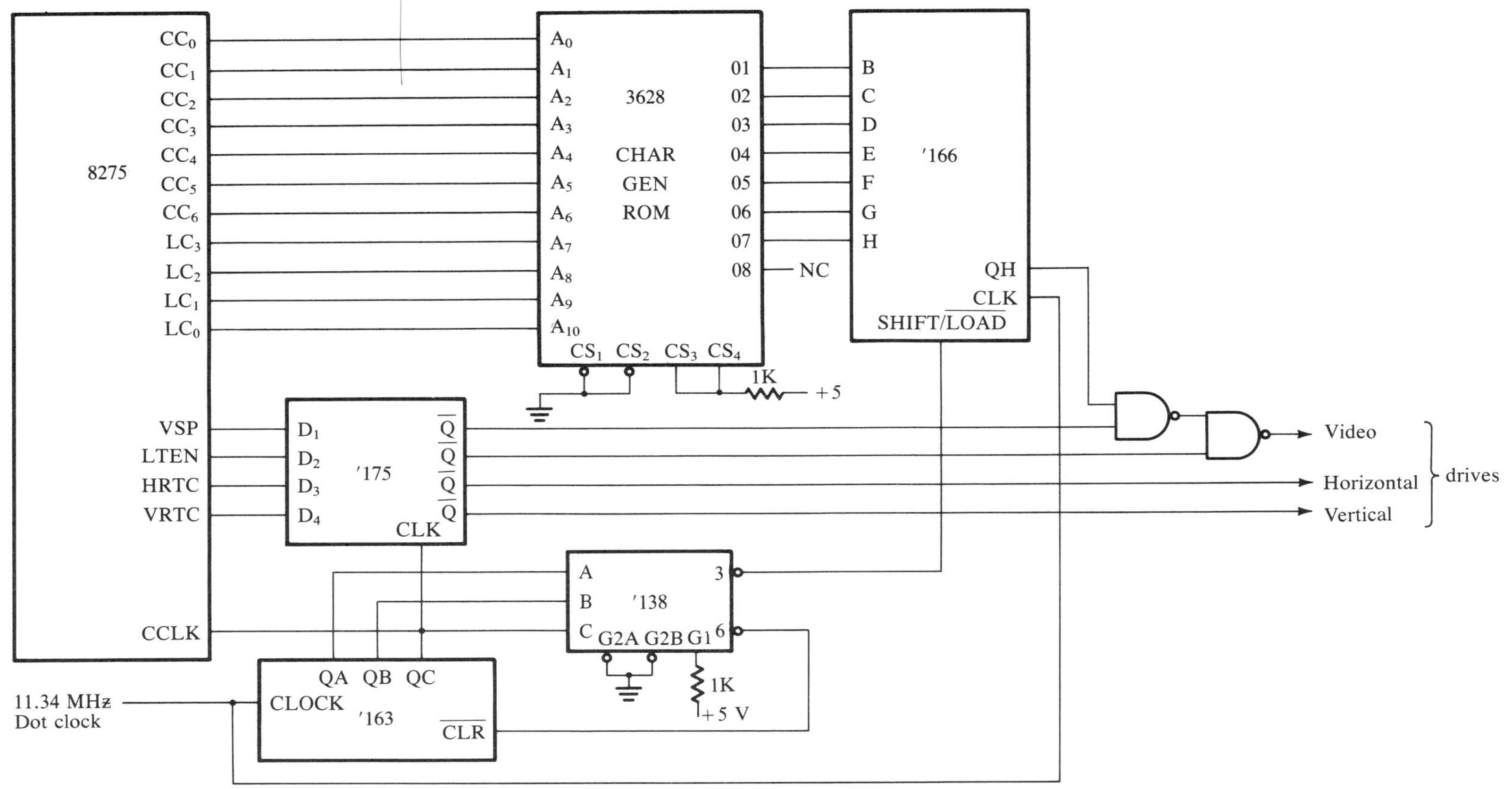

FIGURE 10–15 The 8275 CRT controller interfaced to a CRT.

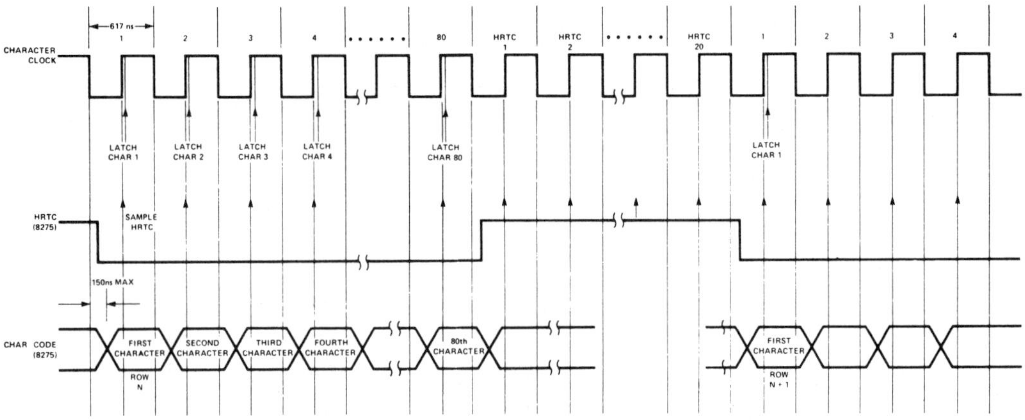

FIGURE 10–16 The timing diagram of the CRT interface illustrated in figure 10–15.
SOURCE: Reprinted by permission of Intel Corporation, Copyright 1978.

```
          OUT   81H
          MVI   A,4FH    ;SETUP 80 COLUMNS
          OUT   80H
          MVI   A,57H    ;2 RETRACE ROWS, 24 LINES
          OUT   80H
          MVI   A,78H    ;UNDERLINE ROW 8, 9 TOTAL
          OUT   80H
          MVI   A,68H    ;CURSOR = BLOCK, RETRACE = 9
          OUT   80H
          MVI   A,80H    ;HOME CURSOR
          OUT   81H
          SUB   A        ;COLUMN = 0
          OUT   80H
          OUT   80H      ;ROW = 0
          MVI   A,0E0H   ;PRESET COUNTERS
          OUT   81H
;INITIALIZE 8257 DMA CONTROLLER
          MVI   A,80H    ;SET AUTO LOAD MODE
          OUT   98H
          MVI   A,RRL    ;SETUP DMA BLOCK ADDRESS
          OUT   94H
          MVI   A,RRM
          OUT   94H
          MVI   A,SSL    ;SET COUNT TO 1919
          OUT   95H
          MVI   A,SSM
          OUT   95H
          MVI   A,23H    ;START 8275 CRT CONTROLLER
          OUT   81H
          MVI   A,84H    ;START DMA CONTROLLER
```

```
35          OUT   98H
             .
             .              (SYSTEM PROGRAM FOLLOWS)
             .
```

The CRT controller has been initialized to display 80 columns per line with a total of 24 lines displayed. This is pretty much a standard today in most CRT terminals. Each character is to be displayed in a five by seven matrix with the underline occurring in row eight; the cursor character type, which has been selected, is a nonblinking inverted video block.

The DMA controller displays the contents of memory block RRRR; and the character count is set at 1919 decimal, which is one less than the total of 1920 (as required by the controller). Once DMA action begins, the controller automatically updates the DMA address for the beginning of each frame of displayed data.

The entire process of displaying memory begins when the CRT controller is commanded to start with bursts of 8 bytes of DMA information at one time. In this way, there is quite a bit of processing time between direct memory accesses.

SPECIAL DMA TECHNIQUES 10-5

Up until this point, DMA transfer has consisted of single byte or burst transfers, but there are still other and sometimes more efficient methods of transferring the data. One such method is *cycle stealing,* or *hidden DMA.*

Hidden DMA

Hidden DMA is accomplished during the normal execution of the instructions. For example, in the 8085A microprocessor during an op-code fetch, there is at least one clocking period in which the system bus is unused or idle. Unfortunately this is not enough time in most memory systems to accomplish a read or write. In some instructions, though, there are actually two or three clocking periods at this time that allow the bus to be used for external events. It is during these longer instructions and the accompanying idle bus time that a DMA can take place.

In the 8085A the best instruction to use for this purpose is either the DCX or INX; each instruction has three unused clock cycles during execution. These three cycles can be used for a completely hidden or transparent DMA.

To signal when either of these instructions is occurring, it is necessary to decode the instruction as it is being pulled out of the memory. This is possible because the 8085A indicates an op-code fetch with status bits S0 and S1. This operation is illustrated in figure 10–17, along with a circuit for decoding any DCX or INX instruction.

The output of this circuit signals an external device that it can access the 8085A memory directly.

The $\overline{RD}$ signal is used as a clock pulse to the flip-flop to capture the output of the NOR gate. The NOR gate's output can only become a logic one when

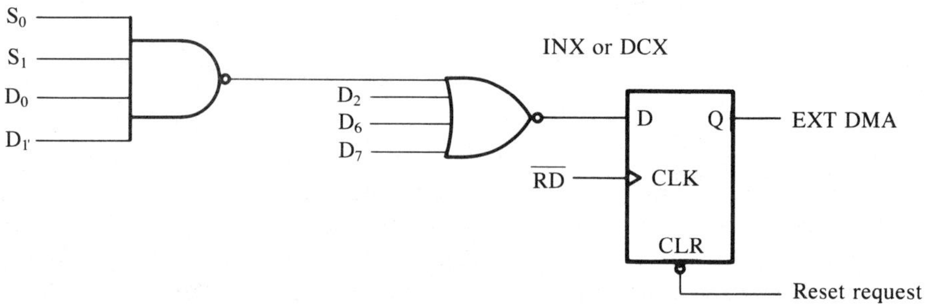

FIGURE 10–17 A circuit that will implement a hidden DMA request for any INX or DCX instruction.

its inputs are all logic zero. This condition occurs when D7, D6, and D2 are low and D0, D1, S1, and S0 are high. S1 and S0 are only high for an op-code fetch, so we are decoding op-codes. In this case the op-code must have the bit pattern 00XX X011. This bit pattern is unique to the eight INX and DCX instructions in the 8085A.

Summary

This chapter introduced the technique of directly accessing the memory for information. This technique is the most complicated of the techniques discussed in this book, and it is also the most efficient.

Using DMA, it is possible to reduce the software overhead to control a device to almost zero. This is demonstrated with the CRT terminal. Other applications include high-speed printers and disk drives.

In multiprocessing systems, DMA is also often used to share information between various microprocessors and/or sophisticated peripheral components. These techniques, although based on DMA techniques, are beyond the scope of this text.

Glossary

CRT controller A programmable device that develops and maintains all of the signals related to a CRT terminal, such as video, vertical synchronization, horizontal synchronization, and light pen position.

Character generator A ROM that contains information to display each possible character on the CRT screen.

CRT A cathode ray tube is a device that displays information visually. The picture tube in a television is a CRT. This abbreviation is sometimes used to indicate a cathode ray terminal (or tube, as it is known in the field).

Cursor An indicator on a video terminal that depicts the current screen update position.

DMA Direct memory access is a technique used to store or retrieve information directly from the memory without intervention from the microprocessor.

DMA burst This is a multiple byte direct memory access, as opposed to a single byte transfer.

DMA controller A device that is dedicated to the management of the DMA system.

Frame In video a frame is one complete sweep of the screen with the electron beam. In TV, a frame is two sweeps of the screen.

Hidden DMA Whenever the DMA occurs while the microprocessor is busy processing other data, also referred to as *cycle stealing*.

Inverse video Normal video is white characters on a black background; inverse video is black characters on a white background.

Screen refresh The act of periodically redisplaying information on the screen of a CRT. This normally occurs at the rate of 60 times per second.

Terminal count The final count or terminating count of a counter.

Questions and Problems

1 Define DMA.

2 List two applications that would benefit from DMA processed I/O.

3 What occurs when a microprocessor is forced into its DMA or hold state?

4 Which has higher priority in a microprocessor, the DMA input or the interrupt input?

5 What is the maximum number of bytes that can be transferred by the 8257 DMA controller without reloading its counter?

6 Describe the way the auto load feature in the 8257 DMA controller functions.

7 What does the F/L flip-flop do in the 8257 DMA controller?

8 Write the software to program the channel zero address register with memory location 1000H and the channel zero counter with a read command and a count of 100 decimal. (The initial state of the F/L flip-flop is unknown.)

9 If the terminal count (TC) pin connection is connected to an interrupt pin, is it possible to use more than one of the DMA channels? Explain.

10 Connect an 8155 to an 8257 DMA controller so that a DMA cycle will be requested whenever data is strobed into the port A input port.

11 For the hardware in question 10, develop software that will program the controller and I/O device to store the information at memory location 2000H. Only 1 byte will be transferred before the controller must be reinitialized.

12 Develop a subroutine to test the status of the 8257 to determine whether or not any channel has reached its terminal count. For a terminal count on channel zero, jump to the program that begins at location 1100H; for channel one at location 1130H; for channel two at location 1190H; and for channel three at location 12A0H.

13 Explain how the CRT controller is programmed to display an inverse video cursor.

14 Would it be possible to connect the 8275 CRT controller to the 8085A without the use of a DMA controller? Explain.

15 Develop software that will scroll the contents of the area of memory displayed in the CRT application in this chapter. To scroll the screen, the software would move the contents of the display memory up one line.

16 Using the CRT cursor registers, develop a subroutine that will allow the cursor to be moved to any screen position. The D register should contain the X coordinate, and the E register should contain the Y coordinate when the subroutine is called.

11

8085A Application Examples

Since understanding anything is best fostered by applying one's knowledge, two applications for the 8085A are listed in this chapter. These applications are meant to be used as examples of what can be accomplished with this microprocessor and the interfacing that has been discussed throughout this textbook. These examples can provide new ideas on ways to handle the many different hardware/software interactions illustrated here.

11-1 DISHWASHER CONTROL CIRCUIT

A dishwasher control circuit is a simple application of a "real-time" microprocessor based system. In this example, time delay subroutines develop the proper timing sequence for a simple one cycle dishwasher.

Figure 11–1 illustrates the circuitry required to control the dishwasher. Included is a 1K-byte ROM, 1K-byte RAM, an address latch to demultiplex the address/data bus of the 8085A, and an output latch for the control of the internal circuitry of the dishwasher.

Looking at the different devices in this circuit, you will notice that the ROM is active whenever address bit A15 is low and therefore will respond to memory addresses 0000H through 7FFFH. The RAM is active whenever address bit A15 is a logic one, so it has an address range of 8000H through FFFFH. Finally, the output port will respond to any OUT instruction; but you should only use a port number of 00 through 7FH. This will prevent the writing of output data to the RAM in this system.

Figure 11–2 pictures the interface circuitry required to drive the motor, heating element, drain solenoid, water inlet solenoid, and soap dispenser solenoid. These parts were chosen so that a reliable system could be developed for long-term operation.

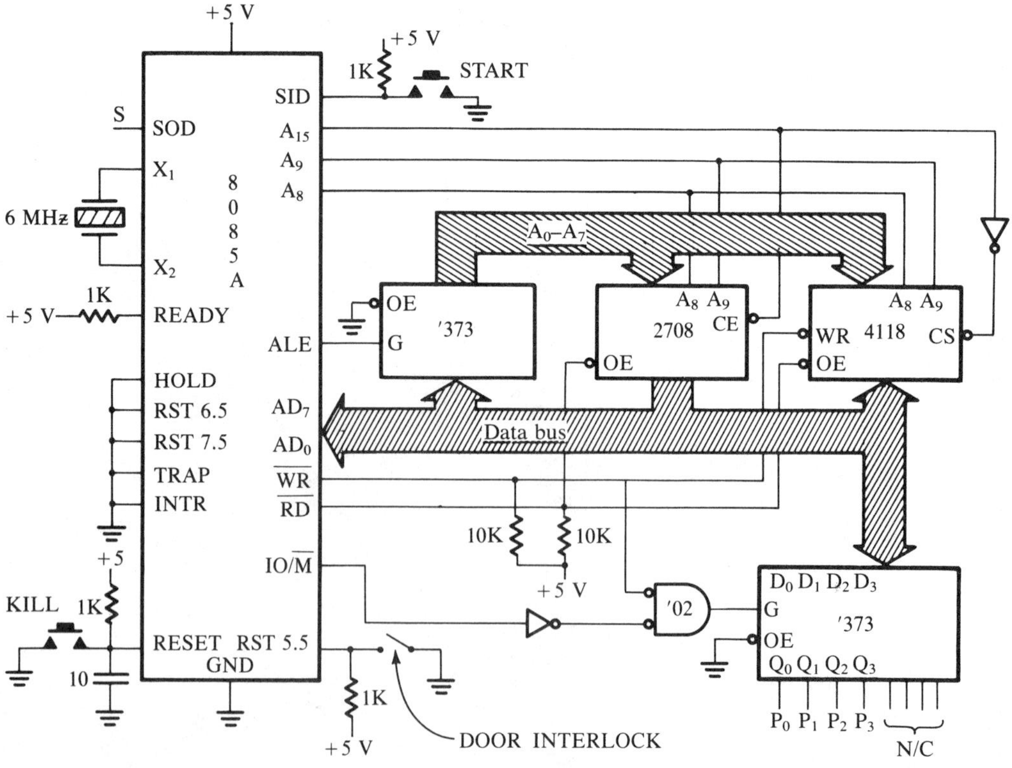

FIGURE 11–1 The schematic diagram of an Intel 8085A based dishwasher controller.

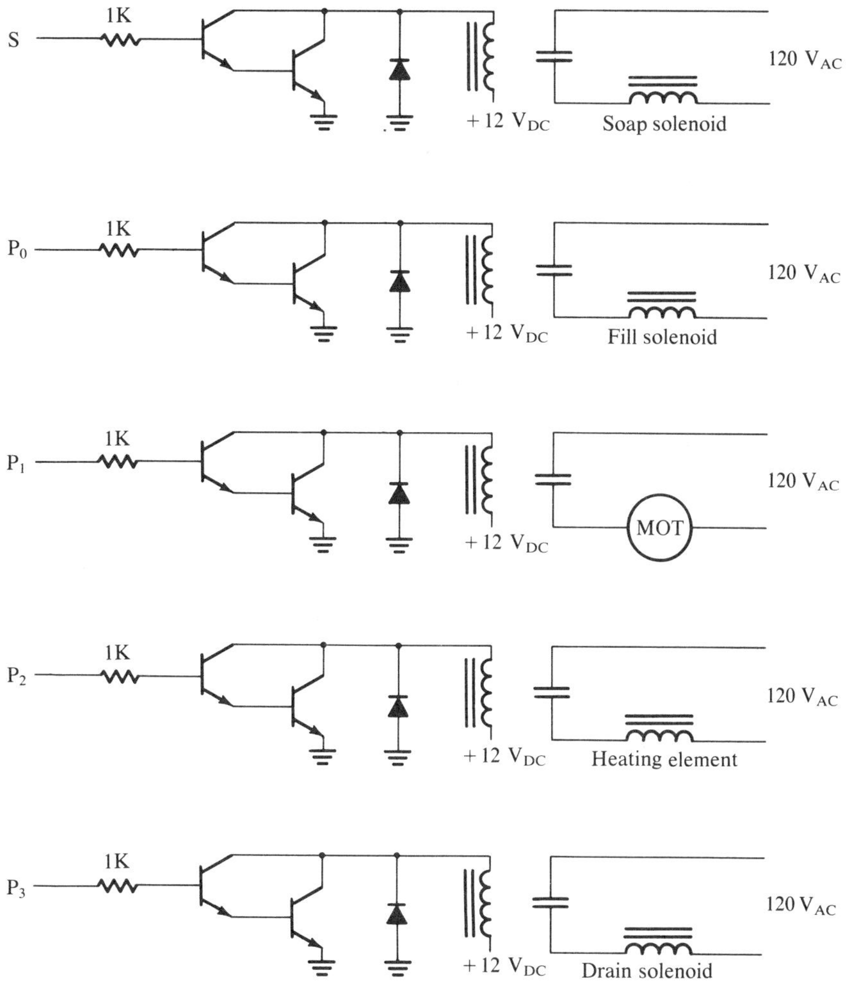

FIGURE 11–2 The solenoid and motor drivers for the dishwasher controller.

The front panel of this washer was chosen so that it contained a minimum number of operator controls for ease of use, as illustrated in figure 11–3.

The kill push button resets the microprocessor so that the current sequence can be aborted. Since it is connected to the $\overline{\text{RESET}}$ input of the 8085A, it forces the microprocessor to begin the program over again.

The start push button causes the dishwasher to begin sequencing through its washing cycle. This input is tested by the software by polling the SID pin on the microprocessor.

The only other input signal to the microprocessor is the door interlock switch, which is open circuited whenever the door of the dishwasher is opened. Since this signal is connected to an interrupt input on the microprocessor, it causes the current program to be interrupted, suspending all function until the door is closed.

FIGURE 11–3 A front view of the door and control panel of the dishwasher.

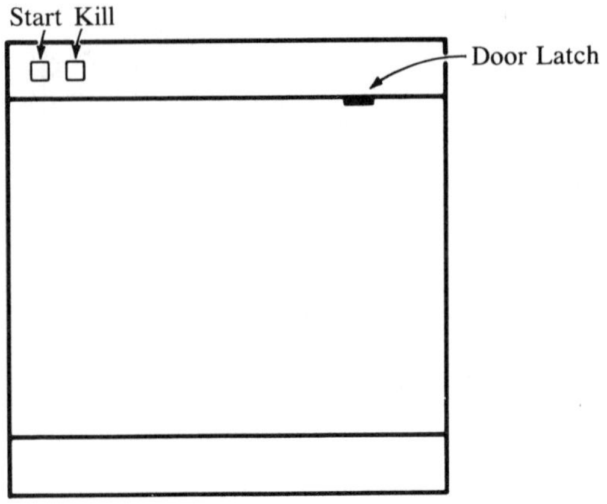

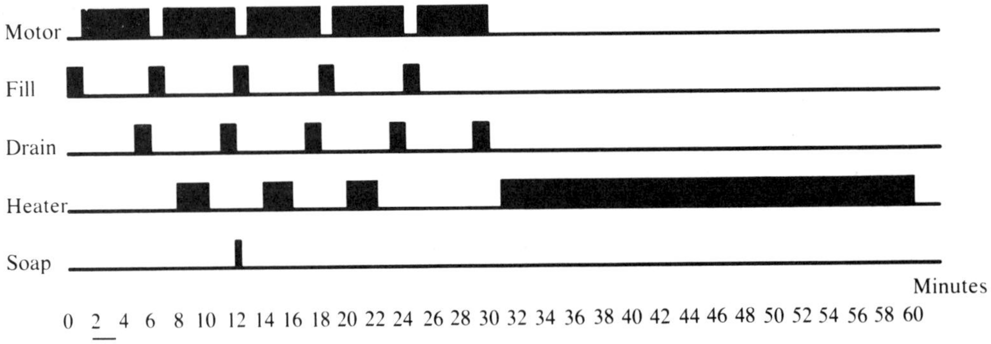

FIGURE 11–4 The timing sequence for the microprocessor controlled dishwasher.

The basic timing sequence for this machine is depicted in figure 11–4. The entire washing sequence requires 60 minutes to be completed. The first timing event is a prewash, which in theory removes dried food particles from the dishes. This is followed by a heated rinse cycle, heated wash cycle, two rinse cycles, and finally a drying cycle.

The program is depicted in the flowchart of figure 11–5, and the listing follows:

```
;MAIN DISHWASHER CONTROL PROGRAM
;
RESET:  LXI   SP,8400H    ;SET STACK AREA
        MVI   A,0EH       ;ENABLE RST5.5
        SIM
        RIM               ;READ SID
        RLC               ;START BUTTON TO CARRY
        JC    RESET       ;IF NO START
        CALL  D50         ;WAIT 50 MSEC.
        RIM               ;READ SID
        RLC               ;START BUTTON TO CARRY
        JC    RESET       ;IF NOISE THEN RESET
        EI                ;ENABLE DOOR INTERRUPT
        CALL  MOTOR       ;TYPE 1 SEQUENCE
```

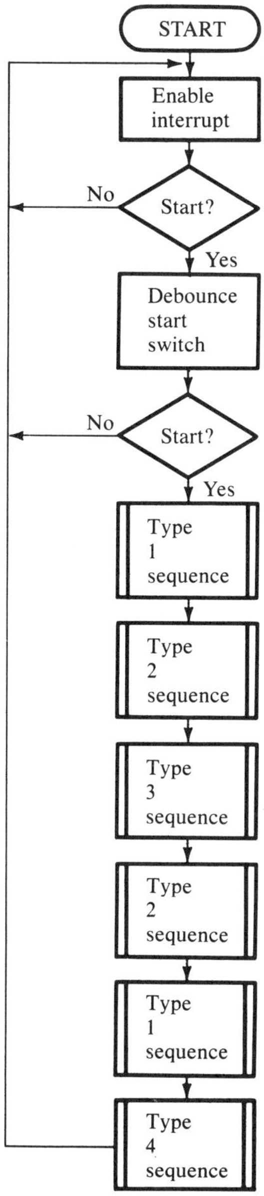

FIGURE 11–5 The flowchart of the microprocessor based dishwasher system program.

```
        CALL MOTORH     ;TYPE 2 SEQUENCE
        CALL MOTORHS    ;TYPE 3 SEQUENCE
        CALL MOTORH     ;TYPE 2 SEQUENCE
        CALL MOTOR      ;TYPE 1 SEQUENCE
        CALL HEAT       ;TYPE 4 SEQUENCE
        JMP  RESET      ;END OF CYCLE
```

In the preceding program if the start button is held down for at least 50 ms, the dishwasher begins its sequence. This, of course, is contingent on the door's being closed.

Once the machine is started, it sequences through four basic modes of operation. The first mode, the type 1 mode, causes the machine to fill with water, run the motor that sprays water on the dishes, and empty the water from the machine. The type 2 mode is identical to type 1, except that the heater is operated to make sure that the water temperature is high enough to kill germs on the dishes and to ensure that they are cleaned properly. The type 3 mode is identical to type 2, except that the soap is dispensed in the middle of the cycle. And type 4 is the heater cycle.

The time delay software, which is used in all modes of operation, consists of two subroutines. One delay subroutine causes a 50 ms delay (D50), and the other a 1 min delay (D1M).

```
;50 MILLISECOND TIME DELAY SUBROUTINE
;
D50:   LXI  B,186AH ;LOAD COUNT FOR 50 MSEC DELAY
D50A:  DCX  B       ;DECREMENT COUNT
       MOV  A,B     ;CHECK FOR ZERO
       ORA  C
       JNZ  D50A    ;IF COUNT IS NOT ZERO
       RET
;
;ONE MINUTE TIME DELAY
;
D1M:   LXI  D,04B0H ;LOAD COUNT FOR 1 MINUTE DELAY
D1MA:  CALL D50     ;WASTE 50 MSEC OF TIME
       DCX  D       ;DECREMENT COUNT
       MOV  A,D     ;CHECK FOR ZERO
       ORA  E
       JNZ  D1MA    ;IF COUNT IS NOT ZERO
       RET
```

A close examination of the timing chart indicates that the machine must be filled with water for 1 min in all types of operations, so a subroutine for filling would be useful. The output condition for each step of the dishwasher sequence is stored in a memory location so that the interrupt, which occurs whenever the door is opened, can suspend the operation until the door is closed. This is illustrated in this subroutine and all subsequent subroutines that control an external event.

```
;SUBROUTINE TO FILL THE DISHWASHER
;
FILL:   MVI  A,01H      ;SET UP FILL PATTERN
        STA  IOB        ;SAVE FOR INTERRUPT
        OUT  00H        ;START FILL PROCESS
        CALL D1M        ;WAIT ONE MINUTE
        SUB  A          ;CLEAR FILL PATTERN
        STA  IOB        ;SAVE FOR INTERRUPT
        RET
```

The next routine to be developed will cause the machine to fill with water; run the motor for 4 min; and, during the fifth minute of motor operation, empty the machine of all water. The motor activates a pump that empties the machine when a solenoid is held open for the last minute of operation. This sequence is the type 1 sequence identified in the main program as MOTOR.

```
;TYPE 1 SUBROUTINE SEQUENCE
;
MOTOR: CALL FILL      ;FILL MACHINE WITH WATER
       MVI  A,02H     ;SET MOTOR PATTERN
       STA  IOB       ;SAVE FOR INTERRUPT
       OUT  00H       ;START MOTOR
       MVI  H,04H     ;LOAD COUNTER
MOT1:  CALL D1M       ;WAIT ONE MINUTE
       DCR  H         ;DECREMENT COUNT
       JNZ  MOT1      ;WAIT FOUR MINUTES
DRAIN: MVI  A,0AH     ;SET MOTOR & DRAIN PATTERN
       STA  IOB       ;SAVE FOR INTERRUPT
       OUT  00H       ;RUN MOTOR AND DRAIN MACHINE
       CALL D1M       ;WAIT A MINUTE
       SUB  A         ;CLEAR PATTERN
       STA  IOB       ;SAVE FOR INTERRUPT
       OUT  00H       ;STOP MOTOR AND DRAIN
       RET
```

The type 2 mode of operation is identical to type 1, except that the heater is turned on for 3 min in the middle of the sequence. In the main program this is identified as subroutine MOTORH, which follows.

```
;TYPE 2 SUBROUTINE SEQUENCE
;
MOTORH: CALL FILL      ;FILL MACHINE
        MVI  A,02H     ;SET MOTOR PATTERN
        STA  IOB       ;SAVE FOR INTERRUPT
        OUT  00H       ;START MOTOR
        CALL D1M       ;WAIT ONE MINUTE
        MVI  A,06H     ;SET MOTOR & HEATER PATTERN
        STA  IOB       ;SAVE FOR INTERRUPT
        OUT  00H       ;RUN MOTOR WITH HEATER ON
        MVI  H,3       ;SET 3 MIN. COUNTER
MOTH1:  CALL D1M       ;WAIT ONE MINUTE
        DCR  H         ;DECREMENT COUNT
        JNZ  MOTH1     ;WAIT FOR THREE MINUTES
        MVI  A,02      ;SET MOTOR PATTERN
        STA  IOB       ;SAVE FOR INTERRUPT
        OUT  00H       ;RUN MOTOR & HEATER OFF
        CALL D1M       ;WAIT ONE MINUTE
        JMP  DRAIN     ;GO DRAIN THE MACHINE
```

The next subroutine is very short because it uses the MOTORH subroutine to perform all of its tasks except the dispensing of soap.

```
;TYPE 3 SUBROUTINE SEQUENCE
;
MOTORHS: CALL  MOTORH    ;DO A TYPE 2 MODE
         MVI   A,0C0H    ;SET SOAP PATTERN
         STA   IOB       ;SAVE FOR INTERRUPT
         SIM             ;SET SOD TO DISPENSE SOAP
         CALL  D50       ;WAIT 100 MSEC.
         CALL  D50
         SUB   A         ;CLEAR PATTERN
         STA   IOB       ;SAVE FOR INTERRUPT
         MVI   A,40H     ;SET SOAP OFF
         SIM             ;SOAP OFF
         RET
```

The next subroutine controls the heating cycle, which lasts for 0.5 hr.

```
;TYPE 4 SUBROUTINE SEQUENCE
;
HEAT:    MVI   A,04H     ;SET HEATER PATTERN
         STA   IOB       ;SAVE FOR INTERRUPT
         OUT   00H       ;HEATER ON
         MVI   H,1EH     ;LOAD 30 MINUTE COUNTER
HEAT1:   CALL  D1M       ;WAIT 1 MINUTE
         DCR   H         ;DECREMENT COUNTER
         JNZ   HEAT1     ;FOR 30 MINUTES
         SUB   A         ;SET EXTERNALS PATTERN
         STA   IOB       ;SAVE FOR INTERRUPT
         OUT   00H       ;HEATER OFF
         RET
```

The last and most important part of the software is the interrupt service subroutine for the door interlock. This routine must be able to turn off all external operations while the door is ajar and must reenable them when the door is closed. This is all handled through the IOB information that is stored in the RAM.

```
;INTERRUPT SERVICE SUBROUTINE
;
RST55:   PUSH  PSW       ;SAVE ACC & FLAGS
         PUSH  B         ;SAVE B & C
         CALL  D50       ;DEBOUNCE DOOR SENSOR
         MVI   A,40H
         SIM             ;SOAP OFF
         SUB   A         ;CLEAR PATTERN
         OUT   00H       ;ALL EXTERNALS OFF
RSTA:    RIM             ;GET I5.5
         ANI   10H       ;ISOLATE I5.5
         JNZ   RSTA      ;WAIT FOR A CLOSED DOOR
```

```
            LDA   IOB      ;GET IOB PATTERN
            ORA   A        ;TEST FOR SOAP
            JM    SOAP
            OUT   00H      ;RESTART EXTERNALS
     OUT:   EI             ;ENABLE FUTURE INTERRUPTS
            POP   B        ;RESTORE B & C
            POP   PSW      ;RESTORE ACC & FLAGS
            RET            ;RETURN FROM INTERRUPT
     SOAP:  SIM            ;SOAP ON
            JMP   OUT
```

This circuit and its associated software illustrate quite a few principles of the real-time control of a machine. They also illustrate the usefulness of an interrupt in halting or temporarily suspending the control system.

The entire system would have on one 8755A combination I/O and EPROM device, but subroutines have not been incorporated, since no RAM is present in this device. The space required to implement that system in this text is prohibitive because of the length of the program. The industrious student may want to try the suggested problems at the end of this chapter.

POINT OF SALES TERMINAL 11-2

Point of sales (POS) terminals or cash registers can be simple devices that handle simple entries or complex devices that are linked to larger computer systems. The latter type of POS terminal can keep track of inventory and look up the price of any item that the store might sell. To do this, it must contain some form of interface to the larger system and a vast amount of internal data storage. Some newer POS terminals can also verify the credit of the purchaser by contacting the credit department's computer or even a commercial bank's computer system.

This section deals with the simpler form of POS terminal—one that might be found in the corner Mom and Pop food market. Since this type of store cannot afford an inventory computer and since it has a limited stock of items, it can manage with a simpler POS terminal. The type discussed in this section would cost well under three hundred dollars and maintain accurate records of tax and sales data for the owners of the market.

Point of Sales Terminal Hardware

A basic POS terminal contains a keyboard for data entry, a set of numeric displays, and a cash drawer. The last item is not present in the simplest types of POS terminals but is included in the terminal in this discussion.

Figure 11–6 depicts the basic keyboard and display layout of the POS terminal developed in this section. There are the numeric keys 0 through 9 for data entry; a void key to erase erroneous entries; a clear entry key; a taxable department key; a nontaxable department key; a tax key; and a total, or final sales, key. In addition to the keyboard entry keys, there is also a keyswitch that allows the owner to program the tax table into the machine and another

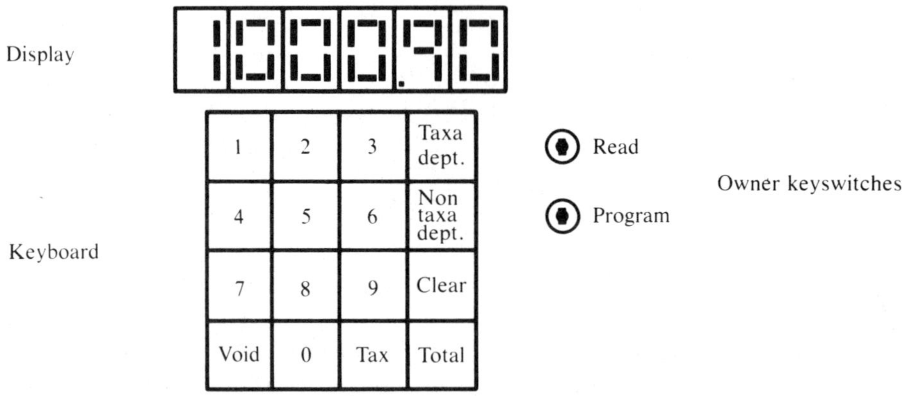

FIGURE 11–6 The keyboard and display layout for the 8085A based point of sales terminal.

to read the department keys, tax data, and total sales key at the end of each day.

The Display Section

The display section consists of six seven-segment numeric displays that allow sales of up to $9999.99 in a single day, large enough for most small stores.

Figure 11–7 illustrates the flowchart for the program of this POS terminal. The displaying of data does not appear in this flowchart because display data is handled by a periodic interrupt and appears on a separate flowchart in figure 11–8.

The Memory

The RAM read/write memory is used for the system stack and also to store such information as the display data and the sales totalizers for the register. A complete schematic diagram for the memory and the rest of the hardware is illustrated in figure 11–9. Following is a complete listing of the data locations in the RAM:

```
DISP:      DS   3    ;DISPLAY DATA
TEMP:      DS   3    ;TEMPORARY STORAGE
TAX:       DS   3    ;TAX TOTAL
NTX:       DS   3    ;NONTAXABLE TOTAL
TTAX:      DS   3    ;TAX TEMP
NTXT:      DS   3    ;NONTAXABLE TEMP
TXT:       DS   3    ;TAXABLE TEMP
TX:        DS   3    ;TAXABLE TOTAL
TOTAL:     DS   3    ;TOTAL SALES
RATE:      DS   1    ;TAX RATE
LOOK:      DS   20   ;TAX LOOKUP TABLE
```

The tax lookup table is used by the program to determine the tax breaks for the cents column below and above one dollar. The tax rate on whole dollars is determined by the value stored at memory location RATE when the machine is programmed by the user. This is necessary because the tax

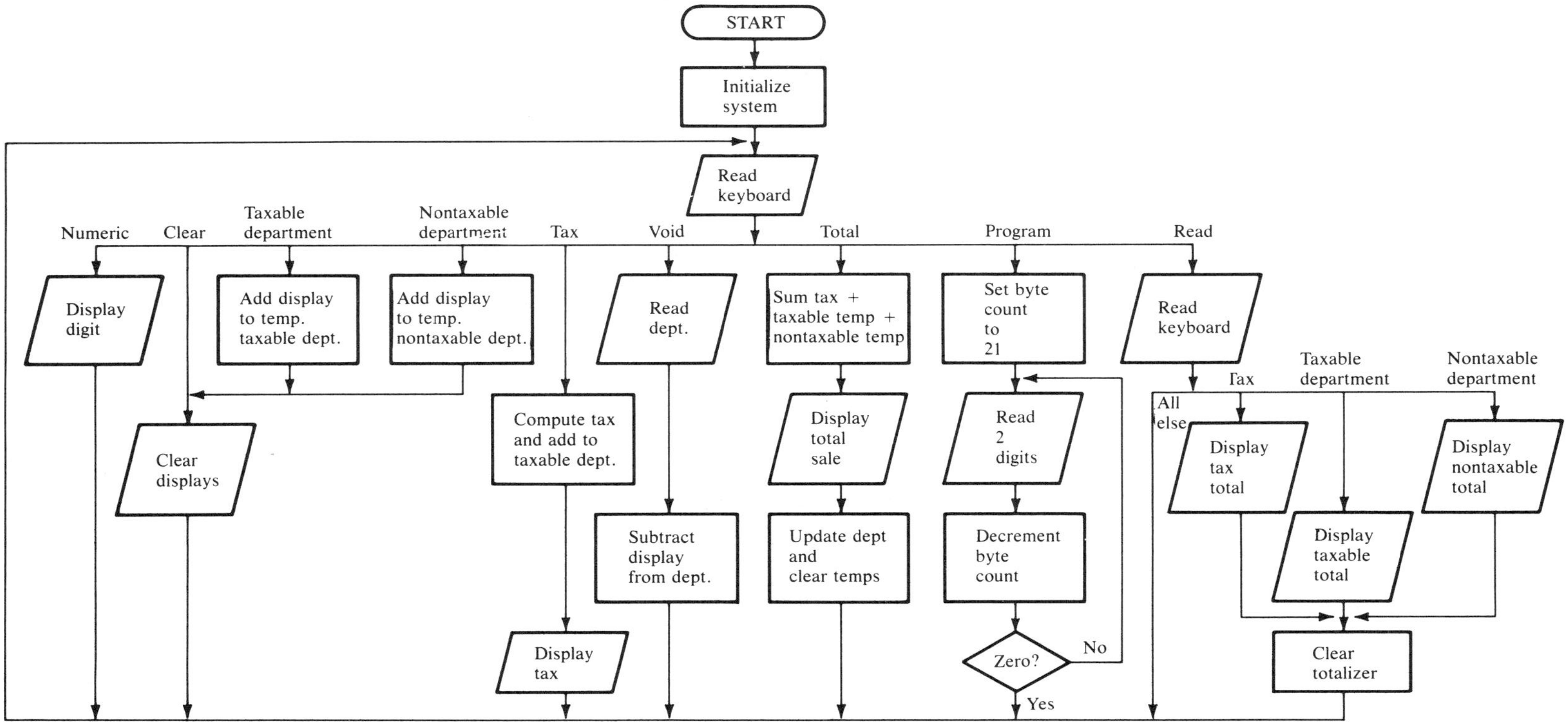

FIGURE 11–7 The system flowchart for the 8085A based point of sales terminal.

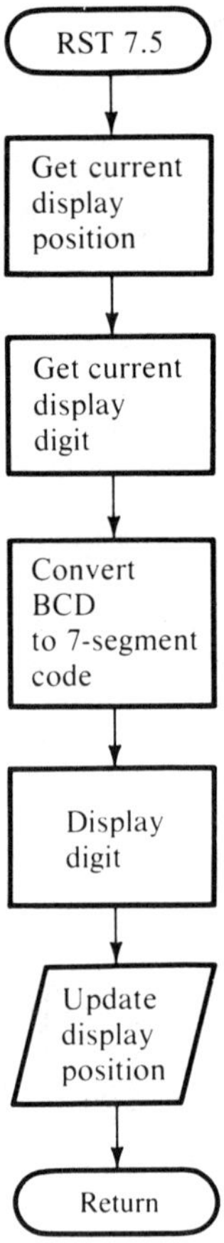

FIGURE 11–8 The flowchart of the interrupt service subroutine that handles the displaying of data.

breaks below and above a dollar are not the same, and some states even charge a different percentage tax on an amount of less than one dollar. The tax rate can be programmed in mills so that stores in various states, counties, and cities can adjust the rate to the exact amount of the local tax.

System Initialization Dialog

When power is first applied to this system, the programmable I/O device must be initialized along with the interrupt structure of the 8085A. In addition to this, the display memory and totalizers must also be cleared to zero. It is assumed that the system power supply is backed up by battery in case of a power failure.

```
;INITIALIZATION DIALOG
;
RESET:   LXI   SP,8100H   ;INITIALIZE STACK AREA
         LXI   H,8030H    ;POINT TO STORAGE
         SUB   A          ;CLEAR ACCUMULATOR
RESETA:  MOV   M,A        ;CLEAR A MEMORY LOCATION
         DCR   L          ;DECREMENT COUNT & POINTER
         JP    RESETA     ;REPEAT UNTIL CLEARED
         MVI   A,0DCH     ;PROGRAM TIMER TO
```

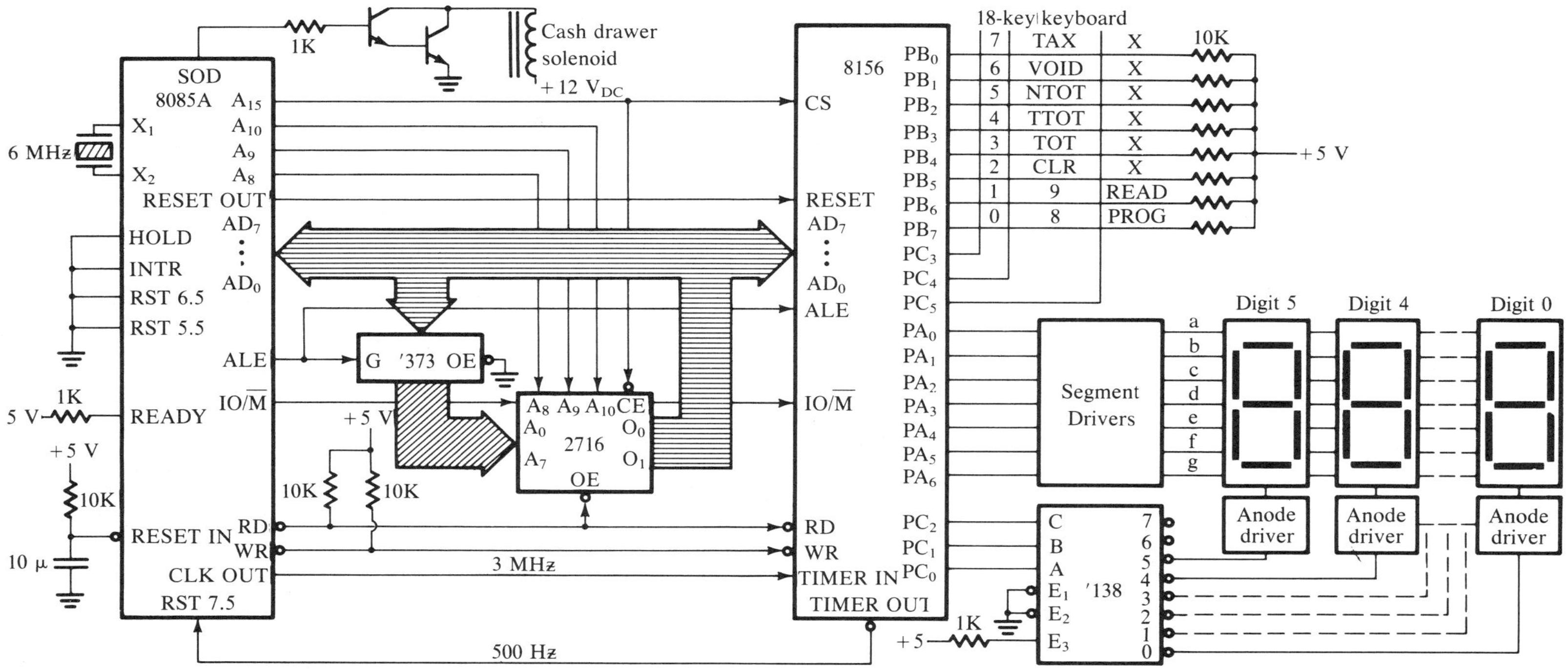

FIGURE 11–9 The 8085A based point of sales terminal schematic diagram.

```
        OUT  84H        ;DIVIDE BY 1500
        MVI  A,45H
        OUT  85H
        MVI  A,0CDH     ;PORT A & C = OUTPUT
        OUT  80H        ;PORT B = INPUT
        MVI  A,0BH      ;ENABLE RST 7.5
        SIM
        EI              ;START DISPLAY
        JMP  SYSTEM     ;JUMP TO SYSTEM PROGRAM
```

The initialization dialog illustrated has cleared the system memory, initialized the programmable I/O device, enabled the display interrupt, and jumped over the RST 7.5 interrupt service subroutine to the system software. The last step is necessary because the RST 7.5 interrupt service subroutine must be located beginning at memory location 003CH.

System Software

The system software has been implemented directly from the flowchart of figure 11–7.

```
;MAIN SYSTEM PROGRAM BEGINS HERE
;
SYSTEM: CALL INKEY      ;GET A KEYSTROKE
        MOV  A,B        ;GET KEY CODE
        SUI  10         ;IS IT A NUMBER?
        JC   NUMB       ;IF A NUMBER
        ADD  A          ;FORM TABLE LOOKUP
        MOV  E,A        ;BIAS
        MVI  D,0
        LXI  H,JTAB     ;POINT TO TABLE
        DAD  D          ;COMPUTE ADDRESS
        MOV  E,M        ;GET JUMP ADDRESS
        INX  H
        MOV  H,M
        MOV  L,E
        PCHL            ;JUMP TO ROUTINE
;
;LOOKUP TABLE FOR VARIOUS SPECIAL KEYS
;
JTAB:   DW   CLEAR      ;CLEAR ENTRY KEY
        DW   TOT        ;TOTAL SALE KEY
        DW   TTOT       ;TAXABLE ENTRY KEY
        DW   NTOT       ;NONTAXABLE ENTRY KEY
        DW   VOID       ;VOID KEY
        DW   TAX        ;TAX KEY
        DW   PROG       ;PROGRAM TAX RATE KEY
        DW   READ       ;READ DEPARTMENT TOTALS KEY
```

The system software is rather simple since its main purpose is to look at the keyboard and sort out the information as it is entered.

Display Interrupt Service Subroutine

The interrupt service subroutine is called once every 2 ms by the timer located inside the 8156. This periodic interrupt displays the next digit on the LED display.

```
;DISPLAY INTERRUPT SERVICE SUBROUTINE
;
RST75:  PUSH PSW     ;SAVE ALL REGISTERS USED
        PUSH H
        LDA  TEMP    ;GET DIGIT LOCATION
        ORA  A       ;CLEAR CARRY
        RAR          ;DIVIDE BY TWO
        MOV  L,A     ;SET DATA ADDRESS
        MVI  H,80H   ;POINT TO DISPLAY DATA
        MOV  A,M     ;GET DISPLAY DATA
        JC   RST7A   ;IF RIGHT HALF
        RRC          ;IF NOT MAKE IT THE
        RRC          ;RIGHT HALF
        RRC
        RRC
RST7A:  ANI  0FH     ;MASK OFF LEFT HALF
        LXI  H,DTAB  ;LOOKUP 7-SEGMENT CODE
        ADD  L
        MOV  L,A
        MOV  A,M
        OUT  81H     ;SEND DISPLAY DATA
        LDA  TEMP    ;GET DIGIT LOCATION
        INR  A       ;ADD TO DIGIT LOCATION
        CPI  6       ;CHECK FOR LAST DIGIT
        JNZ  RST7B   ;IF NOT LAST
        SUB  A       ;CLEAR ACC
RST7B:  STA  TEMP    ;SAVE NEW DIGIT LOCATION
        MOV  H,A     ;HOLD IT
        IN   83H     ;READ PORT C
        ANI  0F8H    ;CLEAR RIGHT THREE BITS
        ORA  H       ;INSERT DIGIT SELECT BITS
        OUT  83H     ;SELECT DISPLAY DIGIT
        POP  H       ;RESTORE REGISTERS
        POP  PSW
        EI           ;ENABLE NEXT INTERRUPT
        RET          ;RETURN TO POINT OF INTERRUPTION
;
;BCD TO 7-SEGMENT LOOKUP TABLE
;
DTAB:   DB   01111110B     ;   "0"
        DB   00110000B     ;   "1"
        DB   01101101B     ;   "2"
        DB   01111001B     ;   "3"
        DB   00110011B     ;   "4"
```

```
90          DB      01011011B       ;   "5"
91          DB      01011111B       ;   "6"
92          DB      01110000B       ;   "7"
93          DB      01111111B       ;   "8"
94          DB      01111011B       ;   "9"
```

The software illustrated for the display section requires that the code conversion lookup table is located at a memory location that does not cross a page boundary. If the table does cross a page boundary, the software will require some modification.

The time required to service the displays is approximately 100 μs, which occurs once every 2 ms. This means that the display software only uses about 5 percent of the microprocessor's time, which creates no problem in a point of sales terminal.

Keyboard Scanning Software

The keyboard on this particular cash register consists of ten numeric, six exposed function, and two hidden special function keys. The special function keys allow data to be entered into the taxable or nontaxable departments and control the outcome of the sale.

The hidden special purpose keys allow the register to be programmed for the state sales tax and also allow totals for each department to be read at the end of the day or at a change of operators. These keys are often controlled with a locking keyswitch to prevent tampering. See figure 11–10 for a detailed flowchart of this subroutine.

```
 95 ;KEYBOARD SCANNING SUBROUTINE
 96 INKEY:  LXI    B,03F0H ;SET COUNTER AND SELECT PATTERN
 97         IN     83H     ;READ PORT C
 98         ANI    7       ;MASK ALL BUT DISPLAY SELECT
 99         ADD    C       ;SELECT KEY COLUMN
100         OUT    83H
101         IN     82H     ;READ A COLUMN
102         INR    A       ;CHECK FOR A KEYSTROKE
103         JZ     INKEY1  ;ON A KEYSTROKE
104         DCR    B       ;LAST COLUMN?
105         JZ     INKEY   ;IF LAST COLUMN
106         MOV    A,C     ;GET NEW SELECT CODE
107         ADD    A       ;SHIFT LEFT
108         ORI    B       ;SET ACC BIT 3
109         MOV    C,A     ;SAVE NEW SELECT CODE
110         JMP    INKEY+3 ;CHECK NEXT COLUMN
111 INKEY1: HLT            ;WAIT 10 TO 12 MSEC,
112         HLT            ;FOR KEY DEBOUNCE
113         HLT
114         HLT
115         HLT
116         HLT
117         IN     82H     ;READ COLUMN
```

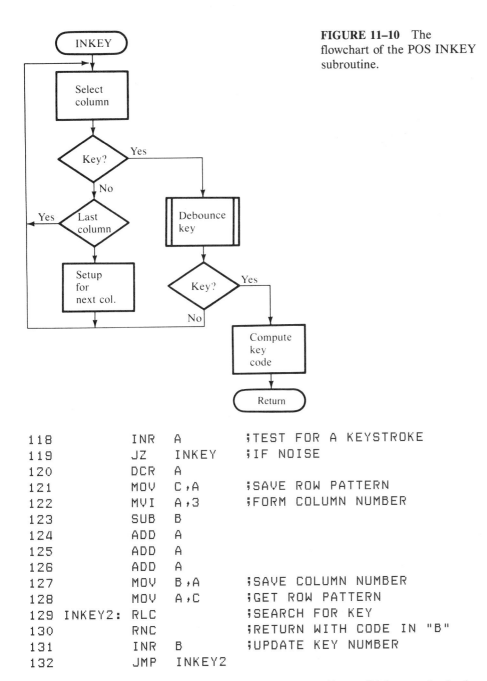

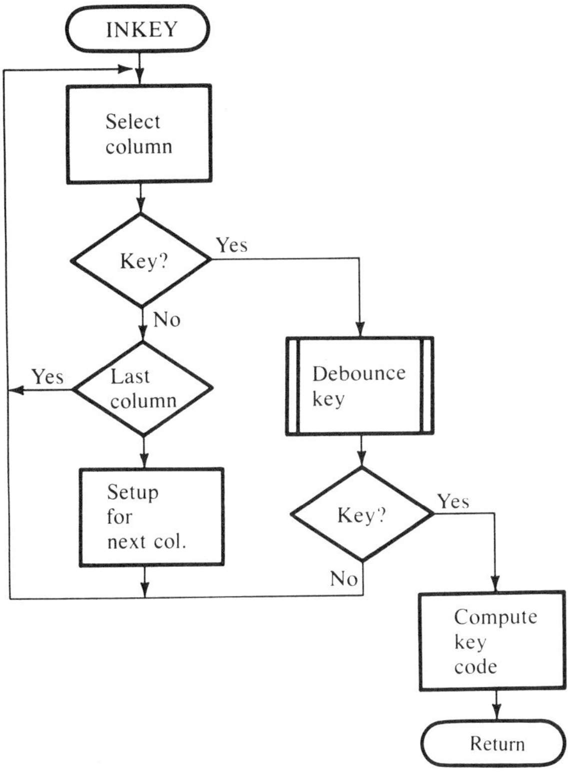

FIGURE 11–10 The flowchart of the POS INKEY subroutine.

```
        INR   A        ;TEST FOR A KEYSTROKE
        JZ    INKEY    ;IF NOISE
        DCR   A
        MOV   C,A      ;SAVE ROW PATTERN
        MVI   A,3      ;FORM COLUMN NUMBER
        SUB   B
        ADD   A
        ADD   A
        ADD   A
        MOV   B,A      ;SAVE COLUMN NUMBER
        MOV   A,C      ;GET ROW PATTERN
INKEY2: RLC            ;SEARCH FOR KEY
        RNC            ;RETURN WITH CODE IN "B"
        INR   B        ;UPDATE KEY NUMBER
        JMP   INKEY2
```

The INKEY subroutine scans the keyboard until a valid keystroke is detected. Once detected, the subroutine waits for the key to stop bouncing, since noise could have triggered a response. This procedure is accomplished by a series of six HLT instructions. The HLT instruction waits until an interrupt occurs before execution continues. Since an interrupt occurs every 2 ms, the amount of time delay caused by the HLT instructions will be 10–12 ms. In general, this is ample time for a keyswitch to be debounced.

Once debouncing is completed, the exact key location is determined, and a return occurs with the code of the keystroke in the B register.

Clear Function Key

Because the clear function is the easiest to understand, it is presented first. This function merely clears the display register in memory locations 8000H through 8002H. Included with the clear function is the return to system point, RETSY, which checks the keyboard for a key release.

```
133 ;CLEAR FUNCTION KEY SUBPROGRAM
134 ;
135 CLEAR:   CALL CLRD      ;CLEAR DISPLAY
136 RETSY:   IN   82H       ;GET KEY PATTERN
137          INR  A         ;CHECK FOR KEY DEPRESSION
138          JNZ  RETSY      ;IF STILL DEPRESSED
139          HLT             ;DEBOUNCE KEY
140          HLT
141          HLT
142          HLT
143          HLT
144          HLT
145          JMP  SYSTEM ;RETURN TO SYSTEM PROGRAM
146 ;
147 ;CLEAR DISPLAY MEMORY SUBROUTINE
148 ;
149 CLRD:    LXI  H,0       ;CLEAR DISPLAY MEMORY
150          SHLD DISP
151          MOV  A,H
152          STA  DISP+3
153          RET
```

Total Function Key

The total key, which is used to total a sale, must add the contents of the taxable temp location, the nontaxable temp location, and the tax temp location together to form the total sales price. Once this is accomplished, it must then update the totals of all three items and open the cash drawer.

```
154 ;TOTAL FUNCTION KEY SUBPROGRAM
155 ;
156 TOT:     CALL CLRD      ;CLEAR DISPLAY MEMORY
157          LXI  H,DISP    ;POINT TO DISP
158          LXI  D,TTAX    ;POINT TO TTAX
159          CALL SUM       ;ADD TTAX TO DISP
160          LXI  D,NTXT    ;POINT TO NTXT
161          CALL SUM       ;ADD NTXT TO DISP
162          LXI  D,TXT     ;POINT TO TXT
163          CALL SUM       ;ADD TXT TO DISP
164 ;
165 ;UPDATE TAX
```

```
        LXI  H,TAX    ;POINT TO TAX
        LXI  D,TTAX   ;POINT TO TTAX
        CALL SUM      ;ADD TTAX TO TAX
;
;UPDATE NONTAXABLE TOTAL
;
        LXI  H,NTX    ;POINT TO NTX
        LXI  D,NTXT   ;POINT TO NTXT
        CALL SUM      ;ADD NTXT TO NTX
;
;UPDATE TAXABLE TOTAL
;
        LXI  H,TX     ;POINT TO TX
        LXI  D,TXT    ;POINT TO TXT
        CALL SUM      ;ADD TXT TO TX
;
;FORM NEW GRAND TOTAL
;
        LXI  H,TOTAL  ;POINT TO TOTAL
        LXI  D,TXT    ;POINT TO TXT
        CALL SUM      ;ADD TXT TO TOTAL
        LXI  D,NTXT   ;POINT TO NTXT
        CALL SUM      ;ADD NTXT TO TOTAL
        LXI  D,TTAX   ;POINT TO TTAX
        CALL SUM      ;ADD TTAX TO TOTAL
;
;CLEAR TEMPS
;
        LXI  H,TTAX   ;POINT TO TEMPS
        MVI  B,12     ;SET COUNT
        SUB  A        ;CLEAR ACC
TOTAL1: MOV  M,A      ;CLEAR A LOCATION
        INX  H        ;POINT NEXT
        DCR  B        ;DECREMENT COUNT
        JNZ  TOTAL1   ;IF NOT DONE
;
;OPEN CASH DRAWER
;
        MVI  B,50     ;LOAD COUNTER
        MVI  A,0C0H   ;SET SOD
        SIM
TOTAL2: HLT           ;WASTE 2 MSEC.
        DCR  B        ;DECREMENT COUNT
        JNZ  TOTAL2   ;IF NOT DONE
;
;WAIT FOR NEXT SALE
;
        CALL INKEY    ;GET NEXT KEY
        CALL CLRD     ;CLEAR DISPLAY
```

```
216              JMP   SYSTEM+3
217 ;
218 ;SUMMATION SUBROUTINE
219 ;
220 SUM:    PUSH  H          ;SAVE POINTER
221         MVI   B,3        ;LOAD COUNTER
222         ORA   A          ;CLEAR CARRY
223 SUM1:   LDAX  D          ;GET BYTE
224         ADC   M          ;ADD BYTE
225         DAA              ;DECIMAL ADJUST BDC RESULT
226         MOV   M,A        ;SAVE RESULT
227         INX   H          ;INCREMENT POINTERS
228         INX   D
229         DCR   B          ;DECREMENT COUNT
230         JNZ   SUM1       ;IF NOT DONE
231         POP   H          ;IF DONE RESTORE POINTER
232         RET
```

Taxable Function Key

The taxable function key stores whatever value is entered into the keyboard into the temporary taxable department. This value is displayed at the same time on the numeric displays.

```
233 ;TAXABLE FUNCTION KEY SUBPROGRAM
234 ;
235 TTOT:   LXI   H,TXT      ;POINT TO TXT
236         LXI   D,DISP     ;POINT TO DISP
237         CALL  SUM        ;ADD DISP TP TXT
238         CALL  CLRD       ;CLEAR DISPLAY
239         JMP   RETSY      ;RETURN TO THE SYSTEM
```

Nontaxable Function Key

This key is used whenever the customer purchases nontaxable merchandise. As with the taxable function key, the display is added to the temporary nontaxable total and then cleared.

```
240 ;NONTAXABLE FUNCTION KEY SUBPROGRAM
241 ;
242 NTOT:   LXI   H,NTXT     ;POINT TO NTXT
243         LXI   D,DISP     ;POINT TO DISPLAY
244         CALL  SUM        ;ADD DISP TO NTXT
245         CALL  CLRD       ;CLEAR DISPLAY
246         JMP   RETSY      ;RETURN TO SYSTEM
```

Tax Function Key

This key is used just before a sale is complete to compute the sales tax. In other words, to tend the sale, the tax key followed by the total key is the normal sequence.

Whenever this key is depressed, it calculates the amount of sales tax-based programmed tax rate. This is accomplished by looking the amount of sales tax up in a tax table. The table contains the amount of tax on the first dollar, followed by the amount of tax on subsequent pennies of the total amount of the taxable sale.

For example, suppose that a state has a 5 percent sales tax with the tax rate shown in table 11–1.

TABLE 11–1 5% Sales tax breakpoints.

Price	Tax
$0.10 to $0.19	$.01
$0.20 to $0.34	$.02
$0.35 to $0.64	$.03
$0.65 to $0.84	$.04
$0.85 to $1.09	$.05
$1.10 to $1.29	$.06
$1.30 to $1.49	$.07
$1.50 to $1.69	$.08
$1.70 to $1.89	$.09
$1.90 to $2.09	$.10

The lower cent breaks are stored in the lookup table, beginning with a 10. These amounts are stored in the following BCD order: 10, 20, 35, 65, 85, 00, 00, 00, 00, 00, 10, 30, 50, 70, 90, 00, 00, 00 00, and 00. The first ten locations contain the breakpoints under one dollar, and the second set of ten locations contains the penny breakpoints over one dollar. Memory location RATE contains the tax rate in mills; in this example, RATE contains a 50H (50 BCD), or 50 mills for a 5 percent sales tax. Figure 11–11 illustrates the flowchart for the tax function key.

```
;TAX FUNCTION KEY SUBPROGRAM
;
TAX:    LHLD TXT+1      ;GET TAXABLE DOLLAR AMOUNT
        MOV  A,H        ;CHECK FOR NO DOLLARS
        ORA  L
        JNZ  TAX1       ;IF ONE OR MORE DOLLARS
        LXI  H,LOOK     ;POINT TO LOOKUP TABLE
        CALL GETX       ;COMPUTE TAX AND SAVE AT TTAX
        JMP  RETSY      ;RETURN TO SYSTEM
TAX1:   LXI  H,LOOK+8   ;POINT TO LOOKUP TABLE
        CALL GETX       ;COMPUTE TAX ON CENTS
        LDA  RATE       ;GET TAX RATE
        MOV  E,A
        MVI  D,0        ;GET TAXABLE AMOUNT
        LHLD TXT+1
        MOV  B,H        ;COPY TO BC
        MOV  C,L
TAX2:   MOV  A,C        ;COMPUTE DOLLAR TAX
        ADD  L
        DAA
        MOV  L,A
        JNC  TAX3
```

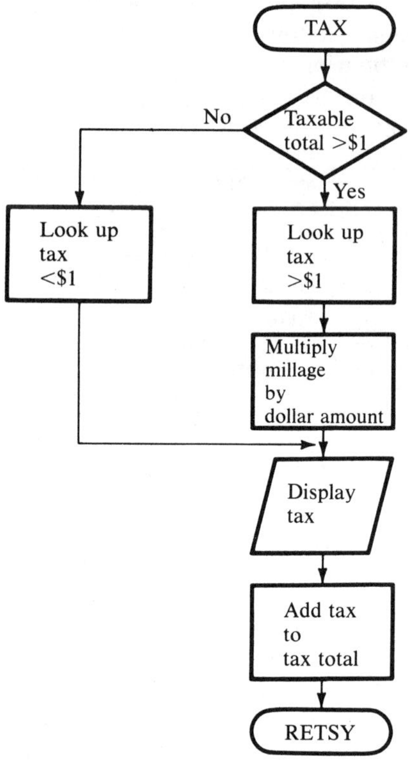

FIGURE 11–11 The
flowchart of the TAX
subprogram.

```
269              MOV    A,B
270              ADC    H
271              DAA
272              MOV    H,A
273              JNC    TAX3        ;IF NO OVER FLOW
274              MOV    A,D
275              ACI    0
276              DAA
277              MOV    D,A
278  TAX3:       MOV    A,E         ;DECREMENT MILLAGE
279              ADI    99H
280              DAA
281              MOV    E,A
282              JNZ    TAX2
283              LXI    B,TTAX      ;POINT TO TAX
284              LDAX   B
285              ADD    L
286              DAA
287              STAX   B
288              INX    B           ;POINT TO NEXT
289              LDAX   B
290              ADD    H
291              DAA
```

```
        STAX B
        INX  B        ;POINT TO LAST
        LDAX B
        ADD  D
        DAA
        STAX B
        CALL GETX3    ;DISPLAY TAX
        JMP  RETSY    ;RETURN TO SYSTEM
;
;LOOKUP TAX AND DISPLAY IT
;
GETX:   MVI  B,0      ;SET CENTS COUNTER
GETX1:  LDA  TXT      ;GET CENTS
        CMP  M        ;CHECK TABLE
        JC   GETX2    ;IF FOUND
        INX  H        ;POINT TO NEXT ENTRY
        INR  B        ;BUMP A PENNY
        MOV  A,M      ;CHECK FOR LAST
        ORA  A        ;TEST ACC
        JNZ  GETX1    ;IF NOT LAST
GETX2:  MOV  A,B      ;GET TAX
        STA  TTAX     ;SAVE IT
        LXI  H,0      ;GET ZERO
        SHLD TTAX+1   ;CLEAR OUT DOLLAR TAX
GETX3:  LXI  H,TTAX   ;DISPLAY TAX
        LXI  D,DISP
        MVI  B,3
GETX4:  MOV  A,M      ;GET DATA
        STAX D        ;SAVE DATA
        INX  H        ;INCREMENT POINTERS
        INX  D
        DCR  B        ;DECREMENT COUNT
        JNZ  GETX4    ;IF NOT DONE
        RET           ;IF DONE
```

Void Function Key

The void key erases erroneous data from either of the two departments in this register. The void key voids the displayed amount when it is depressed if it is followed by the taxable or nontaxable entry key. The void subprogram is pictured in the flowchart of figure 11–12.

For example, if the display indicates one dollar and that is the amount to be erased from the taxable department, the void key is depressed and followed by the taxable function key. This procedure erases one dollar from that total.

```
;
;VOID FUNCTION KEY SUBPROGRAM
;
VOID:   CALL INKEY    ;GET KEY
```

FIGURE 11–12 The flowchart of the VOID subprogram.

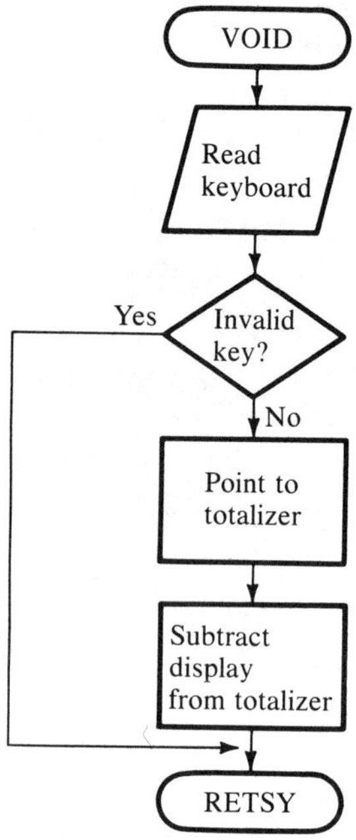

```
330              MOV    A,B          ;GET CODE
331              CPI    14           ;CHECK FOR VOID
332              JZ     VOID         ;IF STILL VOID KEY
333              LXI    H,TXT        ;POINT TO TAXABLE
334              CPI    12           ;CHECK TAXABLE FUNCTION KEY
335              JZ     VOID1        ;IF TAXABLE
336              CPI    13           ;CHECK NONTAXABLE
337              JNZ    RETSY        ;RETURN ON ERROR
338              LXI    NTXT         ;POINT TO NONTAXABLE
339 VOID1:       MVI    C,3          ;LOAD COUNTER TO SUBTRACT
340              LXI    D,DISP       ;POINT TO DISPLAY MEMORY
341 VOID2:       LDAX   D            ;GET DISPLAY DATA
342              MOV    B,A          ;SAVE IT
343              MVI    A,9AH        ;GET BIAS
344              SBB    B            ;FORM 10's COMPLEMENT
345              ADD    M            ;FORM DIFFERENCE
346              DAA                 ;ADJUST ANSWER
347              MOV    M,A          ;SAVE IT
348              CMC                 ;ADJUST BORROW
349              INX    H
350              INX    D
351              DCR    C
352              JNZ    VOID2        ;IF NOT DONE
353              JMP    RETSY        ;RETURN TO SYSTEM
```

This software will not detect an underflow condition of the targeted department. In practice it is included to prevent voiding too much money from any department.

Special Function "Program Tax Rate"

This function, which is usually controlled by a locking keyswitch, is used only after a massive power failure depletes the energy stored in the batteries used for backup or if a change in the sales tax is legislated. The flowchart for this subprogram is depicted in figure 11–13.

To program the register, this keyswitch is activated and followed by exactly 42 numeric entries on the keyboard. The first 2 are the tax rate in mills up to 99 mills (or 9.9 cents), followed by the 40 numeric keystrokes for the tax break table. The dealer normally supplies this information to the end user.

```
;SPECIAL FUNCTION "PROGRAM TAX RATE KEY"
;SUBPROGRAM
;
PROG:   LXI   H,RATE     ;POINT TO RATE
        MVI   D,21       ;SET BYTE COUNTER
PROG1:  CALL  INKEYX     ;GET DIGIT
        MOV   A,B
        CPI   10         ;CHECK FOR ERROR
        JNC   RETSY      ;IF ERROR
        RLC              ;SHIFT TO PROPER POSITION
```

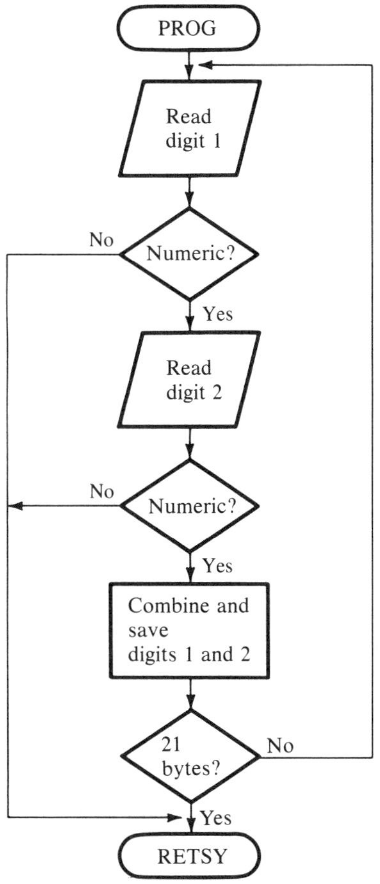

FIGURE 11–13 The flowchart of the PROG subprogram.

```
364             RLC
365             RLC
366             RLC
367             MOV   E,A          ;SAVE IT
368             CALL  INKEYX       ;GET DIGIT
369             MOV   A,B
370             CPI   10           ;CHECK FOR ERROR
371             JNC   RETSY        ;IF ERROR
372             ORA   E            ;FORM BYTE
373             MOV   M,A          ;SAVE IT
374             INX   H            ;POINT TO NEXT BYTE
375             DCR   D            ;DECREMENT BYTE COUNTER
376             JNZ   PROG1        ;IF NOT DONE
377             JMP   RETSY        ;IF DONE
378  INKEYX:   IN    82H          ;CHECK DONE
379             ORA   A
380             JNZ   INKEYX       ;LOOP UNTIL FREE
381             HLT                ;DEBOUNCE SWITCH
382             HLT
383             HLT
384             HLT
385             HLT
386             HLT
387             JMP   INKEY        ;GET KEY
```

Special Function "Read Department Totals"

This key allows the operator to read out the daily totals from the total tax, total taxable, or total nontaxable sales departments. It allows the owner to keep accurate records of the daily receipts and tax information for the government. See figure 11–14 for a flowchart of this subprogram.

This key displays the totals in each department by striking each department key. After the amount is displayed, the totalizer is automatically cleared to zero for the next sale day. A normal sequence of usage is to strike the read key, tax key, taxable key, and nontaxable key. You would of course want to pause between reads to write down the amounts.

```
388  ;SPECIAL FUNCTION "READ DEPARTMENT TOTALS"
389  ;SUBPROGRAM
390  ;
391  READ:     CALL  INKEYX       ;GET KEY
392             MOV   A,B          ;GET KEY CODE
393             CPI   12           ;CHECK FOR TAXABLE DEPT,
394             LXI   H,TX         ;POINT TO TAXABLE
395             JZ    READ1        ;IF TAXABLE
396             CPI   13           ;CHECK FOR NONTAXABLE DEPT
397             LXI   H,NTX        ;POINT TO NONTAXABLE
398             JZ    READ1        ;IF NONTAXABLE
399             CPI   15           ;CHECK TAX
400             LXI   H,TAX        ;POINT TO TAX
```

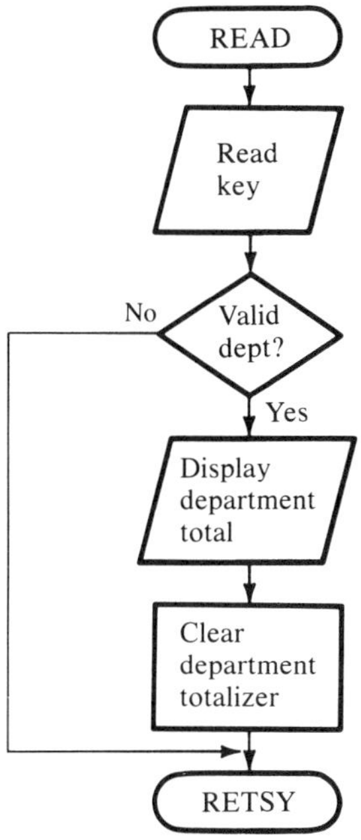

FIGURE 11–14 The flowchart of the READ subprogram.

```
             JNZ   RETSY     ;IF NOT ANY
    READ1:   LXI   D,DISP    ;POINT TO DISPLAY
             MVI   B,3       ;LOAD COUNTER
    READ2:   MOV   A,M       ;GET BYTE
             STAX  D         ;SAVE BYTE
             MVI   M,0       ;CLEAR TOTALIZER
             INX   D         ;INCREMENT POINTERS
             INX   H
             DCR   B         ;DECREMENT COUNTER
             JNZ   READ2     ;IF NOT DONE
             JMP   READ      ;AGAIN
```

Numeric Keyboard Data

The numeric data from the keyboard is always moved into the display memory for display and used with the function keys. The display software is written so that numeric data enters the displays from the right-hand side, or by the "right entry method". The flowchart for the numeric keyboard data is pictured in figure 11–15.

```
;SUBROUTINE TO PROCESS NUMERIC KEYBOARD DATA
;
NUMB:    PUSH  PSW       ;SAVE CURRENT DIGIT
         LHLD  DISP+1    ;GET MOST SIGNIFICANT FOUR
         DAD   H         ;SHIFT LEFT ONE BCD DIGIT
         DAD   H
         DAD   H
         DAD   H
         LDA   DISP      ;GET LEAST SIGNIFICANT TWO
```

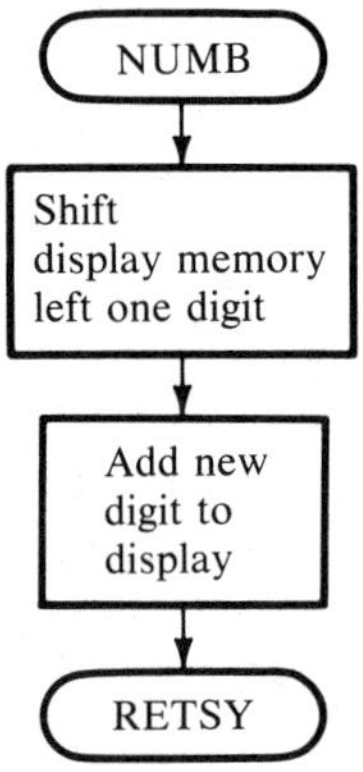

FIGURE 11–15 The flowchart of the NUMB subprogram.

```
        RLC             ;ROTATE DIGITS
        RLC
        RLC
        RLC
        PUSH PSW        ;SAVE IT
        ANI  15         ;MASK OFF MOST SIGNIFICANT
        ORA  L
        MOV  L,A        ;MOVE IT TO L
        SHLD DISP+1     ;SAVE IT
        POP  PSW        ;GET LEAST SIGNIFICANT TWO
        ANI  0F0H       ;MASK OF LEAST SIGNIFICANT
        MOV  C,A        ;SAVE IT
        POP  PSW        ;GET ORIGINAL KEY CODE
        ORA  C          ;FORM NEW LEAST SIGNIFICANT TWO
        STA  DISP       ;SAVE IT
        JMP  RETSY      ;RETURN TO SYSTEM
```

Software and Hardware Design Highlights

Some important features of this software are BCD arithmetic, interrupt processed display, and interrupt timed delays. These features have led to a very simple hardware configuration and a very structured software.

BCD arithmetic was selected for this application because the information is already in this form as it comes back from the keyboard, and it is required to be in this form for the display. Converting the data from BCD to binary and from binary to BCD would be a waste of effort since no complex arithmetic is performed on the data. This is also the case in many other applications. A general rule of thumb to follow is that if no complex arithmetic is to be performed in a system, it is better to keep the data in BCD form.

Interrupt processing the display frees the programmer from the drudgery of periodically updating the displays. The interrupt service subroutine completely handles this task. In fact, in this design example, all that is required to change the display information is to change the contents of three memory locations.

Since a periodic interrupt is used in this system, time delays are extremely easy to implement by using the halt (HLT) command. The halt command waits until an interrupt occurs before processing proceeds with the next contiguous instruction. This feature allows a fairly accurate time delay to be created by stringing together a series of halt instructions.

Summary

This chapter presented two design examples using the 8085A microprocessor. A dishwasher sequencer and a point of sales terminal were used as illustrative examples of microprocessor based controllers.

These examples illustrate many common programming techniques such as real-time control, interrupt driven displays, BCD arithmetic, keyboard scanning, and time delays.

From this handful of basic programming and hardware interfacing techniques, a wide variety of other useful products can be designed and implemented. At the end of this chapter is included a group of suggested design examples to hone the reader's abilities with both the hardware and the software. Be aware that some of the examples may require an extensive amount of time to complete. They illustrate some practical applications of the microprocessor.

Suggested Projects

1 Using the 8085A and any other device required, develop a traffic light controller for the intersection pictured in figure 11–16. This traffic light is to run at the times indicated in the example 24 hr per day. The lamp drivers are TTL compatible and depicted in figure 11–17.

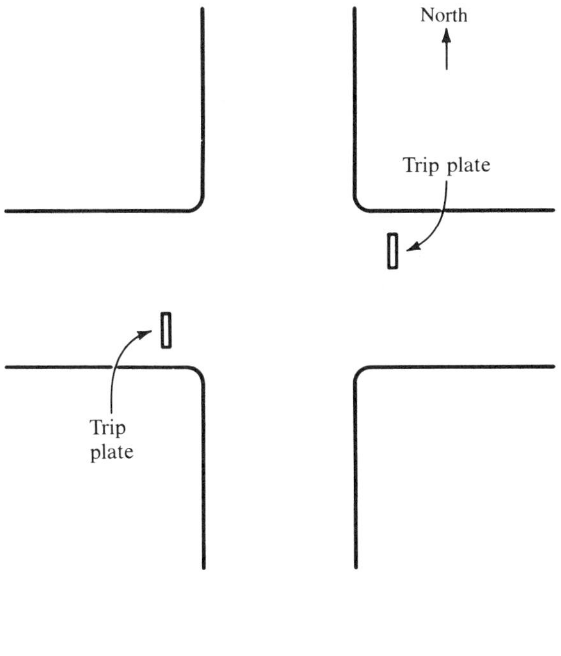

FIGURE 11–16 The traffic light intersection.

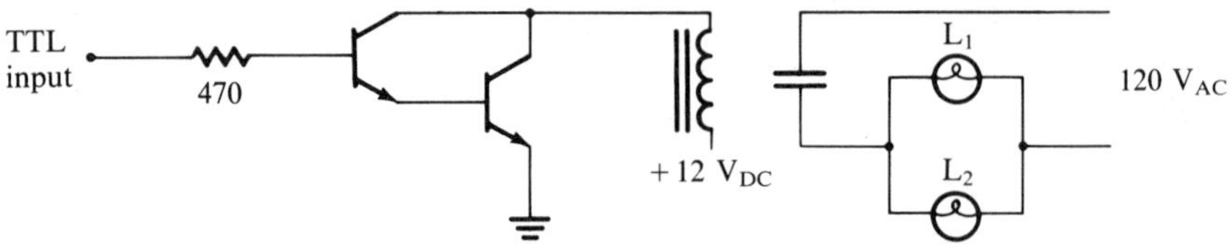

FIGURE 11–17 The traffic light lamp driver circuit.

EXAMPLE 11–1

Timing North-South		Timing East-West	
Green	75 seconds	Green	28 seconds
Yellow	2 seconds	Yellow	2 seconds
Red	30 seconds	Red	77 seconds

2 Modify the system developed in question 1 so that the traffic light will flash red in all directions between the hours of 1 AM and 5 AM. The rate of flashing should be on for a second and off for a second. To obtain the time of day, develop a real-time clock and interface it to the 8085A.

3 Modify the system of question 1 so that a trip plate can be used to modify the traffic flow pattern from the east or west direction. The trip plate may only work after the light has been red for 15 seconds (s) and then may only hold this intersection green for up to 80 s before turning the light yellow and then red.

The trip plate section of the software must be able to detect a car and—if another car hits the plate within 5 seconds—extend the green time for up to 80 seconds maximum. Figure 11–18 illustrates a TTL compatible trip plate with an active high output.

4 Develop the 8085A hardware and software for a coin changer mechanism. It must be able to accept coins in any denomination from 1 cent to 50 cents and dispense change in the fewest number of pennies, nickels, and dimes. The amount of money to be accepted is programmed through a set of switches located inside the vending machine. The programmable amount can be anything from 1 cent to $1.99.

Your software must accept coins until the amount indicated on the internal switches has either been reached or exceeded; if it has been

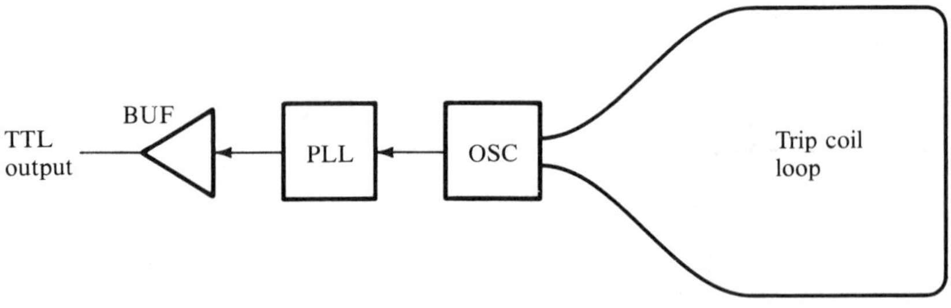

FIGURE 11–18 The block diagram of the trip plate sensor circuit for the traffic light problem.

exceeded, it must dispense the fewest number of coins as change and send an active low pulse out the $\overline{\text{VEND}}$ pin for 20 ms.

As coins are inserted, a mechanical assembly that sorts them signals the microprocessor with a pulse indicating the denomination of the coin.

Once your program has detected and remembered the coin, it must drop it into the internal coin box by pulsing the $\overline{\text{DROP}}$ line for 100 ms. There is also a "bent coin" signal in case a defective coin is inserted into the machine. If a bent coin is detected, you must pulse the $\overline{\text{EJECT}}$ line for 120 ms to clear the coin slot.

To dispense change, the appropriate $\overline{\text{CH}}$ control line is activated for 100 ms to drop a coin out of the change slot of the vending machine. You must only return one coin at a time with a pause of at least 50 ms between coins for the mechanical ejection mechanism to function properly.

Table 11–2 illustrates all of the TTL input and TTL output connections that are to be interfaced to the 8085A.

TABLE 11–2 Signal lines for the coin changer.

Signal	Function
$\overline{\text{VEND}}$	Used to vend merchandise from the machine attached to this changer
$\overline{\text{DROP}}$	Used to accept a coin that has been placed into the mechanism
$\overline{\text{EJECT}}$	Used to return a bent or defective coin
1C	One cent program input switch
2C	Two cents program input switch
5C	Five cents program input switch
10C	Ten cents program input switch
20C	Twenty cents program input switch
50C	Fifty cents program input switch
100C	One dollar program input switch
$\overline{\text{CH1}}$	Returns a penny as change if pulsed for 100 ms
$\overline{\text{CH5}}$	Returns a nickel as change if pulsed for 100 ms
$\overline{\text{CH10}}$	Returns a dime as change if pulsed for 100 ms
$\overline{\text{CH25}}$	Returns a quarter as change if pulsed for 100 ms

5 Develop an IC test fixture that will automatically test the 7490 TTL decade counter. The pinout of this decade counter is pictured in figure 11–19 with a brief description of its operating characteristics.

Your system must completely test this device; if it is found faulty, the red LED must be lit and if good, the green LED must be lit. This test sequence must test the clear to zero, clear to nine, and count sequence of the counter at least 20 times without failure for a good indication. The test socket and two LED indicators are pictured in figure 11–20.

6 If the above system is to be able to test any 14-pin integrated TTL circuit, which changes must be made to the hardware?

FIGURE 11–19 The pinout, block diagram, and truth table for the 7490 decade counter.

SOURCE: Courtesy of Texas Instruments, Inc.

'90A, 'L90, 'LS90 (TOP VIEW)

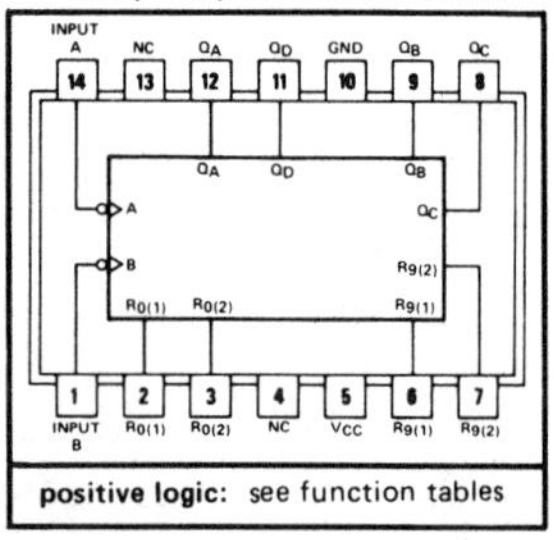

'90A, 'L90, 'LS90
BCD COUNT SEQUENCE
(See Note A)

COUNT	OUTPUT			
	Q_D	Q_C	Q_B	Q_A
0	L	L	L	L
1	L	L	L	H
2	L	L	H	L
3	L	L	H	H
4	L	H	L	L
5	L	H	L	H
6	L	H	H	L
7	L	H	H	H
8	H	L	L	L
9	H	L	L	H

'90A, 'L90, 'LS90
BI-QUINARY (5-2)
(See Note B)

COUNT	OUTPUT			
	Q_A	Q_D	Q_C	Q_B
0	L	L	L	L
1	L	L	L	H
2	L	L	H	L
3	L	L	H	H
4	L	H	L	L
5	H	L	L	L
6	H	L	L	H
7	H	L	H	L
8	H	L	H	H
9	H	H	L	L

'90A, 'L90, 'LS90
RESET/COUNT FUNCTION TABLE

RESET INPUTS				OUTPUT			
$R_{0(1)}$	$R_{0(2)}$	$R_{9(1)}$	$R_{9(2)}$	Q_D	Q_C	Q_B	Q_A
H	H	L	X	L	L	L	L
H	H	X	L	L	L	L	L
X	X	H	H	H	L	L	H
X	L	X	L	COUNT			
L	X	L	X	COUNT			
L	X	X	L	COUNT			
X	L	L	X	COUNT			

NOTES: A. Output Q_A is connected to input B for BCD count.
B. Output Q_D is connected to input A for bi-quinary count.

FIGURE 11–20 The control panel of the microprocessor based TTL integrated circuit tester.

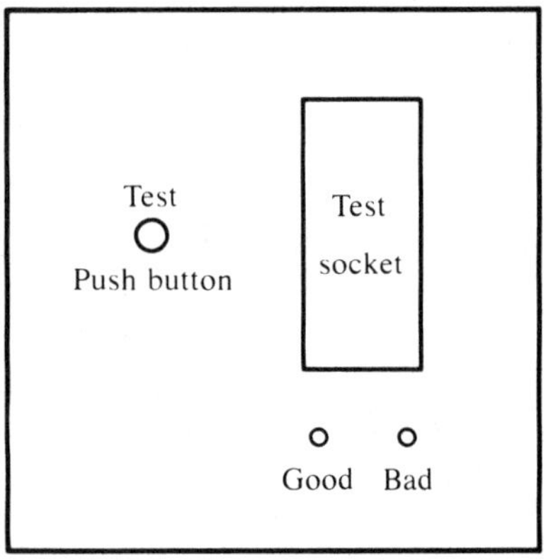

7 Create a darkroom timer to control the length of time that the enlarger exposes the paper. The timer must be capable of exposing the paper in increments of 0.1 seconds, up to 10 min.

Time settings are dialed in on a series of rotary switches labeled in one-tenth seconds, seconds, and minutes (as illustrated in figure 11–21). The push button starts the timing sequence that applies AC power to the lamp in the enlarger for the preset amount of time.

8 Redevelop the dishwasher system presented in this chapter, using the 8755A combination EPROM and I/O interface adapter. Data on this device may be found in the Intel 8080A/8085A User's Manual.

No, you may not use any read/write memory to accomplish this task. Your circuit may only include the 8085A and the 8755A. (Hint: Subroutines can be developed without the use of the stack if the PCHL instruction is used correctly.)

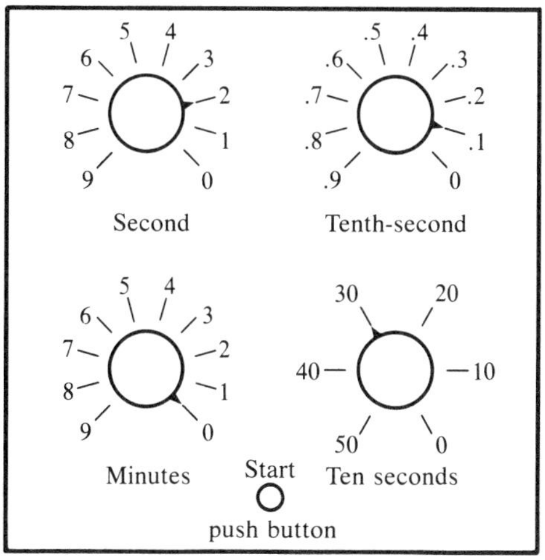

FIGURE 11–21 The control panel of a microprocessor based darkroom timer.

12

MC6800 Application Examples

This chapter collects all of the separate techniques that were learned throughout this textbook. Example problems that include memory interface, various forms of I/O interface, and digital communications have been illustrated. It is very important that the student go through each of the example problems for ideas on hardware and software implementation.

For more examples, see the end of this chapter, which contains a series of projects that illustrate many of the techniques discussed in this text.

12-1 DATA CONCENTRATOR

Data concentrators are used in data communications environments to pack many slow channels of digital data onto one high-speed channel. For example, a department store may have 20 point of sales terminals that must be connected to a computer in another city. Instead of leasing 20 telephone lines for the fairly intermittent data from these in-store terminals, a data concentrator can be connected between the POS terminals and the computer in the other city. This connection does not reduce the speed of the system as far as the user is concerned; it only reduces the total system cost by replacing the 20 leased lines with 1.

6800 Data Concentrator Example

In this example two low-speed channels are concentrated onto one higher-speed channel for transmission to another system. The data on the low-speed channels is serial asynchronous data transmitted at 300 baud, and the data on the high-speed channel is asynchronous data transmitted at 4800 baud. For this example, we will only consider one way communications between the two terminals and the remote system.

Figure 12–1 illustrates the protocol between the concentrator and the larger computer system. The data is preceded by an ID byte that indicates which terminal is transmitting the data. The ID byte is always followed by 15 bytes of information, allowing for a fairly efficient means of data transmission between each terminal and the remote computer system.

6800 Data Concentrator Hardware

The hardware for this application is pictured in the schematic of figure 12–2. The 6800 is surrounded by three 6850 ACIAs that receive serial data from the terminals and transmit serial data to the remote computer system. In addition to the ACIAs, a 128-byte RAM for data storage and a 1K-byte EPROM for program storage exist.

The decoder selects the EPROM for memory locations $FXXX, the RAM for locations $0XXX, and the ACIAs for locations $BXXX, $CXXX, and $DXXX. Data channel one uses $BXXX; data channel two uses $CXXX; $DXXX is used as the link between the remote computer and the data concentrator.

Data Concentrator Initialization Dialog

In this system the three ACIAs must be initialized to start the communications between the terminals and the remote system. This dialog resides at the location pointed to by the restart vector in locations $FFFE and $FFFF.

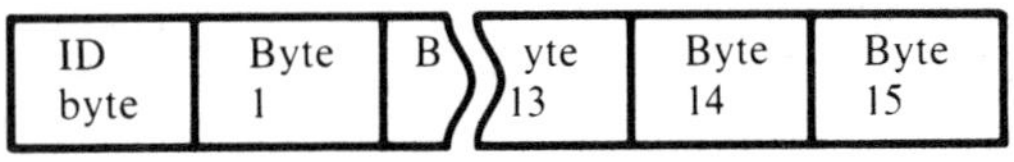

FIGURE 12–1 The protocol for the MC6800 based data concentrator.

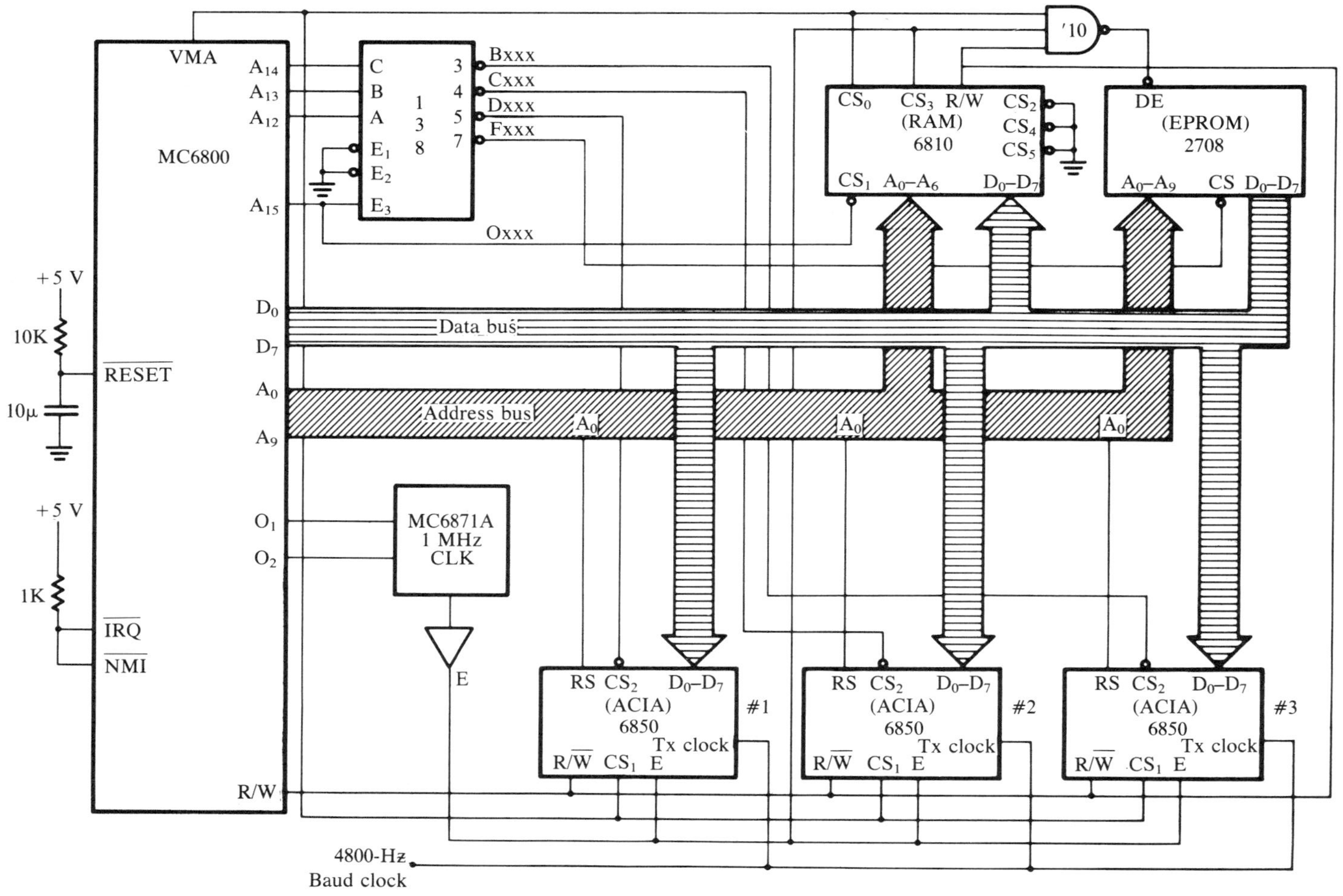

FIGURE 12–2 The schematic diagram of the MC6800 microprocessor based data concentrator.

```
*DATA CONCENTRATOR INITIALIZATION DIALOG
*
START LDDA #$09       SETUP ACIA COMMAND WORD
      STAA $B000      PROGRAM THREE ACIAs
      STAA $C000
      CLR  $D000      SETUP COMMAND FOR ACIA THREE
      LDS  #$007F     SETUP STACK AREA
      LDX  COUNT      POINT TO BUFFERS, POINTER AND FLAGS
LOOP  CLR  X          CLEAR BUFFERS, POINTERS AND FLAGS
      DEX
      BNE  LOOP
      CLR  X
      LDAA #32        SETUP QUEUE TWO POINTERS
      STAA IPNT2+1
      STAA OPNT2+1
        .
        . (System software begins here)
        .
```

The terminal ACIAs are programmed to divide the external clock source by 16, to transmit 7 data bits with even parity, and to send 1 stop bit. The high-speed ACIA is programmed with the same data format, except that its internal divider is setup to divide by 1. The resulting transmission speed is 4800 baud.

Data Storage for the Data Concentrator

The data storage consists of two separate buffer areas in the memory. These hold data as it comes from the two terminal devices and function as FIFOs, or queue memories.

```
*RAM STORAGE
*
BUF1   RMB  32  TERMINAL ONE BUFFER
BUF2   RMB  32  TERMINAL TWO BUFFER
IPNT1  RMB  02  QUEUE ONE POINTERS
OPNT1  RMB  02
IPNT2  RMB  02  QUEUE TWO POINTERS
OPNT2  RMB  02
FLAG   FCB  00  TRANSMIT FLAG
COUNT  FCB  00  BYTE COUNTER
```

The queue pointers are all initialized for the empty condition; that is, both the input and output pointers are equal in value. A full condition is indicated when the IPNT is one less than the OPNT.

ACIA Status Scanning Software

The purpose of this software is to determine when an ACIA has received information or when it is ready to transmit information. This software immediately follows the system initialization dialog presented earlier. Figure 12–3 illustrates the flowchart of this software, which is the main program for the data concentrator.

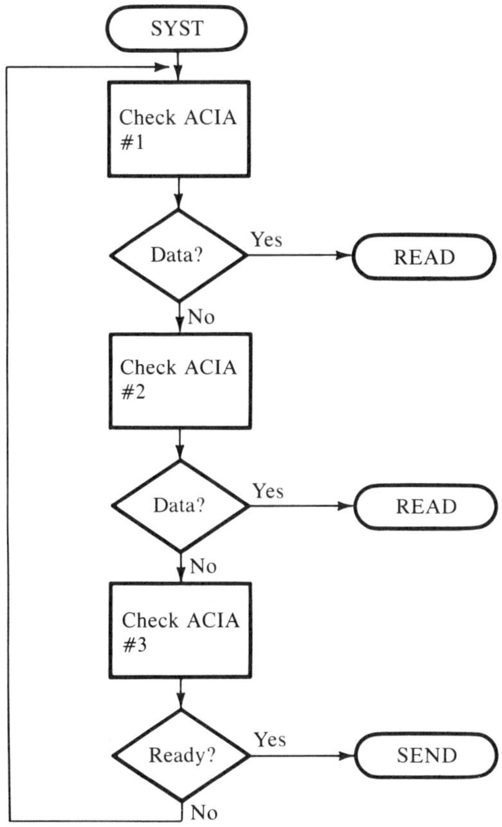

FIGURE 12–3 The flowchart of the SYST program for the MC6800 based data concentrator.

```
26 *STATUS SCANNING SOFTWARE
27 *
28 SYST    LDDB  #1        SET ACIA NUMBER
29         LDAA  $B000     GET STATUS ONE
30         JSR   CHKI      GO CHECK ACIA STATUS
31         INCB            SET ACIA NUMBER
32         LDAA  $C000     GET STATUS TWO
33         JSR   CHKI      GO CHECK ACIA STATUS
34         LDAA  $D000     GET STATUS THREE
35         JSR   CHKO      GO CHECK ACIA STATUS
36         BRA   SYST      KEEP CHECKING
```

The software is looped through continually until a ready condition on any receiver is detected or a ready condition in the transmitter is detected. Once detected, data is transmitted or received by subroutines presented later in this text.

```
37 *SUBROUTINE TO CHECK ACIA RECEIVER STATUS
38 *
39 CHKI  RARA       RDRF INTO CARRY
40       BCS   READ
41       RTS        IF NO DATA IN THE RECEIVER
```

The subroutine illustrated above checks the receiver of the selected ACIA to determine if it is ready with data. If it is not ready, a return from the subroutine occurs. If it is ready, the subroutine continues at location READ.

Reception Software

As the data is read from each terminal, it is stored in the terminal's queue, where it is held for later transmission by the high-speed ACIA. No attempt is made to detect a queue full condition, since this can never happen because of the speeds involved. Refer to figure 12–4 for a complete flowchart of this subroutine.

```
*SUBROUTINE TO READ DATA FROM AN ACIA
*AND SAVE IT IN THE APPROPRIATE QUEUE
*
READ  CMPB #2          CHECK FOR ACIA 2
      BEQ              READ2
      LDX  IPNT1       POINT TO QUEUE ONE
      LDAA $B000       GET DATA
      BRA              READ3
READ2 LDX  IPNT2       POINT TO QUEUE TWO
      LDAA $C000       GET DATA
READ3 STAA X           SAVE DATA
      JSR  UPDAT       INCREMENT AND WRAP POINTER
      STX  IPNT2       SAVE IPNT2
      RTS
```

FIGURE 12–4 The flowchart of the READ subroutine.

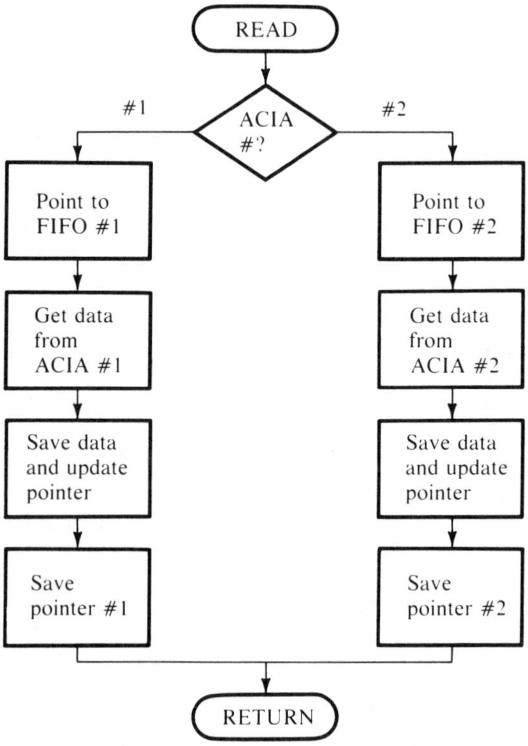

Transmission Software

```
*SUBROUTINE TO CHECK TRANSMITTER STATUS
*
CHKO   BITA #$02       TEST TDRE
       BNE  SEND
       RTS
```

This short subroutine determines if the transmitter in the high-speed ACIA is ready for another byte of information. If it is not, a return from the subroutine occurs so that the remaining ACIAs can be tested.

The SEND subroutine transmits data to the remote system through the high-speed ACIA. The flowchart for this routine is pictured in figure 12–5, and the program itself follows.

```
*SEND SUBROUTINE FOR TRANSMITTING DATA THROUGH
*THE HIGH SPEED ACIA
*
SEND   LDDA FLAG       GET TRANSMITTER BUSY FLAG
       BNE  BUSY       IF BUSY
       LDAA IPNT1      GET IPNT1
       CMPA OPNT1      COMPARE WITH OPNT1
       BNE  ST1        IF FIFO ONE IS NOT EMPTY
       LDAA IPNT2      GET IPNT2
       CMPA OPNT2      COMPARE WITH OPNT2
       BNE  ST2        IF FIFO TWO IS NOT EMPTY
       RTS             IF BOTH FIFOS ARE EMPTY
```

This portion of the SEND subroutine checks whether the transmitter is currently sending data; if it is not, it continues on to check whether data is available to transmit. If no data is present to transmit and the transmitter is not busy, it returns to scanning for input data through the two low-speed data channels.

```
*CONTINUATION OF SEND WHEN FIFOS ARE NOT EMPTY
*
ST1    LDAA #01        LOAD TERMINAL ID NUMBER
       BRA  ST         GO SEND IT
ST2    LDAA #02        LOAD TERMINAL ID NUMBER
ST     STAA $D001      SEND TERMINAL ID NUMBER
       STAA FLAG       SAVE TERMINAL NUMBER IN FLAG
       LDAA #15        SETUP BYTE COUNTER
       STAA COUNT      SAVE IN COUNT
       RTS             CONTINUE SCANNING
```

If the transmitter is not busy but data is available to transmit, this portion of the software sends the terminal number through the high-speed ACIA and also sets a byte counter to 15. The byte counter contains the number of bytes that must follow the ID number. After transmitting the ID number, a return to scanning occurs so that additional data may be received.

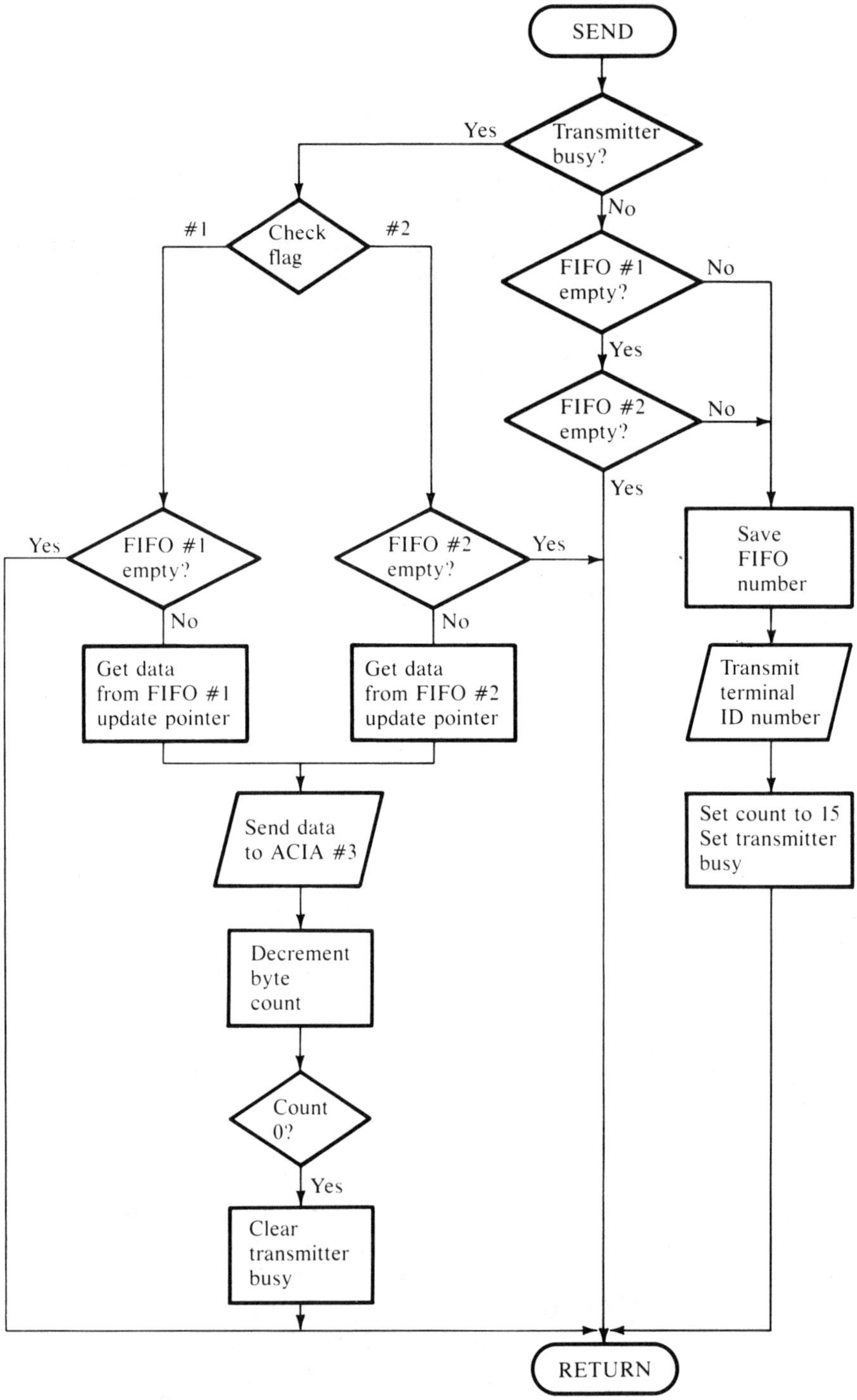

FIGURE 12–5 The flowchart of the SEND subroutine.

```
*CONTINUATION OF SEND
*
BUSY  LDAA FLAG       CHECK TERMINAL NUMBER
      TSTA #02        CHECK FOR TERMINAL TWO
      BNE  T1         GO TO TERMINAL ONE
      LDAA IPNT2+1    GET IPNT2
      CMPA OPNT2+1    COMPARE WITH OPNT2
      BNE  SEN2       GO SEND A BYTE FROM TWO
      RTS             CONTINUE SCANNING
T1    LDAA IPNT1+1    GET IPNT1
      CMPA OPNT1+1    COMPARE WITH OPNT1
      BNE  SEN1       GO SEND A BYTE FROM ONE
      RTS             CONTINUE SCANNING
```

If the transmitter has been sending data, it arrives at this section of the software to determine whether any data has been received. If it has, a transfer occurs to either SEN1 or SEN2 to send the information. If it has not, control is returned, and it continues to search for more input data.

```
*DATA TRANSMISSION PORTION OF SEND
*
SEN1 LDX  OPNT1       GET OPNT1
     LDAA X           GET A BYTE OF DATA
     STAA $D001       SEND THE DATA
     JSR  UPDAT       INCREMENT AND WRAP POINTER
     STX  OPNT1       SAVE OPNT1
SENX DEC  COUNT       DECREMENT BYTE COUNT
     BNE  RETS        RETURN FROM SUBROUTINE
     CLR  FLAG        CLEAR BUSY FLAG
RETS RTS              CONTINUE SCANNING
SEN2 LDX  OPNT2       GET OPNT2
     LDAA X           GET DATA
     STAA $D001       SEND DATA
     JSR  UPDAT       INCREMENT AND WRAP POINTER
     STX  OPNT2       SAVE POINTER
     BRA  SENX        FINISH UP
```

This software sends information through the high-speed ACIA and then decrements the byte counter. If the byte counter reaches zero, which indicates that all 15 bytes have been transferred, the FLAG is cleared so that the transmitter can start transmitting the next 15 bytes of data.

```
*INCREMENT A POINTER AND WRAP IT IF NEEDED
*
UPDAT STX  COUNT+1   SAVE TEMP
      LDAA COUNT+2   GET POINTER
      ANDA #$E0      STRIP MOST SIGNIFICANT
      PSHA           SAVE IT
```

```
        LDAA COUNT+2   GET POINTER
        INCA           INCREMENT IT
        ANDA #$1F      MASK MOST SIGNIFICANT
        STAA COUNT+2   SAVE IT
        PULA           RESTORE IT
        ORAA COUNT+2   COMBINE
        STAA COUNT+2
        LDX  COUNT+1   LOAD INDEX REGISTER
        RTS
```

This subroutine increments the index register and stores the result back into the index register. It is a simple task, except that in this case the number must be a 5-bit cyclic number, which requires all of the special coding listed in the above subroutine. Only the least significant 5 bits are incremented in this subroutine.

System Limitations

This system has one important limitation that should be noted. The low-speed data must continue in increments of 15 bytes. If this does not happen, the system hangs up with no output ever for one of the two channels. If this result is not acceptable, the system can be modified to send a byte at a time, preceded with the terminal number. The only problem with this is that the system's efficiency suffers.

12-2 TRAFFIC LIGHT CONTROLLER

Traffic light control by microprocessors is becoming commonplace in many large cities because these units are easily adjusted for different timing sequences and can be controlled by an external computer system. External computer control has increased traffic flow during peak hours and reduced the number of accidents in the cities where it has been tested.

The system illustrated in this text receives its timing sequence through a keyboard located at the controlled intersection. The keyboard also enters the time of day and other information, such as the times the traffic light should flash. This system also includes a set of trip plates to trip the light for one direction.

Traffic Light Controller Hardware

The hardware for this controller includes an MC6821, which scans the keyboard and controls the traffic lamps. In addition to the MC6821, an oscillator is included to provide the MC6800 with its clock and to act as a timing source for the nonmaskable interrupt input ($\overline{\text{NMI}}$). Also included is a trip plate sensor that causes an interrupt to occur whenever a vehicle is in proximity with the trip plate. The trip plate itself is a loop of wire located just below the surface of the roadbed. When a vehicle sits over it, the metal in the vehicle changes the inductance of the loop, which can be sensed by the interface.

Figure 12–6 illustrates the MC6800 controller hardware, including the memory required and the appropriate device selection logic. The outputs of

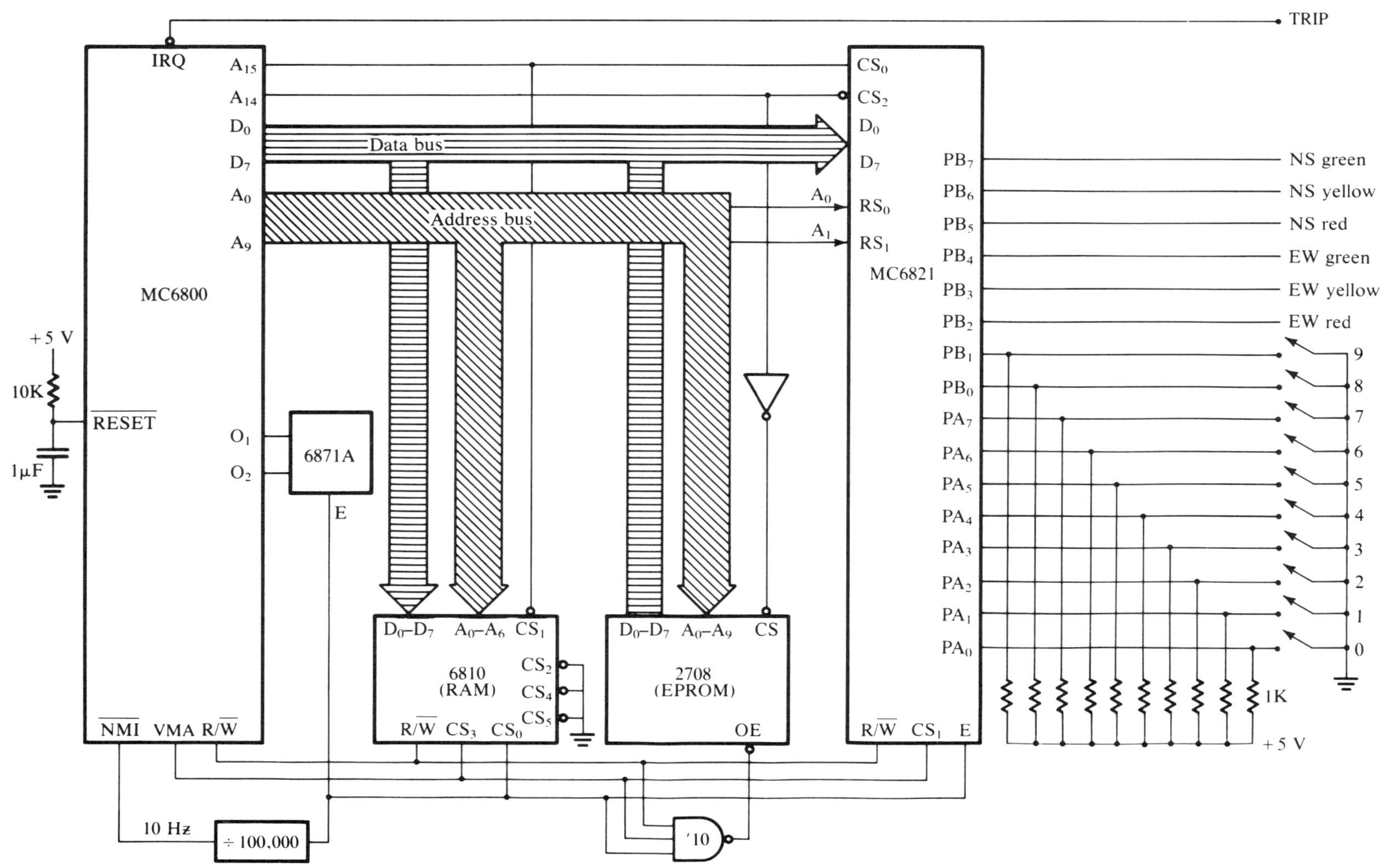

FIGURE 12–6 The schematic diagram of the MC6800 based traffic light controller.

the decoder select the 1K-byte EPROM at address $FXXX, the 128-byte RAM at address $0XXX, and the MC6821 at address $EXXX.

RAM Storage Assignment

```
*RAM STORAGE ASSIGNMENT
*
CLOCK RMB  7        CLOCK STORAGE
TIME  RMB  1        TIMER STORAGE
NSRED RMB  1        NORTH-SOUTH RED
NSGRE RMB  1        NORTH-SOUTH GREEN
NSYEL RMB  1        NORTH-SOUTH YELLOW
EWRED RMB  1        EAST-WEST RED
EWGRE RMB  1        EAST-WEST GREEN
EWYEL RMB  1        EAST-WEST YELLOW
MAXTR RMB  1        MAXIMUM NUMBER OF TRIPS
MINTR RMB  1        MINIMUM TRIP TIME
FLSTR RMB  6        FLASH START TIME
FLEND RMB  6        FLASH END TIME
```

The basic clock timer is allocated 7 bytes of memory: 6 to keep track of the time (in hours, minutes, and seconds) and 1 to divide the 10 Hz input signal into 1-second pulses. The time is kept in unpacked BCD form for ease in software development.

Memory location TIME is used as a down counter that is decremented once per second. TIME is used by the software to time a particular light and is in standard binary form.

The six locations for light timing, NSRED, NSGRE, and so on, are each programmable for times of up to 255 seconds, which should be more than enough time for a lamp in any direction.

Minimum trip time and maximum number of trips indicate how long a light may remain tripped and the minimum amount of time required to cause a trip. A typical minimum time may be 20 seconds, and a typical maximum number of trips may be five. This, of course, depends on the traffic flow pattern at the intersection.

In many cases it is normal to remove a light from service in the wee hours of the morning by programming the start and end flash times into the 12 bytes of memory allocated for this purpose.

Initialization Dialog

Since this is a programmable device, it must be initialized whenever power is applied or whenever a change in the sequence of the lights is to be effected. The dialog that follows is executed whenever the microprocessor is restarted. The initialization dialog programs the PIA and branches to the keyboard entry portion of the software.

```
*INITIALIZATION DIALOG
*
RESET  LDS  #$007F    SET STACK AREA
       LDAA #$FC      SETUP PORT B
       STAA $E002     CONFIGURE PORT B
```

```
          LDAA #$04     SELECT PERIPHERAL DATA REGISTERS
          STAA $E001    SEND TO PIA
          STAA $E003    SEND TO PIA
            .
            .
            .(Continues at the SETUP program)
```

Traffic Controller Setup

The controller must be programmed to function after a restart. Programming is accomplished through the keyboard and consists of entering the time of day, the duration of each light, trip times, and flash times.

Each one of these pieces of information must be entered without visual feedback, since this unit contains no display. A display is unnecessary because the sequence is relatively short and can be entered again if an error is detected.

An example programming sequence is illustrated in figure 12–7.

```
*PORTION OF THE SYSTEM PROGRAM THAT SETS ALL OF
*THE PROGRAMMABLE FEATURES
*
SETUP   LDX   CLOCK+1    POINT TO TIME OF DAY
        JSR   INTIM      GET TIME OF DAY
        CLR   CLOCK      CLEAR CLOCK
        LDX   NSRED      POINT TO NSRED
        JSR   INSEC      GET SECONDS COUNT FOR NSRED
        JSR   INSEC      GET SECONDS COUNT FOR NSGRE
        JSR   INSEC      GET SECONDS COUNT FOR NSYEL
        LDAA  NSYEL      GET NSYEL
        STAA  EWYEL      SET EWYEL
        ADDA  NSGRE      DEVELOP EWRED
        STAA  EWRED      SAVE EWRED
        LDAA  NSRED      GET NSRED
        SUBA  NSYEL      DEVELOP EWGRE
        STAA  EWGRE      SAVE EWGRE
        LDX   MAXTR      POINT TO MAXTR
        JSR   INSEC      GET COUNT FOR MAXTR
        JSR   INSEC      GET SECONDS COUNT FOR MINTR
        LDX   FLSTR      POINT TO FLSTR
        JSR   INTIM      GET FLASH START TIME
        JSR   INTIM      GET FLASH END TIME
        LDAA  MAXTR      CHECK FOR A TRIP PLATE
        BEQ   SYST       IF NO TRIP PLATE
```

Time of day HH/MM/SS	North south red xxx	North south green xxx	North south yellow xxx	Maximum trip count xxx	Seconds for minimum trip xxx	Start flash time HH/MM/SS	Stop flash time HH/MM/SS

FIGURE 12–7 The setup sequence that programs the traffic light controller.

```
47 SET1    CLI              ENABLE TRIP PLATE INTERRUPT
            .
            .               (Continues at SYST program)
            .
```

This software accepts all of the programming data from the keyboard and stores it in the appropriate memory locations. See figure 12–8 for a flowchart. It also calculates the duration of each of the traffic lamps facing east-west and determines whether or not a trip plate is connected to the system. If MAXTR is a zero, it is assumed by the software that no trip plate is connected in the system, and the trip plate interrupt is left disabled.

INTIM Subroutine

The INTIM subroutine reads the time through the keyboard for the time of day, flash starting time, and flash ending time. It stores the time in the format HH/MM/SS. HH is a two digit number for hours, MM is for minutes, and SS

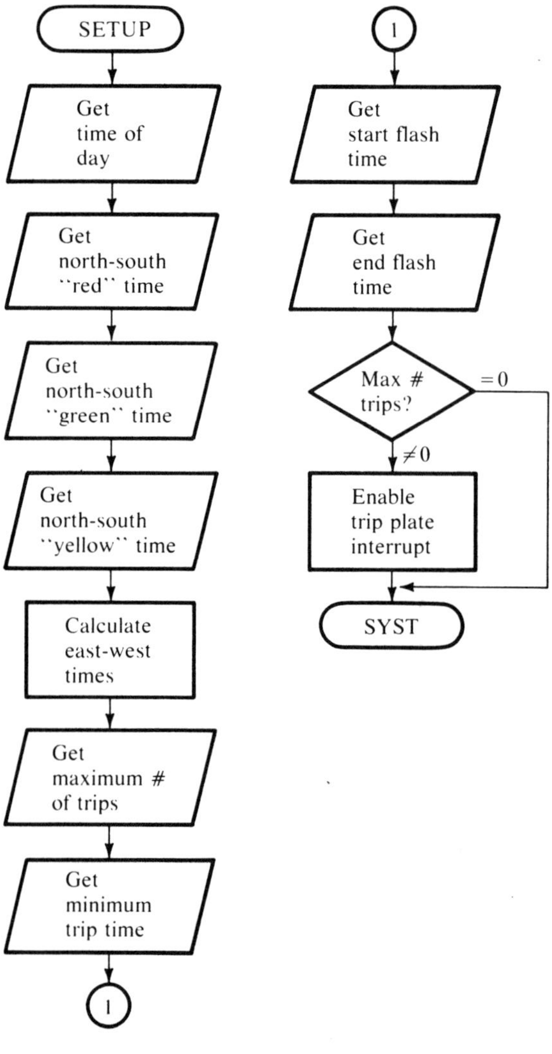

FIGURE 12–8 The flowchart of the SETUP portion of the traffic light controller system program.

for seconds. This six digit number is stored in six contiguous memory locations, which are indexed by the X register in unpacked BCD form.

```
*SUBROUTINE TO SAVE THE TIME IN UNPACKED BCD FORM
*
INTIM  LDAB #$06     SETUP COUNTER
INTIS  JSR  INKEY    GET A DIGIT
       STAA X        SAVE IT
       INX           POINT TO NEXT LOCATION
       DECB          DECREMENT COUNT
       BNE  INTIS    REPEAT UNTIL SIX DIGITS
       RTS           RETURN FROM SUBROUTINE
```

INSEC Subroutine

The INSEC subroutine, illustrated in the flowchart of figure 12–9, accepts a three digit number from the keyboard and converts it from BCD to binary. It is then stored in the memory location that is indexed by the X register. INSEC is used to get and save data for the timing on the lights and the trip times, if required.

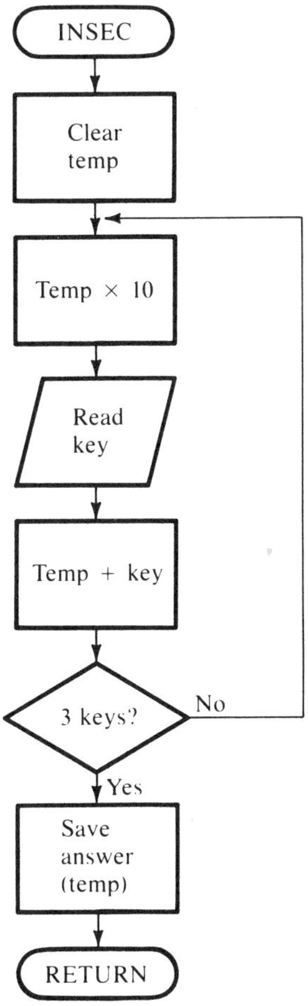

FIGURE 12–9 The flowchart of the INSEC subroutine.

```
*INPUTS DATA IN BCD FROM THE KEYBOARD THEN
*CONVERTS IT TO BINARY AND SAVES IT
*
INSEC  LDAB #$03       SETUP COUNTER
       CLR  FLEND+6    CLEAR TEMP
INTI1  LDAA FLEND+6    MULTIPLY BY 10
       ASLA            DOUBLE ACC
       STAA FLEND+6
       ASLA
       ASLA
       ADDA FLEND+6
       STAA FLEND+6
       JSR  INKEY      GET DIGIT
       ADDA FLEND+6    CREATE BINARY NUMBER
       STAA FLEND+6
       DECB            DECREMENT COUNT
       BNE  INTI1      REPEAT FOR THREE DIGITS
       LDAA FLEND+6    GET BINARY VERSION
       STAA X          SAVE IT
       INX             POINT TO NEXT
       RTS             RETURN FROM SUBROUTINE
```

This subroutine converts from BCD to binary by multiplying the previous binary number by ten and then adding in the new BCD digit. This will generate a binary number for a BCD number of up to 255. In example 12–1, a 103 is converted to binary using this algorithm.

EXAMPLE 12–1

		FLEND+6		
	×10	0000 0000	×	0000 1010
First	+1	0000 0000	+	0000 0001
	×10	0000 0001	×	0000 1010
Second	+0	0000 1010	+	0000 0000
	×10	0000 1010	×	0000 1010
Third	+3	0110 0100	+	0000 0011
	RESULT	0110 0111		

INKEY Subroutine

The INKEY subroutine is used to retrieve information from the ten key numeric keypad interfaced to the MC6800 through a MC6821 PIA. This procedure is accomplished by using the basic INKEY subroutine that was discussed in chapter 7. A flowchart for this subroutine is depicted in figure 12–10.

```
*SUBROUTINE TO READ A CHARACTER FROM THE KEYBOARD
*
INKEY  JSR  CHECK      CHECK FOR A KEYSTROKE
       BNE  INKEY      IF A KEYSTROKE
```

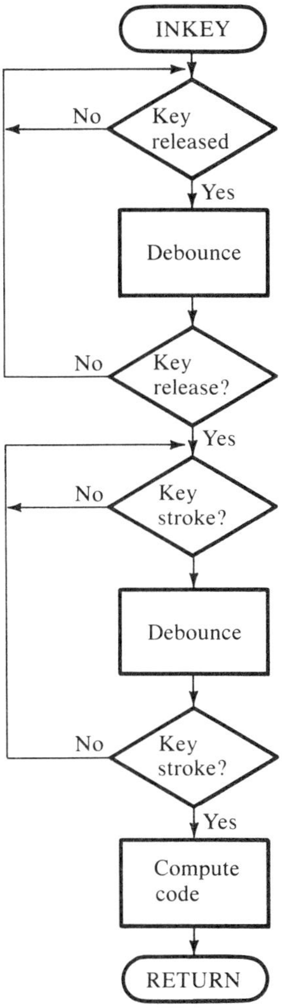

FIGURE 12–10 The flowchart of the INKEY subroutine.

```
        JSR   DELAY       DEBOUNCE
        JSR   CHECK       CHECK FOR A KEYSTROKE
        BNE   INKEY       IF A KEYSTROKE
INKEY1  CALL  CHECK       CHECK FOR A KEYSTROKE
        BEQ   INKEY1      IF NO KEYSTROKE
        JSR   DELAY       DEBOUNCE
        JSR   CHECK       CHECK FOR A KEYSTROKE
        BEQ   INKEY1      IF NOISE
        PSHB              STACK ACC B
        LDAB  #$FF        SETUP BCD CODE
        LDAA  $E000       GET 0 TO 7
        INCA              CHECK FOR ANY
        BNE   INKEY3      IF 0 THROUGH 7
        LDAB  #07         IF 8 OR 9
        LDAA  $E002       GET 8 AND 9
INKEY3  INCB
```

```
         RORA
         BCS   INKEY2      IF NOT FOUND
OUT      TBA               GET BCD CODE
         PULB              RESTORE ACC B
         RTS               RETURN FROM SUBROUTINE
CHECK    LDAA  $E000       GET 0 TO 7
         INCA
         BNE   CHK1        GET A 0 TO 7
         LDAA  $E002       GET 8 AND 9
         ORAA  #$FC
         INCA
CHK1     RTS               RETURN FROM SUBROUTINE
DELAY    PSHB              SAVE ACC B
         LDAB  #$14        CAUSE 10 MSEC. DELAY
         CLRA
DEL1     DECA
         BNE   DEL1
         DECB
         BNE   DEL1
         PULB              RESTORE ACC B
         RTS               RETURN FROM SUBROUTINE
```

Nonmaskable Interrupt Service Subroutine

This subroutine is used for keeping the correct time by modifying CLOCK; it also, once per second, decrements whichever number happens to be in location TIME. This feature provides the traffic light controller with a real-time clock that not only contains the time of day but can also time events. Location TIME is used as a timer and can time events in 1 second intervals. See figure 12–11 for a flowchart of the interrupt service subroutine.

```
*NONMASKABLE INTERRUPT SERVICE SUBROUTINE FOR
*THE REAL TIME CLOCK
*
NMI      INC   CLOCK       GET DIVIDE BY TEN
         LDAB  #$0A        CHECK FOR A TEN
         CMPB  CLOCK
         BNE   NMI3        EXIT
         CLR   CLOCK       CLEAR COUNT
         LDX   TIME        POINT TO TIME
         DEC   X           DECREMENT TIME
         DEX               POINT TO SECONDS
         JSR   INCR        GO INCREMENT SECONDS
         BNE   NMI3        RETURN FROM INTERRUPT
         LDAB  #$06        SET WRAP
         JSR   INCR        GO INCREMENT TENS OF SECONDS
         BNE   NMI3
         LDAB  #$0A        SET WRAP
         JSR   INCR        GO INCREMENT MINUTES
```

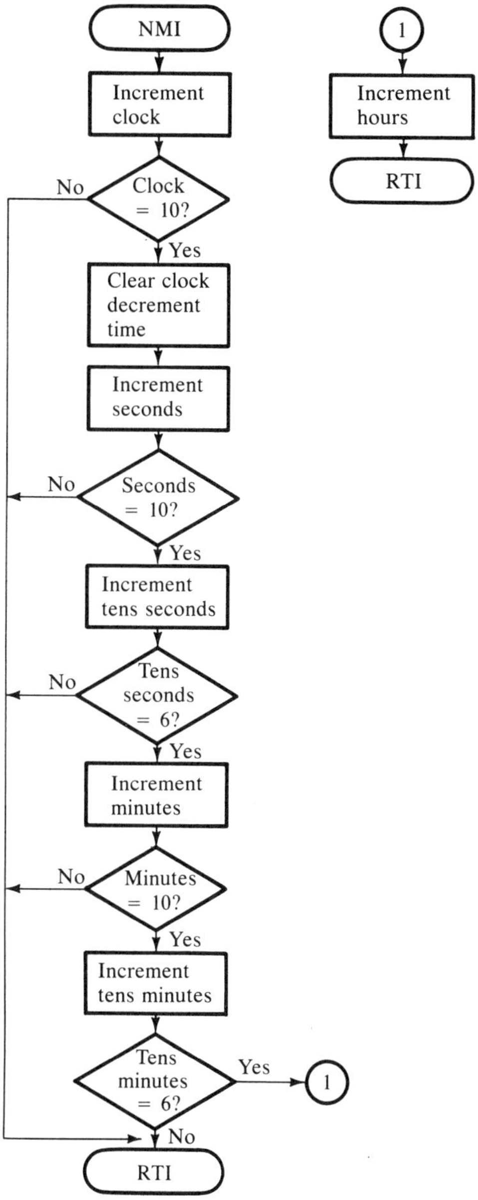

FIGURE 12–11 The flowchart of the nonmaskable interrupt service subroutine.

```
        BNE  NMI3
        LDAB #$06      SET WRAP
        JSR  INCR      GO INCREMENT TENS OF MINUTES
        BNE  NMI3
        DEX
        LDAA X         GET TENS OF HOURS
        LDAB #$0A      SET WRAP
        INX
        CMPA #02       CHECK FOR 20 HOURS
```

```
        BNE   NMI2       IF NOT 20 TO 23 HOURS
        LDAB  #$04       SET WRAP
NMI2    JSR   INCR       GO INCREMENT HOURS
        BNE   NMI3
        LDAB  #$03
        JSR   INCR       GO INCREMENT TENS OF HOURS
NMI3    RTI              RETURN FROM INTERRUPT
INCR    INC   X          GET COUNTER
        CMPB  X          CHECK FOR A WRAP
        BNE   INCR1      IF NO WRAP AROUND
        CLR   X
INCR1   DEX
        TST   X
        RTS              RETURN FROM SUBROUTINE
```

The subroutine INCR has been developed to increment the count in the memory location indexed by the X register. If the count equals the number in ACC B, or wrap, the count is cleared. Number wrap indicates the modulus of the counter to the subroutine. A return with the CCR indicating an equal condition means that the next higher order digit of time must be incremented. If a return with the CCR indicating a not equal condition occurs, it means that no further counters need be updated.

Traffic Light System Software

The purpose of this segment of the software is to change the traffic lights. The software scans through the times programmed into the controller and changes the indicator lamps at the appropriate time. You might call this the system software, since most of the controller's time is spent here. Figure 12–12 illustrates the flowchart for the system software.

```
*SYSTEM SOFTWARE
*
SYST    LDAA  #$01       SYNCHRONIZE WITH CLOCK
        STAA  TIME
SYST1   TST   TIME
        BNE   SYST1      WAIT FOR SYNC
SYST2   LDAA  #$84       SET NS-GREEN, EW-RED
        STAA  $E002      CHANGE LIGHTS
        LDAA  NSGRE
        JSR   TIMO       GO TIME OUT LIGHT
        LDAA  #$44       SET NS-YELLOW, EW-RED
        STAA  $E002      CHANGE LIGHTS
        LDAA  NSYEL
        JSR   TIMO       GO TIME OUT LIGHT
        LDAA  #$30       SET NS-RED, EW-GREEN
        STAA  $E002      CHANGE LIGHTS
        LDAA  EWGRE
        JSR   TIMO       GO TIME OUT LIGHT
        LDAA  #$28       SET NS-RED, EW-YELLOW
```

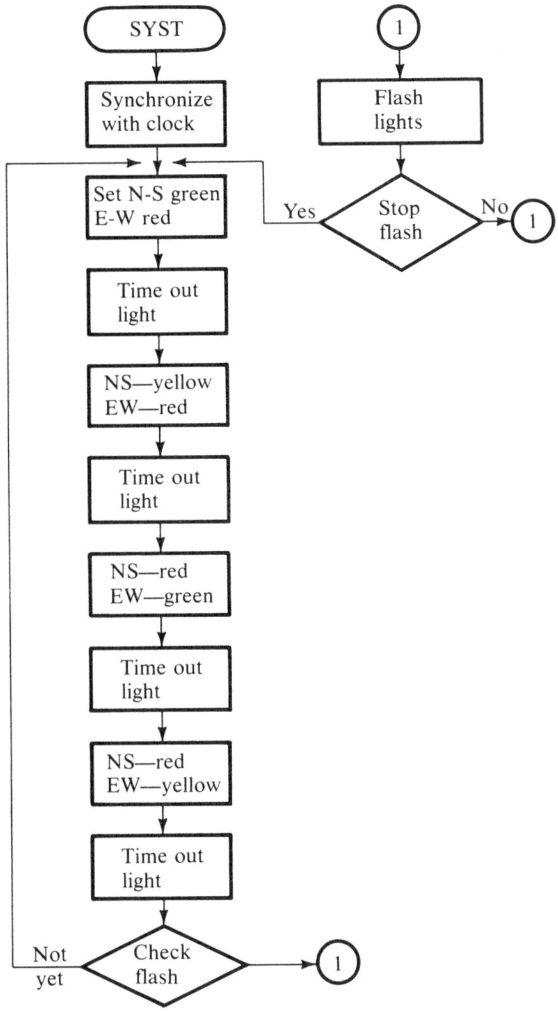

FIGURE 12–12 The flowchart of the main traffic light system program.

```
179         STAA  $E002      CHANGE LIGHTS
180         LDAA  EWYEL
181         JSR   TIMO       GO TIME OUT LIGHT
182         LDX   FLSTR      POINT TO FLASH START TIME
183         JSR   COMPX      COMPARE FLASH START WITH CLOCK
184         BCS   STST2      CONTINUE SEQUENCE
185  SYST3  LDAA  #$28       SET NS-RED, EW-YELLOW
186         STAA  $E002      CHANGE LIGHTS
187         LDAA  #$01       SET COUNT TO ONE SECOND
188         JSR   TIMO       TIME IT OUT
189         LDX   FLEND      POINT TO FLASH END
190         JSR   COMP       CHECK END FLASH TIME
191         BCC   SYST2      CONTINUE NORMAL SEQUENCE
192         CLR   $E002      CHANGE LIGHTS
193         LDAA  #$01       SET COUNT TO ONE SECOND
```

```
194        JSR  TIMO      TIME IT OUT
195        LDX  FLEND     POINT TO FLASH END
196        JSR  COMP      COMPARE FLASH END WITH CLOCK
197        BCC  SYST2     CONTINUE NORMAL SEQUENCE
198        BRA  SYST3     CHECK FOR FLASH END
199 TIMO   STAA TIME      SAVE TIMEOUT TIME
200 TIMOA  TST  TIME      TEST TIME
201        BNE  TIMOA     CHECK FOR TIMED OUT
202        RTS            RETURN FROM SUBROUTINE
203 COMP   LDAA CLOCK+1   GET CLOCK
204        CMPA X         CHECK TIME (SECONDS)
205        BNE  COMP1     IF NOT THE SAME END IT
206        LDAA CLOCK+2   CHECK TIME (TENS SECONDS)
207        CMPA 1,X
208        BNE  COMP1     IF NOT THE SAME END IT
209        LDAA CLOCK+3   CHECK TIME (MINUTES)
210        CMPA 2,X
211        BNE  COMP1     IF NOT THE SAME END IT
212 COMPX  LDAA CLOCK+4   CHECK TIME (TENS MINUTES)
213        CMPA 3,X
214        BNE  COMP1     IF NOT THE SAME END IT
215        LDAA CLOCK+5   CHECK TIME (HOURS)
216        CMPA 4,X
217        BNE  COMP1     IF NOT THE SAME END IT
218        LDAA CLOCK+6   CHECK TIME (TENS HOURS)
219        CMPA 5,X
220 COMP1  RTS            END IT
```

The only feature of the above software that may be a little difficult to understand is the very first portion. Line numbers 162 to 165 are used to synchronize the internal interrupt processed clock with the software listed. If this is not accomplished, timing may be inaccurate by 1 second occasionally.

Trip Plate Software

The trip plate interrupt service subroutine only takes effect if a maximum number of trips is programmed into the controller. If the maximum number is zero, the interrupt remains disabled, and the sequence illustrated in SYST takes complete control. The plate itself produces a pulse on the $\overline{IRQ}$ pin of the MC6800 every time that a vehicle rests on or crosses the plate.

This interrupt service subroutine must be able to determine if the east-west light is in the red condition; if it is, it must then determine how much time remains before the light changes to green. If this time is equal to or less than the minimum time for tripping, no action is taken.

Once tripped, the software must continue to trip the light for up to the maximum amount of time before changing back to red. This is accomplished by counting how many times the light has been tripped during the on cycle. A flowchart for this interrupt service subroutine is illustrated in figure 12–13.

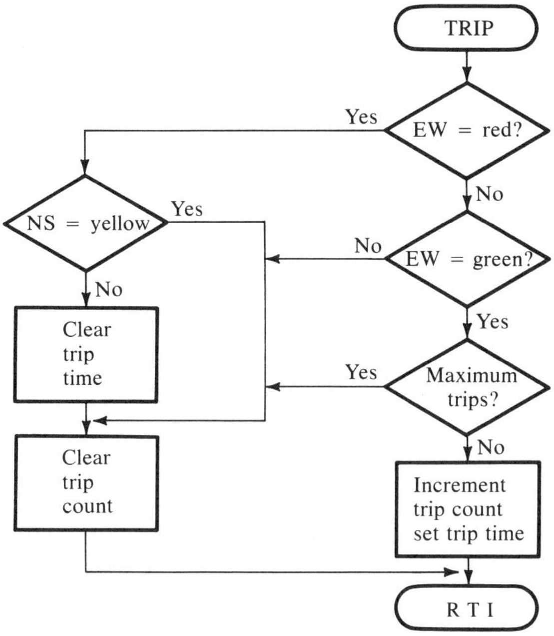

FIGURE 12–13 The flowchart of the trip plate interrupt service subroutine.

```
221  *TRIP PLATE INTERRUPT
222  *
223  TRIP  LDAA  $E002        READ LIGHT POSITIONS
224        BITA  #$04         TEST EW-RED
225        BNE   TRIP1        IF LIGHT IS RED
226        BITA  #$10         TEST EW-GREEN
227        BEQ   TRIP2        IF LIGHT IS YELLOW
228        LDDA  FLEND+8
229        CMPA  MAXTR        CHECK FOR MAXIMUM TRIPS
230        BEQ   TRIP2        IF DONE
231        INC   FLEND+8
232        LDAA  MINTR        GET TRIP TIME
233        STAA  TIME         MODIFY TIME
234        RTI
235  TRIP1 BITA  #$40         TEST NS-YELLOW
236        BNE   TRIP2        IF YELLOW
237        CLR   TIME         END GREEN FOR NORTH-SOUTH
238  TRIP2 CLR   FLEND+8      CLEAR TRIP COUNT
239        RTI
```

Summary

This chapter applies the Motorola MC6800 series microprocessor in two fairly typical examples, a data concentrator and a traffic light controller. Both applications are important, since they use some of the fundamental hardware and software techniques presented earlier in this text.

The data concentrator illustrates the use of ACIAs in an actual example problem including programming and a hardware interface. The traffic light controller uses a PIA with a keyboard and some traffic lamps. This second example employs a real-time clock through the nonmaskable interrupt pin on the MC6800 and a trip plate attached to the maskable interrupt input.

The problems at the end of this chapter include several more examples to be worked on as homework or laboratory projects. Whatever their results, the student will learn a great deal about both hardware and software by attempting them.

Suggested Projects

1 Develop the MC6800 hardware and software to implement a coin changer mechanism. It must be able to accept coins in any denomination from 1 cent to 50 cents and dispense change in the fewest number of pennies, nickels, and dimes.

The amount of money to be accepted is programmed through a set of switches located inside the vending machine. The programmable amount can be anything from 1 cent to $1.99.

Your software must accept coins until the amount indicated on the internal switches has been either reached or exceeded. If the amount has been exceeded, dispense the fewest number of coins as change and send an active low pulse out the $\overline{\text{VEND}}$ pin for 20 ms.

As coins are inserted, a mechanical assembly sorts them and signals the microprocessor with a pulse indicating the denomination of the coin. Once your program has detected and remembered the coin, it must drop it into the internal coin box by pulsing the DROP line for 100 ms. There is also a "bent coin" signal in case a defective coin is inserted into the machine. If a bent coin is detected, you must pulse the $\overline{\text{EJECT}}$ line for 120 ms to clear the coin slot.

To dispense change, the appropriate $\overline{\text{CH}}$ control line is activated for 100 ms, dropping a coin out of the change slot of the vending machine. You must only return one coin at a time with a pause of at least 50 ms between coins for the mechanical ejection mechanism to function properly. Table 12–1 illustrates all of the TTL input and TTL output connections that are to be interfaced to the MC6800.

2 Develop an IC test fixture that will automatically test the 7490 TTL decade counter. The pinout of this decade counter is pictured in figure 12–14 with a brief description of its operating characteristics.

Your system must completely test this device. If it is found faulty, the red LED must be lit; if good, the green LED must be lit. The test sequence must test the clear to zero, clear to nine, and count sequence of the counter at least 20 times without failure for a good indication. The test socket and two LED indicators are pictured in figure 12–15.

TABLE 12–1 Signal lines for the coin changer.

Signal	Function
$\overline{VEND}$	Used to vend merchandise from the machine attached to this changer
$\overline{DROP}$	Used to accept a coin that has been placed into the mechanism
$\overline{EJECT}$	Used to return a bent or defective coin
1C	One cent program input switch
2C	Two cents program input switch
5C	Five cents program input switch
10C	Ten cents program input switch
20C	Twenty cents program input switch
50C	Fifty cents program input switch
100C	One dollar program input switch
$\overline{CH1}$	Returns a penny as change if pulsed for 100 ms
$\overline{CH5}$	Returns a nickel as change if pulsed for 100 ms
$\overline{CH10}$	Returns a dime as change if pulsed for 100 ms
$\overline{CH25}$	Returns a quarter as change if pulsed for 100 ms

FIGURE 12–14 The block diagram, pinout, and truth table for the 7490 decade counter.

SOURCE: Courtesy of Texas Instruments, Inc.

'90A, 'L90, 'LS90 (TOP VIEW)

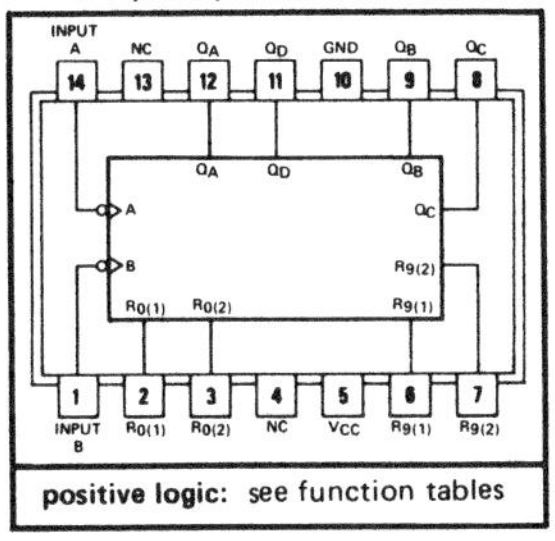

'90A, 'L90, 'LS90
BCD COUNT SEQUENCE
(See Note A)

COUNT	OUTPUT			
	Q_D	Q_C	Q_B	Q_A
0	L	L	L	L
1	L	L	L	H
2	L	L	H	L
3	L	L	H	H
4	L	H	L	L
5	L	H	L	H
6	L	H	H	L
7	L	H	H	H
8	H	L	L	L
9	H	L	L	H

'90A, 'L90, 'LS90
BI-QUINARY (5-2)
(See Note B)

COUNT	OUTPUT			
	Q_A	Q_D	Q_C	Q_B
0	L	L	L	L
1	L	L	L	H
2	L	L	H	L
3	L	L	H	H
4	L	H	L	L
5	H	L	L	L
6	H	L	L	H
7	H	L	H	L
8	H	L	H	H
9	H	H	L	L

'90A, 'L90, 'LS90
RESET/COUNT FUNCTION TABLE

RESET INPUTS				OUTPUT			
$R_{0(1)}$	$R_{0(2)}$	$R_{9(1)}$	$R_{9(2)}$	Q_D	Q_C	Q_B	Q_A
H	H	L	X	L	L	L	L
H	H	X	L	L	L	L	L
X	X	H	H	H	L	L	H
X	L	X	L	COUNT			
L	X	L	X	COUNT			
L	X	X	L	COUNT			
X	L	L	X	COUNT			

NOTES: A. Output Q_A is connected to input B for BCD count.
B. Output Q_D is connected to input A for bi-quinary count.

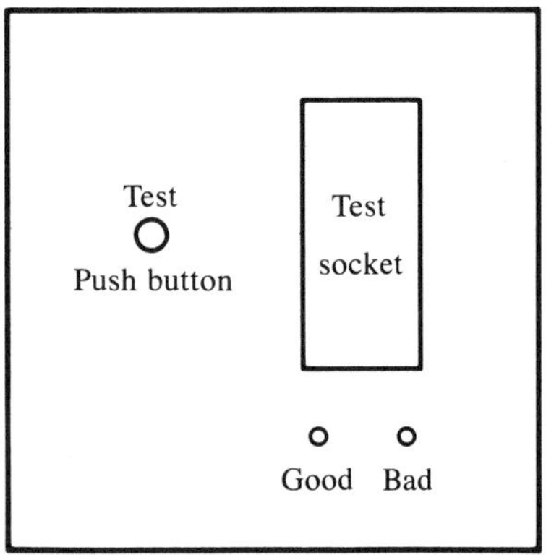

FIGURE 12–15 The control panel of the microprocessor based TTL integrated circuit tester.

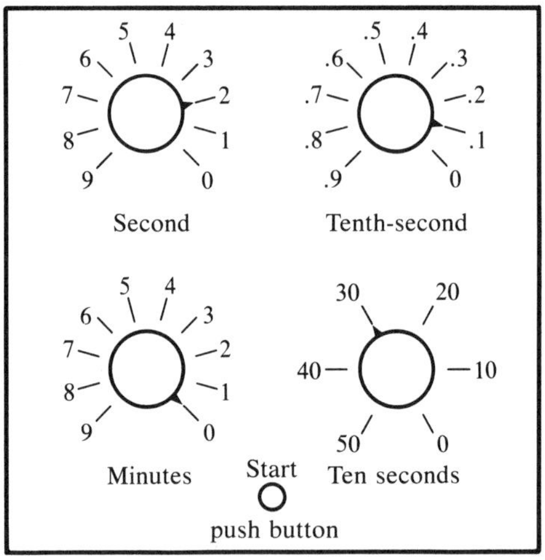

FIGURE 12–16 The control panel of the microprocessor based dark room timer.

3 If the above system is to be able to test any 14-pin integrated TTL circuit, which changes would have to be made to the hardware?

4 Create a darkroom timer that will control the length of time that the enlarger exposes the paper. The timer must be capable of exposing the paper in increments of 0.1 second up to 10 min.

Time settings are dialed in on a series of rotary switches that are labeled in one-tenth seconds, seconds, and minutes (as illustrated in figure 12–16). The push button starts the timing sequence that applies AC power to the lamp in the enlarger for the preset amount of time.

5 Your neighbor's son is a cub scout and wants you to build a timer for the annual pinewood derby. This box must be able to determine who wins each heat and to display the winning time on a set of LED numeric readouts.

Figure 12–17 pictures the ramp, which accommodates two cars at one time, and the location of the beginning and ending trip points.

Your software should start timing when either of the first trip points is tripped and continue timing until either of the second trip points is tripped. The hardware should indicate who has won the race and should light up the elapsed time on a set of displays.

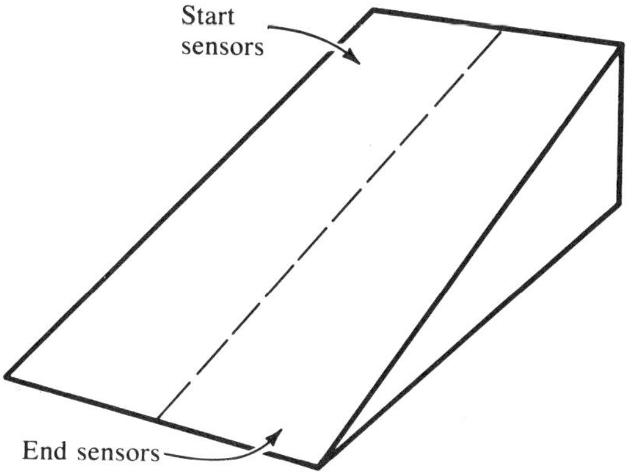

FIGURE 12–17 The ramp for the pine wood derby.

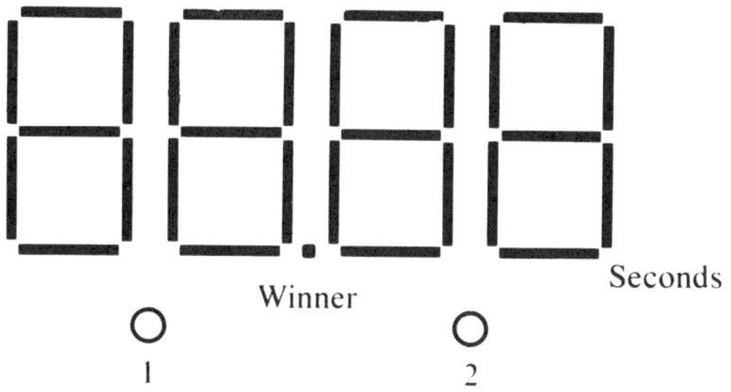

FIGURE 12–18 The display panel on the microprocessor based pine wood derby.

Figure 12–18 pictures the layout of the displays and the winner indicator light.

6 Modify the system developed in question 5 so that it can accommodate a four lane ramp.

Appendices

APPENDIX A:
THE ZILOG Z80
MICROPROCESSOR

APPENDIX B:
DATA SHEETS

APPENDIX C:
SELECTED
ANSWERS TO THE
ODD-NUMBERED
PROBLEMS

A The Zilog Z80 Microprocessor

The Z80 CPU is packaged in an industry standard 40 pin Dual In-Line Package. The I/O pins and the function of each are shown in the figure below.

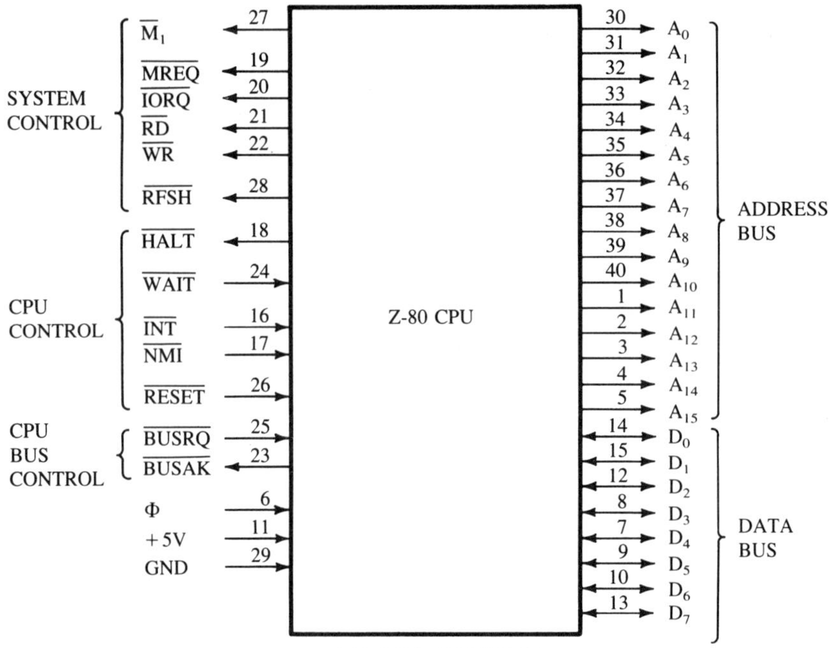

Z-80 CONFIGURATION
FIGURE 3.0-1

A_0-A_{15} (Address Bus) Tri-state output, active high. A_0-A_{15} constitute a 16-bit address bus. The address bus provides the address for memory (up to 64K bytes) data exchanges and for I/O device data exchanges. I/O addressing uses the 8 lower address bits to allow the user to directly select up to 256 input or 256 output ports. A_0 is the least significant address bit. During refresh time, the lower 7 bits contain a valid refresh address.

D_0-D_7 (Data Bus) Tri-state input/output, active high. D_0D_7 constitute an 8-bit bidirectional data bus. The data bus is used for data exchanges with memory and I/O devices.

$\overline{M_1}$ (Machine Cycle one) Output, active low. $\overline{M_1}$ indicates that the current machine cycle is the OP code fetch cycle of an instruction execution. Note that during execution of 2-byte op-codes, $\overline{M_1}$ is generated as each op code byte is fetched. These two byte op-codes always begin with CBH, DDH, EDH or FDH. $\overline{M_1}$ also occurs with $\overline{\text{IORQ}}$ to indicate an interrupt acknowledge cycle.

$\overline{\text{MREQ}}$ (Memory Request) Tri-state output, active low. The memory request signal indicates that the address bus holds a valid address for a memory read or memory write operation.

$\overline{\text{IORQ}}$ (Input/Output Request) Tri-state output, active low. The $\overline{\text{IORQ}}$ signal indicates that the lower half of the address bus holds a valid I/O address for a I/O read or write operation. An $\overline{\text{IORQ}}$ signal is also generated with an $\overline{M_1}$ signal when an interrupt is being acknowledged to indicate that an interrupt response vector can be placed on the data bus. Interrupt Acknowledge operations occur during M_1 time while I/O operations never occur during M_1 time.

$\overline{\text{RD}}$ (Memory Read) Tri-state output, active low. $\overline{\text{RD}}$ indicates that the CPU wants to read data from memory or an I/O device. The addressed I/O device or memory should use this signal to gate data onto the CPU data bus.

$\overline{\text{WR}}$ (Memory Write) Tri-state output, active low. $\overline{\text{WR}}$ indicates that the CPU data bus holds valid data to be stored in the addressed memory or I/O device.

$\overline{\text{RFSH}}$ (Refresh) Output, active low. $\overline{\text{RFSH}}$ indicates that the lower 7 bits of the address bus contain a refresh address for dynamic memories and the current $\overline{\text{MREQ}}$ signal should be used to do a refresh read to all dynamic memories.

$\overline{\text{HALT}}$ (Halt state) Output, active low. $\overline{\text{HALT}}$ indicates that the CPU has executed a HALT software instruction and is awaiting either a nonmaskable or a maskable interrupt (with the mask enabled) before operation can resume. While halted, the CPU executes NOP's to maintain memory refresh activity.

$\overline{\text{WAIT}}$ (Wait) Input, active low. $\overline{\text{WAIT}}$ indicates to the Z-80 CPU that the addressed memory or I/O devices are not ready for a data transfer. The CPU continues to enter wait states for as long as this signal is active. This signal allows memory or I/O devices of any speed to be synchronized to the CPU.

$\overline{\text{INT}}$ (Interrupt Request) Input, active low. The Interrupt Request signal is generated by I/O devices. A request will be honored at the end of the current instruction if the internal software controlled interrupt enable flip-flop (IFF) is enabled and if the $\overline{\text{BUSRQ}}$ signal is not active. When the CPU accepts the interrupt, an acknowledge signal ($\overline{\text{IORQ}}$ during M_1 time) is sent out at the beginning of the next instruction cycle. The CPU can respond to an interrupt in three different modes.

$\overline{\text{NMI}}$ (Nonmaskable Interrupt) Input, negative edge triggered. The nonmaskable interrupt request line has a higher priority than $\overline{\text{INT}}$ and is always recognized at the end of the current instruction, independent of the status of the interrupt enable flip-flop. $\overline{\text{NMI}}$ automatically forces the Z-80 CPU to restart to location 0066_H. The program counter is automatically saved in the external stack so that the user can return to the program that was interrupted. Note that continuous WAIT cycles can prevent the current instruction from ending, and that a $\overline{\text{BUSRQ}}$ will override a $\overline{\text{NMI}}$.

$\overline{\text{RESET}}$ Input, active low. $\overline{\text{RESET}}$ forces the program counter to zero and initializes the CPU. The CPU initialization includes:

1) Disable the interrupt enable flip-flop
2) Set Register I = 00_H
3) Set Register R = 00_H
4) Set Interrupt Mode 0

During reset time, the address bus and data bus go to a high impedance state and all control output signals go to the inactive state.

$\overline{\text{BUSRQ}}$ (Bus Request) Input, active low. The bus request signal is used to request the CPU address bus, data bus and tri-state output control signals to go to a high impedance state so that other devices can control these buses. When $\overline{\text{BUSRQ}}$ is activated, the CPU will set these buses to a high impedance state as soon as the current CPU machine cycle is terminated.

$\overline{\text{BUSAK}}$ (Bus Acknowledge) Output, active low. Bus acknowledge is used to indicate to the requesting device that the CPU address bus, data bus, and tri-state control bus signals have been set to their high impedance state and the external device can now control these signals.

Φ Single phase TTL level clock that requires only a 330 ohm pull-up resistor to +5 volts to meet all clock requirements.

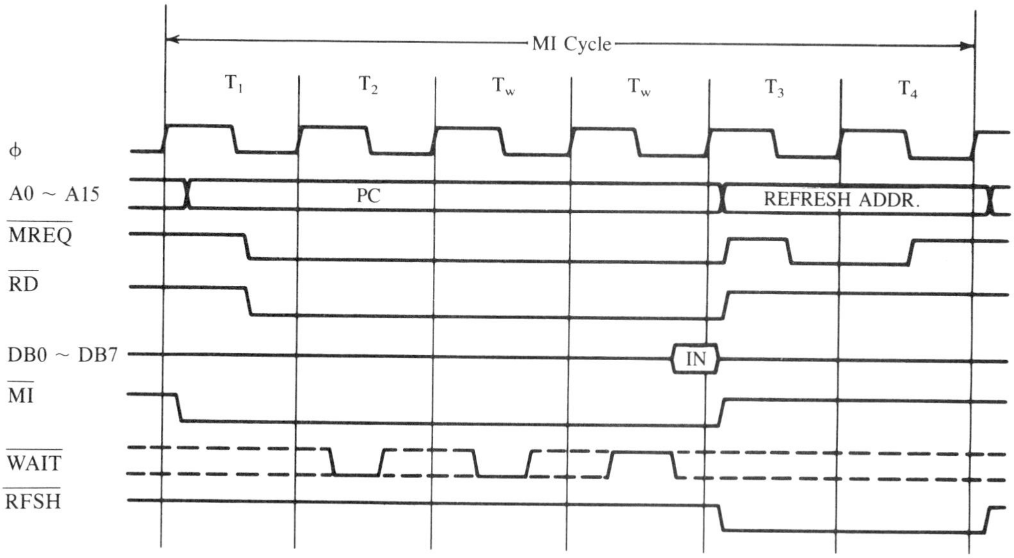

INSTRUCTION OP CODE FETCH WITH WAIT STATES

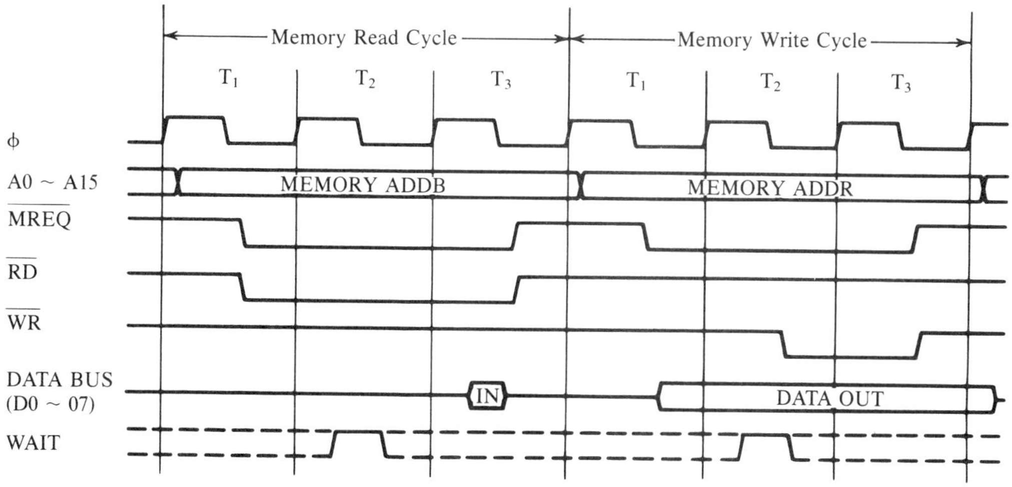

MEMORY READ OR WRITE CYCLES

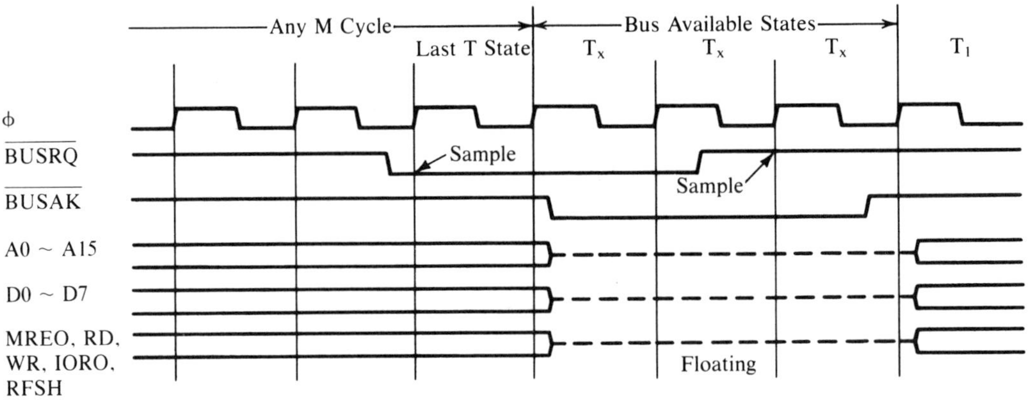

BUS REQUEST/ACKNOWLEDGE CYCLE

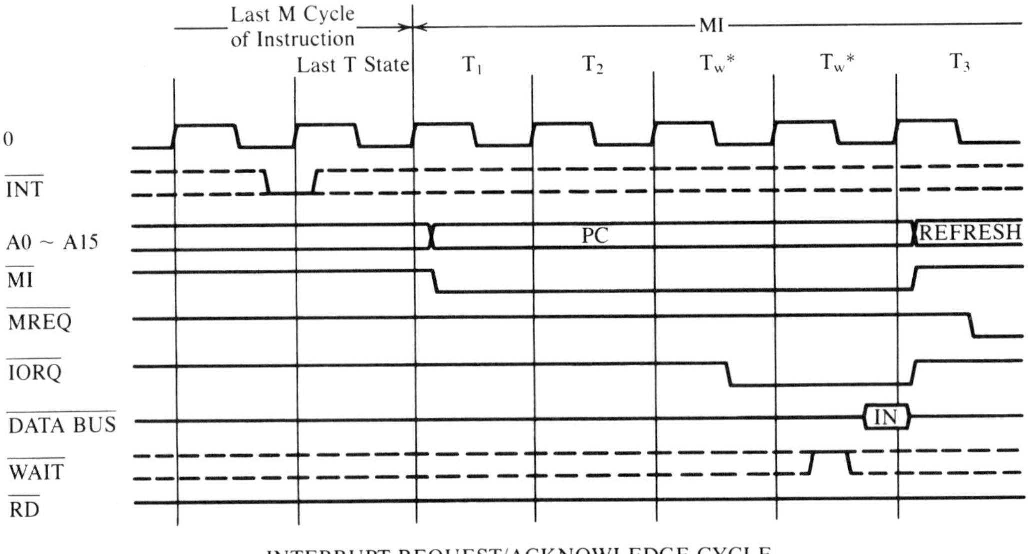

INTERRUPT REQUEST/ACKNOWLEDGE CYCLE

ELECTRICAL SPECIFICATIONS

ABSOLUTE MAXIMUM RATINGS

Temperature Under Bias	0°C to 70°C
Storage Temperature	−65°C to +150°C
Voltage On Any Pin with Respect to Ground	−0.3V to +7V
Power Dissipation	1.4W

• Comment

Stresses above those listed under "Absolute Maximum Rating" may cause permanent damage to the device. This is a stress rating only and functional operation of the device at these or any other condition above those indicated in the operational sections of this specification is not implied. Exposure to absolute maximum rating conditions for extended periods may affect device reliability.

• D.C. CHARACTERISTICS

T_A = 0°C to 70°C, V_{cc} = 5V ± 5% unless otherwise specified

Symbol	Parameter	Min.	Typ.	Max.	Unit	Test Condition
V_{ILC}	Clock Input Low Voltage	−0.3		0.45	V	
V_{IHC}	Clock Input High Voltage	V_{cc} [1]		V_{cc}	V	
V_{IL}	Input Low Voltage	−0.3		0.8	V	
V_{IH}	Input High Voltage	2.0		V_{cc}	V	
V_{OL}	Output Low Voltage			0.4	V	I_{OL} = 1.8mA
V_{OH}	Output High Voltage	2.4			V	I_{OH} = 100μA
I_{CC}	Power Supply Current			200	mA	t_c = 400nsec
I_{LI}	Input Leakage Current			10	μA	V_{IN} = 0 to V_{oc}
I_{LOH}	Tri-State Output Leakage Current in Float			10	μA	V_{OUT} = 2.4 to V_{CC}
I_{LOL}	Tri-State Output Leakage Current in Float			−10	μA	V_{OUT} = 0.4V
I_{LD}	Data Bus Leakage Current in Input Mode			±10	μA	$0 \leq V_{IN} \leq V_{cc}$

• CAPACITANCE

T_A = 25°C, f = 1 MHz

Symbol	Parameter	Typ.	Max.	Unit	Test Condition
Cϕ	Clock Capacitance		20	pF	Unmeasured Pins Returned to Ground
C_{IN}	Input Capacitance		5	pF	
C_{OUT}	Output Capacitance		10	pF	

(1) Clock Driver

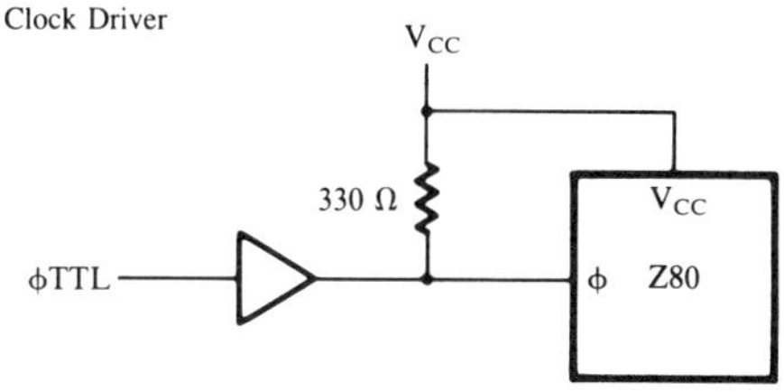

An external clock pull-up resistor of (330Ω) will meet both the A.D. and D.C. clock requirements.

A.C. Characteristics — Z80-CPU

T_A = 0°C to 70°C, V_{cc} = +5V ± 5%. Unless Otherwise Noted.

Signal	Symbol	Parameter	Min	Max	Unit	Test Condition
Φ	t_c	Clock Period	.4	[12]	μsec	
	$t_w(\Phi H)$	Clock Pulse Width, Clock High	180	∞	nsec	
	$t_w(\Phi L)$	Clock Pulse Width, Clock Low	180	2000	nsec	
	$t_{r,f}$	Clock Rise and Fall Time		30	nsec	
A_{0-15}	$t_D(AD)$	Address Output Delay		160	nsec	C_L = 100pF
	$t_F(AD)$	Delay to Float		110	nsec	
	t_{acm}	Address Stable Prior to $\overline{MRFQ}$ (Memory Cycle)	[1]		nsec	
	t_{aci}	Address Stable Prior to $\overline{IORQ}$, $\overline{RD}$, or $\overline{WR}$ (I/O Cycle)	[2]		nsec	
	t_{ca}	Address Stable From $\overline{RD}$ or $\overline{WR}$	[3]		nsec	
	t_{caf}	Address Stable From RD or $\overline{WR}$ During Float	[4]		nsec	
D_{0-7}	$t_D(D)$	Data Output Delay		260	nsec	C_L = 200 pF
	$t_F(D)$	Delay to Float During Write Cycle		90	nsec	
	$t_{S\Phi}(D)$	Data Setup Time to Rising Edge of Clock During MI Cycle	50		nsec	
	$t_{S\overline{\Phi}}(D)$	Data Setup Time to Falling Edge of Clock During M2 to M5	60		nsec	
	t_{dcm}	Data Stable Prior to $\overline{WR}$ (Memory Cycle)	[5]		nsec	
	t_{dci}	Data Stable Priorto $\overline{WR}$ (I/O Cycle)	[6]		nsec	
	t_{cdf}	Data Stable From $\overline{WR}$	[7]			
	t_H	Any Hold Time for Setup Time	0		nsec	
$\overline{MREQ}$	$t_{DL\overline{\Phi}}(MR)$	$\overline{MREQ}$ Delay From Falling Edge of Clock, $\overline{MREQ}$ Low		100	nsec	C_L = 50pF
	$t_{DH\Phi}(MR)$	$\overline{MREQ}$ Delay From Rising Edge of Clock, $\overline{MREQ}$ High		100	nsec	
	$t_{DH\overline{\Phi}}(MR)$	$\overline{MREQ}$ Delay From Falling Edge of Clock, $\overline{MREQ}$ High		100	nsec	
	$t_w(\overline{MRL})$	Pulse Width, $\overline{MREQ}$ Low	[8]		nsec	
	$t_w(\overline{MRH})$	Pulse Width, $\overline{MREQ}$ High	[9]		nsec	
$\overline{IORQ}$	$t_{DL\Phi}(IR)$	$\overline{IORQ}$ Delay From Rising Edge of Clock, $\overline{IORQ}$ Low		90	nsec	C_L = 50 pF
	$t_{DL\overline{\Phi}}(IR)$	$\overline{IORQ}$ Delay From Falling Edge of Clock, $\overline{IORQ}$ Low		110	nsec	
	$t_{DH\Phi}(IR)$	$\overline{IORQ}$ Delay From Rising Edge of Clock, $\overline{IORQ}$ High		100	nsec	
	$t_{DH\overline{\Phi}}(IR)$	$\overline{IORQ}$ Delay From Falling Edge of Clock, $\overline{IORQ}$ High		110	nsec	
$\overline{RD}$	$t_{DL\Phi}(RD)$	$\overline{RD}$ Delay From Rising Edge of Clock, $\overline{RD}$ Low		100	nsec	C_L = 50pF
	$t_{DL\overline{\Phi}}(RD)$	$\overline{RD}$ Delay From Falling Edge of Clock, $\overline{RD}$ Low		130	nsec	
	$t_{DL\Phi}(RD)$	$\overline{RD}$ Delay From Rising Edge of Clock, $\overline{RD}$ High		100	nsec	
	$t_{DH\overline{\Phi}}(RD)$	$\overline{RD}$ Delay From Falling Edge of Clock, $\overline{RD}$ High		110	nsec	

[12] $t_c = t_{w(\Phi H)} + t_{w(\Phi L)} + t_r + t_f$

[1] $t_{acm} = t_{w(\Phi H)} + t_f - 75$

[2] $t_{aci} = t_c - 80$

[3] $t_{ca} = t_{w(\Phi L)} + t_r - 40$

[4] $t_{caf} = t_{w(\Phi L)} + t_r - 60$

[5] $t_{dcm} = t_c - 180$

[6] $t_{dci} = t_{w(\Phi L)} + t_r - 180$

[7] $t_{cdf} = t_{w(\Phi L)} + t_r - 50$

[8] $t_{w(\overline{MRL})} = t_c - 40$

[9] $t_{w(\overline{MRH})} = t_{w(\Phi H)} + t_f - 30$

Signal	Symbol	Parameter	Min	Max	Unit	Test Condition
$\overline{WR}$	$t_{DL\Phi}$ (WR)	$\overline{WR}$ Delay From Rising Edge of Clock, $\overline{WR}$ Low		80	nsec	$C_L = 50pF$
	$t_{DL\overline{\Phi}}$ (WR)	$\overline{WR}$ Delay From Falling Edge of Clock, $\overline{WR}$ Low		90	nsec	
	$t_{DH\Phi}$ (WR)	$\overline{WR}$ Delay From Falling Edge of Clock, $\overline{WR}$ High		100	nsec	
	t_w ($\overline{WRL}$)	Pulse Width, $\overline{WR}$ Low	[10]		nsec	
$\overline{M1}$	t_{DL} ($\overline{M1}$)	$\overline{M1}$ Delay From Rising Edge of Clock, $\overline{M1}$ Low		130	nsec	$C_L = 30pF$
	t_{DH} ($\overline{M1}$)	$\overline{M1}$ Delay From Rising Edge of Clock, $\overline{M1}$ High		130	nsec	
$\overline{RFSH}$	t_{DL} (RF)	$\overline{RFSH}$ Delay From Rising Edge of Clock, $\overline{RFSH}$ Low		180	nsec	$C_L = 30pF$
	t_{DH} (RF)	$\overline{RFSH}$ Delay From Rising Edge of Clock, $\overline{RFSH}$ High		150	nsec	
$\overline{WAIT}$	t_s (WT)	$\overline{WAIT}$ Setup Time to Falling Edge of Clock	70		nsec	
$\overline{HALT}$	t_D (HT)	$\overline{HALT}$ Delay Time From Falling Edge of Clock		300	nsec	$C_L = 50pF$
$\overline{INT}$	t_s (IT)	$\overline{INT}$ Setup Time to Rising Edge of Clock	80		nsec	
$\overline{NMI}$	t_w ($\overline{NML}$)	Pulse Width, $\overline{NMI}$ Low	80		nsec	
$\overline{BUSRQ}$	t_s (BQ)	$\overline{BUSRQ}$ Setup Time to Rising Edge of Clock	80		nsec	
$\overline{BUSAK}$	t_{DL} (BA)	$\overline{BUSAK}$ Delay From Rising Edge of Clock, $\overline{BUSAK}$ Low		120	nsec	$C_L = 50pF$
	t_{DH} (BA)	$\overline{BUSAK}$ Delay From Falling Edge of Clock, $\overline{BUSAK}$ High		110	nsec	
$\overline{RESET}$	t_s (RS)	$\overline{RESET}$ Setup Time to Rising Edge of Clock	90		nsec	
	t_F (C)	Delay to Float ($\overline{MREQ}$, $\overline{IORQ}$, $\overline{RD}$ and $\overline{WR}$)		100	nsec	
	t_{mr}	$\overline{M1}$ Stable Prior to $\overline{IORQ}$ (Interrupt Ack.)	[11]		nsec	

[10] $t_{w(WR)} = t_c - 40$

[11] $t_{nr} = 2t_c + t_{w(\Phi H)} + t_f - 80$

NOTES:

1. Data should be enabled onto the CPU data bus when $\overline{RD}$ is active. During interrupt acknowledge data should be enabled when $\overline{M1}$ and $\overline{IORQ}$ are both active.
2. All control sitnals are internally synchronized, so they may be totally asynchronous with respect to the clock.
3. The $\overline{RESET}$ signal must be active for a minimum of 3 clock cycles.
4. Output Delay vs. Loaded Capacitance
   TA = 70°C V_{cc} = +5V ±5%
   (1) ΔC_L = +100pF ($A_0 - A_{15}$ and Control Signals, add 30 ns to timing shown.
   (2) ΔC_L = −50pF ($A_0 - A_{15}$ and Control Signals), subtract 15 ns from timing shown.

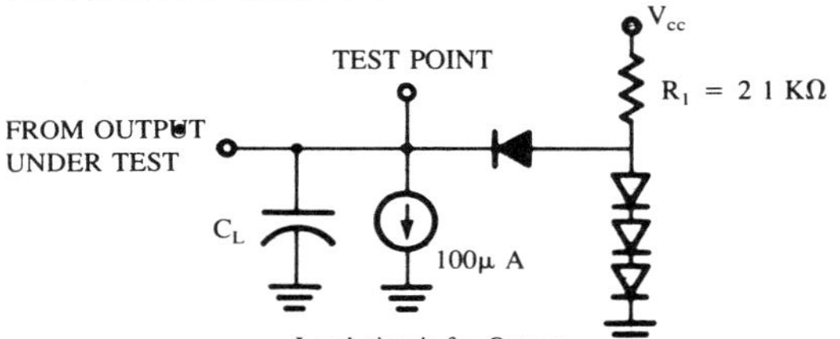

Load circuit for Output

A.C. Timing Diagram

Timing measurements are made at the following voltages, unless otherwise specified:

	"1"	"0"
CLOCK	4.2V	.8V
OUTPUT	2.0V	.8V
INPUT	2.0V	.8V
FLOAT	ΔV	±0.5V

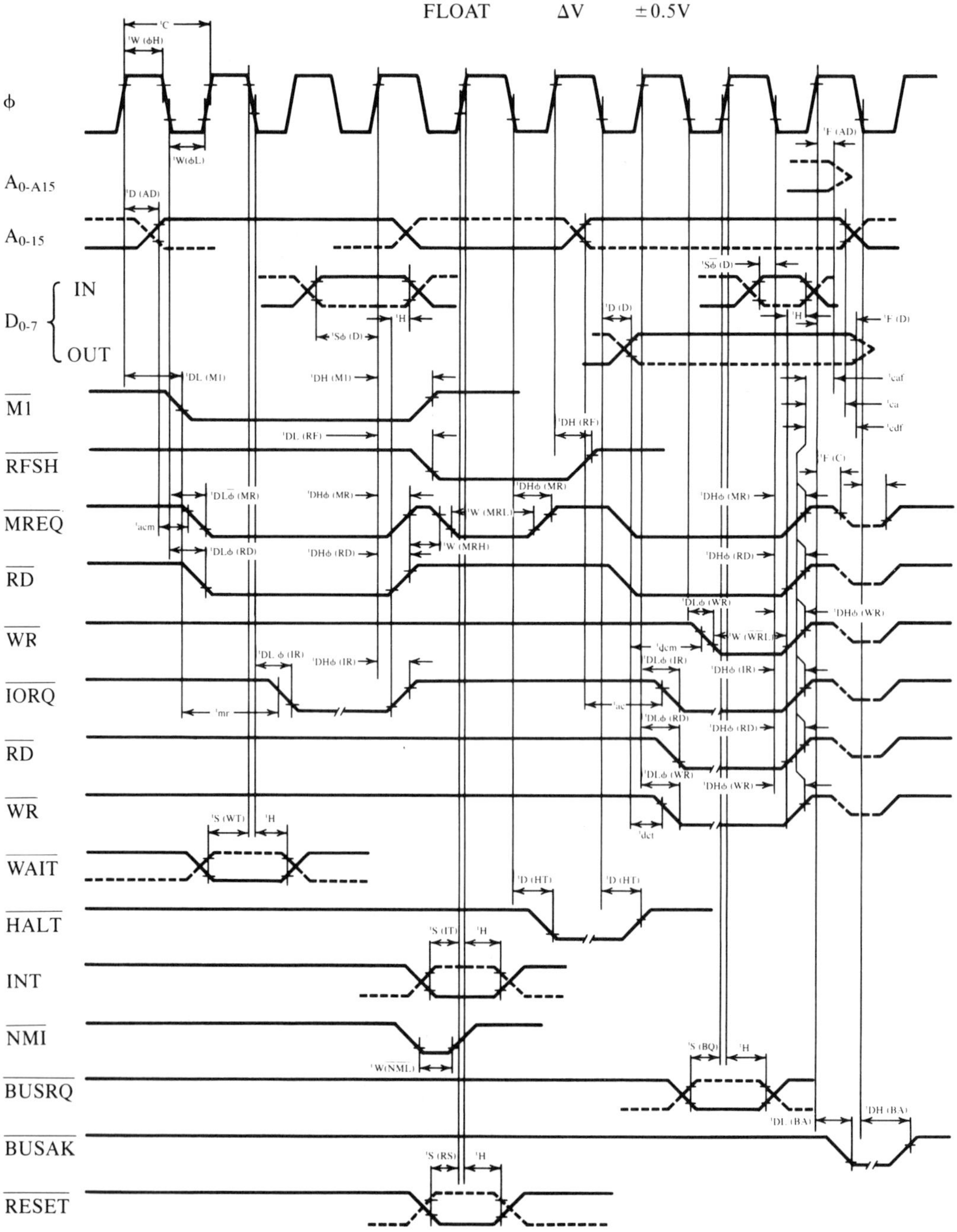

Data Sheets B

SN54LS138, SN54S138 . . . J OR W PACKAGE
SN74LS138, SN74S138 . . . J OR N PACKAGE
(TOP VIEW)

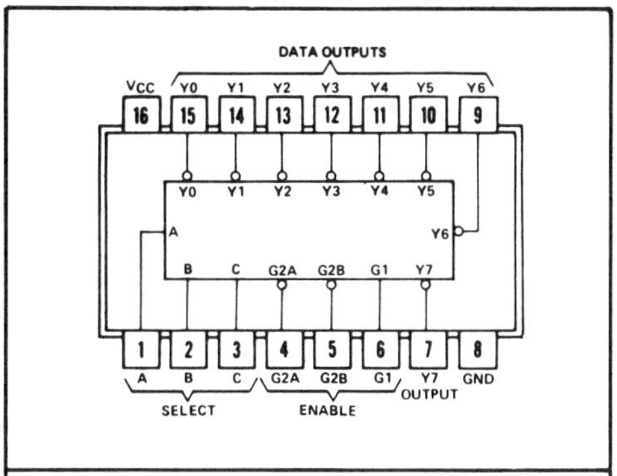

positive logic: see function table

SN54LS139, SN54S139 . . . J OR W PACKAGE
SN74LS139, SN74S139 . . . J OR N PACKAGE
(TOP VIEW)

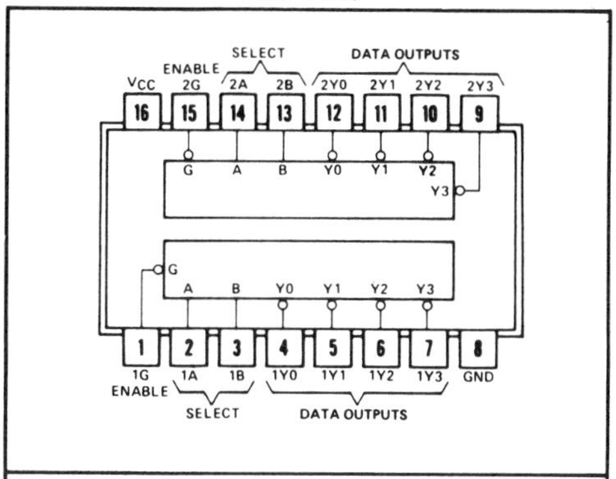

positive logic: see function table

functional block diagrams and logic

'LS138, 'S138

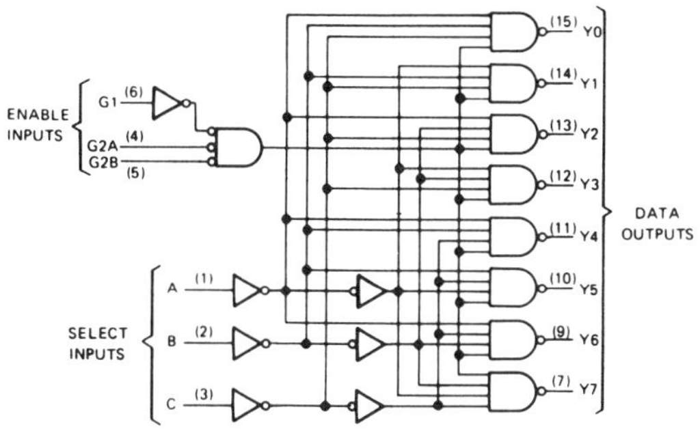

'LS138, 'S138
FUNCTION TABLE

INPUTS					OUTPUTS							
ENABLE		SELECT										
G1	G2*	C	B	A	Y0	Y1	Y2	Y3	Y4	Y5	Y6	Y7
X	H	X	X	X	H	H	H	H	H	H	H	H
L	X	X	X	X	H	H	H	H	H	H	H	H
H	L	L	L	L	L	H	H	H	H	H	H	H
H	L	L	L	H	H	L	H	H	H	H	H	H
H	L	L	H	L	H	H	L	H	H	H	H	H
H	L	L	H	H	H	H	H	L	H	H	H	H
H	L	H	L	L	H	H	H	H	L	H	H	H
H	L	H	L	H	H	H	H	H	H	L	H	H
H	L	H	H	L	H	H	H	H	H	H	L	H
H	L	H	H	H	H	H	H	H	H	H	H	L

*G2 = G2A + G2B

H = high level, L = low level, X = irrelevant

'LS139, 'S139

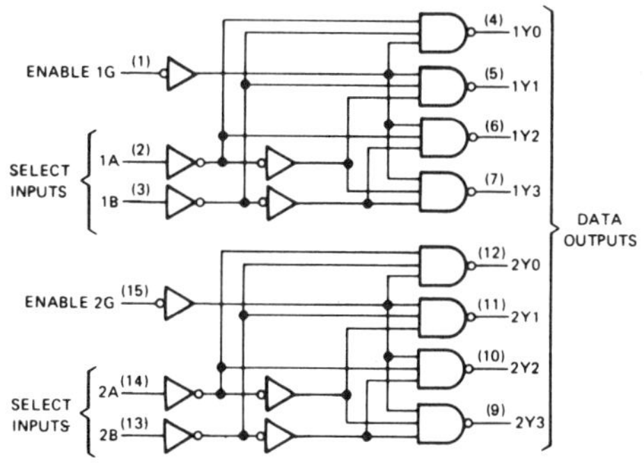

'LS139, 'S139
(EACH DECODER/DEMULTIPLEXER)
FUNCTION TABLE

INPUTS			OUTPUTS			
ENABLE	SELECT					
G	B	A	Y0	Y1	Y2	Y3
H	X	X	H	H	H	H
L	L	L	L	H	H	H
L	L	H	H	L	H	H
L	H	L	H	H	L	H
L	H	H	H	H	H	L

H = high level, L = low level, X = irrelevant

FIGURE B–1 74138 and 74139 data specifications.
(SOURCE: Courtesy of Texas Instruments, Inc.)

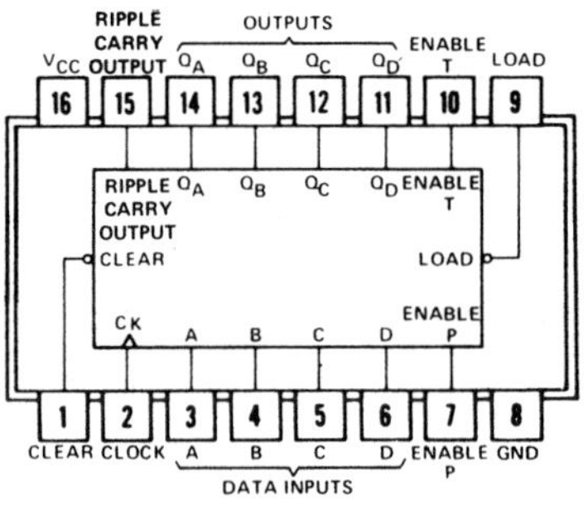

'161, 'LS161A, '163, 'LS163A, 'S163 BINARY COUNTERS

typical clear, preset, count, and inhibit sequences

Illustrated below is the following sequence:

1. Clear outputs to zero ('161 and 'LS161A are asynchronous; '163, 'LS163A, and 'S163 are synchronous)
2. Preset to binary twelve
3. Count to thirteen, fourteen fifteen, zero, one, and two
4. Inhibit

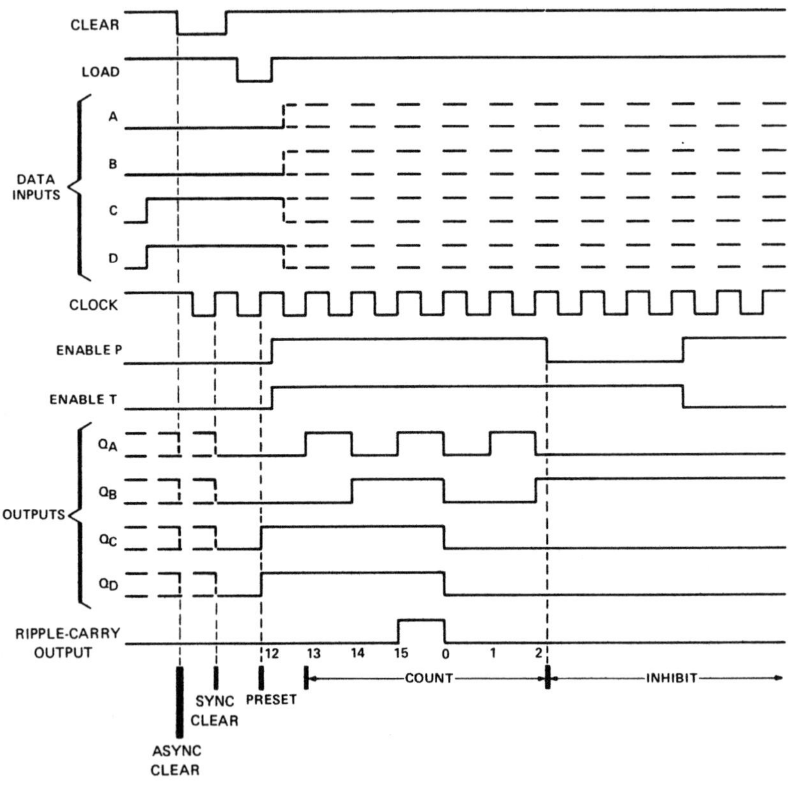

FIGURE B–2 74163 data specifications.
(SOURCE: Courtesy of Texas Instruments, Inc.)

SN54LS245 . . . J PACKAGE
SN74LS245 . . . J OR N PACKAGE
(TOP VIEW)

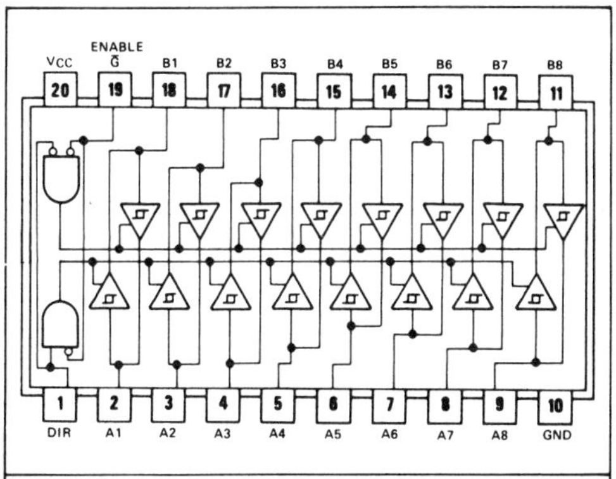

positive logic: see function table

FUNCTION TABLE

ENABLE $\overline{G}$	DIRECTION CONTROL DIR	OPERATION
L	L	B data to A bus
L	H	A data to B bus
H	X	Isolation

H = high level, L = low level, X = irrelevant

FIGURE B–3 74LS245 data specifications.
(SOURCE: Courtesy of Texas Instruments, Inc.)

SN54LS373, SN54S373 . . . J PACKAGE
SN74LS373, SN74S373 . . . J OR N PACKAGE
(TOP VIEW)

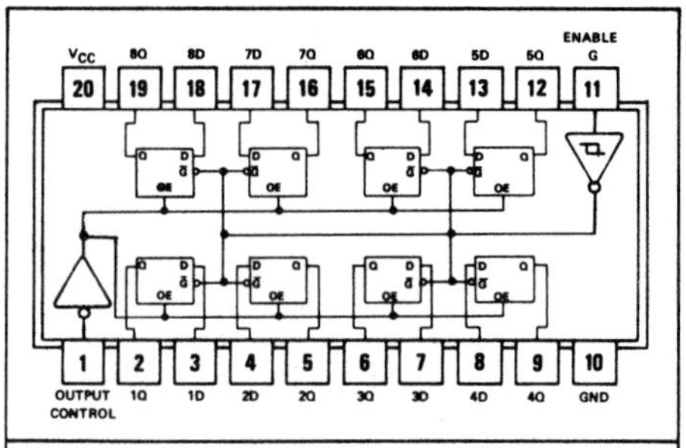

logic: see function table

'LS373, 'S373
FUNCTION TABLE

OUTPUT CONTROL	ENABLE G	D	OUTPUT
L	H	H	H
L	H	L	L
L	L	X	Q_0
H	X	X	Z

SN54LS374, SN54S374 . . . J PACKAGE
SN74LS374, SN74S374 . . . J OR N PACKAGE
(TOP VIEW)

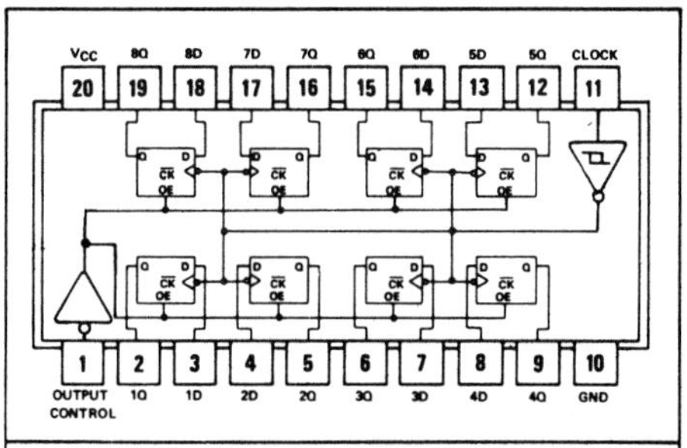

logic: see function table

'LS374, 'S374
FUNCTION TABLE

OUTPUT CONTROL	CLOCK	D	OUTPUT
L	↑	H	H
L	↑	L	L
L	L	X	Q_0
H	X	X	Z

See explanation of function tables on page 3-8.

FIGURE B–4 74LS373 and 74LS374 data specifications.
(SOURCE: Courtesy of Texas Instruments, Inc.)

Selected Answers to the Odd-Numbered Problems C

Chapter 1

1 **Memory size** This is probably the most significant difference between a mainframe and a micro since the micro normally can address 64K to about 16M bytes of memory, while the mainframe can often address billions of bytes of memory.

Word size The microprocessor can normally manipulate either 8 or 16 bits of data, the mainframe can manipulate 32 or more bits.

Speed The mainframe is many times faster than the microprocessor. (The CRAY computer reputedly can execute an instruction in a few nanoseconds.)

3 If arithmetic operations are being developed for a particular application, a compiler would be much more useful than an assembler, because it already contains all of the arithmetic routines.

5 The text lists PL/M and PASCAL, which are currently found in many places where microprocessor software is being developed. These languages are ideally suited to microprocessor software development.

7 The software module allows a system program to be divided or structured into more manageable segments, enabling programmers to develop systems more efficiently.

9 The software development task begins when the engineering department sends a new product specification to the software development manager. The manager develops an estimate of the amount of memory required to implement the system and the number and type of I/O devices required. This information is returned to engineering for development.

The manager now develops a system flow-chart and assigns programming tasks or modules to the people in the department. At this point, the software for each module is developed. When all of the modules are debugged, the manager links them together and tests the system with software drivers and/or an emulator.

11 Sewing machine, washing machine, microwave oven, printer, CRT terminal, and various other simple digitalized devices.

13 Word processing systems would be ideal since they handle ASCII characters, which are 8-bit numbers if you include parity.

15 The secretary with a word processor. The bank teller with the computer. (I know, you still seem to wait as long or longer in the line at the bank.)

Chapter 2

1 The CPU or MPU, memory, and input/output comprise all digital computer systems.

3 The memory stores the instructions and data for a program.

5 Programs are normally stored in one of the read only types of memory.

7 A transparent latch is a device constructed with gated D-type flip-flops. The term *transparent* is derived from the fact that gated D-type flip-flops appear transparent whenever the gate input is at its active level.

9 Propagation delay times are usually short enough that they can be ignored, but not always. It is important that these times be checked if a memory device or external I/O device functions at a speed approaching the upper limit of the microprocessor's operating speed.

11 In a system that uses memory mapped I/O, the I/O devices are treated exactly as if they were memory.

13 The microprocessor disconnects itself from its address, data, and control buses, allowing an external device to gain access to the microprocessor's memory and I/O equipment.

15 The main differences between these two buses are:

S100	STD-BUS
Local regulation	Remote regulation
16-bit data bus	8-bit data bus
24-bit address bus	16-bit address bus
Vectored interrupts	Single interrupt
Multiple channel DMA	Single channel DMA

17 Power supply decoupling is extremely critical in a digital system because digital circuitry generates a tremendous amount of power supply noise. Without adequate decoupling, it is doubtful that a digital system will perform as designed.

Chapter 3

1 The noise immunity of the Intel series of microprocessors is 350 mV.

3 Five lower-power TTL loads may be attached to one output pin. Each load draws a maximum of 0.4 mA of sink current.

5 Since the clock cycle frequency is one-half of the crystal clock frequency, the clock cycle frequency would be 2 MHz for a 4 MHz crystal. This makes the clock cycle time equal to 500 ns.

7 The 8284A clock generator divides the crystal frequency by a factor of three.

9 Since the 8088 contains 20 address pins, it is capable of directly addressing 1M bytes or 512K 16-bit words of memory.

11 Adding buffering to the data bus decreases the amount of access time allowed for the memory.

13 The $\overline{WR}$ signal is a strobe to the I/O or memory that must be used to cause the write. The data from the data bus is only valid during this strobe; the trailing, or positive in this case, edge would be used to transfer the data.

15 **DT/$\overline{R}$** This signal selects the direction of data flow through an external bus transceiver.

$\overline{DEN}$ This signal enables the bus transceiver.

17 The 8085A always powers up executing instructions beginning at memory location 0000H.

19 The amount of access time allowed the memory by the 8085A is 575 ns at its maximum clock frequency.

21

Pin Name	Vector Location
TRAP	0024H
RST 7.5	003CH
RST 6.5	0034H
RST 5.5	002CH
INTR	*

*This interrupt vector is determined by the hardware (refer to Chapter 8).

23 See figure C–1

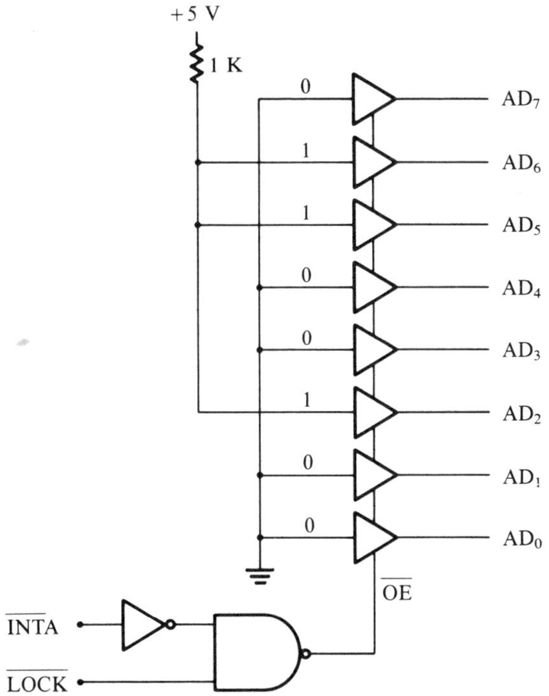

FIGURE C–1

25 During a HOLD condition, the microprocessor <u>floats (or open circuits)</u> the address, data, and control bus connections $\overline{RD}$, $\overline{WR}$ and IO/$\overline{M}$.

27 The READY input can be used for the implementation of the RUN/STOP or the single-step functions.

29 Since the clock cycle time is equal to 1 μs, it would take 231 μs to execute the sequence in problem 28.

31 The logic analyzer can grab onto op-codes from the system data bus as they are actually executed in a system. This would test the system software under normal operating conditions.

Chapter 4

1

Device	Number of Pins
6800	40
6809	40
68000	64

3 It depends on which pins: some of the pins can supply 3.0 mA of sink current, and some can supply 5.0 mA. The 3.0 mA pins can drive 2 standard or 8 low-power TTL loads. The 5.0 mA pins can drive 3 standard or 13 low-power loads.

5 A 1 MHz input clock frequency would operate the MC6800 at a 1 MHz rate.

7 Either of these microprocessors can directly address 64K bytes of memory.

9 The MC68000 handles data transfers either 8 bits or 16 bits at a time through its 16-pin data bus.

11 The $\overline{\text{AS}}$ connection on the MC68000 indicates that the address bus contains a valid memory address.

13 The $\overline{\text{BERR}}$ signal indicates to the MC68000 that a bus error has occurred. It is usually developed by a memory error in order to request a repeat of the current bus cycle.

15 $\overline{\text{BREQ}}$ requests a DMA cycle, and a combination of BA and BS acknowledges it.

17 The reset vector is stored in the first eight memory locations in the MC68000 based system.

19 The MC68000 allows 290 ns of time for memory access.

21 The $\overline{\text{DTACK}}$ signal indicates that the memory or I/O has received a request for an operation.

23 The $\overline{\text{FIRQ}}$, $\overline{\text{IRQ}}$, and $\overline{\text{NMI}}$ interrupt inputs are present on the MC6809.

25 The main difference between these two inputs is the data that is automatically stacked by the processor whenever either request is honored.

$\overline{\textbf{FIRQ}}$ This input will stack the contents of the program counter and the condition code register when honored.

$\overline{\textbf{IRQ}}$ This input will stack all of the internal registers when it is honored.

27 It takes 2–5 μs, depending on the addressing mode.

29
```
*SUBROUTINE TO TEST I/O LOCATION $C000
*
TEST LDAA $C000     READ LOCATION
     STAA $C000     WRITE LOCATION
     BRA  TEST
```

Chapter 5

1 **ROM** Mask programmable read only memory.
PROM Fuse link programmable read only memory.
EPROM Erasable programmable read only memory.
EEPROM Electrically erasable read only memory.
EAROM Electrically alterable read only memory.
NOVRAM Nonvolatile RAM

3 If such a device could be found, it would contain 14 pins for memory addressing.

5 A bus contention, or conflict, occurs whenever two devices drive a bus line at exactly the same instant in time.

7 In a memory device that has common I/O, the same pin is used to read and write information; in a device that has separate I/O, there is a pin for each function.

9 One reason is that the dynamic cell contains one-half the number of inverters of a static cell. Another, and possibly more important, reason is that the amount of power dissipated in the dynamic cell is much lower than in a static cell. This allows the manufacturer to place the MOSFETS closer together on the IC substrate, thereby increasing the packaging density.

11 See figure C–2.

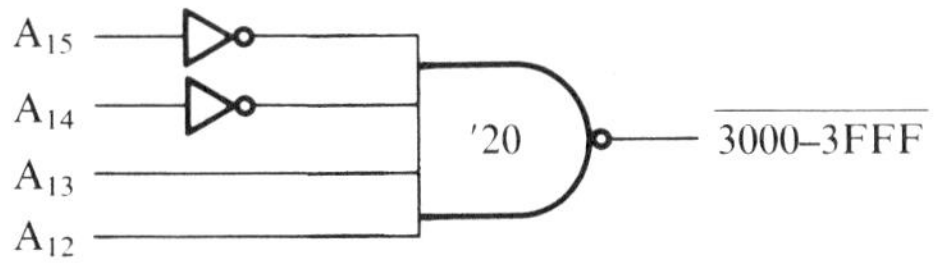

FIGURE C–2

13 GOODLUCK!!! (74LS139 sometime)

15 See figure C–3.

17 See figure C–4.

19 See figure C–5.

21 Integrated circuits that contain totem pole outputs, which are constructed of CMOS circuits or dynamic memory elements, must be bypassed because they produce switching transients on the power supply connections that would be coupled to another circuit in a system, causing faults.

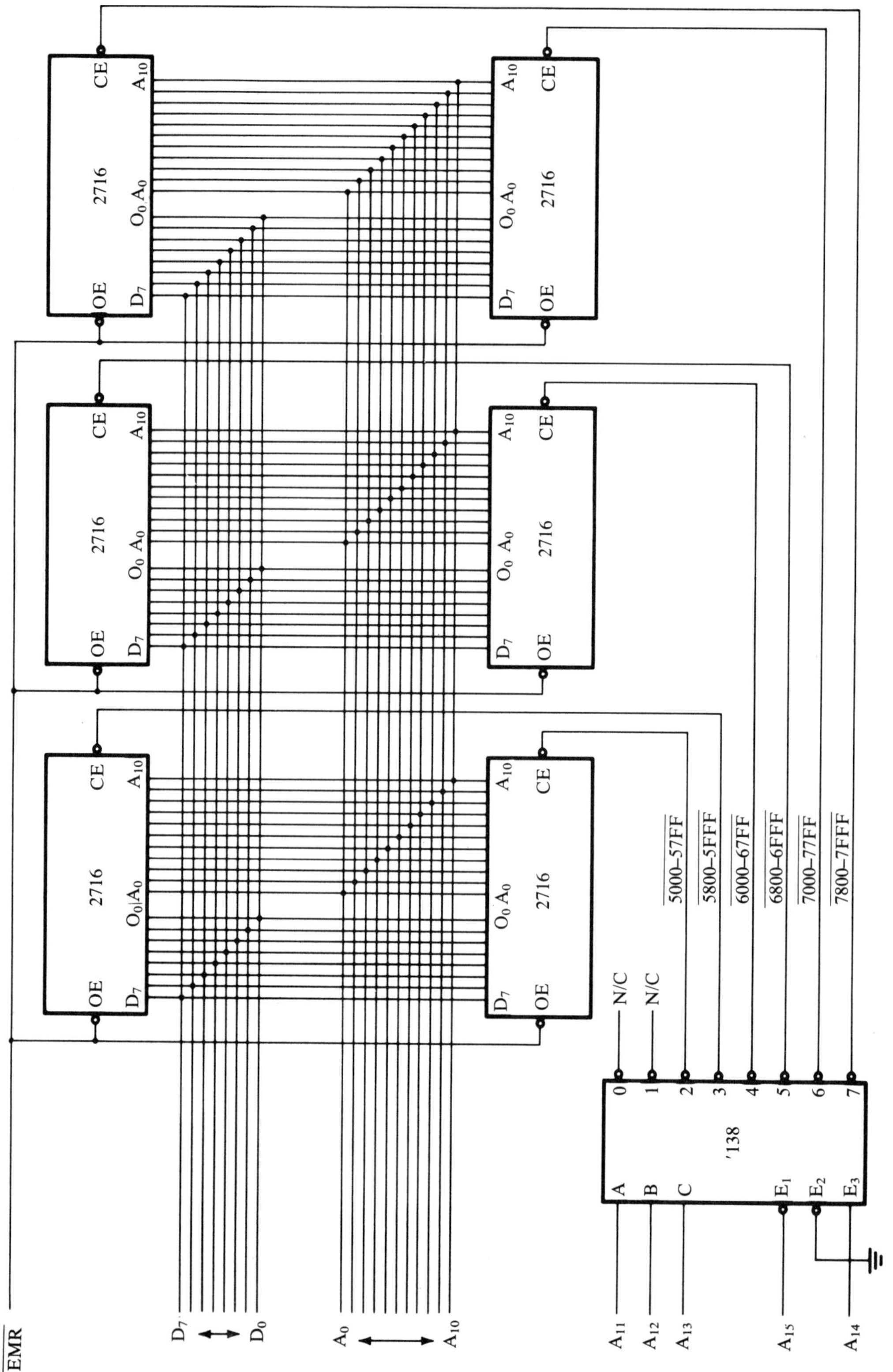
2716
CE
OE
A_{10}
O_0 A_0
D_7
'138
0
1
2
3
4
5
6
7
A
B
C
E_1
E_2
E_3
N/C
N/C
$\overline{5000–57FF}$
$\overline{5800–5FFF}$
$\overline{6000–67FF}$
$\overline{6800–6FFF}$
$\overline{7000–77FF}$
$\overline{7800–7FFF}$
$\overline{MEMR}$
D_7 ↔ D_0
A_0 ↔ A_{10}
A_{11}
A_{12}
A_{13}
A_{15}
A_{14}

FIGURE C–3

*NOTE: Only the selection and control logic have been illustrated.

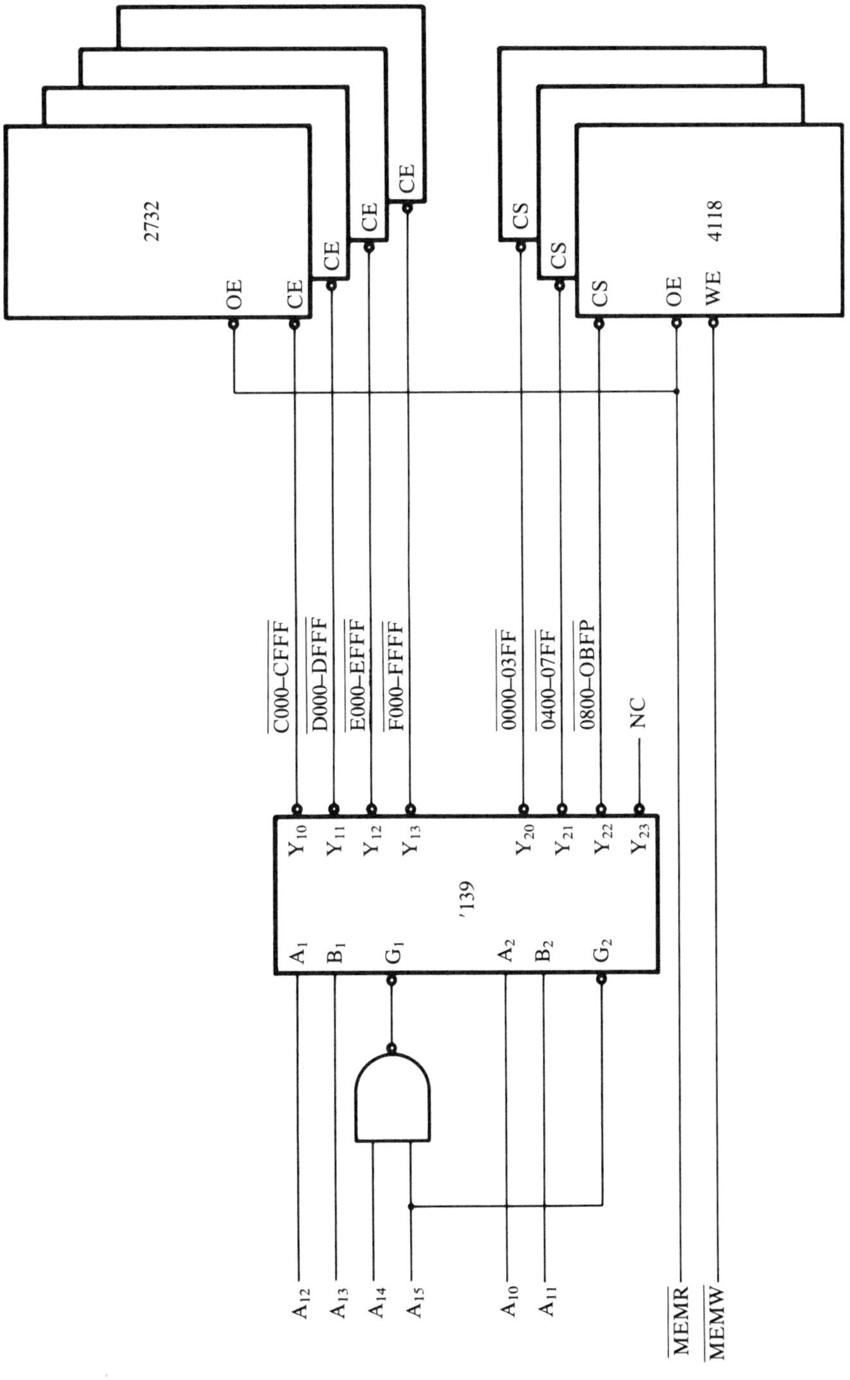

FIGURE C–4

NOTE: Only the selection and control logic have been illustrated.

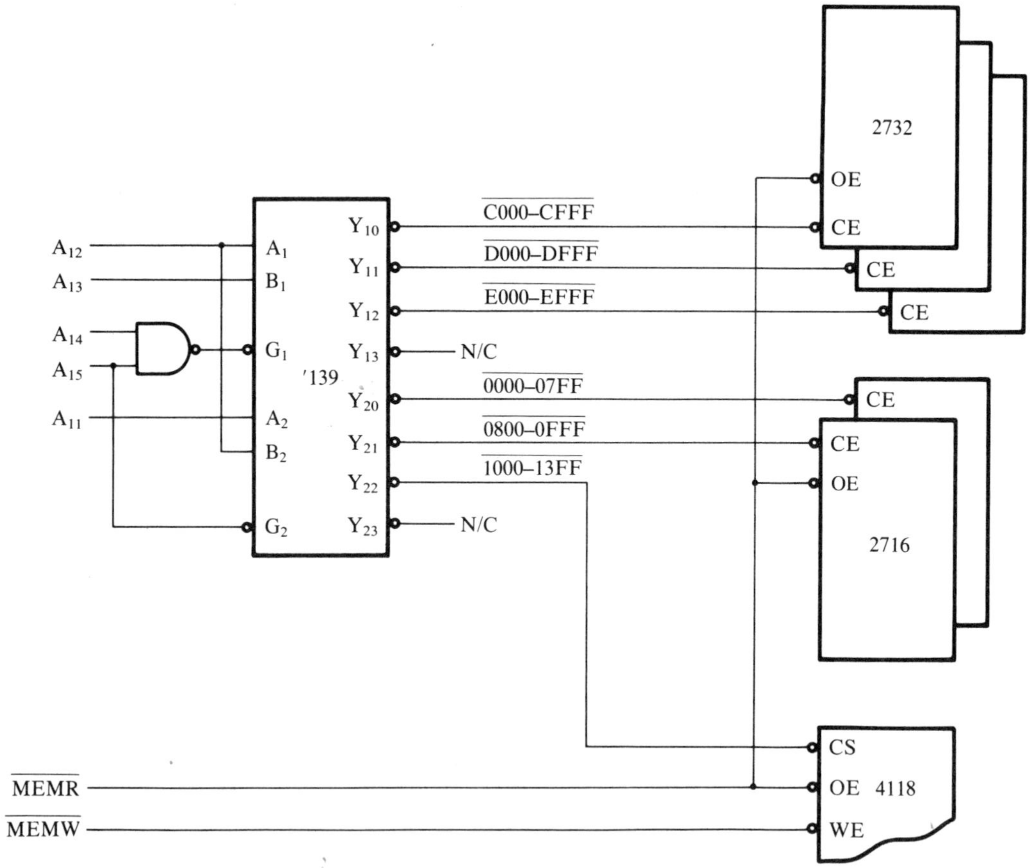

FIGURE C–5

23 This input strobes the address from the address pins into an internal row address register. It is also used for refreshing.

25 7FFFFH.

27 The end of the $\overline{RD}$ or $\overline{WR}$ strobe from the microprocessor, which occurs after the counter reaches its terminal count of 1100.

29
```
;8085A ROM TEST ROUTINE
;
TEST-ROM:   LXI  H,0700H     ;POINT TO ROM
            SUB  A           ;CLEAR CHECKSUM
TEST-LOOP:  XRA  M           ;ACCUMULATE CHECKSUM
            INR  L
            JNZ  TEST-LOOP
            DCR  H
```

```
JP    TEST-LOOP
LXI   H,07FFH
CMP   M
JNZ   ERROR          ;IF BAD
RET                  ;IF GOOD
```

Chapter 6

1 If the switch remains at the indicated position, ground is applied to the uppermost input of gate A, which forces its output to a logic one. This one is coupled to the uppermost input of gate B; along with the logic one at the other input, the output becomes a logic zero.

Once the switch is thrown, as it approaches the other contact, the outputs of both gates remain unchanged. Gate A has a zero on its bottom input, so its output remains a one; gate B has a one on both inputs and its output remains a logic zero. The instant a connection is made, the logic states of the NAND gates reverse; once they have reversed, they can only be changed again if the contact physically bounces back to the other contact. This, of course, is practically impossible.

3 An input device must use a set of three-state buffers between the TTL compatible device and the microprocessor data bus.

5 The I/O strobe is produced by combining the read or write signal with the output of either a memory address decoder for memory mapped I/O or a port decoder for isolated I/O.

7 A page of memory is by definition 256 bytes.

9 All memory reference instructions may be used with memory mapped I/O.

11 See figure C–6.

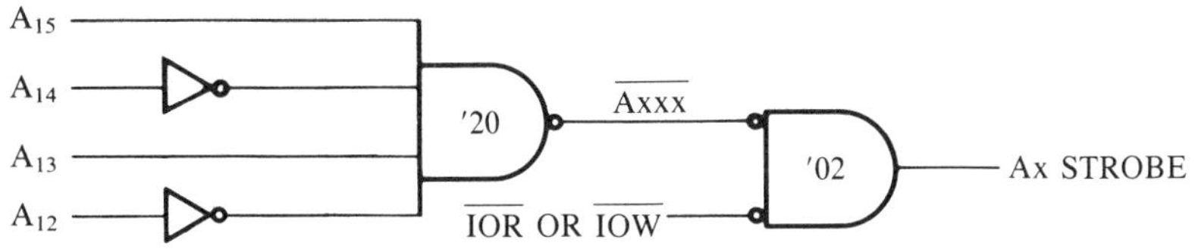

FIGURE C–6

13 See figure C–7.

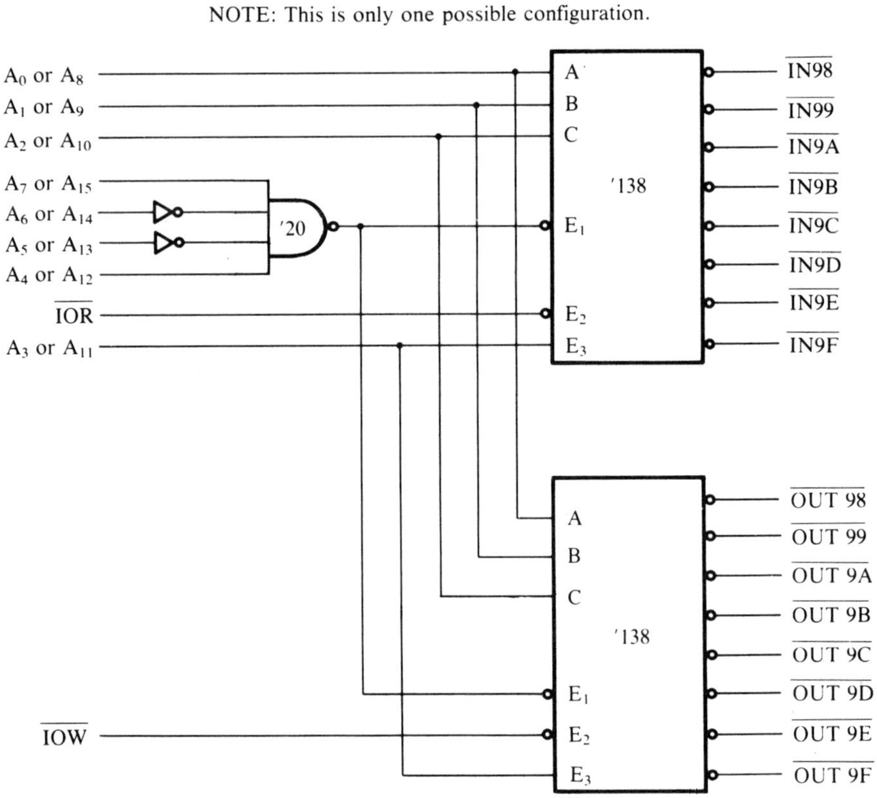

FIGURE C–7

15 See figure C–8.

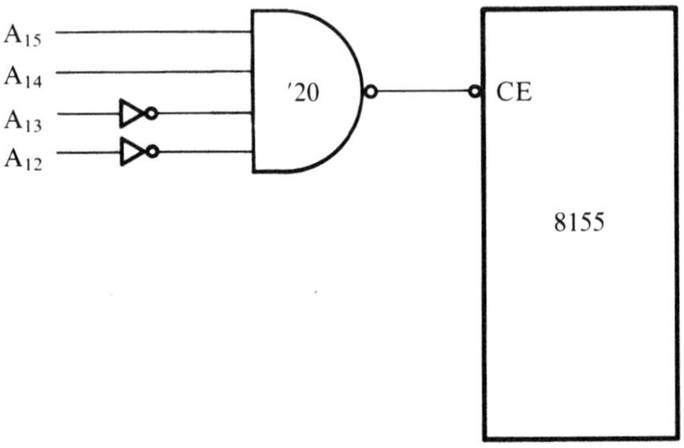

FIGURE C–8

17 See figure C–9.

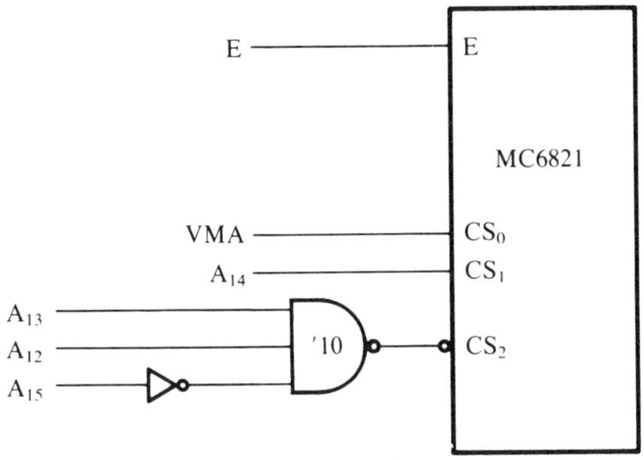

FIGURE C–9

19

```
START:  MVI    A,76H    ;LOAD LSB OF TIMER
        OUT    0C4H
        MVI    A,41H    ;LOAD MSB OF TIMER
        OUT    0C5H     ;AND MODE
        MVI    A,0C2H   ;START TIMER AND SETUP
        OUT    0C0H     ;PORTS A, B AND C
               .
               .
```

21 See figure C–10.

NOTE: This is only one possible decoder.

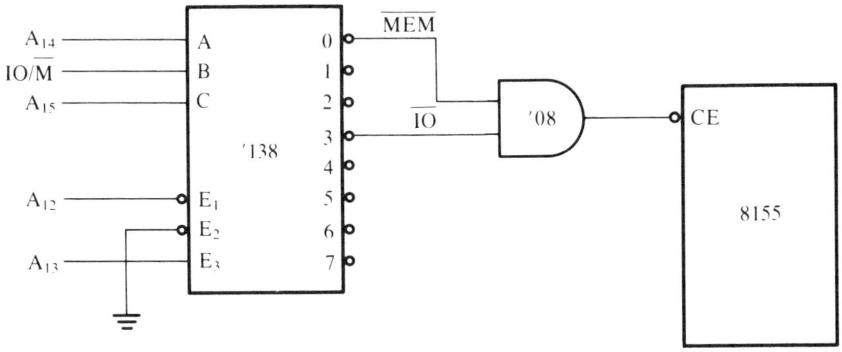

FIGURE C–10

23 The BF, or buffer full, flag bit indicates that the internal holding register contains data. For an input operation, it indicates that information has been strobed into the port; in an output operation, it indicates that information is available to the external device.

25 HARDWARE: See figure C–11.

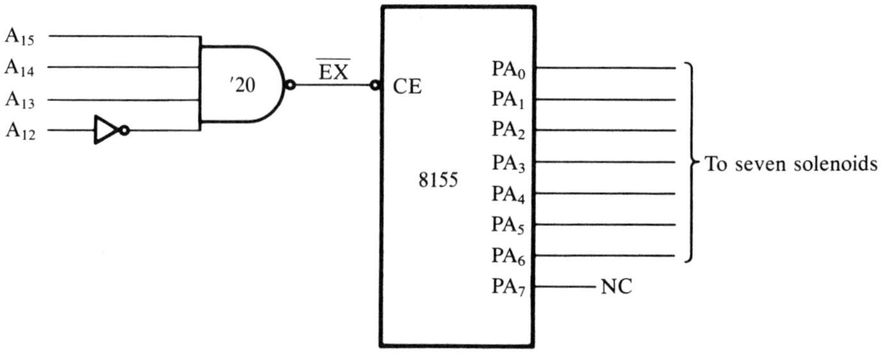

FIGURE C–11

```
 INITIALIZATION DIALOG:
INIT:  MVI  A,01H      ;PROGRAM PORTA AS AN OUTPUT
       OUT  0E0H
       SUB  A          ;TURN OFF SOLENOIDS
       OUT  0E1H
       .
       .
       .
;SUBROUTINE TO FIRE THE SOLENOIDS
FIRE:  OUT  0E1H       ;SEND PATTERN TO SOLENOIDS
       MVI  A,10       ;WASTE 10 MSEC.
FIRE1: CALL DEL1
       DCR  A
       JNZ  FIRE1
       SUB  A          ;TURN OFF SOLENOIDS
       OUT  0E1H
       RET
;
;ONE MILLISECOND TIME DELAY (CLOCK CYCLE = 333 NSEC.)
;
DEL1:  MVI  B,0CFH     ;LOAD COUNT
DEL2:  DCR  B
       JNZ  DEL2
       RET
```

Chapter 7

1 HARDWARE: See figure C–12.

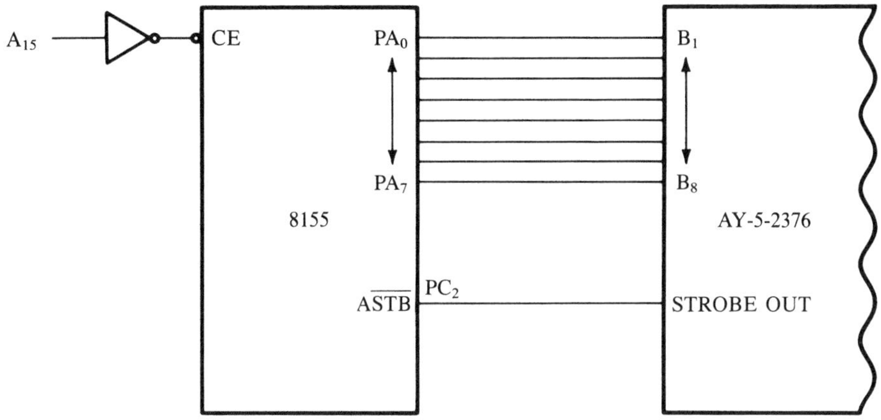

FIGURE C–12

3 SOFTWARE:

```
;INITIALIZATION DIALOG
;
INIT:  MVI   A,04H     ;SETUP PORT A FOR STROBED INPUT
       OUT   80H
;DATA TRANSFER SUBROUTINE
;
GET:   IN    80H       ;GET ABF
       ANI   02H       ;ISOLATE ABF
       JZ    GET       ;IF NO DATA
       IN    81H       ;GET DATA
       RET
```

5

```
*ACTUAL DELAY TIME = 7.816 MSEC.
DELAY     LDAB $#4B  THIS TIME INCLUDES
DELAY1    LDAA $#10  THE JSR COMMAND.
DELAY2    DECA
          BNE   DELAY2
          DECB
          BNE   DELAY1
          RTS
```

7

```
;STEPPER MOTOR CONTROL PROGRAM
;
RPM:      MVI  A,01H    ;MOVE CLOCKWISE ONE STEP
          CALL STEP     ;STEP THE MOTOR
          MVI  B,4
LOOP1:    CALL DELAY    ;WAIT 1 MSEC.
          DCR  B
          JNZ  LOOP1    ;WAIT TOTAL = 4 MSEC.
          JMP  GORPM    ;KEEP STEPPING
```

9 Since the subroutine causes one step in approximately 1 ms, the maximum rotation speed is 300 rpm.

11 Since it takes 4 ms to program a byte, the total programming time is 16.384 s.

13 It would be possible for a program to run wild, possibly causing an erroneous write to the port. This possibility can be prevented by using a key to modify the contents of the bank selection port. This key can be one OUTPUT to enable the bank latch and a second OUTPUT to send data into the bank latch. The bank latch can then be disabled by a third OUTPUT. This additional protection would make the system almost foolproof.

15
```
;THIS SUBROUTINE WILL MULTIPLY NUMB1 BY NUMB2
;BOTH NUMBERS ARE DOUBLE PRECISION NUMBERS.
;
DMULT:   SUB  A           ;CLEAR COMMAND
         OUT  0E1H        ;CLEAR STATUS WORD
         LXI  H,NUMB1     ;POINT TO NUMBERS
         CALL LOAD        ;LOAD MULTIPLICAND
         CALL LOAD
         CALL LOAD        ;LOAD MULTIPLIER
         CALL LOAD
         MVI  A,2BH       ;DMUL COMMAND
         OUT  0E1H        ;START TO MULTIPLY
         CALL STAT        ;TIME OUT COMMAND
         PUSH PSW
         CALL UNLOAD      ;GET ANSWER
         CALL UNLOAD
         POP  PSW
         RET
NUMB1:   DS   8
NUMB2:   DS   8
ANS:     DS   8
```

Chapter 8

1 An interrupt is exactly what the word implies: The program that is currently executing in the microprocessor is interrupted by an external hardware event.

3 If the interrupts are not enabled, there can never be a future interrupt. If the user were to forget to include this instruction, one and only one interrupt could ever occur. The exception is the TRAP interrupt; TRAP interrupt service subroutines should not contain an EI instruction.

5 Real-time clock, queue, printer interface, multiplexing displays, reading keyboards, and so forth.

7 RIM allows the following 8085A information to be read from the internal interrupt register:

SID - Serial input data
I7.5 - RST 7.5 input
I6.5 - RST 6.5 input
I5.5 - RST 5.5 input
IE - interrupt enable status
M7.5 - RST 7.5 mask
M6.5 - RST 6.5 mask
M5.5 - RST 5.5 mask

9 In any case in which it is critically important for the interrupt always to remain active. Examples could include power failure detection, display multiplexing and a real time clock.

11
```
;TURN RST 6.5 ON
;
ONG5:      RIM              ;GET CURRENT MASKS
           ANI  00000101B   ;M6.5 ON
           ORI  00001000B   ;MSE ON
           SIM              ;SET MASKS
            .
            .
            .
```

15
```
;INITIALIZATION DIALOG
;
INIT: MVI  A,00010010B     ;ICW1
      OUT  60H             ;SELECT EIGHT
      MVI  A,00010000B     ;ICW2
      OUT  61H             ;ADDRESS 1000H
      MVI  A,00000000B     ;OCW1
      OUT  61H             ;ENABLE ALL INTERRUPTS
      MVI  A,10100000B     ;OCW2
      OUT  60H
       .
       .
       .
```

17 Figure C–13 illustrates a polled interrupt scheme for the MC6800 microprocessor.

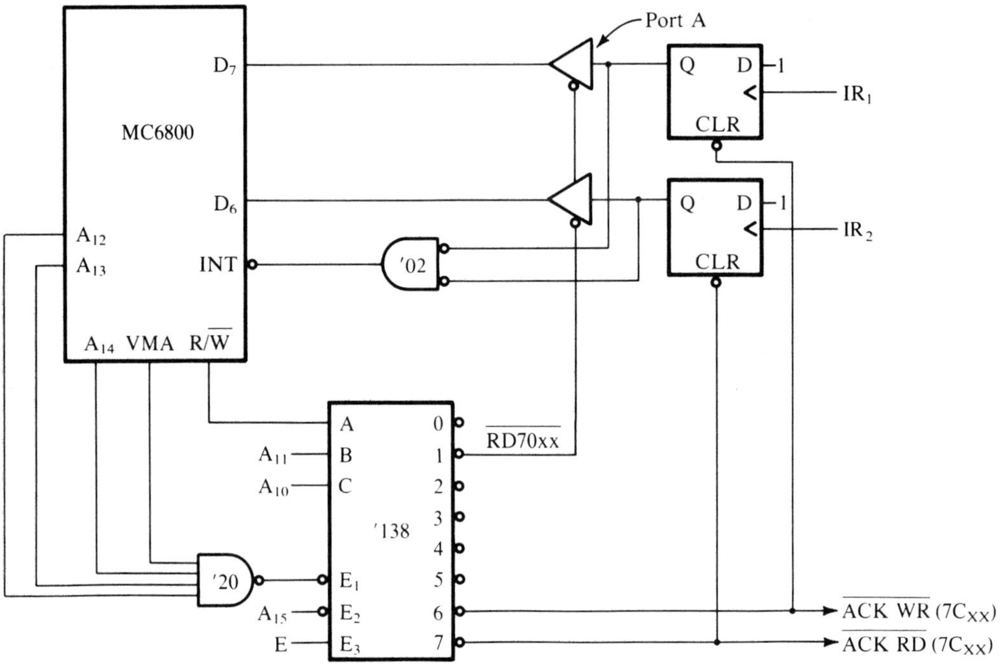

FIGURE C–13

```
*INTERRUPT SERVICE SUBROUTINE
*
INTS      LDAA PORTA      GET INTERRUPT BITS
          ADDA #$40       CHECK IF BOTH TRUE
          BCS  BOTH       IF BOTH ON
          TST  PORTA      CHECK LEVEL
          BMI  LEVEL1     IF LEVEL ONE
          BRA  LEVEL2     IF NOT LEVEL ONE
BOTH      LDAA PRIOR      GET PRIOR INDICATOR
          BMI  LEV1
          ASLA            SELECT OTHER LEVEL
          STAA PRIOR
          BRA  LEVEL2     DO LEVEL TWO
LEV1      ASRA            SELECT OTHER LEVEL
          STAA PRIOR
          BRA  LEVEL1
*PRIOR WOULD BE INITIALIZED AS A 10000000
```

19 Given the following program in which ACCB equals the byte count and the index register points to the data, the transfer rate would equal 50,000 bytes per second.

```
TRANS    LDAA X     ;GET DATA
         STAA IO    ;SEND DATA
         INX        ;POINT TO NEXT BYTE
```

```
        DECB        ;DECREMENT COUNT
        BNE         TRANS
          .
          .
          .
```

Chapter 9

1 In asynchronous digital communications, the data is transmitted without a clock and contains synchronization bits with each byte of data. In synchronous digital communications, a clock signal is sent with the data; and a sync character or two is transmitted with each block of data.

3 One.

5 4800 baud is the normal maximum, but data can be transmitted at higher rates, using leased lines.

7

```
;INITIALIZE THE 8251A
;
INIT:       MVI  A,11111010B     ;PROGRAM PATTERN
            OUT  COMMAND
```

9 25

11 2 V because of the difference between the −5 V level and the −3 V threshold.

13 The main disadvantage of the current loop is its relatively low speed.

15 FSK data is basically generated by steering two different tones: one tone for a logic one condition and the other for a logic zero.

17 PSK.

19 $\overline{\text{CTS}}$ and $\overline{\text{DSR}}$.

21 The synchronous connection uses timing or clock signals and also a sync detect signal; the asynchronous system does not use these signals.

23

```
;CHECK THE MODEM FOR TRANSMISSION
;
CHKT:       MVI  A,00100111B
            OUT  COMMAND
;TURNS TRANSMITTER AND RECEIVER ON AND ALSO
;SETS RTS AND DTR LOW.
            IN   STATUS      ;GET 8251A STATUS
            RLC
            JNC  CHKT        ;WAIT UNTIL DSR = 0
;THE CTS SIGNAL IS CHECKED WITH INTERNAL
;HARDWARE THAT CONDITIONS THE TxRDY OUTPUT PIN
;BUT NOT THE TxRDY STATUS BIT
              .
              .
              .
```

25 The talker checks the NRFD signal to determine whether all of the bus devices are ready to receive data. When they are ready, the talker places the data on the data connections and issues the DAV signal. DAV indicates that data is available to the listeners connected to the bus. The listeners in response to DAV accept the data and respond with the NDAC signal. NDAC indicates that the listeners have all received the information and that it is alright for the talker to continue with its next cycle.

Chapter 10

1 DMA, or direct memory access, is an I/O technique that stops the microprocessor from executing its program so that data can be directly extracted from or stored into the memory.

3 The microprocessor effectively disconnects itself from the address, data, and control buses by floating, or tri-stating, them.

5 16K bytes.

7 The internal F/L, or first last, flip-flop tracks whichever half of an internal register receives data.

9 More than one DMA channel can use the TC interrupt if the interrupt service subroutine polls the 8257. During the poll the channels that are active can be determined, and the counter can be read to see which one has reached zero or the terminal count.

13 The field attribute code determines the logic level on the RVV pin connection. This pin, through an external inverter, can cause reverse or inverse video.

15

```
;SUBROUTINE TO SCROLL THE SCREEN ONE LINE.
;SCREEN MEMORY EQUALS LOCATION RR
;
SCROLL:     MVI   B,23       ;LOAD LINE COUNTER
            LXI   H,RR       ;POINT TO TOP LINE
            LXI   D,RR+80    ;POINT TO 2ND. LINE
SCROLL1:    MVI   C,80       ;LOAD LINE CHARACTER COUNT
SCROLL2:    LDAX  D          ;TRANSFER A LINE
            MOV   M,A
            INX   D
            INX   H
            DCR   C
            JNZ   SCROLL2    ;IF NOT 80 CHARACTERS
            DCR   B
            JNZ   SCROLL1    ;IF NOT 23 LINES
            MVI   C,80       ;BLANK BOTTOM LINE
            MVI   A,' '     ;LOAD ASCII SPACE
SCROLL3:    MOV   M,A
            INX   H
            DCR   C
            JNZ   SCROLL3    ;IF NOT 80 CHARACTERS
            RET
```

Index